Managing Microsoft Exchange Server

Managing
Microsoft Exchange Server

Paul Robichaux

O'REILLY®

Beijing · Cambridge · Farnham · Köln · Paris · Sebastopol · Taipei · Tokyo

Managing Microsoft Exchange Server
by Paul Robichaux

Copyright © 1999 O'Reilly & Associates, Inc. All rights reserved.
Printed in the United States of America.

Published by O'Reilly & Associates, Inc., 101 Morris Street, Sebastopol, CA 95472.

Editor: Robert Denn

Production Editor: Madeleine Newell

Printing History:

July 1999:   First Edition.

This book is printed on acid-free paper with 85% recycled content, 15% post-consumer waste. O'Reilly & Associates is committed to using paper with the highest recycled content available consistent with high quality.

ISBN: 1-56592-545-9

Table of Contents

Preface

Welcome to the Brave New World

Exchange has earned a reputation as a large and complicated product. However, it's also very flexible, with lots of mix-and-match components you can use to build a messaging system that meets your specific needs. Because of its complexity, Exchange requires that you understand in detail how it works and how to configure and manage it. This is especially important since email has become a truly critical application for many businesses, and users who depend on Exchange are pretty unforgiving about outages and interruptions in service.

Exchange was designed to be easy to administer, and to work well out of the box with minimal adjustments. In large part, it achieves those goals, but knowing when (and when not to!) change your configuration is a key part of keeping your Exchange network up and running. The accessibility of the Exchange interface sometimes tempts inexperienced or untrained administrators into making changes that turn out to have a negative impact.

Who's This Book For?

My experience has been that there are relatively few really experienced Exchange administrators, compared to the zillions of grizzled Unix sendmail masters. Since Exchange itself has only been around for about six years, and since the biggest growth in Exchange sales has come in the last two years, there are plenty of people running Exchange who want to know more about how to install, configure, manage, and recover their Exchange servers.

This book is for beginning to advanced Exchange administrators. Super-gurus probably won't find much new material here, but I've tried to structure each chapter so that there's a smooth progression from introductory concepts (what's an MTA?) to detailed information for those who already understand the basics.

To get the most out of this book, you should be familiar with the Windows user interface: you should know how to right-click on things, run programs, and so on. Some background as an NT administrator would be useful, too. In particular, you should be comfortable with the use of the NT registry editing tools.

What's Not in This Book

There are a number of books already on the market that claim to cover every aspect of Exchange. Some are more successful at this than others. Rather than writing a 1500-page book that covers every obscure piece of Exchange, I decided to write a shorter, smaller book that focuses on what administrators need to know to get their day-to-day jobs done. To that end, I purposefully chose not to cover some topics in depth, because my own observations and experience lead me to believe that they're not on the "gotta know" list for the majority of Exchange sites:

- The Microsoft Mail, Lotus Notes, and Lotus cc:Mail connectors. Most sites that have these are using them as crutches to keep mail flowing until they finish migrating to Exchange.

- The mainframe mail connectors (IBM PROFS and Office Vision, Digital All-in-1, Verimation Memo). Configuring and running these connectors requires special expertise with the mainframe mailers that's outside the scope of this book.

- Migration planning. When you migrate to Exchange, if you do it right you only have to do it once. There are entire books dedicated to the many tiny details necessary to do a successful migration.

- Exchange scripting and application development. You can do a ton of neat things with Exchange's scripting capabilities, all of which require some programming.

How This Book Is Organized

This book is broken into 18 chapters and 2 appendixes. In general, the chapters start with the most common tasks and concepts—things that apply to everyone who runs Exchange—and become increasingly specialized as they go.

- Chapter 1, *Introducing Exchange Server*, introduces Exchange by explaining its background and some of the underlying concepts on which it depends.

- Chapter 2, *Exchange Architecture*, focuses on Exchange's database and security architectures. You can think of this as an extension of the first chapter.

- Chapter 3, *Exchange Planning*, discusses the things you need to consider when planning and deploying Exchange, including selecting hardware, planning your network and Internet connectivity, and choosing the right version of Exchange.

- Chapter 4, *Installing Exchange*, describes the Exchange installation process and tells you how to tame it, whether you're installing a single server and site or dozens.

- Chapter 5, *Using Exchange Administrator*, explains how the Exchange Administrator application works, what you can do with it, and how to use it to import and export directory data.

- Chapter 6, *Mailboxes, Recipients, and Distribution Lists*, covers the creation and maintenance of mailboxes, distribution lists, and custom recipients.

- Chapter 7, *Managing Connectors and the MTA*, exposes the Exchange Message Transfer Agent (MTA) and its relationship to Exchange connectors; it includes a discussion on how to create, manage, and configure both connectors and the MTA itself.

- Chapter 8, *Managing the Internet Mail Service*, is all about the Internet Mail Service (IMS), and how you can use it to interconnect your Exchange network with the worldwide Internet.

- Chapter 9, *Managing the Directory*, describes the processes and concepts you need to understand in order to maintain your Exchange directory databases and their contents.

- Chapter 10, *Managing Public Folders*, explains the Exchange public folder architecture, including replication, configuration, and permission assignments.

- Chapter 11, *Managing the Information Store*, covers managing the Information Store (IS) service and its associated databases.

- Chapter 12, *Managing the Internet News Service*, guides you through the process of installing, configuring, and maintaining the Internet News Service (INS), the component of Exchange that allows it to interoperate with Network News Transfer Protocol (NNTP) servers.

- Chapter 13, *Managing Exchange Clients*, explains how to integrate the Outlook client family with your Exchange servers.

- Chapter 14, *Managing Exchange Servers*, discusses the day-to-day maintenance tasks necessary to keep your servers working properly and your mail flowing.

- Chapter 15, *Troubleshooting Exchange Server*, deals with troubleshooting connector, client, service, and NT problems.

- Chapter 16, *Exchange Security*, discusses Exchange's security mechanisms, including the cryptographic underpinnings of Exchange advanced security.

- Chapter 17, *Recovery and Repair*, is a complete guide to recovering and restoring damaged Exchange servers and data.

- Chapter 18, *Managing Exchange Performance*, delves into the mysterious world of Exchange performance tuning.

- Appendix A, *BORK Tools*, describes the Exchange-related tools included in Microsoft's BackOffice Resource Kit (BORK).

- Appendix B, *Useful Performance Monitor Counters*, enumerates the Performance Monitor counters that you can monitor to see what your Exchange server is doing.

Conventions in This Book

The following typographical conventions are used in this book:

`Constant width`
> Used to indicate command-line computer output, commands, code examples, registry keys, executable commands, utilities, and switches

`Constant width italic`
> Used to indicate variables in examples and in registry keys, as well as placeholders for which the user will substitute a real name or value

Italic
> Used to introduce new terms and to indicate URLs, variables or user-defined files and directories, file extensions, filenames, directory or folder names, and UNC pathnames

The following icons appear throughout this book:

> The owl icon indicates a supplementary note related to the surrounding text.

> The turkey icon indicates a cautionary note related to the surrounding text.

We'd Like Your Feedback!

The information in this book has been tested and verified to the best of our ability, but mistakes and oversights do occur. Please let us know about errors you may find, as well as your suggestions for future editions, by writing to:

> O'Reilly & Associates, Inc.
> 101 Morris Street
> Sebastopol, CA 95472
> 800-998-9938 (in the U.S. or Canada)
> 707-829-0515 (international or local)
> 707-829-0104 (fax)

You can also send us email messages. To be put on our mailing list or to request a catalog, send mail to:

> *nuts@oreilly.com*

To ask technical questions or comment on the book, send email to:

> *bookquestions@oreilly.com*

Acknowledgments

Writing the acknowledgments is always difficult, because I live in fear of leaving someone out. In this book's case, my fear is multiplied by the large cast of smart people who contributed to the final product you're holding. This book began as the result of discussions with Robert Denn, my editor at O'Reilly, about whether the world really needed another Exchange book. I'm glad he agreed to do this book, and I remain convinced that David Rogelberg of StudioB, my agent, had a lot to do with his decision.

At O'Reilly, an entire production crew labored to turn my original drafts into a finished product. Steven Abrams cleaned up the manuscript and kept track of everything; Rob Romano did his usual outstanding job of redrawing my junky-looking line art to make it more appealing and clearer.

I was fortunate to be able to work with a number of very knowledgeable contributors on this project. Andy Webb of Simpler-Webb wrote the chapter on the IMS, and Lee Hadfield of LHAD Consulting wrote the chapter on the INS. Ben Schorr provided Chapter 13, which deals with the Outlook client family, and heavy hitter Stephen Gutknecht chipped in with the original versions of Chapters 14, 15, and 17. Missy Koslosky dug deep into the BORK to produce Appendix A. I am grateful for the effort and professionalism that they displayed.

Once the contributors and I finished our work, the technical reviewers pored over the manuscript looking for errors, omissions, and other bogosities. In addition to Missy Koslosky and Andy Webb, the reviewer group for this book included Doug Hampshire, Dougal Campbell, Bob Montgomery (a benchmark guru at Hewlett-Packard), Charles Festel, Richard Dann, and the world-famous Ed Crowley. Their efforts and suggestions made this a vastly better book. (I should also mention the members of the *msexchange* mailing list and the readers of my monthly column in the *Exchange Administrator* newsletter, both valuable sources for figuring out what people need to know about Exchange.)

A number of vendors provided equipment and technical assistance, including Wayne Pendley and Choon-Sim Kim of Dell Computer, Bob Montgomery at Hewlett-Packard, Tom Grubb at Bluecurve, and Martyn Davies and Alan Bach at Eicon. My thanks to them.

I would be remiss if I didn't mention that this book was entirely written on Power Macintoshes, including my Powerbook laptop. I always enjoyed being able to fire up Exchange Server using the Virtual PC emulator while flying from one location to another; the Powerbook enabled me to write portions of this book in Gulf Shores, Mobile, New Orleans, Dearborn, San Diego, Atlanta, St. Louis, Huntsville, Charlotte, and points in between.

My wife and family were extremely supportive during what turned out to be my longest project thus far; I am grateful to them for their love, support, and regular reminders to leave my workroom to come out and play. Lastly, I am thankful to the Lord for the many blessings he has granted my family and me, not least the opportunity to finally finish this book.

1

Introducing
Exchange Server

Things are always at their best in their beginning.
—Blaise Pascal
Lettres Provinciales

It's fair to start out this book by talking about some (but not all!) of the things Microsoft Exchange Server can do—there are a lot of them, and many administrators who are suddenly faced with running Exchange want to know what it can do and what its strengths and weaknesses are.

Exchange Capabilities

Exchange Server is a database-backed messaging, groupware, and collaboration system. It allows clients to exchange messages with one another across a variety of network transport protocols, including X.400 and TCP/IP. These messages can be mail messages like those you're accustomed to seeing; they can also contain directory and scheduling data. You can write your own Exchange-based applications that use Exchange messages to transport pretty much any kind of data you'd like: custom forms, "voting booths" for polling users, and so on.

 To save us both trouble, I'm going to stop calling the server product "Microsoft Exchange Server" and just call it "Exchange" from now on. This is less confusing than it may seem, since the original Exchange client software has been made largely obsolete by the Outlook client. If I'm talking about the client, I'll use the word "client" to make that clear.

Let's look at some specific things Exchange does well:

It's flexible

Exchange offers a dazzling array of choices and protocols. For example, clients can retrieve mail using Microsoft's own Exchange and Outlook clients or with the widely deployed POP3 and IMAP4rev1 protocols; they can also use Outlook Web Access to access their mailboxes from any JavaScript-capable web browser. The administrative interface offers direct (if not always easy) access to a seemingly endless smorgasbord of configuration settings and parameters—so many that the biggest challenge in administering Exchange can be just finding the option you know must be there somewhere!

It plays well with others

Exchange is tightly integrated with the Windows NT authentication system, so each user account can have single-sign-on access to mailbox resources from anywhere in the organization. Exchange ships with connectors that allow it to interoperate and exchange messages with the Internet (via SMTP and NNTP), Microsoft Mail, Novell GroupWise, Lotus Notes, and a variety of mainframe systems. Third-party connectors add voice mail and fax connectivity.

It scales well

Exchange itself is highly multithreaded and self-tuning, and its overall performance is quite good. On a capable multiprocessor machine like the Dell PowerEdge 2300 I used when writing this book, it can easily handle several hundred concurrent users. The hierarchical server-site-organization design (more on that in a bit) makes it possible to group large numbers of users and servers sensibly. Exchange can also take advantage of Microsoft and third-party clustering solutions. For really, really large applications, there's always Exchange running on DEC/Compaq AlphaServers, which can support tens of thousands of users. The Enterprise Edition of Exchange 5.5 supports message stores of up to 16 terabytes, which should be adequate for almost all uses.

It's a complete development platform

Exchange is built on top of a relational database engine. All messages are stored in this database, and (as of Exchange 5.5) you can write custom scripts that process, send, filter, or otherwise modify messages automatically. You can write plugins that run on the server and do server-side tasks like checking inbound mail for viruses, and you can write clients that use Exchange components to transfer mail, schedule appointments, or do almost anything else that can be done manually with the Exchange or Outlook clients.

However—and you knew this was coming—there's a Dark Side to Exchange. Like any other software, it has limitations and faults, some of which can be real problems if you're not forewarned.

It's picky and unforgiving

When you're setting up an Exchange installation, you have to make a number of choices. Once you've made them, in some cases you're stuck with them. For example, there's no way to change the name of an Exchange organization once it's created. This limitation means you need to do thorough and careful planning before you rip open your Exchange CD and start installing.

It's complex

Compared to a relatively simple single-process mail system like *qmail*, Exchange is a huge beast more akin to an oil refinery than a piece of software. The capability and power that Exchange offers comes at the cost of a large number of interconnected pieces, all of which you must understand (or at least be aware of) to administer Exchange well.

It's easy to do trivial things, and hard to do some desirable things

If all you want to do is set up a small Exchange server for a few dozen clients, using only Microsoft's client software, that's no problem. As soon as you want to do anything more—say, exchange mail with the Internet, or perhaps allow HTTP access to mail—the difficulty level starts climbing steeply. This is largely because there's so much to know, but some blame must go to the user interface of the Exchange Administrator application.

It's expensive

Every client requires an access license, and the server software itself is expensive relative to simpler SMTP/POP3 server products. Depending on the client load you plan to support, the server hardware itself can become a significant expense, too. However, Exchange pricing is generally competitive with its two major groupware competitors, Novell's GroupWise and Lotus Notes.

A Little Exchange History

Exchange is Microsoft's entry into the groupware and collaboration server software markets. Microsoft actually has a significant amount of experience with mail software, having shipped its Microsoft Mail product since the early 1980s. However, the confluence of two factors helped push Microsoft into the large-scale messaging server market. The first factor was the availability and capability of Windows NT, which makes a pretty good server operating system for most applications. The second factor was the increasing and lucrative market for groupware and collaboration software, which until that point was owned almost 100% by Lotus Notes.

Exchange 4.0

Exchange 4.0 debuted in 1993; it included the first release of the Exchange client, but it also worked with existing 16- and 32-bit Microsoft Mail and Schedule+ clients. Initial adoption was slow, in part because Exchange was perceived as difficult and expensive to install, configure, and maintain. However, Microsoft targeted the initial release mostly at large customers like Intergraph and Boeing, where the support infrastructure existed to set up servers, migrate users, and keep everything working properly.

Exchange 5.0

Exchange 5.0 added many capabilities (and a ton of bug fixes) to 4.0. The Internet mail connector was better integrated with other Exchange components, and the database schema was changed to make replication more efficient. Exchange 5.0 also included a wider variety of protocols and connectors, enabling it to coexist with a wider range of LAN and mainframe mail systems. This expansion included support for the NNTP, LDAP, and POP3 protocols, as well as the ability to use SSL connections with Internet protocols.

Windows NT Small Business Server

Small Business Server (SBS) is a Microsoft bundle that combines NT 4.0 with an Exchange server, a fax module, and a number of other useful pieces. SBS is supposed to make it possible to deploy a single NT box for Internet access, mail, calendaring, and fax service. In that role, it works pretty well. The first version of SBS included Exchange 5.0; the currently shipping version includes Exchange 5.5 and a 50-user license. The contents of this book also apply to SBS.

Exchange 5.5

Exchange 5.5 was a bigger release than the ".5" might indicate. The biggest internal change was the move away from the Jet Blue database engine to a new database, the Extensible Storage Engine (ESE; you'll see that acronym again and again, so don't forget it). Jet Blue imposed a 16GB size limit on message stores; the Enterprise version of ESE removes that limit and allows message stores to grow up to 16TB (the Standard Edition still has the original 16GB limit). A number of other internal changes were also made:

- The memory allocator was rewritten; the new one uses what Microsoft calls "dynamic buffer allocation" (DBA) to manage the amount of memory Exchange uses. DBA is basically designed to hog all available physical RAM but to release it when other applications need it (as evidenced by upticks in virtual memory paging). This allows Exchange to take much better advantage of servers with more than 64MB of RAM by keeping more of the Information Store databases in RAM.

- The Internet Mail Connector (IMC) of previous versions was replaced by a new Internet Mail Service (IMS). Like its predecessor, the IMS handles SMTP mail exchange, but it adds features for controlling SMTP relaying and is both more robust and faster than the Exchange 5.0 IMC.

- Support for the LDAP version 3, IMAP version 4rev1, and S/MIME version 1.0 protocols was added to various components of the Exchange package, including the directory and Information Store services and the IMC.

- The Active Directory Services Interface (ADSI), allows you to write programs that query the Exchange directory. ADSI is one of the major components of Windows 2000, and its introduction as part of Exchange was a purposeful attempt to give developers a head start on the Windows 2000 learning curve.

- The Enterprise version of Exchange 5.5 supports clustering with Microsoft's Cluster Server product.

- The Information Store was significantly updated to give better performance; it also includes a feature that caches deleted items so users can recover them later—a great antidote to the "Help! I just deleted an important message" telephone calls mail administrators are prone to receive. See the section "The Dumpster" in Chapter 11, *Managing the Information Store*, for details.

The 5.5 release also includes connectors for Lotus Notes and the PROFS and SNADS mainframe mail systems. The X.400 connector was moved to the Enterprise Edition, and Microsoft made a number of changes to their licensing policy, which are covered in more detail in Chapter 3, *Exchange Planning*.

Service Pack 1 (SP1) was released in mid-1998; it added a number of new features to Exchange 5.5, including the ability to record all sent messages* to a file (*message journaling*) and to move users between servers in different sites. In keeping with Microsoft tradition, SP1 also included a large number of bug fixes. It also added better support for version 2.0 of the S/MIME protocol.

Service Pack 2 was released in December 1999; it includes all of the features and fixes that were bundled into SP1, plus more fixes and some interesting new features. Probably the most immediately interesting change is that SP2 makes Exchange 5.5 completely year 2000-compliant (at least, according to Microsoft). In

---

* This sounds like a serious privacy infringement, and it may be, depending on how it's used. However, lots of sites (notably securities firms, financial institutions, and legal firms) are legally required to keep an archive of all messages sent outside the organization, and message journaling is one way to deliver this.

addition, there are several new tools bundled in SP2, including the InterOrg Replication Utility, which allows public folder and schedule replication between sites in different organizations, and a pair of utilities to ease migration from Unix mail systems that use LDAP and IMAP for directory lookup and mail service. SP2 also includes several components that were made available after SP1 shipped, including the Move Server Wizard (which finally allows you to move a server from one site to another without reinstalling Exchange), the Notes connector, and an importer that can pull in cc:Mail archives.

Platinum

As of this writing, no one knows exactly what the next version of Exchange, code-named "Platinum," will include. The Platinum directory will be based on the Windows 2000 Active Directory, so there may not be a separate Directory Service (DS) database (but then again, there might be). It's likely that the Platinum administrative user interface will be overhauled to use the Microsoft Management Console and fit in better with other Windows 2000 components. Furthermore, Microsoft has announced their intention to make SMTP a full peer of X.400 for use by the MTA; that offers a welcome respite from the overhead and difficulty of X.400 addressing. Based on occasional public statements by Microsoft, you'd probably be safe to assume that the Platinum IS and DS will feature some performance and safety improvements.

Exchange Server Concepts

Exchange is a big, complicated set of interconnected components. There are servers and services, transfer agents and system attendants—a whole passel of pieces that combine to move messaging traffic. Understanding what these pieces are, what they do, and how they work together is critical to understanding how to *do* anything with Exchange once you get it installed.

Single-Instance Storage

Let's start with a simple but important concept—how messages are stored on the server. Some systems use *multiple-instance* storage. Each client gets its own copy of a message, even if that message is sent to many recipients. This type of storage is best exemplified by Unix-based mail systems, which usually deliver individual messages to users' private mailbox files.

Most PC-based mail servers are *shared-file* servers: each client attaches to a shared set of directories on a central server and transfers mail by putting it in, or retrieving it from, certain directories. Shared-file servers are basically glorified file servers, because the mail client is in charge of address resolution and mail transport (though some systems run periodic tasks on the shared-file server to move mail between users on different servers).

Exchange uses *single-instance storage*. All public and private messages are kept in database files. Each message is kept only once in each server's database; if you send a message to two hundred users who all have accounts on the same server, there's only one copy of the message in the database. Each user's mailbox contains a pointer to that message.* This is a great savings for systems that support large numbers of users, especially if those users are mailing each other large files.

Servers, Sites, and Organizations

Exchange networks are organized in a containment hierarchy that's different from both Windows NT domains and DNS-style domains. Let's look at them in order, from smallest scope to largest.

Servers

Servers are individual computers running Exchange. These machines have to be running NT Server 4.0 or later; you can't run Exchange on NT Workstation although you can use the Exchange Administrator application on any NT system. Each server must also be a member of an NT domain. Each server normally runs a full set of the key Exchange components discussed in the next section; however, you can dedicate individual servers as mailbox or public folder servers if your network requires it.

At the individual server level, you can control which protocols the server will accept, what connectors are installed, and what properties apply to various Exchange components. If this description seems vague, it's only because there are so many different items you can control.

Sites

A site is a group of servers connected by a network. All servers in a site share the same directory information. Within the site, all directory replication and mail routing is automatic. Networks used to connect a site must have three characteristics:

Permanent

Sites must be based on permanently connected networks because the site connector expects the network to always be available.

---

* This is actually a bit oversimplified, since users can store mail in personal mail folders on their workstations. In this case, each user's personal folder gets a copy of the message. For more on personal folders, read on.

High-bandwidth

Microsoft's documentation says that sites must be connected by high-band-width networks. That means at least 64Kbps of bandwidth available to Exchange—not a total bandwidth of 64Kbps. Most sites are connected with links in the 56–128Kbps range, although I know of sites that run over X.25 connections at 9600 baud. The bandwidth required to connect servers in a site will vary widely depending on how you've set up intrasite replication and how much mail is flowing between servers in the site.

Able to pass remote procedure call (RPC) traffic

Exchange servers in a site communicate with each other through Microsoft's implementation of the Distributing Computing Environment (DCE) RPC model. (The Exchange and Outlook clients, and the Exchange Administrator application, can also use RPCs to talk to Exchange servers.) RPC traffic normally travels over TCP/IP. Port 135 is the service locator port, which clients and servers use to determine which port a desired service is available on. At a minimum, you'll need to unblock ports 137 and 139 to enable RPC traffic within your site. (See Chapter 16, *Exchange Security*, for more details on port configurations.) Microsoft says that site networks must be synchronous, meaning that the network must be able to pass RPC traffic.

Apart from these guidelines, you can group servers into sites however you like. For example, you can put all your North American servers into a single site, or you can group servers by business unit. You can use *locations* to further subdivide servers in a site. Locations are optional, but public folder replication and mail routing can take advantage of any locations you define.

There's no physical server associated with a site—sites are just objects in the organization's directory. When you install an Exchange server, you either create a new site or join an existing site. In either case, the new server is affiliated with one, and only one, of these site objects. You can't directly move a server from one site to another, though you can use the Move Server Wizard if you're running Exchange 5.5 SP1 or later (as discussed in Chapter 14, *Managing Exchange Servers*).

A site can contain servers from one or more Windows NT domains. The *site services account* is a Windows NT account used by all services that run within the site—it's the Exchange equivalent of the NT *Administrator* or Unix *root* accounts. If you're using multiple NT domains, you must either have proper interdomain trust relationships set up or use a site services account with the same password in each domain.

At the site level, you can control defaults that apply to all objects of a particular class in the site. For example, you can set a value for the deleted item retention period for all private Information Stores in a site; this setting will apply to all servers in the site that don't have overriding settings specified at the server level.

Organizations

An organization is a collection of site objects. Like sites themselves, there's no physical server that acts as the organization server. Instead, the organization is represented as a set of directory objects that are replicated among all sites (and servers) in that organization. Just as an organization like Boeing or Ford will have an organization-wide directory, so do Exchange organizations (even if they're not that large). The entire organization shares a single replicated set of directory data. You're free to partition an organization into any number of sites and servers, depending on your needs, and there are no restrictions or suggestions on how sites may be connected to form an organization—anything goes.

 You can replicate public folder data between organizations, but Exchange doesn't provide an automatic way to replicate directory data. See Chapter 10, *Managing Public Folders*, for information on some workarounds you may find useful.

Key Exchange Components

Exchange is a complicated set of interrelated pieces, but, in the tradition of George Orwell's *Animal Farm*, where some animals were more equal than others, some pieces are more important than others. Before planning an Exchange rollout or (heaven forbid!) installing Exchange without planning, you'll find it helpful to know who the key players are and what they do.

Exchange Administrator

Exchange Administrator is the control center for your entire Exchange organization. While you can start and stop the Exchange component services described earlier by using the Services control panel or the `net stop` and `net start` commands, the only way to twiddle the majority of Exchange's settings is to use Exchange Administrator. The interface (shown in Figure 1-1) looks much like most other Microsoft management applications. The left-hand pane (the *container area*) holds *containers*, or objects that can hold other objects. For example, organizations and sites appear in the container pane because they contain other nested objects. All of these container items are actually directory objects. The right-hand pane (the *contents area*) shows you the *leaf nodes* of the selected container object. A leaf node is just an item that doesn't contain anything; mailboxes are a good example. Confusingly, the container area sometimes shows leaf objects; you'll quickly learn through experience which items are leaves and which are nodes.

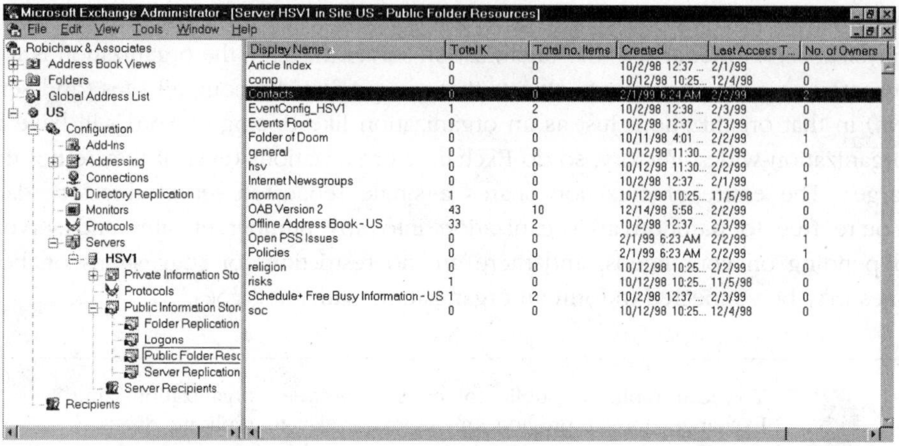

Figure 1-1. Exchange Administrator's interface looks pretty much like Explorer and most other Microsoft management applications

You can install and use Exchange Administrator on any Windows NT machine in your organization. As long as the machine where it's installed has RPC connectivity to the server you want to manage, you can twiddle to your heart's content. In fact, you can even install non-English versions of Exchange Administrator and use them to administer a server. Let's say your data center in San Francisco must be managed around the clock—your Tokyo and Paris offices can install localized versions of Exchange Administrator and manage the San Francisco servers with no trouble.

The System Attendant

The System Attendant (SA) watches over the health and status of all Exchange services on a particular server. It also performs a number of other critical functions—in fact, if the SA isn't running, no other Exchange service will start. To be more specific, the SA is in charge of:

- Maintaining the message tracking logs (if message tracking is enabled)
- Monitoring the other services and providing status information that link and server monitors on other machines can use
- Supervising messaging connections and reporting their status to any active link monitors
- Building routing tables that govern how mail flows between servers in a site
- Cross-checking directory information for inconsistencies, and fixing any that are found

The SA is also involved in setting up advanced security for individual mailboxes, as you'll learn in Chapter 16.

The Directory Service

The directory is the backbone of Exchange's hierarchy and mail transport systems. It contains information about all recipients, public folders, distribution lists, servers, and sites in an organization. Various other parts of Exchange use this data; for example, you can build custom address book views that show administrator-defined subsets of the entire directory. (See Chapter 5, *Using Exchange Administrator*, to find out how.)

The Directory Service is a service process that maintains and replicates the directory data itself. It provides the server-based address book, though users can build their own personal address books. It controls the structure and contents of the directory, and it handles both sending and receiving directory data for replication.

The directory contents are stored in a single database file, *dir.edb*. The contents of the directory database are automatically replicated to all servers in an organization, although you have some control over exactly what contents are replicated, as you'll see in Chapter 9, *Managing the Directory*.

The Information Store

The Information Store (IS) does what you'd infer: it stores mailbox and public folder data. The IS service actually manages two independent databases. The public IS (*pub.edb*) holds public folder messages—the folder hierarchy is stored in the directory. The private IS (*priv.edb*) stores user mailboxes and messages. The IS has the following responsibilities:

- It stores public folder messages in the public IS (but not the folder hierarchy; that lives in the directory).
- It stores users' messages and mailbox data in the private IS.
- It enforces storage, age, and deleted item retention limits for the public and private IS.
- It enforces mailbox access and security restrictions.
- It provides the engine that runs mailbox rules and custom views.
- It assists in message delivery.

 The names of these services and databases all seem to run together. To keep things clear, I'll always specify the Directory Service and the IS service. If I'm talking about the directory or Information Store databases, I'll refer to them as simply the IS or directory.

The Extensible Storage Engine

The Extensible Storage Engine (ESE) is the database engine Exchange uses to manage the directory and IS databases. ESE rates its own section here because of the way it works. It's designed to provide fault-tolerant storage, and it does so by using *database transactions*. Each transaction represents some change to the state of the database—a newly arrived message, an old public folder message due to expire, and so forth. Each database change is represented by one transaction.

As change requests arrive, ESE processes them twice. First, it spools the changes to a *transaction log file* on disk; it also makes the appropriate changes to the copy of the database held in RAM. The underlying master copy of the database isn't changed until the first transaction is complete; this keeps the master database in a consistent state. If you've disabled circular logging, log files are kept around, so in the event of a crash, power failure, or other interruption, you can often restore the entire database to its pre-crash state by playing back the log files. As each transaction is recovered from the log file, it's applied to the database; when all the transactions have been applied, the database will be fully restored.

Log files should be stored on a separate physical disk (and, if possible, on a separate controller) from the databases themselves, for two reasons. The first is so that any failure that kills the database won't affect the log files. The second involves performance: transaction log files are always written sequentially, and the database files are accessed randomly. Distributing the I/O load across two separate disks gives a noticeable performance improvement.

The Message Transfer Agent

The Message Transfer Agent (MTA) is in charge of moving messages between servers. Each server has an MTA process. The MTA is responsible for handling much of the message traffic originating at or bound for that server. It routes each message to the appropriate destination: the local IS, a connector or gateway, or a remote MTA. The MTA also expands all distribution lists (DLs), converting the DL address into a list of recipient addresses.

Whenever a message has to transit outside of the server's site, the MTA must route it accordingly. It does so using something called the *Gateway Address Routing Table*, or GWART. The GWART is a big table, not unlike the routing tables in *sendmail*; it lives in the directory, so it's automatically replicated throughout the organization. The GWART contains information about all the connectors and address spaces configured for the entire organization. The SA and MTAs update the GWART whenever a new address space is added or when Exchange recalculates its routing information.

Normally, the MTA doesn't touch messages that aren't bound outside the server's site; however, if you turn on message archiving (see Chapter 7, *Managing Connectors and the MTA*, for details), the MTA has to process every message sent or received on the server.

As you'll see in Chapter 2, *Exchange Architecture*, the MTA uses the GWART to find the best route for any outgoing message. "Best" is a relative term, of course.

The Exchange Event Service

The Exchange Event Service (EES) allows you to write scripts that run on the server. These scripts can do practically anything: send mail, look up things in databases, connect to web servers, or anything else you can code in VBScript, ECMAscript, or Perl. Scripts can be attached to public folders or mailboxes and triggered when something happens—say, when a new message arrives, or when someone posts a new message to a public area.

The Internet Mail Service

The Internet Mail Service (IMS) moves SMTP mail into and out of your Exchange network. Most people think of it as strictly for use with the Internet; in fact, it also works well when used to connect Exchange sites or organizations. The IMS allows you to configure how your Exchange servers will handle SMTP mail. For individual DNS domain names, you can control whether Exchange will send mail to and/ or accept mail from a given domain. You can also turn relaying on or off on a per-domain basis.

The IMS can also be used to route mail through outbound gateways; for example, you could configure your Exchange IMS to route all SMTP mail sent by Exchange users through a Unix box running *sendmail*. Doing so would allow you to offload all Exchange SMTP traffic bound for the Internet to another machine, presumably outside your firewall.

Connectors

Connectors make it possible for Exchange to communicate with other mail systems. I have already mentioned the IMS, but there are several other connectors available, depending on whether you install the Standard or Enterprise editions of Exchange. In general, each connector has a specific purpose, and you should only install those connectors you actually need:

Site connector
> The default communications method used between sites in an organization. It operates automatically—there's relatively little you can do to configure it. It's included in both flavors of Exchange.

The Dynamic RAS (DRAS) connector

Allows Exchange to establish connections to other Exchange hosts or sites on demand or according to a preset schedule. It's included with the Standard and Enterprise editions.

Microsoft Mail connector

Since Microsoft Mail is still widely used, it shouldn't come as a surprise that Exchange includes a Microsoft Mail connector. This conector can interchange mail with Microsoft Mail (for the PC) and Quarterdesk Mail (the Mac equivalent of MS Mail) post offices; it also allows MS Mail clients to talk to the Exchange server.

cc:Mail

Lotus cc:Mail is widely used, and Exchange Enterprise includes a cc:Mail connector. Microsoft also has a free importer that can move mail from cc:Mail mailboxes into an Outlook mailbox; it's available from the Microsoft web site or as part of Exchange 5.5 SP2.

Lotus Notes connector

Mesa Software originally started shipping a Lotus Notes connector for Exchange in 1997. Microsoft liked it so much they bought the company, and the Notes connector now ships with the Enterprise Edition of Exchange 5.5. Mesa also wrote the cc:Mail importer.

Microsoft Schedule+ Free/Busy connector

Often used in conjunction with the MS Mail connector, translates busy and free times from users' calendars between Exchange and Schedule+. This is required if you want MS Mail users to be able to schedule meetings with Exchange users, and vice versa.

The X.400 connector

Included with the Enterprise Edition, lets Exchange communicate with X.400 hosts. It's often used in place of the site connector since X.400 connections may be scheduled, and their bandwidth usage throttled, to fit the network bandwidth available.

Advanced security components

Earlier versions of Exchange offered digital signatures and encryption for messages. These features protect messages from tampering or interception. The advanced security components in pre-5.5 versions of Exchange were based on the Entrust security product from Nortel (now Entrust Technologies). Exchange 5.5 includes that same functionality, but it also supports the issuance and use of X.509 certificates for the industry-standard S/MIME security protocol.

The advanced security components include a key management server (KMS) that issues user certificates, a set of property pages in the Exchange Administrator that let you control whether individual users can participate in advanced security, and version 4.0 of Internet Information Server (IIS), which acts as a certificate distribution server.

Outlook Web Access

Outlook Web Access (OWA) is Microsoft's attempt to package the most-used functions of the Outlook 97 client in a browser-friendly form. The idea is that you can use OWA to access mail and public folders from any web browser that supports JavaScript and frames. Once you log on to OWA, you can do much of what you could do from your standard Outlook client, without actually having to install and run Outlook itself.

OWA is implemented as a set of Active Server Pages (ASP) that run on a machine running Microsoft's IIS. This machine may be the Exchange server or any other machine in the organization that has RPC connectivity to the Exchange server. You can customize the OWA scripts to change the look and feel that OWA presents to your users.

2

Exchange Architecture

*The art of building, or architecture, is the
beginning of all the arts that lie outside the person.*

—Havelock Ellis
The Dance of Life

In Chapter 1, *Introducing Exchange Server*, you got a gentle introduction to Exchange. Now it's time to dig deeper and tear into the underlying Exchange architecture, including the process by which mail is addressed and routed, where it's stored, and how Exchange security works. Understanding the underpinnings of the Exchange services is a prerequisite to planning your Exchange implementation, since you need to know how everything works to get an accurate idea of what network and server configuration will meet your needs.

Exchange Message Addressing

If you're used to ordinary DNS-style *user@host.domain* names, you may find Exchange addressing confusing at first. Let's start with the reassuring basic fact that every addressable object—mailboxes, public folders, and servers—has at least one address, and may have more depending on which connectors you've installed and how they're configured.

Each server in a site has a *site address*, and each mailbox or public folder has a *recipient address*. These addresses must be unique. Site addresses are built by concatenating the organization and site names you provide; recipient addresses may be automatically generated using a number of prebuilt styles, or you can customize them using a variety of templates and tools. No matter how they're generated, recipient addresses combine a mailbox address with a site address.

Exchange identifies every object with a *distinguished name*, or DN. DNs are so called because they distinguish objects from one another; Exchange DNs include whatever combination of organization, site, and recipient names exists for a particular object. All Exchange components try first to use DNs for address resolution. If a DN can't be resolved, Exchange will try to use the X.400 address for the object instead.

> At some point, you may be tempted to remove the X.400 address for a mailbox or public folder. Don't succumb to the temptation— Exchange requires those addresses to be present and correct even if you're not using the X.400 connector.

Custom Recipients

As long as your mail system only includes Exchange servers, you can get by with using only Exchange addresses. As soon as you mix in SMTP or other mail systems, though, you'll encounter *custom recipients*. A custom recipient address is nothing more than an address in the Exchange directory that uses some other mail system format. For example, let's say you're setting up an Exchange server for a company that frequently works with outside consultants. You could add a custom recipient for each consultant's SMTP address so that those addresses would appear in the organization directory, along with their human-readable names.*

When a message is addressed to a custom recipient, the originator and recipient DNs (which originally came from the Exchange directory) are rewritten with equivalent addresses using the format of the custom address. For example, if you send a message to a custom recipient with an SMTP address, the Exchange MTA will rewrite the addresses in SMTP format.

Address Spaces

Each connector defines an *address space*, or range of addresses it knows how to handle. Microsoft's documentation says that the "address space represents the path a connector uses to send messages outside the site." This is correct, but it might be more helpful to say that address spaces define which addresses the connector *will* send to, not just the path used.

Each address space represents a range of addresses, like *.com* or *OREILLY/ MSMAILPO/*.* The address space has an associated routing cost, which is used by

---

* You can always just type an address into your client, and Exchange will attempt to handle it. Depending on how address spaces are configured, though, custom recipient addresses may be necessary.

the MTA to find the lowest-cost path to a message destination. Each connector must have at least one address space, but it can have more, with different address ranges and costs.

When the MTA prepares to deliver a message, it will use the address space data in the gateway address routing table to find all the connectors that have address spaces matching the address. If you define an SMTP address space of *.org, the connector that owns that space will accept messages sent to any address in the .org domain, but it won't match addresses in any other domain. You can use this feature to control message routing. You can also define address space restrictions, which are applied to keep messages from being sent over a particular connector.

Exchange Message Routing

Now that you know how Exchange addresses work, let's move on to the nitty-gritty of getting mail from point A to point B. When a user composes a message and hits the Send button, what happens next depends on the relative locations of the sender and recipients. Understanding how mail flows between users and servers will be handy later. It's also important to note that directory and public folder data are replicated using mail messages. The discussion in this section covers both user-to-user and server-to-server traffic, since it's all carried as messages.

When All Recipients Are on the Same Server

The simplest case is when the sender (or *originator,* in Exchange parlance) and all recipients are on the same Exchange server. I'll call the server where the originator's mailbox is located the *local server.* Figure 2-1 illustrates the process, which works like this:

1. The originator's mail client connects to the local server using MAPI or any supported Internet protocol. MAPI connections actually establish a connection to the IS service; Internet protocol connections deliver the message to the IMS, which in turn hands it to the MTA. When the message is transmitted, the client may disconnect, because its work is done (although MAPI clients normally stay connected until you force them to log off).

2. The local server's IS service checks the local copy of the directory to see which message recipients are on the local server.

3. Because the recipients are all on the local server, the IS service places a single copy of the message into the server's private IS. It then notifies each connected recipient that new mail has arrived (but only if they're using a MAPI client).

   If any recipient address is a distribution list, the IS service asks the local MTA to expand the distribution list, and the process restarts at step 2. If any recipi-

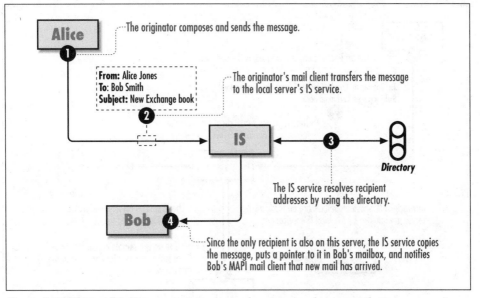

Figure 2-1. Message flow between originator and recipients who are on the same server is straightforward

ents on the distribution list have mailboxes on other servers, the process follows the steps outlined in the following section.

Note that the MTA doesn't have anything to do in this scenario unless one or more recipient addresses point to distribution lists. The IS service, and the private IS, handle all message transit between users whose mailboxes are on the same server. This is an important point to remember when you're trying to troubleshoot mail delivery problems.

Recipients on Multiple Servers Within One Site

The routing scheme used when the originator and all recipients are on the same server is very straightforward. What happens when one or more recipients have mailboxes on *other* servers? The overall process is much the same, except that the local server's MTA gets into the act. Here are the steps in the routing process (shown in Figure 2-2). Note that steps 3–7 are repeated once for each recipient:

1. The originator's mail client connects to the local server and delivers the message.

2. The local server's IS service checks the directory to see which message recipients are on the local server. It delivers mail to any local recipients per the steps outlined in the preceding section.

3. For every recipient whose mailbox is not on the local server, the IS service hands the message over to the local MTA.

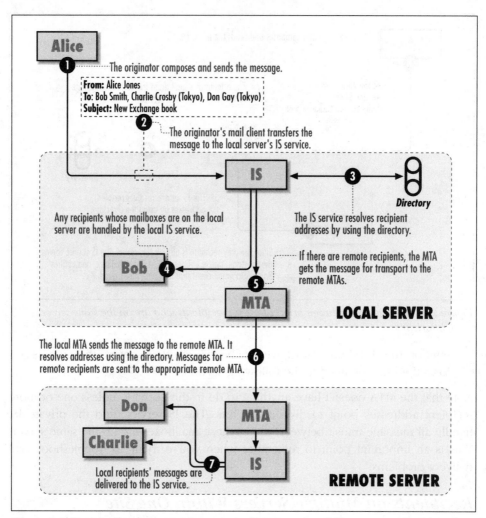

Figure 2-2. Message flow between originator and recipients on different servers involves the MTA

4. The MTA resolves the remote recipient's address in the directory and finds the remote server that hosts the recipient's mailbox.

5. The local server's MTA opens an RPC connection to the remote MTA and transfers the message.

6. The remote MTA accepts the message and resolves the recipient address to find out where the recipient's home server is. If the remote MTA belongs to the user's home server, the message is delivered to the IS service. If not, the remote MTA transfers it to the correct home server's MTA, and the process begins again at step 5.

7. Once the message arrives at the IS service of the recipient's home server, the IS puts a single copy in the message store, as in step 3 in the single-server example.

The remote MTA will resolve any recipient addresses that aren't real Exchange addresses—say, SMTP addresses or other custom recipients—by turning them into distinguished names, then using the DNs to decide which connector should carry the message.

You may also have noticed that step 6 allows multiple hops between MTAs. This allows Exchange to route messages between sites according to routing rules that you establish. You can allow Exchange to make its own routing calculations, or you can specify routing costs to force messages into particular paths.

Users on Multiple Servers in Different Sites

When a message is addressed to recipients whose home servers are in different sites, the routing process gets still more complicated. In this case, the MTAs must use the GWART to figure out how to get the message to its destination. This is a two-step process. The first step, *routing*, requires the MTA to enumerate all routes that can get the message to its destination. The second, *selection*, requires the MTA to choose the path with the lowest total cost, as expressed by the routing costs in the GWART. Here's how the process (shown in Figure 2-3) works:

1. The originator delivers the mail to its local server, which then turns around and uses the directory to attempt to resolve all recipient addresses.

2. Local recipients get copies of the message per the steps outlined in the earlier section "When All Recipients Are on the Same Server."

3. Recipients whose home server is within the site get copies according to the steps outlined in the preceding section.

4. For each recipient whose home server is outside the site, the MTA searches the GWART for a match between the recipient's address and the address spaces in the GWART, then it uses the list of matches to build a list of all potential routes. This is the routing step.

5. Once routing is complete, the MTA chooses the lowest-cost connector from the list of available connectors. This is the selection step.

6. The MTA uses the selected connector to transmit the message to the remote server. The server may be an Exchange MTA or another type of server, like an SMTP server or a cc:Mail post office.* Once connected, the remote server

---

* The remote MTA may be on the destination server, or it may be on a messaging bridgehead. Bridgehead servers are discussed in the "Bridgeheads" section of Chapter 7.

delivers the message (using the steps outlined in the preceding section if it's an Exchange MTA), and it eventually ends up in the recipient's mailbox.

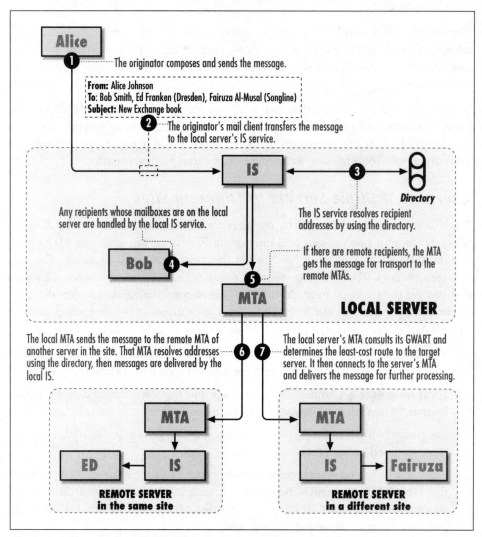

Figure 2-3. Message flow when originator and recipient are in different sites

Address types

Step 4 in the preceding list says "the MTA searches the GWART for a match between the recipient's address and the address spaces in the GWART." However, that's a highly compressed version of what actually happens. The MTA actually compares the *address type* of the recipient address with the GWART. There are three sets of address types:

distinguished name (DN)

> Searched when the MTA finds a DN for the recipient in the directory. This address type shows up in the GWART as "EX."

Domain Defined Attribute (DDA)

> Indicates a custom recipient address. The exact format of an address of this type can vary; for example, an SMTP DDA address contains only the RFC-822 address, but an MS Mail DDA address contains the post office name and some other stuff that MS Mail needs. Each DDA type is listed in the GWART as a distinct type.

Originator/Recipient (O/R)

> An X.400 address; in the GWART, it's marked as "X400."

When the MTA uses the GWART to resolve an address, it scans the GWART from beginning to end, looking for an address space whose type matches the recipient address type. When it finds a matching address space, it adds the connector that owns it to the list of available connectors for this particular message. Once the GWART has been completely scanned, the MTA still has to choose the lowest-cost connector to actually carry the message.

The selection process

The selection process that the MTA uses has six distinct steps. As each step finishes, all connectors that meet that step's criteria are passed on to the next step. At the final step, if there's still more than one connector on the available list, the MTA chooses one at random; this provides load balancing if there are several connectors with similar availability and cost.

The selection steps are as follows:

1. *Comparing the open retry count to the maximum permitted retry count.* Each connector has a setting that controls how many times the MTA may try to use it to transfer a message before giving up. This step effectively throws out any connector that has exceeded its maximum retry count.

2. *Choosing active connectors.* Some types of connectors are always active (the MS Mail, IMS, and site connectors), while others (like the X.400 and Dynamic RAS connectors) allow you to schedule when they're active. As you'll learn in Chapter 7, *Managing Connectors and the MTA*, scheduled connectors can be activated by the local or remote servers. In this step, the MTA first chooses active connectors. If there aren't any whose address types match, it chooses from the list of connectors that will become active according to their schedules. If there aren't any of *those*, it selects connectors that are remote-initiated.

3. *Selecting connectors whose open retry counts are low.* The MTA prefers not to use connectors with open retries, so in this step it selects the connectors with the lowest open retry counts.

4. *Skipping connectors that have previously failed.* Each connection failure triggers a timer that waits until the next permitted opening interval before reopening the connector and retrying the connection. In this step, the MTA rejects any connector that has had a recent failure; it also skips any connector whose timer is still going.

5. *Choosing the lowest-cost connector.* Each address space you attach to a connector has an associated cost. The MTA will choose the connectors with the lowest cost at this step.

6. *Staying local.* Local connectors are those running on the same server as the MTA; remote connectors are those running on a messaging bridgehead server. Whenever possible, the MTA will use a local connector to send the message. If no local connectors are available, the MTA will choose a messaging bridgehead server, albeit reluctantly.

If no connectors can be found using these rules, the MTA will try to reroute the message by repeating the routing and selection steps to find a usable route. However, the MTA doesn't reroute messages sent over foreign connectors (like the IMS, MS Mail, and Notes connectors); it considers its job done once the message is delivered to the connector, even if the connector can't deliver the message. If repeating the rerouting process doesn't find any connector to deliver the message, the MTA returns it with a nondelivery report.

Directory Replication

Each server in a site maintains its own writable local copy of the site directory. That means that each server can accept changes to the directory's data, but it requires that replication and synchronization take place on all servers in a site. Fortunately, intrasite replication is automatic. It takes place in a four-step process:

1. When data in a server's local copy of the directory changes, that server (the *sending* server) starts a five-minute countdown. Every change that occurs resets the countdown timer, so changes can be accumulated without causing unnecessary replication traffic.

2. When the countdown timer expires, the sending server DS sends an RPC notification to every other DS in the site. This notification contains information about the change, but not the changed data.

3. Each DS that receives the notification checks its payload against its own copy of the directory. If it doesn't already have the changes, it sends an RPC request back to the sending server DS asking for the changes.

4. Once the sending DS has transmitted the changes, the receiving DS makes the changes to its own local copy of the directory.

This replication process is a big part of the reason for the requirement that sites have permanent and RPC-capable network connections; intrasite replication happens automatically, and it uses RPCs.

Directory replication between multiple sites

Replication between sites won't happen unless you configure it. This is a feature, not a bug; many organizations don't want or need sites to share directory information. Those that do usually want to schedule and control replication instead of letting it happen automatically, which is why intersite replication happens according to a schedule you specify.

The first thing to know about intersite replication is that it depends on mail connectivity. Before you even think about trying to establish replication, you must ensure that mail flows properly between the sites. If you don't, replication traffic will quickly fill up the queues on either side of your site connection.

To enable intersite replication, you must add a *directory replication connector* between the sites you want replicated. There can only be one of these connectors for each pair of sites. The connector copies directory updates from its local directory (which in turn are received from other site servers according to the four steps above) and transfers them as messages. The steps involved in intersite replication are as follows:

1. Changes arrive and accumulate in the sending server's directory.

2. When the schedule calls for it, the receiving server sends a mail message to the sending server asking for any updates. This message contains information on what updates the receiving server already has.

3. When that message arrives at the sending server (which may take some time, depending on how the site-to-site communications are configured), it sends all the requested updates back to the receiving server as mail messages.

4. The replication messages eventually arrive at the receiving server, which applies the changes to its local copy of the database.

5. Changes are replicated from the receiving server to other servers in its site using the same intrasite replication mechanism explained previously.

Exchange Security

Microsoft has implemented four categories of security features in Exchange:

Windows NT security
> These features depend on the NT user database (in one domain or many). They provide access control and authentication to workstations and servers.

Since each mailbox is assigned to an NT user account, these features also provide a first level of access control to mailboxes.

Exchange access controls

Allow you to assign individual sets of Exchange permissions to Exchange objects and containers. The available Exchange roles and permissions are quite different from NT's built-in sets, and there's not necessarily any correspondence between the two categories.

Auditing

Makes a permanent record of security-related events (and, optionally, Exchange configuration changes) in the system's event log.

Exchange advanced security

Uses public-key cryptography to provide authentication, privacy, and data integrity. The origins of messages can be verified; messages in transit can be protected from tampering or snooping; and recipients can verify that messages they receive are identical to what was sent.

Windows NT Security Features

Exchange relies on Windows NT security for most of its access control and authentication. However, Exchange maintains its own set of access permissions, which are separate from those granted to NT users. An account in the Domain Admins group, for example, won't have administrative permissions in Exchange unless you manually grant them. The only account that gains these privileges in Exchange is the account you're logged on with when you install Exchange. Since that account must have Administrator rights on the install machine, that one account—and that account only—will have administrative access for both Exchange and NT. After you've installed Exchange, you'll have to run Exchange Administrator and give other accounts whatever permissions you want them to have.

NT user accounts and mailboxes

In most cases, users must be able to log on to an NT domain before they may access Exchange resources. You can allow anonymous NNTP, IMAP4rev1, and LDAP traffic; however, by default the NNTP and IMAP4rev1 protocols require authentication too. The account used to log on controls which resources the user may access, in both NT and Exchange.

Each private mailbox on an Exchange server is owned by one Windows NT account; one Windows NT account may own many mailboxes. Because Exchange uses NT's domain account database to control mailbox access, you can build Exchange environments on top of NT domains. Doing so requires you to use domain trust relationships to grant interdomain resource access. For example, you might put your Exchange servers in their own domain, then import user accounts from a single master domain. This is fairly straightforward and doesn't require any extra configuration in Exchange: when a user from the FINANCE domain logs on to a workstation in the STLOUIS domain, she can access her Exchange server normally as long as a proper trust relationship exists between FINANCE and STLOUIS.

There are three ways to get permission to open a user's mailbox:

- Present credentials from that user's account by logging on with it. This is the most commonly used method.

- Open it while logged on as the site service account.

- Give other accounts permission from within Exchange Administrator.

Exchange also allows users to delegate mailbox access, so that individual users can have assistants or others send and receive mail on their behalf. You'll learn how to control this in Chapter 13, *Managing Exchange Clients*.

The site service account

When you install Exchange, you're prompted to specify the name of a *site service account*. Exchange uses this account to provide a security context for its services, so as far as Exchange is concerned, this account is all-powerful. Since the service account provides the security context, it owns all of the mailbox and server configuration data. In fact, you can log on with that account and use it to run Exchange Administrator.

 Be very careful with the site service account—it can be used to read anyone's mail or reconfigure the Exchange services. Protect it accordingly! At a minimum, choose a very difficult (or, better still, completely random) password. Write it down and store it in a sealed, tamper-evident envelope, then store the envelope wherever you store sensitive materials. Don't use the Administrator account as your site service account.

Before you install Exchange on the first server in a site, you must create the site service account using the User Manager, assign it a password, and set the "Password cannot be changed" and "Password never expires" flags on the account. Once you've done so, you need to supply the same account name *and password* as you install each additional server in the site. If you're using multiple domains, you'll also have to be sure that the site service account is available to each server that needs it. This is necessary so that services can use a common set of authentication credentials.

It may be that your site and domain layouts don't correspond—perhaps you put all your user accounts in a single master domain, but you have separate sites for each business unit in your company. If you want to combine servers from multiple domains into a single site, you must ensure that each domain has access to a common trusted domain, and the site service account must live in that trusted domain.

Using Exchange Access Controls

Exchange offers its own set of permissions. Apart from the restriction that users must provide valid Windows NT credentials to talk to the server, you can use Exchange permissions to fine-tune what users can do once they've successfully attached to the server. This is useful both for controlling what end users can do (for instance, allowing some users, but not others, to create and manage public folders) and to allow different levels of administrative privilege to different classes of users. For example, you might entrust one group of administrators with the responsibility of creating mailboxes, but not with the ability to delete them.

Permissions

In Exchange, you use permissions to grant access on an object to a user account or group. Permissions have three parts that specify which account has the permission, what permission it is, and what object it applies to. For example, I might grant the group RA\ExchangeAdmins administrative privileges on the site configuration container.

The permissions themselves fall into three categories. We've already covered *mailbox permissions*; they're granted to one or more NT accounts or groups, which may then use them to log onto the mailbox and use it. *Public folder permissions* govern what users may do to public folders; you can control read, write, and modify access to user mailboxes, distribution lists, and other public folders. Finally, *directory permissions* control read and write access to the Exchange directory. (In Exchange 6.0, which uses the Windows 2000 directory, the two directories will probably be one and the same.) By default, anonymous LDAP users can read the directory, while MAPI users must log on to the server. Only accounts which have been granted specific write access may modify the directory's contents.

Exchange permissions are hierarchical; objects inherit permissions from their parent containers. In practice, this means that normally you'll apply permissions to container objects like the Recipients container. For example, assigning a given account the Permissions Admin role on the Recipients container would grant that account Permissions Admin privileges on all mailboxes, public folders, distribution lists, and custom recipients.

The permissions shown in Table 2-1 normally apply to directory objects and containers. In most cases, the permissions can only be used from within Exchange

Administrator or by a service that holds them; however, the Outlook 97 and 98 clients can take advantage of some permitted operations at the client level.

Table 2-1. Exchange Permissions

Permission	What It Does
Add Child	Users with this permission can add new children of the directory object on which they hold this permission. For example, granting a user this permission on the Recipients container allows them to add new mailboxes.
Modify User Attributes	This permission allows users to change user-level attributes like membership in distribution lists or visibility in the Address Book.
Modify Admin Attributes	Some directory attributes, like job title, display name, and custom attributes, can only be modified by users who hold this permission.
Modify Permission	This permission allows users to modify permissions on an existing object; it doesn't affect granting permissions on new objects.
Delete	Users who hold this permission can delete items from the directory.
Send As	When a user holds this permission, she can send messages with another user's return address. For example, the CEO of a company can grant his executive secretary "Send As" permission so that he can send mail that appears with the CEO's address. Users always have this permission on their own mailboxes. Server objects also have it—they grant it to the site service account so that servers can talk to each other.
Mailbox Owner	This permission enables users to act as the owner of a mailbox; they can read, delete, and modify the mailbox contents, not just send messages from it. Like "Send As," user mailboxes and server objects get this permission by default.
Logon Rights	This permission controls access to the directory; without it, users can't access any directory data. Exchange services need this permission, and it must be granted to any user account that will be running Exchange Administrator.
Replication	Only the site service account should have this permission; holders can replicate directory information between servers.
Search	When you apply this permission on an object, you're giving the holder permission to search it. Its main use is customizing search permissions on address book views; see "Using Container-level Search Controls" in Chapter 9, *Managing the Directory*, for more details.

Roles

In Exchange, a role represents a group of permissions you want to grant. While you can assign individual permissions to user accounts, roles speed up the process and reduce the likelihood that you'll accidentally give someone permissions you don't want them to have or, contrariwise, forget to give them a right they need. Table 2-2 shows the predefined Exchange roles; you can also define custom roles and apply them in Exchange Administrator.

Table 2-2. Exchange Roles

Role	Included Permissions	Usually Granted To
User	Modify User Attributes, Mailbox Owner, Send As	Individual user accounts
Search	Modify User Attributes, Search	Individual user accounts
Send As	Send As	Mailbox delegates
Administrator	Add Child, Modify User Attributes, Modify Admin Attributes, Delete, Logon Rights	Administrators
Permissions Administrator	Add Child, Modify User Attributes, Modify Admin Attributes, Delete, Logon Rights, Modify Permissions	Administrators whom you want to be able to modify permissions
Service Account Administrator	Add Child, Modify User Attributes, Modify Admin Attributes, Delete, Logon Rights, Modify Permissions, Replication, Mailbox Owner, Send As	Site service account
View-Only Administrator	Logon Rights	Administrators whom you want to view, but not change, Exchange settings in Exchange Administrator

The Permissions tab

You assign permissions to containers and individual objects using their various properties dialogs. Each object that can have permissions assigned to it can display a Permissions tab in its properties dialog. Figure 2-4 shows an example; you can see which accounts have inherited permissions and which accounts have been granted specific permissions.

By default, Exchange Administrator will only show this tab for container objects. You can turn it on using the Permissions tab in the Exchange Administrator Options dialog (see "Setting Exchange Administrator Preferences" in Chapter 5, *Using Exchange Administrator*, for complete details).

Auditing

Exchange logs a wide variety of security events to the system's event log (more specifically, in the application section of the event log). For example, if you grant a user or group administrative privileges on a recipient container, you'll see an event log message noting the change. You can use the NT Event Viewer or a variety of third-party tools to automatically scan the event log and notify you of changes. Exchange also logs messages about backup status and database integrity to the event log, so reviewing it periodically—or, better yet, automatically—is a very good idea. See *Windows NT Event Logging*, by James Murray (O'Reilly &

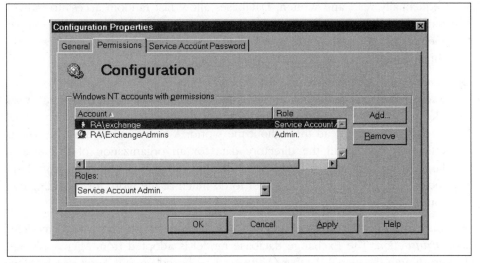

Figure 2-4. *The Permissions tab in Exchange Administrator summarizes which accounts have what access to the selected object*

Associates) for more details on how NT's event log works. Chapter 15, *Trouble-shooting Exchange Server*, will tell you how to interpret the various events that Exchange can log, as well as how to fix the problems that caused the event in the first place.

The Exchange Databases

Exchange uses a set of databases to store its directory, mail, and public folder data. This approach may seem a little unusual; after all, most Unix-based mail systems (and many other PC-based LAN mailers) store messages in either individual files or plain-text message collections. A relational database may seem like overkill, but there are three good reasons to use a database for the message store:

Reliability

> The Exchange transaction logging architecture records each transaction to a log file before it's put into the database. If the database is damaged or corrupted, the transactions can be replayed. This can often restore a database to its original pristine state without requiring a full restore from a backup. As a bonus, it also makes it much easier to keep the databases consistent with one another.

Performance

> In an ordinary file-based mail store, one of two things has to happen. The store must be indexed to allow quick retrieval and insertion of messages, or users have to pay the performance penalty of dealing with files that are always

sequentially read and written. Databases allow fast random access to individual messages and items, along with indexing. The Exchange database implementation has particularly good performance because it is heavily multi-threaded and because it uses transaction logging.

Scalability

Exchange is designed to scale to large environments. Some Exchange sites, like General Electric, Boeing, and Compaq/Digital, handle more than 50,000 Exchange users spread throughout the world. A single server must be able to efficiently handle all the directory data for an organization of that size or larger. Database storage also allows efficient retrieval of user mail from large message stores. It allows the server to do much of the work for providing custom address book and message views.

As you may remember from Chapter 1, every change to the database is modeled as a *transaction*. The Exchange database model is adopted from Microsoft's SQL Server, though the actual database software isn't based on SQL Server and doesn't require an SQL Server license. SQL Server is a fairly robust SQL database with some useful properties, which together go by the nifty acronym of ACID:

Atomicity

Every transaction is an indivisible unit, like an atom. When a transaction is posted, one of two things may happen: either *every* result of the transaction is committed to the database, or *no* results are. Atomic operations may not be interrupted by other system activities; atomic database updates thus either succeed completely or fail completely; there's no half-done state. This property ensures that once a transaction is committed, all its side effects are properly registered in the database.

Consistency

Every posted transaction leaves the database in a valid state. No transaction is allowed to leave the database in an inconsistent or partially complete state.

Isolation

Every transaction is treated as though it were the only transaction being handled. In a system like Exchange, where many concurrent threads may be posting transactions, isolation ensures that the results of each transaction are properly stored in the database and that there are no hidden side effects or linkages between transactions. Any transaction can extend or undo changes made by another one, since at the start of each transaction the database assumes that every other transaction has already been handled.

Durability

Once a transaction is posted, its effects are permanent, unless they are undone by another transaction. Ideally, a durable database is one that can happily survive (or at least recover from) media failures or database corruption. Exchange uses its transaction logs to make its databases more durable. As long as you can recover the complete set of transaction logs, you can completely restore a damaged database. If you can only recover part of the log set, you can at least restore a portion of the database, which is usually better than nothing.

All About Logging

Exchange transaction logging is often misunderstood, both because it's confusing and because the Exchange documentation makes it even more so. The fundamental idea behind logging is simple: the logs store copies of all transactions. These stored transactions can be played back later to restore a corrupted database, or even to retry a transaction that didn't complete successfully. Logging is a mainstay of relational database engines because it provides a backup mechanism for transactions to help preserve the ACID properties.

Log and checkpoint files

Exchange logs transactions. Although Exchange treats the log as a single entity, it's actually a set of files. Each log file is exactly 5MB (that's 5,242,880 bytes, for you purists) in size, even if there aren't any transactions in it. If you see a log file that's any other size, it's probably corrupted. The DS and IS maintain their own log files, each named *edb.log*. As transactions for each service occur, they're written to the appropriate log file. When the log file fills up, the DS or IS service renames it, using a sequential hexadecimal ID (the first file is *edb00001.log*, the second is *edb00002.log*, and so on). These renamed log files are called *generations*; *edb.log* represents the highest, or most recent, generation. Note that just because a log file is full doesn't mean its transactions have been committed—all commitments happen according to the rules outlined in the section "The logging process," later in this chapter.

The log files contain a number of tidbits that are useful if the logs have to be played back during server recovery, including the full path to the database files, information about which generation of log data is in the file, a signature and timestamp for the data, and a signature for the database. This header information enables the store to make sure that each log file is replayed into the correct database file, and to balk if you do something like try to restore files from one machine onto another.

Of course, the log files also contain information about the transactions themselves. For each transaction, the log records the type of transaction (i.e., whether the transaction represents a change, a rollback of a previous change, or a commit of a previous change). These transactions record the low-level modifications to individual pages and tables within the database.

When the DS and IS services are shut down normally, any transactions that have been made to the in-RAM copy of the database are committed to the disk version, and the checkpoint file is updated to reflect which transactions have been committed. If the service is shut down abnormally (say, by a power failure), when it restarts it will scan its inventory of log files and play back any uncommitted transactions from the log files to the database. This means that it's very important not to move, delete, edit, or otherwise disturb the log files until their transactions have been committed.

How do the services know which transactions have been logged? The IS and DS services maintain checkpoint files named *edb.chk*. Whenever a transaction is committed, the checkpoint file is updated to point to that transaction. The services use the checkpoint file at startup time; if this file is present, transactions are played back from the checkpoint to the end of the last available log file. The checkpoint files tell the store which transaction log files contain uncommitted transactions, and would be needed in case of a crash. If the checkpoint file is missing or damaged, Exchange can scan each log file and check whether its transactions have been committed, but this is much slower than using the checkpoint files.

Reserve logs

Since transaction processing depends on log files, it's a fair question to wonder what would happen if there wasn't enough space to start a log file. As a last-ditch defense against running out of space, the DS and IS services each maintain two reserve log files named *res1.log* and *res2.log*. When *edb.log* fills up and is renamed, if there's not enough space to create a new file, the store services will use the reserve file instead. If this happens, ESE will send a remote procedure call to the service. When the service gets this special emergency message, it will flush any uncommitted transactions from memory into the reserve log files, then shut down cleanly. The service will also log an event in the system event log; if your DS or IS service won't start, check the event log to make sure you have adequate free space.

The logging process

Logging transactions is a good way to keep the database unsullied and consistent; however, there may be performance costs involved. A simplistic logging mechanism would just log transactions to a file, then periodically inject them into the database. The Exchange logging process is quite a bit smarter; it works like this:

1. Something happens—a message arrives, directory data changes—and a new database transaction is created by the directory or IS services. The transaction only reflects data that has changed; for example, if you open a draft message in your mailbox, edit it, and resave it, the transaction will contain only your changes, not the entire draft.

2. The timestamp on the page that will be changed by the new transaction is updated.

3. The transaction is logged to the current generation of log file for the service that owns it. Transactions are written to the log file in sequence, with no random-access seeking. Once the transaction has been logged, the caller assumes that it will be properly registered in the database and goes about its business.

4. The transaction is applied to the version of the store database cached in RAM. The store never, ever records a transaction to the cached database until the transaction has been logged.

5. When the log file hits its maximum size, the service that owns the log file renames it and creates a new log generation. This log file will stay on disk until it's purged during an online backup.

6. Exchange copies the transactions from the cached copy in RAM back to the disk version of the database. This so-called "lazy commit" strategy means that at any point in time the "real" database consists of data from the database file on disk, data from the database copy in RAM, and as-yet-uncommitted transactions.

When the DS or IS services are shut down normally, they attempt to commit any outstanding transactions from the in-memory database, but not from the log files. If the service shuts down abnormally, and the transaction files remain intact, when the services restart they'll replay transactions starting at the checkpoint. If the transaction files are missing or partially damaged, the DS and IS services will do the best they can to commit any transactions that can be recovered.

 You can speed up your Exchange server's shutdown time by manually stopping the Exchange services before shutting down the server; see Chapter 14, *Managing Exchange Servers*, for details. *Never* power down your Exchange server instead of shutting it down cleanly. That's a fast route to corrupting your Information Store databases.

Circular logging

Since a new log file is created whenever the current one fills up, log files can potentially take up a large amount of space on your disk. One solution is to put them on a dedicated disk (more on that in Chapter 3, *Exchange Planning*); another is to enable *circular logging*. Normally, every log file is kept until its transactions have been committed; the files are usually purged when backups are made. However, when you enable circular logging, Exchange will keep a fixed number of log files, rolling from one to another as transactions arrive. The default number is four, but Exchange may use extra log files if a large set of transactions

Databases and Caching

For most applications, disk caching provides a big performance win with little or no overhead—applications request disk I/O and it's handled by the cache, if possible. Windows NT includes disk caching that's smart enough to order disk writes so that overall disk head motion is minimized. Many server systems also include caching disk controllers. Caching is especially popular when combined with controllers that provide hardware RAID.

Here's the killer question: if a caching disk controller has data in its cache, and the power goes out, where does the data go? The answer is most likely to be "nowhere," and that's bad news. Exchange depends on transaction logs and lazy commits, so an unexpected power failure can trash both the log files and the database. It's probably obvious that you should equip your Exchange servers with uninterruptible power supply (UPS) units, but you must make sure that your UPS has sufficient capacity to keep the server up long enough for NT to shut down properly and flush its caches.

If you're using a caching controller, you have several options. For a long time, Microsoft recommended turning off write caching on the controller. This reduces the likelihood that data will be lost, but why buy a caching controller if you can't use write caching? More recently, Microsoft, Compaq, Dell, Intergraph, and most other server vendors have endorsed the position that it's OK to use write caching on your controllers as long as they're equipped with a battery backup. This type of controller has a small onboard battery that keeps the cache memory alive until system power is restored; the controller can then write out the cached data before the next reboot. The Dell PowerEdge 2300 I used to write this book has a PowerRAID II controller with a battery backup; it easily survived the severe thunderstorms and power outages common in an Alabama summer.

arrives. As the fourth log file fills up, Exchange will commit transactions from the first file; when the fourth file is completely full, all transactions will be flushed from the first file and it will be reused. However, since these additional log files are never deleted, a very busy server can still use more than the default 25MB circular logging allocation.

Circular logging is turned on by default in Exchange. This is actually a Bad Thing, since with circular logging on, you only have the most recent transactions in the log files—older data is lost as the circle rolls around. Without a complete record of all transactions posted to the database, recovering the entire database may be difficult if you don't notice that it's been corrupted or damaged for a while. Circular logging also limits your backup choices, as you'll see in the next section. In Microsoft's defense, circular logging does keep log files from filling the entire disk, making it possible for novice administrators to run Exchange without being aware of its disk space or backup needs.

Having said that, you should immediately turn circular logging off as soon as you install Exchange. When it's on, it's *much* more difficult to recover the IS from a backup. With 10GB disks selling for less than US$150, there's no excuse for not having enough disk space for the log files.

You should acquire the habit of looking through the event logs regularly. The Exchange services all log helpful messages that will tell you your database is corrupt *before* you've overwritten the good version on your backup tapes with the corrupted version.

Log files and backups

Exchange comes with an updated version of the standard NT backup application, *ntbackup*, which can back up the DS and IS databases without stopping the Exchange services. This is a real boon, since you normally don't want to shut down your server to back it up. Depending on the type of backup you select (see the section "Backup Considerations" in Chapter 17, *Recovery and Repair*), various things may happen to your log files. Full and incremental backups will purge log files whose transactions have all been committed—both of these backup types record all changes to the IS and DS databases, so the log files are no longer needed. Differential backups require a complete set of all log files since the last full backup, so differential backups don't purge any files. If you enable circular logging, you won't be able to do incremental or differential backups. (If you stop the Exchange services and do an offline backup, you can do incremental and differential backups, but you lose the Exchange-aware features of *ntbackup*.)

One cool feature of the Exchange-*ntbackup* integration is the way incoming transactions are handled during a backup. Here's how the process works for a full backup:

1. The backup starts. Any transactions that are in the transaction log but haven't been committed to the database are committed. The various checkpoint (*.chk*) files are updated to reflect which transactions have been committed and which are still outstanding.

2. The backup proceeds. Each database file is backed up in turn, in 64KB chunks.

3. If new transactions arrive for a database that's currently being backed up, they're stored in two places: in the transaction logs for that database and in the corresponding *patch file* (*priv.pat*, *pub.pat*, or *dir.pat*—one for each database).

The patch files hold copies of incoming transactions that would ordinarily apply to database pages that have already been backed up.

4. When the database file is completely backed up, *ntbackup* backs up the patch files. While it's doing so, new transactions are stored in the log files.

5. When the patch files are completely backed up, the remaining log files are backed up, too. Normally, the last log file will be partially full; each log file is exactly 5MB, but there can be fewer transactions in the last file.

Incremental backups work differently: they just copy the log files, not the main databases. This five-step process allows Exchange to continue running while a backup is in progress. Incoming transactions generate log files; on an active system, there may be several log files generated during the backup. There's nothing wrong with this, because the backup process is designed to handle it. However, it can make the patch files grow pretty large, so they take extra time to back up and restore.

Where Everything Lives

Exchange keeps its data in four separate but interrelated databases. These databases store all the contents of Exchange's directory and public folder data; they may also store some or all of your users' mail data. Each database is stored in its own file and is self-contained, though relationships between tables will exist.

Table 2-3 shows the four databases, their contents, and their usual locations. When you install Exchange on a server, the installer will put the database files in subdirectories of the main Exchange installation directory. For a variety of reasons, these locations aren't always optimal (though in Chapter 3 you'll find a set of recommendations for disk layout). The final step in the Exchange installation process according to Microsoft is to run the Performance Optimizer, which will automatically determine what it thinks is the best location for each of the three primary databases. However, it's better to wait and run Performance Optimizer manually after you've finished installing and configuring any connectors you need (see Chapter 4, *Installing Exchange*, for more details).

Table 2-3. Exchange Database Files

Database	What's in It	Filename	Usual Location
Public Information Store	Public folder messages	*pub.edb*	*exchsrvr\mdbdata\pub.edb*
Private Information Store	User mailbox data, including messages, rules, and views	*priv.edb*	*exchsrvr\mdbdata\priv.edb*

Table 2-3. Exchange Database Files (continued)

Database	What's in It	Filename	Usual Location
Directory store	Addresses for every addressable object, public folder hierarchy, permissions	*dir.edb*	*exchsrvr\dsadata\dir.edb*
Temporary	Transactions that are in progress but not yet committed; this file only exists while it's in use	*temp.edb*	*exchsrvr\mdbdata\temp.edb*

Transaction log files live in the same directory as their respective databases; for example, the default location for directory transaction logs is *exchsrvr\mdbdata*.

Mail storage

Did you notice the weasel words in the second sentence of this section? Databases *may* store *some or all* of your users' mail data. The cynical reader is probably wondering, "Well, where's the *rest* of it stored?" The answer: it depends. Exchange offers several different methods of mail storage. Which ones are available depends on which mail clients are in use.* The default, which is probably most desirable for the majority of sites, is to keep all user mail in the private IS on the server. This affords you the benefits of single-instance storage, the recoverability and performance features of the database, and an easy way to back up all mail at one time.

Some users prefer to store mail on their local clients. There are serious reasons *not* to take this approach (see Chapter 13 for more details), but it's sometimes necessary or even desirable. Microsoft's mail clients support local client storage using two types of stores. The *offline store file* (OST) is a replica of selected folders from the server. Think of an OST as a portable copy of part of the server's message store; it normally contains the *Inbox, Outbox, Sent Items, Calendar, Journal, Tasks,* and *Contacts* folders. You can customize your OST so that it contains whatever private and public folders you want to use offline. OSTs must periodically be synchronized with the server; once that's done, though, they're self-sufficient and can be used offline.

The *personal store file* (PST) is a client-based message store that contains the user's messages. Exchange and Outlook both support PST files. Users may open several PSTs, and PSTs may be used in addition to server-based storage, not just as a replacement. When using a PST, new mail may be delivered directly to the PST

---

* Which ones are *sensible* depends on your organization's needs. This topic is covered in more detail in Chapter 13.

(actually, it's sent to the client's Inbox and then moved to the PST), although this isn't the default. There may still be a copy on the server if the message was also sent to other recipients; however, for mail sent only to the PST user, the server doesn't maintain a copy if the user has selected to have all new mail sent straight to the PST. This places the burden of data integrity, security, and backup squarely on the PST user. It also means that corruption or damage to the PST may not be recoverable, though Microsoft does provide a tool for PST repair.

Both OST and PST files are subject to two size limits. The total file size for a single OST or PST can't exceed 2GB, and no single file can have more than about 65,000 items.

Database Maintenance

All this database magic comes with a price. The database itself must be periodically maintained. The good news is that this maintenance is largely automatic and invisible. You probably won't notice it unless you reschedule the automatic tasks to happen during working hours on your server.

As with most other databases, the ESE holds on to space once it's allocated and reuses it internally instead of returning it to the filesystem. For example, if you create 50 10MB Word documents, then delete 20 of them, you'll regain 200MB (20 × 10) of space. If your Exchange stores grow to 2GB and you delete 500MB worth of mailbox data, the stores will still take up 2GB, but Exchange will be able to recycle the 500MB of free space. The Exchange databases are like a balloon with a one-way valve attached—you can blow it up bigger and bigger, but it doesn't normally get any smaller.

Defragmentation

Over time, your Exchange database files will become fragmented. This fragmentation is internal; as transactions occur, the contents of the database file itself are split into little islands of free space. Since the database must index each message component, along with the free space chunks, fragmentation slows down database performance. The more fragmented the store files become, the bigger the performance hit.

The DS and IS services automatically defragment their databases. This process, known as *online defragmentation*, is a scheduled maintenance task that runs nightly, or whenever else you schedule it. During an online defragmentation, the DS and IS services shuffle data in the private, public, and directory databases to minimize fragmentation and keep mailbox, public folder, and directory data in contiguous blocks.

You can also use the *eseutil* tool (covered completely in Chapter 17) to do an *offline defragmentation*. The difference is that during an offline defragmentation, the IS and/or DS services must be stopped, and *eseutil* can do a more thorough job of defragmenting and recovering space. Offline defragmentations can actually shrink the size of the database files to match the actual size of the data in them; they return the unused space to the filesystem. Contrast this with online defragmentations, which move data around but don't shrink the database size. The offline defragmentation process actually creates a temporary database and moves data from the original database to the new one, defragmenting and compacting as it goes. When the defragmentation is done, the new database replaces the old one.

The scheduled online defragmentation process will do its thing unobtrusively, and in most cases, you won't need to run an offline defragmentation. However, there are times when you might want to force Exchange to defragment the database more thoroughly. For example, let's say you've just moved two hundred users from one server to another, and you want to reclaim the space those two hundred mailboxes were taking up on the old server, instead of waiting for the private IS to grow into the space. You'll need to run an offline defragmentation to regain the space.

Compaction

Exchange will automatically *compact* database entries, removing deleted items and periodically sweeping away expired public folders and views. This process is akin to opening a filing cabinet and removing any outdated or unnecessary files; it doesn't increase the total amount of filing space, but it does increase the amount you can actually use. Exchange's compaction process attempts to consolidate partially full pages into a smaller number of completely full pages. This consolidation speeds reading and writing to the database as transactions arrive.

Automatic maintenance tasks

Because the public, private, and directory stores are integral to Exchange's operation, you probably won't be surprised to see all the background maintenance tasks that take place. These tasks primarily do housekeeping, cleaning out expired data and flushing data from caches into the database. (We've already discussed the lazy commit system, which isn't really a maintenance task anyway.) Tasks fall into two categories: those that run according to the schedule set on the IS Maintenance tab of the Server Properties object (see Table 2-4) and those that run either when Exchange needs them or when a separate schedule fires (see Table 2-5).

Table 2-4. Tasks That Run on the IS Maintenance Schedule

Task	When It Runs	What It Does
Index aging	Controlled by registry values (see Chapter 11, *Managing the Information Store*, or KB article Q159157)	Clients can create custom views, each of which is stored as an index in the database. Once these indices hit a certain age without being used, Exchange purges them to free up table space.
Tombstone aging	Minimum of every 24 hours unless overridden by the registry (see Chapter 11)	Deleted public folders are marked with a "tombstone." This tells replication partners that the marked item no longer exists and shouldn't be replicated. After the tombstone reaches a certain age, it's removed to keep the tombstone list from growing infinitely large.
Tombstone maintenance	Minimum of every 24 hours	This task compacts deleted items and replaces them with tombstones, which are then aged.
Public store expiration	Minimum of 24 hours unless overridden by `Replication Expiry` registry value	Public folders may have a message age limit. Messages older than this limit are deleted as part of the maintenance process.
Public store version updates	Minimum of every 24 hours	Each server stores the version of Exchange that it's running in its directory; this allows any two servers to agree on a common schema and feature set. Once per day, the IS maintenance task updates this version number to reflect any changes to Exchange.

Table 2-5. Other Automatic Maintenance Tasks

Task	When It Runs	What It Does
Background cleanup	Controlled by the `BackgroundCleanup` registry values (see Chapter 11).	Reclaims empty space formerly used by deleted items. Space is marked as unused and can be moved or reallocated by the compaction task.
Storage warning notification	Controlled by values set on the IS Site Configuration object's Storage Warnings tab.	Checks each mailbox and public folder, sending "you're using too much storage" warnings to users who are over their assigned quotas.
Database grooming	Main task runs every 10 minutes; each grooming subtask has its own scheduled interval.	Reloads and reapplies storage and per-user quotas from the directory; flushes cached directory information back to the DS.
Database compaction	Nightly at 1 a.m., unless changed.	Moves all unused and reclaimed space to the end of the database.

DS/IS Consistency

The DS and IS databases are closely entwined. For example, the directory contains information on which users exist and which mailboxes they own, but the mailboxes and their contents belong in the private IS. It's important to keep the directory and IS stores synchronized and consistent; remember the "C" in ACID? Without consistency between these two, it may become impossible to tell who owns an object, or even which objects exist. For example, if data in the directory and in the IS don't match, the global address list might show recipients that couldn't receive mail because they had no actual mailboxes in the private IS!

The DS and IS services normally keep their databases consistent without any help from you. As transactions arrive, they're posted to the appropriate services. When directory changes are replicated, the receiving server can apply them without fear—they won't apply to the private IS, and there are guaranteed to be matching transactions for any changes to the public IS.

It's possible for the three databases to end up in an inconsistent state, though. If you restore the DS without the corresponding public or private IS, or if for some reason your IS files are corrupt, you have to manually tell Exchange to readjust its associations. You may also need to do this if you lose your domain controllers, since restoring the SAM database may result in the loss of some account information. The DS/IS Consistency Adjustment page (covered in detail in Chapter 17) allows you to force Exchange to make these adjustments, using the directory as the master and adjusting the public and private IS contents as needed.

Exchange Advanced Security

Exchange advanced security provides message protection for some or all of your users. It does so by using *public-key* cryptography. Each user is assigned a public and a private key; the keys are mathematically related, but it's practically impossible to derive one from the other. Table 2-6 outlines the basic cryptographic operations, signing and encryption, and shows how they work in a conversation between two hypothetical Exchange users, Alice and Bob.

Table 2-6. Basic Public-Key Cryptographic Operations

Desired Result	Sender Uses	Recipient Uses	What Happens
Alice wants to send a digitally signed message	Alice uses her private key to sign the message	Bob uses Alice's public key to verify	Exchange computes a digest of the message and encrypts it with Alice's private key. It can only be decrypted with Alice's public key.

Table 2-6. Basic Public-Key Cryptographic Operations (continued)

Desired Result	Sender Uses	Recipient Uses	What Happens
Bob wants to verify a message from Alice			When Bob gets the message, his Outlook or Exchange client computes its own digest of the message. The client then uses Alice's public key to decrypt the digest Alice originally signed. If the digests match, the signature is authentic.
Alice wants to send Bob an encrypted message	Alice uses Bob's public key to encrypt	Bob uses his private key to decrypt	Alice's client fetches Bob's public key from the Exchange server, then uses it to encrypt the message to him only.
Bob wants to read encrypted mail sent to him			When the message arrives, Bob's client attempts to use his private key to decrypt it. If the message was encrypted to him, he'll be able to read it. If Alice chose to sign the message, the client will verify it only if the decryption succeeds.

The key management server

The Exchange advanced security system requires the use of a *key management server*, or KMS. This server is an NT machine running Microsoft's Certificate Server (included with the Internet Information Server 4.0 package) and the Exchange KMS software. You may have zero or one KMS machines per Exchange site.

The KMS' main job is to issue keys to clients. Overall, here's what the KMS is required to do:

- Generate temporary keys so that users requesting new keys can get them securely from the KMS

- Issue signature and encryption certificates to individual users enrolled in advanced security

- Keep backup copies of public signature keys and private encryption keys

- Manage the master copy of the certificate revocation list (CRL)

When the KMS receives a client request, it archives the provided keys and creates a new digital certificate for the user. This certificate is signed by the KMS, and it attests that the KMS believes that the user's keys are authentic. Other users within the same organization can verify both the user's certificate and the KMS signature; this provides an additional level of trust, since normally the KMS is the only entity able to issue keys within an organization.*

---

* How many KMSs you have in your organization will depend on your site and organization design. In general, one KMS per organization is enough for most uses. See Chapter 16 for more details.

The KMS has to be well protected, for two reasons. First, if it's offline, you won't be able to use it to issue new certificates, revoke existing certificates, or recover archived keys. Worse still, if it's compromised you won't be able to trust its signatures or revocation lists—meaning you might potentially have to build a new KMS installation and reissue all your users' certificates!

Advanced security steps

The detailed process of enrolling users in advanced security and keeping the KMS healthy is discussed in Chapter 16, *Exchange Security.* However, now is a good time to outline the steps you must take in order to provide advanced security for your organization.

First, you have to install your Exchange servers. Once that's done, you need to install the KMS, which in turn requires setting up IIS 4.0. You must also configure the KMS as appropriate for your organization's security needs. Once that's done, here's what happens:

1. You enroll users in advanced security, either *en masse* or individually.

2. You ask the KMS to generate temporary keys for each user. The temporary key is used only once; it safeguards the communication channel from the client back to the KMS. Ideally, you give each user his or her temporary key in person. If you absolutely must, you can distribute them electronically, although this raises the possibility that a malicious user may steal the key and use it to masquerade as the real user and steal her keys.

3. The user uses her client to generate whatever type of key pair (encryption-only, signature-only, or dual-purpose) you've enabled on her mailbox. The client generates the keys and uses the temporary key to establish a secure channel to the KMS.

4. Once the secure channel is open, the client registers its keys with the KMS. The user's public keys are added to the Exchange directory and can be freely replicated; the KMS also keeps an archival copy. Optionally, the KMS can also archive a copy of the private key from the user's encryption certificate.

5. The client uses its private keys when requested by the user. Other users who want to send encrypted mail to, or verify mail signed by, a user can get the necessary keys from the Exchange directory. Certificates may be revoked or rekeyed at any time by the Exchange administrator.

3

Exchange Planning

*There is always something to upset the
most careful of human calculations.*

—Ihara Saikaku
The Millionaires' Gospel, Book II

Building an Exchange network is like building a house. You could just run over to
Home Depot, pick up a truckload of lumber and materials, then go back to your
site and start hammering, but your house would probably be lopsided and fall
down. On the other hand, if you prepare the ground, dig a foundation, pour a
slab, add electrical and plumbing, and *then* start hammering you're much more
likely to be pleased with the final result.

If you're setting up Exchange for a small organization, you can probably get away
with just setting up a single server and using it, at least for now. However, for
optimal performance, you'll be better off doing some careful planning before you
start your rollout. Of course, if you're deploying Exchange for a larger group (say,
for your entire company, spread across twelve states, five time zones, and two
countries), prior planning can save you a lot of unnecessary aggravation, expense,
and wasted time.

Before You Start Planning

The first actual step in your Exchange deployment planning is simple: you have to
answer a bunch of questions. The answers to these questions will guide you
through the planning and deployment process. It's perfectly all right to say "I
dunno" to any of these questions, but the more answers you can ferret out now,
the better.

Geography

The first—and probably easiest—question to answer: where are you going to put Exchange? You'll need to know the number of physical locations (buildings on a campus, offices in different cities, or whatever) that will need access to your servers and the approximate number of users at each site. Take this information and use it to draw a map of your organization's geographic layout. It doesn't have to be complicated, and it doesn't have to reflect the actual geography; a block diagram (like the one in Figure 3-1, which shows the O'Reilly & Associates offices, with made-up numbers of users) will do fine. Your goal is to capture the total number of places and users you need to support. If you plan to have one or more of your Exchange servers talk to the Internet, go ahead and draw the Internet as a site on your map, too.

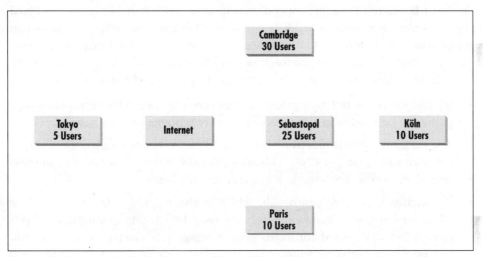

Figure 3-1. Draw a simple map to start off your planning process

Organizational Factors

Large organizations are usually pretty diverse. It's not uncommon for a company to have subsidiaries, business partners, research groups, or other entities that have or want their own separate mail servers. If your organization falls into this category, now is the time to subdivide your basic map so that it shows political (as opposed to physical) divisions. For example, a government contractor working on an Army base might be legally required to maintain a separate Exchange server so that contractor employees don't use government computers.* If possible, as you

---

* No, I'm not making this up. The rules that apply to government computer systems in the U.S. are so Byzantine that it would take a whole book—which would immediately be obsolete—to describe them accurately.

split the map up, include the approximate number of users in each subdivision; that will come in handy later.

While you may be tempted to give each department, workgroup, or business unit in your company its own Exchange server, you should resist that particular temptation. As you'll see in the section "Planning Your Servers: More Than Buying the Right Hardware," later in this chapter, you can achieve significant economies of scale by building a few large servers as opposed to many small ones.

Network Topology

Now that you know where your users are, the next step is to figure out how the various offices are connected. As you may recall from the previous chapters, Exchange can communicate over LAN, WAN, or modem links, but servers within a site must be linked by a high-speed, synchronous, RPC-capable network. You'll need to know how your network is configured because that will affect how you group your servers into sites. In addition, the number and kind of network links you have will influence what connectors you can (and should) use to move traffic between the various sites. For each network link, you'll need to know:

- Its endpoints, or the two places it connects together. This tells you which paths can be used to get data between any two points on your network.

- The maximum bandwidth available on the link (sometimes called the committed information rate, or CIR*). This tells you how fast the link between the two sites is, thus how much traffic it can theoretically support.

- The normal *available* bandwidth, which is the maximum bandwidth minus whatever amount of bandwidth is being used by existing applications. If you have a T-1 that's used for video conferencing, you can't expect to get full bandwidth for Exchange's use.

- The link type. This tells you whether the network is synchronous (X.25, frame relay, T-1/E-1, and so on) or asynchronous (modem-based connections), which in turn tells you which connectors you can use over the link.

- Any extra costs associated with the link. For example, many ISDN lines are metered on a per-minute basis. You'll need this cost information to set up the routing costs for the gateway address routing table, or GWART.

Once you've gathered all this information, update your map to reflect what you've learned. It might look something like Figure 3-2.

---

* Astute readers will recognize that CIR actually has a more precise technical meaning: the amount of bandwidth the service provider is willing to *guarantee*. A CIR of 128KB means that you're assured of getting 128KB at all times, even if you may be able to get more bandwidth from time to time.

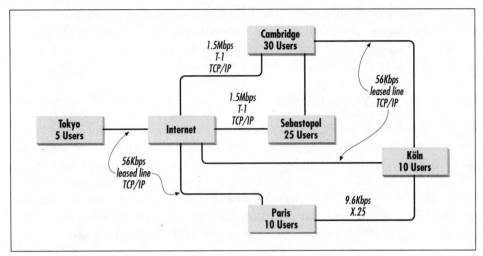

Figure 3-2. Update the map to show how sites are linked together

User Requirements

Hopefully, you already have some idea of why you're installing Exchange. If you don't, now is a great time to find out, particularly because you need to know what services your users need. Virtually every Exchange installation is used for vanilla email, but you also need to know which Internet protocols you need to support, whether your users will need to migrate from, or coexist with, other LAN mailers, and so on. The more detailed a list of user needs you have, the better you'll be able to plan your architecture and server capacity to meet them. In particular, you need to carefully consider your users' security requirements. Now is the time to find out if they will need to use Exchange advanced security, since it imposes additional infrastructure requirements.

You may also find that your users (or management) want to deploy more sophisticated solutions that build on top of the base Exchange capabilities. These solutions include:

- Information sharing by using public folders, both as discussion forums and as a way for moderated or structured communication between groups

- Customized applications that use Exchange forms to gather and process data

- Document management, lead tracking, or other workflow management tools

- Integrated voice mail* or fax transmission and delivery

---

* Some of the cooler products, like Lucent's Unified Messenger, will either let you listen to voice mail using your PC's sound card or have the PBX read your email to you over the phone.

As you might infer from the list, all of these solutions require some amount of additional planning. We'll deal with the resource usage implications in the section on sizing server hardware; you're on your own when it comes to choosing and deploying third-party products for any of these tasks.

Connectivity Requirements

Each little block on your map may have unique connectivity requirements. For example, field sales offices frequently install RAS servers so their salespeople can dial in and get access to the LAN. It's important to do two things: document what connectivity exists right now (which you've already done) and plan what connectivity might be desirable. For example, wouldn't it be nice to have a redundant modem link available between sites that are joined by leased lines? Now is the time to consider what additional connectivity you could productively use.

As you mull it over, consider that X.400 and Internet connectivity in Exchange can be centralized into a single location, or it can be distributed over many servers. Each approach has its pros and cons, which we'll examine more in the section titled "Putting Everything in Its Place," later in the chapter.

Boring Administrative Stuff

Well, maybe it's not *that* boring. I'm going to assume that you'll figure out who's going to pay for your hardware, who it belongs to, and so on without my help. Instead, let's drag a few last issues onto the table before moving on.

The first involves naming conventions. Microsoft recommends that you pick a standardized format for naming all of your Exchange servers, sites, and users. This is probably a good idea, as long as you pick decipherable names. One company I worked with in the past had a simple naming convention: first initial, middle initial, last name for mail accounts and the three-letter International Civil Aviation Organization (ICAO) airport code for the server. For example, their servers in Huntsville were named *HSV1*, *HSV2*, and so on. The organization and site names are limited to 64 characters; server names are derived from the server computer's NetBIOS name, so they're limited to 15 characters. For maximum compatibility with the rest of the world, you should probably stick to this 15-character limit for all your names, and you should avoid using any characters other than A–Z, a–z, and 0–9. In particular, avoid the underscore (_) character, since it's not legal in DNS names.

When it comes to naming user accounts, you have a variety of options. The one I usually recommend is to name mailboxes according to whatever standard you have for naming Windows NT accounts. In some cases, each user chooses her own account name; in others, there's a standard policy that everyone is stuck with.

Fortunately, you can create mailboxes *en masse* if necessary; there are also tools that allow you to quickly create NT accounts, and matching mailboxes, from an existing directory. Some large sites, like Lockheed-Martin, have written their own customized utilities, using the Exchange Active Directory Services Interface (ADSI), to read their existing X.500 directories and automatically populate an Exchange directory.

You should also give some thought to how you plan to group your users together in the Exchange Global Address List. By default, all mailboxes will end up in the same recipient container. You're free to create multiple recipient containers, but there are good reasons not to, and there are other ways to achieve the same functionality. See Chapter 9, *Managing the Directory*, for more details on grouping users; for now, just be mindful that it's something you need to consider before you start madly creating mailboxes.

Next step: setting administrative policies. These policies should govern who has which permissions on your Exchange servers. You can designate specific individuals to have Administrator and Permissions Admin access, or you can delegate that access to domain groups and put the people you want to have permissions into the groups. Whichever approach you choose, make sure you have at least two people with administrative access; that way, you're protected against their sudden absence or unavailability.

The last boring administrative topic is scheduling. You need to allow time for scheduled maintenance tasks, replication, and backups. Exchange will perform some maintenance tasks when it thinks they're necessary, and others will only run during the time periods you specify. You can limit the time periods when Exchange will replicate public folder data to avoid having replication suck up valuable bandwidth during peak usage hours. Backups, of course, will run according to your schedule. Preferably, both backups and scheduled maintenance should be left to run when your users are at home asleep, unless your users are spread across many time zones. In that case, you'll have to find the least inconvenient time for the majority of users.

Licensing, or How to Keep Microsoft's Lawyers Away from Your Cubicle

I know a number of people who earn their living installing and running Exchange networks for large and small companies. Almost without exception, they will not publicly discuss Exchange licensing! While I can give you a general outline of the current licensing policies, please remember that you and Microsoft are always free to make your own deals. Most large companies that use Microsoft products have (confidential) licensing agreements, and the best advice I can give you boils down to "talk it over with whomever you buy your Exchange licenses from." Having said that, let me share a few specifics. Of course, I disclaim all responsibility if you use this information and end up running afoul of the License Police.

Three parts of the Exchange network require licenses: clients, servers, and connectors. The server license is the easiest: it gives you the right to run Exchange Server on a single computer. Server licenses may or may not include client and connector licenses as part of a package deal; it all depends on which Microsoft product stock number you buy.

Connector licenses are a little more complicated. The Standard Edition of Exchange includes the IMS, the site connector, and the DRAS connector. X.400, MS Mail, cc:Mail, and Notes connectors are available either as add-on products or as part of the Enterprise Edition version of Exchange. If you add connectors to the Standard Edition package, the connectors are licensed to you under a "connector addendum," so called because it's a set of changes to your Exchange Server license as connectors can only run on a server. It's easy to figure out how many connector licenses you must buy: one per server in a site. Microsoft's documentation says that if you buy, say, the X.400 connector for one server in a site, you must also buy it for every other server in the site! If you buy the Enterprise Edition instead, you get licenses for all the connectors on one server. Microsoft claims (in a document titled *Concise Guide to Selling MS Exchange*, available on the Technet CD) that you must do something even more expensive:

> Once Microsoft Exchange Server, Enterprise Edition, has been installed on one server in an organization, subsequent servers must run the Enterprise Edition or licenses for its connect components must be acquired for each Microsoft Exchange Server in the same Microsoft Exchange Server organization.

This says that if you install Enterprise Edition *anywhere*, you must either buy licenses for all the connectors for every server in your site or install licensed copies of Enterprise Edition on every server—there's no middle ground. (Microsoft, if you're reading this and I've misunderstood, corrections would be very welcome.)

As part of the server license, you can legally install the Exchange Administrator tool and source extractors on as many computers as you like. For example, if you bought one Exchange Server license, you could install Exchange Administrator on the desktops of all twenty of your network support team. It's worth pointing out again that the server license is good for *one* server on *one* computer. If you want to run seven sites with one server each, you'll need seven separate server licenses.

If you're a careful reader, you may be wondering why I skipped over client licenses. I would if I could, because client licensing is one of the most confusing parts of the whole mess. You need one client access license (CAL) for each client who could log on to a server. If your servers have 2,500 accounts on them, you need 2,500 CALs, even if you only have 100 simultaneous users. The CAL covers connections to the server, not the use of the Outlook client—POP3 and IMAP4rev1 users need CALs too, just like Outlook, Exchange, and MS Mail clients do. The only exception is for Outlook Web Access (OWA) users who use OWA only to browse anonymous public folders or who use OWA to get their mail less than 15% of the time. However, OWA users who depend on it for more than 15% of their mail time need a CAL just for OWA access.

Designing Your Exchange Organization

You may not be able to redesign your company's organization to make it best fit your business needs, but you certainly can design an Exchange organization that takes three things into account: who's going to use it, where they're located, and what they want to do. The answers to these three (admittedly broad) questions will drive the design of your Exchange organization and its sites and servers.

Choosing a Site Model

If you only use one site, you might think that you don't need to do any topology planning; but read this section anyway, so you'll understand how to grow your network when it's time. The number of Exchange sites in an organization has a profound impact on how much traffic will go over the connections between those sites. If you only have one site, you have no problem, but as soon as you add a second site, you'll find that you need to have the two sites connected for directory replication, and that directory and public folder replication generate lots of traffic on your network links.

There are two ways to structure your Exchange sites. The *mesh* model looks like what you saw earlier in Figure 3-2. Sites are linked to each other, not to a central site. You can have mesh site models wherein every site talks to every other site, or where each site talks only to one or two others. As long as you have some sort of network connectivity between two sites, they can take part in the mesh.

The hub-and-spoke topology is more like the arrangement shown in Figure 3-3. Notice that each site has only a single connection: to the hub. The hub, in turn, is responsible for all message routing, so that a message bound from Cambridge to Tokyo first must travel to Sebastopol. This is similar to the arrangement that FedEx uses: no matter where your package comes from or goes to, it has to stop at the hub in Memphis.

Figure 3-3 shows a hub-and-spoke airport topology, where the hub site has multiple servers connected via a LAN. A variation on the hub-and-spoke model has the hub servers connected via a medium-bandwidth WAN (say, a 128KB frame relay line) and placed in the regional offices, with each local office using its own hub. This approach can reduce the amount of directory replication traffic on the network, but it requires careful attention to how hub servers' routing tables are configured.

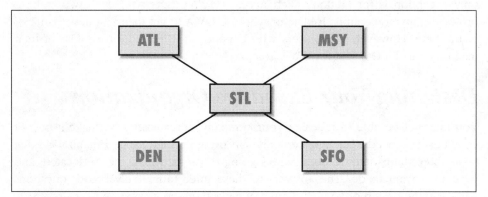

Figure 3-3. The hub-and-spoke site model

How do you choose the right model? The hub-and-spoke model is much more scalable, since adding new sites only requires adding one more link back to the hub. By adding servers to the hub, and distributing the workload by using dedicated mailbox, connector, public folder, and DL expansion servers, you can support a very large number of users on the spokes and still get reasonable performance. This scalability is particularly important when you start thinking about directory replication (see Chapter 9 for more details on why this is so). The mesh model provides better routing flexibility, since there can be several different routes that will get a message from point A to point B. The downside, of course, is that the GWART grows exponentially as you add routes, and it doesn't take long to grow such a big GWART that routing performance is unacceptable.

If you plan on having more than 40 sites, Microsoft strongly recommends the hub-and-spoke model. Actually, though, if you plan on having that many sites, you should carefully reconsider your design. The fewer sites you have, the better, since each site requires a finite amount of administrative work. If you're going to have more than 15–20 sites, you need to be very careful about scheduling public folder and directory replication, because you can quickly get to the point where there are so many updates pending that the MTA can never process all of them.

Planning for Users

No one wants to spend time deploying a large product like Exchange only to find that the intended users hate the end result. At one client of mine, users were very unhappy about having to switch from a Unix-based server—which they could tel-net into to read mail—to an Exchange solution. Fortunately, a little exposure to the public folder, POP3/IMAP, and calendaring features of Exchange changed their minds.

The best way to avoid this particular pitfall is to have a good idea of who your users are and what they will be doing. You need to know the following:

How many users are there?

This is probably the easiest question to answer: all you need to know is how many mailboxes you need to support on your servers. With this number, you can estimate how much disk space you'll need. Pick an arbitrary mailbox size and multiply by the mailbox count to get a total figure for mailbox storage.

How much mail do users send?

This question is a little harder. The total message volume you have to support will vary according to a seemingly infinite number of factors (just wait until the first Internet chain letter hits your network). You may be able to get semi-accurate statistics from your existing mail system, or you may need to make a wild guess and multiply the number of users by the number of messages you guess each one will send. Multiply that number by your guess for the average message size, and you'll have a rough estimate of the total volume in KB.

Who talks to whom?

Because of the way Exchange routes messages, you'll get maximum efficiency if users who need to communicate with each other are grouped on the same server whenever possible, but to do that you need to know who they are.

What other systems do users need to talk to?

The easiest way to roll out Exchange is to not have it talk to any other sys-tems. Adding Internet connectivity is pretty easy too, and even X.400 connec-tions are straightforward. As you get further away from these ideals and start talking about coexisting with Notes, Microsoft Mail, cc:Mail, or a mainframe mail system, the complexity and administrative overhead of your organization increases accordingly. In fact, Microsoft's Exchange documentation lists sev-eral pages of consultants you can hire to help you with migration, whether it's from mainframe or competing LAN mail systems.

How much shared data is there?

Exchange public folders provide a pretty nifty way to share data. Since each folder has its own email address, and since you can attach scripts to process incoming items, you can develop some fairly sophisticated capabilities. The Exchange infrastructure also handles replication and distribution for you—at the cost of bandwidth and storage space. You can come up with a reasonable estimate of user storage requirements by picking a mailbox size and multiply-ing by the number of users.

Are there any other restrictions?

For example, most firms in the securities industry have to meet SEC requirements that force them to review all communications—including email—with customers. If your business, or users, have special legal or security requirements, find out what they are. (Chapter 16, *Exchange Security*, discusses ways to meet these and other requirements.)

What applications do users need?

Out of the box, Exchange provides vanilla email, public folders, NNTP news, calendar and scheduling tools, and LDAP access. Since you can write or buy add-on tools for everything from voice mail to document and workflow management, you need to find out what your users want to do with this snazzy new system you're rolling out. Application needs will drive your server CPU, disk, and RAM sizing.

Planning Your Servers: More Than Buying the Right Hardware

First of all, let's get it out in the open: Exchange performance is extremely dependent on your hardware. For good performance, you're going to have to spend some money, whether you build your own servers or order prebuilt boxes. You'll get maximum performance from fast multiprocessor machines with RAID controllers; you can still get tolerable performance out of less exalted machines, but to go really fast, you'll have to write some big checks.

There's a table in the *Exchange Concepts and Planning Guide* that sets out what Microsoft thinks are reasonable configurations for various server loads. I've reproduced it in Table 3-1 for your edification.

Table 3-1. Microsoft's Server Sizing Recommendations

Server Type	Processors	RAM	Disks	Users
Small	1 Pentium	32MB	2 × 2GB	100–300+
Medium	1 Pentium	64MB	5 × 2GB	250–600+
Large	3 Pentiums	256MB	8 × 2GB	500–1000+

Taking into account that Microsoft also claims that Windows NT can be run in 12MB (it can, but not at a pace that allows you to *do* anything), let's take a look at these recommendations and how they stack up against reality.

Disk

First off, Microsoft's disk space suggestions are inadequate. A 16GB disk set allows you about 28MB per user mailbox, assuming 500 users and a single 2GB disk dedicated for the OS and transaction logs, a measly 14MB per user on a 1,000-user

How Fast Do You Want to Go Today?

All this information about performance ignores one critical variable: how fast you *want* things to run. While you might first say "Hey, I want things to go as fast as possible!," the cost of getting optimum Exchange performance may cool your ardor a bit. Microsoft's own planning and deployment documents indicate the server sizes necessary to achieve a particular response time goal under various loads. For example, the *Exchange Concepts and Planning Guide* includes a graph of response time for light users on a low-end server; this graph indicates that you can support about 300 users and still get average response times of around one second.

As with many other products, Exchange performance and benchmarking analysis is somewhat of a black art. You can use the LoadSim tool included with the BackOffice Resource Kit to build your own Exchange testbed. With LoadSim, you configure clients to be "light," "medium," or "heavy" users, then gang as many clients as you want to up on your server to see how well it handles the load. Dynameasure, from Bluecurve Software (*http://www.bluecurve.com*), offers similar functionality in an easier-to-use and more flexible (albeit more expensive) package. Chapter 18, *Managing Exchange Performance*, offers more detail on these tools.

When it comes to hardware configuration, don't take my word for it. If you're contemplating a large Exchange rollout, the best thing you can do is to size a single server according to these guidelines (or by using Dell's PowerMatch tool, described in Chapter 18), install it, and use LoadSim, Dynameasure, or real users to see how the server's real-world performance measures up before you order 25 more just like it.

server. If you factor in the space used by public folders and the deleted item retention cache, the possible mailbox size shrinks further. There are a few guidelines to remember when choosing and sizing disks for your servers:

More spindles are better

The more physical disks you have, the better Exchange can spread out the I/O load. For example, if you've set up a five-disk array, each physical disk can service a different I/O request.

Buy the fastest disks you can afford

If you're spending money on hardware, spending it on the disk system is usually the best way to improve your overall server performance. If you have to choose between the number of disks and their speed, the preceding rule wins—more slower disks are usually better than a smaller number of faster ones.

Everything has a place

For maximum performance, put transaction logs and the IS databases on separate physical disks. Put the public and private IS database files on a striped set,
then put the system's page file on the same volume as the OS. If you can, it
also helps to put the MTA and IMS queues on a separate physical disk.

Redundancy is good

If you can afford it, use RAID for your Information Stores and transaction logs.

Leave enough room for growth

It's only a matter of time until you run out of space. However much disk
space you have now, your users will absorb it all and demand more. If you
add users, that just speeds up the space crunch. If you set per-mailbox quotas, and you know how many users you want to put on a server, you can estimate how much mailbox space each server needs. Once you have that number, add a generous reserve (50% is probably reasonable) to cover future
expansion. Single-instance storage will help you some here. In the same vein,
if you're using a RAID set, don't allocate all the space in your RAID array to
Exchange now; if you do, when it's time to expand you'll have to replace
disks and rebuild the array, instead of just resizing the logical volume.

Disks keep getting bigger and less expensive, so don't be surprised if sometime
during the life of your server you end up removing its original disks and replacing
them with newer, faster, larger ones. That's the nature of the beast.

Now, what about RAID? As you learned in the preceding chapter, hardware RAID
controllers can offer significantly better performance than using either software
RAID or none at all. As the number of users on a server increases, so does the
likelihood that the I/O subsystem—not just the disks—will become Exchange's
bottleneck. Most server vendors, including Dell, Compaq, and Intergraph, normally configure their Exchange server bundles with a hardware RAID controller,
and I recommend you include one in your configuration if at all possible. See
Chapter 18 for more details on what RAID levels are appropriate for the various
databases.

RAM

Exchange 5.5 uses a technique called *dynamic buffer allocation* to manage its
memory. In short, it will always grab as much physical RAM as possible and use it
as long as no other system component needs it. You probably remember that
Exchange will cache as much of its database in RAM as possible. The more it can
cache, the faster overall performance will be. I did some brief tests with a Dell
OptiPlex (using a single 200MHz Pentium and 32MB of RAM) and Exchange 5.5
and found that its response time in Exchange Administrator (not to mention MAPI
clients!) dropped by half when I added another 64MB of RAM. As of this writing,
adding RAM is the least expensive way to boost your servers' performance; even if

RAM prices trend upward, you'll still find that moving to 128MB or more of RAM on your servers will yield a noticeable performance increase. Of course, you must run the Performance Optimizer after any hardware changes, including adding or removing RAM or physical disk drives.

CPU

Exchange is not always as CPU-intensive as you might think. I/O speed and memory size are much more likely to be bottlenecks for most mailbox servers. However, when you start adding connectors, RAS, routing, public folder scripting, or advanced security to your servers, you'll notice the increased toll these features take on the CPU. In fact, MTA servers (like the ones you find at the hub of a hub-and-spoke architecture) tend to be heavily CPU-bound. Exchange is multithreaded so that it can take advantage of multiple processors; in Exchange 5.5, there's almost (but not quite) a linear gain in performance as you scale up from one processor. This is a significant improvement over previous versions, which had a much smaller per-processor improvement factor. For CPU-bound servers, you'll get better performance from newer processors: a dual Pentium-II 300 will beat a quad Pentium Pro at 200MHz.

In general, the CPU won't be a bottleneck until you've added enough RAM and a fast enough I/O subsystem to let Exchange run full-throttle. You may want to consider buying multiprocessor-capable machines, but not adding more processors until the CPU load increases beyond 50% or so.

Network

Exchange is dependent on network communications, period. The amount of bandwidth between each client and its home server, as well as the amount of bandwidth between servers, has a direct impact on your servers' performance. This is particularly true if your network interface cards (NICs) can't process data without involving the CPU. As with RAID controllers, most server vendors ship high-quality 100BaseT NICs with their Exchange servers; if you build your own server, don't scrimp on the NIC! Adding multiple network adapters is a relatively inexpensive way to get more use out of your existing servers, especially for multiprocessor machines, since they can spawn multiple threads for each NIC.

Server roles

A single Exchange server can hold several distinct roles, as described in the following list. A single server can participate in any or all roles, but in general, the more the server does, the bigger a load will be placed on it by ancillary functions.

Connector servers

Host Exchange connectors, including the site, X.400, and IMS connectors. A single server can run several types of connectors without having any public folders or mailboxes; this is a good way to offload work from your mailbox servers to a less expensive, less-redundant machine—no mailboxes means less damage if data's lost. You can also configure several different servers to run a particular connector; this provides added redundancy in case of a failure. You'll learn more about using connector servers, or messaging bridgeheads, in Chapter 7, *Managing Connectors and the MTA.*

Domain controllers

Serve up the domain security database and authenticate logon requests. There's nothing stopping you from putting Exchange on your domain controllers, but there are two factors you should consider carefully. First is the amount of RAM and CPU time required for the domain controller's work; this overhead can be substantial if you have a large domain. The second, and scarier, concern is disaster recovery. If you put Exchange on a primary domain controller, and the machine fails, you may have a difficult time restoring Exchange. In general, I recommend using dedicated machines as domain controllers and Exchange servers instead of mixing the two.

Key management servers

Generate advanced security keys. The load on these servers is very low, since they're not used that often, but the security consequences of a compromise are high, so it's best to dedicate a small, cheap machine as the KM server. You should only have one KM server per organization, and Microsoft recommends that you put the KM server in its own Exchange site. As with any other valuable server, put it in a physically secure place, run NTFS on it, and make regular backups.

Mailbox servers

Hold mailboxes for end users; this means that they have a private IS database. By default, whenever you install Exchange, it'll be able to host mailboxes; you may want to split your servers so that one or more servers are dedicated to mailboxes, with dedicated public folder and connector servers. By doing so, you move much of the ordinary load imposed on all-purpose servers to the connector and public folder servers, which decreases the load on the machines to which your users directly connect.

Public folder servers

These servers have a public IS, but not a private one. They don't store any user mailboxes; instead, all they do is host, replicate, and serve public folders to clients. Dedicating a public folder server can greatly reduce the load on your mailbox servers; as a bonus, it lowers your administrative workload by centralizing all your public folder management. One oddity: if you're using server-side scripting to build applications around public folders, public folder servers may have heavier CPU loads than mailbox servers do. If every new public folder message triggers a script, make sure you have enough CPU horsepower to keep up.

Don't forget third-party products: for example, there are Exchange-based solutions that allow you to integrate your voice mail and/or faxes so that everything appears in a client's inbox. There are also Exchange virus scanners, workflow routing packages, and content scanners that check incoming and outbound mail for forbidden (or sensitive) words and phrases. All of these products require additional resources; many of them are implemented as services or connectors that must run on the Exchange server itself. That means that you need to do adequate research into the requirements of whatever third-party packages you plan to run before you buy and install them.

Planning Your Server Groupings

Now that you've figured out how to configure your servers, you have to decide how to group them together, both logically and physically. The process of moving servers, sites, and mailboxes around ranges from easy (for mailboxes moved between servers in the same site) to involved (moving servers from one site to another with the Move Site Wizard, as detailed in Chapter 14, *Managing Exchange Servers*), so it pays to think carefully about how your servers will be grouped.

Network placement

It's more important to have high bandwidth between the server and its clients than to have high bandwidth between servers. This is because most network traffic in an Exchange network passes between mail users and their home servers. Accommodate this fact by putting your servers on the same network segment with their users whenever possible. By reducing the number of hops between client and server, you localize traffic, thus keeping it out of other parts of your network and clearing the way for clients and their servers to talk.

If you have users spread across a WAN, you have two choices: installing a server at each location served by the WAN, or letting users access Exchange servers across the WAN. The latter approach is easy to set up and administer, but it requires a share of your WAN bandwidth. The former approach requires a server at each location, but it keeps the majority of each site's Exchange traffic off the WAN.

Sites

Exchange allows you some flexibility in your organization's site design. You can have one large site with many servers, or you can have many small sites, with at least one server apiece. Microsoft, Compaq, Boeing, and a number of other very large companies use the "one big site" model, even though they have operations flung all over the world. Why one site? There are some big advantages, including:

Ease of administration

When all servers are in a single site, you avoid the potential pitfalls involved in setting up intersite connectors and service accounts. In addition, the fewer sites you have, the less per-site configuration you have to do, since many of Exchange's settings are controlled through site-level containers.

Ease of maintenance

It's trivial to move mailboxes and public folders between servers in the same site. If you frequently have to move users who have migrated to different business units, or if you'll need to relocate public folders to handle changes in your organizations, the single-site model greatly eases the process.

Freedom from "uh-oh"

This factor's a little harder to quantify, but I'll give it a shot. You can't easily change the directory replication topology, and it's not trivial to move servers from one site to another. If you put everything into a single site, you don't have to worry about changing your site architecture in the future.

This is not to say that single-site organizations are perfect. The biggest argument against putting all servers in a single site is the volume of intrasite network traffic. Remember that Microsoft says servers in a site must have permanent, high-bandwidth, RPC-capable connections; this is because intrasite replication can take place at any time and can be very bandwidth-intensive. If your physical locations are joined by slow, busy, or unreliable links, you may be better off putting a separate site at each location and joining them with the X.400 or Dynamic RAS connectors. If you do, you can use the connectors to schedule replication and connection times to avoid burning up bandwidth during peak hours—something you can't do with the standard site connector. This is particularly useful if your sites are joined by X.25 or asynchronous dial-up links, which is still the case throughout much of Europe, Africa, and Asia.

All these factors add up to my suggestion that you use the smallest possible number of sites, preferably one.* In North America, and in many countries in other parts of the world, bandwidth is cheap compared to the cost of a human administrator. One person can easily administer even a large site, but the workload scales up as the number of sites in the organization increases. *E pluribus unum,* or "out of many, one" is the official motto of the United States of America, and you may as well adopt it for your Exchange site planning. However, there are

---

* Okay, you caught me. If you follow my earlier recommendation and put the KM server in its own site, you'll end up with two sites.

often good business reasons to use multiple sites, and Exchange Administrator allows you to administer any number of sites from a central location, so if your situation calls for multiple sites, you can use them without fear.

Sites and networks: plan them together

The design of your Exchange organization has a major impact on its day-to-day performance. The site design you choose dictates what connectors will work best for you and how much bandwidth will be required to move data between your servers—not to mention how much data will need to be moved in the first place. Some factors may dictate a particular site and network arrangement:

- If your users are in different Windows NT domains, you must take into account Exchange's requirement that all users in a site have access to a controller for their home domain.

- If you have relatively low bandwidth connections between servers, the servers probably shouldn't be in the same site. Exchange servers in the same site communicate using RPCs, which can't be scheduled or throttled. Likewise, the site connector expects to have as much bandwidth as it wants, when it wants it.

- Conventional wisdom says that directory replication requires lots of bandwidth. It can—if you're replicating lots of changes to lots of places. If there are no changes to the directory, there won't be much to replicate. Of course, extremely large operations, such as importing thousands of entries into the GAL, can cause unforeseen traffic loads, but you can schedule these mass modifications.

- Users' email traffic can be unpredictable. Grouping users who work together on the same server is essential for best performance. If necessary, you can move mailboxes between servers in the same site to facilitate this grouping. It's more difficult to move a user between sites, but it can still be done.

- In low-bandwidth islands on your network, it may actually make more sense to keep your servers in a central site and have users on the island access the server using something besides the standard online Outlook client. You can use Outlook Express (in IMAP mode) or OWA, both of which work pretty well with low-bandwidth connections. Alternatively, you can use the regular Outlook client with offline OST files to provide an efficient way to move mail without sucking up all the bandwidth.

Growth aside, there may be other factors that point to a need to redesign your organization from time to time. If you've been running Exchange for a while, consider that changes in your network infrastructure or Windows NT domain model may moot the reasons why you chose your current site design. This "oops" factor will strike more sites when Windows 2000 ships, because its new directory model allows things that older versions of Windows NT do not. For example, Exchange has always allowed a disconnected site, even one that dials up occasionally, to share the same global access list (GAL) with other sites in an organization. NT, prior to Windows 2000, does not allow this kind of sharing for user accounts, as the connections between servers in a domain must be up at all times to enable logon validation. Periodically consider how changes in the OS and Exchange feature set, along with any changes in your WAN or LAN configuration, may suggest (or require) changes to your Exchange site design.

Locations

You can group servers within a site into *locations* based on their proximity to one another. For example, all my servers in Huntsville have a location of "HSV," and all the ones in St. Louis have a location of "STL." Exchange uses location information to efficiently find the "nearest" public folder replica that a client can use. A server will always look for a folder replica within its location first, then query other servers outside its location (but still within the site) if it can't find one. By designating one public folder server per location, you can effectively throttle public folder replication so that it only takes place on the designated machines.

You can also use locations to restrict access to connectors; see the section "The Address Space tab" in Chapter 7.

Choosing the Right Connectors

So far, you've drawn physical and network maps of the places where you need Exchange capability. You know how many users you have, where they're located, and what they need to do. You've sized your servers to handle the user loads you expect, and you're ready to plan out how your servers and sites will talk to one another. That means you're ready to dip into your Exchange toolbox and pick a set of connectors.

Exchange's connectors move mail between Exchange servers and other mail systems (including SMTP-based systems). Each connector type imitates some non-Exchange system; for example, the Notes connector makes the Exchange server appear to Notes clients as a standard Notes server. Connectors function as bridges between Exchange and other systems; messages and directory data flow over the bridge, subject to schedules and constraints you apply to the connector. Table 3-2 summarizes some pertinent features of the major Exchange connectors. The "Scheduling" column indicates whether the connector can be made to connect only at times you specify, and the "Throttling" column indicates whether you can restrict inbound or outbound message size.

Table 3-2. Exchange Connectors Compared

Connector	Connects To	Scheduling	Throttling	Works Over
MS Mail for PC Networks	MS Mail post offices running on Win3.x/Win32	No	No	LAN, dial-up, X.25
MS Mail for Apple-Talk Networks	MS Mail or QD Mail post offices running on MacOS	No	No	LAN
Lotus Notes Connector	Lotus Notes 4.x	No	No	LAN
Lotus cc:Mail connector	Lotus cc:Mail 6.x or 8.x	No	No	LAN
Site Connector	Exchange 4.0, 5.0, 5.5	No	No	LAN
X.400 connector	Exchange or any other 1984 or 1988 X.400 system	Yes	Yes	LAN, dial-up, X.25, Internet
Dynamic RAS connector	Exchange 4.0, 5.0, 5.5	Yes	Yes	Dial-up
Internet Mail Service	Any SMTP server	Yes	Yes	LAN, dial-up

The site connector

The site connector connects two Exchange sites (surprise!). In Microsoft parlance, site connectors join a server in a local site (which I'll call the local server) with a list of *target servers* in a remote site. When the local server has a message for any server in the remote site, it tries the least-cost entry in the target server list for that site. If that doesn't work, it will proceed to the next most expensive target and try that. Eventually, either the connection will succeed or Exchange will run out of targets; in the latter case, the message is queued for later redelivery.

Site connectors are independent little critters. You can't schedule or throttle them; Exchange will merrily use them whenever a message needs to be routed. You can establish *messaging bridgehead servers*, which concentrate intersite connections into a single server at the local site. Figure 3-4 shows a two-site network with bridgeheads. When a message needs to travel from a user on *HUNTSVILLE\charger* to a user at *NEWORLEANS\jazz*, it will first be routed from *charger* to *HUNTSVILLE*'s bridgehead server, *bigspring*. In turn, *bigspring* will open a connection to the *NEWORLEANS* bridgehead and transfer the message. In this example, the *HUNTSVILLE-NEWORLEANS* site connector only has one server in the target list; to provide additional redundancy, you could add *charger* and *gumbo* to the sites' target list.

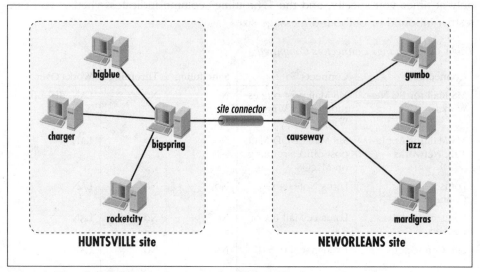

Figure 3-4. Bridgeheads concentrate intersite message flow

When you want to control site-to-site message transfer, the messaging bridgehead server is the place to do it. There's also a type of server called a *replication bridgehead server*; that's just a server that uses the directory replication connector to share directory information with other sites. You'll learn more about the role of both types of bridgehead in Chapter 7.

The Dynamic RAS connector

The Dynamic RAS (DRAS) connector joins two Exchange sites over a standard dial-up link (via either modem or ISDN). When you install DRAS on a server, that server gains the ability to connect to and exchange messages with another DRAS-capable server in another site. As part of the DRAS configuration process (covered more fully in Chapter 7), you have to specify which servers you want to call, which entry in the system's RAS phone book to use for each one, and what MTA parameters you want to use.

You can regulate DRAS usage in three ways:

- You can schedule DRAS connections to occur at regular intervals (say, once per hour every day), whenever outbound message traffic is queued, or only when another DRAS server calls your server. This allows you to tailor your DRAS schedule to minimize communications cost or delivery latency.

- You can set limits on the maximum size of messages carried over the DRAS connector. This is particularly useful if you use the DRAS connector as a backup for another connector, since you probably don't want to send multi-megabyte video clips or PowerPoint presentations over a little bitty 28.8 modem if you can avoid it.

- You can apply delivery restrictions. These restrictions make it possible to grant or deny access to the DRAS connector to any entry in the address book, including distribution lists. For example, you could allow messages from your company's engineers and manufacturing staff, but not from your legal, finance, or HR departments, to use the DRAS connector.

The DRAS connector is particularly useful as a backup connector. By setting your DRAS routes to a higher cost than your normal WAN or LAN connectors, you can tell Exchange not to use DRAS unless the other connectors aren't available. This approach lets you keep mail flowing between sites even if the bridgehead or connector servers are down, albeit at a slower rate.

 It's worth pointing out that you can also assign permissions to connectors. By doing so, you can effectively control who can use them to send messages.

The X.400 connector

As its name implies, the X.400 connector links systems that use the X.400 protocol. Exchange uses X.400 as the basis of its MTA operations;* in fact, the acronym "MTA" comes from the X.400 standard! Even as standards go, X.400 is big and complicated. It defines the way messages should be encoded for transport, how messages and directory information should be structured, and how two systems may communicate to exchange message traffic. As with most other complex standards, though, it's very flexible, a large number of configuration options. Some of them are pretty obscure, so I'm going to save discussion of how you configure and use the X.400 connector until the section "Creating X.400 Connectors" in Chapter 7.

You use the X.400 connector to define a message route between two X.400-compliant systems. Either or both systems may be running Exchange, or you can configure Exchange to talk to any non-Exchange X.400 service that uses either the 1984 or 1988 versions of the standard. Because it was designed for use in environments where network links are slow, have high latency, or are unreliable, X.400 includes a number of adjustable settings that control retransmission times, connection timeout values, and the number of open connections that can be in use at one time. By tweaking these settings, you can get fine control over the performance of your X.400 connections.

---

* Exchange 6.0, which is projected to be available "90 days after Windows NT 5.0 ships," will switch to using SMTP as its MTA protocol.

As with the DRAS connector, you can schedule X.400 connector connections* to take place at specified times, when needed, or only after a remote request from another X.400 connector system. You can also apply delivery restrictions on the connector. Also as with the DRAS connector, you'll normally install X.400 connectors on bridgehead servers in each site, not on every server. The X.400 connector isn't included in the standard version of Exchange Server (it's available as an add-on or as part of Exchange Server Enterprise Edition), so this may factor into your decision on whether or not to use it.

The Internet Mail Service

The Internet Mail Service (IMS) is a key component of Exchange; almost every Exchange site I've ever seen runs it to allow interchange of mail with Internet users and hosts. IMS is a connector that makes Exchange able to send and receive messages using the Internet-standard Simple Message Transfer Protocol (SMTP). IMS is actually a separate Windows NT service that coexists with the MTA and IS. Incoming SMTP mail is passed to the IS; it goes to the MTA if it's destined for a recipient on another server somewhere. In turn, the MTA moves outbound messages destined for SMTP hosts from its own queue into the IMS queue. The IMS translates incoming and outgoing mail to and from Internet standard formats, according to the Multipurpose Internet Mail Extensions (MIME) standard.

The IMS can be used to move mail between any combination of Exchange servers and SMTP hosts. The only absolute requirements for the IMS are that you have TCP/IP installed and properly configured. If you're using DNS for address resolution, you also need valid DNS mail exchange and address records for your Exchange servers, and access to a DNS server that can resolve the addresses of any servers you want to talk to.

Like the DRAS connector, the IMS can use NT's built-in RAS to dial into an ISP or remote access point for mail transfers. You can specify how often IMS opens RAS connections and how long they stay open. You can schedule these connections to happen periodically, at particular times, or after outbound mail has been sitting in the queue for a certain interval. One neat feature is that you can set separate schedules for weekdays and weekends (although there's no way to set a different schedule for any day during the week). You can also apply delivery restrictions and message size limits for both inbound and outbound message traffic.

The Exchange 5.5 IMS also includes some new—and very welcome—features that reduce the likelihood that your server will have spam problems. *Spam,* or "unsolicited commercial email" as it's more politely known, is commercial junk mail often sent via the use of SMTP relays. In an SMTP relay, a spammer connects to a

---

* Try saying "X.400 connector connections" ten times fast.

third party's server and uses it—without permission—to send the spam. When angry users trace the spam back, the finger points at the innocent server owner. You can turn off SMTP relaying in Exchange 5.5, and you can block incoming mail from particular high-spam domains to keep some junk mail from reaching your users.

Service Pack 1 for Exchange 5.5 (and, naturally, SP2, which includes all of SP1's features) also includes support for message journaling. When journaling's turned on, every message—incoming, outbound, or both—is archived. While this might seem like a terrible invasion of privacy, many organizations have legal requirements to track their interactions with clients, and journaling provides a simple-to-administer (as long as you don't mind editing the registry) solution. See Chapter 7 for more details on how journaling works and how you administer it.

The Microsoft Mail connectors

There are actually three connectors that fall into this group: one for Microsoft Mail for PC Networks, one for the Macintosh version, and one for sharing Schedule+ information. All three work in basically the same way: they make Exchange look like an MS Mail post office to other post offices. Each connector is implemented as a separate NT service; these services are collectively called *connector MTAs*. Incoming mail arrives at the connector post office and is translated from MS Mail to Exchange format by the connector interchange. Once the translation has completed, the mail is handed off to the Exchange MTA for further processing. Outgoing mail follows the same process, but in reverse.

The MS Mail connectors also include *directory synchronization* capability. Dirsync is just a fancy way of saying that changes to either the MS Mail or Exchange directory can be mirrored in the other directory. Notice that this is not the same as directory replication; in a dirsync setup, changes are made to both directories so they're identical, whereas a replication setup just copies changes from one directory to another.

Microsoft is pushing Exchange as a replacement for, not a partner with, MS Mail. Configuring MS Mail connectors can be a difficult and time-consuming endeavor, and this section is about the last time you'll see MS Mail mentioned in this book—I've mostly ignored it in favor of more detailed coverage of the IMS and all the nifty administrative tricks you can do with various Exchange components. However, in "Migration and Coexistence," later in this chapter, I'll discuss using the Migration Wizard and other tools to move users and mail data from MS Mail to Exchange.

The Lotus cc:Mail and Notes connectors

Not content with its current lot, Microsoft is pushing Exchange as a replacement both for Notes, which has more installed seats than Exchange, and for cc:Mail, which is still the number one LAN mail package, despite its confusing and clunky interface. Accordingly, Exchange has two separate connectors that allow coexistence with Lotus products: one for cc:Mail and one for Notes. These connectors operate as separate NT services; the services transfer mail between the Exchange IS (which is where the MTA puts it) and the connector store. Along the way, the connector services will translate the message and any attachments. The translated message is delivered to the cc:Mail or Notes server via the Import/Export service, which also copies messages from the Lotus post office to the connector store, where it's picked up by the service and delivered to the IS.

The directory replication connector

The directory replication connector (DRC) allows you to set up directory replication between two sites, even if they don't have LAN connectivity. When you create a DRC between two sites, you're creating a logical pathway that the DS can use for replication. The DRC requires you to have an established and working way to move messages between sites; you can use the site, X.400, or IMS connectors.

When you set up a DRC at a site, you specify a *directory replication bridgehead server.* These bridgeheads work just like messaging bridgeheads: directory replication traffic within Site A is concentrated at A's bridgehead, where a DRC transfers it to the bridgehead of Site B. Once the B bridgehead has assimilated the replicated data, it's replicated within Site B using the normal intrasite replication methods described in Chapter 2, *Exchange Architecture.* You can schedule DRC replication traffic in the same way you schedule other connectors; you can allow it to take place when needed, or you can relegate it to a preset schedule, which can be different on each day of the week.

DRCs and their associated bridgeheads always come in pairs: when you create a new DRC in one site, you must specify which remote bridgehead server in the other site the local bridgehead will talk to. This is required because replication traffic is always two-way (though you can selectively filter replication traffic using trust levels, as described in Chapter 9).

Planning for Public Folders

As an administrator, you ordinarily won't have much interaction with public folders. Once you've assigned top-level permissions, users create new public folders directly from their mail clients, and your work will revolve around setting aging, replication, and storage limits on folders that need them. You may also create public folders from Network News Transfer Protocol (NNTP) newsfeeds, and as you'll see later on, you can build fairly complex applications that use public folders as their storage mechanism. Before you can put your feet up and relax, you have some up-front work to do: you need to plan where your public folders will be stored and how they'll be replicated.

When users look at their organization's public folders, they see the entire public folder hierarchy. This hierarchy is replicated as part of the directory, so every server has the list of folders available. The actual folder contents are stored on various servers—you can host a single public folder on a server, or one server can hold all the folders in your organization. No matter how you distribute and replicate public folders, users will always see the entire hierarchy.

Planning public folder distribution

The easiest method of planning public folders is just to put all folders on a single server. This removes any need for distribution or replication, since all the data is on a single box. However, this can impose quite a load on that server, and if you have users in many different physical locations you'll burn a lot of bandwidth just getting folder data from its home in Denver to clients in Dakar, Dresden, and Durban.

The obvious solution to the load problem is to put different folders on different servers. Since the public folder hierarchy is automatically replicated, the mail client can automatically figure out which server holds whatever folder the user's trying to read. This doesn't solve the bandwidth problem, though; it just spreads it out. Instead of having all your remote users banging on the cable to Denver, now you have the same total load split (evenly or not) between Atlanta, Chicago, Dallas, and Frankfurt.

So, on to the next solution: *public folder replication*. Each item in a public folder is just a message, and Exchange can use its replication process to copy folder data between servers, whether or not they're in the same site. A *source folder* can be replicated to one or more *public folder replicas*. Each replica is an exact copy of the original; all the forms, permissions, and messages in the source folder are faithfully preserved. A change in any replica—say, a new message posted to a replica in Moscow—will be propagated to all other replicas. This makes all replicas equal, as there's no central master copy. Since folder updates are just messages, they're subject to the vagaries of message flow, so there's no guarantee that folder updates will happen in any predictable order or interval. The good news is that you can schedule replication to happen only when you want it to, and you can set a ceiling on replication message size to keep replication from choking your network links.

To affinity... and beyond

Even though each client can see the entire folder hierarchy, a public folder client will usually be able to see contents of folders that are hosted within the client's local site,* but not those that are hosted in other sites. (If you have directory replication turned on, the folder hierarchy will be replicated even if the folder contents aren't.) Exchange does this on purpose, to avoid flooding the network with folder traffic; the order in which clients search for and use public folder replicas is at least partly under your control. When a user opens a public folder, the Exchange/Outlook client will first contact the public folder server for that user's home server and look for folder contents there. If it can't make the connection, Outlook will try connecting to each server in the site that has a replica of the desired folder. The first successful connection is used to retrieve the requested folder contents. If no connection succeeds, ordinarily the folder retrieval would fail and the user would be left staring at an empty folder. Fortunately, you can stamp out this sorry state of events by using *public folder affinity*.

"Affinity" means "attraction to or relationship with," so you might guess that public folder affinity specifies a preferred relationship between public folder clients and servers. That's exactly what it does: an affinity relationship allows clients in one site to connect to public folder replicas in another site without replicating the folders themselves. Each affinity relationship includes a connected site cost, so you can specify a particular search order for intersite public folder access. For example, if you configure the *HOUSTON* site to have affinity with *DENVER* at a cost of 20 and with *LA* at a cost of 35, clients in *HOUSTON* will always try to fetch their folder data from *DENVER* first, then *LA*.

To set up affinity between two sites, the sites must be connected via an RPC-capable network, and there must be a trust relationship between the user's site and the affinity site. As long as you meet these conditions, public folder affinity is a simple way to improve your users' access to public folder data without scattering replicas all over the place. (For more information about configuring public folder affinity, see the section "How Do Clients Get Public Folder Data?" in Chapter 10, *Managing Public Folders*.)

Public folder scripting and the Exchange Scripting Agent

Exchange 5.5 introduces the capability of attaching scripts to public folders. These scripts can do just about anything: send mail, make appointments, look up things in databases, and so on. Scripts can be run when items in a public folder are added or deleted. This capability is implemented by the Exchange Scripting Agent (ESA). ESA runs alongside the Exchange Event Service (EES), which watches for folder changes and fires the appropriate ESA script.

---

* Clients who read public folders via NNTP don't have this restriction.

There are two areas where forethought in implementing ESA will save you trouble later. The first is security. By default, only folder owners can create, save, or edit scripts, and only users with permission to use EES can run scripts manually. Scripts run with the permissions of the last account to save the script, so they never have more access than the account that created them. This means that you have to closely monitor which users have permissions to create scripts and what permissions their accounts have. Since ESA scripts are just programs, you also have to be wary of poorly written, buggy, or malicious scripts, since they can chew up CPU time or cause other undesirable damage.

The second thing to plan for is resource usage. Since ESA scripts fire whenever the public folder's contents change, busy public folders can cause your servers to burn lots of CPU time just processing scripts. If you plan on deploying ESA-based applications, consider using a separate public folder server, preferably one with multiprocessor capability. That'll save you from having to rehome your public folders later on.

Planning Internet Connectivity

By this point in the chapter, you've probably decided how much Internet connectivity you want. Most Exchange sites run the IMS so they can interchange mail with Internet hosts, and there's relatively little planning necessary to get the IMS up and going—but that's not the same as *no* planning. There are a few things you should consider before rolling Internet access out to all your users.

How mail gets moved

When an Exchange user sends mail to an Internet user, the mail flows according to the steps outlined in Chapter 2. When the Exchange server sees an address that falls into an address space assigned to the IMS, it copies the message from the MTA queue to the IMS queue, provided that the delivery restrictions on the connector allow the message to go through. Eventually, perhaps at the next scheduled connection, the IMS will reach that message in the queue and the message will be processed. For each outbound message, the IMS looks up the DNS MX records for the target host. If that succeeds, it will then open an SMTP connection to port 25 of the matching IP address. If the connection succeeds, it will identify itself, possibly using Extended SMTP (ESMTP) if the remote end supports it, and deliver the message. If the recipient address is unknown, a nondelivery report (NDR) will be returned to the sender, following the process for inbound mail. If the DNS resolution fails, the message bounces and an NDR is generated. If the SMTP connection fails, the message will sit in the queue until the next delivery attempt.

Inbound messages follow pretty much the same trail, but in reverse. A host opens an SMTP connection to the IMS, which accepts the connection if the IMS restriction list allows incoming mail from that domain. Once the connection is established, the sending server will send the list of message recipients to the IMS, and the IMS will accept the message. If the recipient address doesn't exist, or if a routing restriction prevents delivery, the IMS will return an NDR to the sender. If the address is okay, the IMS converts the message from MIME format to Exchange format, then hands it over to the MTA, which will then move and route the message as necessary to get it to the recipient's mailbox. For a lot more detail on this process, see Chapter 8, *Managing the Internet Mail Service.*

The IMS can consume a significant amount of CPU time and network bandwidth on moderately to heavily loaded servers because it has to reformat every incoming and outbound message. For that reason, and because the IMS has to be stopped and restarted whenever you change its configuration, I recommend putting it on a connector server, either by itself or with other connectors. Even if bandwidth isn't a concern, large sites will generate lots of IMS traffic. The number of messages in the inbound and outbound IMS queues will fluctuate, depending on your traffic, so you may need to allocate extra space for the queues if your connection intervals are long.

How clients connect

Even though Outlook 97/98 has lots of really cool features, not everyone can or will run it. In recognition of this fact, Microsoft has made Exchange 5.5 support other protocols for retrieving mail. You can use standard POP3 or IMAP4rev1 clients like Eudora, Netscape Communicator, or *pine* to pick up messages, but you lose many of the features available with the Outlook and Exchange clients, like access to the Exchange address book. (With an LDAP-capable mailer, you can use LDAP to access the directory, as you'll see.)

You can control whether individual servers and sites accept POP3 and IMAP4rev1 connections, and what type of authentication and encryption clients may use with those protocols. About the only decision you have to make is whether or not to support these protocols in your system; the IMS automatically handles properly authenticated incoming requests, so the client never knows it's not talking to a Unix box.

Providing Outlook Web Access

Exchange 5.5 also includes another useful feature for people who aren't running Outlook. Known as Outlook Web Access (but universally called OWA), this add-on is a set of HTML pages and scripts that run on an IIS server in your domain. With these pages, you can do most of what you can do with the Outlook client, including accessing public folders, using the Exchange global address list, and scheduling things with the calendar. The screen shot in Figure 3-5 shows OWA in use; it's interesting to note that you can customize the HTML and scripts that OWA uses to give OWA the interface you prefer.

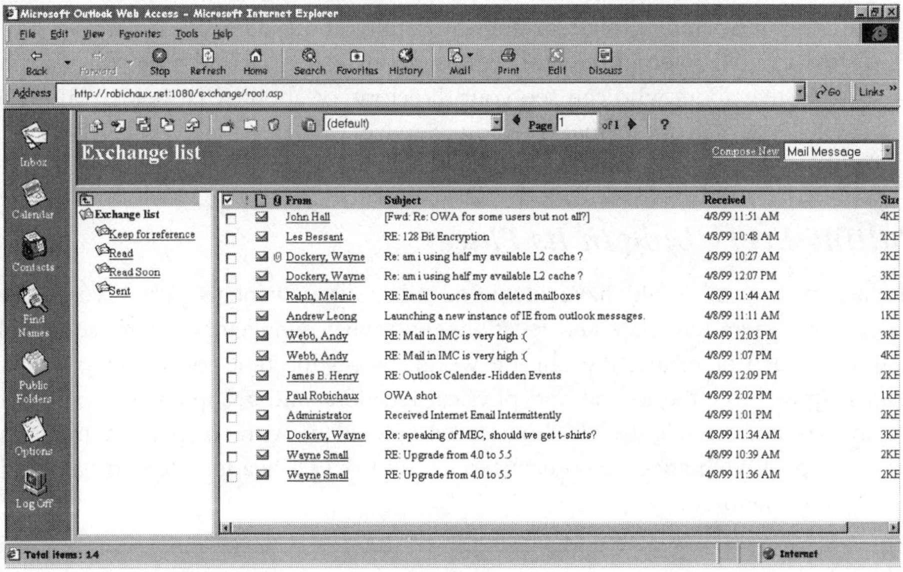

Figure 3-5. OWA in action

If you decide to install and run OWA, you'll need to plan on having a server running version 4 of Microsoft's Internet Information Server. It's probably a good idea to put this on a separate machine (or perhaps on the connector server) so that it doesn't tie up your mail servers.

Handling NNTP, chat, and LDAP access

Exchange 5.5 also supports two useful Internet protocols:

Network News Transfer Protocol (NNTP)
> Used to carry Usenet articles from place to place. You can allow authenticated or anonymous NNTP connections to your public folders, and you can use Exchange to send and receive Usenet feeds via NNTP. Usenet can consume literally gigabytes of space per day, and the CPU load required to handle a feed scales directly with the number and size of incoming articles. If you intend to use Exchange as a heavy-duty NNTP server, plan to put extra RAM and disk space into a multiprocessor box to handle it.

Lightweight Directory Access Protocol (LDAP)
> Provides a standard way for clients to query directories. Exchange's directory is fully exposed for anonymous read access via LDAP; you can optionally

require authentication for read access, and with Exchange 5.5 you can enable authenticated or anonymous write access, too. Since only Exchange/Outlook clients can access the native Exchange directory, LDAP access is a real boon to people who are using alternate clients or who are outside the organization. As part of your planning process, think carefully about who you'd want to have access to your internal directory information; you may find that you want to be selective about who can see your directory, or about what fields you make visible. You can force the Directory Service to hide some, or all, directory fields when anonymous LDAP users connect, as described in Chapter 9.

Putting Everything in Its Place

At this point, you should have identified where you want to put servers, how you'll group them into sites and locations, and what connectors you'll use to link them with each other and the outside world. Now's the time to update your network map to show the logical and physical locations and groupings of your servers and connectors. Figure 3-6 shows a completed network map for a medium-sized company with about 1900 users spread out over a headquarters in San Francisco and six field offices.

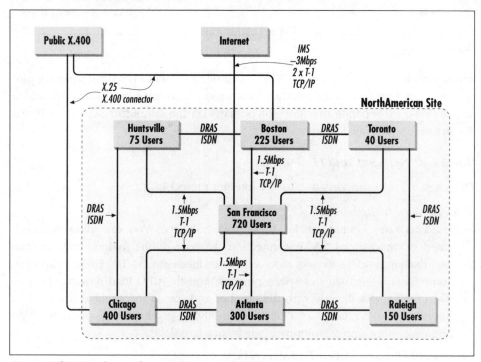

Figure 3-6. Network map for a medium-sized company

Some interesting features in this particular map are the result of points mentioned earlier in the chapter:

- All seven offices are in a single site. Since the offices are all linked to head-quarters with high-speed links, putting all servers into a single site reduces the workload on the Exchange administrators. They can easily move user mail-boxes and public folders between servers. Because all servers at each office are in the same site, there are no site connectors.

- Each site has an ISDN line. These lines are used in conjunction with the DRAS connector to provide both redundancy and an alternate message path. By adjusting routing costs, administrators can selectively reduce congestion over the field office-to-headquarters links.

- The San Francisco, Chicago, and Boston offices have separate connector serv-ers. The San Francisco connector server hosts the IMS for the entire organiza-tion, while Chicago and Boston run X.400 connectors. The only single point of failure in this design is the IMS, since there's only one, but for this organiza-tion that's an acceptable tradeoff.

- Although it's not explicitly shown, the servers in each office are grouped into locations. This reduces the overhead of retrieving public folder replicas, since offices with multiple servers will look first within their own location before tying up bandwidth to fetch folder data from other offices' servers.

When you have finished your planning process, the end result will be something like Figure 3-6. You may find it helpful to show individual servers at each loca-tion or site so you can designate public folder locations, show which servers will be hosting connectors, and so forth.

Migration and Coexistence

The fastest and easiest way to get Exchange going is to install it *before* you have lots of users, then add new users as they arrive—remember that strategy if you start your own small business! For companies with established mail systems, though, an abrupt move from the current mail system to a brand-new one is a non-starter. Users want to be able to access their old mail from the new system, and in most organizations there will be pockets of users who for whatever reason are stuck with (or stick themselves with) the legacy mail systems. In addition to the drastic "everyone gets Exchange right now" strategy, there are two alterna-tives: *migration* and *coexistence*.

Let's take migration first. When the Mormon pioneers migrated from Illinois to Utah in the 1840s, they did so under threat of extermination from the governor of Illinois. They moved from one area to another, taking their belongings with them and seeking a better place to live. Like those pioneers, when mail users migrate they usually do so under threat from their administrators, and they move as many of their belongings—mail messages, contacts, and collaboration data—as possible. Also like those hardy trailblazers, users can migrate in phases, with one group moving at a time, or they can migrate all at once. Exchange includes a variety of tools to ease the migration process, including the Migration Wizard.

Coexistence is the process of keeping your existing mail systems around and making them talk to Exchange. The connectors we've already discussed in this chapter are designed to facilitate coexistence with various LAN-based mail systems, the Internet, and X.400 systems; there are also other connectors for SNADS, PROFS, ALL-IN-1, and other mainframe mail systems. Most organizations that choose to keep both Exchange and another mail system on the payroll do so for one of two reasons. The first is the cost of the installed base: for a company like Ford, which has an extremely large amount of money invested in a PROFS mail system, the cost of moving everyone to Exchange is prohibitive. The other is the cost of upgrading; by the time you buy licenses for all the Exchange seats you need, buy adequate server hardware for all those users, and upgrade any older machines that can't run whatever client software you standardize on, you've spent a pretty penny.

How Migration Works

Out of the box, Exchange includes migration tools for importing mail and user data from six different mail systems:

- Microsoft Mail for PC Networks (version 3.x)
- Microsoft Mail for AppleTalk Networks, version 2.x, 3.x, and 4.x (known now as Quarterdeck Mail)
- Lotus cc:Mail (version 2.x, 6.x, or 8.x)
- Novell GroupWise (version 4.1)
- Netscape/Collabra Collabra Share (versions 1.x and 2.x)
- Compaq/Digital Equipment's ALL-IN-1 (version 2.3 or later)
- IBM's PROFS and OfficeVision (all versions)
- Verimation's MEMO for MVS, version 3.2.1 or later

Of course, that doesn't mean that you can migrate only from these systems. Third-party companies, like Simpler-Webb (*www.swinc.com*) offer migration tools for systems including Hewlett-Packard's OpenMail and Spry's AirMail. If you have a mail system that's not supported by Microsoft, spend a few minutes checking the Web to see if there's a third-party tool to ease your migration.

Each of these systems can be used as a migration source from which Exchange will import some amount of data. Exactly what gets imported varies from source to source; for example, the MS Mail importer is smart enough to import messages, attachments, and schedule data, but the GroupWise importer (for example) only handles mail and address book entries.

There are three tools involved in the migration process: source extractors, the Migration Wizard, and the Exchange Administrator tool. Each of them has its own role to play in the grand scheme of things:

Source extractors

Extract data from the migration source and reformat it so the Migration Wizard can handle it. What data you can extract from a migration source depends entirely on how clever the extractor is; each of the systems listed above has its own source extractor. The output of the extractor is usually an ASCII file full of comma-separated values (CSVs); if need be, you can edit these values yourself to modify the data sent to the Migration Wizard.

Migration Wizard

Takes the output from a source extractor and bulk-loads it into the Exchange directory. The Wizard also includes the source extractors for MS Mail, Collabra Share, GroupWise, and cc:Mail. If you're using one of these four systems, the Wizard will extract the data and load it into the directory; if you're not, and you've generated a migration file using a source extractor, the Wizard will ingest it and use it.

Exchange Administrator

Turns a list of Windows NT or NetWare accounts into a set of mailboxes. You can also use Exchange Administrator to edit the directory schema by adding custom attributes that appear in each directory record. For example, you could add an employee ID number or security clearance field as a custom attribute. You also use Exchange Administrator to set the default addresses for each address type your site supports. Properties and permissions on individual distribution lists and mailboxes are set using the Administrator program.

The actual migration process looks something like this:

1. You identify a set of users who are going to migrate and schedule their migration. While you certainly could migrate all your users at once (a so-called single-phase migration), that approach is best for small numbers of users. If you were moving 15,000 users from MS Mail to Exchange, it would be best to break up the migration into multiple phases and move one bunch at a time.

2. You identify the migration source and run the appropriate source extractor (or the Migration Wizard, if you're using one of the four supported systems). This produces a CSV file that the Migration Wizard can import. If you're using one of the systems supported by the Migration Wizard, it will handle the process of importing information, but you can still generate a CSV file if you want to.

3. If you need to massage the CSV data—perhaps to add attributes that the source extractor didn't handle—you can edit it, then use the *header.exe* tool from the BackOffice Resource Kit (BORK) to register your changes in the directory schema.

4. You use the Migration Wizard to import the CSV file if you have one. If you're migrating users from one of the magic four systems, the Wizard will automatically import data straight from the mail system, with no intervening CSV file.

Of course, these steps don't take into account all of the skull sweat expended before the migration starts!

Planning a Migration

Migration planning can be nerve-wracking. The prospect of doing something wrong and losing all of your CEO's mail is pretty daunting for most administrators. The cost and difficulty of a migration is proportional to the number of users you're migrating; for large projects (say, more than 5,000 users), you might consider reading Tony Redmond's excellent book, *Exchange Server 5.5 Planning, Deployment, and Implementation* (Digital Press), to get a more in-depth view of the planning process that Digital consultants use when migrating Fortune 500 companies to Exchange.

For the moment, though, I'll assume you're ready to press on with your planning without reading another 500-page book. There are nine relatively simple steps to planning a happy and successful migration; each step has its own section below. However, before you read over the steps and charge off to do your own migration, consider whether you would be better off to hire a third party to do it. A good consulting organization will have done dozens or even hundreds of migrations before they tackle yours, meaning that they'll bring some very useful experience to your side of the table. They're less likely to make critical mistakes during the process than you are, and that's welcome too.

Choose a migration type

You can migrate everyone at once in a massive single-phase migration, or you can take smaller steps and migrate one small group at a time. Single-phase migrations work best under these conditions:

- You have a small number of users. Migration takes time, and large migrations take more time.

- Your users are reasonably close to each other; it's hard to coordinate a large migration across multiple time zones, continents, and so on.

- You have time to build, install, and shake down your Exchange servers well before the migration period. You'll need enough time to avoid later surprises.

- You either don't want to or cannot keep your existing mail system around for a coexistence period while you slowly move users over in little clumps.

Multiple-phase migrations are popular because they reduce the overhead, time, and risk involved with a "big bang" single-phase migration. As you prepare to migrate each group of users, you can set up and test their servers and clients, fixing any problems you find with less deadline pressure. Of course, multiphase migrations require that your legacy mail system will remain available as long as you need it to, and that this migration type also allows you to go through the migration process several times, fine-tuning as you go.

Build your servers

The sooner you have your servers up, the better—you can begin installing and configuring your connectors, setting up test accounts, and so on. If your servers are set up well before the migration, you'll have enough time to verify that your Exchange servers can talk to the outside world and any systems you want to coexist with.

Build your applications

If you're deploying new Exchange-based applications, the best time to build them is before your migration starts. That way, they're ready and tested on Day 1 of the new regime. If you're converting older applications to run with Exchange, you may need extra time to design new forms, write ESA scripts, or rebuild your MAPI/Extended MAPI client software.

Migrate user accounts and mailboxes

When you're satisfied that your servers, connectors, and applications are ready, you can start migrating users from the old system. This may involve creating new NT domain accounts, writing your own tools to move data that the source extractor for your mail system doesn't handle, or even hiring outside help. Most users won't consider a migration successful unless their old mail makes it over to the new system, so this step is particularly important.

Provide coexistence

As you migrate users, make sure you can keep mail flowing to, and from, the old system. This is super-important for multiphase migrations, since a user who's migrated already may still need to talk to users who remain on the old system.

Migrate calendar and contact data

Microsoft's messaging products keep calendar and contact data as entries in special folders. Other systems have their own conventions. The MS Mail, Notes,

GroupWise, and mainframe system extractors all have some capability (ranging from robust to rude) for migrating this data, too. However, this stuff takes a back seat to getting mail migrated and making sure that Exchange and the old system can coexist.

Migrate lists, public folders, and bulletin boards

The Migration Wizard may or may not correctly handle all your users' old distribution lists and public data-sharing areas. If it doesn't, you can easily recreate the public folders you need (say, a public folder for sales lead tracking), then forward messages from the old system's store to the email address of the public folder. You can also build your own source extractor (as described in Appendix A of Microsoft's *Exchange Migration Guide*), but that's probably overkill for most needs.

Provide remote access

If you have users who depend on remote access, don't forget them! If you need to offer POP3 or IMAP4rev1 access, turn it on where necessary. Make sure you have enough Internet and RAS capability to handle the expected user load, and remember to migrate mail and data stored on laptops and other systems that may not be permanently connected to your network.

Do lots of testing

Look for volunteers. That's the single best suggestion I can make. Migrate your own account first. Once you're satisfied that your mail is intact, migrate the accounts for all the other workers who are helping to plan and execute the migration. Once any glitches have been resolved, find some ordinary users and use them as guinea pigs. Thorough early testing will prevent those dreaded phone calls and user visits asking "Where did all my old mail go?" or "Why can't I send mail to Ferguson & Bardell any more?"

A Word About Coexistence

Coexistence planning revolves around connectors. That's because the connectors you use are what allow messages to flow between Exchange and your legacy mail system. If you want your Exchange server to coexist with Microsoft Mail, cc:Mail, Notes, or GroupWise, it's largely a matter of setting up the connectors and sitting back to watch the mail move around. Actually, that's somewhat of an oversimplification, but in this book I'm not going to devote any time to coexisting with these older systems. Exchange itself provides some gateways and connectors, as you've seen; for connecting to other systems, the usual solution is to use SMTP and the Exchange IMS.

## 4

Installing Exchange

> *A monkey could install Exchange.*
> —Charles Eliot, Microsoft program manager
> "Deploying Exchange, Part 1," presentation
> at the 1998 Exchange Conference

It follows that before you can do anything with Exchange, you'll have to install it. The tricky part is installing the first server in a site; once you have one functioning server, it's fairly easy to add additional servers to that site. Things get interesting again when you want to add more sites and configure them to talk with one another.

Of course, as with any installer that meets the Windows logo requirements, the Exchange installer offers some choices for deciding what you install and where it goes. The Exchange installation process also has its own workflow, which you'll understand by the time you get done with this chapter.

Before You Start Installing

If you were paying attention in the preceding chapter, you know how important it is to plan out your Exchange installation process before you actually dive in and start ripping the shrink-wrap off your CDs. By now, you should already have planned the topology of your Exchange organization, set up your user accounts (or at least figured out how you'll migrate them), and purchased appropriately sized servers. The last thing you need to do before installation is review the installation process; this will help insulate you from unpleasant surprises during the actual installation.

Understanding What You Can Do with the Installer Utility

The installer has to install the actual Exchange software; this covers a myriad of modifications to various parts of your system, including a ton of new registry entries and a big load of new and modified system DLLs. Of course, all this is in addition to the actual Exchange components that go in the installation directory! The installer also has some other tasks:

- It has to validate the service account to make sure that the credentials you supply are valid.

- After installing the core components and their support files and registry entries, it has to start the system attendant and the DS.

- It has to create and populate an empty set of DS and IS databases for that machine. They're not entirely empty, since the directory will be populated with objects representing the new server, along with site and organization objects if the server is the first one installed in a new site. When you join an existing site, the setup program connects to the target server you specify and modifies its directory, adding objects that represent the new server. When the changes are completed, the new server requests a partial replication update from the remote server. Making the changes this way means that, if setup fails on the new server, its directory information still exists in the site directory.

- It has to start the newly installed Exchange services. Without this step, your new server would just sit there like a big lump instead of processing traffic. In one case, as will be explained in the later section "Replacing a failed server," you don't want the services started, and there's a way to skip this step.

- Once all the necessary components are installed, it has to request a full directory replication update if there are other servers in the site. This step pulls in the contents of the GAL and other information that wasn't replicated during the earlier replication.

There are other steps that may be required, depending on whether you install any optional connectors or components like the key management server (KMS).

Installing the first server in a site

When you install the first server in a site, the setup application asks you for a site name. It may also ask you for an organization name, if it doesn't detect any other sites available. The installer will create new directory objects for the site and organization. Once you've named these objects, you *cannot* rename them, so choose your names carefully! (You can, however, change the display name used in Exchange Administrator, which is mostly equivalent to renaming.)

Installing a server in an existing site

When you install a server into an existing site, you'll have to supply the name of a server in the site. The installer will contact the site and register the newly created server. For this connection to succeed, you'll have to have a working intrasite network connection, with RPC capability. If you don't, the new server won't be able to register itself and installation will fail.

A secondary side effect of this registration is that an aborted installation can result in an orphaned server name in the directory. Let's say you're installing a new server named *operations*. The first time you install Exchange, the install fails. When you run Setup again, the name *operations* is already registered in the directory, and Exchange will complain that you're trying to use a duplicate server name. The workaround is simple: delete the offending object from the directory on the other site's server, then wait one full replication cycle to make sure the change took.

If you're going to install several servers into a new site, make sure you have all of them up and exchanging regular mail traffic before you start changing things. Abstaining from settings tweaking makes it easier to pinpoint problems. If you start with a known set of defaults, finding what's wrong is much easier. The same advice goes double if you're installing a new site that needs to communicate with existing sites. If you turn on directory replication and there's some obstacle that blocks normal mail flow between the sites, you'll quickly choke the MTA queue with undeliverable replication messages.

Reconfiguring or removing Exchange

The installer can also be used to selectively add and remove Exchange components—you can even use it to remove Exchange altogether. While this might seem the equivalent of using a hammer to saw apart a piece of plywood, nonetheless it's the supported way to de-Exchange your server. If you run Setup on a machine that already has Exchange on it, you'll be given three choices:

- You can add or remove individual components. This is the option you use to add components like the ESA or OWA to an existing server.

- You can reinstall all currently installed components. This can often fix problems caused by accidentally deleted or corrupt DLLs or configuration files; all it does is scan to see what components and connectors were installed, then it recopies them from the CD.

- You can remove all traces of Exchange Server. Note that this won't have any effect on Outlook or IIS. If you use this option to remove Exchange before you reinstall it, make sure you back up any data files (including any OWA scripts you've modified *and your store and directory databases*) before you use the removal option. Setup will remove all of the DS and IS data as part of the removal.

There's actually a fourth option: if you run Exchange 5.5 Setup on an older machine, you'll be given a chance to upgrade the installation instead of replacing or reconfiguring it. More on that in a bit.

Replacing the only server in a site with another server

One scenario happens often enough to warrant its own section here: you have only one server in a site, but you want or need to replace it with another machine. The most common cause for this problem is that an organization finds out that it's outgrown its existing server and wants a smooth transition to a new server. The easiest and most seamless way to accomplish this is a little surprising: add the new server to the site, let the original server replicate the site directory to the new machine, move the user mailboxes and public folders to the new server, and remove the first server.

There are some caveats you need to be aware of, though. There's a specific procedure you have to follow to actually remove the original server, and the entire process of adding the new server, twinning the existing directory, and getting rid of the old box is very sensitive to the order in which you do the required steps. A bit later in this chapter (in the section "If you're removing the first server in a site"), I'll discuss exactly what you need to do.

Replacing a failed server

Normally, one of the final steps in the installation process is for Setup to kick off the Exchange services. The System Attendant service starts first, followed by the DS, IS, MTA, and connector services. As the DS and IS services start, they attempt to replay any uncommitted transactions they find in transaction logs. This may not actually be what you want to do; when you recover a failed Exchange server, in some cases the preferred recovery method is to reinstall Exchange, reload the database files from a backup, run the database maintenance tools, and restart the services only when the database is found to be clean and whole.

To reach this happy state of affairs, you have to start the Setup program with the /r switch, which tells it not to restart the services. Once Setup is finished, you can manually start the services when you need them, or you can reboot the server and let the newly installed software do what comes naturally after the reboot.

Automating installation

You probably know that you can install NT using what's called an *answer file.* This file is just a bunch of name-value pairs; the NT setup program reads them and uses the values instead of asking a human for them. Answer files allow you to install and configure NT without any human intervention—just type a command on the command line and go eat lunch while the computer does all the work.

Exchange's Setup utility supports the same capability. You can install any mix of Exchange Server and its components (including KMS, individual connectors, Exchange Administrator, and the documentation) by writing the appropriate answer file. This is really handy: once you've built an answer file that installs a particular type of server (say, a public folder or connector server) you can reuse it to speed up the process of deploying other servers of the same type. It's also a great aid to disaster recovery. Need a brand-new server? Pop in the Exchange CD and run your answer file. Voilà! (Actually, it's a bit more complicated; see the section "Automating installation," later in this chapter.)

What to Know About Upgrading

Not everyone who installs Exchange 5.5 is starting from scratch. A large number of sites have adopted earlier versions of Exchange,* but found the new features—particularly the unlimited message store size and the ability to recover deleted items—too good to resist. The standard Exchange installer is smart enough to detect the presence of a prior version of Exchange, and to convert the DS and IS databases into the format used by Exchange 5.5. From Chapter 1, *Introducing Exchange Server*, you may remember that the Exchange database schema changed between 4.0 and 5.0 and again between 5.0 and 5.5. In addition, the database engine itself was replaced as part of the 5.5 changes.

In defense of previous versions of Exchange, I should note that all the various flavors of Exchange interoperate perfectly well, with the stipulation that sites running older versions have applied all the appropriate service packs for their version of Exchange. There are also some known problems with intermixing different versions of Exchange as bridgehead servers. You can administer 4.0 and 5.0 servers with the Exchange 5.5 version of Exchange Administrator. The new features in Exchange 5.5 (not to mention the hundreds, if not thousands, of bug fixes and performance improvements) make it a worthwhile upgrade, though.

---

* In this context, I mean Exchange 4.0, Exchange 5.0, or Small Business Server 4.0.

When you upgrade an Exchange database, you take its life in your hands. Never start an upgrade until you have a backup of that machine's data that you know is good. If the upgrade fails, it can leave the database in an inconsistent state, and without a backup you may not be able to restore it to health.

How do you actually execute an upgrade? Good question. When you run Exchange Setup on a computer that has an older version of Exchange, Setup detects it and asks you if you want to upgrade the existing installation. Remember that the upgrade process has to convert the entirety of the public and private Information Stores, so the length of time it takes is sensitive to the size of those stores and the speed (particularly the I/O speed) of your server. Don't expect upgrades to happen instantly.

General upgrading tips

Here are several things you should do before you start in on your upgrade. Some of them are obvious, but others are a little more subtle.

- Make a complete backup of any server you're upgrading. While this should go without saying, I'll say it anyway, since people are often tempted to skip this critical step. For maximum safety, take two backups: one online backup (made while the Exchange services are running) and one offline.

- Exchange 5.5 requires NT 4.0 with Service Pack 3 or later. You really should be running at least SP4 anyway, since it fixes a large number of bugs. You must perform this upgrade before you install IIS 4.0 or upgrade your Exchange server. Don't forget that Exchange clustering requires NT 4.0 Enterprise Edition; if you plan to cluster your new 5.5 servers, you'll have to upgrade NT first.

- If you want the upgraded server to run OWA, it will require either IIS 3.0 or 4.0. If you're planning on using IIS 4.0, you must install all the necessary components in a fixed sequence: first Internet Explorer 4.01, then IIS 4.0. After you install IIS 4.0, you have to reinstall SP4 (if you're using SP3, reinstall it, then add the *asp-memfix* and *rollup* hotfixes). Finally, you install Exchange 5.5. Don't deviate from this sequence or you'll suffer the consequences, which usually involve some or all of the new components failing in interesting and spectacular ways.

- Don't switch languages; if you're running the Exchange version localized for French, upgrade it using the same language. This seems obvious, but Microsoft explicitly warns against mixing languages at upgrade time in the upgrade release notes, so *somebody* must have been doing it incorrectly.

- If you're going to upgrade an Enterprise Edition server, upgrade it to 5.5 Enterprise, not 5.5 Standard. The only way to move from Enterprise back down to Standard is to back up your databases, use Setup to remove the older Enterprise version, then use 5.5's Setup to install the new version.

- When you upgrade a system, turn off anything that monitors it, including link monitors, server monitors, and NT's Performance Monitor and Server Manager tools. The Exchange monitors will try to restart services when they stop, and the upgrade process has to stop them to perform the upgrade, so it can't continue if the monitors interfere.

The best way to make sure that you don't get any complaints about busy files during an upgrade is simple. Use the Services control panel to set the startup type of *every* BackOffice service on your machine—Exchange, IIS, SQL Server, etc.—to manual or disabled, then reboot the machine. When the machine restarts, none of those pesky services will come up, and you'll be able to do your installation. If you still get complaints about busy files, just rename the existing version of the problematic file and let the installer try again.

Upgrade space and time requirements

The amount of disk space and time it takes to do an upgrade varies, depending on what version you're upgrading from, what you're upgrading to, and how big your private and public IS databases are. Microsoft says that a standard upgrade requires enough free space to equal approximately 17% of the largest database you want to upgrade. That means that for a 4GB private IS, you'll need about 713MB of free space. Fault-tolerant upgrades take a lot more space—you must have as much free space as the combined total size of all your databases. For a 4GB private IS, a 2GB public IS, and a 250MB directory, you'll need 6.25GB free!

One other factor to consider: it takes longer to move a database with lots of small messages than an equal-size database with fewer but larger messages in it. That argues in favor of running the Mailbox Cleanup Agent or otherwise clearing deadwood out of the public and private IS before you do the upgrade (but after you take a usable backup).

Upgrades and server configurations

The easiest configuration to upgrade is the simplest: one server in one site. Beyond that, things get more complicated. If your existing Exchange topology uses servers in separate roles, there are some additional things you need to consider when planning which machines get updated in what order. The first and most important thing to remember is that while the upgrade is in progress, your servers will be unavailable to the world: no mail will flow, users won't be able to log on, and no services will be available. Overall, your goal will probably be to minimize the total upgrade time, and you'll probably want to do upgrades at night or on the weekends, so that you don't bring down your users' mail during working hours.

In pursuit of this goal, the first thing to think of is your public folder (PF) servers. If you're using dedicated PF servers, they must be upgraded before you upgrade the mailbox servers that point to them. If you've split up your server loads this way, upgrade all your PF servers before upgrading any mailbox servers. Next, you may want to take advantage of the fact that bridgehead and connector servers have very small IS and DS databases, since they don't contain any mailboxes or public folders. Small databases make for fast updates, so you can quickly upgrade these servers with minimal downtime.

Depending on the number of mailboxes you have, you may want to consider moving user mailboxes (as described in the later section "Moving users and connectors as part of an upgrade") as an alternative back-door upgrade method; this allows you to leave the users' mail server up and move mailboxes individually. Instead of locking out all users while the server is upgraded, you lock them out one at a time. Most of the time, users aren't even aware that their mailboxes have been moved.

A final word about server configurations: if you're moving to Exchange 5.5 to take advantage of its clustering features, you can't upgrade directly from 4.0 or 5.0 to a clustered installation of 5.5. You'll have to set up the new clustered server, then move mailboxes, public folders, and connectors to the new server.

Upgrading from Exchange 4.0

The first step in upgrading from Exchange 4.0 to Exchange 5.5 is understanding what has changed. Exchange 5.0 introduced new database schemas for the IS and DS databases, as did Exchange 5.5. When you upgrade directly from 4.0 to 5.5, your database may need to be converted twice, meaning that a 4.0 to 5.5 upgrade may take twice as long as an upgrade from 5.0. Microsoft claims that the processing can take up to 75 minutes per GB of data in the original store. There's nothing you can do to speed it up, so be prepared to wait.

If you only have one server in your site, and you want to upgrade it, you can move straight from 4.0 to 5.5 without any special planning. However, if you've got more than one server in your site, Microsoft recommends that you upgrade *all* your 4.0 servers to Service Pack 2 before attempting to upgrade any 4.0 server to 5.0. This is a good idea, since SP2 includes the 5.0 schema design. If you don't do this, the directory schemas for your SP2 or 5.0 and non-SP2 machines will vary, and directory replication will break. If you can't do this, at least upgrade to 4.0 SP2 on your directory replication bridgehead servers. Once replication completes, reboot all your 4.0 servers and they'll begin using the new schema; at that point, it's safe for you to upgrade any of your 4.0 servers to 5.5.

When you run 5.5's Setup on an older system, it will detect the presence of the earlier version and ask whether you want to upgrade or remove the older version. Make sure you tell it to upgrade the existing installation, since this preserves your DS and IS databases. Once you've selected the upgrade option, Setup will alert you that the database format will be changed. Once you acknowledge that alert, the fun begins.

It's important to point out that a 4.0 to 5.5 upgrade is an in-place operation: the actual in-use versions of your database files will be upgraded, so if the upgrade fails, your database will be unusable. (Exchange Setup calls this a "standard upgrade," which is not very reassuring.) Before you start an upgrade of 4.0, make sure you have a good, clean, offline backup. Setup will upgrade the databases before it installs the Exchange 5.5 binaries, so if the upgrade *does* fail you can restore the databases from your backup and bring the 4.0 version of the server up again.

After the upgrade finishes, Setup will restart the Exchange services and give you a chance to run the Performance Optimizer, just like it does in a normal installation. Once you've completed the upgrade, you may need to run Setup again to install the EES, OWA, or KMS components, since the upgrade installation doesn't include them.

One final note: once you start upgrading your 4.0 servers to 5.5, don't install any new 4.0 servers. While you can make this work by following a convoluted proce-dure, it doesn't make sense to do it at all.

Upgrading from Exchange 5.0

When you move from 5.0 to 5.5, you have a choice about how the database is upgraded. The 4.0 to 5.5 upgrade just updates the database where it sits on disk, putting it at risk if the upgrade process fails. You can do that same type of upgrade from 5.0 if you want to, or you can perform a *fault-tolerant* upgrade. As its name suggests, a fault-tolerant upgrade is resilient enough not to fail in the event of a setup or conversion failure. At the start of the fault-tolerant upgrade, Setup makes a copy of the database files. Instead of converting the real database files, it then converts the copies. If anything goes wrong, you can restart Setup and it will restart the conversion at the point of failure. Once the conversion com-pletes without error, the modified copies replace the original files.

This tolerance comes at a price, though. Microsoft says that the 5.0 to 5.5 upgrade can process about 1.7GB per hour. You need at least twice as much disk space as your databases currently occupy. For example, if your private IS weighs in at 7GB, you'll need 14GB of free space to complete the conversion. Fortunately, the upgrade procedure allows you to select the directory you want to use for the temporary database copies. You can specify a volume with enough free space, or you can use a network volume, but be forewarned that using a network disk will significantly slow down the conversion process.

Moving users and connectors as part of an upgrade

If you're doing wholesale upgrades to 5.5, there's a relatively straightforward way to ease the potential upheaval. You can upgrade a small number of servers, or build completely new ones, then move user accounts and connectors to the new servers. While the total time required for this process is usually longer than the time needed to upgrade a database, it offers some benefits. The biggest is that you can move users in small groups, and their mail will only be unavailable during the short time when the mailbox is actually being moved. This is often more palatable than telling all users on a server that their mail will be offline for a few hours while you upgrade the databases and reinstall Exchange.

Moving users one at a time is simple; moving them *en masse* is more complicated. When you use Exchange Administrator to move a mailbox from one server to another, in essence, you're forcing the servers to replicate the entire mailbox, deleting the original when the replication succeeds. As you might expect, this can generate a noticeable amount of network traffic. What you may not expect is that all the traffic generates transactions in the log files—if you move a 250MB mailbox, you'll be generating 250MB *or more* of log traffic on the receiving server. If you're moving lots of mailbox data, remember to leave enough disk space for your transaction logs, and don't forget that you can always do an online backup, which will remove the log files for you. I don't recommend turning on circular logging, but you may be able to get away with it.

There are some other things you need to do as well:

- Use the Exchange Administrator Tools → Move Mailbox command to move mailboxes. It automates the process relatively well. Sure, you could accomplish the same result by exporting the user's mail to a PST file and reloading the PST on the new server, but that's a big pain in the neck to do for more than one user.

- Whenever possible, run Exchange Administrator on the server to which you're moving mailboxes. This minimizes the amount of network traffic, since Exchange Administrator will request the mailbox data from the original server and then resend it to the receiving server. If you can't do so, at least try to run Exchange Administrator on the same subnet as the receiving server.

- Move users one group at a time. Don't even *think* about using multiple copies of Exchange Administrator to move multiple groups at once; that's a remarkably easy way to trash your directory and private IS.

- After you've moved all the mailboxes off the old server, leave it on the network long enough for your users to log onto it. When they do, their MAPI clients will helpfully update their profile settings to point to the new, correct location.

Moving connectors is often easier than moving users, since Exchange is happy to have lots of connectors of the same type within a site. However, if you remove the old connectors too soon, you'll disrupt service to your users, so the easiest route is usually to upgrade a server, designate it as the new connector server, and put connectors on it. As soon as the connectors are operating, set connection costs on them that are lower than the old connectors' cost values. This forces Exchange to try to use the new connectors first, falling back to the old ones if the new ones fail for some reason. When you're satisfied that everything still works, you can remove the old connectors, or even leave them in place for additional redundancy.

Pre-Installation Checklist

By now, you're probably wondering if I'm ever going to get around to the actual installation. While all of this preliminary stuff may be making you impatient, there are some things that, once done, are hard to undo, so "measure twice, cut once" is an excellent, if clichéd, principle to apply here.

Check your NT domain mappings

Tony Redmond, the Compaq (née Digital) Exchange guru, likes to talk about what he calls "legacy NT." While this might seem to be an oxymoron, what he means is that many early NT networks were designed with domain architectures that are much less elegant than they could be. Once you establish a set of domains, and people start using them for access control, the die is cast, and you're usually stuck with that system, at least until Windows 2000 forces everyone to redesign everything.

This isn't the place for a lecture on NT domain design, so I won't harangue you. However, the right time to make sure your domains have proper trust relationships, and that they have the structure you actually want to use, is *before* you install Exchange. Part of your planning process should be to make sure that your domains are all squared away. If they're not, you should fix them before you proceed with the installation.

Create a site service account

You need a service account so the services have a security context to run in. There's nothing magic about the account or its name; you can create the account with User Manager, give it any name and password you want, and merrily use it, as long as you follow a few simple rules:

- Don't install Exchange while logged in as Administrator. The account you log in as gets permissions on the organization, site, and configuration containers, and Setup uses that account as the default choice for the service account. Create a separate account and use it for installations instead; don't use the service account.

- The account must be available to every domain that will contain an Exchange server in a site. If you have one big domain, this is no problem. If every site has its own domain, that's no problem either. If, however, you have multiple domains, you have to be very careful to make sure that all servers either have trust relationships with a common domain (into which you put the service account) or are configured with appropriate trust relationships.

- When you create the account, make sure the "Password never expires" checkbox is turned on and that the "User must change password at next logon" checkbox is turned off. If the service password ever expires, or is changed, your Exchange services will keep running until the next time they're restarted—then they'll be *kaput.*

- Make sure all members of your Administrators, Domain Admins, and Account Operators groups know that they should leave the site service account alone. If the account is renamed, has its password changed, or (worst of all) is deleted, your Exchange services will fail to start, probably when you need them the most.

- Don't fool with the user rights on the service account. Exchange Setup will modify the account rights to grant the minimum required level of access. If you try to outsmart the Exchange designers by tailoring the account's rights, you'll be sorry in the end.

The site service account is all-powerful in Exchange. If you log on as that account, you can read mailboxes, reconfigure anything on any server in the site, and generally wreak all kinds of havoc. Treat the account with the respect it deserves. Don't make it part of any local or global groups, and make sure to choose a strong password. In contravention of every security policy ever written on paper, it's okay to write down the site service password, but split it into two halves, seal each half in an envelope, and keep the envelopes in two very safe but separate places. This helps protect you against compromise while still allowing a reasonable chance of recovering the password if it's lost.

Check your clustering setup

Chapter 3, *Exchange Planning*, should have given you some useful background on Exchange clustering. If you've decided to go ahead and cluster your Exchange installation, there are a couple of differences in the installation process. First of all, you must use Exchange Enterprise Edition if you want a cluster, since the Standard Edition doesn't support clustering. You must have NT4 Enterprise Edition installed and set up on both nodes in the cluster, and you must have the cluster hardware configured with a shared disk set before you build the cluster itself. You also have to create all the cluster resource groups manually before trying to install Exchange, as it expects to see the disk, network addresses, and so on already in place.

Once the cluster is established, you have to create several virtual resources before you can install Exchange Server on the cluster. The process for doing this is covered thoroughly in the Exchange documentation, so I won't duplicate it here. Once you've set up your virtual resources, you install Exchange on the first cluster node, just as you would on a single machine. When that installation succeeds, you then have to install Exchange on the second cluster node. After that installation finishes, you can use Cluster Administrator to set the failover and failback parameters that best suit your needs.

Check that you meet the resource requirements

Have you ever left home to make a quick trip somewhere, then noticed that your gas gauge was frighteningly close to "E"? In an ideal world, we'd all remember to check the gauge before going somewhere,* but sometimes that doesn't happen. The Exchange analogue of forgetting to check your fuel tank before driving off is forgetting to check the Exchange resource requirements before starting an installation. Unlike your car, which will happily run out of gas and leave you stranded, the Exchange Setup application fails gracefully when there isn't enough of some resource or other.

What resources must you have to successfully install Exchange? First of all, you need lots of disk space—at least 250MB of free disk space just to install the Exchange components, plus whatever space you want to use for public folders and mailboxes. If you're adding a server to an existing site, you'll also need enough room to import the site directory. (Remember that how you arrange your physical disks can have a significant performance impact; see Chapter 3 for more details.) Finally, don't forget to allow enough space for a generous page file— Microsoft recommends that you set your page file size to the amount of physical RAM plus 125MB. You should make sure to set the page file size to a fixed amount to keep the file from growing and shrinking.

---

* Actually, in an ideal world, we'd all be riding Harleys, but I digress.

The other requirements are all software or network prerequisites:

- You must be running NT4 with Service Pack 3 or later, or Windows 2000. If you intend to use clustering, you'll need the Enterprise Edition of NT 4.

- If you want to provide OWA to your clients, you must have either version 3.0 or 4.0 of IIS installed *before* you install Exchange.

- If you're going to use the Dynamic RAS or IMS dial-up connectors, you must install the Remote Access Service (RAS) or Routing and Remote Access Service (RRAS) before installing those connectors.

- If you're going to use the IMS, you must have TCP/IP correctly configured and installed, and you need to have DNS MX and A records for all your IMS servers. (Actually, you can install the IMS without these records, but it won't work until you've established them.)

- If you want to install Exchange on a cluster, you must have the cluster configured and running before you try to install Exchange on it.

Once you've completed these preflight checklist items, you're finally ready to install Exchange.

Installing Exchange

As the epigraph on the first page of this chapter points out, installing Exchange is easy when everything goes well—and that's most of the time. Still, it's helpful to understand the process even if you could probably get through it on blind luck and a sufficiently large stack of donuts, so let's peer under the hood of the installation process to see what you need to do.

Running the Setup Program

I alluded to the fact that the Exchange installation program is a standard Windows logo-compliant installer. If you've ever installed any Microsoft software other than Windows NT itself, or almost any third-party package, you already know what it looks like. The overall install process follows a fairly simple flow, as shown in Figure 4-1. (Note that this diagram doesn't show the steps for upgrading a previously installed Exchange server.)

Now that you've seen the big picture, let's delve into the details. Each step in the installation has a purpose. First, you have to read Microsoft's license agreement. Before you can install Exchange, you're supposed to read and agree with the license agreement. The purpose of this particular step is to protect Microsoft by helping them claim that you agreed to whatever terms they put in the agreement. I recommend that everyone read the agreement once, just so you understand what's in it.

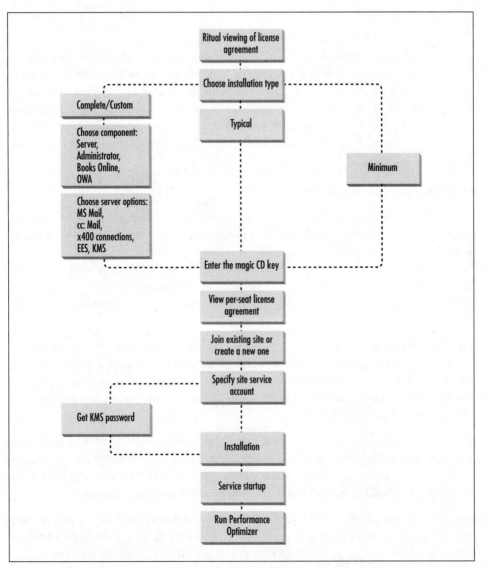

Figure 4-1. The Exchange installation map is fairly linear

Installation types

Once you've accepted the license agreement, you next have to choose an installation type. The standard Windows paradigm offers you three options: install everything that Microsoft thinks you need ("Typical"), install only the bare minimum ("Minimum"), or let the user choose ("Complete/Custom"). Perhaps tellingly, Typical is the default installation option in this installer. If you choose the Typical or Minimum options, you won't have any control over what gets installed. Neither of these options installs any connectors,* and neither includes the very useful online help.

Which installation option you choose will depend on what you want your server to do. If you want a vanilla public folder or mailbox server, or don't need any connectors other than the IMS, you can stick with the Minimum or Typical installations. If you just want to install the "trial size" version of Exchange, do a Minimum install. If you need connectors, or if you want to pick out components as though you were ordering from the Sears catalog, use Complete/Custom or do an automated installation.

Typical installation, step by step

The Typical installation takes place in seven discrete steps, as you saw in Figure 4-1. (This doesn't count the step of choosing "Typical" as your installation type.) The first step after choosing the installation type is providing the CD key; this is simple enough that I won't go into it in more detail. The only potential complication is if you're installing a version of Exchange that you got from an OEM or through a special licensing agreement with Microsoft; in that case, you'll enter the product ID code instead of the CD key.

The next step is to agree that you're using Exchange in per-seat licensing mode. As mentioned in Chapter 3, you need one client access license for each user that can access Exchange, regardless of how many simultaneous users you have. By checking the "I agree that" checkbox, you're asserting that you've bought the correct number of licenses already.

As soon as you've done that, the *real* installation process can start! The next step after the second licensing dialog is to tell Exchange whether you want to join an existing site or create a new one. The dialog you'll see is shown in Figure 4-2; in this case, the installing administrator is creating a new site and organization.

To join an existing site, you'll need to know the name of any server in the site, and you'll need an RPC-capable network connection to that server. To create a new site, all you need is the ability to make up an organization and site name, making sure to follow the naming plan you developed in response to the suggestions in Chapter 3. When you create a new site, Setup will ask you to confirm your choice before it does anything.

The next step is to tell Exchange which service account to use. You do so with a simple dialog box that contains a field showing the account name, a text entry field where you type the password, and a button labeled Browse.... Use the

---

* To be accurate, I should say that all options install the IMS, but it's not active or configurable until you create a new IMS instance in Exchange Administrator. No *other* connectors are installed, though.

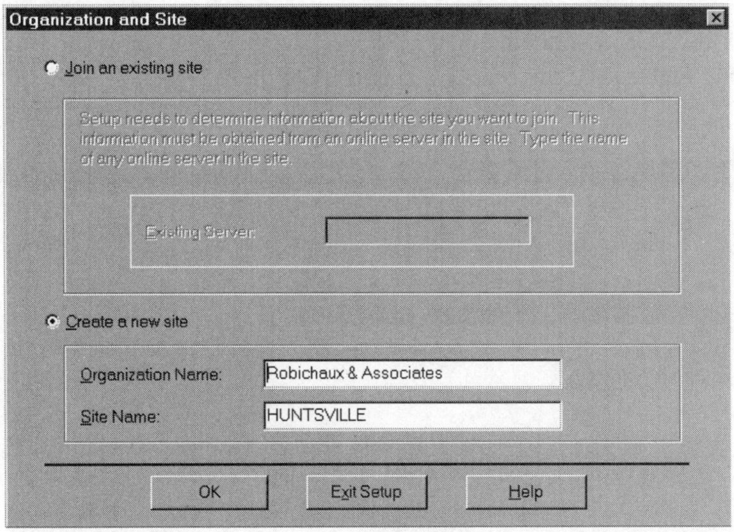

Figure 4-2. You can either join an existing site or create a new one

Browse... button to bring up the standard NT user and group browser dialog box. Once you've chosen an account in that dialog box and clicked its OK button, type the account password into the appropriate field and click the OK button. Setup will verify the password; if you get the password or the account name wrong, you'll get a warning dialog and another chance to get things right.

Once you've chosen the site service account, Exchange will warn you that it's modifying the user rights granted to the account. It does so by adding the "log on as a service," "restore files and directories," and "act as part of the operating system" user rights to the account; these rights are required by some of the services which run in the service account's security context.

Now that Setup knows what service account to use, it begins doing the actual installation work, creating the databases and copying files as described earlier. When it finishes, it will start the Exchange services, then prompt you to run the Performance Optimizer. This is a good idea; you'll get a quick look at how the Performance Optimizer works in the section "A Word About the Performance Optimizer," later in the chapter.

Custom installation, step by step

If you choose to do a Complete/Custom installation, there are a few additional steps that Setup interposes before the Typical installation steps I just described. First of all, you'll be presented with the dialog box shown in Figure 4-3. Use the checkboxes next to each item to control what gets installed. For example, you can uncheck everything except "Exchange Administrator" to get only the Exchange Administrator application and the Exchange backup client on a machine, or you can install the documentation on your laptop to give you something to read on long, boring flights (like the one I'm on as I write this).

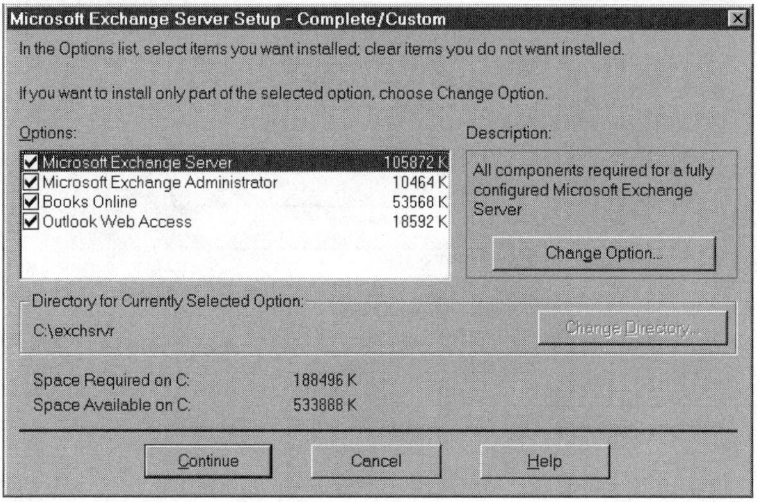

Figure 4-3. The Complete/Custom dialog lets you specify Exchange components to be installed

Notice the Change Option... button to the right of the options list? It's useless for three of the four options; you can't customize exactly which parts of Exchange Administrator, the documentation, or OWA are installed. Normally, if you choose a Complete/Custom installation, Setup will install all the connectors it can find. Luckily, you can tailor which connectors and optional services are installed by selecting the "Microsoft Exchange Server" checkbox in the Options list, then clicking the Change Option... button. When you do, you'll see a dialog box like the one in Figure 4-4. The list of connectors and components you see will vary, according to whether you have the Enterprise or Standard editions of Exchange.

In Figure 4-4, you'll notice that I've selected the X.400 connector, the EES, and the KMS. You can mix and match any combination of items in this list. Future versions of Exchange may add even more default connectors. Attentive readers will also notice that the X.400 connector is shown as requiring no disk space (if it's shown at all; it's only part of the Enterprise Edition). That's because the X.400 connector and IMS are always installed, but they're not activated or available until you add a new instance of the connector. Exchange just installs it now to save having to ask for its installation CD at a later time. Once you've made your choices in this dialog, click the OK button; you'll be swept along to the next installation step, which happens to be entering the CD key.

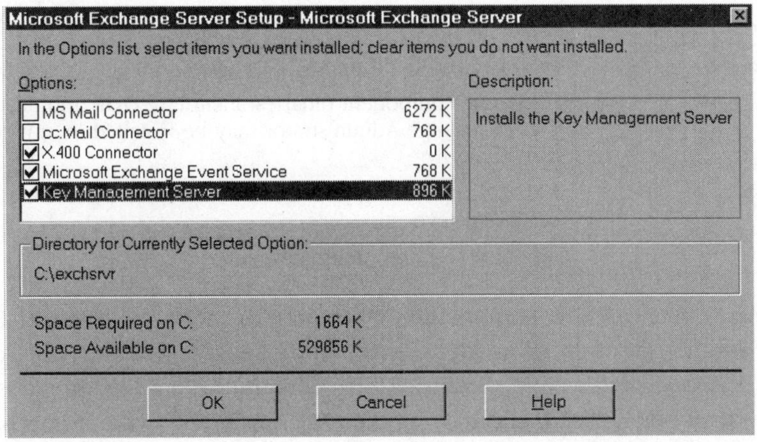

Microsoft Exchange Server Setup - Microsoft Exchange Server

In the Options list, select items you want installed; clear items you do not want installed.

Options:

☐ MS Mail Connector	6272 K
☐ cc:Mail Connector	768 K
☑ X.400 Connector	0 K
☑ Microsoft Exchange Event Service	768 K
☑ Key Management Server	896 K

Description:

Installs the Key Management Server

Directory for Currently Selected Option:

C:\exchsrvr

Space Required on C: 1664 K
Space Available on C: 529856 K

[OK]   [Cancel]   [Help]

Figure 4-4. This dialog allows you to select connectors and optional components

From this point on, a Custom installation proceeds just like a Typical or Minimum installation, with one exception. If you choose to install KMS, Setup will perform one extra step before it starts installing DLLs and executables. It'll generate a KMS password (a long string of random letters and numbers) and give you two options: you can write the password down, then manually type it in each time the KMS starts, or you can make a pair of special password floppies. This step is critical, because without that password the KMS can't be started; if you lose it, you're hosed, because you'll never be able to use that KMS installation to issue or revoke a certificate. Make sure you write the password down properly; better yet, use the password floppies instead.

After you complete the password assignment step, the installation, service start, and Performance Optimizer phases will continue normally.

What gets installed where

Exchange is a big product, and it installs tentacles in several places. By default, Setup will install Exchange in the \exchsrvr directory, but you can change the directory with the Change Directory button. Whatever directory you choose, Exchange will create a number of subdirectories under it, each with its own unique and useful contents as shown in Table 4-1.

Table 4-1. Exchange Installation Subdirectories

Subdirectory	What's in It
dsadata	Directory database and log files
mdbdata	Public, private, and temporary databases and their log files
%systemroot%\system32	Exchange DLLs used by multiple components

Table 4-1. Exchange Installation Subdirectories (continued)

Subdirectory	What's in It
mtadata	Inbound and outbound MTA queues
bin	Exchange component binaries, including DLLs and executables (Exchange Administrator may be installed in any directory, though)
kmsdata	KMS data, including public keys, encrypted private keys, and certificate revocation lists
imcdata	Inbound and outbound IMS queues

If necessary, you can use Performance Optimizer to move the DS and IS databases to another location. Don't ever move them manually; not only will you confuse the services, but the transaction log files contain the hardcoded paths to the databases they belong with, and moving them manually will make it impossible to replay the logs.

Special Considerations

If you're doing a Typical install, then you've probably stopped reading by now and gone off to actually do the installation. If you're still here, it's probably because you want to do something that you intuit as being more troublesome than a standard installation, like running OWA or an Exchange cluster. This section is here to point out any quirks or traps involved in these special situations, so that you can join your fellow readers in gleefully installing your new messaging system.

If you're clustering Exchange

Exchange clustering is surprisingly popular, considering what you can't (or aren't supposed to) do with it. You're required to have two identical servers; there's no way to use Microsoft Cluster Server (MSCS) to do load balancing, and your servers have to share a single point of failure, the disk system. As a further insult, Microsoft doesn't support running the Notes, MS Mail for AppleTalk, DRAS, or SNADS connectors; OWA; or X.500 over either X.25 or TCP/IP under MSCS. That limits what you can do with a clustered server, on top of the resource requirements.

The overall installation process for putting Exchange on your cluster is pretty straightforward. There's an entire document on the Exchange 5.5 CD (see *docs\ word_docs\clustering\cluster.doc*) that goes into great detail, so I'll just present a summary. If you need further explanation, see the Microsoft document.

1. Install your cluster servers so that they share a physical disk array. Test the cluster by trying to fail over NT services and make sure that the resource manager is working okay before you go any further. Fix any failover problems you find.

2. Create a cluster resource group on the cluster, then create three resources in it: an IP address resource, a network name resource (which is the equivalent of an Exchange server name, but for a cluster), and a physical disk resource. Test the cluster again.

3. Install Exchange on the primary or active node. When you run Setup, it will ask you to identify the cluster you want to install on. You can choose where you want Exchange installed, as long as you choose a clustered drive. As installation proceeds, you'll notice that the files Exchange normally installs in *exchsrvr* go to the shared physical disk, while files that would normally go in *%systemroot%* end up on the active node's system disk.

4. Run Performance Optimizer on the active node. This is necessary because the disk system is shared and you can't run Performance Optimizer on the secondary node.

5. Run Exchange Setup on the secondary node. When prompted, click the Update Node button to tell Exchange that you want to use this node as the secondary node in a cluster.

Once you've completed this process, your clustered server is ready to go. If you change the active node's configuration by adding or removing components (including the IMS, the Internet News Service, the KMS, the MS Mail or cc:Mail connectors, and the Exchange Scripting Agent), you'll need to reinstall Exchange on the secondary node.

You can move an existing server into a cluster using the disaster recovery procedures outlined in Chapter 17, *Recovery and Repair*. However, it's much safer (not to mention easier) to move users from one server into a cluster group; this greatly eases the migration process, and it takes less time to boot.

If you're installing OWA

You can run OWA with IIS 3.0 or 4.0. However, you have to be careful to install IIS first. If you install IIS 3.0, then install Exchange, and later upgrade to IIS 4.0, OWA will suddenly screech to a halt. You'll have to reinstall it to bring it back up again. One little-known fact: you don't *have* to have IIS and Exchange on the same server. You can install OWA and Exchange on separate computers, and everything will work just fine. In fact, you'll probably be better off doing so, since the load imposed by IIS/OWA users can drag down your Exchange server performance.

If you're removing the first server in a site

When you install the first server in a site, it becomes home to several invisible *site folders*. These folders hold data that all servers in the site share, like the Schedule+ free/busy table, the organization's forms library, and the offline address book. When you remove the first server ever installed in a site, those folders will be orphaned unless you follow a special procedure to move those folders to another server. Before you worry about the site folders, though, you must move any mailboxes and public folders off the server you're removing. Do this first, after taking a backup; that way you'll know that the only data remaining on the server is the site folders.

The remaining steps are pretty straightforward. For a more in-depth explanation, see Microsoft Knowledge Base article Q152959 (available at *http://support. microsoft.com/support/kb/articles/q152/9/59.asp*). If these instructions don't make sense now, just stick a bookmark in the book and come back to them once you're more comfortable with using Exchange Administrator.

Your first task is to move the offline address book (OAB) folder to another server:

1. Decide which server in the site will be the new home for the OAB.

2. Run Exchange Administrator and select the DS Site Configuration object within the configuration container.

3. Open the DS Site Configuration properties dialog. Click the Offline Address Book tab.

4. Select the server you want to host the OAB from the Offline Address Book server pulldown.

5. Click the Generate All button. Exchange Administrator will update the OAB and move it to the server you've selected.

Next, you have to designate another server as keeper of the GWART. By default, the first server in a site is responsible for calculating routing costs for use in the GWART, and you have to manually reassign that role to another server before you can remove the first one. Here's what to do:

1. Decide which server you want to be the new routing calculation server.

2. Open Exchange Administrator, find the configuration container, and open the Site Addressing properties dialog.

3. Use the Routing calculation server pull-down to identify the server you want to take over the job.

4. Toggle the "Share address space with other X.400 systems" checkbox. Why? Because if you don't, Exchange Administrator is too dumb to notice the change in the pull-down selection. This is a longstanding and stupid bug.

5. You'll notice that once you toggle the checkbox, or make a change on any of the other property pages, the Apply button becomes active. Click it to start the process of moving the routing calculation responsibility to the new server.

6. Click the Routing tab, then click its Recalculate Routing button. This forces the new server to recalculate the routing costs and update the GWART.

Finally, you have to move the Schedule+ Free/Busy and organization forms library site folders. The steps for doing this are pretty simple, too, especially since these two items stick together and move as a unit:

1. Decide which server in the site will be the new home for the Schedule+ and forms library folders.

2. Run Exchange Administrator and expand the Servers container until you can select the server you identified in step 1.

3. Open the server's Public Information Store properties dialog, then click the Instances tab.

4. Select the *Schedule+ Free Busy Information* and *Organization Forms* public folders from the public folders list.

5. Click the Add button to tell Exchange to replicate the folders on the new server, then click the OK button.

Once you've done all three of these things, and waited long enough for the site folders to replicate to their new home, Microsoft recommends that you disconnect the old server from the network and make sure that everything still works okay. (One caveat: most Schedule+ users won't see free/busy times until they've made an appointment.) Once you're satisfied that the GWART and site folders are present and accounted for, use Exchange Administrator to delete the old server from the site and you're done!

A Word About the Performance Optimizer

The final step in the installation process is running the Exchange Performance Optimizer. The setup application configures Exchange using its own set of comfortable defaults. While this is great for the setup program, it may not be so great for your server's performance. As you learned in Chapter 3, Exchange performance is sensitive to which sets of files go on which physical disk drives. In addition, there are a ton of internal parameters that Exchange uses to allocate resources among its various components. Setup assigns default values for these parameters, but the defaults may not be adequate for your particular configuration.

There's a simple way to fix this: run the Performance Optimizer. However, don't do it when Setup prompts you after it's done installing. Instead, wait until you've installed and configured any additional connectors (like the IMS), since it can't adjust things that aren't installed. Instead of blindly accepting the default locations Performance Optimizer suggests for database files, make sure you understand where you want your database files to go based on your knowledge of the disk configuration, since Performance Optimizer looks only at timing test results, not at the RAID level (if any) or drive configuration. Be sure to correctly fill out the wizard page that asks you how many users are on your server and what it's doing. (If you want to know what it's actually doing, see Chapter 18, *Managing Exchange Performance.)*

Installing Service Packs

When you get ready to install a service pack, the first thing that should immediately leap to your mind is a strong urge to make two backups of your server: an online backup (preferably made with *ntbackup*) and a separate offline backup. Only after doing both of these should you pop in the SP CD and start installing it.

This section describes how to install Exchange 5.5 SP2. Since SP2 includes the contents of SP1, you'll find that the overall process is similar (and it'll still be similar when, or if, Exchange 5.5 SP3 hits the streets). The first step is to obtain the service pack itself. Microsoft makes them freely available for download, but they tend to be large (SP2 was about 25MB), so you may find it more convenient to order the CD for the US$15 or so that Microsoft charges.

Because Exchange includes encryption and security components, you should also be aware that there are two separate versions of the SPs. One is intended for use outside North America. Its encryption is weaker than the North American version.* When you download the SP from Microsoft, you're getting the weak version, even though the web site doesn't say so.

Once you have the CD or downloadable version, and you're ready to install it, begin the installation by launching the appropriate updater for your machine. For most of the world, it'll be the *eng\server\setup\i386\update.exe* executable; for those running servers with Alpha CPUs, try *\eng\server\setup\alpha\update.exe*. Once Setup launches, it will warn you that it's about to update your currently running Exchange server; at this point, you can cancel without having touched anything on your server. After a little bit of poking around, Setup will return to tell you that it plans to update some installed components, and that to do so it has to stop the running Exchange services, but that your database files will be left intact. Once you click the OK button, the SP installer starts in on the update.

---

* This is because the U.S. government seems to think that no one outside North America is capable of writing good cryptographic software. Of course, they're totally wrong. See the Electronic Frontier Foundation's *Cracking DES* (O'Reilly & Associates) for more details on these policies and their impact.

You may notice that Setup installs updated versions of the documentation, too. For an overview of what's new in the SP, see the file *eng\docs\relnotes\misc\default.htm.*

When the update finishes, Setup makes all needed changes to the registry and restarts the Exchange services. Once the update is complete and Setup quits, I recommend that you make another online backup, just in case. Be sure to check the event logs once the services are restarted; they'll indicate any hidden problems that you may have missed in the past because you didn't restart your servers very often.

Automating Server Installation

I've already mentioned automated installations a couple of times in this chapter. It's really a neat feature: you can literally build a "silent" installer that will install Exchange for you and do rudimentary configuration of some services, all in just a few lines of plain ASCII text. If you're an experienced NT administrator, you can skip over the next couple of paragraphs, since you're probably already familiar with unattended answer files and how they work.

The standard tool for installing NT, BackOffice components, and most third-party products is the Setup application. It's designed to ease the installation process for people who aren't necessarily experts, but it requires that a human sit there in front of the machine and make choices. As you've seen from the description of the Exchange installation process earlier in this chapter, a number of items normally require manual intervention. The good news is that you can build an *unattended answer file*, also known as a UDF file, that tells Setup everything it needs to know about the installation. With a correctly written UDF file, you can install any combination of Exchange, its connectors, OWA, and KMS. When you run Exchange Setup, just add the /q switch, along with the full path to your UDF file. For example, the following code launches Setup from a network share and uses the UDF file *standard.ini* to do the installation:

```
\\tornado\exchange\setup\setup.exe /q \\tornado\exchange\udf\standard.ini
```

Why might you want to use unattended installations? For one thing, they can be a real time-saver: you can launch Setup on a server and let it work while you do something more interesting than watching the progress bar creep towards the 100% mark. You can also use UDF files to quickly deploy a standard server configuration in many places, either concurrently or in sequence. This is particularly useful when you install Exchange from a network installation point, since you can do many installs at once. There's a third benefit, too: as long as you have a copy of the UDF file (which is fortunately short, legible, and easy to print out), you have a permanent record of how your server was configured.

The UDF file format

If you've ever seen a Windows NT UDF file or any *.ini* file, then you know what an Exchange UDF file looks like. The file format is very simple. Each parameter or choice that you can specify with a UDF file is called a setting. Settings are specified as name/value pairs. Related settings are clustered into sections. Section names are marked with brackets, and setting names and values are separated by a single equal sign, with no spaces. Here's a short snippet from a UDF file:

```
[Components]
Services=TRUE
Administrator=TRUE
MSMailConnector=FALSE
cc:Mail=FALSE
```

This section specifies which components Setup should install: the basic Exchange services (the system attendant, IS, DS, and MTA), the Exchange Administrator application, but not the MS Mail or cc:Mail connectors. The order of sections and settings isn't important, but the setting names and values are case-sensitive, so beware. The available Exchange UDF settings are grouped into nine sections; there are a total of 37 settings that you can combine in various ways. I've indicated which sections and settings are mandatory.

The ProductID and Licensing sections

Naturally, the first sections in most of Microsoft's example UDF files are ProductID and Licensing. These sections tell Setup what the serial number of your product is and how you're going to license it. In the case of ProductID, there are two pertinent settings:

cdkey=*key*
> Use this setting if you have a 10-digit CD key (usually found on a sticker on the back of your Exchange Server CD jewel box.)

pid=*productID*
> Use this setting if you have a 20-digit product ID. If your company is an OEM, has bought a computer that includes an OEM version of Exchange, or has a Select license with Microsoft, you'll have a product ID number instead of a CD key.

The Licensing section is a little simpler, because there's only one setting you can use. Exchange 4.0 and 5.0 had both per-server and per-seat licensing, but 5.5 only allows per-seat mode. In the Licensing section, you must include the setting PerSeat=TRUE.

The Service Account section

You no doubt remember the site services account from our earlier encounters with it. You can use the Service Account (note the space between the two words) section to provide Windows NT account credentials for the account, so you don't have to interrupt your installation to browse the domain account list. Remember that the service account is all-powerful, and that the UDF file is plain text—anyone who has access to your UDF file will have the plain text version of the service account password. Since these settings are mandatory when you install the core services, be careful with your UDF files.

AccountName=*domain\account*
> You can specify the account (and, optionally, the domain) you want used as the site service account.

AccountPassword=*password*
> Use this setting to provide the password for the account you've specified.

The Components section

With this section, you can specify which individual components Setup installs. More precisely, you can tell Setup whether to install, or not, the Exchange server core, the Exchange Administrator application, and various add-ons, including the standard set of connectors.

Active Server Components={TRUE | FALSE}
> Although this setting is labeled "Active Server Components," it could more precisely be named "OWA," since that's what you get when you install this item. You can create OWA-only installation scripts; in fact, this is a handy way to roll out OWA to an existing Exchange infrastructure.

Administrator={TRUE | FALSE}
> Controls whether Exchange Administrator is installed. You may want to not install it on every server, then use a separate UDF to install Exchange Administrator alone on servers and workstations that you want to use as administrative machines.

Books Online={TRUE | FALSE}
> This setting controls whether or not you get the voluminous online documentation. While you may want to install it on the same machines where you install Exchange Administrator, you might not want to install it *everywhere*.

cc:Mail={TRUE | FALSE}
> This setting controls whether the cc:Mail connector is installed or not. If you install it, you'll still have to configure it manually from Exchange Administrator.

`Event Service={TRUE | FALSE}`

Controls whether or not the EES is installed. When you upgrade a 4.0 or 5.0 server, EES isn't installed as part of the upgrade, so you might consider using a UDF to install just the event service on your upgraded machines.

`KMServer={TRUE | FALSE}`

Controls whether or not the 5.5 KMS is installed. If you specify that you do want the KMS, Setup will interrupt its installation to ask you what to do with the KMS password. There's no way to silence this portion of the installation, so whenever you install KMS you'll have to manually intervene to complete the installation.

`MSMailConnector={TRUE | FALSE}`

This setting controls whether the MS Mail connector is installed or not. As with the cc:Mail connector, you'll have to configure the connector manually after it's installed.

`Sample Applications={TRUE | FALSE}`

Controls whether the sample Exchange applications included on the CD are installed or not.

`Services={TRUE | FALSE}`

Controls whether the core Exchange service set—the System Attendant, store, directory, and MTA services—is installed. Normally, you'll need this, unless you're updating an existing installation or installing Exchange Administrator by itself.

`X400={TRUE | FALSE}`

Controls whether the X.400 connector is installed or not. There's also a separate section that controls some of the X.400 connector parameters.

The Paths section

The two settings in the Paths section control where Exchange installs the server components and the Exchange Administrator program. No matter what paths you specify here, some DLLs and files will be installed in various places under *%systemroot%*.

`ServerDest=path`

Use this setting to tell Exchange where you want the *exchsrvr* directory to be installed. You can safely leave this setting out; if you do, Setup will default to *c:\exchsrvr*. This setting is ignored if you're not installing server components.

`AdminDest=path`

Use this setting to tell Setup where you want Exchange Administrator installed. By default, Exchange Administrator goes in the *exchsrvr\bin* directory. This setting is ignored if you're not installing Exchange Administrator.

The Organization and Site sections

The Organization and Site sections let you tell Setup what site and organization names to use for your server. The easiest case is when you're installing a server into an existing site; in that case, you use the `ExistingServerName` setting in the Site section to specify the target server, without anything in the Organization section. The final result looks like this:

```
[Site]
ExistingServerName=ENGINEERING
```

If you're installing a new site in an existing organization, you use the Site section with some additional settings:

`SiteName=name`
> This setting is the directory name to be used for the new site. Once you set this, it can't be changed.

`SiteProxyName=proxyName`
> As you'll learn in Chapter 5, *Using Exchange Administrator*, connectors use proxy address generators to generate appropriate addresses. For example, when you add or import a user account on a server with the cc:Mail and X.400 connectors, the cc:Mail and X.400 proxy address generators are called to create suitable cc:Mail and X.400 addresses for the new account. You can specify the root proxy name passed to these generators with the `SiteProxyName` setting. Usually, you'll use the same site and proxy name, but you may need to make them different if your site name somehow violates the proxy address generator's restrictions.

`InternetSiteName=internetName`
> You can specify the DNS name of the site with `InternetSiteName`. This is often useful, since Exchange will happily take a name like "Robichaux & Associates" and turn it into a monstrosity like *exchange.robichaux&associates.com*. The Internet site name is used when Exchange constructs SMTP proxy addresses, so you can just use the organization's name here (as in *oreilly.com*) instead of the site address.

If you're creating the first site and server in a new organization, you can also use the Organization section to specify an organization name and a proxy name to go with it. `OrganizationName` and `OrganizationProxyName` work just like `SiteName` and `SiteProxyName`.

The X400 section

The first thing you should know about this section is that, for once, there's no period in "X.400." The Microsoft documentation says that your section name should be "[X.400]," but if you include the period, Setup will ignore your settings! Apart from that, there are five settings you can use to configure an X.400 connector setup.

They work together to build a complete distinguished name, or DN, for your X.400 connection:

`Organization=`*`orgName`*

> This setting lets you specify the X.400 DN for the organization name. It's equivalent to the `o=` specifier.

`Country=`*`countryName`*

> This setting lets you specify the country in which your X.400 connector lives; you must use the CCITT-standard two-letter abbreviations, like "uk" for the United Kingdom and "at" for Austria; it is equivalent to the `c=` specifier.

`OrgUnit1=`*`orgUnitName`*

> This setting lets you specify the X.400 DN format for the organizational unit that owns the X.400 connector. It's the same as the `ou=` specifier.

`PrivManDomName=`*`prmdName`*

> This setting lets you specify the X.400 PRMD name for the connector.

`AdminManDomName=`*`admdName`*

> This setting lets you specify the X.400 ADMD for the connector.

If you're wondering how this works, consider the following UDF sample for an organization whose X.400 DN is `c=US`, `o=`Mighty Big Airlines, `ou=`Operations, `ou=`Los Angeles:

```
[X400]
Organization=Mighty Big Airlines
Country=us
OrgUnit1=Operations
OrgUnit2=Los Angeles
PrivManDomName=
AdminManDomName=
```

Using unattended installation files

The only trick to building a usable UDF file is to make sure that you have the correct combination of mandatory sections and settings, and that all the critical parameters (like the CD key and the site name) are spelled correctly. Here's a sample UDF file taken from the one I routinely use to install new servers:

```
[Product ID]
cdkey=xxx-yyzzaabb

[Paths]
ServerDest=c:\exchsrvr
AdminDest=c:\exchsrvr

[Components]
Services=TRUE
Administrator=TRUE
MSMailConnector=FALSE
```

Automatically Configuring Connectors

Since the IMS, X.400, cc:Mail, MS Mail, and Notes connectors all require hand configuration, you might wonder if there's a way to automate not only their installation but their configuration. The answer is a resounding "sort of." This ambiguity arises because the connector configuration data is stored in the directory, where it occupies a number of binary blobs in the database. In theory, you should be able to configure a connector the way you want it, then export the configuration blob and import it elsewhere. How much success you have at this will probably vary by connector.

The good news is that you have some other alternatives. You can use the Windows Scripting Host (WSH) to set properties for connectors that expose their interfaces to WSH; you can use WSH, Perl, or even Visual Basic to change connector settings for those few connectors that use the registry. You can even write applications that use the Active Directory Services Interface, or ADSI, to modify entries in the Exchange directory.

Unless you have a lot of connectors to configure, you're probably best off just doing it by hand instead of risking your directory, and possibly your sanity, by trying to automatically blast settings all over your organization.

```
cc:Mail=FALSE
X400=FALSE
Active Server Components=FALSE
Sample Applications=FALSE
Books Online=FALSE
Event Service=FALSE

[Site]
SiteName=ATL

[Organization]
OrganizationName=RA

[ServiceAccount]
AccountName=RA\exchange
AccountPassword=secret

[Licensing]
PerSeat=TRUE
```

As you can see, there's nothing in this sample that's not discussed earlier in this section (there are similar samples on the Exchange Server CD; look in *server\support\batsetup*). All you have to do is put the file somewhere that Setup can find it, use Setup with the /q switch, and relax while it does all the work. If you misspell or omit something important, Setup will catch it and tell you that something's wrong with the file. At that point, you'll have to fix it.

5

Using Exchange Administrator

It's the biggest mess I've ever seen.

—Larry Layten, owner of LJL Enterprises
and my former boss, immediately after
installing Exchange 4.0 and running
Exchange Administrator for the first time

Exchange is a complicated product, with myriad features and options that you can twiddle. This complexity is manifested in the Exchange Administrator application, since it's your primary interface with all the major Exchange components. Learning to use the application is pretty easy; it follows the standard Windows Explorer paradigms, and it's easy to learn the Exchange-specific terminology. Once you're familiar with the Exchange Administrator interface, you'll be ready to start exploring the property pages that control how the MTA, stores, IMS, and so forth actually work.

Exchange Administrator Basics

Exchange Administrator is the primary tool you'll use to manage your Exchange organization, no matter how large or how small it is. In fact, with the few exceptions noted in this chapter and in Appendix A, *BORK Tools*, there aren't any command-line tools you can use—you're stuck with Exchange Administrator. Because you can install Exchange Administrator on any computer running NT 4.0, you can put it wherever your administrators are, then use it to connect to, monitor, and manage any server in your organization, provided that the connection between you and the server you want to manage is RPC-capable.

Basic Concepts

Exchange Administrator is organized around a few simple concepts, which I'll get to in a minute. First, it's important to realize that what you see in Exchange Administrator is actually a reflection of the contents of the directory. Every container and leaf object you see has a corresponding object in the directory. When you change the properties or permissions of an item, you're actually modifying the object's settings in the directory. This may be confusing if you're accustomed to tools that change the registry or configuration files tucked away somewhere on disk. In Exchange, the vast majority of configuration data lives in the directory;* as such, it's automatically replicated throughout the site and organization.

The following list describes the fundamental Exchange Administrator concepts:

Leaf objects
> These objects have no subordinate items. For example, a mailbox is a leaf node because it's the smallest indivisible part of the private store. A server isn't a leaf node because each server has its own set of connectors and containers.

Container objects
> These objects can hold other containers or leaf nodes. Each container appears in the containers pane; most containers are expandable, so you can see their leaf nodes.

Every object has properties
> You access these properties in three ways. You can double-click the object in either the container or contents panes; you can select the item and use the File → Properties… command, or you can use the Alt-Enter accelerator. The properties dialog for each item range in complexity from manageable to absurd, but the general mechanism for setting properties remains the same. (Unfortunately, you can't right-click objects in Exchange Administrator—a rather baffling oversight.)

Most objects have permissions
> By carefully assigning permissions on connectors, mailboxes, and other components, you can achieve fine-grained control over who may do what on your Exchange network. In addition to these permissions, you can control access to specific protocols and services at the mailbox, server, and site levels.

Figure 5-1 shows the Exchange Administrator main window. As you can see, the application uses the same familiar pattern as most other NT administration tools: each server you connect to appears in its own window, and each window is split vertically into two panes. This makes it easy to monitor and administer multiple servers from within a single Exchange Administrator session on your desktop

---

* The IMS is a welcome exception to this trend; many of its settings are stored in the registry.

workstation. The pane on the left is the *container pane*; the Exchange documentation calls it that because that's where the organization-site-server-object hierarchy is displayed, and I'll stick with the official Microsoft terminology. The pane on the right is the *contents pane*; it displays the contents of whatever item is selected in the container pane.

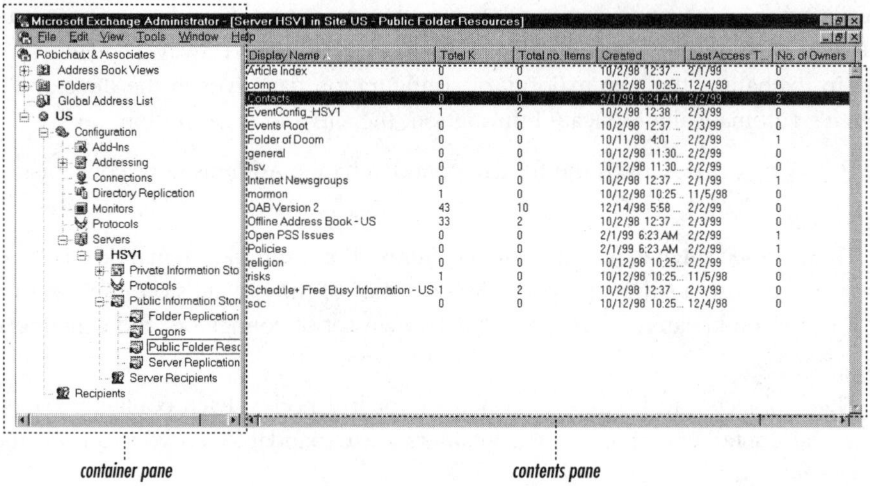

Figure 5-1. Exchange Administrator's main window

Types of Containers

It helps to know what the most common containers are, since you'll often have to select a particular container in Exchange Administrator to accomplish some action. The overall container hierarchy is shown in Figure 5-2; as you can see, some containers encapsulate other containers and some don't.

The organization container

The organization container appears at all servers in all sites within an organization. As you might expect, this container shows directory data that's global to the entire organization. Within the organization container are the following three containers, as well as a container for each site. All site containers appear in the organization container, since sites belong to a single organization.

Address Book Views (ABVs)

These containers allow you to group mailboxes and custom recipients into unique groups. For example, you could quickly build a group of ABVs by city, so that each city has its own local address book. The Address Book Views container holds all the address book views defined for an organization.

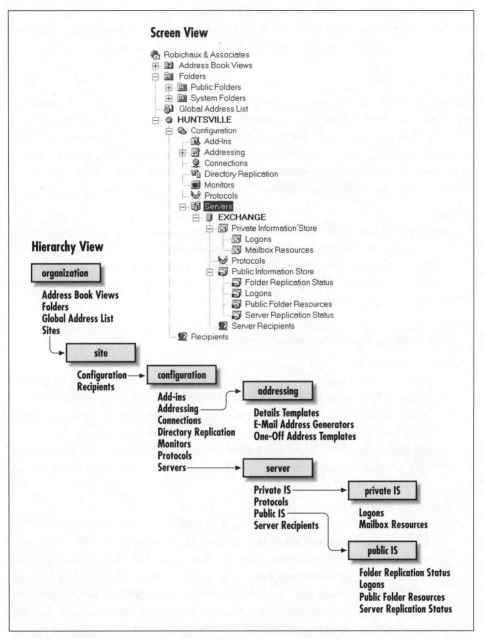

Figure 5-2. Exchange's container hierarchy

Folders

Holds all public folders in the organization. These folders include any public folders defined by your users, any Usenet newsgroups your servers carry, and system folders, like the *Schedule+ Free/Busy* and OAB folders, that Exchange uses internally.

Global Address List

The master address book for the entire organization. It's automatically updated and doesn't contain any subordinate items.

The site containers

Each site in an organization has its own container. These containers contain directory data that's local to the site, including configuration data that applies only to servers within the site. There are two primary containers: the Recipients container holds all mailboxes and custom recipients in the site (including custom recipients), and the Configuration container, which has all the interesting stuff in it. Here's what the Configuration container holds:

Add-ins

Optional services that don't require their own mailbox live in this container. For example, the Schedule+ Free/Busy connector, which is implemented as a Windows dynamic link library (DLL), appears here, as does the MS Mail connector. If you install third-party products like reporting tools, fax servers, and the like, chances are good they'll end up here.

Addressing

This container has its own set of contained items:

Details Templates

This container holds the definition for each address space's address templates. These templates control what data you're asked to provide (and what the directory stores) for each type of recipient, including custom recipients and standard Exchange mailboxes. You'll see one set of details templates for each language module you have installed; for example, if you have Canadian French and US English servers, you'll see two items in the Details Templates container.

E-Mail Address Generators

This container holds entries for each automatic email address generator. Each installed connector has the opportunity to set up an address generator that turns X.400 addresses into its own native format. For example, the cc:Mail address generator turns my address into "Robichaux, Paul at HUNTSVILLE." Each time you do something that causes a new address to be generated, like adding a mailbox or importing data to the directory, these address generators are called to build addresses in their native formats. You can't modify them.

One-Off Address Templates

This container holds the templates that define how users enter addresses they only want to use once. For example, when you use Outlook to create a new message to an X.400 recipient who's not in the GAL, you use the X.400 Address template in your host language (English/USA on my server).

Connections

Connectors that tie Exchange to other sites and foreign systems live in this container. The DRAS, X.400, site, MS Mail, and cc:Mail connectors all appear here, as do the IMS, MS Mail directory synchronization, and NNTP newsfeed connectors.

Directory Replication

This container has one leaf node for each directory replication connector you've configured. Since these connectors link one site with another, each site for which you've defined a DR connector will have a leaf entry in this container.

Monitors

This container contains one leaf entry for each defined link or server monitor. You can configure these monitors to periodically test connections to a remote site, server, or mailbox and raise alerts if the remote server doesn't respond within a specified period.

Protocols

This container has leaf entries for the HTTP, IMAP4, LDAP, NNTP, and POP3 protocols. Whatever settings you apply to the protocol leaves in this container apply to all servers in the site unless you override them at the individual server or mailbox level. For example, if you allow IMAP4 access at the site level but deny it on one server in the site, users on that server won't be able to use IMAP4 to read their mail.

The site-level Configuration container also has five leaf nodes. Confusingly, when you run Exchange Administrator and select a site in the container pane, the contents pane will show the six real containers I just listed, plus the following five leaf items, which the Exchange online help calls containers despite their lack of contained items. These leaf nodes hold much of the most useful site-level configuration data. The settings in these leaf nodes apply to all servers in the site, but they can be locally overridden at the server level.

DS Site Configuration

This leaf is where you set site-wide parameters for the Directory Service, including what custom attributes the site maintains in its schema, what directory data is exposed to LDAP queries, and when and how OABs are generated.

Gateway

Exchange can use connectors and gateways to route messages to and from foreign systems like PROFS, SNADS, Lotus Notes, and SAP. Microsoft calls their own connectivity products "connectors"; third-party products are called "gateways." The Gateway container acts like the site's Connectors container—it shows which gateways are installed in your site and allows you to configure them. If you're not using any gateways, this container will be empty.

Information Store Site Configuration

This container is where you set parameters for the public IS. These parameters include which recipient container public folder addresses go into, who may create top-level public folders, and what public folder affinity settings you want to use.

MTA Site Configuration

You configure MTA connection behavior for all MTAs in the site with this MTA Site Configuration container. These settings govern how the MTA makes and retries connections, as well as what timeout values apply to MTA sessions; they can be overridden on individual servers.

Site Addressing

This container gives you control over how servers in the site build addresses for recipients in the site. For example, you can tweak the addressing defaults to change the right-hand side of the SMTP address for site recipients, or you can turn cc:Mail addresses off. The Site Addressing container is also where you define the schedule you want Exchange to use for recalculating the GWART's routing information.

Finally, there are two additional leaf nodes that appear only when you have a key management server (KMS) installed in your site. For the complete lowdown on the KMS, and the changes introduced with 5.5 SP1 and SP2, see Chapter 16, *Exchange Security*.

CA

This container is where you configure the KMS settings, including designating which users may act as KMS administrators and what password policies to use; you also use it to bulk-enroll new advanced security users.

Site Encryption Configuration

This container lets you specify where the site KMS is located; you can also specify that you want a site to use a KMS in another site.

The server containers

Just as the organization container has one entry for each site, site containers have one subordinate container for each server in the site. Each server in a site appears in that site's Servers container. As with the site container itself, there are two sets of containers: one set appears only in the contents pane, while the other appears in both panes. There are four real containers:

Private Information Store

This container is your gateway to controlling the server's private IS, including deleted item retention periods and per-mailbox storage limits. Beneath this container are two leaf nodes: Logons shows a summary of who's logged on to the server at the current time, and Mailbox Resources shows a summary of how many items and how much disk space each mailbox contains. You can customize what these two nodes display, as you'll see in the section titled "Customizing column view contents," later in the chapter.

Protocols

This container has leaf nodes for the four Internet protocols: HTTP, LDAP, NNTP, and POP3. Each of these leaves has its own set of protocol-specific property pages. If you want servers to use the site-wide defaults for protocol settings, you can leave the "Use site defaults for all properties" checkbox on the server protocol property pages set to "on" (its default), and the servers will inherit the site protocol settings. For any or all protocols on each server, you can clear this checkbox and set independent defaults if you want the server's behavior to be different.

Public Information Store

This container gives you control over the public IS settings, including the replication schedule, age and storage limits, and which public folder replicas go where. (For details on configuring the public IS, see Chapter 10, *Managing Public Folders*.) This container has four subcontainers, each of which expands into a columnar view in the contents pane. Like all other columnar contents views, you can change which columns are displayed, as described later in this chapter.

Folder Replication Status

This view shows which folders are replicated on the server, when the last update for each folder was received, and the current status of the folder's replication.

Logons

This view displays a summary of who's logged on to the public folders; if you've set up anonymous public folder access, this view will be empty (except for the System Attendant) most of the time.

Public Folder Resources

This view shows you how many items are in each public folder and how much space each folder occupies.

Server Replication Status

This view shows the state of replication for each server that the current server talks to, including the last time replication data arrived.

Server Recipients

> This container is a special class of recipient container; it holds only the recipi-
> ents whose mailboxes are homed on the selected server. The only way to get
> someone out of this container is to move their mailbox to another server or
> delete it entirely.

In addition to these four containers, each server has five additional items that
appear in the contents pane when the server is selected:

Directory Service

> This leaf lets you force this server's DS to synchronize itself with other servers
> in the site or to check for consistency between the DS and IS.

Directory Synchronization

> This leaf controls directory synchronization with Microsoft Mail post offices.

System Attendant

> This leaf sports a minimal set of configuration options; about all you can do
> with it is change the amount of time that old message tracking log files are
> maintained.

Message Transfer Agent

> This leaf is where you set this server's MTA parameters. You can set message
> size limits and force the local MTA to recalculate its local routing information.
> You can also view some of the MTA's work queues, so you can get a quick
> idea of what's in them.

Transport Stack leaves

> Each MTA transport stack you install will have a leaf entry here, represented
> by the display name of the stack. For example, if you have a TCP/IP stack
> named "TCP/IP: Denver-SF," that's what you'll see here. By opening the prop-
> erties dialog, you can change the OSI address information for the stack and
> see which connectors are currently running on top of it.

Making Connections

Before you can see anything on a server, you have to establish a connection to the
server. When you connect to a server, Exchange Administrator communicates
directly with the server's DS and IS using RPCs. That means that the channel
between your instance of Exchange Administrator and the server you want to
manage must be RPC-capable. (The good news is that you can manage Exchange
servers quite well over dial-up modem connections, provided that all your network devices are configured to allow RPCs to reach the remote server.)

When you connect to a server, Exchange Administrator opens a window for that
server. The window basically shows you most of what's in the server's local directory, but it's structured into a nice, pretty hierarchy so you can make better sense

of it. You can connect to many servers at once, whether they're in the same site or not. The only restrictions on these connections are that the account you're running Exchange Administrator under must have permission to connect to the target server and it must have adequate permissions in the Exchange directory.

Each server appears in its own window. You can create multiple windows to a single server and use them to view different parts of the directory. The connection to a server remains active until the last window to that server is closed. Remember this if you're using any type of network connection that's metered by time or by usage, since as long as the window is open, Exchange Administrator will keep sending packets to the server.

Getting Around in Exchange Administrator

If you're familiar with the Windows NT Explorer or DNS Manager, you already know what to expect from Exchange Administrator: expand the tree in the container pane until you find the thing you're looking for, then select it and use the File → Properties command to bring up its properties dialog. You can also use all the standard keyboard shortcuts, as shown in Table 5-1.

Table 5-1. Navigational Keys for Exchange Administrator

Key	When Used In…	Action
Alt-Enter	Content or container panes	If selected object has a properties dialog, opens it
Backspace	Content or container panes	Returns the focus to organization container in the container pane
Ctrl-Shift-C	Anywhere	Sets the focus to the first site's Configuration container
Ctrl-Shift-E	Anywhere	Sets the focus to the first site's Recipients container
Ctrl-Shift-N	Anywhere	Sets the focus to the first site's Connections container
Ctrl-Shift-S	Anywhere	Sets the focus to the first site's Servers container
Ctrl-Tab	Properties dialog	Switches to next tab
Home and End	Content or container panes	Moves to top or bottom of pane's contents
Keypad -	Container pane	Collapses the selected container
Keypad +	Container pane	Expands the currently selected container
Left/right arrows	Container pane	If selected item has subcontainers, expands (left arrow) or collapses (right arrow) it; if not, moves to next or previous item

Table 5-1. Navigational Keys for Exchange Administrator (continued)

Key	When Used In...	Action
Left/right arrows	Contents pane	Scrolls the contents pane left or right
PgUp/PgDn	Content or container panes	Moves up or down one pane's worth of data without changing focus
Return	Content pane	Opens properties dialog of selected item
Tab	Content or container panes	Switches focus between the content and container panes
Up/down arrows	Content or container panes	Moves focus to the next or previous item in the current pane

Connecting and Disconnecting

When you start Exchange Administrator for the very first time, you'll be asked to specify what server you want to connect to. (You'll get the same result from choosing the File → Connect to server... menu command.) While you might think Exchange Administrator would be smart enough to look for a server running on the same machine, it's not. The "Connect to server..." dialog is so simple I won't show it here; you can do only three useful things with it. First, you can type in the name of your server directly and either hit the Return key or click the OK button. If you're not sure of the exact name of the server you want to connect to (see? I told you in Chapter 3, *Exchange Planning*, that naming standards were important!), click the Browse... button and you'll see the server browser dialog. It looks just like the container hierarchy: sites appear beneath the organization, and each site's servers appear below the corresponding site. Pick a server from the Servers list and click OK; the server you select will appear in the text field of the original dialog.

Remember, I said there were three useful features available from this dialog. The "Set as default" checkbox is the third. Select a server, then click this checkbox before clicking the OK button, and Exchange Administrator will automatically connect to the specified server when you launch it.

Once Exchange Administrator contacts the server you want to talk to, a new Exchange Administrator window will appear. The window title contains the server, site, and container names, for example, "Server HSV1 in Site US—Public Folders." You can switch between windows, open additional windows to the same server, and do several other tricks that you'll learn about in the next section. You can also close your connection to a server by closing the associated window. When you close the last window connected to a server, that ends your connection to it.

In addition to the File → Connect to server... command, there are two other commands pertinent to server connections. Both live in the Tools menu. The Save Connections on Exit command (which is on by default) tells Exchange Administrator to save a list of your connections when you quit the application; when you restart it, your connections will reappear. The Save Connections Now command does the same thing with the currently active set of connections. Be aware that there's no way to keep Exchange Administrator from reopening your saved connections when you relaunch it, so you might not want to save your connection list if any of the servers you're connected to are on the other side of a modem or on-demand WAN link.

Controlling What You See

First, let's dispense with the Window menu. As with most other Microsoft-developed applications, you use the commands on this menu to sort and switch between multiple windows in Exchange Administrator. Because each server you connect to appears in its own window, you may have several windows open at once if you're managing several servers from one Exchange Administrator session. You can tile, cascade, or arrange the windows with the corresponding commands; you can also switch to any server window by selecting it from the bottom half of the menu. The New Window command lets you open additional windows to the currently active server; this is a helpful way to view more than one container of data at once. When you close the last window connected to a server, you're actually breaking Exchange Administrator's connection to that server.

The View menu offers the standard Win9x-style commands for controlling which user interface elements appear in Exchange Administrator. Here's what you can do with it. First of all, let's cover the mostly useless commands. You can show or hide the toolbar and status bar with the (surprise!) Toolbar and Status Bar commands, and you can move the vertical splitter that separates the contents and container panes with the Move Split Bar command, although why you'd want to do this instead of just dragging the splitter with the mouse is beyond me. You can use the Font... command to change the display font Exchange Administrator uses, and you can change the sort order of items displayed in the contents pane with the Sort by submenu: you can sort items by their display name or their modification date, but you can't choose any other criteria or change the sort from ascending to descending.

Moving on to something a little more useful, you can filter out recipient types you don't want to see. The View → All setting is the default; it shows mailboxes, distribution lists, public folders, and custom recipients in recipient containers. You can use the corresponding View menu commands to see any one of these item types by itself; this is a good way to quickly isolate DLs or public folders that you're interested in without having to wade through other recipient items. These commands are only active when you've selected a recipient container in the container pane.

Some recipient items are invisible; for example, when you create a new DL, you can keep it from appearing in the GAL, and (by extension) in Exchange Administrator. If you need to modify it, though, you'll want to see it. The View → Hidden

Recipients command toggles the visibility of these items. By default, it's off, so hidden items will remain hidden.

Customizing column view contents

One extremely useful feature of Exchange Administrator is the View → Columns… command, which lets you customize which columns are displayed in the contents pane. By default, Exchange Administrator tries to show you what Microsoft's engineers thought was the most useful data for each view, like the mailbox resources view available in the Private IS container. When you use View → Columns…, you'll see a dialog (see Figure 5-3) that allows you to add and remove columns from the display list, so you can customize what appears in the list view.

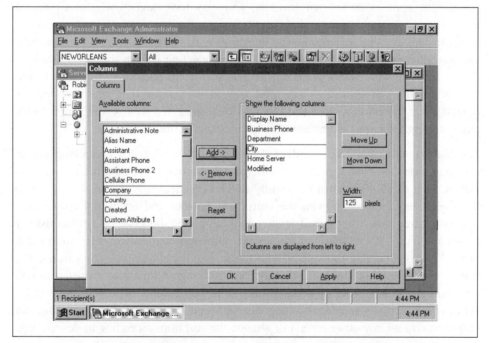

Figure 5-3. Use the Columns dialog to customize the contents pane's display

The dialog features two columns: the left-hand column lists all the attributes that can be attached to a mailbox, and the right-hand column lists the attributes that will appear in the contents pane. By judicious use of the "Add ->" and "Remove <-" buttons, you can build a list that contains only those attributes you want to see. The Move Up and Move Down buttons let you reorder the right-hand list (the first list item appears in the leftmost column of the contents view, the second item in the second column, and so on). You can also select an attribute and change its default column width with the Width field. These settings are saved, so they'll persist between runs of Exchange Administrator.

Viewing Object Properties

Each object in the directory has properties associated with it. Some object properties can be modified through Exchange Administrator's user interface, while some are privately held by the DS and IS. Objects that have properties you can change expose these properties through a properties dialog. Remember that you can open this dialog in three ways: by double-clicking an item in the contents pane, by selecting an item in the contents or container pane and using the File → Properties... menu command, or by selecting an item in either pane and using the Alt-Enter accelerator.

The exact contents of the properties dialogs vary from object to object; however, there are three common tabs that you'll see in several different dialogs. Let's see what they are so you'll be prepared to use them later.

The Permissions tab

The Permissions tab, one incarnation of which appears in Figure 5-4, lets you set permissions on an object. You probably remember from Chapters 1 and 2 that Exchange permissions don't have anything to do with NT permissions; you can take any NT account and give it as many, or as few, administrative privileges on your Exchange network as you want. Each account that has permissions is shown in the list box in the "Windows NT accounts with permissions" group. Each account is shown with its home domain and the role it plays. (See Table 2-2 for a recap of Exchange's roles.)

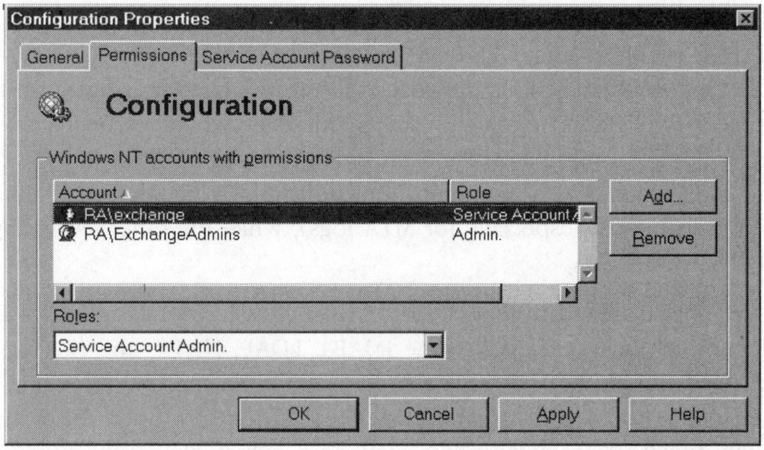

Figure 5-4. The Permissions tab lets you control access to individual objects

You can use the Add... and Remove buttons to change the list of accounts in the box; after you select an account, you can change its role with the Roles pull-down. When you add an account, it takes on the Admin role, so make sure you change it to whatever access level you want it to have. Changes to the account list or role assignments are immediately visible, but they're not made permanent in the directory until you click the OK or Apply buttons. As extra protection, if you change permissions so that the account you're using would lose administrative access, Exchange will warn you.

Note that using this tab only allows you to assign permissions based on Exchange's standardized roles. If you want to assign rights (as described earlier in Table 2-1) to each account instead of using roles, you can force Exchange Administrator to display those rights by changing an Exchange Administrator preference. See the section "Setting Exchange Administrator Preferences," later in this chapter, for the details.

It's worth pointing out something subtle about permissions: just like every other attribute, they're stored in the directory, and propagate via directory replication. This means that permission changes won't be instantly available on every server in a site, much less at every site in an organization. Be forewarned that these changes take a little time to make the rounds to all servers.

The Diagnostics Logging tab

Many of Exchange's services have diagnostic logging built in. For example, the MTA has twelve different categories of things it can log, including security events, directory access, and what its internal state is at various checkpoints. It's often useful, even crucial, to capture this diagnostic information when you're trying to isolate and fix a problem somewhere in your server network. However, diagnostic logging has a potentially serious drawback: all those logged messages can take up lots of space. By default, logging is turned off everywhere. Actually, saying it's turned off is a bit of a misnomer; the truth is that the logging level is set to "none." There are three other levels: minimum, medium, and maximum. Maximum gives you lots of trivial detail (especially for MTA logs), while the other levels have progressively less detail.

Server-level objects that can generate diagnostic logs have a Diagnostics Logging tab; these objects include the MTA; the IMAP4, LDAP, NNTP, and POP3 protocol containers; and the public and private IS services. You can control logging only at the server, not at the site or organization level. When you open the Diagnostics Logging tab, you'll see something like Figure 5-5, which shows the public IS version. The Services list box shows all the services whose log settings can be controlled from this property page; the Category list box on the right shows what the currently selected service can log and what each category's current logging level is set to.

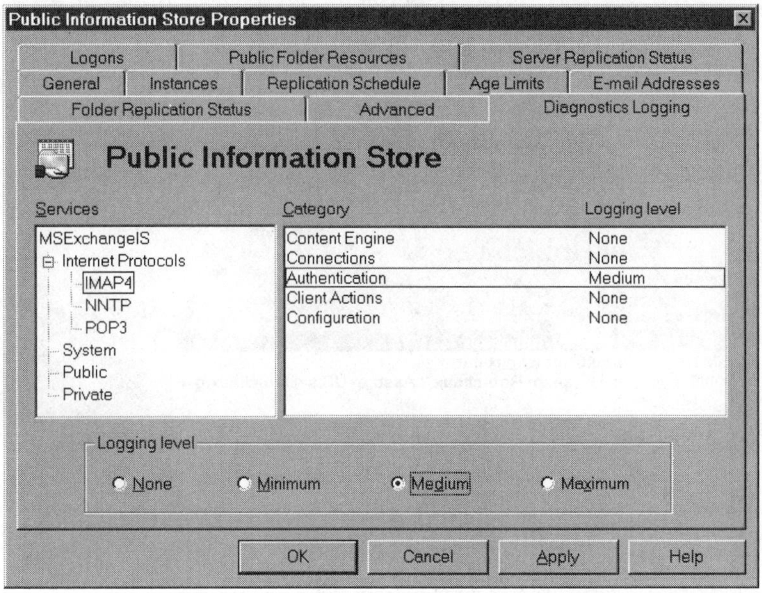

Figure 5-5. The Diagnostics Logging tab lets you control what gets logged for each logging-capable object

The E-mail Addresses tab

Some objects (including mailboxes, distribution lists, and public folders) have email addresses associated with them. When you create a new object, all installed address generators get a crack at the object and can generate appropriate addresses. For example, if you have the cc:Mail and Notes connectors installed, when you create a new mailbox, both address generators will be called to generate additional addresses for the mailbox. Objects with associated email addresses have an E-mail Addresses tab in their properties dialogs; Figure 5-6 shows the tab for an ordinary mailbox. As you can see, the "E-mail addresses" list shows three addresses: one in X.400 form, one in SMTP, and one in MS Mail. You can add, edit, or remove addresses using the buttons on the right-hand side of the dialog:

New...

> When you click this button, you'll see a list of all the address types the system knows how to generate. Once you choose a type, the new address is generated (courtesy of the proxy address generators) and will appear in the "E-mail addresses" list.

Edit...

> You can edit an existing address with this button. The resulting dialog lets you change the address however you want; however, it doesn't validate your entry or constrain it in any way, so be careful.

Remove

> You can remove addresses with this button; changes don't take effect until you close the properties dialog or click the Apply button.

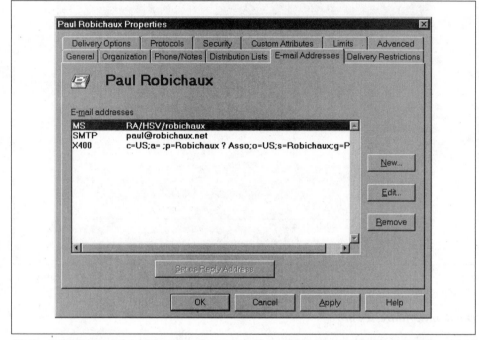

Figure 5-6. The E-mail Addresses tab shows you what addresses are associated with an object

You can specify which address is used as the default return address by selecting it and clicking the Set as Reply Address button—just make sure the address is correct and properly spelled, or replies to the object will bounce as clients try to use the (bogus) return address.

> Don't remove or change the X.400 addresses you see in the E-mail Addresses tab of these property dialogs! Since Exchange 5.5 uses X.400 DNs internally, if you change the address of any item, the MTA won't be able to route mail to it.

Setting Exchange Administrator Preferences

Microsoft applications almost always feature a toolbar, and it's usually customizable, to an extent. Exchange Administrator is no different; you can customize the toolbar with the Tools → Customize Toolbar... command. However, since most of the useful commands available in the application are already on the toolbar, and not every menu command can be added, you may not find this feature very useful.

Some more significant settings are lurking, however. When you use the Tools → Options... command, you get the Options dialog box, which has three tabs: Auto Naming, Permissions, and File Format. Each of these tabs controls some aspect of how Exchange Administrator behaves.

The Auto Naming tab, shown in Figure 5-7, lets you control the names Exchange Administrator supplies when you create a new mailbox. These settings are stored in the registry, so each user who runs Exchange Administrator can have her own set of autonaming options. When you fill out the first name, last name, and middle initial fields in the mailbox properties dialog, Exchange Administrator will construct two names from what you enter. The display name is what's listed in the GAL and on the mailbox properties pages—that's the human-readable tag associated with the mailbox's actual DN. The alias name serves as a secondary identifier for the mailbox. For example, my mailbox display name is "Paul Robichaux," and the alias is "paul"; these names both refer to (and are associated with the directory entry for) the same mailbox.

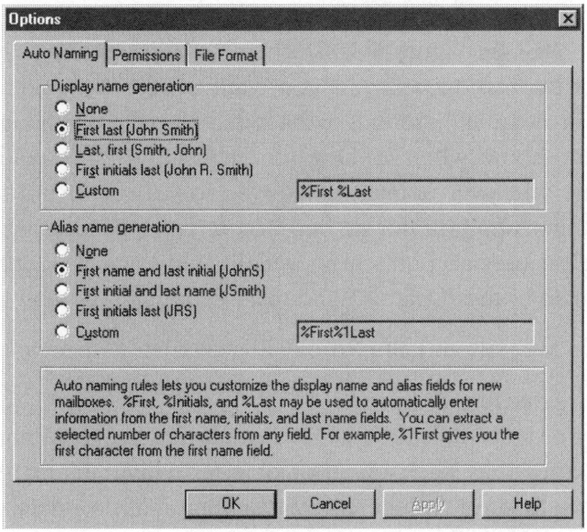

Figure 5-7. The Auto Naming tab gives you control over how display names and alias names are generated

The two groups of controls in the Auto Naming tab give you control over this behavior. Both sets work the same way; you can leave the default behavior as is, or you can set independent preferences for alias and display name generation, as follows:

- You can turn off automatic name generation altogether with the None button.

- You can choose from three prefabricated naming styles with the three middle buttons; these assemble display and alias names based on various combinations of first name, last name, and initials.

- You can build a customized name by selecting the Custom button and typing a naming specifier into the associated text field. The format of these specifiers is simple: %First, %Initials, and %Last all do what you'd expect, so that typing in "%Last (%First)" will turn "John Smith" into "Smith (John)." You can also pull out only part of the field by including the number of characters you want in the format specifier: "%Last, %1First (%2Initials)" turns "George H.W. Bush" into "Bush, G (H.)."

 If you're going to change the autoname generation settings, do it before you create any mailboxes, since the new settings only affect mailboxes created after they have been changed.

The Permissions tab (see Figure 5-8) is where you instruct Exchange Administrator in the default permission behavior you want to see. The controls in the "Windows NT domain defaults" group govern what domain Exchange Administrator tries to use as the home when looking for or creating NT accounts. The default behavior is to use whatever domain the server you're connected to is in, but you can force Exchange Administrator to find accounts in the domain you specify by selecting the "Select user accounts from default Windows NT domain" button and specifying a domain in the "Default Windows NT domain" combo box.

Each checkbox in the bottom half of the dialog box has a specific meaning:

Show Permissions page for all objects
    This checkbox does what it says. By default, Exchange Administrator doesn't show the Permissions page on most objects, which simultaneously makes it harder for you to screw things up by assigning inappropriate permissions and makes it harder for you to secure individual objects from tampering. Turn this checkbox on and you'll see a Permissions tab on every object in the directory. You may not want to leave this on by default; when you do, every time you select a Permissions tab, Exchange Administrator will look up all of the accounts that have permissions all the way up to the organization container— and this may take longer than you expect.

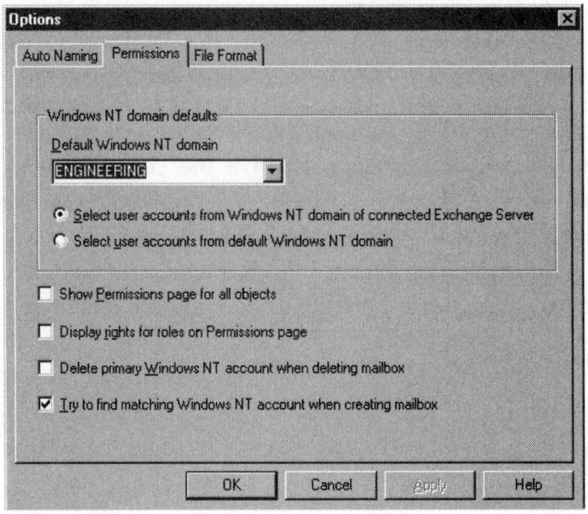

Figure 5-8. The Permissions tab is where you specify default permission behavior for Exchange Administrator

When you install Exchange Administrator on a new machine, this setting isn't propagated. If all of a sudden you don't see permissions pages when you expect to, this is the setting to check.

Display rights for roles on Permissions page

This checkbox adds a new list box to the Permissions tab you saw earlier in Figure 5-4. The list box allows you to change the individual rights assigned to each account listed on the Permissions tab. Normally, you have to take all of the rights lumped together in a role; by checking this box, you can grant very specific permissions to accounts and groups with considerably finer precision than by just slapping them into one of the predefined roles.

Delete primary Windows NT account when deleting mailbox

This checkbox is dangerous; when checked, it instructs Exchange Administrator to remove (not disable) the NT account attached to the mailbox. Once the account is deleted, all permissions based on that account (for files, shares, and so on) will be invalidated. If you really want to disable access to an account, use the User Manager to disable it. Leave this checkbox off so Exchange Administrator will only delete mailboxes, not their associated accounts.

Try to find matching Windows NT account when creating mailbox

This checkbox is turned on by default, and with good reason. When you create a new mailbox, and this option is on, Exchange Administrator will search for an account that matches the alias name on the mailbox properties tab; if it finds a close match, it will offer to let you use that match instead of forcing you to manually search for the correct account. This option is most useful if you create mailboxes after their user accounts are available; if you create both at the same time (and you probably will, after reading Chapter 6, *Mailboxes, Recipients, and Distribution Lists*), it's not quite so worthwhile.

The File Formats tab is worth a mention, too (but not a picture—sorry!). When you import or export directory information or save the contents pane's data to a text file using the File → Save Window Contents... command, you can choose which separator character is used to delimit columns (the default is a comma, but you can choose the tab, space, or semicolon characters), whether single or double quotes are used to quote text, and what punctuation character is used to flag directory properties (% is the default). As a last tweak, you can choose whether to save the files with Unicode or ASCII characters. It's unlikely you'll ever need to use this tab for anything, since the default settings (comma as delimiter, double quotation marks for quoting, and % as a property flag) work fine for almost any conceivable use.

Creating and Deleting Objects

Now that you know how to move around in Exchange Administrator, you're probably wondering what you can do with it. I'll cover the myriad property pages and options for the MTA, IS, and other components in later chapters; right now, it's time to see how you create and delete directory objects from within Exchange Administrator. The File menu contains several commands that you can use to create new mailboxes, distribution lists, address book views, and other goodies. This section is just an overview of what commands exist; each command is discussed in more detail in the appropriate chapter.

Deleting Things

In the science fiction novel *Mindkiller*, Spider Robinson points out that if you don't know anything about the technology, it's easier to build the erase head of a tape recorder than the recording head. The same is true for Exchange Administrator: it's easier to delete things than to create them. The Edit → Delete command deletes the currently selected item in the contents or containers pane. You can delete some things, but not others, as shown in Table 5-2. Exchange Administrator will never delete something without asking you to confirm your command, and when your request has consequences (like the loss of all mailboxes on a server) Exchange Administrator will warn you as part of the confirmation.

Table 5-2. *What You Can and Can't Delete*

Object	Deletable?	Consequences
Address book view	Yes	If you delete an ABV, it has no effect on the recipients in it, since they really live in a recipient container.
Public folders	No	Users who have permissions may delete folders from their mail client, but you can't do it in Exchange Administrator.
GAL	Of course not	
Add-Ins	No	This container is automatically maintained; to remove an add-in, use its setup program.
Addressing items	No	
Connections items	Yes	If you delete a connector, it stops all mail flow over the connection.
Directory Replication items	Yes	You can delete directory replication connectors, but read Chapters 7 and 9 before you do.
Monitors items	Yes	Deleting a link or server monitor immediately stops it from working.
Protocols items	No	If you want to turn off individual protocols, use the site or server configuration containers.
Servers	Sort of	You can only delete servers that Exchange Administrator thinks are inactive. If you delete a server and it comes back up, you'll have backfill problems.
Public and private IS on a server	Yes	You can remove the public and/or private IS databases on a server to turn it into a mailbox-only, public folder-only, or (if you delete both) connector-only server. Exchange Administrator will warn you that deleting either IS requires you to copy any data you want to keep, because it deletes the databases too.
Recipients containers	Sort of	You can't delete the master Recipients container. If you've created your own containers, you can remove them, but when you do, all their recipients will be deleted, too.

Creating Mailboxes

When you create a mailbox, you're actually creating a new entity in the private IS (that's where the mail goes) *and* a new address entry in the organization's directory. Creating mailboxes is easy: the File → New Mailbox... command does the deed, and you can use the Ctrl-M accelerator to speed the process further. When the General tab of the mailbox properties dialog appears, you can fill out as much of it as you want to; at a minimum, you have to supply a display name and an alias, both of which will be generated for you if you supply a first name or last name. You should also tell Exchange Administrator what NT account should be associated with the mailbox. If the urge strikes, you can fill out settings on the

twelve other tabs stuffed into this dialog. For complete details on what all those
tabs mean and what you can do with them, see Chapter 6.

 You nominally have to have a recipient container selected to add a
mailbox, DL, or custom recipient; if you have something else
selected, Exchange Administrator will ask you if you want to switch
to the Recipients container to create the object. The correct answer is
yes.

If you want to create many mailboxes at once, you'll probably need to use the
directory import features discussed later in the chapter. You may also be able to
use the `net user /add` command, as described in Chapter 6.

Creating Distribution Lists

An Exchange DL is a convenient way to group users so you or anyone you give
permissions to can send mail to many users at once. When you create a DL, it
goes into the organization's directory and is visible in the GAL by default. To create a new DL, use the File → New Distribution List... command or the Ctrl-D accelerator. The DL properties dialog requires you to enter a display name and an alias
name for the DL, from which its address is automatically generated. You can also
specify who's on the DL, what server is responsible for expanding mail sent to it,
and who owns it—and that's just on the General tab; there are five other tabs that
control attributes, delivery restrictions, and so forth. All these items are discussed
in the section "Creating and Managing Distribution Lists" in Chapter 6.

Creating Custom Recipients

You probably remember that a custom recipient in Exchange is what you use to
address mail to a non-Exchange recipient. When you create a custom recipient,
you're creating an address record in the directory, but there's no associated
mailbox data—just an address that maps to an outside address. That address in
turn may be in one or more address spaces in the GWART. Custom recipients
appear in the GAL just like regular Exchange recipients, and users anywhere in the
organization can use them without doing anything special.

You create custom recipients with the File → New Custom Recipient... command
or the Ctrl-R accelerator. The next thing you'll see is a small dialog box that asks
you to choose an address type: MS Mail, SMTP, fax, and so on. The list of address
types you see will vary according to what connectors you've got installed (remember, connectors install address generators, which are what Exchange uses to create
custom recipient addresses). Once you select the address type, you'll see a dialog

specific to that type of address. For example, if you create an MS Mail custom recipient, your dialog will have spaces for the post office name, the mailbox name, and the location. That's pretty much it; for somewhat more detail, see the section "Creating and Managing Custom Recipients" in Chapter 6.

Creating Recipient Containers

You might think that you should group your users together by putting each group in its own recipient container; after all, why would Microsoft include such a seemingly handy feature as the File → New Other → Recipients Container... command if they didn't want you to use it? Don't succumb to this particular temptation, or (as with many other kinds of temptation) you'll almost certainly regret it later.

Creating multiple recipient containers seems like an easy way to assemble, say, all of the users in your Dallas office in one place. It *is* easy. The heartache begins when you want to move a user from one container to another. Guess what? You can't. This means that if one of your users moves from Dallas to Dublin, and you've put her in the Dallas recipient container, her mailbox will stay there unless you remove and recreate it. Yuck.

Ignore this feature—just pretend it's not there. Instead of grouping users with recipient containers, use address book views. Since ABVs are dynamically generated based on user attributes, when you change a user's record, all ABVs that the user participates in will be updated automatically; you can also use the Tools → Add To Address Book View... command to instantly put one or many users into a specific ABV. (See the sidebar "A Sneaky Way to Do Bulk Attribute Changes" in Chapter 9, *Managing the Directory*, for full details.)

I should leaven the foregoing by saying that you can use recipient containers as long as you don't mind the inability to easily move users between containers. For example, you can put DLs, custom recipients, shared resource mailboxes for things like conference rooms, and "regular" mailboxes into separate containers, since the Exchange Administrator export/import features work on entire containers. This lets you handle each of these item types independently of the others.

Creating Link and Server Monitors

Link and server monitors are valuable trouble-prevention tools. They periodically monitor the state of a server or a connection and report back to you when response time exceeds the bounds you set or when the remote system fails to respond at all. You can watch multiple servers in one Exchange Administrator session, but each monitor can only watch one server; if you want to monitor ten servers in a site, you'll need ten separate monitors.

Server monitors watch any set of services you specify (by default, this set contains only the DS, IS, and MTA). If any service fails to respond to a query from the monitor, the monitor can restart it, reboot the machine, or do nothing; in any of these three cases, the moniter can notify you via email or an alert message, or you can have it launch an external process (like a program to dial your alphanumeric pager and send a message).

Link monitors work a little differently. If you're monitoring an Exchange server, the monitor sends periodic RPC pings to the monitored server and notifies you if it doesn't get an answer in time. If you prefer, you can also set the monitor to send mail messages to a specified recipient; this allows you to monitor Unix servers and other non-Exchange mail systems by sending messages and waiting for an automatically generated reply. Like server monitors, link monitors can alert any combination of accounts you specify.

Both types of monitors let you provide a list of NT accounts to notify when the monitor reaches either its warning or alert states. If a monitored system doesn't respond within the allowed interval, the monitor moves that server to its warning state list; if it still doesn't respond in the interval after that, the server is moved to the alert list. You can set the polling interval in seconds, minutes, or hours, and you can specify that servers on either list be polled more frequently.

You create these monitors using the File → New Other → Link Monitor... and Server Monitor... commands, which are covered in more detail in Chapter 14, *Managing Exchange Servers*.

The New Other Submenu

You can create thirteen other items from Exchange Administrator's File → New Other submenu. We've already discussed link and server monitors and recipient containers, and in Chapter 9, you'll see the two commands related to ABVs, but that still leaves us with eight other items. Here's what they do and where to learn more about them:

MTA Transport Stack...
    Creates a transport protocol stack for the X.400 connector. You may create a TCP/IP, X.25, RAS, or TP4 (an X.400-specific transport) stack, and you must create a stack using one of these protocols before you can create an X.400 connector. For more details, see the section "Creating site connectors" in Chapter 7, *Managing Connectors and the MTA*.

X.400 Connector...
    Creates a new X.400 connector atop a previously created MTA transport stack. Once you've created the connector, you'll need to configure it using the directions in Chapter 8, *Managing the Internet Mail Service*, before mail will start to flow.

Dynamic RAS Connector...

Creates a new DRAS connector, which you can then use to transfer mail to other sites via an on-demand RAS connection. Before you can create a DRAS connector, you have to create a RAS MTA transport stack, and before you can do that, you'll have to install and configure NT's RAS service.

Site Connector...

Creates a new site connector. Once you specify a server in the target site, Exchange Administrator will connect to the specified server and configure both ends of the site connector at once. You must have RPC-capable connectivity to the other site, and you must have administrative permissions in the site you're connecting to; if the two servers are in different domains, this means you'll also need administrative rights in the foreign domain. See the section "Creating site connectors" in Chapter 7.

Directory Replication Connector...

Creates a replication connector between two sites. Directory replication traffic just rides on top of a mail connection, so you can't create any DRCs until you've established a connection between two sites using one of the standard connector types. Once you've done that, you can establish a DRC to form directory replication bridgeheads in each site.

Information Store...

Creates a public or private IS on a server that doesn't have one. For example, let's say you took one of your servers and deleted its private IS to turn it into a public folder server. Six months later, you decide that you need an additional mailbox server, so you want to restore the private IS to your public folder server—you'd use this command. Oddly, the command is enabled on all servers, but if you open the dialog box on a server that already has both types of IS, you'll find that you can't do anything except cancel the dialog.

Newsfeed...

If you want to snag NNTP news from other sites and offer it to your users via public folders or NNTP, this command creates a new instance of the Internet News Service (INS) and configures it to exchange news articles with your upstream NNTP providers. Note that this command has nothing to do with allowing NNTP access to your public folder hierarchy and contents. For more details on how this works, see Chapter 12, *Managing the Internet News Service.*

Internet Mail Service...

Exchange Setup always installs the IMS, even if you don't need it. Once it's installed, it just sits inertly on your disk until you use the Internet Mail Service... command. This command runs the Internet Mail Wizard (described in gory detail in Chapter 8) so you can configure the IMS for inbound and outbound mail transfer.

Using the Duplicate Command

Sometimes you want to copy an object and retain most of its properties. For example, if one of your departments adds a new employee, wouldn't it be nice to copy an existing employee's mailbox, including the department name, mail stop, fax number, and so on, and just change the name? The File → Duplicate… command does exactly that for mailboxes and DLs. Select the object you want to duplicate in the contents pane, and it creates a duplicate and displays the duplicate's properties dialog, copying most of the mailbox or DL properties except the names. Just give the duplicate the name you want it to have (and the NT account, in the case of mailbox objects), change any other properties that differ, and voilà!—a duplicate is created.

Interestingly, you can duplicate other objects besides mailboxes and DLs, including link and server monitors (select the Monitors container of a site, then select the monitor in the contents pane) and public folders (select the Public IS container of a server, then its Public Folder Resources subcontainer, then the folder in the contents pane).

Exporting and Importing Directory Data

Exchange Administrator offers you a very useful capacity: you can import and export information from the organization directory. This offers a wonderful way to load the contents of your Exchange database into an external application; better yet, you can bulk-load existing legacy databases (say, the contents of your employee records database) into Exchange Administrator and let it do the work of creating new mailboxes and populating their attributes. This export/import capacity is at the heart of the Migration Wizard; all the source extractors do is convert information from its original format into a CSV file that the import utility can read.

When you export data, you can import it into any application that can read a CSV file; this makes it possible to export directory information to another email system or a database. You can also use export files to keep a list of mailbox properties; this can be helpful in the event you lose your mailbox server or domain controllers. Going in the other direction, importing files into Exchange gives you an easy way to quickly build distribution lists, make bulk changes to many mailboxes (like changing mailbox storage limits or the deleted item retention period), or import data generated by an external system.

Understanding the CSV Format

If you've ever used a spreadsheet or database program, you probably already understand the CSV format pretty well; after all, there's not much to it. Unfortunately, you can't just slap a bunch of data in a file, sprinkle it with a few commas, and expect Exchange to ingest it without complaining. Exchange writes (and expects to read) CSV files that have two distinct sections: a header and a set of contents. The following code shows what a header looks like; this header specifies that each line of the contents that follow will have thirteen properties, starting with Obj-Class and ending with Hide from AB. Each property may have zero or more values, although the directory only allows zero or one value for most properties.

```
Obj-Class,First Name,Last name,Display Name,Alias Name,Directory Name,Primary
Windows NT Account,Home-Server,E-mail address,E-mail Addresses,Members,
Obj-Container,Hide from AB
```

Notice that there aren't any spaces between items, just commas. Although you can't see it here, the header all has to be on the first line of the CSV file. When you export a CSV file, Exchange Administrator can generate a header for you, or you can provide a header that specifies exactly which fields you want exported. (After all, there's no sense in exporting stuff you don't plan to change before you reimport the file, is there?) If you make up a property name that doesn't match any directory attributes, the import will fail with a warning message, but you can cheat by using the Import Header tool, as described in Appendix A.

Let's see the header again, this time followed by the first contents line, which is emphasized:

```
Obj-Class,First Name,Last Name,Display Name,Alias Name,Directory Name,
Primary Windows NT Account,Home-Server,E-mail Address,E-mail Addresses,
Members,Obj-Container,Hide from AB
Mailbox,Paul,Robichaux,Paul Robichaux,PaulR,PaulR,RA\Paul,HSV1,,
MS:RA/HSV/robichaux%SMTP:paul@robichaux.net%X400:c=US;a= ;p=Robichaux ?
Asso;o=US;s=Robichaux;g=Paul;,,/ou=US/cn=Recipients,
```

The combination of these two lines tells us that this entry is for a mailbox assigned to Paul Robichaux; the mailbox's alias and directory names are both PaulR, and the primary NT account for this mailbox is *RA\paul*. The mailbox is hosted on the *HSV1* server and has three email addresses: an MS Mail address, an SMTP address, and an X.400 address. The Members field is blank, since this isn't a distribution list, and no value is assigned to the Hide from AB field. If you edit any of these fields, say, the X.400 address, and reimport this contents line, the attributes you edited will be added to the existing values.

 Some useful values for Obj-Class: "Mailbox" and "DL" are self-explanatory, and "Remote" means custom recipient.

There are two other things to notice about the contents line. First, and most importantly, in properties with multiple values, like E-mail Addresses, those values are separated by % characters, unless you specify a different character in the File Formats tab of the Exchange Administrator options dialog. The values aren't escaped or quoted in any way; they're just jammed in together unless there are commas in a property, in which case they must be enclosed in double quotes. Second, values that are blank, like the Members property in the previous example, must be empty, with no spaces, tabs, or other characters in them.

Of course, CSV files may contain thousands of records; each content record has to be on a single line, but apart from that, there's no restriction on their size. Once you get Exchange Administrator to export a file for you, you can edit it with any tool you choose. Excel is popular because it understands how to read and write CSV files and it has good macro programming tools, so it's not hard to whip up a quick macro to make some required change to all 20,000 entries in your GAL. You can also write scripts to do repetitive tasks like reformatting data from a legacy database; Perl is particularly useful for these tasks, since it's good at pattern matching and text processing. Of course, you can always open up Notepad and use it if you feel masochistic.

Most Exchange books, and many demos, use Excel as the editor of choice for CSV files. As long as no field in your data is longer than 255 characters, you can use Excel; if any are longer (as may happen if you have long secondary addresses, or if you're working with DLs) you need to find another editor.

The mode property

There's one major difference between import and export files. When you create an export file, it just contains directory data; it doesn't specify what action Exchange Administrator should take with each record when the file's imported again. A special property called the *mode property* controls what happens when an import record is processed. This property *must* follow the Obj-Class property in the header, or Exchange Administrator will complain and refuse to import your file.

The default value for **Mode** is **modify**. That tells Exchange Administrator to create any object that has an import record but that isn't already in the directory, and to modify any existing entry based on the import record's properties. Most of the time, **modify** will solve your needs, since it'll automatically create any objects that don't exist. You can also use the **create** mode to create new objects or the **delete** mode to remove existing objects. Here's a short sample that removes one mailbox and adds a new one:

```
Obj-Class,Mode,First Name,Last name,Display Name,Alias Name,Directory Name,
Primary Windows NT Account,Home-Server,E-mail address;E-mail
Addresses,Members,Obj-Container,Hide from AB
```

```
Mailbox,create,Jim,Hood,Jim Hood,JimH,JimH,RA\JimH,HSV1,,MS:RA/HSV/hood%
SMTP:jim@robichaux.net%X400:c=US;a= ;p=Robichaux ? Asso;o=US;s=Hood;g=Jim;,,
/ou=US/cn=Recipients
Mailbox,delete,Chuck,Farnsworth,Chuck Farnsworth,ChuckF,ChuckF,,,,,,,
```

Of course, if you try to delete an object that doesn't exist, or if you use the
create mode and specify an object that does exist, the operation will fail.

Exporting Data

The basic procedure for exporting data is very simple: use the Tools → Directory
Export... command, fill out a dialog box, and scoop up the CSV file for later use.
The actual process is a bit more complex, but only because filling out the dialog
box properly takes some knowledge of what data you want in the output file.
Figure 5-9 shows the Directory Export dialog.

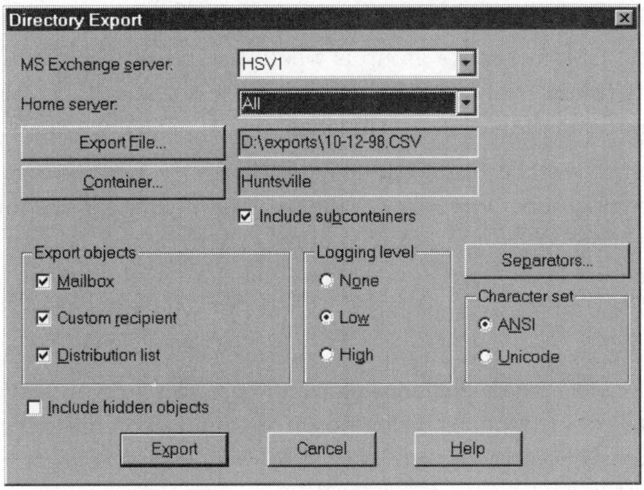

*Figure 5-9. The Directory Export dialog box controls what data is exported from your
directory and how it is formatted*

Here's what the Directory Export dialog controls do:

* The MS Exchange server pull-down controls which server Exchange Administrator retrieves the directory data from. Choose this server wisely, since
  retrieving a lot of data will place an extra load on the export server. The
  Home server pull-down lets you tell Exchange Administrator what server has
  the data you want on it. The difference between these two is subtle: the
  former is the server Exchange Administrator will query for the data, and the
  latter is where the data actually comes from.

- The Export File... button lets you tell Exchange Administrator what export file to use. If you want to create a blank file, you can; if you supply the name of an existing file, the exporter will look in the file and use whatever header it finds. This makes it easy to recycle one set of fields and use it again and again.

- When you first use the Directory Export command, the Container... field indicates that Exchange Administrator will export the contents of the Recipients container. If you want to change that, use the Container... button, which displays a dialog showing a hierarchy of all the recipient containers in your directory. This hierarchy includes the GAL, the standard Recipients container, and any ABVs or additional recipient containers you've added. Pick the container you want Exchange Administrator to export from.

  The "Include subcontainers" checkbox tells Exchange Administrator whether you want to export all subordinate items of the container you chose, or just those items immediately below the container itself.

- The Export Objects control group is where you select what items you want to export. By default, only the Mailbox checkbox is selected, but you can export any combination of mailboxes, DLs, and custom recipients you want.

- Specify what level of diagnostic logging (if any) you want with the Logging Level control group. Once you get the hang of it, your exports probably won't encounter any errors; the default setting of Low is still good to use, just in case. The log file is written to the same directory as the export file you specify, and it has the same name as the export file, with an extension of *.err.*

- The Separators... button and the "Character set" controls together provide a way to override the default separator and character set you define in the File Formats tab of the Options dialog box. The settings you make here only apply to this export and aren't saved.

- The "Include hidden objects" checkbox does what its name implies: when set, it exports hidden DLs, recipients, and mailboxes. By default, it's off.

The export process, then, boils down to these five steps:

1. Open the Directory Export dialog and choose which servers you want to handle the export.

2. Choose an export file, either by typing in a new filename to create a new file or locating an existing file.

3. If you don't want to export the entire Recipients container, use the Container button to select whatever container you do want to export.

4. Use the Export Objects group to select only those objects you want in the output file.

5. Optionally, you can change the logging level, separator, and character set with the corresponding controls.

That's it—follow these steps and you'll end up with a CSV file that you can edit, tweak, and massage in preparation for importing it back into the directory.

Importing Data

Once you've rearranged, edited, added to, and deleted from your CSV file, you're ready to reimport it and repopulate the Exchange directory. Interestingly, importing data imposes a greater load on your server than exporting data. The biggest bottleneck in the import process is the use of proxy address generators. As each record is imported, if Exchange Administrator has to generate new email addresses it has to call the proxy address generator DLLs, each of which has to construct a valid address and make sure it doesn't duplicate an existing address. This can take a long time, so it's important to turn off address generation for address types you don't need.

You import data into Exchange Administrator with the Tools → Directory Import... command, which produces the Directory Import dialog shown in Figure 5-10.

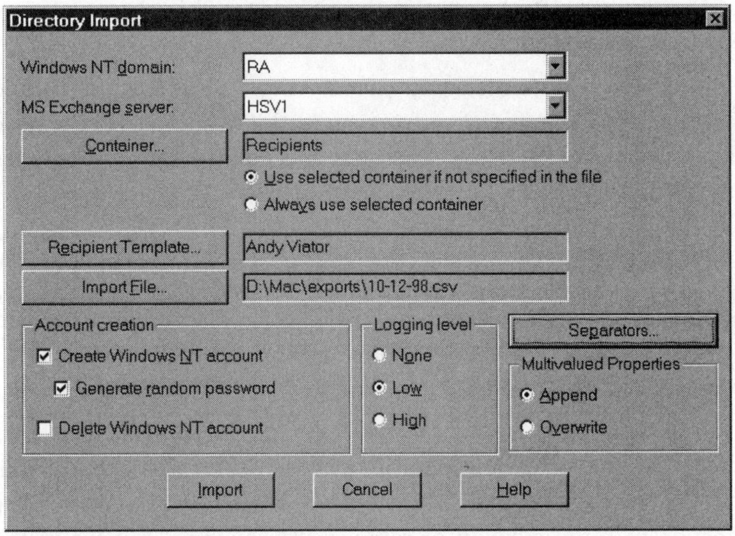

Figure 5-10. The Directory Import dialog box controls how Exchange Administrator processes incoming data

Here's how to use the Directory Import dialog:

- Use the Windows NT domain pull-down list to select the domain Exchange Administrator should use when it creates new accounts. If you uncheck the "Create Windows NT account" box, this setting is ignored.

- Use the MS Exchange server pull-down to indicate what server you want the newly created (or updated) directory information to go to first. That server will replicate to its peers in the organization through the normal directory replication process.

- The Container... button allows you to specify what container incoming records go into. Each content line in the import file can specify a container for that record. If you want to honor that setting, choose the "Use selected container if not specified in the file" radio button and Exchange Administrator will use the import file's specified container unless none is specified. If you choose the "Always use selected container" button instead, all imported records will be created in the container you specify.

- The Recipient Template... button is pretty useful; it allows you to specify a template mailbox whose attributes will be copied to the new mailbox. For example, you can create a template mailbox for each department in your organization, naming each of them after the corresponding department. By filling out the template's address, phone number, department name, and so on, then specifying it as the template when you do an import, any property that's defined in the template but not in the CSV file will be copied from the template item to the newly created object.

- The Import File... button lets you choose what CSV file to use for the import. You must select a file that already exists, and if it doesn't have a header (or if the header is invalid, perhaps because it specifies a bogus attribute name), the import will fail.

Beware: the Directory Import dialog remembers what import file you selected last time, but it forgets your choice of template. Make sure to select a template before doing an import, or you'll find out all the fields you wanted from the template are empty.

- The Account creation group controls what happens when the CSV file specifies that an account should be created or deleted, which always happens in conjunction with the creation or removal of a mailbox, not for custom recipients or DLs.

    — If you're creating a new mailbox, and want to automatically generate a new account to go with it, check the "Create Windows NT account" checkbox and Exchange Administrator will create new accounts in the domain specified by the Windows NT domain pull-down. Normally, Exchange Administrator will generate a password for each account based on the mailbox name. Names shorter than four characters are padded with "x" characters, names longer than 14 characters are truncated to 14 characters, and names in between are used as is. This is simple, but not particularly secure. If you check the "Generate random password" box instead, Exchange Administrator will generate random passwords instead of basing them on the account name—you should probably use this option.

In either case, your passwords will be saved in a file in the same directory as the import file you specify. It will have the same name as the import file, with an extension of *.psw*; if a file with that name already exists, Exchange Administrator will use *.p01*, then *.p02*, and so on. Each account will be listed, along with its password. If the import file's directory is on an NTFS volume, Exchange Administrator helpfully sets the password file's NTFS permissions so that only the account that was active during the Exchange Administrator import has access to the file.

— If you're deleting a mailbox and you want Exchange Administrator to automatically remove the corresponding NT account, check the "Delete Windows NT account" box. I strongly recommend disabling accounts rather than deleting them; unfortunately, there's no way to do so automatically as part of an import operation.

• Some properties, like the E-mail Addresses property you saw earlier, may have multiple values. The Multivalued Properties control group controls what happens when the CSV file specifies new values for a multivalued property. The default setting, Append, tells Exchange Administrator to add the CSV file's new values to the existing values, while Overwrite replaces the directory entry's values with whatever it finds in the file.

• The Logging level controls and Separators... button work just as they do for the Directory Export dialog; their settings apply only to this import and aren't persistent.

The overall process for importing data is largely similar to the one for exporting it:

1. Edit your CSV file as desired. Don't forget to add a mode property column if you need one (and you will if you're deleting things, at a minimum).

2. Open the Directory Import dialog.

3. Choose the domain where you want accounts created (if any) and the server where you want the imported information sent.

4. Use the Container... button and its associated radio buttons to select where newly created recipients should go.

5. If you want to use a recipient template, select it with the Recipient Template... button.

6. Select an import file with the Import File... button.

7. Choose whether you want Exchange Administrator to create and delete NT accounts as it creates or deletes objects. If you enable account creation, choose whether or not you want to have Exchange Administrator generate random passwords for you.

8. Decide what you want done with import records that have multivalued properties: Exchange Administrator can overwrite the properties' values with what's in the import file, or it can add the new values to the existing ones.

9. Optionally, you can change the logging level and separators used to read the file.

Nifty Exchange Administrator Tricks

"Okay, fine," you say. "When do I learn how to do something useful with Exchange Administrator?" Buckle up, because that time has arrived. While real Exchange Administrator wizardry comes only from knowing how and when to adjust all 5,739,222* property page settings, you can accomplish quite a bit just based on what you know right now.

Creating Mailboxes from Account Lists

Exchange Administrator can vacuum in an NT or NetWare account list and create a CSV file from it. This is the equivalent of migrating a group of users from a foreign mail system. Exchange Administrator reads the NT or NetWare directory server, extracts a list of accounts and whatever attributes it can find, and generates a CSV file with an appropriate header.

Extracting NT accounts

The Tools → Extract Windows NT Account List... command can pull an entire domain's worth of account information and turn it into a CSV file. There's no way to filter out accounts; every account entry in the SAM, including the Exchange service account, the guest account, and the administrator account, will be included in your CSV file. Plan on editing it by hand to remove the extraneous accounts. Groups aren't transferred, so you'll have to manually create any distribution lists you want either from Exchange Administrator or with another import file.

---

* I admit to making this number up, but it's probably close.

When you use the Extract Windows NT Account List... command, you'll see a dialog box that asks you for three things: the domain you want to extract accounts from, the name of the domain controller you want to use, and the location of the output CSV file. Once you supply those parameters and click OK, Exchange Administrator will repetitively query the domain controller (DC) you specify and generate the CSV file. The file itself contains only five properties for each account: the object class, the common and display names, the home server (which will be *~SERVER*, indicating that Exchange Administrator should honor the settings you choose in the Directory Import dialog), and a comment taken from the comment field in the User Manager for Domains properties dialog for the account. Once you've exported the account list, you can either edit the CSV file to add more attributes, or you can supply a recipient template for the import process. Either way, you're not constrained to using only those five properties.

When you use this command in conjunction with the "Create Windows NT account" checkbox in the Directory Import dialog, you end up with a quick and easy way to add an entire domain's worth of accounts and mailboxes to your existing domain. This combination is a real blessing for those who have to switch from an architecture with several domains into a single-domain model.

Extracting NetWare accounts

Since Microsoft devoutly hopes that every NetWare shop on the planet will migrate to NT and Exchange, they've included a command to ease that migration: Tools → Extract NetWare Account List.... To use this command, you need a NetWare 3.x or 4.x server running bindery emulation, and you need supervisor access to that server. When you select the command, the NetWare User Extraction dialog will appear; you'll need to supply the name of the NetWare server you want to talk to, the supervisor name and password, and the location of your output file.

Just like its NT counterpart, the extracted NetWare file contains relatively little information, but it's enough to let you bulk-create mailboxes and accounts to move some or all of your NetWare users over to NT and Exchange, which is all it's designed to do.

Exchange Administrator Command-Line Switches

There are seven documented command-line switches you can use when you launch Exchange Administrator; all seven of them are actually useful. Let me first dispense with the switch you'll probably use the most, initially: the /H switch launches Exchange Administrator and displays the help topic that describes the command-line switches themselves! Think of it as a built-in cheat sheet. The other switches are a bit more involved. Table 5-3 describes all the switches.

Table 5-3. Exchange Administrator Command-Line Switches

Switch	What It Does
/H	Displays the help topic that describes the command-line switches
/E	Runs the command-line export utility (see "Exporting and importing directory data")
/I	Runs the command-line import utility (see "Exporting and importing directory data")
/M	Starts the link or server monitor you specify (see "Starting and suspending monitors")
/R	Starts Exchange Administrator in raw mode (see "Raw Mode: Not For Sissies")
/S	Connects to the server you specify in addition to whatever default connections Exchange Administrator makes at startup
/T	Temporarily stops monitoring the specified server (see "Starting and suspending monitors")

For those of you who are hooked on Unix-style command descriptions, here's the full-blown version:

```
admin [/H ]
          | /E exportFile /D dirServerName [/N] [/O optionsFile]
          | /I importFile /D dirServerName [/N] [/O optionsFile ]
          | /M [site ] monitorName server
          | /R
          | /S serverName
          | /T { r | n | nr }
```

The raw mode switch, /R, is pretty simple to use (but raw-mode Exchange Administrator isn't). The subtleties of using Exchange Administrator in raw mode are covered later in this chapter, in the section "Raw Mode: Not for Sissies." In the meantime, feel free to make a desktop shortcut to Exchange Administrator with /R on the command line—you'll probably use it a lot in the future.

The next-simplest switch is /S, which you use to connect to a server directly from the command line. Its only parameter is the server name:

```
admin /S serverName
```

Exchange Administrator will resolve whatever name you provide and attempt to use it. You may supply either a NetBIOS or TCP/IP name.

Starting and suspending monitors

You can start or stop Exchange Administrator link and server monitors from the command line. This is useful, since putting an appropriately built script or *.bat* file in your *Startup* folder makes it trivial to automatically start the same set of monitors each time you log on. To start a monitor, you need at least two things: the name of the monitor you want to run and the name of the server you want to monitor. Here's how the /M switch works:

```
admin /M [ site ] monitorName serverName
```

site

Specifies the site whose directory contains the monitor. For example, if the monitor you want to run is in the *NorthAmerica* site but you want to monitor a server in the *Europe* site, you'd just include *NorthAmerica* as the site name.

monitorName

Specifies the directory name of the monitor you want to run.

serverName

Tells Exchange Administrator what server you want to monitor.

You may also suspend monitors. In fact, you'll have to: if you've set up a monitor to watch a server, and then take that server down for maintenance, the monitor will go berserk as soon as it notices that the monitored server is down. To prevent this problem, you need to suspend monitoring when you want to perform maintenance, do an offline backup, or do anything else that requires you to stop the monitored services. You accomplish this with the /T switch, which you use from the console of the server being monitored. It works like this:

```
admin /T {r | n | nr }
```

/T n

Keeps the monitor from sending any notifications that a monitored server is down, but still allows any corrective action (like restarting services) to occur.

/T r

The opposite of /T n; this switch tells the monitor to send notifications, but not to attempt any corrective actions.

/T nr

Shuts up the monitor altogether by preventing it from sending notifications or undertaking repair actions.

If you use /T with no arguments, it restores the active monitors to their normal state, allowing them to send notifications or initiate repairs normally.

Exporting and importing directory data

The /E and /I switches let you run batch import and export operations from the command line or from scripts. This is a very useful capacity, since it allows you to automate moving data into and out of the Exchange directory with minimal fuss. The export command, /E, looks like this:

```
admin /E exportFile /D dirServerName [/N] [/O optionsFile]
```

/E *exportFile*

Specifies the full path to the output CSV file you want to use. If the export file exists, Exchange Administrator will use its header; if not, you'll get the default set of export headers.

/D *dirServerName*

Tells Exchange Administrator what Exchange directory server to talk to. This is equivalent to the "MS Exchange server" pull-down in the Directory Export dialog box.

/N

Forces Exchange Administrator to keep quiet and not show its progress dialog.

/O *optionsFile*

Provides the full path to a file of options that control what gets exported and how the output is processed.

These settings are all pretty self-explanatory; your real opportunity to control how the export works comes from what you put in the options file, which I'll talk more about in the next section. In the meantime, let's see what the import command looks like; it's very similar to the export command:

```
admin /I importFile /D dirServerName [/N] [/O optionsFile]
```

/I import*File*

Specifies the full path to the input CSV file, which must contain a valid header.

/D *dirServerName*

Tells Exchange Administrator which Exchange directory server to send the imported data to.

/N

Forces Exchange Administrator to keep quiet and not show its progress dialog.

/O *optionsFile*

Provides the full path to a file of options that control how the imported data is processed on its way to the directory.

The options file format

The import and export options files are very important, since they're the only way you can control the behavior of a command-line import or export. First, let me show you a sample export options file so you can get a feel for the format:

```
[Export]
DirectoryService=SFO3
ExportObject=Mailbox
InformationLevel=None
```

You'll probably notice that this looks just like the familiar old *.ini* file format. The file begins with the [Export] keyword, which tells Exchange Administrator what type of options file this is; if it instead started with [Import], it would be treated as an import file. Following this keyword, there may be one or more name-value assignment pairs. Each pair specifies the name of an Exchange Administrator setting and the value you want it to have. In this case, there are three settings: the DirectoryService line tells Exchange Administrator to export data it finds in the server named *SFO3*, the ExportObject line indicates that we want to export mailboxes only, and the InformationLevel line tells Exchange Administrator not to log any information about the export.

You can build a single options file that contains both [Export] and [Import] sections and reuse it every time you do a command-line export or import; this is an easy way to ensure the consistency of your exported and imported data.

Table 5-4 shows the keywords that are common to both import and export options files.

Table 5-4. Keywords That Work for Both Export and Import Options Files

Keyword	Default Value	Legal Values	Description
Basepoint	Empty (e.g., use the local site)	DN of base-point object	The basepoint for an export or import is the root item used: for example, Recipients/cn=US Employees is a basepoint that points to a DL named "US Employees" in the Recipients container.
CodePage	0	0 (ANSI), −1 (Unicode), or any legal code page ID	Tells Exchange Administrator what code page to use when exporting or importing text data.
Column Separator	44 (the ASCII code for ,)	Any printable ASCII character	Tells Exchange Administrator to use this ASCII character as the column separator.
Container	Recipients	Any legitimate DN that points to a recipient container	DN of the container to use when exporting or importing.
Directory Service	NULL (e.g., talk to the local server)	Any Exchange server name	The name of the Exchange server to which directory queries or changes should be sent.
Information-Level	Minimal	None, Minimal, or Full	Amount of information Exchange Administrator should log during an import or export.

Table 5-4. Keywords That Work for Both Export and Import Options Files (continued)

Keyword	Default Value	Legal Values	Description
MVSeparator	37 (the ASCII code for %)	Any printable ASCII character	Tells Exchange Administrator to use this ASCII character as the separator between values in properties that have multiple values.
Quote Character	34 (the ASCII code for ")	Any printable ASCII character	Tells Exchange Administrator to use this ASCII character as the quote delimiter.
RawMode	No	Yes or No	Indicates whether you want the export or import to use raw mode. Files that can normally be imported or exported will often fail in raw mode because Exchange Administrator is much stricter about checking for conformance to the database schema.

Table 5-5 shows the keywords specific to import options files, and Table 5-6 shows specific export options keywords.

Table 5-5. Keywords That Work Only with Import Options Files

Keyword	Default Value	Legal Values	Description
ApplyNTSecurity	Yes	Yes or No	Yes: apply NT security settings to the imported object. No: leave the objects unsassoci-ated.
CreateNTAccounts	No	Yes or No	Yes: create new accounts for new objects. No: don't ever create NT accounts.
DeleteNTAccounts	No	Yes or No	Yes: delete NT accounts when deleting mailboxes. No: leave existing accounts alone.
GeneratePassword	No	Yes or No	Meaningless unless CreateNT-Accounts=Yes. Yes: create random passwords instead of using the account name. No: use the account name as the password.
NTDomain	None	Any domain name where the account you're using has permission	Specifies what domain you want newly created accounts to go into; if blank, newly created accounts will go into the domain where the account you're using to run Exchange Administrator is homed.

Table 5-5. Keywords That Work Only with Import Options Files (continued)

Keyword	Default Value	Legal Values	Description
OverwriteProperties	No	Yes or No	Yes: overwrite existing values in multivalued properties. No: append new values from the import file to the existing set.
RecipientTemplate	None	Any DN that points to a mailbox	DN that points to the mailbox you want to use as a template (e.g., `Recipients/cn=Huntsville Template`).

Table 5-6. Keywords That Work Only with Export Options Files

Keyword	Default Value	Legal Values	Description
BasepointOnly	No	Yes or No	Yes: export only items that are immediate descendants of the basepoint object. No: export from the basepoint all the way downward.
ExportObject	Mailbox	Mailbox Remote DL Recipients All	Export only the named type of item. `Remote` means custom recipients; `Recipients` includes all DLs, custom recipients, and mailboxes; `All` means all directory objects. You can only use one `ExportObject` command per file; if you say `ExportObject= Mailbox,DL` you'll only get mailboxes.
HiddenObjects	No	Yes or No	Yes: export objects that are normally hidden. No: Don't export hidden objects.
HomeServer	Empty	Any name that points to an Exchange server	Tells Exchange Administrator what server to query for the data to be exported.
Subcontainers	No	Yes or No	Yes: export all objects in subcontainers beneath the target container. No: export only objects in the target container.

Using these three sets of keywords, you can duplicate any combination of options that you could assemble in the Directory Import and Directory Export dialog boxes. Well, that's almost true; in reality, you can only export one type of item at a time using options files, while if you use the Directory Export dialog you can choose to export DLs, mailboxes, and custom recipients, in any combination. This minor flaw notwithstanding, you can still get a lot of mileage out of automating your imports and exports.

Raw Mode: Not for Sissies

Deservedly or not, Microsoft products have a reputation for obscuring deep technical details from the user. This is in strong contrast to Unix tools, which usually force those deep technical details down your throat whether you want them or not. Exchange Administrator falls into this obscuring mold; despite the fact that the Exchange directory is actually a complex relational database, in Exchange Administrator it looks like a set of harmless, friendly lists, trees, and properties dialogs.

If you lift the hood, though, you'll find that there's a lot more detail that Exchange Administrator hides from view. When you run Exchange Administrator in raw mode, you can see details of the database schema that are normally hidden from view. This exposure can be very educational, since it lets you see the exact property names and values that Exchange stores in its directory. However, a little knowledge is a dangerous thing; if you're careless about editing data while in raw mode, you can easily hose your directory. Remember, mistakes are automatically replicated!

Before we dive in to talking about what you see in raw mode, it's important to mention that the Exchange directory has an internal hierarchy of object classes. Classes may inherit attributes from other classes; each attribute in a class may be mandatory or optional. Exchange Administrator normally takes care of deciphering the relationships between objects and tracking which class attributes are required; however, in raw mode, you can see *everything*. It's like X-ray spectacles for your directory data.

When you run Exchange Administrator in raw mode, most of the interface looks the same. Eagle-eyed users will notice that there's a new command in the File menu: Raw Properties…, with Shift-Enter as its accelerator. That command allows you to view the raw properties for any object, as described in the next section. There are also some other new commands:

- The File → New Other → Raw Object… command lets you create a raw object with exactly the attributes and values you want, within the limits imposed by the object hierarchy and the mandatory object attributes.

- The Edit → Delete Raw Object command lets you remove raw objects. Microsoft warns that you should never use this command unless Microsoft's Product Support Services (PSS) group tells you to; if you accidentally do a raw delete on an object, the changes are immediate and irreparable, so I'd avoid this command unless PSS recommends it.

- The View → Raw Directory command tells Exchange Administrator to add raw objects (like the site directory schema) to the normal set of displayed containers and objects. At the same time, it hides the "fake" directory objects and containers that Exchange Administrator normally displays for your convenience.

X.500: The Empire Strikes Back

If you've ever worked with an X.500 Directory Service agent (or DSA; that's X.500-speak for "directory server"), you probably recognize the concepts that underlie Exchange's raw mode. The X.500 standard sets out some basic object classes, along with their mandatory and optional attributes. A DSA that follows the standard properly won't allow you to create or modify an object without specifying values for all of its mandatory attributes. Since some of these attributes can be obscure, Exchange Administrator normally removes this burden from you; however, when you use raw mode you end up with what looks remarkably like a real X.500 DSA. This means that the DS is obligated to honor the X.500 standard and will impose the same restrictions that any other DSA would.

What does this mean in practice? Well, if you try to modify data in the directory, you'll have to get its object class and mandatory attributes correct—that's why I warned you earlier about turning on raw mode during command-line imports and exports. If you try to import a file that usually imports normally, it may fail in raw mode because required attributes are missing. If you write programs that use LDAP to modify information in the Exchange directory, you have to make sure to honor the mandatory attributes and object class restrictions, though if you use ADSI this problem solves itself, because the ADSI layer automatically validates the parameters you pass it before attempting a directory change.

If you *really* like raw mode and want to use it all the time, you can add a registry key that will force Exchange Administrator into raw mode all the time. If you add a REG_DWORD value named RawMode to the Exchange registry tree under HKCU\Software\Microsoft\ Exchange\MSExchangeAdmin\Desktop and set its value to 1, Exchange Administrator will always start in raw mode. Set this value back to 0, or remove it altogether, to return Exchange Administrator to its normal behavior. Note, however, that if you use this tweak, there's no way to switch back to normal mode from within Exchange Administrator.

Viewing raw properties

The raw properties dialog looks quite a bit different from the standard properties dialogs you've gotten accustomed to seeing. Figure 5-11 shows a raw properties dialog for a mailbox. The most obvious difference is that there's only one tab—the mailbox display name still appears at the top of the content area, but the rest of the dialog is different.

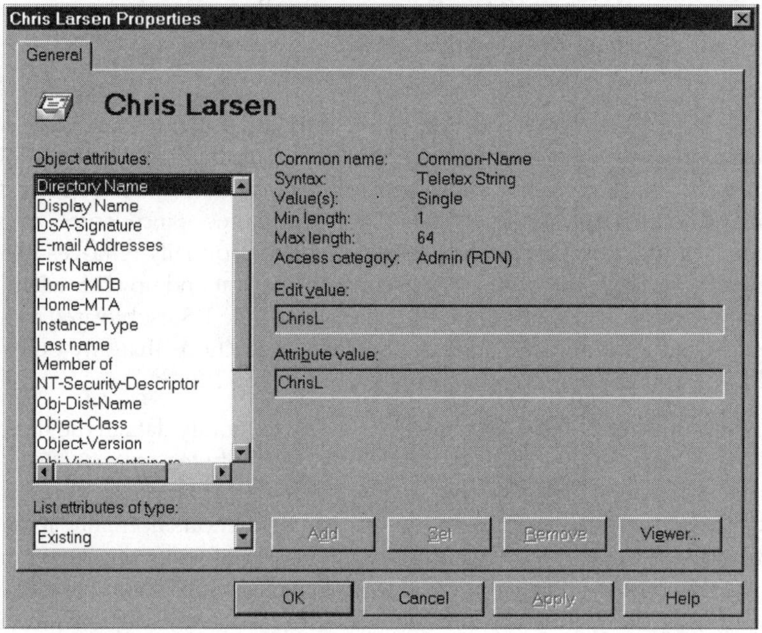

Figure 5-11. The Properties dialog looks different in raw mode

Here's what's in the dialog:

- The "List attributes of type" pull-down lets you specify which set of attributes you want to see for this object. There are eight categories: existing (attributes that currently have values assigned), nonexisting, required (attributes that must be present in the object), optional (attributes that may be present but aren't required), all, added, modified, and removed. The latter three reflect changes you've made while the properties dialog has been open.

- The "Object attributes" scrolling list shows all attributes of this object that match the type you've selected in the pull-down. Selecting an attribute here will display its value and attributes to the right of the list box.

- The "Attribute value" field displays the actual value for whatever attribute you've selected, and "Edit value" lets you edit the value, if it's editable. For example, the directory name isn't editable, so you can see it, but the Edit value field will remain inactive. For attributes with multiple values (like "Member of" or "Accept messages from"), the Attribute value field changes to a list box that shows all the values. You can edit any value by selecting it in the list box and using the Edit value field as you normally would.

The buttons at the bottom of the property tab let you make changes to the attribute list. These changes aren't actually written to the directory until you click the dialog's Apply or OK buttons, so you can enjoy a few small experiments without fear of trashing your directory. Here's how to use the buttons:

- To add a new attribute, select it in the list on the left and type the desired value into the Edit value field, then click the Set button. You can add attributes from the optional, all, and nonexisting lists.

- To edit an existing attribute value, just edit the value in the Edit value field, and click the Set button. If you want to edit one value of a multivalued property, first select the value you want to change, then change it and click Set.

- To add an additional value to a multivalued attribute, type the new value you want to add into the Edit value field and click the Add button.

- To remove an attribute's value, select the attribute from the "Object attributes" list and click the Remove button. If you want to remove one value from a multivalued attribute, select that value only and click Remove.

- The Viewer... button allows you to see an attribute's values in a text editor–style dialog window. If you've selected an attribute that may be edited, you can also click the Editor... button to open an editing dialog that gives you an interface for editing single or multiple values.

Creating raw objects

You can use the File → New Other → Raw Object... command to create a new object almost anywhere in the directory hierarchy. You first have to select a container in the container pane, since you want to create a child object under some existing container. When you use this command, you'll see a dialog that lists all available object types. For example, if you select the organization container, you'll find that you can create a new organizational unit or a new object view. If you instead select a site's configuration container, you can create any attribute from an Add-In to an X.400-Link.

When you select an object type, you'll see the raw properties dialog for the new object. All of its required attributes will be there, but not all of them will have legal values. At a minimum, you should expect to supply a directory name; depending on the object, you may also have to supply values for other attributes.

Be careful with this command. When you create a new object, you may be inadvertently adding it in a place that will confuse the Exchange Directory Service (DS). I can't think of any reason why you'd need to create a new raw object, so my recommendation would be to leave it alone unless PSS tells you to use it.

Customizing Address Templates

Now that you've taken a look at raw mode, you know that Exchange Administrator must have some way to interpret the directory contents and generate those spiffy property pages that you normally use to edit object properties. In fact, it does, and you can customize some of the templates. You may remember the Addressing container (it lives under the site Configuration container). If you expand it, you'll see two interesting items: the Details Templates container and the One-Off Address Templates container. Both of these containers hold templates that Exchange Administrator uses for properties dialogs; the major difference is that items in the One-Off Address Templates container can't be edited.

Under the Details Templates container, you'll see one container for each language you have installed; most of you will only see "English/USA" under here, but you can import additional languages from your Outlook product CD. These languages allow you to support localized clients; for example, you can install the French, German, and Spanish templates so that clients using those languages will see items titled in the appropriate language for their installation. When you select a language container, you'll see seven items in the contents pane: Custom Recipient, Distribution List, Exchange Send Options, Mailbox, Mailbox Agent, Public Folder, and Search Dialog. These items allow you to customize their addressing dialogs except for Exchange Send Options, which you can't change. For each item, you can adjust the contents of its properties dialog, including adding or removing user interface controls for retrieving attributes from the user. Each control is linked directly to a directory attribute, so whatever the user puts in the field goes to the designated attribute slot in the new object.

General address template properties

When you open any of the address templates, the first thing you'll see is the General tab. This tab is pretty featureless; you can change the display name for the template, and you can specify an administrative note. The only interesting thing you can do is attach a Windows help file to the address template so that when the user clicks the Help button they see your help file instead of the default one that Exchange provides. There are actually two separate buttons: "Import 16 Bit Help File" lets you attach a help file for 16-bit DOS and Win 3.1x clients, and "Import 32 Bit Help File" is for Win32 clients. That's it.

The Templates tabs

The Templates tab is where the action begins. Actually, there are two tabs: Templates and MS-DOS Templates. They work identically; Templates is for building templates for the MacOS, Win16, and Win32 Exchange and Outlook clients, and MS-DOS Templates is for the MS-DOS Exchange client. I'll stick with discussing the Templates tab in this section, but everything I say applies equally to both. When you open either of the Templates tabs, you'll see a big mess (see Figure 5-12 if you don't believe me). Here's what's inside:

- The list box shows six items of information for each control in the template: its upper-left coordinate (the X and Y columns), its width and height, the type of control, and the control's value. The value column has two separate meanings: for label and page break controls, the value is displayed, but for other controls, the value specifies what directory attribute is tied to the field. Exchange Administrator automatically handles getting and setting directory attributes, and it's even smart enough to disable fields whose values can be displayed but which aren't editable.

- The six buttons along the right side of the list box allow you to add, change, remove, and reorder individual template controls. The Test... button displays the entire template as it's currently defined. All the fields will be empty, but you can still see where the fields are and whether the overall design is usable or not.

- The Original button at the bottom of the dialog is your escape hatch. Pressing it will remove all your changes and restore the directory definition of the template back to its original condition.

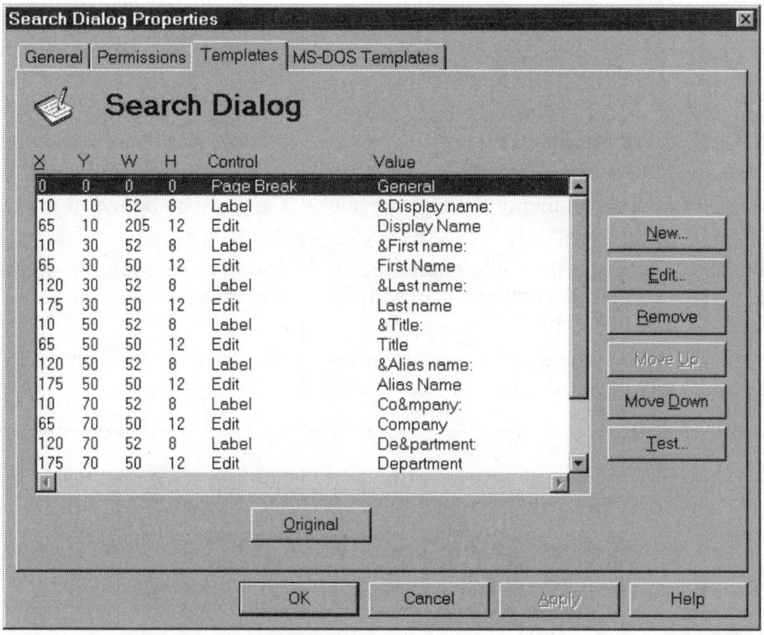

Figure 5-12. The Templates tab of the Search Dialog object

Editing templates

So, how do you actually use this dialog? Since you have pre-made templates to work with, the overall process is pretty easy: decide which fields you want each directory entry to have, open the template, see what attributes you need to add and remove to match your design, then start pushing buttons. Before you get too far into the process, though, it might help to know what types of controls you can use. Table 5-7 shows the supported control types you'll see in templates.

Table 5-7. Control Types Available for Building Address Templates

Control Type	What Is It?	Restrictions and Notes
Button	Standard button; causes an action when clicked	You can't create or modify buttons, but you may see them in some templates.
Check Box	Checkbox bound to a specific on/off property	Value text is what gets stored in named attribute when checkbox is set to on.
Edit	Editable text field that accepts one or more lines of text	You can set the maximum length and whether or not the control accepts multiple lines.
Group Box	Static rectangle with a text label; used to group related controls	
Label	Static text label that displays its value as a caption	Use an ampersand to indicate the accelerator letter for the associated field (e.g., &First translates to First).
List Box	Standard free-text list box (not a list of preloaded choices like a dropdown)	Can control whether horizontal & vertical scroll bars appear.
Multivalued dropdown	Dropdown menu that lists specific value entries	Can only be bound to multivalued properties.
Multivalued list box	List of specific value entries; each entry is a separate choice, with no free-text entry	Can only be bound to multivalued properties.
Page break	Dialog tab, used to separate property pages; displays its value as the tab caption	May have an associated help context.

Each data entry control (checkbox, edit field, both types of list box, and dropdown) must be bound to a specific directory attribute. This cuts down on what you have to know to design a template; all you really have to do is use the dropdown list in the control creation dialog to pick the field you want to use.

For some reason, when you edit a search dialog, you can only use labels, edit fields, page breaks, and group boxes. My guess is that it's because there's no need for any of the other control types, but it's still a little odd.

When you use Outlook to find mail recipients, the form you get (shown in Figure 5-13) is drawn from this template, but in my humble opinion, it doesn't include some of the most useful search criteria, like notes or mail stop. (Searching for custom attributes is useful, too, but since we haven't discussed defining them yet, just imagine how you can apply this process to your own custom attribute usage.)

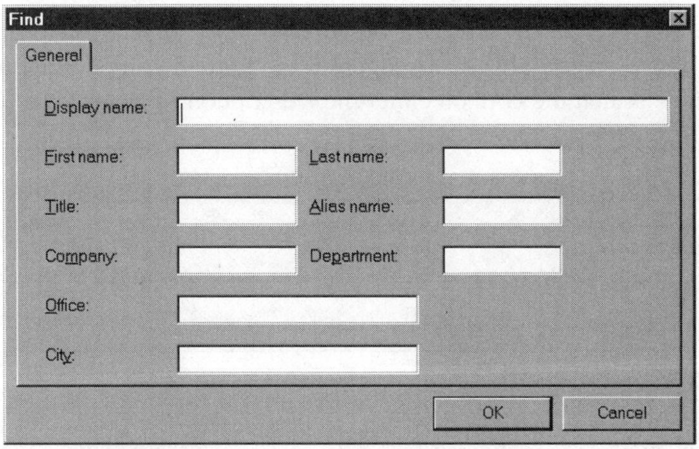

Figure 5-13. The original search dialog

Let's walk through the process of customizing the search dialog template to make it more useful by adding a Notes tab that lets you search for notes:

1. Open the Search Dialog addressing template (it's in the Addressing container of the site Configuration container; open any of the installed language containers and you'll see it there) by selecting it and using the File → Properties... command.

2. When the Search Dialog Properties dialog opens, switch to the Templates tab.

3. Scroll to the end of the control list, select the last item in it, and click the New... button. The Select Control Type dialog will appear. Choose Page Break and click OK. When the Page Break Control dialog appears, type "Notes" in the Text field, then click OK. The new page break control will appear just above the item you'd previously selected.

4. Click the Move Down button to move the page break to the end. Notice that it's still selected. Click New... again. This time, add an Edit field. You can leave the X and Y coordinates at (0,0); specify a more generous height and width (I used 320×50).

5. Use the Field dropdown to select Notes as the attribute bound to this control, then click OK.

6. Use the Move Down button again so that your new Edit control is the last item in the list.

7. If you're curious to see how it looks, click the Test... button and you'll see a mockup of the dialog. When you're done admiring your work, click the Cancel button.

8. Click the OK button to save your changes, or the Original button to throw them away.

To see the finished product (plus a description field, which you can easily add using the above steps), check out Figure 5-14. With this modification in place, users can now search the GAL on either the Description or Notes field.

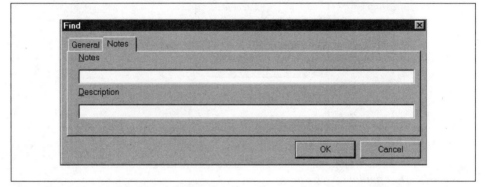

Figure 5-14. The modified Find dialog, thanks to the Search Dialog template

Save Some (Data) for Later

The tabular views that Exchange Administrator uses in its contents pane are pretty useful; they summarize things like mailbox resource usage in a customizable format. If you want to use that data in another application, like a database or a spreadsheet, you'll first need to extract it from Exchange Administrator in a usable format. While taking screen shots with Alt-Print Screen works fine, it's sort of laborious. There's a better way, even though it's seldom used. The File → Save Window Contents... command can save the contents of any of the tabular views to a CSV file that you can archive or process however you need to. For example, to get a snapshot of how much space user mailboxes are taking up on your server, just expand the Mailbox Resources object of the Private IS container of your server, then save the window contents. The resulting data can easily be parsed by a VBScript, a Perl script, an Excel macro, or even by hand.

One caveat: the data written out depends on what's displayed. Use the View → Columns... command to get just the data items you want on screen; once you've done so, you can save the tabular data and use it however you need to.

Taming the Import and Export Features

You might think that I have now covered everything you need to know about importing and exporting directory data. That's half true. I have included everything you need to know about how the commands work, but not about how you actually use them. Bulk import and export provide a great way to massage the contents of your GAL, but there are some subtleties that aren't apparent at first glance.

Getting the Right Headers

Getting the correct headers in your export file is critical, because that's what Exchange Administrator uses to decide what fields it's going to export. Just as in elementary school, spelling counts in Exchange. When you export using Exchange Administrator, it reads the header file you supply to decide which fields to copy into the export CSV file; that, in turn, will determine what you can import, unless you build a custom header file for the import step. Since most batch processing follows the export-edit-import cycle we discussed earlier, you have to get the headers right from the start. Even if you're just importing a bunch of new data, you still have to get the attribute names right or Exchange Administrator will ignore them.

What to do? Well, there are several sources for attribute information. You can use the BORK *header* tool (see Appendix A), which reads the directory and shows you a list of all available attributes for the object type you select. You can quickly point-and-click your way to a properly built header file. If you're more adventurous, you can start Exchange Administrator in raw mode and look at the raw properties of an object to get the names of the attributes it supports. If you're less adventurous, you can use the sample CSV files included with Exchange—look on your Exchange CD in the *server\support\samples\CSVS* directory.* For example, the *mailbox.csv* file contains a header with all the attributes supported by a mailbox. Just specify it as the export header file and your CSV file will contain every attribute for each exported mailbox.

Creating and Removing Things en Masse

One way that the bulk import/export commands can help make your job easier is by providing a way to add or remove lots of similar items at once. For example, if your company sells a subsidiary, it would be nice to automatically remove all the mailboxes of the people who worked for the the subsidiary; likewise, you may

---

* This directory isn't on my Exchange 5.5 Enterprise Edition CD, but I've seen it on others. I don't know where mine went.

find it necessary to remove a particular attribute value, say, a custom attribute you were using to keep track of employee ID numbers. As a happier example, perhaps you've just bought out a competitor and need to add new mailboxes and NT accounts for them. You can do all these things, but it's not as straightforward as you immediately assume.

The Mode property

The key to creating or removing entire items is using the Mode property discussed earlier in the chapter. Removing items is easy. Let's say you want to remove all of your distribution lists:

1. Create a header file that looks like this:

   ```
   Obj-Class,Mode,Directory Name
   ```

2. Use that header file with the Tools → Directory Export... command. Make sure the Distribution list checkbox is the only checked item in the Export objects group.

3. Open the header file and fill "delete" into each of the item entries, like this:

   ```
   Obj-Class,Mode,Directory Name
   DL,delete,Managers
   DL,delete,HuntsvilleEmployees
   DL,delete,FalconsFans
   ```

4. Reimport the file. Poof! All the items you specified are now gone.

Since the default mode is "modify," you don't have to do anything special to change existing attribute values, but you must specify the right mode property to create or delete them.

 If you remove mailboxes, you should probably leave the "Delete Windows NT" account option turned off so the accounts stay around. Why? In NT, when you delete an account, any items that had permissions for that account lose their memory of those permissions. It's better to use User Manager or the `net user` command to disable the account instead of removing it.

Creating new mailboxes

The key to successfully using the directory import tool to create new mailboxes is getting the right options file set up. You must use an options file to tell Exchange Administrator what options to use; if you're creating new NT accounts along with the mailboxes, you must ensure that the PDC for the domain is available. You also have to be picky about where you do the import; it has to occur on the server where you want the new mailboxes to be homed.

If you're creating new Windows NT accounts as part of your mailbox import process, be aware that account creation is pretty slow, and will slow down the overall process quite a bit.

Let's take a look at an example options file:

```
[Import]
ApplyNTSecurity=yes
CreateNTAccounts=yes
GeneratePassword=no
NTDomain=RA
```

This tells Exchange Administrator that I want to use NT security on the files, that I want to create new NT accounts for the new mailboxes, and that I don't want random passwords generated. The accounts will all go in the domain named RA. The actual import file might look like this:

```
Obj-Class,Mode,Directory Name,Alias Name,Display Name,E-Mail Address,
Home-Server Mailbox,Create,Jason McNamara,jason,Jason
McNamara,SMTP:jason@robichaux.net,HSV1
```

Note that this file specifies a mode, and that for each recipient the file contains a directory name, an alias, a display name, an email address, and a home server. These are all required. You can specify more attributes if you'd like, or you can specify a recipient template in the import options file to allow Exchange Administrator to copy the account details for you.

Removing attribute values

One common way to remove something is to replace it with blank space. At first glance this seems like a good way to remove things from the Exchange directory—just export the GAL, edit the header so you only touch the field you want to clear out, and tweak the file accordingly. There's a hitch, though: if you just leave the field blank, Exchange Administrator won't replace the existing value. For example, this won't work:

```
Obj-Class,Directory Name,Issue warning storage limit,Outgoing message size
limit Mailbox,TomZ,,
```

No problem—you can just replace the existing value with a space, right? You sit down and try this approach, only to find that it doesn't work either:

```
Obj-Class,Directory Name,Issue warning storage limit,Outgoing message size
limit Mailbox,TomZ, ,
```

Why doesn't this work? Because Exchange Administrator won't replace an existing value with an empty value, like the ones in the two preceding examples. Instead, you have to use a blank space in double quotes, like this:

```
Obj-Class,Directory Name,Issue warning storage limit,Outgoing message size
limit Mailbox,TomZ," ",
```

This will do what you want, but it's a little cumbersome. There's a better way to remove individual fields from mailboxes: use the ~DEL operator, like this:

```
Obj-Class,Directory Name,Issue warning storage limit,Outgoing message size
limit Mailbox,TomZ,~DEL,
```

Whenever Exchange Administrator sees ~DEL in a field, it removes the existing value from the field. If the field has multiple values, it removes all the values. If you want to be a little more selective—so you can remove a single address from a mailbox's E-Mail Addresses field, perhaps—you can do a little extra work. Include the value you want to delete after the ~DEL keyword, like this:

```
Obj-Class,Directory Name,E-mail Addresses
Mailbox,TomZ,~DEL<SMTP:TomZ@robichaux.net>
```

This would remove only the SMTP address, without touching any other items. (Note that this only works with Exchange 5.5 SP2 or later.)

Importing and Exporting Custom Attributes

You can import and export custom attribute values, too. The Exchange directory holds ten custom attributes for each recipient item; these attributes are named "Custom Attribute 1" through "Custom Attribute 10" by default. If you leave those names as is, you can import and export their values by using the appropriate name. If you change the names (say, by changing "Custom Attribute 3" to "Employee ID"), you can still import and export using the names, but you may run into problems. According to Microsoft, in some circumstances, you may not be able to import custom attribute data after changing an attribute name. Changing the name back doesn't fix the problem. To make matters worse, Knowledge Base article (Q185578), which documents this flaw, doesn't specify who it might bite. There is a fix, though: in your import file, use the directory name (not the display name) of the attribute. In the example a few sentences ago, that would call for using "Extension-Attribute-3" as the attribute name instead of either "Custom Attribute 3" or "Employee ID."

Importing and Exporting Permissions

This is a really nifty feature in Exchange 5.5: you can import and export permissions on objects! This means you can quickly specify who has User, Admin, and Permissions Admin roles for any mailbox, DL, or custom recipient. This makes it trivial to do things like assign a new secretary permissions to the mailboxes she needs access to, or to control who can twiddle access to a DL. There are three pseudo-attributes you need to know about: Obj-Admins, Obj-Perm-Admins, and Obj-Users. They're not really attributes; instead, the directory import/export code intercepts them and applies the values you specify to the permissions data stored on the target item.

These are the only permissions values you can import or export; you can't alter Search, Send As, or custom permissions using this method. In fact, if you list the same account in more than one of the pseudo-attributes, you'll find that you can no longer export or import the permissions attributes! Furthermore, it's important to understand that you can't change who owns an object (the Primary Windows NT Account for a mailbox or the Owner for a DL) through this mechanism.

To export permissions settings on an item, just add whichever pseudo-attributes you want to see for the specified item to your export header file. For example, this header will tell Exchange Administrator to admit whoever has the Permissions Admin role on an item:

```
Obj-Class,Directory Name,Obj-PermAdmins
```

Each account is shown with its domain and account name. If there are multiple accounts with the specified permission, Exchange Administrator will include them all, delimited with a percent sign between each entry. For example, this shows who has the User privilege on a particular mailbox:

```
Mailbox,Feedback,RA\paulr%RA\arlener%RA\chrisl
```

Importing permissions data is pretty easy: just list the accounts you want to have permissions, separated by percent signs if there's more than one for any attribute. If you want to remove permissions, you can do that too, using the ~DEL keyword.

Importing and Exporting Secondary SMTP Addresses

One common question I hear from Exchange administrators is how to use Exchange Administrator to add multiple SMTP addresses. For example, let's say you're the administrator at BigCorp. You've set up autonaming so that a new user named Joan Smith will have an SMTP address of *joan.smith@bigcorp.com*. Because you know that it's hard to remember the exact naming details when you're trying to send someone mail, you also want to allow Joan to get mail at *jsmith@bigcorp. com*, and *smith.joan@bigcorp.com*. You hunt around in Exchange Administrator, but can't find what you're looking for; that's because there isn't any way to do this from within Exchange Administrator.

The trick is to use the Secondary-Proxy-Addresses attribute. This might not seem obvious at first, but that's where Exchange actually stashes these proxy addresses.

Export the mailboxes you want to modify, then open the CSV file and add the attribute and appropriate values. For Joan Smith, here's what you'd do:

```
Obj-Class,Directory Name,Secondary-Proxy-Addresses
Mailbox, Joan Smith,smtp:smith.joan@bigcorp.com%smtp:jsmith@bigcorp.com
```

Notice that "SMTP" here is in lowercase; that's because these addresses aren't usable as reply addresses. Exchange Administrator displays address types you can't reply to in lowercase and without bolding them.

Exporting the Entire GAL

If you want to export the entire GAL to an export file, you can, but it requires a little extra work. You need an export options file that specifies the correct starting point for the export operation. Here's the file I use to export the GAL from my organization, whose name is RA:

```
[export]
basepoint=/o=RA
exportobject=mailbox
informationlevel=full
subcontainers=yes
```

This tells Exchange Administrator to start from the organization level and export all information for all mailboxes, including any subcontainers of the organization. Try it—you'll like it.

6

Mailboxes, Recipients, and Distribution Lists

Beginning of the teaching for life /
The instructions for well-being...
Knowing how to answer one who speaks /
To reply to one who sends a message.

—Amenemope, Egyptian king c. 1100 B.C.

In the previous chapter, you learned how to use Exchange Administrator to surf around the Exchange directory, and how to create and manage some of the most common object types. You even got a brief primer on how to create mailbox objects, but there's a lot more to managing mailboxes than just filling out the General tab of the mailbox properties dialog. In this chapter, you'll learn all the ins and outs of creating, modifying, and maintaining recipient items, the things to which mail can be addressed. Mailboxes, distribution lists, and custom recipients are the most common recipient items; public folders can receive mail too, but they're covered in Chapter 10, *Managing Public Folders*.

Creating and Managing Mailboxes

The mailbox is the fundamental object Exchange users interact with, no matter what client they're actually using. The mailbox stores users' personal mail messages; if they're using a client like Outlook that supports additional item types (notes, contacts, and so forth), these items are also stored in the private store and attached to the mailbox. Accordingly, knowing how to create mailboxes and set their properties is a critical part of the day-to-day work you'll probably have to do.

In Chapter 5, *Using Exchange Administrator*, you got a tiny taste of how the mailbox creation process works: you use the File → New Mailbox... command to create the mailbox itself and display its properties dialog. If all you want to do is create simple mailboxes with a minimum of identifying information, you already know how. However, the thirteen tabs of the mailbox properties dialog give you a lot more flexibility and capability than you might suspect, so let's explore what you can do with them. The Permissions and E-mail Addresses tabs have already been covered in Chapter 5, so I won't discuss them again here.

Identifying the Mailbox Owner

There are three tabs whose primary purpose is to give information about the mailbox owner, like what her phone number is and who she manages.

The General tab

The General tab is the first tab of the mailbox properties dialog, and it's the only one some administrators ever see. It's shown in Figure 6-1. By and large, what you put in this dialog is up to you; the data you enter here are mostly for human use. There are size limits: the first name, last name, and alias are limited to 64 characters; the initials field will accept 6 characters, and the display name can be up to 256 characters long. The display name and alias are usually generated automatically when you enter a first and last name; at a minimum, all you have to do is provide either a first *or* last name to create a new mailbox. If you're creating a mailbox for someone who already has a Windows NT domain account, you can use the "Primary Windows NT Account..." button to pick an account from the domain database (including any domains your domain trusts). If you don't select an account, when you click the properties dialog's OK button you'll be faced with another dialog that asks you whether you want to select an existing account or create a new one. If you don't want this mailbox to have an account associated with it, just click the Cancel button and the mailbox will be created without an account association—but no one will be able to log onto Exchange and read its mail, so be forewarned.

Exchange 5.5 caches mailbox account information for two hours. While this makes mailbox ownership checking more efficient, it also means that it takes up to two hours for any change to take effect. If you want to shorten the caching time, add a new `REG_DWORD` value `Mailbox Cache Age Limit` to the `HKLM\CurrentControlSet\ Services\MSExchangeIS\ParametersSystem` key. This setting is the number of minutes in hex that you want the cache to persist for.

When you look at this dialog, you'll probably notice that all of the fields are plain text entry fields except the "Primary Windows NT Account..." field. That's because the information you enter here isn't subject to any validation or checking; you're free to enter your title as "Grand Poobah and Emperor of E-Mail" and Exchange

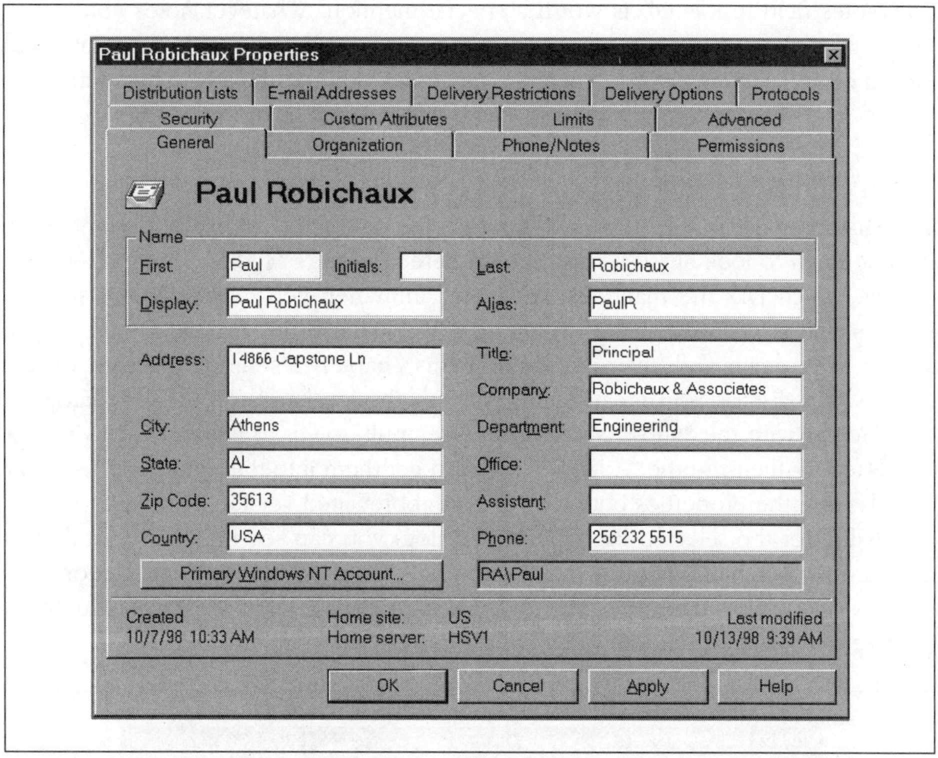

Figure 6-1. The General tab of the mailbox properties dialog is where you identify the mailbox holder

Administrator will happily record it as such in the directory. This argues that you should be careful about what you type in; even though you can always go back and change it, it's easier to be accurate at the beginning.

A brief word about the pane at the bottom of the tab: it shows when the mailbox was created, what its home site and server are, and when the mailbox was last modified. This is a handy reference, since there's no other place to see the mailbox modification or creation dates; you can see what site and server the mailbox is in by eyeballing each server's Server Recipients container, but this is inefficient.

The Phone/Notes tab

The Phone/Notes tab allows you to enter a total of eight phone numbers for the mailbox: two business numbers and two home numbers, plus a pager, mobile phone, and fax number, not to mention the mailbox owner's assistant's phone number. Like the fields in the General tab, Exchange Administrator doesn't make any attempt to check this data for validity, so make sure whatever you enter is reasonable, since it's what users will see in the directory.

The Notes field in this tab is worth a special mention. Whatever notes you put in here are globally visible to directory users, and (using the right templates, as described in Chapter 5) you can make the notes field searchable. This is an easy way to let users search for other users with particular skills or knowledge.

The Distribution Lists tab

The Distribution Lists tab shows which DLs the selected mailbox is a member of. It's not much to look at, so it's not shown here. The tab's Modify... button lets you change which DLs the mailbox participates in. When you click it, you'll see the address selection dialog shown in Figure 6-2; you'll see this dialog, or others very similar to it, again and again throughout this chapter. It's simple enough to use that I won't discuss it in great detail: you use the left-hand side of the dialog, in conjunction with the "Show Names from the" pull-down, to show the DLs you're interested in, then use the "Add ->" button to get them into the right-hand list. You can also use the Properties button to see an abbreviated version of the DL proper-ties dialog for the selected list; from this dialog, you can see the display and alias names, membership lists, and email addresses for the DL. The Find button dis-plays a find dialog based on the stored search dialog template, so if you don't know exactly what DL you're looking for, you can do a broader search.

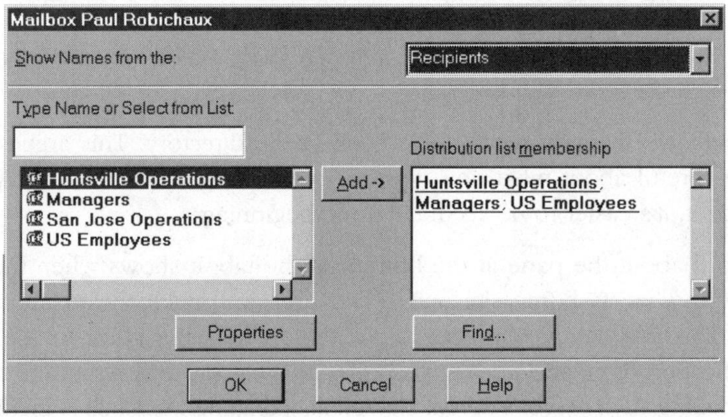

Figure 6-2. The address selection dialog

The Organization tab

Most organizations follow a hierarchical model: people work for managers, who in turn work for other managers, and on up the food chain. If your organization hap-pens to fall into this category, you'll probably want to use the mailbox properties dialog's Organization tab, shown in Figure 6-3. Of course, the mailbox doesn't manage anyone itself; instead, this tab shows you who the human that owns the mailbox manages, as well as who that human's manager is. Here's what the Organization tab controls do:

Manager

This group lets you view, and set, the manager of this mailbox's owner. Click the Modify... button to see an addressing dialog, from which you can choose the custom recipient or mailbox who manages this mailbox's owner.* You can use the Clear button to clear the Manager field and return this mailbox to its native manager-less state.

Direct reports

This list shows the list of mailboxes that have this mailbox shown as their manager. You can use the Modify... button to display another addressing dialog, from which you can add or remove direct reports. When you modify the direct reports list, you're actually editing the Manager attribute of other mailboxes; for example, if you open your boss's mailbox and add yourself as a direct report, you're actually setting your mailbox's Manager field, as you'll see if you open it.

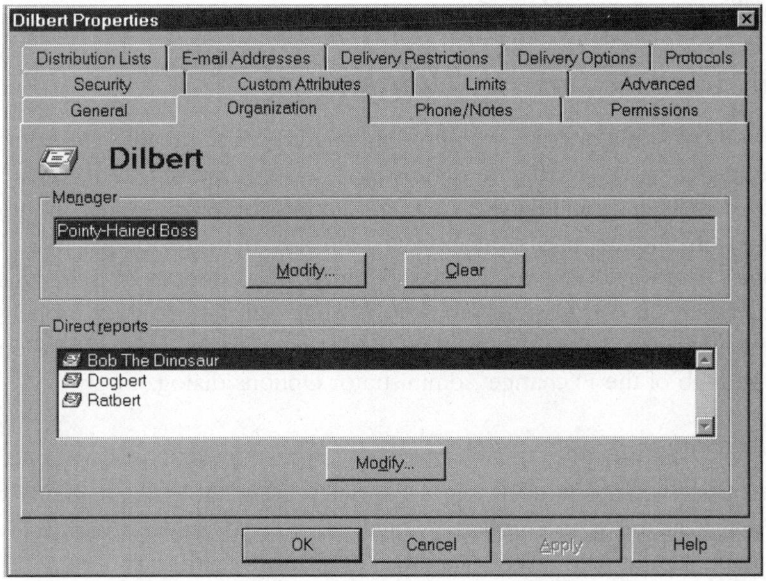

Figure 6-3. The Organization tab shows you who a mailbox owner reports to and who reports to the mailbox owner

---

* This dialog also allows you to select distribution lists, but if you try to make a DL a manager, you get a dialog pointing out your error and asking if you want to try again.

If you plan on making lots of changes to the organizational structure, do it with the directory import and export features. It's easy to export a list of people in each department, then edit the exported file to get the right manager listed.

The Custom Attributes tab

You may want to define custom attributes for your recipients, as detailed in Chapter 9, *Managing the Directory*. The most common application for these is when importing data from some other directory system or database that has fields missing from Exchange's default schema; they're also useful for keeping track of any other information that you want replicated as part of each mailbox's directory information. The Custom Attributes tab of the mailbox properties dialog is pretty straightforward: for each attribute (whether you've explicitly defined it or left it as "Custom Attribute *N*"), there's a matching text entry field. As with all the other text entry fields, Exchange Administrator doesn't validate what you type in here. Since most sites use custom attributes in conjunction with the directory import feature, this usually isn't a big problem.

Setting Mailbox Security Options

You can set two categories of security settings through the mailbox properties dialog. The first category, Exchange permissions, are set through the familiar Permission tab. Most often, you'll have to use the Permission tab to grant one user User permission on another user's mailbox; if you ever need to log on to or recover data from a user's mailbox, you'll have to add your account as a user by using the tab. Remember, the Permissions tab doesn't appear in the mailbox properties dialog unless you turn on the "Show Permissions page for all objects" option in the Permissions tab of the Exchange Administrator Options dialog.

The Security tab

If the Permissions tab is familiar, the Security tab is probably like something out of *The X-Files*. You use it to enroll individual users in advanced security, revoke or recover their security certificates, and see when those certificates expire. This may sound a little buzzword-ish, so let's take a look at what these individual functions actually do. The security tab dialog is shown in Figure 6-4.

Before users can take advantage of the advanced security features, they must be *enrolled*. This enrollment has two distinct steps: an administrator must enroll the mailbox in advanced security, and the mailbox user must generate a key pair and send it to the certificate server for processing. The result of enrollment is a security

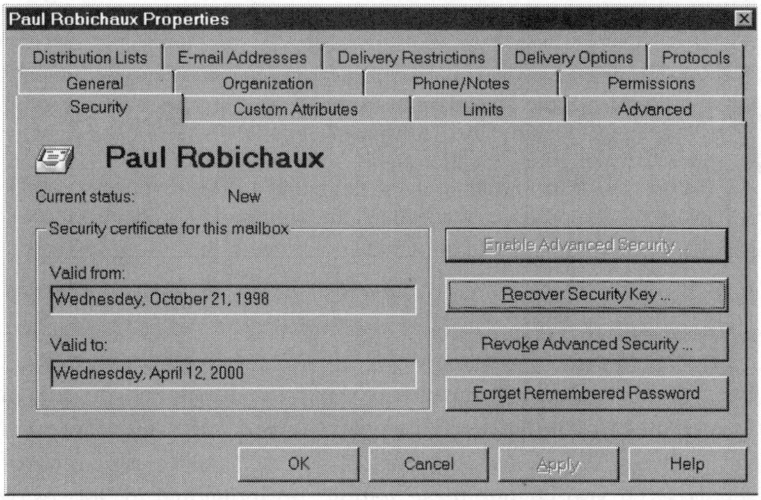

Figure 6-4. The Security tab allows you to enroll, revoke, and recover security certificates

certificate that has been digitally signed by the certificate server. To enroll a user, use the Enable Advanced Security... button in the Security tab. You'll be prompted to enter the KMS password for whatever account you're running Exchange Administrator under, then Exchange Administrator will generate a temporary enrollment key. The setting of the "Allow email to be sent to the user" checkbox on the Enrollment tab of the CA properties dialog governs whether you have to write this key down and convey it to the user by hand or whether it can be emailed to the user. In either case, once the user has that temporary key they have to follow the steps described in the section "The Enrollment tab," in Chapter 16, *Exchange Security.*

After the user completes the enrollment process, the certificate server issues a signed certificate, which lives in the directory and is available to anyone in the organization. Access to the private part of the certificate is controlled by a password. If the user loses the password, or if the private part of the certificate file is damaged or lost, an administrator can generate a new temporary key, which the user can use to regenerate the missing information. Clicking the Recover Security Key button generates the new key token and either displays it or emails it to the user, just like the Enable Advanced Security... button.

Finally, you can choose to revoke a user's advanced security certificate, either because the user is no longer associated with the organization or because the key has been (or may have been) compromised. Clicking the Revoke Advanced Security button immediately revokes the user's certificate and tells the certificate server to add it to the revocation list. Once you revoke a certificate, you can't recover, reissue, or reuse it—you'll have to re-enroll the mailbox and have the user generate a new pair of keys.

 As Gus Baird, the legendary instructor in Georgia Tech's College of Computing, would say, "Advanced security is serious bidness." Please make sure you thoroughly read the material in Chapter 16 before you start enrolling users; there are a number of very subtle potential compromises you can fall into in innocent ignorance.

Controlling Mail Transfer

The biggest chunk of tabs in the mailbox properties dialog are the ones that deal with various facets of mail transfer. This probably isn't surprising, since mail transfer is what Exchange is for. You can control several aspects of mail transfer on a per-mailbox basis. If you change these settings on individual mailboxes, your settings will override the site and server defaults.

The Limits tab

The Limits tab, shown in Figure 6-5, allows you to change the individual mailbox's storage, retention, and message size limits. Normally, all mailboxes inherit their deleted item retention and storage limit settings from the server and site, in that order. If you need to, you can override these settings by clearing the appropriate "Use information store default" checkbox and filling in the limits yourself.

Deleted item retention time
> This group controls how long deleted items are stored in the dumpster, from which they can be recovered. Normally, using the IS default values will work fine, but if you have users who are prone to deleting items and forgetting to undelete them before the standard retention period expires, you can increase the item retention period for their mailbox only. If you want more detail on exactly how deleted item retention works, see "Recovering Deleted Items" in Chapter 11, *Managing the Information Store.*

Information Store storage limits
> This group lets you override the mailbox size limits set at the IS level. You can set three separate limits. The first limit triggers a warning email message when the mailbox grows beyond the specified size. You may also set limits that, when exceeded, cut off the sending and receiving of mail; users can still log in to delete old messages and clean their mailbox, but no mail can be sent or accepted. You may find it helpful to assign different storage limits to some users (for example, users who routinely need to send large files like Power-Point presentations).

The Prohibit Send option has no effect on POP3 and IMAP4 clients; they can always send mail, no matter what you've set this field's value to.

Message sizes

These control groups let you set a high-water mark for incoming and outgoing messages. By default, there's no size limit on either type of message, though most sites impose limits by setting them on their connectors. If you want to, you can set maximum sizes for incoming and outgoing messages. Messages that exceed this limit fail with an NDR explaining that they're over the preset limit.

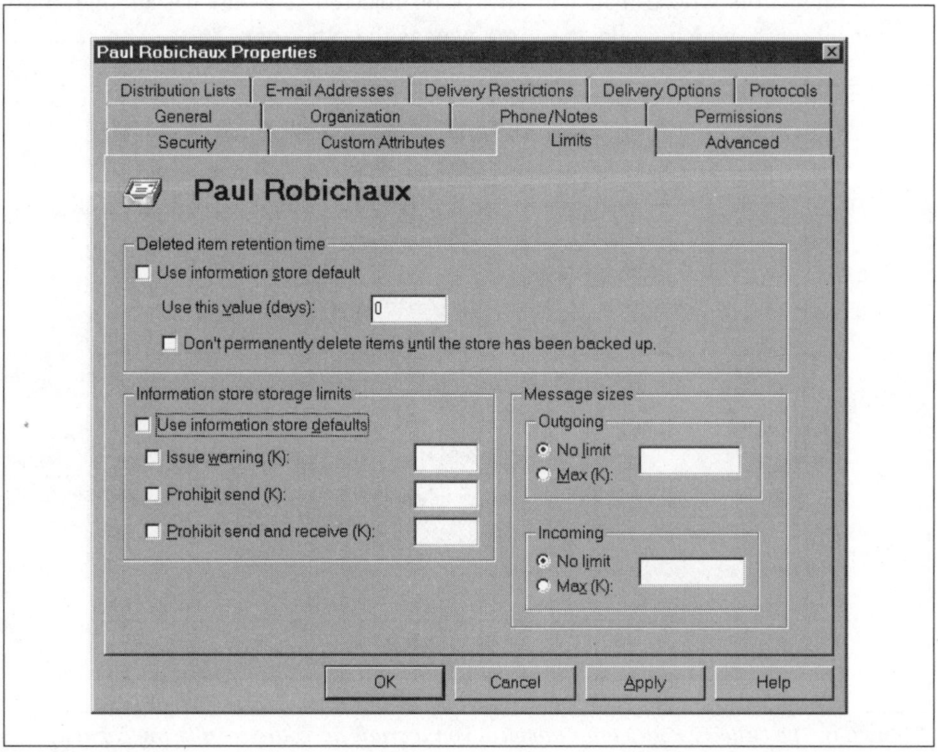

![Paul Robichaux Properties dialog box showing the Limits tab. Tabs include Distribution Lists, E-mail Addresses, Delivery Restrictions, Delivery Options, Protocols, General, Organization, Phone/Notes, Permissions, Security, Custom Attributes, Limits, Advanced. The Limits tab shows "Paul Robichaux" with sections: Deleted item retention time (Use information store default, Use this value (days): 0, Don't permanently delete items until the store has been backed up.), Information store storage limits (Use information store defaults, Issue warning (K):, Prohibit send (K):, Prohibit send and receive (K):), Message sizes (Outgoing: No limit / Max (K):, Incoming: No limit / Max (K):). Buttons: OK, Cancel, Apply, Help.]

Figure 6-5. The Limits tab lets you apply gentle but firm pressure to your users' mailbox habits

The Delivery Restrictions tab

Like the Limits tab, the Delivery Restrictions tab gives you one more tool you can use to control what users can do with their mailboxes. The tab, which appears in

Figure 6-6, lets you establish the following two separate categories of delivery restrictions:

Accept messages from

This list shows all the mailboxes, DLs, and custom recipients from which this mailbox will accept mail. If you leave the radio button set to All, anyone can send to this mailbox; if you turn on the List button instead, any mail sent by anyone *not* shown in the list will be returned to the sender with an NDR. The Modify... button shows the address selection dialog that you saw earlier in Figure 6-2 so you can add or remove list items.

Reject messages from

This list works the same way; when the None button is selected, no message will be rejected. If you instead select the List button, you can selectively specify originators whose mail will always be rejected. This list has its own Modify... button, which works the same way as the other one.

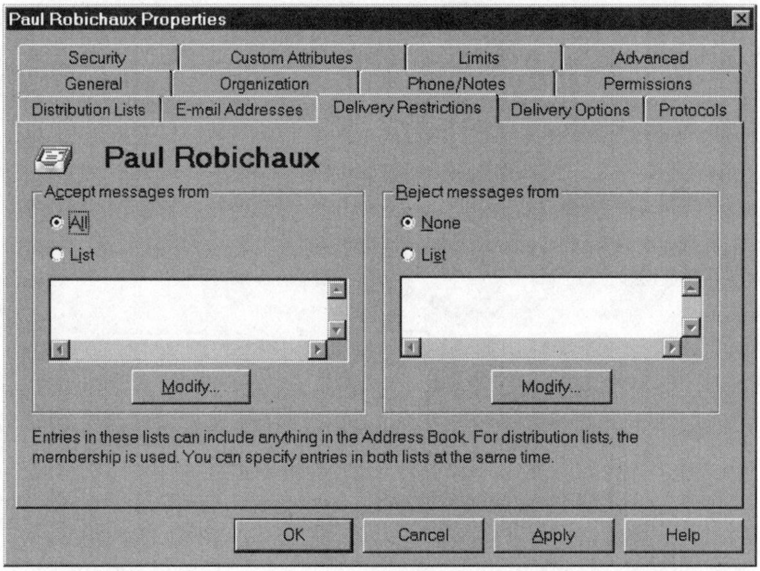

Figure 6-6. The Delivery Restrictions tab gives you a crude accept/reject filtering capacity

The difference between these two lists is subtle: anyone whose name is on the Accept list can send mail to the mailbox, and no one whose name is on the Reject list can. For example, to set up a mailbox that only one person in the organization can send to, open its Delivery Restrictions tab and set the "Accept messages from" radio button to List. Add the desired sender to the Accept list, and leave the Reject list empty—that does it. (In fact, the mailbox can't even send messages to itself using this combination!) You can combine accept and reject filters to fine-tune exactly who may send mail to a particular mailbox.

 Don't confuse these filters with Outlook's filtering rules or with the anti-spam filters you can add in Exchange 5.5. The accept/reject filters only apply to one mailbox, and you can only accept or reject mail based on entries from the GAL. If you want to block mail from originators outside the organization, you'll have to create custom recipient addresses for them first.

The Delivery Options tab

Exchange allows you to designate a *delegate* for any mailbox. The delegate can act as a proxy for the mailbox owner, sending mail with the owner's name and accepting meeting requests on their behalf. You have to set up delegates for each individual mailbox; in most environments, the only people who use them will be those who have assistants or other real-life delegates who routinely carry out tasks for them.

The Delivery Options tab, shown in Figure 6-7, lets you delegate two separate types of power. The first type is permission to send on behalf of the mailbox. For example, let's say that my wife is also my office manager. I want her to be able to send mail with my name on it; that way, she can handle email interaction with our ISP, our suppliers, and so on, just as she does on the phone. To accomplish this, I granted her mailbox "Send On Behalf Of" permission to my mailbox. That way, she can generate messages that appear to come from me.

 You can assign delegates from within the Outlook client, too; see the Delegates tab of the Options dialog in Outlook 97 or 98.

By default, mail for a mailbox goes only to that mailbox. The "Alternate recipient" control group allows you to specify someone else who receives all mail sent to the mailbox (note that this isn't the same as giving delegate access to the mailbox). Depending on the setting of the "Deliver messages to both recipient and alternate recipient" checkbox, mail will either go to both the original and alternate recipients or to the alternate only. When would you use this? Let's say your boss is going on maternity leave, and she's not planning on being around the office to collect her email. You agree to pinch-hit for her and notify her of anything important, so you open her mailbox properties dialog and set yourself as an alternate

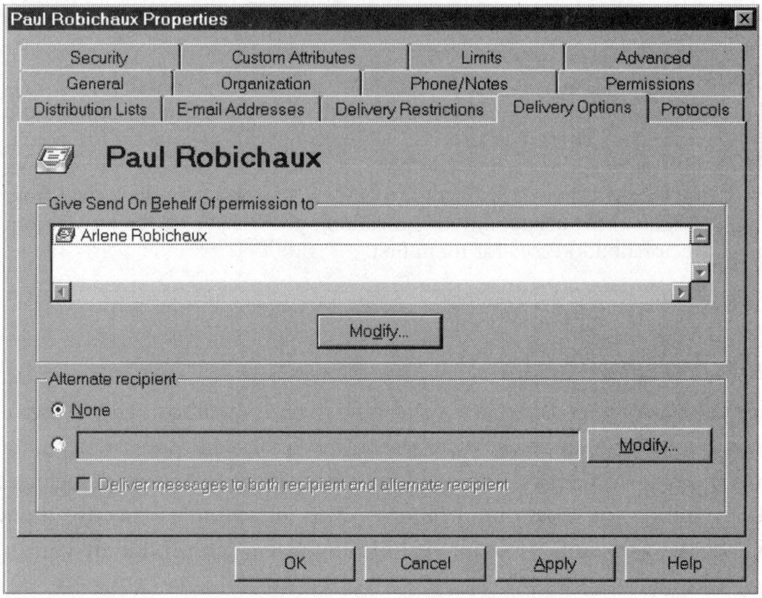

Figure 6-7. The Delivery Options tab allows you to set alternate recipients for any mailbox

recipient for her mailbox. Presto! Her mail now goes to you, and you can answer it as yourself (or as her, if you've also got "Send On Behalf Of" permission).

The Protocols tab

Normally, you enable or disable mail access protocols *en masse* at the site and server level. For instance, once you decide to allow some of your users to use IMAP4 or POP3, you may as well allow all of them the same privileges. In some cases, though, you might need to override protocol settings for an individual mailbox. This overriding can cut both ways: you can turn an individual protocol on or off, and the mailbox-level setting takes precedence over the site and server settings. Let's say that you don't want anyone to have POP3 or IMAP4 access to your help desk mailbox: a few seconds of poking around on the Protocols tab of its properties dialog will solve that problem posthaste.

The Protocols tab is shown in Figure 6-8. Each protocol is shown on one line of the Protocol list; you can also see whether the protocol is enabled on the recipient mailbox and on the server. The HTTP and LDAP protocols don't have any settings; the only thing you can change in this dialog is whether the protocol is enabled for the mailbox or not. The NNTP, IMAP4, and POP3 protocols have additional settings, which you access via the Settings... button. These settings control how outgoing messages are encoded, what message format Exchange uses, and (for IMAP) what IMAP retrieval options are available.

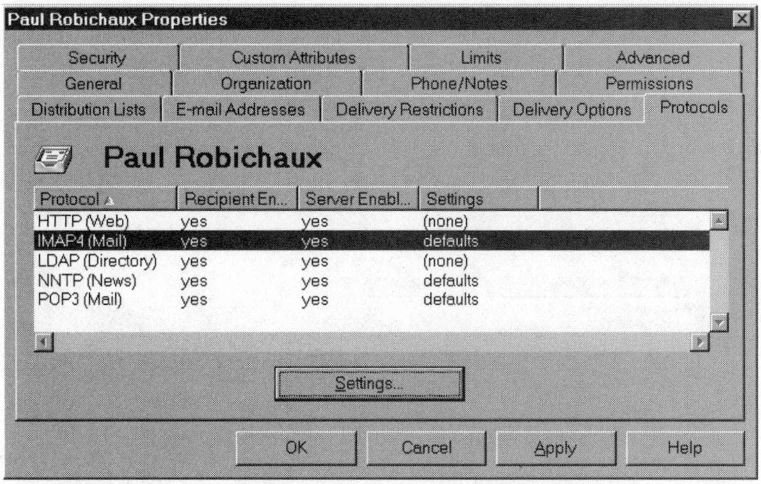

Figure 6-8. The Protocols tab lets you detail which protocols you want an individual mailbox to handle

How to Let Other People Read Your Mail

If you want to completely reroute mail from one mailbox to another, the Alternate recipient control group will do this. Sometimes, though, you need to enable one user to read mail in more than one mailbox. For example, in some companies it's common to have one administrative assistant shared between several managers or executives. The assistant could make good use of delegate access to the calendars and mailboxes of the entire group (though most managers I know would blanch at the thought of letting someone else read their entire mailbox, dirty jokes and all).

You can delegate access in several ways. First, you can give the "extra" recipients User permission on the desired mailbox. This allows the extra recipients to act just like the mailbox owner; they can do anything that the original owner can do. Sometimes, though, you want to grant more limited access. You can do so by having the original mailbox owner use the Outlook client to grant delegate access to the subordinate mailboxes. If you just want to allow a user to send mail on behalf of another mailbox holder, you can add the Send As permission on the target mailbox. For more on all these approaches, see Chapter 13, *Managing Exchange Clients*.

Figure 6-9 shows the IMAP4 Protocol Details dialog. It's representative of what the other two dialogs look like, except that they have fewer controls.

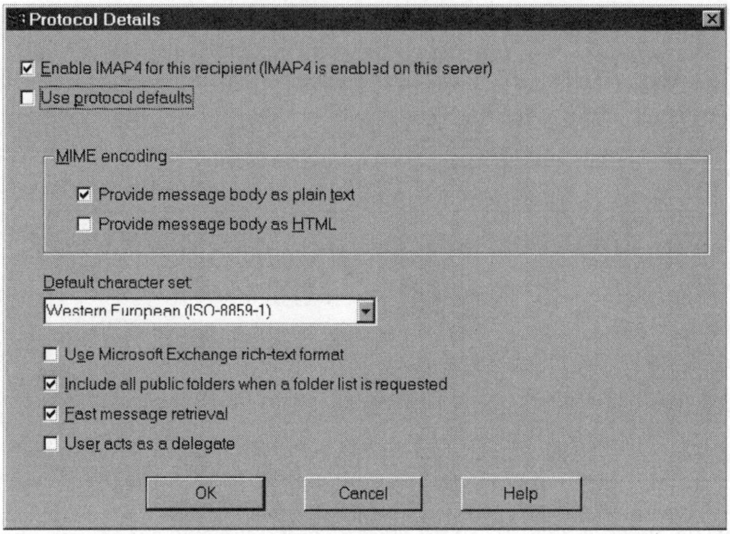

Figure 6-9. The IMAP4, POP3, and NNTP Protocol Details dialogs give you control over protocol settings at the mailbox level

Here's what the controls do; I've noted which controls are specific to which dialogs:

Enable IMAP4 for this recipient

This checkbox lets you override the server and site settings for the protocol. When it (or the POP3 or NNTP equivalents) is checked, this mailbox will have IMAP4 access, no matter what the site and server settings say.

Use protocol defaults

This checkbox specifies whether you want to accept the site and server protocol settings, or override them for this mailbox. While this checkbox is checked, you won't have access to the other controls in the dialog.

MIME encoding

This group controls how Exchange sends the message body. Since the MIME specification allows mail programs to include multiple copies of the same data in different formats, Exchange can deliver the message body as plain ASCII text only, HTML only, or both. Using both doubles the message size, but choosing one of the other formats has its own drawbacks: plain-text messages lose fonts, colors, hyperlinks, and other cool formatting features of modern mail clients like Eudora, Outlook, and Netscape Messenger, but not every mailer knows what to do with HTML parts.

This setting only applies to one protocol, so you can choose different settings for news postings, POP3, and IMAP4 message retrieval. The POP3 and NNTP settings dialogs name the control group "Message encoding" instead of "MIME encoding," and also offer an additional control: instead of using MIME, you can fall back to the older UUENCODE format, which MS Mail and cc:Mail require.

Default character set

This pull-down tells Exchange what ISO character set to use when encoding outgoing messages. The default ISO-8859-1 character set is fine for some languages; others, like Russian, Norwegian, Greek, and most Asian languages, have their own ISO character sets. Adjust this setting with care: if you choose a character set your mail recipients can't handle, they'll get unreadable gobbledygook instead of readable text. The NNTP protocol dialog doesn't have this control.

Use Microsoft Exchange rich-text format

This checkbox lets you rein in Exchange's default behavior of converting everything to RTF. Normally, Exchange will send styled text (i.e., any text that uses multiple fonts, underlining, boldface, italics, colors, and so on) in RTF, which few other mail clients can decode. If you're going to be sending primarily to other Exchange or Outlook users, this setting is okay, but if the mailbox in question mostly needs to talk with other clients, it's safe, and desirable, to turn this off. An alternative is to tell your client users not to use styled text, but this doesn't always work. This option is also missing from the NNTP dialog.

The remaining three checkboxes are specific to the IMAP4 protocol dialog, because the features they control are specific to the IMAP4 protocol:

Include all public folders when a folder list is requested

This checkbox lets you specify whether public folders appear in the list of all folders available to the mailbox user. With other IMAP4 servers, this list contains only those folders in the user's personal mail store, but since Exchange allows IMAP4 access to public folders, it makes sense to show those folders in the list of folders the user can access.

Fast message retrieval

This checkbox controls whether Exchange reports the actual message size, which is slow, since it has to retrieve the message from the store and count the bytes, or reports an approximate size. Approximating the size is faster, but it breaks some IMAP4 clients—notably Simeon, Pine, and Netscape Messenger 4.5. Depending on how many IMAP4 users you have, you may need to clear this flag at the server or site level, not on individual mailboxes.

User acts as a delegate

If you want a mailbox to have delegate access to other mailboxes via IMAP4, you'll have to check this checkbox. All this does is enable the IMAP4 client to see mailboxes to which it has delegate access. You, or the mailbox owners, still have to grant delegate access to the mailbox you're configuring.

Setting Advanced Mailbox Properties

Most of the properties you can attach to a mailbox fall neatly into one of the categories I've already discussed, and they're all fairly straightforward. However, there are a few settings that are more esoteric. Microsoft has lumped these into the mailbox properties dialog's Advanced tab (see Figure 6-10).

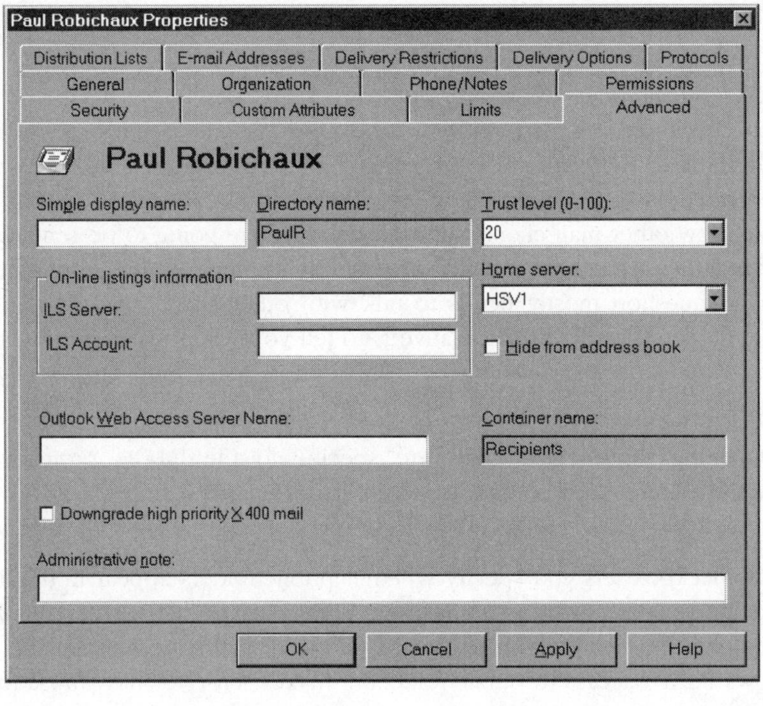

Figure 6-10. The Advanced tab has a bunch of settings most administrators never touch

When you look at this dialog, the absence of group boxes tells you right away that it's a dumping ground for miscellaneous settings that didn't fit in anywhere else. Let's start with the top left and work our way towards the bottom right:

Simple display name

This field allows you to provide an alternate display name for clients that can't handle embedded spaces, dashes, or other characters in their names. This is most commonly used in networks that have to coexist with mainframe mailers, and the field is usually set via a directory import. After all, who wants to type in new display names for every mailbox on the server?

Directory name

    This field shows you the directory name for this mailbox. Once the mailbox is created, you can't change the directory name, because Exchange uses it internally for message routing. However, until the first time you press the Apply or OK buttons while creating a mailbox, you're free to edit this field.

Trust level (0-100)

    This control lets you set the replication trust level for this mailbox. Items whose trust levels are higher than the directory replication connector's threshold won't be replicated through the Microsoft Mail directory synchronization process. This is a simple way to allow some items, but not others, to replicate between sites or organizations, provided you're using MS Mail. You can also set a trust level, then filter on it, when you use directory import and export, as discussed in Chapter 5.

On-line listings information

    If you're running Microsoft's NetMeeting server, which lets users find other users and arrange online meetings through the Internet Locator Service (ILS), you can make an individual mailbox (and its owner) visible to ILS users by filling out the server and account fields in this group.

Home server

    This pull-down shows you what server this mailbox is currently stored on. When you create a new mailbox, you can use this pull-down to specify what server should host the new mailbox. If you're editing an existing mailbox, you can change its value and click OK, which is the same as using the Tools → Move Mailbox... command.

Hide from address book

    By default, every mailbox, DL, and custom recipient appears in the DL. If you want a mailbox to be hidden, so that only people who know its name can send to it, check this checkbox. Be warned: when you use this setting, you can't see the mailbox, DL, or custom recipient anywhere, even in Exchange Administrator.

Outlook Web Access Server Name

    If this mailbox is configured to allow HTTP access, you can specify the name of the OWA server that provides HTTP access in this field. POP3 and IMAP4 clients can use their own mail clients for mail and OWA for calendaring and scheduling. If you provide an OWA server name, meeting requests and other messages that use custom forms will show up in the IMAP4 or POP3 client as URLs that the recipient can use to go straight to the OWA server. If you don't provide an OWA server name, clients will still get meeting request and custom form messages, but they won't contain a URL, so the user will have to manually open OWA and find them.

It's much easier to set the OWA server name in the General tab of the private IS properties dialog—that way you can set the OWA server for all users on a server at once. However, if you have individual users who are on different servers than the IS default, set their correct server name here.

Container name

This field shows you what recipient container this mailbox lives in; this is actually pretty useless, since you can't change it.

Downgrade high priority X.400 mail

Users can send high-priority X.400 mail on their own, but some X.400 gateways disallow it (or, worse, charge extra for it). If you check this checkbox, Exchange will automatically force the priority flag of outgoing messages back to normal.

Administrative note

Last, but not least, is the Administrative note field. If you've just *got* to keep a note about this mailbox, this is the place to do it. Where does it appear? By default, nowhere—but you can use the View → Columns... command to show it in any recipients view, including those for ABVs, the Recipients container, and each server's Server Recipients container.

Moving Mailboxes

Every mailbox has a home—its home server. As long as a user can establish a communications path to that server, she can get her mail. Sometimes you may need to move one or more mailboxes to a different server. This is the easiest way to add more Exchange capacity to your network: build a new server, install Exchange on it, then just move a bunch of mailboxes over to it. In addition, it's the fastest way to move user data from server to server; this might be desirable if you've set up separate servers at each geographic location or department, then find that some users need to move from one location to another.

The Tools → Move Mailbox... command does the move for you. Open a recipient container, select one or more mailboxes, and select the command. You'll see a dialog that lists all the servers within the site; pick the target server and click OK, then wait patiently while Exchange does its thing. In essence, this command replicates the selected mailbox from its current home server to the new one, then deletes the original and updates the mailbox's directory data. Because every message in the mailbox has to be copied to the new server (remember, single-instance storage means that many of the mailbox's messages may already exist in the new home's private IS, preserving the storage savings), moving mailboxes can take quite a while.

In addition, you may find that after you move a mailbox, it appears on the original home server *and* the new server. Don't be alarmed; the mailbox really did move, and it's no longer on the original home server. This is a known but relatively benign bug that lingers on, even in Exchange 5.5 SP1. Sometimes the post-move cleanup code doesn't properly clean all the directory objects associated with the mailbox, so it appears in the directory twice. To fix this, you have to open an Exchange Administrator window to the new server and use Tools → Move Mailbox... to move it *back* to the home server. When you do, you'll see an error dialog that reports that the object exists already, but Exchange will silently clean up the dangling objects on the original server, and the mailbox will remain on the new server where you just put it. You have to repeat this procedure for every dangling mailbox you run into, so be on the lookout.

Cleaning Up Mailbox Litter

Some users are much more diligent than others about keeping their mailboxes clean. It's easy to become an email pack rat, especially when your mailbox is on a remote server and it's not taking up any of *your* disk space. You can gently encourage your users to clean out unneeded messages by using Exchange Administrator's mailbox cleanup feature. This feature, available from the Tools → Clean Mailbox... command, lets you purge messages according to their size, age, sensitivity, and read status. You can also specify whether you want the messages deleted immediately or moved to the user's *Deleted Items* folder; either way, they can be recovered from the dumpster if deleted item retention is enabled.

 There's an automated way to clean mailboxes, too: see "The Mailbox Cleanup Agent" in Appendix A, *BORK Tools*.

Select one or more mailboxes in any recipient container or ABV, then use the menu command. The Clean Mailbox dialog will appear, as shown in Figure 6-11. Here's what its controls do:

Age

This group contains two separate purge criteria. You can remove all messages that are older than a certain number of days, and you can remove messages that exceed a certain size limit. Messages that meet *either* of these thresholds are removed; the criteria cannot be combined. Currently, there's no way to remove messages that are, say, over 180 days old *and* bigger than 2MB.

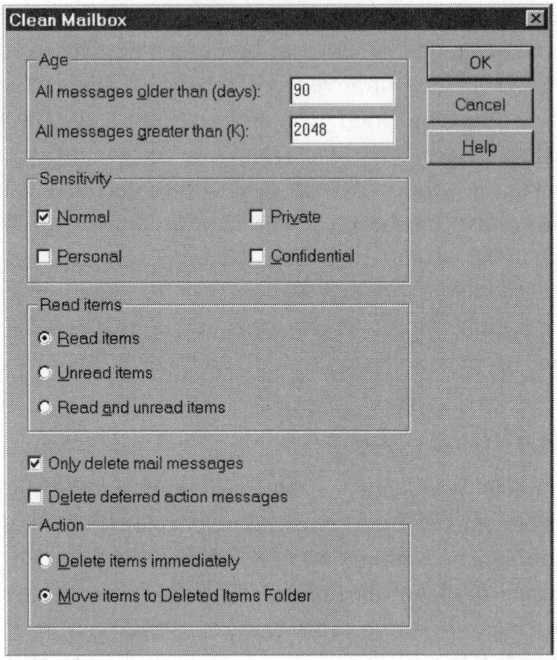

Figure 6-11. The Clean Mailbox dialog lets you selectively purge old messages from one or many mailboxes

Sensitivity

This group lets you purge messages based on the sensitivity class the sender put on the message. All messages flagged with the sensitivity categories you check off will be purged. This is a great way to get rid of personal or confidential mail before granting delegate access to a mailbox.

Read items

You can use this radio button group to purge messages based on whether the mailbox owner has read them or not. Normally, you'll be called on to purge read items only, but you can remove unread items or any item that meets the criteria. This setting is ANDed with the settings in the Age and Sensitivity groups, so you can delete (for example) all read private messages or all unread messages older than 45 days.

Only delete mail messages

This checkbox provides an additional layer of filtering. If you accept the default setting, the cleanup task will remove only mail messages—not calendar items, tasks, or any of the other flotsam that can occupy a mailbox. Turn the checkbox off, and purging the mailbox will delete any item in the mailbox that meets the other criteria you've set.

Delete deferred action messages

This checkbox also acts in conjunction with the other criteria you set. When you're working offline, any server-side mail action that requires a server connection is queued *on the server* for the next connection. For example, a server-side rule that moves messages to a personal folder will generate deferred action messages each time it's executed. If you purge these messages on a mailbox, any deferred actions for the mailbox will be lost.

Action

This last group of controls is arguably the most important: it controls where the purged messages go. If you stick with the default setting of "Move items to Deleted Items Folder," purged items go into the mailbox's trash folder, and users can easily recover them using Outlook's Tools → Recover Deleted Items... command. If you choose the "Delete items immediately" radio button, purged items are deleted in place, so users won't be able to recover them unless you apply the registry change described in the section "The Dumpster" in Chapter 11.

The Tools → Clean Mailbox... command isn't disabled when you select custom recipients or distribution lists, but you can't clean them—Exchange will complain that the selected object isn't a mailbox.

Two Alternate Ways to Create Mailboxes

Apart from using Exchange Administrator, there are two other ways to create mailboxes that you may find useful. Both are implemented as extensions to the standard NT tools used for creating new accounts; Exchange modifies these tools to allow you to create a new Exchange mailbox at the same time.

User Manager for domains

When you run User Manager on a machine where Exchange is installed, you'll notice the addition of the Exchange menu to the menubar. This menu has two useful commands: Exchange → Options... and Exchange → Properties....; we'll get to them in a minute. When you use the modified User Manager to create a new account, you fill in the New User dialog normally. As soon as you hit the Add button, you get the standard mailbox properties dialog, which you fill in as discussed earlier in this section. The Exchange → Properties... command lets you see the mailbox properties of a selected account at any time.

Now, what about that Exchange → Options... command? That's where you set the same options you set from within Exchange Administrator, including what home server you want new accounts' mailboxes to live on, whether you want to auto-matically create and delete mailboxes when you modify NT accounts in User Man-ager, and what recipient container new accounts should go into.

The net user command

Experienced NT administrators know and like the net user commands because they can be used directly from the command line. While teaching you how to use these commands isn't part of this book,[*] you should know that when you add or remove a user account with the net user command you may also be adding or removing a corresponding Exchange mailbox. If you use the User Manager Exchange → Options... command to specify that you want User Manager to create or delete a mailbox when you create or delete an account, those settings will also apply to net user. This is great news, since it allows you to tie mailbox creation and deletion in with whatever automated scripts you've developed for bulk addi-tion and removal of user accounts. If you don't have any such scripts, see *Win-dows NT User Administration*, by Ashley Meggitt and Timothy Ritchey (O'Reilly & Associates).

Creating and Managing Custom Recipients

A custom recipient is a placeholder in the GAL that provides a GAL entry for a recipient who's not using Exchange. In this sense, it's like an alias—it puts an Exchange-friendly directory object in front of a fax number or other foreign address you want your users to be able to send to. The "send to" part is impor-tant—custom recipients don't have mailboxes and can't receive mail.

When you create a custom recipient, you'll have to provide some amount of infor-mation to create the object; once that's done, you can fill in many of the same properties that regular mailboxes offer. Table 6-1 shows what you have to pro-vide for each standard custom recipient type.

To create a new custom recipient, use the File → New Custom Recipient... com-mand or its accelerator, Ctrl-R. You'll see a dialog that lists the custom recipient types you can create; you'll see the six types shown in Table 6-1, plus any others that may have been added by third-party connectors or products. Select an address type, and you'll get a properties dialog, into which you'll enter the required items listed in the table. Once that's done, the custom recipient properties dialog, which looks suspiciously like the regular mailbox properties dialog, will appear.

---

[*] See Æleen Frisch's *Essential Windows NT System Administration* (O'Reilly & Associates) if you want the skinny.

Table 6-1. *What You Need to Supply for Each Custom Recipient Type*

Custom Recipient Type	Required Items	Notes
cc:Mail address	*Display name*: display name you want for this recipient *Mailbox*: name of the cc:Mail mailbox *Post office*: name of the cc:Mail post office server	
Internet address	*E-mail address*: RFC 822 SMTP address for the recipient	Advanced tab offers message format setting similar to POP3 and IMAP protocols dialogs.
MacMail/ QDMail address	*Display name*: display name you want for this recipient *User name*: name of the user mailbox for this recipient *Server name*: network name of the Mac post office	Can select whether or not this recipient always gets Exchange rich-text format messages.
Microsoft Mail address	*Network name*: network name of the post office computer *Post office name*: MS Mail name for the recipient's post office *Mailbox name*: name of the recipient mailbox on the specified post office	
Other address	*E-mail address*: recipient address you want to use *E-mail type*: type of address	This address type is seldom used, and I don't really know what it's for.
X.400 address	*Given name, surname, initials, common name*: name of the person who owns the address *Organization and organizational units*: organization which owns the address *ADMD, PRMD, country*: administrative domain information	The name, organization, ADMD, PRMD, and country data are combined to build an X.400 distinguished name. Advanced tab lets you specify extra parameters, including domain attributes and terminal type information.

What's the Same

The Organization, Phone/Notes, Permissions, Distribution Lists, E-mail Addresses, Delivery Restrictions, Protocols, and Custom Attributes tabs are all the same as their mailbox counterparts. All the same guidelines and restrictions apply. There are a couple of *very* minor differences between the two, though:

- When you look in the E-mail Addresses tab, you'll see two addresses: an X.400 address (the one that Exchange uses internally) and whatever address type you just created. The proxy address generators that get called when you create a new mailbox don't get called when you create a custom recipient.

- Since custom recipients don't have to be associated with an NT account (and usually aren't), you won't see any accounts granted permission in the "Windows NT accounts with permissions" section of the Permissions tab.

What's Different

First of all, you'll probably notice that the Security, Limits, and Delivery Options tabs are missing. Custom recipients can't participate in advanced security. Since there's no mailbox associated with the custom recipient, there can't be any mailbox limits, or any deleted item retention, for that matter. Similarly, custom recipients can't grant delegate access to their (nonexistent) mailboxes. Once you get past these missing tabs, and subtract the eight tabs that are the same, that leaves two: the General and Advanced tabs.

The General tab for custom recipients looks very much like its mailbox equivalent. The name, address, and organizational fields are all there; the primary difference is that the "Primary Windows NT Account..." button/field combination is replaced by one that's labeled "E-mail...". Clicking that button allows you to either change the current custom address or add another one. Surprise! Custom recipients may have more than one address attached to them. For instance, you can create an SMTP custom recipient, then add an X.400 address.

The Advanced tab is also a bit different. There's no way to specify an OWA server for the custom recipient, although you can still provide a simple display name, replication trust level, home server, and ILS information. Three items in the Advanced tab are relegated to other tabs in the mailbox properties dialog:

Message size
> This control group lets you set a maximum size for outgoing messages sent to this custom recipient. By default, there's no limit, but you can specify a maximum size (in kilobytes) that the server will enforce.

Allow rich text in messages
> This checkbox is for controlling whether or not Exchange sends RTF to this recipient or not. By default, it's turned off.

Primary Windows NT account...
> If you want this custom recipient to be able to function as a normal client of the Exchange server—that is, to be able to send messages, look at calendar data, and so on—use this button to assign an account to the custom recipient. Once you do this, the account you select will appear with User permission in the Permissions tab.

Creating and Managing Distribution Lists

Distribution lists are just like their paper equivalents—those lists of names at the top of memos. All a DL does is encapsulate several (or many) recipients into one address; mail sent to that address goes to every DL recipient. Thanks to the magic of single-instance storage, this process is fairly storage-efficient, although the MTA does have to expand the DL to find out who's on it.

Speaking of who's on it: DLs may contain any addressable object, including public folders, other DLs, mailboxes, and custom recipients. If you include DLs inside another DL, they're treated just like every other recipient type, but the designated expansion server will expand them when it's time. Mail clients treat the DL just like any other recipient, and many of the same restrictions you apply to an ordinary mailbox can also be placed on a DL.

Creating a New DL

To create a new DL, you use the File → New Distribution List... command. When you do, you'll immediately see the General tab of the distribution list properties dialog. You'll probably notice that the distribution list properties dialog shares some common tabs with its custom recipient and mailbox brethren. The Custom Attributes, Delivery Restrictions, Distribution Lists, E-mail Addresses, and Permissions tabs are all the same as the ones you've already seen in this chapter. The DL is not a mailbox—it has no storage capacity—but when it comes to using a DL to deliver mail, it acts like a mailbox. However, there are a few differences, as you'll see in a moment.

If you want to create distribution lists based on rules, you can; see "The Rule-Based Distribution List Tool" in Appendix A.

The General tab

The General tab, shown in Figure 6-12, is the DL equivalent of the mailbox and custom recipient dialogs' General tabs; it's where you name the DL and provide an easy-to-remember alias for it. As you can see from the figure, though, there's more to the DL General tab than to the others:

Owner

You may designate an owner for the DL. That owner can then change the DL membership, adding and removing recipients, directly from her Exchange or

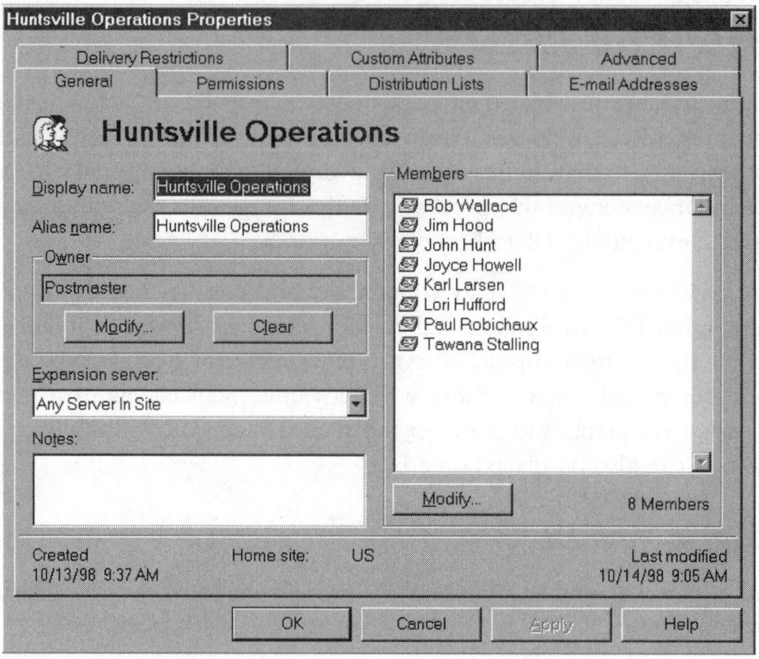

Figure 6-12. The General tab of the distribution list properties dialog

Outlook client. If you want to assign an owner to your DL, use the Modify… button to choose a mailbox; if not, use the Clear button to remove any assigned owner. Whether or not the DL has an owner, administrators may change the list membership from within Exchange Administrator.

Expansion server

This pull-down lets you pick which server in the site will be used to expand the DL membership list. DL expansion can be time-consuming, so one way to boost overall throughput for message flow in a site is to designate the least heavily loaded server as the DL expansion server. Alternately, you can install a small, cheap server, put only a public IS on it, and use it as a combination public folder and DL expansion server. If you're content to let any server do the expansion work, use the default "Any Server In Site" choice; otherwise, pick a server from the list.

Members

This list shows who's currently on the DL. Of course, when you create a new DL this list will be empty, and you'll need to populate it. If you're modifying an existing list, you can update it. Both actions depend on the Modify… button. When you open it, you'll see the familiar addressing dialog, from which you can select DLs, custom recipients, or mailboxes for inclusion in your DL.

Notes

This field allows you to enter a note for the DL. This note is not displayed anywhere in Exchange Administrator, but with appropriate search templates, you can find DLs based on the contents of their Notes field. This allows you to quickly find DLs based on the project or organization they were set up to serve, or whatever other criteria you can shoehorn into the Notes field.

The Advanced tab

The contents of the Advanced tab of the distribution list properties dialog should look pretty familiar by this point (see Figure 6-13).

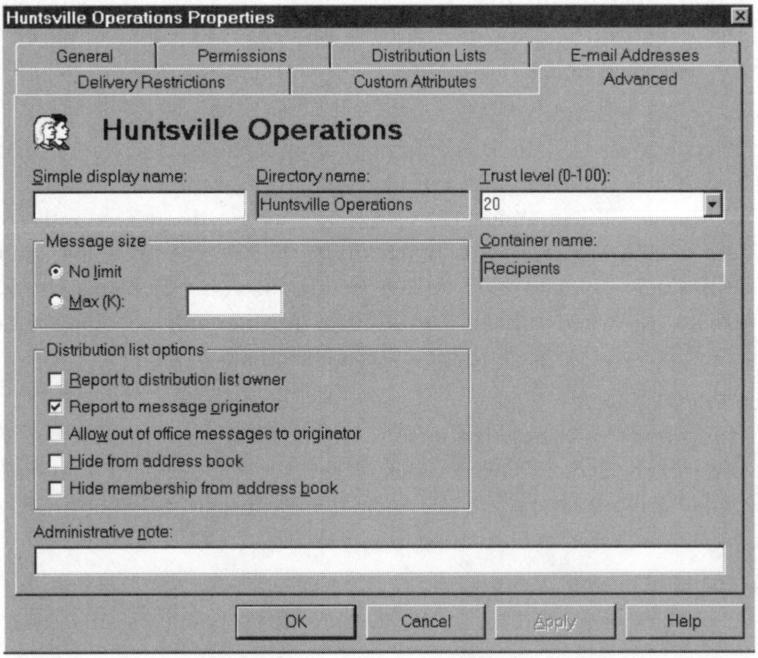

Figure 6-13. The Advanced tab of the distribution list properties dialog looks mighty familiar

The "Simple display name," "Trust level (0-100)," "Message size," "Container name," and "Administrative note" controls all look and work the same as they do in the other property pages, though the corresponding controls aren't necessarily on the Advanced tab in the other dialogs.

The real meat of this dialog is the Distribution list options group. These checkboxes control some of the interaction between the MTA and distribution list messages, to wit:

Report to distribution list owner
Report to message originator

> These checkboxes control where delivery notifications and nondelivery reports go. By default, only the message originator gets a report of delivery or failure. If you want, you can instead have the report go to the list owner, to both places, or nowhere at all. Be careful with this option: if you send out a message with a read receipt or any other delivery report request, and either of these are checked, the victim will get one notification message for each delivery report. That means that a 1,000-member DL could potentially send the message originator and list owner 1,000 delivery receipts each, which may not be what you intended.

Allow out of office messages to originator

> The Exchange and Outlook clients both support automatic out-of-office notification: you tell your mail client you're going out of the office, and it automatically replies to all incoming mail with a message to that effect until you turn it off. DLs usually suppress this behavior so that recipients won't send out-of-office messages back to the message sender. If you check this checkbox, DL users who've turned on the out-of-office feature will generate out-of-office messages that will go back to the message sender.

Hide from address book

> This checkbox does just what it says. Check it and the DL won't be visible in the GAL; uncheck it, as it is by default, and it will appear as an addressable item. Like mailboxes and custom recipients, you can still send mail to a hidden DL if you know its correct address.

Hide membership from address book

> This checkbox keeps the list of DL members from being visible in the GAL.

7

Managing Connectors and the MTA

"Did he ever return, no, he never returned . . ."
—Kingston Trio
Charlie on the MTA

The Message Transfer Agent (MTA) is the Exchange equivalent of your friendly neighborhood U.S. post office: when you deliver mail to it, it automatically chooses the best route to deliver your message, then delivers it in a way that's transparent to you. When you think about the MTA, connectors probably come to mind, since they're inextricably linked to the MTA. Just as your telephone line provides a conduit that you can use to make voice, fax, or data calls, the connectors provide various types of conduits that the MTA can use to do its work.

MTA and Connector Concepts

The most important thing to understand about the relationship between the MTA and connectors is this: the MTA depends on having at least one connector to each target system you want to talk to. That connector can be anything appropriate for the remote system (e.g., you can't use an MS Mail connector to talk to a Notes server), and it must have an underlying transport protocol that allows the connector to do its work. For example, if you want to connect to a site and exchange mail with it using X.400, you need an MTA (already provided as part of Exchange), a properly configured X.400 connector, and a properly configured X.400 transport stack.

This dependency makes sense when you think about it in light of the MTA's function: Mail, directory replication, and public folder data all flow through the MTA as mail messages, so the MTA must have a connection path to whatever remote system you want to talk to. To do its job, the MTA must be able to receive messages, decide which routes are available, choose the best route, and communicate with another MTA on the remote end.

Connections and Associations

The MTA can open one or more *connections* to target servers. Each connection is maintained independently of any others, and each has its own set of parameters. These parameters control how the MTA establishes and uses the connection—how long it waits before timing out, how many times the MTA will try to open a connection before it decides the remote server is unreachable, and so on. It may help to think of a connection like a dial-up PPP connection: once it's established, you can actually have several separate sessions using it simultaneously, just as you could use a PPP connection to simultaneously run two HTTP connections and an FTP download.

In Exchange parlance, each of these separate sessions is called an *association*. A single association ties together one server on each end of the connection. You can control how long associations will remain open after the last pending message is transferred, how many queued items can accumulate before Exchange will attempt to open a new association, and how long the MTA will wait for a response from the remote end before deciding that the association is dead. Via some reasonably clean registry tweaks, you can also control the maximum number of associations that the MTA will attempt to open at one time.

MTA Components

The MTA itself is a single executable, *emsmta.exe*, but there's more to it than that. The MTA runs as an NT service, but it depends on, and communicates with, several other components. From reading Chapter 1, *Introducing Exchange Server*, you know how the MTA talks to the other standard Exchange components; let's look at the MTA-specific items in more detail.

The MTA transport stack

The X.400 and DRAS connectors depend on a separate *MTA transport stack* to do their work. This stack, which is installed from, and only available to, Exchange, provides an underlying communications protocol for the MTA. The MTA passes messages to the stack, which then takes care of transmitting them without error and in correct sequence to the remote system, whose stack reassembles the message and passes it to *its* MTA. When you create a new transport stack, you specify the server it connects to; if it helps, think of each transport stack as a leased communications line that only runs to one place.

Exchange includes support for four MTA transport stacks:

Eicon X.25

Used with Eicon's X.25 packet network cards. You'll use this protocol stack if you're using any of the many X.25 networks that cover literally the entire planet; X.25 coverage is especially pervasive in Europe. Eicon also has some cards that handle ISDN connections.

TP4

Implements the TP4 protocol, which is used to speak pure X.400 to remote X.400 systems. You'll normally use this protocol stack to connect to private (and sometimes public) X.400 networks outside North America over a dedicated or shared Ethernet connection.

TCP/IP

Runs your MTA connections over TCP/IP. To use this protocol stack, you must have the TCP/IP protocol installed on your server and configured properly. One nice thing about this setup: you can use X.400 to connect two systems across the Internet, as long as both of them have port 102 open.

RAS

Works over a standard NTRAS connection; before you can install this protocol stack, you must install and configure NT's RAS server, either by itself or as part of the Routing and Remote Access Service (RRAS) package.

The MTA queues

The MTA maintains several queues. As messages arrive, either from remote MTAs or from the local IS, they go into a queue, where they sit until previously arrived messages have been cleared from the queue. This strict first-in, first-out approach imposes an orderly flow onto message transfer. The MTA maintains two queues that you can watch from within Exchange Administrator: one for private IS messages and one for public IS messages. It also maintains a number of invisible work queues; you can use Performance Monitor to find out how many items are in these queues, but you can't see what they are, where they're bound, or how long they've been waiting. Despite this seeming limitation, just knowing the overall queue length is useful; if the queue keeps growing and growing, something is stopping up the MTA so that it can't transfer outbound messages.

Connectors

It might seem odd to mention connectors as an MTA component, but the MTA is totally dependent on connectors to do its work. As I have already mentioned, it's critical to have the right set of connectors installed and properly configured so that the MTA can do its job. There's a simple rule to follow in this regard: install only the connectors you need, and set them up before turning on directory replication or doing anything that might make the MTA generate large volumes of replication traffic. Since every connector you install represents one more message path that the MTA has to evaluate and route over, the fewer connectors you install, the better. Failing to check the connector configuration before telling the MTA to use it can result in a big backlog of replication or mail messages sitting in the MTA's outbound queue.

Bridgeheads

There are two ways to connect your Exchange sites with each other and with outside systems. One way is to put connectors on several (or even all) of your servers, establishing multiple routes from each site to its peers. This approach provides redundancy, but it imposes higher administrative overhead because there are more connectors to manage. The alternative is to designate a single server in each site as a *bridgehead server*. The bridgehead server in a site runs all the connectors for that site, and all message traffic destined for other sites must flow from its originating server to the bridgehead, then to its destination. Actually, you could split up the connector load by putting different connectors on different machines, so that in each site you had one instance of each connector type.

Figure 7-1 shows the same imaginary organization implemented using each of these two models. In each case, the four sites are connected by the standard Exchange site connector. In each site, the computer that's running the site connector acts as a bridgehead, too. All connections to other sites flow to the site connector server, then on to their destination. Interserver replication and messaging connections all run on top of these connectors, but external connections are handled by the named connectors, shown as arrows.

The top diagram looks sort of like a porcupine; there are connectors in each site, each of which must be managed independently. The bottom diagram, by contrast, concentrates all the connectors into a single site. Messages addressed to address spaces that belong to the X.400, IMS, or cc:Mail connectors must be routed to that site and its bridgehead server (or servers; nothing says that all connectors in a site must be on the same server) for later processing. By adding a small, inexpensive box as a connector server, the connector processing load can be moved off your mailbox and public folder servers, and the administrative overhead of managing connectors drops, because there's only one instance of each connector to manage.

 There's no rule that the sites in Figure 7-1 *must* be connected with the site connector; the theory of bridgeheading still holds if they're connected by X.400 or IMS connections.

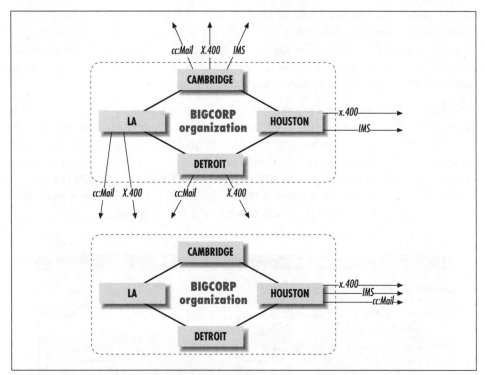

Figure 7-1. The same organization before and after a bridgehead is implemented

Managing the MTA

The Exchange 5.5 MTA is basically a big state machine. Each possible step in the entire MTA communications dance is represented in a large table, along with the inputs that led to that state and the possible states that could occur next, depending on what inputs arrive. All this behavior is hardcoded into the MTA, so there's nothing you can do to change it. You can, however, control some aspects of the MTA's connection behavior by changing various MTA properties. Some of these properties are set at the site level and apply to all MTAs in the site; others are set at the server level and have no effect on other servers in the site.

Setting Site-Level MTA Properties

You use the MTA Site Configuration object (which appears in the contents pane when you select the site's Configuration container) to set permissions on the MTA and to control the connection and association parameters that govern retry attempts. As an added, if minimal, bonus, you can also enable and disable message tracking and change the display name for the MTA Configuration object by using the General tab of the MTA Site Configuration Properties dialog. It's such a simple dialog that I'm not going to show it here; you already know what the Permissions tab does (remember that you won't see it unless you turn on "Show Permissions page for all objects" as discussed in Chapter 5, *Using Exchange Administrator*). The settings you apply here are stored in the site directory, so they're automatically replicated and applied to all MTAs in the site.

That leaves the Messaging Defaults tab, which appears in Figure 7-2. The default values set in this dialog provide a good balance between performance and robustness, but once you know what you're doing, it's perfectly safe to tweak them. The controls in this dialog are organized into four groups, each of which I'll describe below. The values you apply here will be used for all MTAs and X.400 connectors in the site; you can use the Override tab in the X.400 connectors' properties dialogs to change settings for a particular connector if you need to.

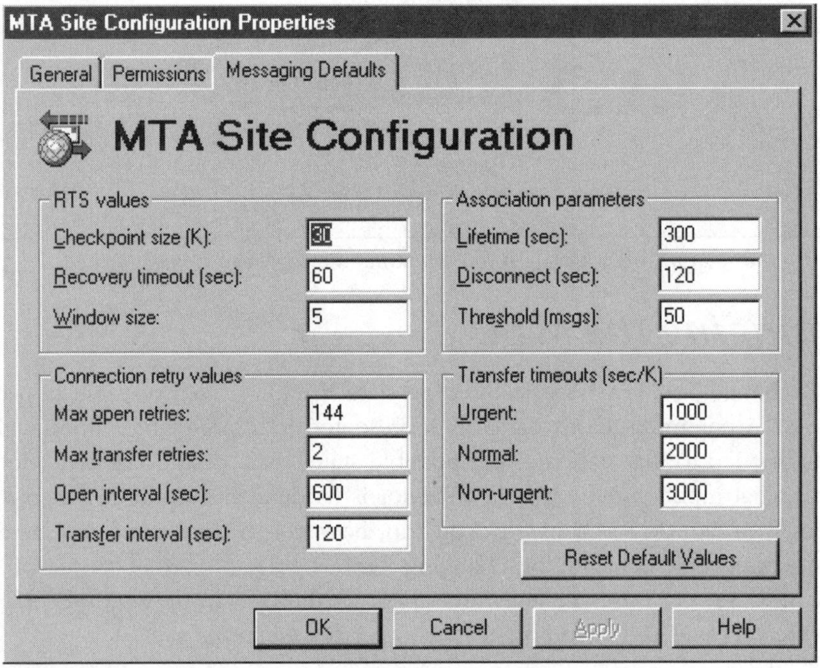

Figure 7-2. The Messaging Defaults tab of the MTA Site Configuration object

The RTS values group

Reliable transfer service (RTS) is what the MTA is designed to provide. When the MTA opens a connection and starts a message transfer, it uses the RTS values you set here to control retransmissions and retries over the connection.

RTS breaks its communication up into checkpoints. If you're familiar with database lingo, you probably already know that a *checkpoint* is a milestone event: at a checkpoint, the database or service records what data has been successfully transferred or recorded. If a failure occurs later, the system can revert to the checkpoint state and reapply any stored transactions.

At the interval you specify in the "Checkpoint size (K)" field (the default is 30KB), the MTA records a checkpoint so that a later failure will restart transmission from the last checkpoint instead of from the beginning. A value of zero tells the MTA never to keep checkpoints; this may speed performance on very reliable links, but it will slow things down as soon as the first error occurs, since the entire transmission will have to start again from scratch.

The "Recovery timeout (sec)" field tells Exchange how long to wait before it drops back to the preceding checkpoint. As each packet arrives at the destination MTA, it sends back an acknowledgment. When the sending MTA doesn't hear an acknowledgment immediately, the recovery timeout determines how long the sender waits before falling back to the checkpoint.

The "Window size" field controls how many checkpoints the sender will allow to go unacknowledged before it marks the connection as a failure. For example, let's say you've set the checkpoint size to 10KB and the window size to 3. The sending MTA will send a total of 30KB before it decides that the connection is unusable and closes the current association to the remote server.

The Association parameters group

Since a single connection can support multiple associations, Exchange needs a way to control what happens to the associations. The Association parameters group provides that control. There are three separate association parameters you may set:

- By default, associations stay active after the last queued message is sent. In most cases, this eliminates the overhead of reestablishing associations when new messages arrive, as long as at least one new message arrives before the activity period expires. The "Lifetime (sec)" field specifies how long the association is kept open after the queue of messages destined for that particular remote server empties.

- MTAs support two methods of breaking a connection. One MTA sends its peer a disconnection request; the sender can wait for an acknowledgment from the remote end, or it can just close the connection. The "Disconnect (sec)" field controls how long the sending MTA waits to hear a disconnect acknowledgment from the other end. Set it to zero to tell the MTA to close connections immediately.

- Each association has its own processing thread. When the size of the message queue exceeds the value of the "Threshold (msgs)" field, the MTA will spawn a new thread and open another association to the remote server. This association will expire and die according to the settings you enter in the other two fields. Since NT thread creation imposes little overhead, you might first think of lowering the threshold value to spawn new threads at a low threshold, but setting up the association takes time and bandwidth, so it's best to let the queue reach a fairly large size (like the default of 50 messages) before spawning new associations.

The Connection retry values group

The settings in the Connection retry values group determine what metrics the MTA uses to decide whether a connection is usable or not. The "Max open retries" field specifies how many times the MTA will try to open a connection before it gives up and marks the attempt as a total failure. The "Max transfer retries" field specifies how many retry attempts the MTA will apply to individual transfers; once that limit is exceeded, the connection will be closed as a failure. The "Open interval (sec)" and "Transfer interval (sec)" fields control how long the MTA will wait before trying again after an open or transfer operation fails. You'll probably find that adjusting these values will have little effect unless your communication links are prone to failure, in which case tweaking these values can achieve the optimum balance between link usage and throughput.

The Transfer timeouts (sec/K) group

The three fields in this group control how long the MTA will wait, in seconds per kilobyte, before it decides the message is undeliverable because the connection is too slow or has failed. For example, the default Urgent value of 1000 means that the MTA will wait 1000 seconds, or 16 minutes, for each 1KB chunk of an urgent message. As you can see, these values can add up quickly for large messages.

Setting Server-Level MTA Properties

You can also set some parameters at the server level. These settings only affect one MTA—the one on the target server. To see and change these properties, you use the Message Transfer Agent Properties dialog, which you'll see when you select a server in the container pane, select its Message Transfer Agent object, and use the File → Properties... command. This properties dialog has three tabs: General, Queues, and Diagnostics Logging (which we won't cover here, since it works the same way as all the other Diagnostics Logging tabs in Exchange Administrator).

The General tab

The General tab is shown in Figure 7-3. Like many of the other General tabs, this one is sort of a dumping ground for miscellaneous MTA options that Microsoft has lumped all together.

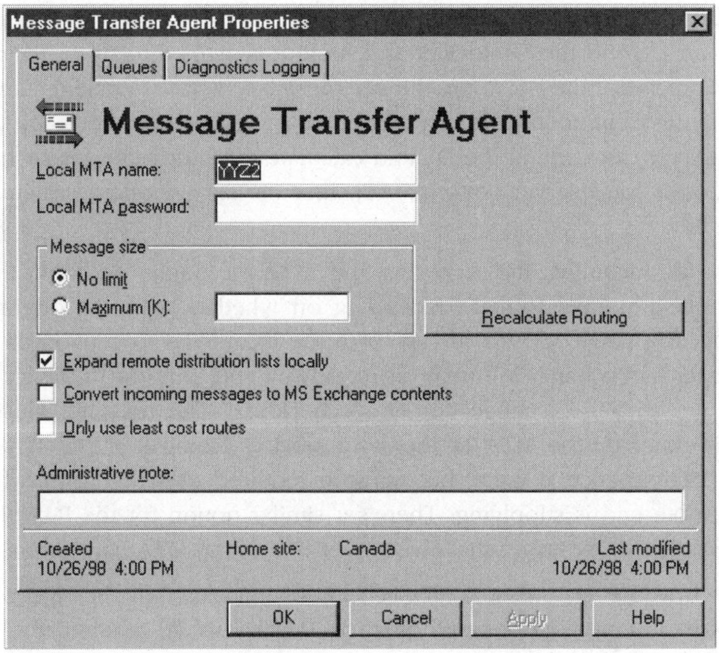

Figure 7-3. The General tab of the server's MTA Properties dialog

From this tab, you can set the MTA name and password, the message size, and some assorted other MTA options:

- The "Local MTA name" and "Local MTA password" fields let you specify a name of up to 32 characters and an optional 64-character password. Remote systems use this name and password to connect to this MTA. Exchange itself doesn't use either of these, but other X.400 systems can. If you change the name or password, bear in mind that any existing connections to foreign X.400 systems may break as a result.

- The "Message size" group lets you dial in the maximum size message you want to allow through this MTA. Messages larger than that size will be bounced back to the sender.

- The Recalculate Routing button forces the local MTA to recalculate all of its routing information and rebuild its local copy of the GWART. The new

GWART will then be replicated throughout the site. Use this button when
you've changed address spaces or connections on a server; forcing a routing
recalculation will make the MTA notice and honor those changes immediately.

- Distribution lists are replicated as part of the organization directory. When a
  message arrives at an MTA addressed to a distribution list that lives on another
  server, the MTA can do one of two things: it can forward the message on to
  the distribution lists' expansion server and let that machine do the expansion,
  or it can expand the DL locally and route messages directly to recipients (or,
  more precisely, the MTA on the recipients' servers). Checking the "Expand
  remote distribution lists locally" box improves routing efficiency, since the
  local server can expand the DL and calculate the best route for each message,
  but it costs some server performance, since the expansion and calculation take
  some time.

- When an incoming message hits the MTA, it might or might not be in
  Exchange's internal format, depending on whether or not it originated with
  another Exchange MTA. You can force the local MTA to convert all incoming
  messages to Exchange's format on receipt by checking the "Convert incoming
  messages to MS Exchange contents" checkbox. The message must be converted either by the MTA or the store service. Doing it at the MTA exacts a
  small performance penalty, but may be required depending on what format
  the remote end is supplying. There's a similar option for the IMS; this setting
  only applies to messages that arrive over one of the MTA connectors.

- The "Only use least cost routes" checkbox controls whether the MTA treats
  least-cost routing as a desirable goal or as an absolute requirement. Normally,
  the MTA will always attempt to find the least-cost route, but if that route's not
  available (perhaps because a connector or communications link is down), it will
  choose the next least expensive route and use that. If that link fails, it moves on
  to the next least expensive route, and so on, until the message is delivered or
  all routes have been exhausted. If you want to force Exchange to either use the
  least-cost route or bounce the message as undeliverable, check this box. This
  option prevents a message from travelling to another site and using its connectors if the originating site can't deliver the message for some reason.

The Queues tab

The Queues tab shows you the contents of some of the MTA's working queues.
Figure 7-4 shows the contents of the MTA queue that holds messages arriving from
the private Information Store. The summary view shows the message originator,
the message size in KB, and the time when the message was first submitted to the
MTA. You can use the buttons on the right side of the queue list to view details of
a queued message, change the priority of a queued message, or remove a message from the queue.

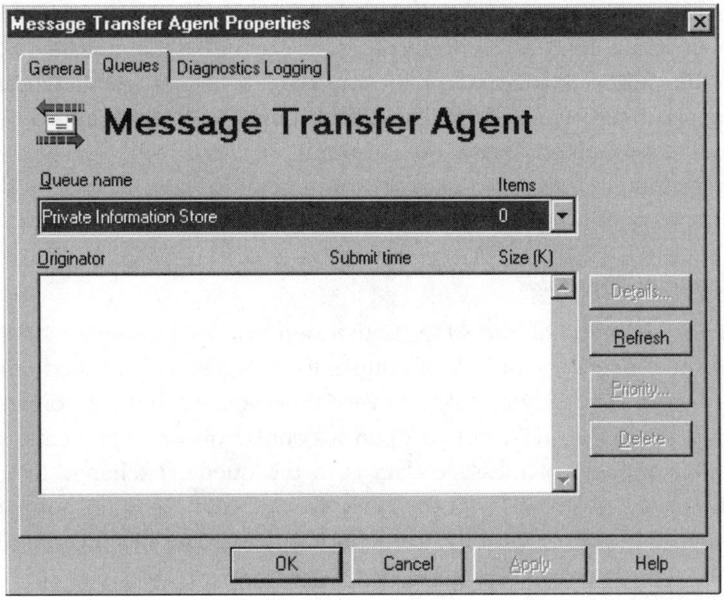

Figure 7-4. *The Queues tab of the server's MTA Properties dialog*

If you're talking to foreign X.400 systems

If your X.400 connectors will be talking to non-Exchange systems, Microsoft recommends making a registry change. The X.400 standard recommends that X.400 mail systems be able to negotiate a mutually agreeable transfer block size, or Transport Protocol Data Unit (TPDU). Exchange can handle this negotiation, but many other systems can't. Older spots may choke when faced with the 16KB default size of an Exchange-generated TPDU, since they usually require a 2KB TPDU. To fix this, you'll need to change the value of `HKLM\System\CurrentControlSet\Services\MSExchangeMTA\Parameters` from its default of 0 to 1.

> This registry setting, and all the others in this chapter, are collected in a system policy template file named *exch-mta.adm,* available from this book's web site at *http://www.oreilly.com/catalog/managexsvr.*

Adjusting message timeouts

The MTA holds messages for a certain period of time before deciding that they're undeliverable and returning an NDR. The amount of time messages are held varies according to their priority: urgent messages can be held for 48 hours, normal messages for 7 days, and non-urgent messages for 10 days. In Exchange 5.5 and later, you can adjust these timeout periods by making a change to the registry.* The timeout value for each priority class is controlled by a REG_DWORD value beneath the HKLM\System\CurrentControlSet\Services\MSExchangeMTA\ Parameters subkey. To override the default timeout, add the appropriate value. The values are named Message timeout (*priority*), minutes, where *priority* is either Urgent, Normal, or Non-urgent. Be sure to specify the time in minutes, not days or hours!

Adjusting queue thresholds

The ordinary behavior of the MTA is to open connections when there's traffic pending for a connector (subject, of course, to the connector's schedule). In some cases, like when it costs you money every time you establish a connection, you may want to force the MTA not to open a connection on a particular connector until a certain volume of message data is in the queue. Exchange SP1 adds this feature, in spades: you can force the MTA to wait until a certain number of messages are in the queue or until the amount of queued data hits a certain level, and you can allow urgent messages to be sent sooner.

You enable these features (in any combination) by adding three registry values:

Content Length Threshold (Kbytes)
> Specifies the value below which the MTA will not initiate a connection, even if traffic is waiting.

Queue Length Threshold
> Specifies the number of messages you want to accumulate in the queue before the MTA initiates a connection.

Urgent Overrides Thresholds
> Controls whether messages with Urgent priority can trump the restrictions and force the MTA to send them as soon as possible. If the value is not present, urgent messages are subject to the controls.

These values are all REG_DWORD values, and they must be added to each individual connector's subkey under the MTA's setting subkey, HKLM\System\ CurrentControlSet\Services\MSExchangeMTA\Parameters. For example, if you want to set a queue length threshold limit on a connector named *Canada*, you'd add the value HKLM\System\CurrentControlSet\Services\MSExchange MTA\Parameters\Canada\Queue Length Threshold.

---

* This is a great candidate for a system policy template.

Setting per-connector message limits

Another nifty feature added in SP1 is the ability to regulate what type of messages can use a particular connector. For example, you might want to allow urgent messages to use any connector, but restrict non-urgent messages to a particularly low-cost route instead. Using this feature isn't for the faint of heart, since it requires you to make a change using Exchange Administrator's raw mode. Here's what to do:

1. Open Exchange Administrator in raw mode, then find the site where the connector you want to modify is installed. Open the site's Connections container, then select the target connector. Choose the File → Raw Properties... command.

2. When the properties dialog appears, change the value of the "List attributes of type" pull-down to All, then select Heuristics from the "Object attributes" list.

3. Find the restrictions you want to impose in Table 7-1. If you want to use multiple restrictions, just add the values for each of the restrictions you want. If you want to allow the MTA to ignore the schedule and send urgent messages immediately, add 131072 to your restriction value.

Table 7-1. MTA Restriction Values

To Restrict...	Use This Value
System messages	4096
Non-system messages	8192
Urgent messages	16384
Normal messages	32768
Non-urgent messages	65536

4. Type the restriction value into the "Edit value" box, then click the Set button to put your change into the directory.

Monitoring What the MTA Is Doing

Since the MTA is such an important part of Exchange's messaging system, it's understandable that you might want to know what it's doing at any given time.

What's in the MTA queues?

In the section "The Queues tab," earlier in the chapter, you saw how to monitor the contents of any of the MTA's work queues. But what if you don't know which queue to look at? Table 7-2 will serve as a handy guide. There are some other MTA work queues that you can't see in Exchange Administrator, notably the queue where deferred items, which you mark to be sent at a future time in your mail client, sit until they're ready to go out.

Table 7-2. MTA Work Queues

Queue Name	Contains
Directory Service	Inbound replication messages bound for the local DS; only visible on directory replication bridgehead servers.
Internet Mail Connector	Outbound messages destined for SMTP recipients.
Private Information Store	Inbound mail destined for local recipient mailboxes.
Public Information Store	Incoming public folder replication messages sent by other servers in the site or organization.
X.400 connector name	Each X.400 connector has a queue entry named after the connector. This queue contains outbound X.400 mail.
DRAS connector name	Each DRAS connector has its own work queue, which contains outbound mail destined for that connector.
Other Servers in the same Site	Outbound mail destined for other servers in the same site.
Servers serviced by a Site Connector	Outbound intersite mail headed for the site connector.

How to get warnings when the queue size rises

If the size of any of your MTA queues suddenly rises, that usually indicates either a sudden sharp spike in traffic (perhaps because your users are circulating the latest Internet chain letter) or a problem with one or more connectors. Unfortunately, the MTA's normal behavior is just to let the queues lengthen, never calling for help or notifying you that things are getting hectic on the inside. You can add some registry values to instruct the MTA what queue length should trigger an event log message. If you care to, you can use a third-party tool like Ipswitch Software's WhatsUp to send you email or pager messages when selected events get logged.

There are four registry values you can tweak. They come in pairs: one value sets the threshold that turns on event log notification, and the other sets the level that turns it off again. There's one pair for the work queue and one for the outbound message queue. The exact value names are shown in Table 7-3; they're case-sensitive. Each of these values must be added to the `HKLM\SYSTEM\CurrentControlSet\Services\MSExchangeMTA\Parameters` registry key.

Table 7-3. MTA Queue Size Warning Keys

Value Name	What It Does
`Work queue alarm on`	Specifies a value for the work queue length threshold. When the queue length exceeds this value, the MTA will log event ID 666[a] in the event log. The event message contains the total number of queued messages.

Table 7-3. MTA Queue Size Warning Keys (continued)

Value Name	What It Does
Work queue alarm off	When the work queue length drops below this value, the MTA logs event ID 667 to the event log.
Outbound queue alarm on	Specifies a value for the outbound queue length threshold. When the queue length exceeds this value, the MTA logs event ID 659.
Outbound queue alarm off	When the outbound queue length drops below this value, the MTA logs event ID 660.

[a] Yes, that really *is* the event ID it logs.

Nothing says you have to specify "alarm off" values. If you don't, the MTA will use half of the "alarm on" value, so if you set "Work queue alarm on" to 350, when the queue length drops below 175, the alarm will shut off. If you prefer, though, you can set the "alarm off" values to any number from 0 up to the corresponding "alarm on" count.

Pumping up the MTA logs

You can always use diagnostic logging on the MTA if you need to trace what it's doing in a particular situation. The MTA also allows you to turn on what Microsoft calls "unbounded logging" (that's short for "it will fill up your disk fast if you forget to turn it off"). There are three `REG_DWORD` values you can add to the `HKLM\` `SYSTEM\CurrentControlSet\Services\MSExchangeMTA\Parameters` registry key, as shown in Table 7-4. Before any of these will work, you'll have to set the `Text Event Log` value on that key to 1 instead of its default value of 0.

The log files generated by these entries will end up in the *exchsrvr\mtadata* directory. However, you won't see any log files unless you turn on diagnostic logging and change the `Text Event Log`; otherwise, the MTA will keep quiet.

Table 7-4. MTA Unbounded Logging Enablers

Value Name	What It Does
Unbounded Event Log	When set to 1, causes the MTA to log every item it logs to the system event log to the file *ev0.log*.
Unbounded APDU Log	When set to 1, and when X.400 Service and APDU Logging is set to maximum on the Diagnostic Logging tab of the MTA object, causes the MTA to log a binary trace of all ASN.1 data it transfers to the *bf0.log* file. You can view this data with the *ASpiriN* tool from the BORK (see Appendix A, *BORK Tools*).
Unbounded Interop Log	When set to 1, and when Interoperability Logging is set to maximum on the Diagnostic Logging tab, causes the MTA to write a text log of all the back-and-forth interchange between the Exchange MTA and the foreign MTA on the other end to the *ap0.log* file.

Managing Connectors

Connectors link your Exchange server with other servers. Servers within a site talk to each other directly, without using connectors, but as soon as you want to link Exchange sites with other Exchange or foreign sites, connectors enter the picture. (I'm including the IMS as a connector, but it's covered in Chapter 8, *Managing the Internet Mail Service*.) Knowing how to create, remove, and manage connectors is critical if you need to exchange mail with the outside world.

Each connector has an associated address space, which describes the range of addresses to which that connector can deliver mail. The address space, as well as other information about the connector, is stored as a directory object so it can be replicated and used by other servers and sites. When you create a connector, you're actually creating this directory object, which appears in Exchange Administrator as a connector in the Connectors container. Removing a connector does the opposite: it removes the connector's address space and directory entry. Adding or removing a connector forces a recalculation of the routes in the GWART, since those routes describe which connectors can move a message from place to place.

 Whenever you add or remove a connector or an MTA transport stack, you'll need to stop and restart the MTA service to force it to notice the changes. The preferred way to do this is manually, using the Services control panel. You can also reboot your server, but that's a lot of time and effort just to restart the MTA.

Managing MTA Transport Stacks

Before you can install an X.400 or DRAS connector, you'll need to install an MTA transport stack. This process is fairly easy, although if you want to run an X.25 or TP4 transport stack, you'll need some relatively exotic hardware and drivers.

Creating MTA transport stacks

Before you can create an X.400 or DRAS connector, you must have at least one MTA transport stack installed. As I mentioned in the beginning of this chapter, there are four flavors of MTA transport stack. The TP4 and X.25 stacks won't install unless you've already installed and configured their respective adapter cards and drivers; the TCP/IP and RAS stacks won't install unless you've appropriately configured their respective network services.

Creating the new stack is simple. I won't discuss the TP4 or X.25 stacks, since they require specialized hardware, so you're on your own there. The basic process for all four stack types is very similar, though, so don't be discouraged if you're using

TP4 or X.25. The action starts with the File → New Other → MTA Transport Stack... command. The New MTA Transport Stack dialog is divided horizontally into two areas: the top area lists the four stack types, and the bottom area lists servers in the local site. Even if you're connected to a server in another site, you can only install transport stacks on local servers.

Select a stack type and a server in the dialog box, then click the OK button. Exchange Administrator will check the server's registry to make sure you've installed any prerequisites like RAS or an X.25 driver; if you pass the test, Exchange Administrator will install the stack and present its properties dialog.

Which properties dialog you see depends on which stack you install, but there are some features common to all of the stacks' dialogs: they all have a Permissions tab (if you've told Exchange Administrator to display it), and they all have a Connectors tab that shows you which connectors currently use the stack. You can't change the connector-to-stack binding on this tab, though you can from the individual connectors' properties dialogs. You can, however, select a connector and use the Edit... button to bring up the connector's properties dialog.

Site Connectors

Site connectors join sites. While that sounds really stupid, it's so simple that it's actually profound. Normally, sites are permanent, not transient. You might change the mix of servers in a site several times a year by adding, removing, and updating servers as your budget and user load dictate. On the other hand, although you might add sites once in a while, it's fairly rare that you remove them (especially if you followed my advice from Chapter 3, *Exchange Planning*, and stuck with the single-site model).

Site connectors also have another interesting property: they work in one direction, like domain trusts. If you run Exchange Administrator, attach to the California site, and add a connector to a target server in the Texas site, the connector flows from California to Texas. If you want mail to flow in the opposite direction, you need to configure a connector from Texas back to California.

 Once you create a connector to join two sites, whether it's a site connector or something else, Exchange Administrator won't let you delete it if that connector is the only link between the two sites and you have a replication connector in place. You've been forewarned.

One common heuristic of user interface design is that you should make common operations very simple; operations that are used infrequently can be more complex. Despite the fact that you rarely need to create a site connector, the actual process is very simple. It's not that Microsoft intentionally violated Occam's Razor; rather, the process of setting up site connectors is simple because there's not much to configure! As long as you've already got a working network connection between the two sites, there's not much else you have to do. The actual steps are simple, but first there's a little matter of service accounts to settle.

Service accounts and the site connector

The site connector works via remote procedure calls, so it depends on the standard NT logon mechanism to gain access to the target server. When you get ready to install a site connector, how you set up the site service account will depend on which of the following basic scenarios best describes your network setup:

- *Both sites are in the same Windows NT domain.* In this case, you don't have to do anything special—just set up the site connector and go about your business.

- *The two sites are in separate Windows NT domains, but a properly configured two-way trust relationship exists between the domains.* This is just like the first case: as long as the trust remains unbroken, the two sites can communicate using their existing service accounts.

- *The two sites are in separate Windows NT domains, with no trust relationship between them.* In this case, you'll need to create a set of credentials that either domain can use, then instruct the site connectors to use them.

The third case is the most interesting (well, it's the most complex, at least). It further divides into two separate subcases, depending on whether you've already created and installed a server in the second site or not.

There's one additional restriction: when you create a site connector between two untrusted domains, at least one of the two servers must be a domain controller. If they're both domain controllers, so much the better. If not, you must install and configure the site connector from the server that's not a domain controller.

To illustrate the first of these two subcases, let's use the following example: your company, WidgetCo, has a single site for your offices across the U.S. called *WidgetUS*. You have a single NT domain, *widgetco*, for all your accounts. Life is fine until your CEO sees an opportunity to exploit NAFTA by buying a Canadian (or Quebeçois, if you prefer) competitor, Widgets et Cie. To ease the transition, your boss plans to leave the new acquisition alone and let the Canadians run their own operations. Let's say that Widgets et Cie is running NetWare. You quickly decide to put a stop to *that* and roll out NT, creating a separate domain called

WIDGETSETCIE so the new branch can manage its own resources. Your next move is to install Exchange. Since you plan to use a site connector to join the new site (to be named *WidgetsCA*), you want to configure the Exchange settings for the new site so the site connector will work. Here's what you need to do:

1. Get the name of the service account you're using in the *WidgetUS* site. You should have it written down in your disaster recovery plan; if you don't, you can get it from the Service Account Password tab of the Configuration object's properties dialog. For the rest of this example, let's pretend the service account is named *exchange*.

2. Create a service account in the *WIDGETSETCIE* domain with the same name as your *WidgetUS* site service account. The password doesn't have to be the same.

3. Use User Manager for Domains to give *WIDGETSETCIE\exchange* the "Access this computer from network" permission on the Exchange servers in both domains.

4. Install Exchange on a server in the *WIDGETSETCIE* domain. When the setup program asks you, tell it to use the *WIDGETSETCIE\exchange* service account.

5. Configure a site connector on either server; use the Override tab of the connector properties dialog to specify the correct service account credentials. When Exchange Administrator asks, don't let it create the "other" site connector.

6. Go to the other server and configure a site connector back to the first site.

These steps cover the case where you're installing a new server into a different domain. What if you want to link two existing servers in different domains? Let's rework our thought experiment from earlier in the section. This time, let's say that you're an email administrator for NASA. Since the Russian Space Agency (RSA) is building some components of the International Space Station, NASA sends a team from Houston to Baikonur Cosmodrome, and you need to ensure that they have messaging connectivity. You need to link Baikonur and the Johnson Space Center in Houston, using two different site service accounts. Here's one way to accomplish this task:

1. Create a new service account in each domain, using the same name (I'll use *rsalink* for this example).

2. Grant the "Access this computer from network" permission to the *rsalink* account on the Exchange servers that will host the site connectors in each domain.

3. Run Exchange Administrator on each domain's Exchange servers. Use the Permissions tabs of the organization, site, and configuration containers to give the

rsalink account "Service Account Admin." permission. You'll need to do this only on the servers that will host the site connectors.

> This isn't the same as replacing the site service account with a different account; all you're doing here is adding a second account that the site connectors can use. For details on how to replace your existing site service account with a different one, see Chapter 14, *Managing Exchange Servers*.

4. Use the *rsalink* account to log on to the server where you're going to put the connector in either domain. When you configure the connector, it is essential that you be running Exchange Administrator as the newly created connector account. Otherwise, the account you use must be part of the local Administrators group, which is normally a bad idea from a security standpoint.

5. Run Exchange Administrator and create the site connector. Before you tell Exchange Administrator to create the connector, drop by the Override tab and fill in the *rsalink* account information, then let Exchange Administrator create the connector on the "other" server when it asks.

There's another case that's worth investigating: what if all your sites use a common master domain for authentication? In that case, you wouldn't establish a new site service account when you add a site; instead, you would just specify the master domain service account when you create the connector, using the Override tab.

Creating site connectors

When you're ready to create a site connector, you'll be pleased to find that it's easy to do. Of course, installing the connector is the easy part; once that's done you have to make sure it actually works! Here's how to install a new site connector; I assume you've read and followed the steps in the preceding section, if your domain setup requires it:

1. Launch Exchange Administrator and connect to a server in one of the sites you want to connect. Choose the File → New Other → Site Connector... command.

2. When the New Site Connector dialog appears, you'll see that the only thing you're asked for is the name of a target server in the remote site you want to connect to. Once you enter the server name, Exchange Administrator will attempt to contact the server you've specified. Be prepared to wait while it makes the connection and exchanges credentials.

3. If the server successfully establishes a connection, you'll see the General tab of the Site Connector Properties dialog. Exchange Administrator will automatically name the new connector "Site Connector (*SiteName*)," where *SiteName* is

the name of the site where the specified target server lives. This name will appear in the "Display name" and "Directory name" fields of the properties dialog. You can edit it if you like, or you can adjust other properties of the connector. In particular, if you're setting up a site connector between two untrusted sites, make sure you configure the Override tab appropriately, as described in the preceding section. (See the next section for more details on site connector properties you can adjust.) Once you're done configuring the connector, click the OK button.

4. If this is the first site connector between your site and the target site, Exchange Administrator will ask you whether you want to create a connector from the target site back to you. If you say no, you're done. If you say yes, you'll see the properties dialog for the other connector, and you can adjust its properties.

Once you've completed these steps, the new connector will appear in the site's (or sites') Connection container, which in turn is inside the site Configuration container.

Setting Site Connector Properties

The Site Connector Properties dialog has only four tabs (or five, if you count the Permissions tab). Most of its operations are automatic—you can't schedule its transfers or set limits on the size of messages it carries—but there are some other adjustments you can make.

The General tab

You had a very brief encounter with the General tab earlier in this chapter; it's shown in Figure 7-5. The "Display name," "Directory name," and "Administrative note" fields should be familiar by now. However, some of the other fields are new, like the "Target site" field, which shows you which site this particular connector is supposed to be communicating with. The Cost field lets you specify the cost of using this connector to carry traffic. The MTA will use whatever cost you enter here when it examines the GWART to find the least-cost way to get mail from point A to point B.

The "Messaging bridgehead in the local site" group is worth a mention. I discussed bridgehead servers earlier in this chapter; as it turns out, to force the site connector to use a bridgehead server in the local site, you select it here: set the radio button to "Specific server," then choose the server you want from the list. This setting applies to all servers in the site; for example, when you change the local site messaging bridgehead to the server named *hsv4,* all other servers in the site will honor that setting and transfer any traffic bound for the site connector to the bridgehead machine. If you want to establish bridgeheads between sites A and B, you need to adjust the "Specific server" setting on both site connectors: the one

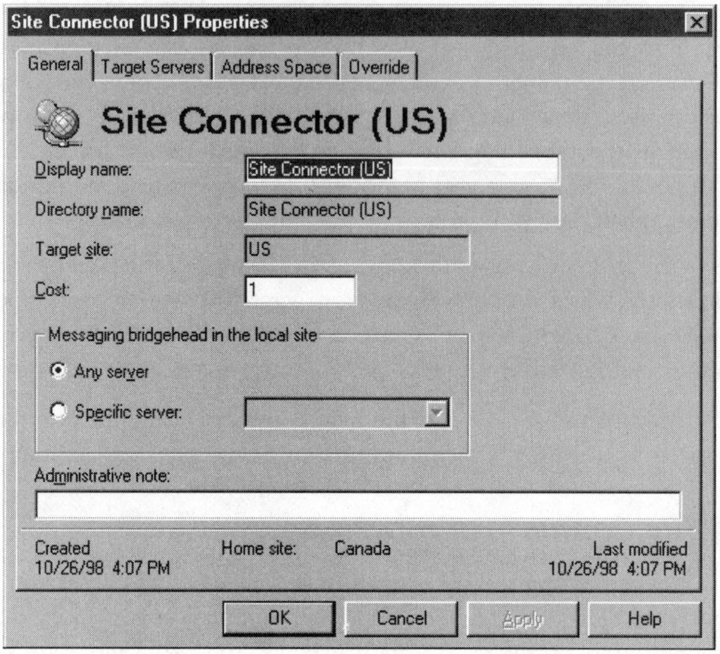

Figure 7-5. The General tab of the Site Connector Properties dialog

in site A named "Site Connector (B)" (or whatever else you may have named it), and the one in site B named "Site Connector (A)."

The Target Servers tab

Site connectors join sites, not servers. You might think that the old nautical chestnut "any port in a storm" would apply, and that it doesn't matter which server in a remote site mail goes to. Whether that's true or not depends on your configuration. When you create a site connector, you specify a target server in the site to get the ball rolling. What you're really doing, though, is designating that server as the only target server in the remote site. You can use the Target Servers tab to add additional targets. If you're using a single bridgehead in each site, you might wonder whether you'd still want to provide additional targets. The answer is a resounding "yes." If you've got more than one target server in each remote site, a failure of one target doesn't stop the mail from moving.

This magic is implemented by assigning a target server cost to each target. The MTA uses the target cost to decide which target to send mail to; it always chooses the lowest-cost route that's actually available. If you specify equal costs for multiple target servers, the MTA will try to balance the load on each target so that it's roughly equal.

The Override tab

The site connector will normally attempt to use its local site's service account credentials to connect to the remote site. If both sites happen to be using the same service account in the same domain, or if there's a properly configured trust relationship between the two sites' domains, this will work fine right out of the box. If the two sites are in different domains, and there's no trust relationship, neither site will be able to validate the other's credentials. The solution to this problem is the Override tab of the Site Connector Properties dialog. The four fields on this tab allow you to specify the domain name, account name, and account password you want to use when connecting to the remote site. Follow the directions in the section "Service accounts and the site connector" earlier in the chapter to figure out what to put here; in brief, you'll need to fill in the service account name and password from the remote domain, but what that name and password are can vary depending on how your site and organization are set up.

The Address Space tab

You've already seen the Address Space tab, and it's not intrinsically very interesting, so I won't show it again, but it's worth a mention here. You can funnel traffic to (or away from) a site connector by properly configuring the connector's address spaces on this tab. Each address space you define should have just enough information to disambiguate the messages you want to go over the connector. For example, if you want all SMTP mail to go over a connector, give it an SMTP address space of "*". If you only want mail to *oreilly.com* and *robichaux.net* to go over the connector, create matching address spaces instead. Any mail destined for a route that doesn't match a defined address space for a connector won't travel over that connector. Thus endeth the lesson.

Actually, there is one additional fillip that's worth describing. When you open the properties of any defined address space, you can restrict who can send messages over that address space. The Restrictions tab in the Address Space Properties dialog lets you specify one of three choices for message delivery via this connector. The Organization radio button, which is the default, tells the connector to accept messages from anyone in the organization. The This Site and This Location radio buttons do the same thing, but at the site and location level.

Why is this useful? Consider a setup where you have users at three sites in three different cities. You probably don't want a user in Vancouver sending Internet mail via the IMS in Boston if you can avoid it, and this setting provides a way that you can avoid it. In fact, with a little creative address space management, you can do neat things like force all traffic to free mail services like HotMail to go over a single connector, freeing your other connectors of the burden.

Creating X.400 Connectors

Now you're ready to install the X.400 connector. Unlike site connectors, X.400 connectors are bidirectional: once you install a connector on one site, the other site can use it to transfer mail as well. This is a nice simplification, because creating X.400 connectors is a bit more complex than creating site connectors.

To start with, if you're using TCP/IP, you must verify that each server can ping the other, either by IP address or by name (though you should use IP addresses, not names, to configure the connector). You'll also need to know the remote MTA's MTA name and password. If you plan to use OSI address information to make connections, you'll need to have that information available also.

Connecting two Exchange servers

Why use X.400 to connect Exchange servers? First of all, X.400 connectors can do their jobs with a lot less bandwidth than site connectors, and—since they don't use RPCs—they're also more reliable on flaky links. Here's how to create an X.400 connector between two Exchange servers:

1. Use the File → New Other → X.400 Connector... command. Exchange will display the New X.400 Connector dialog, which lists all the installed MTA transport stacks. For example, if you have TCP/IP and X.25 stacks in place, this dialog will show both stacks. Pick the stack you want to use for the new connector, bearing in mind that you can easily retarget the connector to another stack after it's created.

2. The X.400 Connector Properties dialog will appear. At the bare minimum, to get the connector up and going you'll need to fill in information on the General, Stack, and Connected Sites tabs. In the General tab, you must fill in the following fields:

   — The "Display name" and "Directory name" fields are where you christen your connector; as with other objects, you can go back and change the display name later, but you're stuck with your choice of directory name.

   — The "Remote MTA name" and "Remote MTA password" fields must contain the name of the remote Exchange server MTA this connector will be talking to and the password required to connect to it. The name isn't case-sensitive, but the password is. If you're connecting two Exchange servers via the X.400 connector, the MTA name will be the name of the remote server, and there won't be a password unless you've assigned one. If there's no password on the remote MTA, you can leave the password field blank.

3. Switch to the Stack tab (shown in Figure 7-6) by clicking it. The contents of this tab may vary depending on what stack you chose in step 1, because the

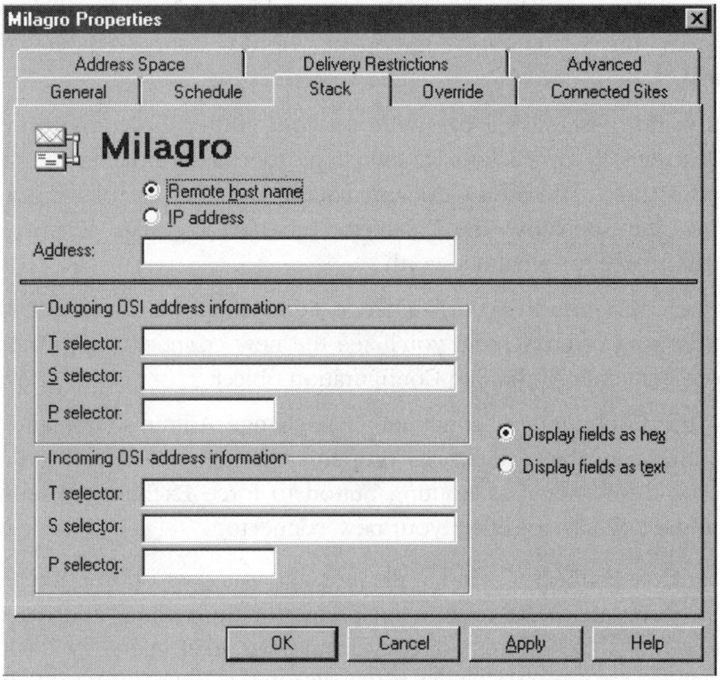

Figure 7-6. The Stack tab of the X.400 connector properties dialog when the connector is running on top of TCP/IP

purpose of this tab is to give you a way to set the stack's properties so the connector can use the stack. In the case of a TCP/IP connector, at a minimum, you must enter the TCP/IP or DNS address of the remote MTA server. Microsoft recommends using the TCP/IP address; under some conditions, the X.400 connector may not successfully transfer mail if you force it to resolve the remote host's name.

If you want to use OSI addresses on your X.400 connector, you can enter the outgoing and incoming T selectors when you first configure the connector. The connector won't work unless the T selectors on both ends of the connection match exactly, so be careful when you enter them. Microsoft recommends that you wait until you're confident the connector is working properly before you use the S and P selectors.

4. Switch to the Connected Sites tab. You may notice that this tab looks suspiciously like the Address Space tabs you've seen in other dialogs; in fact, the X.400 connector properties dialog has both of these tabs. The difference is that the Connected Sites tab lets you specify which organizations and sites you route traffic to—no fooling around with X.400 DNs, OSI addresses, or any of that kind of stuff. Use the New... button on this tab to pop up a properties

dialog that lets you specify the organization and site to which you want to route mail. You can also use the Routing Address tab of the properties dialog to specify the X.400 DN components of the connected sites, but that's optional.

5. If you want to establish a password on your end of the connection, switch to the Override tab by clicking it, then type the password into the "Local MTA password" field. Microsoft's documentation says that establishing a password isn't necessary because "the T selector provides adequate security." You can take that advice for what it's worth.

6. Click the OK button to make Exchange Administrator create the X.400 connector. After a bit of crunching, you'll see the new connector appear in the Connections container of the Site Configuration object.

7. Go to the Configuration container in Exchange Administrator and select the Site Addressing object. Open its properties dialog, switch to the Routing tab, and click the Recalculate Routing button to force Exchange Administrator to update the GWART to reflect your new connector.

To test your new connector, send a test message to a user on the other side of the connection. You can create custom recipients for the remote addressees, or you can just use the X.400 address directly from your mail client by enclosing it in square brackets, for example, *[c=us;o=RobichauxAssociates;cn=Paul Robichaux]*. If the test message arrives successfully, that means your connector is ready for use.

Connecting Exchange to a foreign X.400 system

If you want to use the X.400 connector to link your Exchange server to a non-Exchange X.400 system, you have a little more research to do before you can set up your connector. There are two separate versions of the X.400 standard: the 1984 and 1988 versions. The 1988 version is more capable, and most systems that support the 1988 version of the protocol can interoperate with systems running the 1984 version. An additional wrinkle: the 1988 standard defines two separate modes of operation, the "normal" mode and the "X.410" mode. The differences between these modes aren't as important as knowing what version your remote MTA is using.

Here's how to set up the connector:

1. Use the File → New Other → X.400 Connector... command to create the connector; along the way, you'll have to choose the transport stack you want this connector to use.

2. The X.400 connector properties dialog will appear. At the bare minimum, to get the connector up and going, you'll need to fill in information on the General, Stack, and Address Space tabs. In the General tab, you must fill in the following fields:

— The "Display name" and "Directory name" fields are where you christen your connector; as with other objects, you can go back and change the display name later, but you're stuck with your choice of directory name once you apply your changes.

— The "Remote MTA name" and "Remote MTA password" fields must contain the name of the remote MTA this connector will be talking to and the password required to connect to it, if any. The name isn't case-sensitive, but the password is. This information will normally come from whoever is administering the foreign system.

3. Switch to the Stack tab by clicking it, then enter the TCP/IP address (recommended) or the DNS host name (if you must) of the remote server.

4. Switch to the Address Space tab by clicking it. Once you're there, use the New... button to add at least one address space to this connector. Remember, when you add an address space you can choose between SMTP and X.400 address types, among others. Define address spaces that match the traffic you want carried over the X.400 connector. You can easily route SMTP, MS Mail, or even Notes traffic over an X.400 connector! Note that you only use the X.400 connector's Address Space tab when you're communicating with a foreign system. To talk to another Exchange server via X.400, you'd use the Connected Sites tab.

5. If you want to require a password on your local MTA, switch to the Override tab by clicking it, then type the password into the "Local MTA password field." Once you do, remote MTAs can only connect if they get your local MTA name and password correct.

6. Fill out the Advanced tab if you need to. For details on what fields are in that tab and what they mean, see the section "The Advanced tab," later in this chapter.

7. Click the OK button to make Exchange Administrator create the X.400 connector. After a bit of crunching, you'll see the new connector appear in the Connections container of the Site Configuration object.

8. Go to the Configuration container in Exchange Administrator and select the Site Addressing object. Open its properties dialog, switch to the Routing tab, and click the Recalculate Routing button to force Exchange Administrator to update the GWART to reflect your new connector.

Testing the X.400 connector

Testing the X.400 connector is easy as pie: create a custom recipient on one side of the connector, using the X.400 address of any mailbox on the other side, or the plain X.400 address, if you prefer. The easiest way to find this address is to look at the E-mail Addresses tab of the target mailbox. Once you have that, use it as the custom recipient address, then send mail to the custom recipient.

If the mail arrives safely, great—that means the connector is at least half-working. Create a custom recipient on the other site, pointing back to a mailbox in your local site, then send a test message to it. Chances are good that if your first test worked, the second one will, too. If one or both of these tests fail, see Chapter 15, *Troubleshooting Exchange Server*, to find out how to isolate and fix the problem.

Setting X.400 Connector Properties

The X.400 connector has some additional properties we haven't really talked about yet. You already know what's on the General tab of the X.400 connector properties dialog, and you've had a brief introduction to the Stack, Override, Connected Sites, and Address Space tabs. (In fact, since the Address Space tab is common to several connectors, I won't mention it further in this section.) Now it's time to delve deeper into what's on these tabs, not to mention the as-yet-unexplored Delivery Restrictions, Schedule, and Advanced tabs. Before we go any further, let me mention the rest of the controls on the General tab. You've already met the Display name, Directory name, Remote MTA name, and Remote MTA password controls. There are a few others you should know about.

The MTA transport stack pull-down shows you which installed transport stack this X.400 connector is currently bound to. If you change the set of installed stacks, you can use this pull-down to move the connector to another stack. If you do this, make sure to make any necessary changes to the MTA credentials and the mode settings on the Advanced tab.

The controls in the "Message text word wrap" box let you tell Exchange whether you want it to forcibly wrap outgoing text at a particular column or not. Some receiving MTAs will choke on text lines that exceed 80 or 132 columns, so you can break lines wherever necessary by using the "At column" radio button and field.

The final control in the General tab, the "Remote Clients Support MAPI" checkbox, is worth its own paragraph. If you've ever seen a file called *winmail.dat* pop up on your mail system, you're seeing this checkbox in action. When the Exchange server knows it's sending to a client that supports MAPI, it assumes that it can safely send rich text, embedded OLE attachments, and so forth. This checkbox is on by default, as it should be if you're using the X.400 connector to link two Exchange servers. If you leave the checkbox on, and you're sending mail to a system that doesn't support MAPI, that system's clients will see *winmail.dat* files as attachments to every message—yuck! Turning the checkbox off forces Exchange to strip the attachments out of outbound messages and send them as separate X.400 messages.

Now, on to the Schedule tab. The two most useful properties of the X.400 connector are that it works well over unreliable or low-bandwidth links and that its connections can be scheduled. The Schedule tab is where you specify exactly when you want to transfer mail over the X.400 connector. There's a group of four radio buttons on the tab that controls the schedule mode:

Remote Initiated
> This button tells your MTA to sit tight and wait for a connection from the remote end.

Never
> This button does what you'd expect: it prevents your MTA from sending or receiving X.400 mail over this particular connector, but mail can still flow over others. You normally use this when you need to stop a connector before removing or relocating it.

Always
> This button (the default) tells Exchange that it can transfer mail whenever necessary. You'll probably want to change this default if you're using any kind of on-demand connection (via modem, X.25, or ISDN); otherwise, the connector will feel free to initiate a connection at sporadic intervals.

Selected times
> This radio button activates the familiar grid control that lets you specify exactly what times and what days of the week you want to schedule connections. You can also use the "1 Hour" and "15 Minute" radio buttons to control the time intervals represented by the grid. Remember, the schedule you set here applies only to this X.400 connector.

The Advanced tab

The Advanced tab (shown in Figure 7-7) lets you give the X.400 connector a brain transplant. Not really; it actually allows you to change the settings that govern which version of the X.400 protocol the connector uses, as well as a number of other related parameters. The net effect of these controls is that you can make the connector talk to just about any X.400-capable remote system, although it helps a lot to know exactly what protocol the remote end expects to see before you start sending stuff across.

Here's what's on the Advanced tab:

MTA conformance
> This control group has three radio buttons that let you specify which version of the X.400 standard you want the MTA to follow. This is the most important setting on the entire tab, since it controls how your MTA tries to communicate with the remote side. The original 1984 version of the standard is supported by most existing X.400 products, but its feature set is limited compared to the

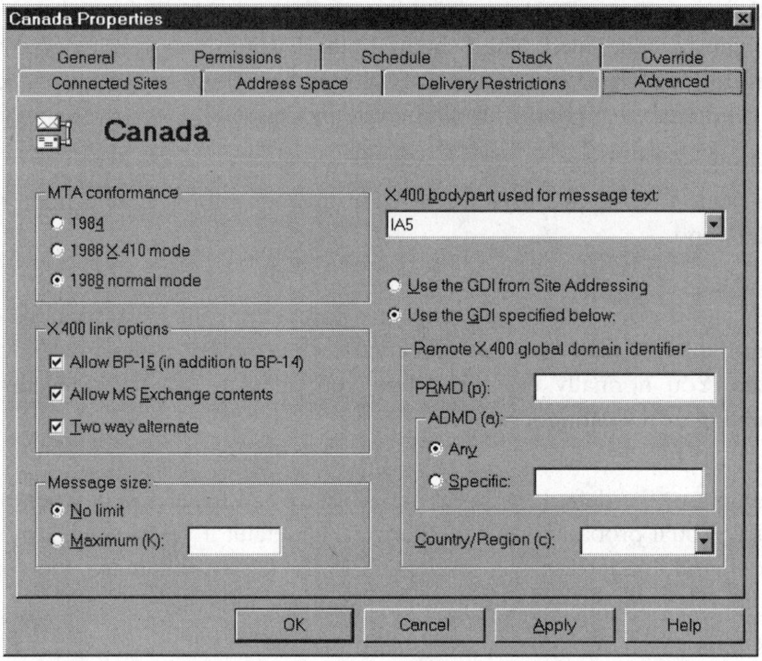

Figure 7-7. The Advanced tab of the X.400 connector properties dialog

1988 version. There are two separate 1988 modes: normal mode is the plain, standard 1988 mode, which is what most 1988-compliant systems expect to see; and the 1988 X.410 mode is for use with systems that implement part, but not all, of the 1988 standard (HP OpenMail is the most notable offender here). How do you know which conformance mode to use? When in doubt, stick with the 1988 normal mode setting (the default) unless the remote system's administrator tells you otherwise. If you pick the wrong setting, you'll know, because your connector won't work at all.

X.400 link options

This control group provides three additional parameters that you can use to adjust how the connector sends mail to its remote peer. These settings don't affect inbound mail.

Allow BP-15 (in addition to BP-14)

This checkbox has a confusing name, doesn't it? The BP series of formats are part of the X.400 standard; they specify how body parts may and should be formatted for interchange. BP-15 is a newer and more flexible version of the body part encoding standard, but not all 1988-compliant X.400 MTAs support BP-15. Most do, though, which is why this checkbox is on by default. Leave it on unless your remote system chokes on BP-15 messages.

Allow MS Exchange contents

The P2 and P22 formats are another set of message-interchange standards included in the X.400 definition. Non-Exchange X.400 systems always use P2/P22, so Exchange may already have to convert incoming P2/P22 messages into its own internal format, MDBEF. This is time-consuming enough, but it may also have to convert outbound messages from Exchange format to P2/P22. This checkbox controls whether an outbound translation is performed or not. If you leave this checkbox on, as it is by default, Exchange will always send using MDBEF. However, if this connector isn't talking to another Exchange server, you must turn it off, since non-Exchange X.400 systems won't be able to convert MDBEF into P2/P22. The "Convert Incoming Messages to Microsoft Exchange Contents" checkbox on the General tab of the server MTA Properties dialog controls whether incoming messages are automatically converted.

Two way alternate

This checkbox regulates whether or not the local and remote MTAs take turns sending messages. When it is checked, one MTA will send a message, then allow the other MTA to send one. When it is unchecked, whichever MTA initiated the connection will send all its mail before allowing the other MTA to get a word in edgewise.

Message size

These controls do what they do everywhere else in Exchange. Use them to set a maximum size on outbound messages sent over the X.400 connector, but remember that this setting has nothing to do with incoming messages—you're at the mercy of the remote connector.

X.400 bodypart used for message text

This pull-down controls what character set is used for outgoing message body parts. The IA5 character set is the default, and it's generally useful for most languages that use the Roman alphabet. The plot thickens, though: there are separate dialects of IA5 for Norwegian, German, and Swedish. If you know that you're primarily talking to servers that use one of these dialects, you can force Exchange to always use that encoding when it sends outgoing mail. There's a related setting on the General tab of the server MTA Properties dialog; if you turn on the "Convert Incoming Messages to Microsoft Exchange Contents" checkbox, incoming messages will be translated to plain old IA5.

The Global Domain Identifier (GDI) is similar to an Internet Domain Name Service (DNS) name. The GDI completely specifies the unique name of a particular domain; no two domains may have the same GDI. Normally, you'll use the GDI that you specify in the Site Addressing object; after all, that object controls what address can be used to reach users on your server. If you're talking with an X.400 peer that's not in the same domain as you, though, you'll need to manually tell your local Exchange MTA what the remote system's GDI is. This usually happens because you're connecting your organization (Private Management Domain, or PRMD) to a public X.400 service (Administrative Management Domain, or ADMD). You control how the GDI is constructed using the GDI controls in the lower-right corner of the Advanced tab, in particular the "Use the GDI from Site Addressing" and "Use the GDI specified below" radio buttons. If you want to use the site addressing GDI, leave the default button set. To explicitly provide the remote GDI, toggle the "Use the GDI specified below" radio button, then fill in the private and administrative domain specifications and the country in the provided fields.

More about the Override tab

The X.400 connector's Override tab is where you specify the name and password you want to use with your local MTA. Remote MTAs must have both the correct password and MTA name to establish a connection to your machine. You can also use this tab to override the RTS, connection retry, association, and timeout values normally set on the MTA at the site level (see the section "Setting Site-Level MTA Properties," earlier in this chapter, for more details on these values). When you use this tab to override connection values, the overridden values apply to this particular X.400 connector instance only. Any site MTA that can use the connector will use the override values only when it uses that connector; any connectors that don't have their own set of override values will revert to using the site MTA defaults.

The Delivery Restrictions tab

The Delivery Restrictions tab lets you tell your connector to accept or reject messages from specific entries in the GAL. The nice thing about these restrictions is that they only apply to one X.400 connector instance; each connector can have its own set of addresses to accept and reject messages from. Since you can provide both accept and reject lists at the same time, you can easily limit access to your connector to only the mailboxes, distribution lists, and custom recipients that you want to be able to send mail through the connector.

By default, the Delivery Restrictions settings are configured to accept messages from everyone and reject messages from no one. See the section "The Delivery Restrictions tab" in Chapter 6, *Mailboxes, Recipients, and Distribution Lists*, for more information on how to use the dialog controls; even though that section covers the tab as it appears on the mailbox properties dialog, its operation is identical.

One final caveat: this tab isn't perfect, as its settings only apply to outgoing messages. That means that you can prevent particular users from using your connectors to send messages to foreign sites, but there's no way to do the same trick for incoming X.400 messages.

Restricting mail from particular recipients

You can instruct the X.400 connector to reject incoming mail from particular addressees, either with or without generating an NDR. To do so, you must add a registry value to each X.400 connector you want to know about the reject list. This value, which is of type REG_MULTI_SZ, should contain the full or partial DNs of originators whose messages you want to block. For example, if you wanted to block out any messages from Singapore or the U.S. Department of Justice, you'd specify *c=SG* and *c=US;o=Department of Justice* as the two values. The value name is Bar P1 Originator; you have to add it to the HKLM\SYSTEM\Current-ControlSet\Services\MSExchangeMTA\Parameters key for each individual connector.

You can also control whether the MTA sends back an NDR or silently rejects the message (the default). To force the MTA to return an NDR for each rejected message, add a REG_DWORD value named NDR to barred originator to the connector's key, then set its value to 1. Whether you set this value or not, the MTA will log an event message each time it rejects an inbound message.

DRAS Connectors

As with X.400 connectors, you can't create a DRAS connector until you've installed the proper transport stack. For DRAS connectors, though, "proper" really means "RAS." You have to install a RAS-capable transport stack, which means that you must have NT's RAS service installed and configured, even if you only want your DRAS connector to make outgoing calls.

DRAS connectors are unidirectional. If you want to exchange mail between two sites, each site needs a DRAS connector pointing to the other site. This is similar to the site connector's capability, but different from how X.400 connectors work.

Bare-bones RAS setup

A complete discussion of how to configure RAS and get it working is outside the scope of this book. The basic setup steps are fairly straightforward, though, so I'll go over them briefly:

1. Use the Network control panel to install the RAS service, then go back and reinstall the latest NT service pack you'd previously installed.

2. Create a new domain account for the RAS connector to use in each domain. Make sure it has the same account name and password in all domains. Why do this? Because it allows you to not use the all-powerful Exchange service

account, thus limiting the spread of its password and the associated risk of compromise.

3. Grant the new connector account the right to dial in to the network. You can use the Users → Permissions... command in the Remote Access Admin application, or the Dialin button on the Account Properties dialog in User Manager for Domains.

4. Use Exchange Administrator to give the connector account Service Account Admin permission on your local Exchange server. You'll need to do this on all your Exchange servers, one at a time.

5. Make a new RAS phone book entry for the site you'll be calling. Make sure the "Use default gateway on remote network" checkbox is off (it's in the PPP TCP/IP Settings dialog, which appears when you click the TCP/IP Settings... button on the Servers tab). If you're dialing into a system that can handle encrypted authentication, make sure that either the "Accept only encrypted authentication" or "Accept only Microsoft encrypted authentication" radio buttons on the Security tab is turned on.

   If you're accepting only Microsoft encrypted authentication, you must make sure to also clear the "Use current user name and password" checkbox. When the RAS service connects to another machine, it must use credentials to log on. It can get these credentials from the process that started the dial-up connection, or it can use a predefined set of credentials. If the checkbox is on, RAS uses the credentials that belong to the MTA: the site service account. If it's off, RAS will use the credentials passed into it; in this case, they come from the RAS Override tab in the DRAS Connector Properties dialog.

6. Set up the RAS IP address pool. Each device you use for DRAS connections needs two IP addresses, which means that each server's address pool needs two addresses per modem, ISDN TA, or other connection device. These addresses must be different from the one(s) you're using for your NICs. Microsoft recommends using a private Class C IP address range (192.168.x.y) defined by the Internic in RFC 1918, Address Allocation for Private Internets.

7. Set up *HOSTS* and *LMHOSTS* file entries for each server on each server. RPC connections depend on TCP/IP name resolution. The entries in these files should point to the actual IP address of the NICs on the other servers, not their RAS pool addresses. For example, if you're creating the *HOSTS* file for a server named *hurricane* whose NIC address is 207.224.135.14 and whose RAS pool address range is 192.168.15.40 to 192.168.15.44, here's what the corresponding *HOSTS* entry would look like:

```
207.224.135.14  hurricane
```

The *LMHOSTS* file entries should use the #PRE keyword to specify that these addresses should be preloaded in the names table.

8. Open the Network control panel, switch to the Protocol tab, and open the TCP/IP Properties dialog. Switch to the WINS Address tab and make sure the "Enable DNS for Windows Resolution" checkbox is checked; this ensures that your *HOSTS* file changes can be used for TCP/IP name queries.

9. From the command line, rebuild the NetBIOS name cache with the nbtstat –R command. This forces NT to read and honor the values in the *HOSTS* file you just changed.

At this point, you should be able to establish a vanilla RAS connection to the other server by using any of NT's TCP/IP or NBT tools, including *net use*, *ping* and *tracert*. Once you've successfully established a connection, you know your RAS setup is solid; if you're having trouble, you might find the Nutshell Handbook *Windows NT TCP/IP Network Administration,* by Craig Hunt and Robert Bruce Thompson (O'Reilly & Associates) to be helpful.

Creating the DRAS connector

There's no law that says you must properly configure RAS before you start creating DRAS connectors, but it's probably a good idea. Having said that, let's see how you actually create a DRAS connector. The first step here is to create a RAS MTA transport stack using the File → New Other → MTA Transport Stack... command in Exchange Administrator. When the New MTA Transport Stack dialog appears, choose the RAS MTA Transport Stack item from the Type list and click OK. When you do, the RAS Stack Properties dialog will appear.

This properties dialog is extremely simple. The General tab lets you enter a display name for the RAS MTA stack; whatever you enter here is what Exchange Administrator will display as the connector's name. You may also enter a callback number; if you do, remote servers that have callback security turned on will call your server back at that number when you try to connect to them. There are two other tabs in the RAS MTA Properties dialog: a Permissions tab (which you've already seen several times) and a Connectors tab, which I mentioned earlier. Click the OK button, and that's it! Your new RAS MTA stack is now available.

The next step is to actually create the DRAS connector itself. You do this via the handy File → New Other → Dynamic RAS Connector... command, which immediately creates the connector and opens its properties dialog. You'll need to fill out several fields on various tabs to complete the connector's birth process:

- On the General tab, you must supply a display name, a directory name, the name of the remote server you're calling, and which RAS phone book entry you want to use. For more details on setting up this tab, see the section "The General tab," later in this chapter.

- On the RAS Override tab, you must provide a set of logon credentials that Exchange can use when it dials up: a username, password, and domain name.

This account must have Send As and Mailbox Owner permissions on the Servers or Configuration container in the remote site. If you don't have an account that meets those criteria, you can use the remote site's service account instead.

- You must specify at least one address space to use with this connector, using either the Address Space tab (if you're talking to non-Exchange systems) or the Connected Sites tab (when you're calling another Exchange server). See the section "The Connected Sites and Address Space tabs," later in this chapter, for more details on creating the address spaces—it's a little different from the usual process.

You can also set a schedule for RAS connections using the Schedule tab. Strictly speaking, this is optional, but the default schedule of "Always" means that your DRAS connector may be in use a lot more than you expect, and that can quickly get expensive if you're using metered ISDN. Instead, you'll probably be better off using the "Selected times" radio button and specifying a fixed schedule that matches your mail traffic patterns. Finally, Microsoft recommends changing the settings on the MTA Override tab, but I'll get to that in a minute.

Once you've filled out the required fields, click the OK button and Exchange Administrator will create the new connector. You can test the connector, or you can proceed with setting its properties and configuring the other site's DRAS connector if you want traffic to flow in both directions.

Testing the DRAS connector

The first step in testing the DRAS connector is to make sure that RAS itself is working properly. If you can route TCP/IP* packets from your server to the other server using RAS, you're in good shape. Once you're sure that the underlying transport is doing what it's supposed to, you can test the DRAS connector itself.

The easiest way to do this is to create an X.400 custom recipient in your local site that contains the X.400 address of a mailbox on the remote site. I usually cheat and use Exchange Administrator to look at the mailbox on the remote site, using its E-mail Addresses tab to get the complete and correct X.400 address. Be especially careful to get the correct value for the "ADMD (a)" field from the remote mailbox; the field may contain a single space, in which case it appears blank but isn't. You can use the left and right arrow keys to check whether the field is blank.

Once you've created the custom recipient, use it to send mail to the remote mailbox. If the mail arrives, your DRAS connector is OK. If not, it can indicate either that the RAS connection itself isn't working right or that the DRAS connector is misconfigured. To test the RAS connection, make certain that you can connect the

---

* You can use DRAS with IPX, too; see Microsoft's Knowledge Base article Q170252.

two servers using RAS and that you can share and view network resources normally. Pay particular attention to the TCP/IP configuration. If you get an NDR from Exchange, note the error it reports. You may find it helpful to turn up MTA diagnostic logging, then check the event log to see whether any specific and useful error messages appear.

 For more detailed information on troubleshooting DRAS connections, see Chapter 15.

If you've configured another DRAS connector from the remote site back to you, follow the same procedure to create a custom recipient on it that points back to one of your mailboxes, then test it to make sure that mail flows from the remote site back to you.

Setting DRAS Connector Properties

Fortunately, the DRAS connector is less complicated than the X.400 connector. (Of course, that's true of pretty much everything in Exchange!) Apart from the ubiquitous Permissions and Schedule tabs, there are six interesting tabs on the DRAS connector properties dialog.

The General tab

This tab is where you name your connector and specify which stack and RAS phone book entry it should use. You already know all about the "Display name" and "Directory name" fields, not to mention the ever-popular "Administrative note," so let's skip to the good stuff:

Remote server name
　　The value in this field must exactly match the remote server's MTA name. To find that name, check the General tab of the remote server's MTA Configuration object.

MTA transport stack
　　This pull-down shows you which RAS transport stack this connector is set to use. You can change this value if you have multiple RAS stacks installed; in effect, this retargets the connector to a different remote server, since you may only have one RAS stack per target server.

Phone book entry
　　Use the controls in this group to choose the RAS phone book entry you want this connector to use. The RAS Phone Book... button will open the phone

book so you can add, remove, or edit entries; before the changes you make will appear in the dropdown list, you'll need to click the Refresh List button.

Message size

This control group lets you set a maximum message size for this connector. Unlike the corresponding value for the X.400 connector, the DRAS connector will apply this value both to inbound and outbound messages.

The RAS Override tab

If you're sharing a service account and its credentials between sites, you won't need to use the RAS Override tab. However, as I recommended earlier, you're much better off creating a separate account for the RAS connector, just as you do for the print spooler and the Services for Macintosh package. Use this tab to specify a full set of logon credentials (domain name, username, and password) for the account you want RAS to use when it attempts to log on to the remote network. For your RAS connection to succeed, these credentials must belong to an account that has permission to dial into the remote network; for the DRAS connection to work, this account must also have permissions as described earlier.

The "Optional phone numbers" group on the RAS Override tab lets you override two different phone numbers. You can use the MTA Callback Number field to pass a callback number to the remote network; if it has callback security enabled, it will hang up and call your server back at the number you provide; so make sure you get the number right! The Overriding Phone Number field lets you provide a phone number that's different from the one in the RAS phone book entry you specified on the General tab. You might do this, for example, if you normally offer RAS access through an 800 number but need to override it so a system inside the 800 number's local area can still call it.

The MTA Override tab

The MTA Override tab lets you overrule the default MTA settings, which control timeout and retry values for the RTS, connection establishment, transfers, and associations. For most dial-up connections, either over asynchronous modems or ISDN, you'll need to adjust these parameters to take the link characteristics into account.

First, set the "Open interval (sec)" field to whatever interval you want the MTA to dial. For example, a value of 120 tells the MTA it can dial every two minutes if it has mail queued for delivery over the connector. Adjust this value to reflect whatever frequency you want to make connections at.

The default value of 144 in the "Max open retries" field tells the MTA it can try up to 144 times before deciding a connection just isn't going to work. This is excessive for most uses; a value of 5–10 is probably more reasonable. Likewise, you should probably bump up the value in the "Max transfer retries" field to allow more than two reconnection attempts. Multiply these two values to calculate the total number of times that the MTA will try to establish a connection before it marks the connection as unavailable.

Next, set the Lifetime and Disconnect values in the "Association parameters" group to 15. Remember these parameters? They control how long the MTA will keep an association open when there's no queued mail; lowering these values reduces the length of time the connections will sit idle but open.

The Connected Sites and Address Space tabs

You already know that both of these tabs are used to provide routing information to the DRAS connector. The MTA needs to know which address spaces it can route mail to via this connector, and these tabs provide this information. Like the X.400 connector, though, the DRAS connector has two tabs. Which one to use? It's simple: use Connected Sites when you're talking to other Exchange servers, and Address Space when you're talking to other systems.

When you create a new address space with the Connected Sites tab, you specify the Exchange organization and site you want to connect to; you must also specify the X.400 address of the remote site with the Routing Address tab. It's critical that you make sure the X.400 address you see here matches the remote site's actual X.400 address. Remember that any character that's illegal in an X.400 address (like "&", "_", "-", and so on) will be replaced by a "?", and that X.400 PRMD names have a shorter maximum length than Exchange names. That turns the legal Exchange organization name "Robichaux & Associates" into "Robichaux ? Asso," and it may do the same thing to you.

 If you want to connect servers that are in two different Exchange organizations via DRAS, you can, but you need to ensure that you fill out the Organization field in the General tab of the Connected Sites properties dialog with the right organization name. Exchange Administrator will fill in *your* organization name by default; put in the *other* organization's name, then go to the Routing Address tab and make sure the X.400 address information matches the remote site.

When you create an address space with the Address Space tab, you can use a wider range of address types (including X.400 and SMTP, plus addresses for other non-Exchange systems), but you must completely specify the address space in the parlance of the selected address type. For an X.400 address space, that means knowing the organization, organizational units, PRMD, ADMD, and country. In the Exchange world, the default is to set the organization to the Exchange site name and the PRMD to the Exchange organization name.

Creating and Configuring Directory Replication Connectors

The directory replication connector (DRC) enables sharing and replication of directory data between sites. Intrasite replication happens automatically after any change to a directory object, but the only way to replicate data between sites is to use the DRC. The DRC provides a bidirectional conduit for the replication; once you install the DRC, designate directory replication bridgehead servers in each of the sites, and schedule when you want replication to occur, the replication process is automatic.

 Don't install a directory replication connector until you're sure that mail is properly flowing between the servers. The DRC generates a ton of messages when it first starts replication, and those messages will quickly stuff your MTA queues to bursting.

Whenever the schedule says it's time, the directory replication bridgehead on your site (which I'll call the *local* site for the remainder of this section) will poll the remote site's bridgehead and ask it for a list of changes. If the two sites are joined by on-demand links, this will cause a new connection to be established. The remote site collects all directory changes that have been posted since the last replication, bundles them into a single, possibly very large, message, and queues that message for delivery to the local site. If there are more than 512 changes, the remote site sends two messages; the first one contains the first 512 changed objects, and the second one is a signal to the local site to request the next batch of changes once it finishes digesting the first 512.

Once the replication message is delivered to the local site's directory replication bridgehead, the local site's directory is updated with the changes, and the normal intrasite replication process spreads those changes throughout the local site. If the remote site sends an "I have more objects" message, the local site will send another replication trigger request to the local site, and the process restarts anew.

Before you can use the DRC to link two sites, you have to know how they're connected. Since DRC traffic is packaged in mail messages, it's important to know what connector those messages will go over. It's a little easier to set up DRCs that use the site connector; since the two sites are guaranteed to be connected, Exchange Administrator can configure both sides of the DRC at the same time. For this to work, you have to know which server in the remote site will act as the bridgehead, and the account you use to run Exchange Administrator and install the local end of the DRC must also have Administrator permissions on the remote site. If your X.400 or IMS-based DRC is run over a permanent network link, you can do the same. If there's no permanent connection, you'll have to configure each end separately.

A word about directory replication bridgeheads

When you connect two sites via a DRC, you have to nominate a directory replication bridgehead server in each site. You already know that a regular bridgehead acts as the point of contact for the site; the replication bridgehead server does exactly the same thing, but for directory replication messages instead of ordinary messages.

Directory replication bridgeheads always come in pairs, and a pair of servers will handle all replication traffic between their respective sites. Let's say you're setting up a DRC between two sites, *ATLANTA* and *BOSTON*, with directory replication bridgeheads named *ATL1* and *BOS2*. Those two servers will handle all of the replication traffic between the sites; there's no way to designate a different bridgehead in either site. If you want to connect *ATLANTA* and *DALLAS*, of course, *ATL1* could be one of the bridgeheads for that DRC, too, but it doesn't have to be. In fact, it's good practice to use separate bridgeheads in your site for each DRC; that distributes the load to multiple servers.

Installing a new DRC

The actual installation steps are painless and fairly straightforward:

1. In Exchange Administrator, use the File → New Other → Directory Replication Connector... command. The New Directory Replication Connector dialog will appear.

2. Use the "Remote site name" pull-down to pick the remote site you want to connect to, then enter the bridgehead server's name in the "Server in remote site" field.

3. The DRC setup process needs to know whether the remote site is currently available on your network or not. If not, use the "No, the remote site is not available on this network" radio button. If it is, choose the "Yes, the remote site is available on this network" radio button instead, and if you want to configure both sides of the connector at once, turn on the "Configure both sites" checkbox.

When you're done, click OK. Exchange Administrator will open the DRC properties dialog. You've already seen the Permissions tab elsewhere, so no need to revisit it.

Setting DRC properties

The "Display name" and "Directory name" fields will already be filled in, so you can accept the defaults or edit the names to taste. You can also use the "Local bridgehead server" and "Remote bridgehead server" pull-downs to change the servers the DRC will use. If you change the local bridgehead, you'll have to update the "Remote bridgehead server" field on the remote bridgehead server. Going back to our earlier example, if you want to change the *ATLANTA* bridgehead to be *ATL7*, you need to change the "Local bridgehead server" field in the *ATLANTA* site and the Remote bridgehead server field on the *BOSTON* site.

Now, on to the Schedule tab. Actually, I don't have anything new to say about how it works; it's the same grid interface as every other Schedule tab in Exchange Administrator. Actually, there is one thing to point out: if you set the detail view to "1 hour," then select a time, you're actually telling the DRC to replicate four times in that hour. If you want to limit replication to once an hour, you'll have to switch to the 15-minute view and select the 15-minute slot you want to use.

The biggest thing to be aware of in the DRC Schedule tab is that you need to tune your replication schedule to two things: the frequency of directory changes and the frequency of connections to the remote site. Since each replication cycle actually collects all the changes since the previous cycle and stuffs them into one big message, the only penalty you pay for having updates scheduled infrequently is that changes take a while to propagate to the other site. On the other hand, scheduling frequent updates costs you some extra overhead, since your server has to scan the directory for updates, package them, and hand the replication message over to the MTA. In addition, if your servers are connected by the site connector, you'll burn more bandwidth with frequent updates. Carefully consider how often your directory data changes and how quickly it needs to be propagated to the remote site, because if you replicate too often you can quickly fall into the dreaded replication death spiral (see the sidebar for more details).

The connection schedule is important, too. If you schedule replication updates every 10 minutes, but have your IMS (for example) set to connect three times a day, each IMS connection is going to spend a fair amount of time just moving the queued replication traffic, since if you schedule replication for a time when there's no connection to the remote server, the messages are queued until the next connection.

The Sites tab of the DRC Properties dialog is worth knowing about, too. It contains two lists: one for inbound sites, and one for outbound sites. The DRC considers any site that gives your local site directory updates as inbound sites. For example, any site that you already have a DRC connection to will appear in the "Inbound sites" list, as will any other sites that share their directory information with the remote site. When your site sends a replication query to the remote site, the remote site will gather and package not only updates to its directory, but also any updates it has received from its inbound sites. When the replication message arrives at your site, it could potentially contain updates from any or all of the sites

The Replication Death Spiral

It may come to pass that your replication configuration will suddenly start slowing down, often to the point where replication updates don't seem to *ever* be processed. I call this the "replication death spiral" because the longer it goes on the worse it gets. Eventually, your replication will fall so far behind that it will never be able to catch up unless you intervene. What triggers the problem? Usually it's one of two things: either there are a large number of changes to the directory in a very short period of time, or some element of the messaging transport fails, causing replication messages to back up like hair in a drain.

You already know that directory changes are bundled in single messages. On request, the remote site packages up the first 512 changes it has and sends that message to the local site. So far, so good: whenever the remote MTA gets around to sending the message, the local MTA can hand it over to the DS and it gets processed. However, if another scheduled replication time arrives before the pending change message has been processed, the connector assumes that the earlier updates never arrived and aren't going to arrive, so it asks for all the changes since the time of the first request. The longer this situation goes on, the more replication data the connector will decide it needs, and the bigger the backlog will get.

The death spiral is exacerbated by the fact that the DS code that sorts, reads, and processes replication messages is contained in a single thread within the DS process. It's possible for so much work to pile up that the thread can never get enough CPU time to catch up. To see whether this is the problem or not, you can use Exchange Administrator to check the number of items in the directory mailbox: open the bridgehead server's Private IS object, then check the "Total no. items" in the Mailbox Resources view. If you see more than a dozen or so messages here, you might be falling into the spiral. You can use the Performance Monitor to look at the % Processor Time counter of the Thread object (select all the instances for the DSAMAIN process); if one thread is sucking up more than 50% of the CPU time, you're probably hosed.

How do you fix the problem? Well, it's better to avoid it—more on that in a minute. If you do get trapped in the spiral, Microsoft recommends doing three things: changing the replication schedule on the backlogged bridgehead server itself, changing the schedule on all the inbound servers of that bridgehead, and moving some sites' DRCs off the backlogged machine. You should do all three of these, not just one or two. The net effect of these changes is to reduce the number of incoming updates that the backlogged server has to process. In extreme cases (say, if you have more than 1,000 or so backlogged messages in the Directory Service mailbox), you'll need to remove them by using the service account to log on to the Directory Service mailbox with an Exchange or Outlook client, then removing the messages manually.

—Continued—

Now, how do you prevent the problem from happening in the first place? One way is to leave the default replication interval of 3 hours alone. Microsoft strongly cautions against making the interval any shorter. For some environments, you may have to make it much longer. One organization I know of has its sites connected by 56Kbps links, and they had to set their replication interval to 72 hours to get acceptable replication performance, even though updates are dog-slow.

Next, you can calculate the minimum number of replication messages that might be generated in a day by using this formula:

numSites × (2 × numMessages × frequency) = messages/day

numSites

> The number of connected sites that participate in intersite replication anywhere in your organization

numMessages

> (*numSites* – 1) × 2; represents the number of messages required to replicate changes in all other sites to your bridgehead

frequency

> The number of times per day that replication is scheduled to take place

The factor of 2 is necessary because each replication message generates a reply message.

Using this formula, you can see that a network of five connected sites will generate a minimum of (5 × (2 × 8 × 3)) = 240 messages per day, if you stick with the default interval. Jump the interval up to once per hour, though, and you'll end up with (5 × (2 × 8 × 24)) = 1920 messages at a minimum.

listed in the "Inbound sites" list. The "Outbound sites" list shows who your local site's directory replication bridgehead server sends updates to.

If you need a directory replication update right now, instead of patiently waiting for the next scheduled connection, you can select one or more of the sites in the Inbound sites list and click the Request Now button. Why would you want to do this? The most common reason is that you know that there's been a major change to an inbound site's directory (like a bunch of moved mailboxes, or even a server moved with Pilgrim), and you want to get it sooner than the next scheduled update. When you use the Request Now button, Exchange Administrator politely asks you whether you want to replicate only items that have changed since the last replication (which is what happens during scheduled replication) or to replicate *everything* in the remote site's directory. The latter option takes a long time and lots of bandwidth; however, it's an easy way to make sure that the local and remote sites' directory data are properly synchronized.

Removing Connectors

Before you even think about removing a connector, consider the consequences. If the connector you've targeted for removal is the only connection to a particular address space or site, removing it will terminate your connectivity to that site. This isn't intrinsically bad, but you need to consider the effect on your other connectors beforehand. For example, if you cut the site connector link to a site that provides your IMS connectivity, none of your users' Internet mail will be able to make it out until you either connect to another IMS-capable site or install your own IMS.

Exchange Administrator will always ask you to confirm your command when you try to delete a connector. Once you confirm the command, Exchange Administrator will remove the connector object from the directory, and mail will immediately stop flowing over the now-deleted connector. It's a good idea to force Exchange to recalculate its routing at this point, even though it will eventually notice the change. If you later want to restore the connector, you can do so and mail will flow over it as before, as long as you properly configure the connector the same way it was previously configured.

There's one other caveat: Exchange won't let you delete the last remaining connector that joins two sites if there's still a DRC linking the sites, even if you've already deleted one side of the DRC. You must remove any DRCs between two sites before you can remove the last mail connector.

Removing DRCs

Removing a DRC is different from removing messaging connectors. When you remove a DRC, Exchange Administrator will try to be helpful and warn you of the consequences. Of course, the obvious consequence is that directory replication will stop. There are some more subtle side effects. First and foremost is that Exchange will return each site's directory to its pre-replication state by removing any objects in the local site that came from an inbound site. While this is often desirable, it's never good to be surprised by the disappearance of your replication information.

When you actually remove a DRC by selecting it and using the Edit → Delete command or by pressing the Delete key, you'll see two warning dialogs. The first dialog warns you that removing the DRC will stop replication with the remote site and that you'll have to create another DRC to restore replication. If you tell it to proceed, it will ask if the remote site's DRC should also be removed—say "yes" to cut off replication completely, or "no" if you want to stop replication only in one direction.

After the connector has been removed, you'll see a confirmation dialog informing you that the site connector has been severed and reminding you to remove the remote site's DRC, too. You may also see another dialog telling you what to do if you plan to reconnect the sites in the future. After you remove a DRC, if you don't intend to reconnect the two sites that were formerly joined, you should run the DS/IS consistency adjuster available from the Check Now button on the General tab of the server's Directory Service object. Doing so forces the directory to discard any formerly replicated data instead of waiting for it to expire. However, if you do intend to reconnect the sites, don't run the consistency adjuster, because that will mess up ownership of any replicated public folders. (When you reconnect the sites, any new or changed public folders in either site will automatically be replicated to the other site.)

Moving Connectors to New Machines

You may find it necessary to move connectors between servers in a site. For example, maybe you started with a mixed architecture and have decided to move all your connectors to a connector server, or maybe you're juggling machines around within the site. You can easily move connectors from one machine to another as long as you follow the move steps in the right order:

1. Create the new connectors between the sites you want to connect. Set up both ends of the connection.

2. Raise the cost of the old connectors higher than the new connectors, so that Exchange will prefer the new connectors to the old ones when routing messages.

3. Force Exchange to recalculate the GWART by using the "Recalculate Routing" button on the General tab of the server's MTA Properties dialog. Once the GWART has been rebuilt, new messages should start moving over the new connectors instead of the old ones.

4. Monitor the new connectors to make sure they're transferring messages the way you expect them to.

5. When the old connectors' queues are empty, delete the old connectors on both ends of their original connection.

6. Recalculate the routing table again to remove all references to old connectors.

Saving and Restoring the Connections Container

Think back to the discussion of directory import and export in Chapter 5. You probably remember that it was mostly about mailboxes and the like, but you can export other items, too. In fact, you can export the entire contents of a container, like the Connections container, and then reload it later. Microsoft warns you not to do this, because when you import the CSV file, you will overwrite the connector configuration information in the directory. However, having the configuration contents in a text file is useful for at least two reasons: it's easier to see all the connectors at once, and it's easier to compare the configuration of connectors on two different machines.

To make this work, you need a custom import/export option file. Microsoft Knowledge Base article Q160971 suggests the following, where *server1* is the server whose connection setup you want to capture, *server2* is the service where you're running Exchange Administrator, and *ORG* and *SITE* are your organization and site names:

```
[Export]
DirectoryService=server1
HomeServer=server2
Basepoint=/o=ORG/ou=SITE/cn=configuration/cn=connections
ExportObject=All
InformationLevel=Full
RawMode=Yes
HiddenObjects=Yes
Subcontainers=Yes

[Import]
DirectoryService=server1
Basepoint=/o=ORG/ou=SITE/cn=configuration
Container=
InformationLevel=Full
OverwriteProperties=Yes
RawMode=Yes
```

Next, you need a header file. The best way to get one is to use the Import Header Tool from the BORK (see Appendix A) to create a header file that contains all attributes for objects of class "Mail-Gateway." This ensures that you'll get all the data the directory holds for your connections. Just select all the items in the Available Attributes list, click Add, then generate the CSV file.

Once that's done, just use the standard export and import commands you learned about in Chapter 5. Since you want to use a custom options file, you'll have to use `admin /E` and `admin /I` to do the trick.

Configuring Site Addressing

The Site Addressing object in each individual site container is where you set up what types of addresses the site will understand and when it will regenerate its mail routing information. If you remember earlier mentions of the GWART, you're right on target; this object controls how and when the GWART is regenerated. The

Site Addressing properties dialog has five tabs, counting the Permissions tab. The other four tabs control how the GWART is maintained and what it does.

The General tab lets you provide a display name for the Site Addressing object (whoopee!) It also lets you specify which server is used for routing recalculation: by default, this will be the first server installed in the site, but you can deputize another server by selecting it from the "Routing calculation server" pull-down. You can also make this site share the same X.400 address space with a foreign system. This is useful if you're migrating from some other X.400 setup to Exchange. Click the "Share Address Space with Other X.400 Systems" checkbox to let Exchange and a foreign system both have access to the same address space.

The Site Addressing tab lets you specify which types of secondary addresses are generated for mailboxes in this site. You'll see a list containing one entry (with a checkbox next to it) for each address type available in the site. The list contents are determined by which proxy address generators are installed; that, in turn, is governed by which connectors and gateways your servers have. For example, in my sites I turn off cc:Mail and MS Mail address generation, since I don't need to talk to those types of systems.

More important, the Site Addressing tab lets you customize the format of the addresses that Exchange Administrator generates for new mailboxes. For example, one common tweak many administrators apply is to change the default SMTP address. By default, Exchange will generate an address of the form *site.organization.domain*, which may or may not be what you want—instead, you might prefer just *organization.domain*, so that all mailboxes answer to *somebody@yourdomain.com* instead of having the unnecessary site information. To edit the address generation settings for an address type, highlight it and use the Edit... button. You'll get a small properties dialog whose contents will vary depending on the address type; no matter what type of address it is, though, you can edit its components so that newly generated addresses conform to your desired format.

Changing the proxy address generation settings here will cause Exchange Administrator to ask you if you want it to update all proxy addresses. This is different from what happens when you use Exchange Administrator's Tools → Options... command. You can also effect a widespread proxy address change by either using the E-mail Addresses tab of individual mailbox properties dialogs or the directory import and export features of Exchange Administrator.

If you change the site address on a site that's connected by a DRC to some other site, you'll need to go to the other site and update the underlying connector's addressing information. For example, if you have two sites connected via the X.400 connector, *US-West* and *US-East*, and you rename them to *NAmerica-West* and *NAmerica-East*, you'll need to open each side's X.400 connector properties dialog and change the remote side's X.400 address to match the new site name.

The Routing Calculation Schedule tab offers the standard schedule grid, on which you draw little boxes to indicate when you want the GWART recalculated. The grid runs from midnight to midnight, which means you can schedule updates at any hour, but not at finer intervals.

The Routing tab itself shows the contents of the GWART. Each address space or connected site you've defined on a connector will appear here, listing the type of address space range that hosts it (EX for Exchange addresses, X.400 for X.400 addresses, and so on), the complete address space, the cost of the route, and the connector that hosts the route. This information comes directly from the GWART; if, for some reason, you want to see it in its raw, unedited, poorly formatted glory, the MTA stores a text copy of the GWART in *\exchsrvr\mtadata\gwart0.mta*. By examining this file, you can see how the MTA has constructed its routing paths.

The most important item on this tab is the Recalculate Routing button; when you click it, the MTA recalculates all routes in the GWART, updating them to incorporate any changes to connector availability, address spaces, or costs that you've made. It's a good idea to use this button to trigger a recalculation any time you add or remove a connector or address space. The MTA will eventually notice the change and honor it, but it never hurts to give it a prod.

Message Journaling

Exchange 5.5 SP1 added a new capability that can either be a boon or a danger, depending on your viewpoint. *Message journaling* allows you to route a copy of every message sent on the system, including system messages generated by the SA and MTA, and archive it in a mailbox, file it in a public folder, or forward it to a custom recipient. The Exchange IMS has always allowed you to archive copies of inbound and outbound messages, as you'll learn in the next chapter, but the process was annoyingly manual. Journaling automates message archiving, except that you can only configure it via changes to the registry.

Why would you want to journal your messages? Many firms, particularly those involved with the U.S. securities industry, are required by law to keep records of all their correspondence. Many other companies want to keep comprehensive records of mail traffic for various reasons, including their use in proving, or disproving, that certain messages were or were not sent.[*]

---

[*] Many of these companies are paranoid about lawsuits for things like racial or sexual harassment, so they want a clear record they can use to identify whether prohibited conduct has taken place.

Without going any further into the legal or ethical quagmire that journaling presents, I would be remiss if I didn't point out that it imposes a performance penalty. In normal operation, the MTA doesn't have to touch every single message sent from a server—just the ones bound for other servers. With journaling on, the MTA has to handle every message, and it can quickly bog down under the load. Microsoft claims that the MTA performance enhancements included in SP1 make up for much of the increased load, but be prepared to reconfigure your servers if you turn journaling on and it proves to be too much for them to handle. In particular, if your site or organization has high message traffic you should consider putting the journaling target mailbox or public folder on a dedicated server.

 Microsoft's release notes for SP1 point out that the mailbox, public folder, or custom recipient selected to receive journaled messages must always be available, or journaling will stop. Make sure you factor that requirement into your decision about where recorded messages will go.

How Journaling Works

When you enable journaling on a server, the MTA saves copies of most types of messages that pass through it. It doesn't archive every message; specifically, it doesn't keep messages posted to public folders, delivery reports, NDRs, directory or public folder replication messages, link monitor messages, or X.400 probe messages. However, it gets all messages that fall into one of these categories:

- Messages sent to, or received by, user mailboxes, including read receipt messages

- Messages relayed through the IMS, including delivery reports for messages sent via the IMS)

- Messages sent directly to public folders

If you have POP3 or IMAP4 clients that send mail directly to an outside SMTP host, or if your users use free services like HotMail, MailExcite!, or Yahoo Mail, you won't be able to journal those messages because they never reach the Exchange server. Most sites that have to turn on journaling have already disabled these routes for mail, though.

You can configure journaling at the server, site, or organization level. Each message may be captured once or twice. For example, if you turn on journaling at the site level, a message sent between two recipients in that site will be captured when it's first sent and when it's received, but the same is not true when you journal messages at the organization level: messages are captured as soon as they hit the first server that has journaling active, but are not recaptured when they arrive at their destination.

Journaling and security

Microsoft identifies two issues with journaling security. First, you don't want anyone to turn off journaling when it's supposed to be on, especially if you're using it because your organization is legally required to. Second, you don't want anyone to turn it on when it's not supposed to be on. There's a third issue that's probably worth raising: you don't want unauthorized people to be able to see what messages have been sent.

Fixing the first two problems is relatively easy. Since journaling is configured in the registry, you need to make sure that your registry permissions are set so that only administrators you want to have access (not necessarily everyone in the local or domain administrators groups) can change these settings. You really should be exercising tight control over the registries of your servers anyway, because there are a lot of other ways to compromise an NT machine's security if you don't. See my Nutshell Handbook *Managing the Windows NT Registry* (O'Reilly & Associates) for more details.

The third problem is manageable, too. The key is to prevent unauthorized people from seeing the message archives. First, hide the message destination from the address list, whether it's a public folder, a mailbox, or a custom recipient. If you're storing messages in a mailbox, make sure that only the authorized user has permission to see the mailbox and that you've secured the site service account password so that it's not easily available. If you're using a public folder to hold the journaled messages, use the folder's Permissions tab to remove everything but the accounts you want to have access. Set those remaining accounts' role to Contributor, then set the folder permissions to allow the accounts to create items.

Configuring Journaling

To enable journaling, you must make four registry changes on your servers. If you only want to enable journaling on one server, you're in good shape. If you want to enable journaling at the site or organization level, you must make these changes on every server in the site or organization. Here's what you need to do to configure journaling:

1. Specify whether you want journaling on at the server, site, or organization level. You do this by adding a new `REG_DWORD` registry value named `Per-Site Journal Required` to the MTA's primary settings key, our old friend `HKLM\SYSTEM\CurrentControlSet\Services\MSExchangeMTA\Parameters`. A value of 0 specifies that journaling should be organization-wide; a value of 1

means that you want journaling active at the site level, and a value of 2 means that you only want journaling at the server level.

2. Specify where you want recorded messages to go. You'll need the full distinguished name of the recipient, which you can get by running Exchange Administrator in raw mode and looking up the Obj-Dist-Name attribute for whatever mailbox, public folder, or custom recipient will be the journaling target. Once you have the DN, create a new string value with it. The value must be named `Journal Recipient Name`, and it goes under the `MSExchangeMTA\Parameters` key.

3. Add the `RerouteViaStore` value (a `REG_DWORD`, set to 1) to the IMS registry settings   (`HKLM\SYSTEM\CurrentControlSet\Services\MSExchangeIMC\Parameters`) to force it to route all its message traffic through the private IS. If you don't do this in conjunction with step 4, your IMS traffic won't be captured in the journal.

4. Force the private IS to route all local messages through the MTA. If you don't do this, messages sent between recipients on the same server and messages sent through the IMS won't be captured. The value you need to add is a `REG_DWORD` named `No Local Delivery`, set to 1.

Once you've made all four of these changes, stop and restart the MTA, IMS, and IS services on each server you have changed. This will force those services to take note of the changes and honor them.

8

Managing the Internet Mail Service

*Having two protocols that do the same thing is
much worse than having one.*
—The Internet Mail Consortium (*www.imc.org*)

You might have noticed that Chapter 7, *Managing Connectors and the MTA*, conspicuously neglected to discuss how Exchange communicates with the Internet. While at its core the task is quite simple, the variations on this theme are broad enough to require a separate chapter. The Internet Mail Service (IMS) is the mechanism through which most Exchange servers communicate with the rest of the world. This chapter covers the details of installing, managing, and troubleshooting the most common IMS configurations.

Throughout this chapter, you'll see the Exchange Internet connector referred to by two names: IMC and IMS. They're the same thing: in Exchange 4.0, the Internet Mail Connector (IMC) provided SMTP connectivity, but starting with Exchange 5.0, the component was renamed to the Internet Mail Service, or IMS. The change in name reflects a change in architecture that made the SMTP connector more of a core service on par with the IS, DS, and MTA. However, not all of the user interface and registry references to IMC were updated—hence the double acronyms.

Understanding the IMS

The IMS is one of the core Exchange services and has only one job: to exchange mail with SMTP hosts on the Internet, on the company intranet, such as Unix hosts, or at other Exchange sites. More generally, it sends messages from Exchange to the Internet, and receives messages for Exchange from the Internet. While mail is routed to the IMS by the MTA's routing tables, the IMS itself is more closely coupled to the IS than to the MTA.

As described in Chapter 1, *Introducing Exchange Server* and Chapter 2, *Exchange Architecture*, Exchange maintains a directory database full of X.400-style objects with lots of modifications to support MAPI. While these technologies are quite powerful, they're not what the Internet uses. The IMS acts as the glue that ties the proprietary Exchange database formats and protocols to the standards-based Internet. In that role, the IMS is responsible for the following tasks:

- Accepting mail from the MTA for delivery to SMTP hosts

- Accepting mail from SMTP hosts and delivering it to the private IS or MTA for further delivery

- Converting messages between Internet-standard formats and the proprietary format used by the private IS database

The IMS and Core Components

Figure 8-1 is a picture of how the IMS integrates with other components, which may help make the integration more clear. The IMS interacts with the store in two ways: it sends and receives mail, and it does content conversion in conjunction with the IMail component. The IMS uses the DS to do address resolution and to store its configuration parameters. Apart from these interactions, the IMS mostly spends its time talking to external systems.

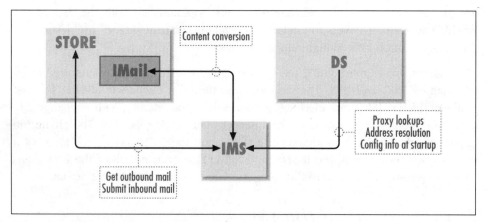

Figure 8-1. IMS integration with core services

In practice, the consequence of this design is that the IS sits between the MTA and the IMS; this improves IMS performance. In Exchange 4.0, the IMC was loosely coupled to the MTA, and it used filesystem queues for all inbound and outbound mail handling, including content conversion. In Exchange 5.0, the queuing architecture was changed so that the IMS could use a pair of folders located inside the IS; this facilitates the content conversion required to communicate with non-MAPI clients.

This is why you'll see an Internet Mail Service mailbox if you look at the Mailbox Resources view of a server with the IMS configured. In Exchange 5.5 SP1, a bug caused the count of messages in this mailbox to display incorrectly, which alarmed many administrators. SP2 corrected this problem.

The IMS Mail Flow

In Chapter 2, you learned how the MTA makes decisions about routing messages to various connectors and how mail flows from sender to recipient. The IMS has its own peculiar mail flow. Actually, it has two flows: one describes how mail moves from a sender to a recipient via the IMS, and the other describes how mail is transferred inside the IMS itself.

Mail sent by clients to the Internet

The IMS accepts mail from Exchange clients in a roundabout way; the exact steps depend on what kind of client is running. Figure 8-2 shows the process, which begins when a client submits mail to the IMS.

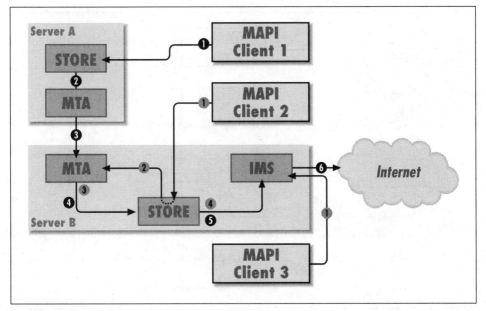

Figure 8-2. IMS outbound message flow

Post Office Protocol (POP3) and Internet Mail Access Protocol (IMAP4) clients submit messages directly to the IMS using the SMTP protocol. MAPI clients submit mail to the private IS on their local servers; if that local server doesn't have an IMS, the message may be rerouted across one or more servers before it finally reaches an IMS. (See Chapter 2 for a recap on how the MTA and IS work together to route mail between servers in a multiserver environment.) From now on, I'll call this process the *outbound flow*, since messages are headed out from your server to the Internet.

Mail sent from the Internet to Exchange recipients

The process works in the other direction, too. When an Internet host has mail addressed to an Exchange recipient, that host will eventually make an SMTP connection to an IMS somewhere in the recipient's organization. Let's call this the *inbound flow*, as shown in Figure 8-3. When an inbound message arrives, it's put into the IMC inbound queue. An Inbound MAPI thread inside the IMS removes messages from that queue (first come, first served) and routes them appropriately. In this case, "appropriate" means that the IMS follows any restrictions you've placed on who may send mail to your IMS, rejecting anything that doesn't fit those rules. The inbound message is then converted to Exchange format and loaded into the IS, which determines if the recipient is local, in which case the message can be delivered immediately, or whether it must be handed over to the MTA for further routing.

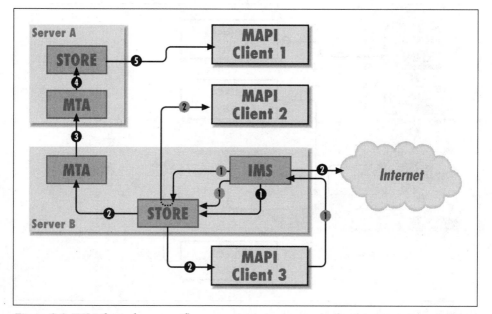

Figure 8-3. IMS inbound message flow

The internal IMS mail flow

Now, let's get deeper into the specifics of what the IMS does internally. Figure 8-4 shows how mail flows inside the IMS: the top half shows outbound mail moving from the MTA to the Internet, and the bottom half shows inbound mail moving from the Internet to the Exchange system.

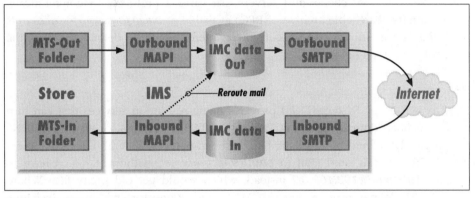

Figure 8-4. IMS internal structure

First, the outbound flow: outbound mail is pulled from the MTA queue by the IS and placed in the *MTS-Out* folder inside the IS, where it's eventually picked up by the Outbound MAPI threads of the IMS. The IMS converts the message contents, resolves all recipient addresses, and expands any distribution lists that weren't handled by the MTA. The result of this process is an RFC 822-compliant message that's ready to be sent via SMTP. This message is placed in the IMC Data Out queue (a filesystem queue located in *\exchsrvr\imcdata\out*), and the queue index file (*\incdata\queue.dat*) is updated to reflect the new message. Once that's done, the message may be deleted from the IS if there aren't any references to it; since most users tell their clients to save sent items in the *Sent Items* folder, most messages actually stay in the IS after being sent. Eventually, the mail is delivered by the IMS via an SMTP connection to the destination host.

What about the inbound flow? When an Internet host has an inbound message, it will establish an SMTP connection to the IMS (see the section "Using Dequeuing," later in the chapter, for a few wrinkles that may occur first). The Inbound SMTP threads of the IMS accept the incoming connection and store the message in the IMC Data In queue (another filesystem queue, which lives in *\exchsrvr\imcdata\in*), where it sits until the Inbound MAPI threads grab it. Those threads pass the message to the IMail process for conversion from the standard Internet format (more on that in a bit) to MAPI format. If the message is accepted, it will be delivered to the *IS MTS-In* folder, where the IS can get it and deliver it either to the recipient or to the MTA for further routing. If the message isn't accepted, it's passed back to the IMC Data Out queue for redelivery as an NDR.

Key Protocols and Standards

Since Exchange is based internally on the MAPI standard, the IMS is responsible for dealing with Internet standards–based products from other vendors. The IMS, along with other components that talk to Internet hosts, has to conform to an extensive set of Internet standards. These standards, or Requests for Comments (RFCs), set out how clients and servers use various protocols to communicate. There's a nifty searchable archive of RFCs available at *www.faqs.org/rfcs/rfcsearch. html*; this is a good place to look if you're interested in the details of any of the protocols discussed below.

DNS

The Domain Name System (DNS) provides name resolution services that can turn a fully qualified domain name (FQDN) into a TCP/IP address, or vice versa. DNS was originally defined by RFC 882, but has been updated several times since then. With DNS, you can send mail to *paul@robichaux.net*; without it, you'd have to send mail to *paul@192.168.0.1* instead, which would get old pretty fast. Where the GWART defines routing between MTAs and connectors within an Exchange organization, DNS and its Mail Exchanger (MX) records define routing instructions among Internet mail hosts.

I have long chanted a mantra to new network and mail administrators that sounds something like "*DNS and Bind* by Paul Albitz and Cricket Liu. *DNS and Bind* by Paul Albitz and Cricket Liu." The new and improved chant is too long to reproduce here in its entirety. It's "*Windows NT TCP/IP Network Administration* by Craig Hunt and Robert Bruce Thompson, *DNS on Windows NT* by Paul Albitz, Matt Larson, and Cricket Liu," repeated until it sinks in. Both books are Windows NT–specific versions of the venerable O'Reilly & Associates DNS and TCP/IP books, and I highly recommend them.

Your Exchange server depends on DNS for several things:

- The IMS performs DNS lookups to determine what mail exchange host should receive outbound mail.

- The IMS performs reverse DNS lookups to determine the names of hosts sending inbound mail; since it already has their network addresses, a reverse lookup will yield the corresponding DNS names.

- All hosts sending mail to your IMS must be able to look it up via DNS so they can find it on the network.

- Other hosts may perform reverse DNS lookups to verify your identity when you connect to deliver mail.

All these items depend on you or your service provider. One of you has to properly configure DNS addresses and MX records for your Exchange server. You also have to correctly specify the hostname and DNS domain name of your Exchange server, plus at least one DNS server, in the TCP/IP properties dialog of the Network control panel.

The third item listed depends on the Exchange server being correctly registered in the public DNS system. Mail delivery relies on two standard DNS record types: the A, or Address, record and the MX, or Mail Exchanger, record:

```
yourcorp.com.            IN   MX   10          yourserver.yourcorp.com.
yourserver.yourcorp.com. IN   A    10.1.1.1
```

There should also be a reverse lookup entry for *yourserver.yourcorp.com* (a PTR, or Pointer record). In the *1.1.10.in-addr.arpa* domain, the record would be:

```
1    IN      PTR      yourserver.yourcorp.com.
```

SMTP

The Simple Mail Transfer Protocol (SMTP) was initially defined by RFC 821. (RFC 822, a companion specification, defines the format that SMTP messages are supposed to be in.) The objective of the SMTP protocol is "to transfer mail reliably and efficiently."* The protocol's success at this goal has made it the *lingua franca* of Internet mail, which is why Microsoft supports it. Mail systems wouldn't be nearly as useful if they could only talk to other servers from the same vendor.

The SMTP standard defines a conversation syntax for systems to transfer mail messages. A sample SMTP session is shown in Figure 8-5; in it, *paul@robichaux.net* is trying to send an RFC 822 message to *robert@oreilly.com*. The dance begins when the mail host *robichaux.net* opens an SMTP connection to the destination host, which responds with a numeric status code of 220. The "Ready" after the code is for humans to use when debugging, but SMTP servers ignore any text in status messages (although ESMTP status messages contain useful information and are processed by ESMTP servers). After that, you can see how the back-and-forth negotiation proceeds: the sender says who the mail is from and who it's for, then sends the message data and indicates that it's done. At each step, the receiving server sends back status messages to indicate that the process can proceed.

The *message data* portion of Figure 8-5 is an RFC 822–formatted message. The actual message data sent during the exchange above looks like this:

```
To: Robert Denn <robert@oreilly.com>
From: Paul Robichaux <paul@robichaux.net>
```

---

* Jonathan B.Postel, "RFC 821—Simple Mail Transfer Protocol," 1982.

```
Subject: I'm too full to work
Date: Sun, 14 Feb 1999 21:18:39 -0600

Robert,

I won't have the IMS chapter done tomorrow like I promised. I ate too much
Valentine's Day candy and can't get up off the sofa.

Cheers,
-Paul
.
```

Figure 8-5. SMTP back-and-forth

An RFC 822 message has two parts:

Header

> The header section is always the first section of the message and is terminated with a blank line. Each header is a key/value pair with a colon (:) separator character.

Body

> The body section is always the second section of the message and is terminated with a period (.) on a line by itself. It is this indicator that terminates the message data section of Figure 8-5.

It's useful to understand how SMTP works, since that knowledge can come in handy when you're trying to debug IMS connectivity problems. You can use a simple telnet client to connect to the SMTP port (TCP port 25) of a remote system and submit a test message to ensure that you can connect and talk to the server.

ESMTP

Exchange also supports the basic Extended SMTP (ESMTP) standard, plus several of its extensions. RFC 1869 defines some of these extensions, including a method for generating delivery status notifications like "message read" and "who gets the return receipt?," a useful feature missing from the original SMTP standard. RFC 1870 defines the SIZE parameter, which can be used by SMTP servers to limit the size of incoming messages. There are others: check the searchable archive I mentioned earlier if you want all the gory details. ESMTP sessions are differentiated from SMTP sessions by the use of the EHLO verb instead of the HELO verb. EHLO tells the receiving machine to generate a list of extensions it supports, something like what you see in Table 8-1.

Table 8-1. ESMTP Feature Negotiation

Open Connection

                    220 ESMTP Server ready

EHLO

                    250-Hello [mauve]
                    250-XEXCH50
                    250-HELP
                    250-ETRN
                    250-DSN
                    250-SIZE 0
                    250-AUTH LOGIN
                    250-AUTH=LOGIN
                    250-STARTTLS
                    250 TLS

The ETRN and TURN extensions

The SMTP TURN command allows any host to connect to a system holding queued mail and request that mail. For example, your home machine could connect to your ISP and say "give me the mail for *myhome.com*." TURN is a useful command, but it's also a security risk, because the queued mail is sent back to the requestor over the same connection, so anyone can ask for your queued mail and get it!

RFC 1985 defines an extension to the ESMTP standard called ETRN, short for Extended TuRN. ETRN was designed as a replacement for TURN; instead of sending queued mail back over the same connection, it sends mail to the DNS registered primary MX address for that domain. This means that anyone can send ETRN `yourdomain.com` to your ISP, but the ISP will always try to send that mail to you when they receive the request.

The **ETRN** command format is:

    ETRN [option] node <CR><LF>

option is an optional modifier with two possible values, **@** and **#**. The meaning of these modifiers is described in Table 8-2.

Table 8-2. Modifiers for the ETRN Command

Command	Meaning
`ETRN yourdomain.com`	Request mail queued for exactly *yourdomain.com*.
`ETRN @yourdomain.com`	Request mail queued for *yourdomain.com* or any subdomain.
`ETRN #yourdomain`	Request mail from the queue named "yourdomain."

MIME

When the SMTP protocol was first written in 1982, mail was restricted to printable ASCII characters and attachments were required to be converted to a 7-bit ASCII printable form. With the advent of rich media like sound, video, and still images, a number of Internet architects realized that these multimedia items could easily be encapsulated and carried in mail messages. RFCs 1521 and 1522 defined the initial set of Multipurpose Internet Mail Extensions (MIME) standards; since then, MIME has become the basis for multimedia, multilingual, and rich-content mail sent over the Internet.

The MIME specifications claim to define "Mechanisms for Specifying and Describing the Format of Internet Message Bodies."[*] In plain English, they define a way to indicate that a message has complex content (e.g., multiple parts, binary attachments, and so on) and to describe the content (e.g., filename, character set, encoding). A simple example is shown here. You'll notice that there are two new headers: "MIME-Version," which defines the version of the MIME specification the message adheres to, and "Content-Type," which defines the content of the message and the boundary indicator that delineates separate message parts.

    From: "Robert Denn" <robert@oreilly.com>
    To: "Paul Robichaux" <paul@robichaux.net>
    Subject: Candy, schmandy
    Date: Mon, 15 Feb 1999 04:00:27 -0600
    MIME-Version: 1.0
    Content-Type: multipart/mixed;
        boundary="----_=_NextPart_000_01BE58CA.036A16F8"

---

[*] N. Borenstein and N.Freed, "RFC 1521 – MIME (Multipurpose Internet Mail Extensions) Part One," 1993.

```
------_=_NextPart_000_01BE58CA.036A16F8
Content-Type: text/plain;
    charset="iso-8859-1"

See attached document.

 <<write-or-die.doc>>


------_=_NextPart_000_01BE58CA.036A16F8
Content-Type: application/msword;
    name="write-or-die.doc"
Content-Transfer-Encoding: base64
Content-Disposition: attachment;
    filename="write-or-die.doc"
```

0M8R4KGxGuEAAAAAAAAAAAAAAAAAAAAAPgADAP7/CQAGAAAAAAAAAAAAABAAAAIQAAAAAAAAA
-snip-
AAAAAAAAAAAAAAAAAAAAAAAAA==

```
------_=_NextPart_000_01BE58CA.036A16F8-
```

SASL, TLS, and SSL

There are three significant security protocols that have something to do with email; Exchange 5.5 supports all three. The first is the Simple Authentication and Security Layer (SASL) protocol, defined by RFC 2222. SASL provides standards-based authentication that clients can use to authenticate themselves to an Exchange server without sending plain-text username/password pairs over the net. If you want to use SASL with Exchange, you'll have to configure the Microsoft Certificate Server (which comes with IIS and is discussed in Chapter 16, *Exchange Security*), then register its certificate with either a public Certificate Authority (CA) like Verisign or your own private CA. Once you've done that, you can turn on SASL authentication.

The Transport Layer Security (TLS) and Secure Sockets Layer (SSL) protocols provide connection security—a TLS- or SSL-encrypted connection can't be eavesdropped on. SSL was the original connection security protocol deployed by Netscape in the Navigator 2.x series of browsers; TLS is the Internet standard based on the SSL protocol, with some extensions and security fixes. TLS is defined in RFC 2246; the particulars of how SMTP and TLS work together are covered in RFC 2487. To use TLS or SSL encryption, you don't have to do anything other than installing IIS 3.0 or 4.0 and specifying that the IMS may use IIS for an authentication method.

S/MIME

S/MIME is an offshoot of the MIME protocols; the S/MIME standard specifies how mail clients and servers can encrypt or digitally sign email to protect it from tampering and disclosure. While SASL authenticates who you're talking to, and SSL/TLS protects the connection between two servers or a client and a server, S/MIME tools like the ones included with Outlook 97/98/2000 and Outlook Express protect the message before it ever leaves the client. To use S/MIME with Exchange, you'll have to set up the clients and server according to the directions in Chapter 16.

Content Conversion

Messages in the Exchange IS are stored as OLE documents in an X.400-like message structure, but the IMS, and the Internet, expect to see MIME. This leads to a chocolate-in-the-peanut-butter situation, since one side or the other has to be made to accept the other's format. That's why part of the Exchange IMS is responsible for content conversion.

In Exchange 4.0, this process, called IMail, was part of the IMC. When Microsoft added POP3 and IMAP support to the IS in Exchange 5.0 and 5.5, IMail was upgraded and moved inside the IS. This new IMail provides content conversion services for both the IMS and for clients that require content conversion for message rendering. The process of converting an OLE document to MIME and back is not an exact science and may, in some cases, produce unexpected results. In an attempt to maintain content integrity, the conversion engine will often attach a body part to the message that Microsoft clients can interpret, which may show up as an attachment named *winmail.dat*, or as an attachment with a MIME type of `application/x-ms-tnef` (short for Transport Neutral Encapsulation Format). This is particularly likely if clients are creating rich text format (RTF) messages by including colors, fonts, or typeface changes (or using the Wordmail option of Outlook), then sending them to clients that cannot handle RTF content. You can configure some IMail behavior, including which domains you want to allow RTF messages to go to, through the IMS property pages.

Installing the IMS

You may have noticed that in Chapter 4, *Installing Exchange*, I didn't talk about installing the IMS as part of the normal setup process. That's because it's not part of the normal setup process; you have to explicitly activate the IMS by installing it from within Exchange Administrator, even though the installer copies all the necessary files as part of the installation process.

Before You Install

There are a few prerequisites before you can install IMS. Lest you be tempted to skip this section, be aware that the IMS installer checks to make sure that the DNS and TCP/IP setup steps have been correctly completed, so you're better off to do all of the following first:

- You must have TCP/IP correctly configured and installed. In this case, "correctly" expands to mean that you must specify a DNS domain name and hostname for your machine in the TCP/IP Properties page of the Network control panel.

- Since SMTP mail requires DNS, you need to configure a DNS server for your Exchange server to use when delivering outbound mail. Exceptions to this rule are noted later in "Using the Internet Mail Wizard."

- To receive SMTP mail, your Exchange server needs its own pair of MX and A records in your DNS server, whether it's your corporate server or one at your ISP. Exceptions to this rule are noted later in the coverage of Exchange security.

- If you will be using Dial-up Networking to connect to your ISP, you must install the Windows NT Remote Access Service (RAS) before installing the IMS. You must also create a phone book entry on the Exchange server for the ISP. I strongly recommend that you test this connection and verify that you can get connected before continuing with the IMS installation.

In previous versions of Exchange, there have been problems with certain RAS phone book entries. To be safe, keep the phone book entry name less than 20 characters, and use only the "A–Z," "0–9," and "-" characters.

It is hard to emphasize enough the importance of getting the DNS configuration right. SMTP mail delivery absolutely depends on correct DNS configuration. Several of the most frequently asked questions on Exchange newsgroups and mailing lists like the one hosted at *www.swynk.com* have root answers involving DNS configuration.

Using the Internet Mail Wizard

When you want to install the IMS, you'll use Exchange Administrator's File → New Other → Internet Mail Service... command, which starts the Internet Mail Wizard (IMW).* As with most other Microsoft wizards, the IMW will lead you by the hand through the process of installing something, but when it's time to configure it you're on your own. (When it's time to configure it, come back and reread this

---

* Why is it called that? Beats me. A better name might be the IMS Wizard, since you don't use the Internet Mail Wizard to actually send mail.

Where to Put Your IMS

The best place for your IMS is on its own server, either with or without other connectors. This is true for a number of reasons, all of which involve the tradeoff between time and resources:

- A heavily loaded IMS can consume a significant amount of resources as it converts incoming and outgoing content between MIME and Exchange format. Putting the IMS on its own server shifts the load away from your mailbox servers.

- As you'll learn in Chapter 15, *Troubleshooting Exchange Server*, when the IMS crashes it can take the IS with it. Separating the IMS and your mailboxes means that you can deal with a crashed IMS at your leisure, not at the breakneck pace required when none of your users can get their mail.

- Mail bombs, mail loops, and spam floods can cause the machine running the IMS to be completely submerged in mail. If the IMS is on its own server, these crises have little impact on your users' normal operations.

- Separating the IMS and your mailboxes allows you to move and reconfigure the IMS (or other connectors) without affecting your users' mail access.

chapter.) In Microsoft's defense, this isn't necessarily different from how real-world processes work; I know we were sure on our own when our first baby arrived.[*]

The first page of the IMW just tells you what the wizard will do; the second page reminds you to do the things I listed in the preceding section before you continue with the installation. The third page is where things start to get interesting, because you have to choose the server in your site on which to install the IMS. Yes, that's right: you don't necessarily have to run the IMW on the machine where you actually want the IMS installed. That's a handy feature, since most often you'll use a small number of IMS servers no matter how many servers and sites you have.

Choose the appropriate server from the pull-down, which lists all the servers in your site, then check the "Allow Internet mail through a dial-up connection" checkbox if you want the server to be able to send and receive mail through a RAS connection to your ISP. If you want to run RAS, though, you have to run the IMW on the machine where you want the IMS installed; you can't do remote

---

[*] Andy Webb pointed out that babies don't come with Books Online or the Exchange Administrator help files, either.

installations with that checkbox marked. If you told the wizard you wanted to use RAS, you'll see an additional page that asks you to select a phone book entry to specify how to call the ISP.

Page 4: Rerouting and relaying

The next wizard page asks you whether you want to enable rerouting, better known as SMTP relaying. This question appears innocuous, but it isn't, because SMTP relaying (where your host is given permission to accept mail for recipients on other servers outside your organization) is a great way to send unsolicited commercial email (UCE, or spam). The default is to leave relaying off. You'll need to turn it on if you're using POP3 or IMAP4 clients, and you might need it if your Exchange server is being used to route mail for other internal SMTP servers. If you do turn it on, make sure to apply routing restrictions, as described later in the chapter.

Page 5: Outbound mail delivery

The next page allows you to control how outbound mail will be delivered by the IMS. The first option, "Use DNS to send mail," indicates that your Exchange server should connect directly to each destination mail host to deliver outbound mail. This is the default for non-RAS connections. The second option, "Route all mail through a single host," forces the IMS to send all outbound mail to some other host (sometimes called a *smart host*) for eventual delivery. This is the default for dial-up connections, and it requires you to specify a hostname or IP address for the smart host. When the IMS NT service starts, it will attempt to resolve the smart host name to an IP address using DNS; the IP address is then used for all mail delivery. If the hostname cannot be resolved, the IMS will fail to start. This often happens with systems that use dial-up connections where the ISP provides the DNS server; the connection, and thus the ability to perform name resolution, isn't active when the system is started. If that sounds like your setup, use the IP address of the smart host instead of its DNS name. It is also a good idea to use the "Forward all mail to host" option if you have a slow connection to your ISP. You effectively offload much of the delivery processing to the ISP's SMTP server and conserve your bandwidth.

Page 6: Address space restrictions

The Internet Mail Wizard will configure a default address space for the SMTP service of * with a cost of 1. This will cause this IMS to be used to route SMTP mail to all domains. If this is a secondary IMS within your organization, or if you need to restrict what Internet domains your users can send to, you may want to limit the addresses delivered by this IMS. You do this on the sixth page of the wizard. By default, the "All Internet mail addresses" radio button is selected. If you instead select the "Only mail destined for a particular set of addresses" option, the wizard won't create an address space for this IMS, so you'll need to manually configure one on the IMS Address Space property page. (If you need a refresher on address spaces and routing, pop back to Chapter 7 for a quick look.)

Page 7: Site addressing

The seventh page is where you tell the IMS what format to use for site addressing. The address format you supply here is what the SMTP proxy address generator will use when you create new mailboxes in Exchange. Whatever address you enter here will be used as the right-hand side of the SMTP address. This address appears on mail you send out to the Internet, and it is the address people must use to send you mail from the Internet. The Internet Mail Wizard makes a guess at the format you want based on the information it knows. Its guess is *@<site>.<org>.com*, where the Exchange site and organization name are used to build the domain. If its guess doesn't match your actual DNS domain, this is the place to set it straight (although you can also change it using the instructions given in "Configuring Site Addressing" in Chapter 7).

If you want to change this setting after setting up the IMS, go to the Site Addressing tab of the Site Addressing Properties page in the site Configuration container (I know, that's a mouthful). Changing the site addressing can change the addresses of all existing mailboxes; Exchange Administrator will ask you if you want to update existing addresses to match the new format when you make changes.

Page 8: Who's the postmaster?

By convention, SMTP hosts have a mailbox called *postmaster* that gets bounce notifications and other types of abnormal mail. Exchange doesn't automatically create such a mailbox; the eighth page of the wizard allows you to specify where NDRs go. By default, they end up in the Administrator mailbox, but you can choose another mailbox (or DL) to receive them instead. I recommend creating a mailbox called *postmaster* and using it, especially since other sites are more likely to send you administrative mail there.

You can assign alternate recipients to your *postmaster* mailbox; for example, I've configured the *postmaster* account on my servers to have each mail administrator as an alternate recipient. That way, no matter who's in (or out of) the office, *postmaster* mail is always visible to some human.

Page 9: Service account credentials

The ninth step in the IMW is assigning the service account and password. You don't get to specify the account, since its name is read from the directory, but you do have to supply the correct service account password so the IMS can log into the DS and make the necessary changes.

Page 10: Finishing up

The last page that the IMW displays gives you a last chance to back out without actually changing anything. If you click the Cancel button, the IMW exits without making any changes to your system. If you click Finish, the IMS will be installed as an active component, after which the wizard will remind you to run the Performance Optimizer. You really should do this, because when you install the IMS there are several configuration parameters that need to be adjusted accordingly. In fact, on servers with the IMS, I recommend that you not run the Performance Optimizer at the end of the Exchange Setup program, but wait until the IMS is installed.

Managing the IMS

The Internet Mail Wizard installs the IMS, so it should conclude by leaving you with a fully functioning IMS, but it by no means configures every IMS option. In most environments, there are other things you need to configure. Instead of covering every trivial item in the property pages, I will cover only the most important items, particularly those that are poorly documented in the online help.

Setting IMS Properties

When you install the IMS, it appears in the site's Connections container. When you open the IMS' property pages, you'll see a daunting array of eleven tabs, most of which seem to have long names. You've already seen the Delivery Restrictions tab, so we'll ignore it here.

The General tab

The General tab is where the IMS global message size limit is applied. In every other kind of Exchange connector, message size limits apply only to outbound mail. On the IMS, however, the message size limit is applied to both inbound and outbound mail, so you can bounce messages that are too big. This value is the source of the ESMTP SIZE parameter setting that the IMS uses to advertise the size limits to other ESMTP servers.

MIME and UUENCODE encoding of binary attachments may increase their size 10%–30%. The message size limit is applied after the encoding, so if you want to limit your users to 10MB attachments, the limit should be 12–13MB to account for the expansion.

The Connected Sites and Address Space tabs

As you saw in Chapter 7, the Connected Sites tab is what you use to configure connector settings used when talking to other Exchange sites. While the IMS has been optimized to be the fastest connector in the Exchange suite, you may find that its overall performance is comparable to that of the X.400 connector. The IMS has the disadvantage of having to do content type conversion—from MAPI to MIME on the outbound side, then back from MIME to MAPI on the inbound side. This conversion, along with the increased message size caused by MIME encoding of binary attachments, imposes a performance hit. If performance is similar, why use the IMS to connect your Exchange sites? There are two primary reasons:

- The IMS comes with the Standard Edition of Exchange, but the X.400 connector doesn't.

- You can use smart hosts to centralize SMTP routing for several sites connected via IMS.

Just as with every other kind of connector, the primary difference between these two tabs is whether you're connecting to a foreign system or to an Exchange site. Let's talk about the Address Space tab for now. It controls what SMTP addresses this IMS is allowed to deliver to, plus the routing cost of this particular connector.

Recall that an address space contains both a path for routing mail and a number representing the cost of that path. The IMS Address Space tab configures the paths and costs for this IMS. The email domain portion of the address space is compared against the recipient address of a message, in the following order:

1. *Exact match*: the recipient address matches the address space range exactly.

2. *Wildcard match*: the recipient address matches the address space range after all wildcards in the address space range are expanded.

3. *Partial substring match*: the address space range is a substring of the recipient address (for example, *robichaux.net* is a substring of *hsv.robichaux.net* (but be careful—*haux.net* is also a valid substring).

4. *No match*: there aren't any common elements between the two.

When you first run the IMW, it will create an Address Space with an address pattern of * and a cost of 1. If you have multiple servers running the IMS installed, you might split the responsibility for delivering mail between them. For example, let's say BigCorp has two offices, one in San Francisco, and one in Boulder. The two offices are connected by a WAN, and the Internet gateway is in San Francisco. The Boulder site, however, has a research community with several Unix workstations, and their users need to send and receive mail. For Internet connectivity, you've installed an IMS in San Francisco with an address space of *. We could leave it at that, but mail from an Exchange user in Boulder to a Unix user in Boulder will have to traverse the WAN, be converted to MIME, and traverse the WAN back to the Unix system. A much better design would be to install an IMS in Boulder with an address space of *boulder.bigcorp.com*. Now mail to the local Unix hosts will be routed through the local IMS, saving the WAN bandwidth. You could also install multiple IMSs at a single location and split the responsibility for an especially busy domain off to a separate system.

A full discussion of how the MTA builds the routing table and chooses the best route for mail can be found in Chapter 7; that discussion holds here, with one exception. Internet mail will only use the lowest cost route that matches the address specification, period. If there's a communications problem, the IMS will not fail over to a higher cost route, so your mail will sit until you get the problem fixed.

As with other connectors, you can restrict an IMS so that it can only be used by users in a particular location or site. See the section "The Address Space tab" in Chapter 7.

The Diagnostics Logging tab

I didn't talk much about this tab in previous chapters, but the IMS log is useful enough that it deserves some coverage here. You'll normally use it when you're trying to debug a problem with inbound or outbound SMTP delivery, though there are some logs you might want to leave on. If you change logging levels, you'll have to restart the IMS before the change takes effect. Here are the most useful logging categories:

Message Archival

Setting Message Archival logging to Medium or Maximum will cause a copy of every message sent or received by the IMS to be saved to disk. When archiving is enabled, the messages are processed from the *exchsrvr**imcdata*\ *in* and *exchsrvr**imcdata**out* directories on disk, then moved to *exchsrvr*\ *imcdata**in**Archive* and *exchsrvr**imcdata**out**Archive,* respectively. Message archiving is most useful when you're in one of two circumstances: you're required to keep logs of traffic you send to and from the Internet,* or you're trying to track down an interoperability problem with the IMS.

 On an active system, message archiving will rapidly consume disk space. Some method of monitoring or regularly deleting the files should be implemented. You might consider using a script that removes archive files older than a certain date or that backs up old archive messages before removing them.

"What are the files in the Archive directories, and can I delete them?" is one of the most frequently asked questions concerning the IMS. The answer is yes. The files in the archive directories may be safely deleted at any time, but it's better to turn Message Archival logging off by setting it to None if you don't need copies of these messages. Message journaling can copy all messages, not just the IMS messages, and the archived messages go into the IS instead of on your local disk. It's faster, too.

SMTP Protocol Logging

The SMTP Protocol Logging function is the other diagnostic tool you may want to run all the time (but only at Minimum or Medium levels!). This logging function generates log files in the *exchsrvr**imcdata**log* directory. Depending on the log level, the file contains connection and SMTP conversation information for every inbound and outbound message. If your mail delivery is failing, and you can't figure out why, this is a good place to start debugging. Problems with the SMTP sessions will often be very apparent here.

You may infrequently want to see the SMTP message envelope information for a particular message, as well. Within Outlook, you can view the SMTP headers, but not the actual delivery envelope. Through the SMTP protocol logs, you can view the exact address used to send mail to a user as well as the connecting system IP address.

The log levels for this counter are:

None (0)
No text logs are created. This is the default setting.

Minimum (1)
Only connection information is written to the log.

Medium (3)
SMTP commands and headers are written to the log.

---

* Even so, message archiving may be less efficient than message journaling (see Chapter 7), and journaling is much more space efficient.

Maximum (5)

Complete, unformatted protocol packets are written to the log.

 These log files grow over time and are never automatically deleted, so you must either clean them manually or start shopping for a bigger disk.

Table 8-3 shows the other logging categories you can use on the IMS, along with a brief description of their functions.

Table 8-3. Other Logging Categories for the IMS

Category	What It Does
Initialization/Termination	Records events relating to starting and stopping the IMS service
Addressing	Records failures to resolve originator and recipient names in the directory
Message Transfer	Records successes and failures of message transfer to or from the IMS queues
SMTP Interface Events	Records successes and failures connecting to SMTP and other hosts and receiving/transmitting mail, binding to TCP/IP, and accepting connections
Internal Processing	Records failures to create temporary files, access temporary resources, and map SMTP headers to Exchange Extended MAPI properties

The Internet Mail tab

This tab allows you to customize settings that govern how the IMS formats outgoing messages and some aspects of how it interacts with the Internet. The tab itself appears in Figure 8-6.

The Administrator's Mailbox group lets you specify where delivery status notifications go. Click the Change button to specify a mailbox or a DL. Click the Notifications button to configure which notifications get sent: every kind of NDR the IMS can generate, or just a subset. This isn't rocket science, but there's a trick that might make your administrative operation a little easier. If you want multiple people to keep track of the notifications sent to the administrator, you have three options:

- You can specify a distribution list as the administrator mailbox. This will send each notification to all your administrators. This may not be the best way to please this group of people, however, since it means that every bounce message goes to every administrator every time. On an active system, that can amount to a lot of mail.

Figure 8-6. The Internet Mail tab lets you control how outgoing mail is processed and encoded

- You can specify a mailbox (like *postmaster*) and add it as an additional mailbox to the Outlook profile of each administrator. This is a pretty good solution, except that it forces your postmasters to use Outlook, and it commingles bounce messages with real mail, though this can be fixed with filters. I usually recommend this for sites that have one or two administrators.

- You can also create a public folder (called *Postmaster*, for example), tell the IMS to use it for delivery notification mail, then grant permissions to the appropriate administrators. Now all the administrators have access, no special client configuration is necessary (beyond setting up access to public folders), and new users can be added, without any configuration of their desktop, by setting permissions on the folder.

The "Attachments (outbound)" group lets you specify how attachments on outbound messages are encoded. These settings control the default encoding; however, the sending client can request a particular type of encoding, or you can specify encoding rules on a per-domain basis. In most cases, the default settings are acceptable. Turning on MIME and selecting both "Plain text" and "HTML" will cause the IMS to create MIME messages with two message parts, so that the message text is encoded in both text and HTML formats, and the receiving client is left to decide which format to use. Note that this can double the size of all outbound IMS mail. HTML mail is most commonly used if you want to exchange richly formatted content (including images, sounds, and styled text) with users who have HTML-capable clients like Netscape Messenger or Eudora Pro 4.0. If your clients are all using Outlook, you can turn off HTML mail. In general, most postmasters find HTML mail to be an unnecessary source of clutter, so I normally recommend leaving it off.

If you need to, you can choose to use the older UUENCODE standard, but its use is more appropriate on a per-domain basis, since most clients now handle MIME For example, the MS Mail SMTP gateway cannot process MIME messages, so if you are sending mail to recipients in a domain served by that gateway, you can specify that messages headed to that domain should be uuencoded. I shouldn't forget to mention Binhex—don't use it, since all modern Mac mail clients now support MIME.

The Character Sets control group lets you control what character set the IMS will use for outbound MIME and non-MIME messages. Leave this alone unless you find that clients using non-Roman languages can't read your mail; changing it may result in garbled-looking messages on the client side.

You can configure options for particular domains with the E-Mail Domain button. When you click it, you get a dialog that lets you add and remove individual domains, then set the maximum message size, attachment encoding, character sets, and advanced options for those domains. This is an easy way to specify, say, that you want all your mail to *microsoft.com* to use RTF and MIME, but that mail to *lotus.com* shouldn't use RTF.

The "Advanced options" button allows you to configure some settings controlling how the IMS processes outgoing mail. You can control whether outgoing mail may use RTF or not* and whether messages should be line-wrapped. This button also allows you to disable autoreplies and out-of-office notices sent to the Internet, which helps your site be a good Internet citizen. These functions are off by default; you can enable them, but if your users subscribe to mailing lists, this can create a real headache for you, the list administrator, and the other members of the list.

The "Clients support S/MIME signatures" checkbox tells the IMS whether its clients know what to do with S/MIME signed messages. In the not-too-distant future,

---

* Normally, RTF and the Internet don't coexist well, but if you're using the IMS to connect Exchange sites you'll probably want to turn this option on.

all mail clients should support S/MIME signed messages, and this option will become superfluous. For now, in mixed environments where not all clients support S/MIME signatures (Outlook 98 does, but Outlook 97, Exchange, and some varieties of Outlook Express and other POP3/IMAP4 clients don't), the Exchange server can extract the content from the signature wrapper so that all clients can read the contents of the message.

The ever-popular "Convert inbound message to fixed-width font" checkbox lets you turn incoming messages into monospaced, difficult-to-read text. I'm sure there's a good reason for it being here (probably so that messages formatted with space and tab characters will be readable).

The Connections tab

The Connections tab, shown in Figure 8-7, is where you control how the IMS does its job. As you can see, there are a number of things you can set here, all of which are fairly important to getting your IMS running properly.

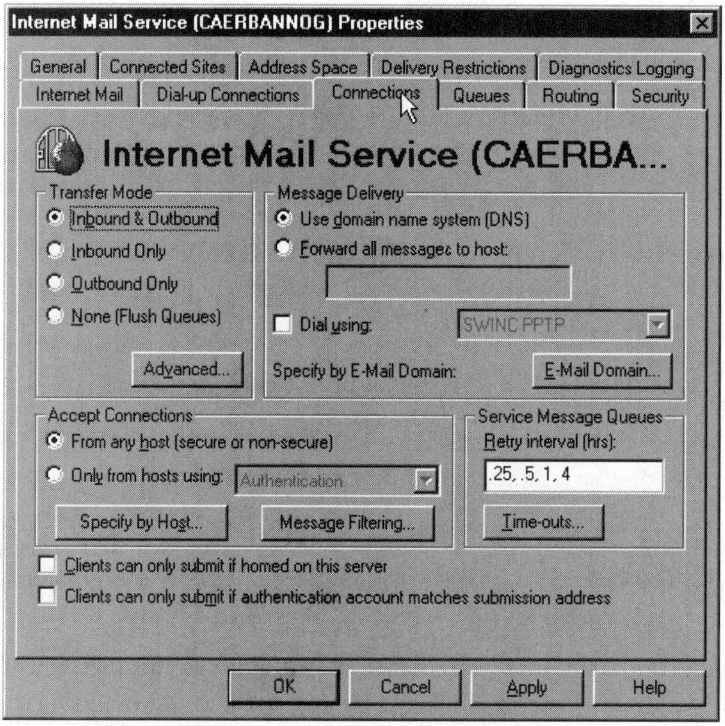

Figure 8-7. The Connections tab controls when and how the IMS connects to other SMTP hosts

The Transfer Mode control group governs what types of traffic the IMS will attempt to pass. The default of "Inbound & Outbound" means that the IMS can both send and receive mail. If your message volume is high, you might want to split the IMS workload in half and use one server for outbound mail and one for incoming mail. You'd accomplish that by adjusting the transfer mode on each server. The "None (Flush Queues)" option is useful for maintenance operations or situations where you are permanently removing an IMS from a server; it allows the IMS to deliver queued mail, but no new mail will be accepted.

The Advanced button in this group lets you adjust the default SMTP connection thresholds of the IMS. Busy sites may need to increase these values to keep the queue from backing up. Dial-up sites, or sites with low bandwidth, may wish to lower the number of connections, while increasing the number of messages per connection, to improve overall efficiency.

The Message Delivery group tells the IMS how to send outbound mail. The default option is "Use domain name system (DNS)," which makes the IMS look up the MX address for each mail recipient in DNS, then connect directly to the destination host to deliver the mail. On dedicated networks with adequate bandwidth, this is the most efficient option. Alternatively, you can set "Forward all messages to host" to specify a single "smart" host and forward all outbound mail to it, letting it do the routing. This may be required if your corporate firewall acts as a mail relay. This option is the best choice if you're using a dial-up connection, since it is more efficient for the mail host to perform all the DNS resolutions and make multiple simultaneous connections for delivery. You can use the "Dial using" checkbox and pull-down to specify a particular dial-up connection to use.

Finally, the E-Mail Domains... button lets you specify these settings for individual domains in the same manner as the corresponding button on the Internet Mail tab. You can specify that a particular domain use DNS, a smart host, or dial-up connections, overriding whatever default choice you originally made. In addition, you can specify that mail for a particular domain be held for ETRN; this causes the IMS to hold mail for the specified domain in the IMS outbound queue until the destination host connects and issues the ETRN command. This may be useful if you are providing ISP-like functions with Exchange (in fact, this feature is used by the ISPs on the Small Business Server referral list to spool and deliver mail to SBS customers) or if you route mail to a subdomain that is only periodically connected.

Now, on to the Accept Connections group. The default setting is to allow connections "From any host (secure or non-secure)." If you want to, you can tell IMS to accept connections only from hosts using SASL, SSL, and/or NT challenge-response authentication; furthermore, by using the Specify by Host... button, you can explicitly reject connections from specific hosts or domains, or require that specific hosts use authentication or encryption. It is important to recognize that if you configure your servers to reject connections from a particular domain, you still may get inbound mail sent from those hosts. If you have a secondary MX configured, then when your server refuses to accept a connection from a banned machine, it will likely fall back to delivering to the secondary MX, which will then deliver the mail unimpeded. You can prevent mischievous users from spoofing mail internally, but it is unlikely you can prevent spoofing from external systems.

The Message Filtering... button (which only appears in Exchange 5.5 SP1 or later) allows you to selectively reject incoming messages; its use is described later in the section "Rejecting Spam." This button is also very useful for stopping mail loops.

The Service Message Queues control group lets you specify the retry schedule for messages whose previous delivery attempts failed. By default, the IMS is configured to retry 15 minutes after the first attempt, then 30 minutes after that, then 1 hour after that, then every 4 hours until delivery is complete or the timeout value is reached (you configure timeouts with the Time-outs... button, surprisingly enough). The default Retry interval for most hosts on the Internet is 30 minutes. In most cases, this is a good balance between wasting time retrying too often and speeding mail delivery. You may want to set the Retry Interval (hrs) field to "0.25, 0.5", or extend the number of retries before the every-four-hour point is reached by using "0.25, 0.5, 0.5, 1, 1, 4."

Mail Delivery from Multiple Hosts

A little-documented option is the ability to specify multiple hosts in the "Forward all messages to host" box by separating them with a comma. This can add redundancy in the case where a single server may go out of service. You would typically only list multiple IP addresses here, but multiple hostnames are acceptable.

You can also specify multiple hosts in the Mail Retrieval dialog ETRN host box by separating them with a comma. If your ISP uses multiple mail hosts to queue your mail, the ETRN command will be sent to each one. If you use the default "Forward all messages to host" value as the ETRN destination, the command will also be sent to all hosts listed there.

The two checkboxes at the bottom of the dialog allow you to control which clients may connect. "Clients can only submit if homed on this server" forces the IMS to reject any message submitted by any sender who doesn't have a mailbox on the IMS server. This provides an additional way to restrict who can send Internet mail. The other checkbox, "Clients can only submit if authentication account matches submission address," tells the IMS to accept mail only from senders whose SASL authentication credentials match the address they're using to send the message.

The Dial-up Connections tab

You use the Dial-up Connections tab, shown in Figure 8-8, to control how the IMS dials up hosts to exchange mail with them. The "Available connections" list box shows all the connections you could potentially use for IMS traffic; before you can change any options for a connection, you must select it from this list. Once you've selected a connection, you can start adjusting parameters.

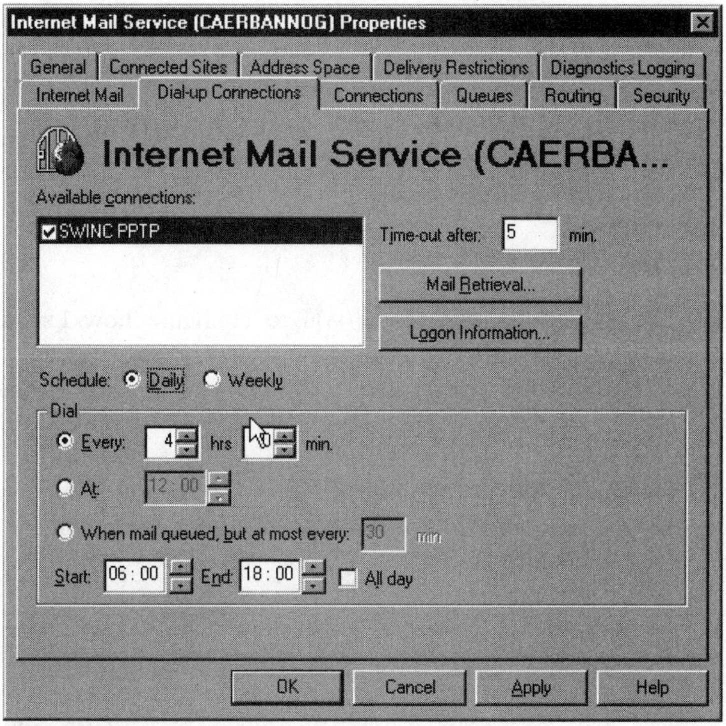

Figure 8-8. The IMS Dial-up Connections tab

Here's what the various controls and control groups on this tab do:

Time-out after X minutes

This field is an idle time counter. After the initial outbound SMTP delivery, the connection will stay open for this period, waiting for inbound mail. If an inbound message is received, the timer restarts. Outbound mail is only sent on the initial connection, so don't set this value too high. If you have lots of incoming mail, the timer will never expire, so the connection will never close and outbound mail will gather dust.

Mail Retrieval

> This button displays the Mail Retrieval dialog so you can choose the method the IMS will use to retrieve queued mail from the ISP mail host. Retrieving queued mail is fully covered in the section "Using Dequeuing" later in this chapter.

Schedule

> This radio button group lets you control whether you want to schedule the IMS connections daily or weekly. The schedule you set applies to every day (or week); there's no way to override it on a day-by-day basis.

Dial

> This control group lets you tell the IMS when you want it to dial out. Most sites set a dial frequency (say, every 2 hours) and leave it alone, but you can schedule outbound calls at a fixed time or whenever mail is queued, if you prefer.

The Security tab

The Security tab (see Figure 8-9) allows you to configure how Exchange uses encryption and/or authentication when making SMTP connections to other servers. This is especially useful when you're using the IMS as a site connector, but you can also protect your connections to business partners, suppliers, or whoever else you want, as long as they're running Exchange or another server that supports the authentication method you choose. For any individual email domain, you have the option of using either NTLM authentication and encryption, or SASL/SSL authentication and encryption.

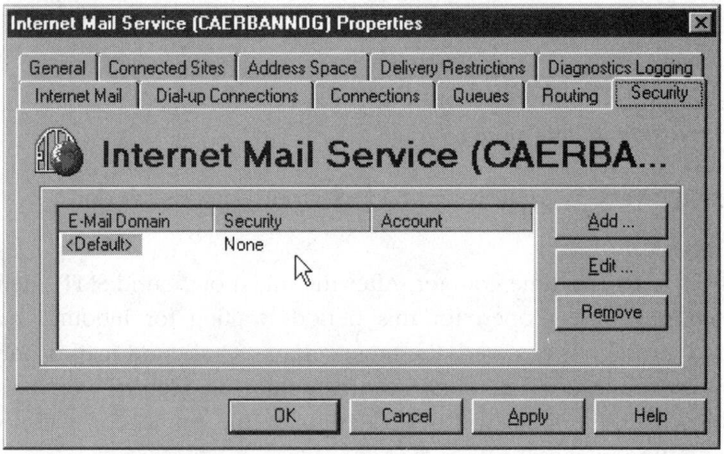

Figure 8-9. The IMS Security tab

Each domain is listed separately. The level of security you choose is shown in the Security column, and the account you've specified (more on that in a bit) shows up in the Account column. To add security for a domain, click the Add... button, and you'll see the dialog shown in Figure 8-10.

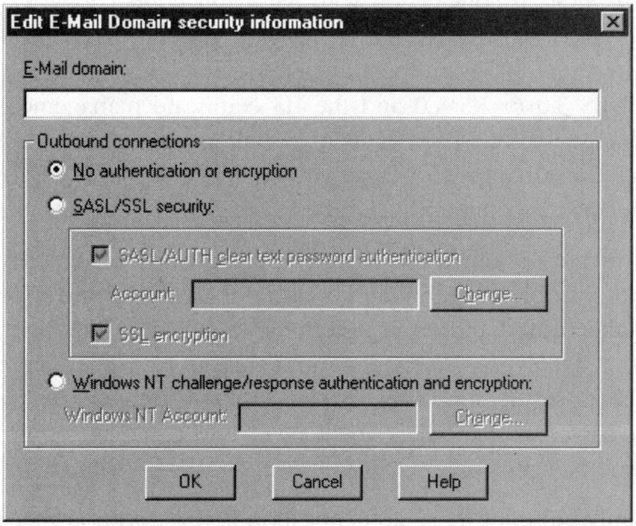

![Edit E-Mail Domain security information dialog box. E-Mail domain field. Outbound connections section with radio buttons: No authentication or encryption (selected), SASL/SSL security (with SASL/AUTH clear text password authentication checkbox, Account field and Change button, SSL encryption checkbox), Windows NT challenge/response authentication and encryption (with Windows NT Account field and Change button). OK, Cancel, Help buttons.]

Figure 8-10. Adding a new security setup for a domain

Start by providing the name of the domain you want to secure. The E-Mail domain field accepts the same wildcard characters as the other IMS dialogs, so configuring security for *.*robichaux.net* will cause security to be used for *zydeco.robichaux.net* also.

Which security settings should you choose? When connecting two Exchange servers, the "Windows NT challenge/response authentication and encryption" option (also called NT LAN Manager, or NTLM) is by far the easiest to configure—all you have to do is turn it on. Unfortunately, you can only use NTLM authentication with other Exchange servers, which may limit its practical usefulness in your setup.

 Once created, the domain entries can't exactly be edited, even though that's what the Edit... button seems to be for. You can change the user and password, but you will need to remove and re-add them to change the domain name the security settings apply to.

When you specify NTLM authentication, you will need to tell your IMS which account to use: this account must come from the NT domain of the Exchange server to which you are connecting. This account does not need to be the Exchange service account—in fact, it shouldn't be! I recommend that you create a separate account specifically for this purpose and strictly limit its permissions.

Using the SASL/SSL options may require some additional work. If you just want to use SSL encryption, you can do so, but that doesn't provide any extra authentication. If you use SASL in conjunction with SSL, your connections will be authenticated and encrypted. To use SASL, you have to generate an X.509 certificate for the receiving host; the SMTP protocol engine uses it. To generate a certificate, you have to install IIS 3.0 or IIS 4.0 and the IIS certificate management tools *before* installing Exchange Server. (The details of installing and configuring the certificate tools are covered in Chapter 16.) Once you've generated an X.509 certificate, you can specify the SASL account and you'll be in business.

A few things to note about these security settings: first of all, they're one-way, because they only apply to outbound connections that your server originates. You can require authenticated and encrypted traffic in one direction, and allow normal traffic in the other direction by enabling authentication or encryption on one end but not on the other. If you want to use SASL to authenticate two-way traffic between your server and another, you'll need two certificates: one for you and one for the remote end.

More significantly, none of these authentication and encryption mechanisms guarantees end-to-end security. You can only force security on the next hop of the SMTP route with these options, so if the server you send the message to relays that message on to another SMTP server, it may not be encrypted at that point. For true end-to-end security, use S/MIME on the client to protect the message before it is submitted to the IMS for delivery.

The Queues tab

The Queues tab allows you to view the list of messages in the various IMS queues. The queues shown in the dropdown list box are the same as those shown earlier in Figure 8-4; Table 8-4 shows what each queue contains and where it's stored.

Table 8-4. IMS Queues

Dialog Selection	Queue	Location
Inbound messages awaiting conversion	IMC Data In	*exchsrvr\imcdata\in*
Inbound messages awaiting delivery	MTS-In	IS
Outbound messages awaiting conversion	MTS-Out	IS
Outbound messages awaiting delivery	IMC Data Out	*exchsrvr\imcdata\out*

As discussed earlier, the MTS queues are integrated with the IS and the IMC Data queues are on disk. The IMC Data Out queue has an entry for each destination host of each outbound message, so there may be more items listed in the queue than files on the disk. Temporary delivery failure information can be found by using the Details... button on a specific message. The display will show the number of retries, a failure description and the next scheduled retry time. A message retry can also be forced through the interface, or a queued message can be deleted.

In extreme cases, you may need to manually remove a corrupt or incorrectly formatted message from a queue. To remove a message from either the IMC Data Out or IMC Data In queues:

1. Stop the IMS through the Services control panel.

2. Remove the bad message file. If you wish to perform further diagnosis, move the file to a temporary directory; otherwise, simply delete it.

3. Restart the IMS.

It's a bit trickier to remove a message from the MTS-In or MTS-Out queues, since they're actually kept in the Exchange private IS. Microsoft Knowledge Base article Q165505 describes how to create a MAPI Profile to access the IS-based IMS queues.

Configuring IMS Routing

Exchange 5.0 allowed its IMC to be used as a generic SMTP routing (or relay) server. POP3 and IMAP4 clients require this feature, since those protocols are only for retrieving mail, and clients still need some protocol to get mail to the server. However, allowing SMTP routing opens up a big can of worms, because the basic SMTP protocol has no authentication mechanism. On a relay server, any outside system can connect and submit a message for delivery—to any destination mail address—and make it appear as if it had been sent by someone else.

The IMS currently supports several types of authentication, but not all mail clients or servers support the authentication methods Exchange supports. The problem is that there are literally thousands of SMTP servers out on the Internet that may try to send you mail, or worse, to relay mail through you. If your domain is hijacked by an unscrupulous user, it may take weeks or months to clean up the mess. Most spam, or UCE (unsolicited commercial email), is sent through mail servers that have not blocked relaying. The spam also is usually forged to appear to have come from the relay host, meaning that all the NDRs (and there might be hundreds of thousands) and nasty replies from the recipients (and there *will* be tens of thousands) will be sent to you. This has been known to shut down even large companies' mail gateways for several days.

If your server is hijacked and used as a spam relay, the long-term impact is that your domain will likely be added to one of the many relay-blocking lists. Many companies and ISPs reject mail from domains on the list out of hand, and clearing your reputation, once tarnished, is no simple task. The easy answer is this: if you don't need SMTP relaying, turn it off. Inbound mail will be delivered if the recipient address matches an entry in the GAL; otherwise, it will generate an NDR.

This doesn't work for all sites, though. If your environment requires you to accept some relay traffic, or if you're using POP3/IMAP4 clients, you'll need to use relaying. If you answered yes when the Internet Mail wizard asked about mail rerouting, then the wizard enabled routing and created an inbound entry for your domain (as configured in the Site Addressing part of the Wizard).

IMS routing exposed

The IMS maintains its own routing table, completely separate from the GWART. This table tells the IMS how to accept and process inbound mail destined for relaying or delivery. Each entry in the routing table consists of a sent-to domain and a route-to domain. The sent-to domain tells you where the mail was addressed; the route-to part tells you (and the IMS) where mail for that particular sent-to domain should go.

The sent-to value is a wildcard domain by default, so a sent-to entry of *microsoft. com* will match mail to the specified domain and all of its subdomains (e.g., *microsoft.com, mail.microsoft.com, exchange.microsoft.com*). You can also use the "#" option character to limit the match to the exact domain, so that *#microsoft.com* will only match *user@microsoft.com*, not *user@exchange.microsoft.com*.

Take a look at Table 8-5, which shows a sample routing table.

Table 8-5. Sample Routing Table

Sent to	Route to
#robichaux.net	*<inbound>*
exchangeheadaches.com	*robichaux.net*
msexchange.org	*<relay>*
robichaux-associates. com	*<inbound>*
bankbuilding.com	*spider.hiwaay.net*

You'll notice that the route-to entries come in three flavors:

<inbound>

Mail sent to a domain whose routing entry is marked *<inbound>* is passed from the IMS MAPI process to the IS for routing. If the address does not match a recipient in the GAL, the message generates an NDR. In the example table, this IMS will attempt to deliver mail to *paul@robichaux.net, david@robichaux-associates.com,* or *arlene@hsv.robichaux-associates.com* to users on the local system; however, it will specifically not route inbound mail to *thomas@hsv.robichaux.net.*

<relay>

Mail sent to a domain marked *<relay>* will be redelivered by the IMS. Relayed messages go from the inbound IMS queue right to the outbound queue, where they're handled as specified on the Connections tab. This entry overrides any relaying restrictions that you've configured. In Table 8-5, mail for *msexchange.org* will be passed to the SMTP outbound delivery queue for delivery based on the configuration of the Connections tab (either via DNS or a smart host).

Domain name

This option allows you to configure a specific destination for mail sent to a particular domain. This option differs from the *<relay>* option in that it rewrites the SMTP envelope with the route-to domain.* This can be quite useful if you want to accept mail for multiple domains, but don't want to maintain Secondary-Proxy-Addresses for all your users. In Table 8-5, mail sent to *jim@bankbuilding.com* will be rerouted to *spider.hiwaay.net* for delivery. Mail to *editor@exchangeheadaches.com* will be rewritten *editor@robichaux.net* and routed inbound.

Configuring routing

You configure the IMS routing behavior with the Routing tab, as shown in Figure 8-11. Once you understand the routing mechanics discussed in the previous section, this tab makes perfect sense. Your first priority is to use the radio buttons at the top of the dialog to turn routing on or off, depending on whether you need it or not. If you turn routing on, the Routing control group becomes active. You can use the Add..., Edit..., and Remove buttons to modify the listed routes and to set their route-to and sent-to portions.

Exchange 5.5 SP2 added an interface for configuring more complex routing rules. The Routing Restrictions... button displays the Routing Restrictions dialog (see Figure 8-12). This dialog allows you to configure a list of hosts that can route based on a set of connection characteristics. For example, you can allow routing from hosts and clients at specific IP addresses, and you can configure a list of hosts that will never be allowed to route mail.

---

* This is similar to the way that Unix sendmail handles address rewriting, only it's not as flexible, or nearly as complicated, as sendmail.

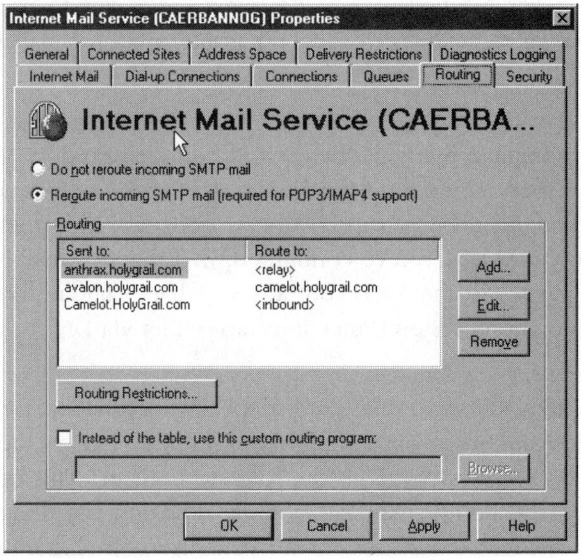

Figure 8-11. The IMS Routing tab

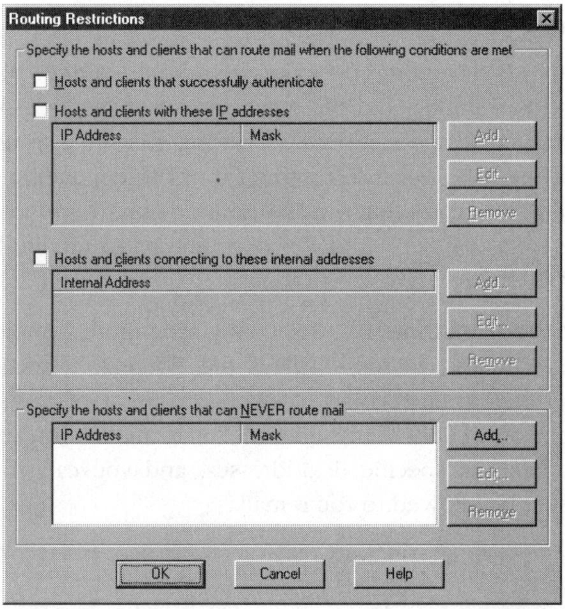

Figure 8-12. The Routing Restrictions dialog is accessible from the IMS Routing tab

If you permit routing at all, you can restrict it to hosts that meet any of the following criteria:

Hosts and clients that successfully authenticate (with SASL or NT challenge/response)

This option effectively covers Outlook Express clients on your network; if you have Unix hosts or other clients that cannot authenticate, you will need to use the second option.

Hosts and clients with these IP addresses

This option allows you to specify specific hosts, or entire subnets. It should cover any client or host on your internal network; specific hosts on a DMZ or the external network could also be configured (firewall for alarm mailing, web server for webmaster or form mailing, etc.).

Hosts and clients connecting to these internal addresses

This option allows you to configure a multihomed server only to accept mail for routing on certain interfaces (internal versus external, for example). IP forwarding must be disabled in the Network control panel for this to function correctly since external users can connect to the permitted IP if forwarding is enabled.

Using Dequeuing

You may have seen the term *dequeuing* used in discussions of the IMS. If so, by now you might be wondering what dequeuing is. It's simple: when you have a dedicated Internet connection, any machine on the Internet that has mail for you opens a connection to your IMS and delivers the mail. The inbound mail doesn't have to be queued anywhere outside your server. On the other hand, let's say you're using a Dial-up Networking connection to your ISP. When you're not actually connected, other Internet hosts can't connect to you to deliver mail. Instead, they connect to your ISP and drop the mail off in a queue. Whenever you connect and pick up mail from that queue, you're dequeuing it. Here's a real-world example: you go on vacation and the FedEx lady tries to deliver a package. Since it requires a signature, she leaves it with your neighbor. When you get home and pick up the package from your neighbor, you've dequeued it.

There's a useful list of dequeuing resources and software on the Simpler-Webb web site at *www.swinc.com/resource/exch_smtp.htm*. Among other things, you'll find the freeware utility *dequeue.exe* and a passel of other useful dequeuing information.

You may remember the earlier description of the ETRN and TURN commands. These two commands instruct your ISP to deliver any mail it's holding, so you'll normally use them to dequeue mail. You control how your server attempts to dequeue mail with the Mail Retrieval dialog box, which you open with the same-named button on the IMS Dial-up Connections tab.

If you're still using Exchange 5.0 without at least Service Pack 1, the only way to send an ETRN to your ISP's mail host when you are not using the Dial-up Connections feature is with an external program. You'll need to schedule the program with *at*, *winat* (reskit), *crond* (shareware), or another scheduling package.

The Mail Retrieval dialog, shown in Figure 8-13, lets you choose whether to dequeue mail with the ETRN command, the TURN command, a custom command, or no command. If you use ETRN, you can choose to have the IMS determine which mail domains should be dequeued, or specify them explicitly yourself. If you let Exchange choose (by selecting the "Derive from Routing property page" radio button), it uses the domains configured as *<inbound>* on the Routing tab, and it assumes that you want to dequeue all the subdomains of any entry in the Routing tab. This setting always uses the @ option of the ETRN command.

Alternately, you can select the "Use these domains" radio button, then list specifically which domains ETRN is used for. Entries here are taken literally, so the option characters listed earlier in Table 8-2 apply.

The ETRN command is sent to the host specified in one of two places. By default, the ETRN command is sent to the outbound mail host as specified on the Connections tab. This requires you to use the "Forward all mail to host" option and specify either an IP address (recommended) or a hostname on the Connections tab. Alternatively, you can specify a specific host by checking the "Send ETRN to specified host instead of outbound mail host" checkbox, then filling in the name of the host you want to use. This option was added in Exchange 5.5 SP2; if you have a previous version and need to send the ETRN to an alternate host, you can either upgrade or use the Custom command radio button (more on that in a few paragraphs) to issue the ETRN.

TURN is also offered as an option for mail retrieval. To overcome the inherent security problems with TURN, Exchange will only send TURN over an authenticated connection. In practice, this means you can use only TURN when connecting to another Exchange server that requires an authenticated connection. As with ETRN, you can require the IMS to send the TURN command to a particular host instead of the outbound mail host.

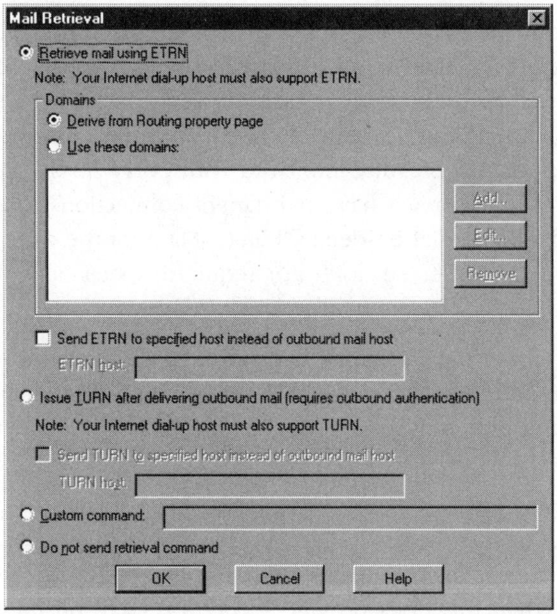

Figure 8-13. *The Mail Retrieval tab*

If your ISP requires some other command or process to initiate mail delivery, you can use the "Custom command" field to launch this process. This can be a batch or command file or executable program. The full path should be specified if the program is not in the PATH environment variable. Also, the program will run in the security context of the Exchange Service Account, so file permissions should be set appropriately.

Last, you have the option to do nothing at all. Some ISPs will initiate the mail delivery automatically when you connect and therefore do not require any sort of trigger.

> Mail retrieval depends on mail queuing. This is not the same as having a single POP mailbox for your company at an ISP, which won't work with Exchange.

Connecting Without a WAN

Many sites don't have a permanent connection to the Internet, so the IMS features that allow on-demand connections are particularly interesting.

Dial-up Connections

Exchange has come a very long way in its support for small companies; in Exchange 4.0, there was little or no support for dial-up users. The flood of small customers who purchased Exchange surprised everyone at Microsoft who had, justifiably, focused on building a product for the enterprise customer. To Microsoft's credit, dial-up support has steadily improved with every service pack and product release. Some Exchange servers have permanent connections to the Internet; others connect via dial-up or dial-on-demand links. Many of the exceptions to the IMS defaults described in earlier sections are required specifically for these dial-up environments.

The requirements for using Exchange over a dial-up connection are not very different from the requirements for using Exchange with a permanent connection, though they are a bit different than those for most basic ISP mail connections.

What you need

Dial-up accounts, such as those provided by companies like AOL, MSN, and CompuServe, are used in small businesses primarily to send and receive mail on an individual basis. While this does provide a way for small businesses to use Internet email, it requires everyone who wants an individual mailbox to have a separate account. Exchange Server provides a much richer solution. By using Exchange Server, small businesses will have a full mail solution for the entire company using a single ISP dial-up account and a single phone line. For small businesses with dial-up accounts, we therefore recommend moving to an ISP that supports the queuing of mail.

It should be noted that small businesses can choose to retain their individual accounts if need be (for example, if they are printed on business cards, and so on), or they can slowly migrate mail being sent to those accounts over to the Exchange Server account.

Now, apart from an ISP account, what else do you need? For dial-up connections, you will need the following:

- The phone number you need to establish a modem connection to the ISP

- A user ID and password to authenticate your connection to the ISP

- An IP address (static or dynamic; it's difficult to find an ISP that can properly set up dynamic IP addresses for use with Exchange, so you're better off with a static address)

- Enough information to correctly configure Dial-up Networking

Configuring DNS

Before you can install and use the IMS, you'll also need DNS service. If you're depending on your ISP for this, you need to have them register a DNS domain name for you and load it into their name server. Once that's done, the ISP still needs to configure several entries in their DNS.

For email service, the ISP should publish two DNS MX records for your domain and a DNS A record for your Exchange host. One MX record points to your Exchange server, and the other points to the ISP's mail host. So DNS excerpts look like this:

```
yourdomain.com              IN    MX    10        yourserver.yourdomain.com
yourdomain.com              IN    MX    20        ISPserver.isp.com
yourserver.yourdomain.com   IN    A     x.x.x.x
```

The ISP should also configure a reverse lookup entry for *yourserver.yourcorp.com* (a PTR record):

```
x.x.x.x      IN     PTR     yourserver.yourdomain.com.
```

In addition, you will need the IP address of the ISP's DNS server for your server configuration, because you'll need it for telling the IMS where to dequeue mail. Come to think of it, you'll also need to know the DNS name and IP address of the ISP's mail host. In some cases, the ISP may have separate hosts for inbound and outbound mail. To configure your Exchange Server, you will need the DNS name and IP address of both hosts.

Configuring your server

To call your ISP, you will need a Dial-up Networking phone book entry for the ISP. You create these with the New Connection icon in the *Dial-up Networking* folder (Start → Programs → Accessories → Dial-up Networking). If this is the first time you have run Dial-up Networking, the DUN wizard will automatically start and lead you through creating a connection.

As I've mentioned, you also have to tell your machine what your DNS domain name is. Open the Network control panel, select the Protocols tab, select TCP/IP, and click the Properties button to bring up the protocol properties dialog. Select the DNS tab and enter your domain name (e.g., *yourcompany.com*) and the DNS name for your Exchange host.

Configuring Exchange

If you used the IMW to configure IMS for a dial-up connection, don't think you can skip this section! It's important to understand what the IMW does so you can duplicate it manually, if necessary. Here's the outline of what you need to do (the specifics are covered in earlier sections):

1. Configure the Dial-up Connections page:

    a. Set the schedule you want to use, according to whatever your mail transfer needs are.

    b. Set the mail retrieval option you want to use. If your ISP supports ETRN, choose ETRN Delivery.

2. Configure the Connections page:

    a. Set "Forward all mail to host" to the IP address of the ISP mail host.

    b. Select Dial Using and choose the appropriate phone book entry.

3. Configure the Routing page:

    a. Disable message routing from outside hosts.

ISDN, DSL, and Cable Modem Connections

Using ISDN, DSL, and cable modems is different from using plain analog modems because the type of hardware you purchase (or are supplied by your ISP) can vary pretty widely. ISDN devices are available as ISA or PCI cards to be installed inside the computer just like an internal modem. These are typically called ISDN terminal adapters (TAs) or ISDN modems. ISDN devices, as well as DSL and cable modems, are also often available as external devices, often called dial-on-demand routers. All of these devices can be typically operated in two modes: dial-up and dedicated. Dial-up is much more common because it's usually less expensive. In a dedicated configuration, the line is up all the time and has the same characteristics as a leased line, including security concerns. The connection type you choose will depend on three factors:

What's available in your area

Where I live, ISDN is ubiquitous but expensive, cable modem service is only available in a few areas, and DSL is being held hostage by BellSouth. Even though DSL would be a great solution for my network, I can't use it, so that makes it somewhat less great.

How much bandwidth you need

If you don't depend on the Internet for your daily business, or if you have a small company, you can probably get by with a relatively slow dial-on-demand connection. If your users depend on fast Internet access, you'll need more bandwidth.

How much money you want to spend

This is often related to what's available; for example, in many places you can get a frame relay circuit for about half the cost of a "real" T-1 line. As long as you don't use the full T-1 bandwidth, frame relay is cheaper; but as soon as you hit that high-water mark, the price goes up sharply. SMTP in and of itself has very modest bandwidth needs, as long as you're exchanging text messages. As soon as you start swapping messages with large attachments, or sharing your Internet connection between HTTP, FTP, and SMTP traffic, your bandwidth requirements are likely to go up.

ISDN terminal adapters

A terminal adapter (TA) is the ISDN equivalent of a modem. As with modems, TA features and pricing vary widely, but all share the same basic feature: they connect your computer to an ISDN line. Optional features include jacks that let you connect standard analog devices, including phones, modems, and fax machines, to your ISDN line, smart firmware that can sniff the ISDN line and configure the TA's settings for you, and the ability to tie two ISDN B channels together to give you 128Kbps throughput.

TAs come in internal and external varieties. External TAs generally require serial ports driven by a 16550 or later UART. Some TAs use drivers that make them appear like network cards, while some impersonate really fast modems. All these devices use a DUN phone book entry to connect to the ISP like an ordinary analog modem, though, so once you get the TA talking to the ISDN line itself you usually don't have to do anything special to use the TA to connect to your ISP—just create the appropriate entry in DUN.

ISDN, DSL, and cable modem routers

These routers are actually dedicated network hardware devices. Even though they're often called routers, they may not actually do any routing—most DSL and cable modem devices are actually bridges. To make things even more confusing, most ISDN devices (like the Ascend Pipeline series) do act as routers. Local traffic stays on your LAN, but packets destined for the Internet (or whomever else you call on your ISDN line) are routed over the ISDN line.

These standalone devices don't normally require you to make any configuration changes to your NT software. Hardware's a different story: with these devices, the Exchange server is typically configured with two network interface cards, one for the internal network, and one for the external network that connects to the router. Whenever there is outbound traffic from the server, the router automatically raises the connection to the ISP. To the clients on the local network and the Exchange server itself, it appears as if there is a full-time connection. What is special about this case is that from the perspective of the ISP hosts, it appears as if there is a normal dial-up connection. There are some special configuration considerations for Exchange Server noted in the next section.

Most DSL and cable modem devices offer permanent connections, but they may assign dynamic IP addresses, so you have to treat them like dial-on-demand devices. If you do get a permanent connection, you must be very careful to ensure that your server security is up to the task. In particular, you need to turn off TCP and UDP ports 137, 138, and 139 on the Internet interface, so you don't expose yourself to incoming NBT traffic. Most security recommendations argue against putting real Exchange servers (e.g., the ones with your important stuff on them) directly on the Internet; it's difficult to get the configuration exactly right, and if you don't, your servers are vulnerable to compromise. Instead, you should probably put an SMTP server outside the firewall. To do this, you can:

- Use the IIS 4.0 SMTP service

- Pass incoming traffic through a proxy server like Microsoft's Proxy Server 2.0 or a firewall like Checkpoint's Firewall-1

- Use an Exchange server with no public or private IS, just an IMS that routes inbound SMTP traffic to your real IMS inside the firewall

- Use a cheap Linux box running sendmail to route inbound traffic to your IMS

Getting your mail

Since there are two different ways to connect—dedicated and on-demand—there are two different ways to set up your Exchange server. Which one you use depends on how you're going to connect.

If you're using a dial-on-demand solution where the network hardware makes the connection for you (like an ISDN router), you're in good shape. Just set the IMS schedules you want to use and specify whether outbound mail should be immediately sent, then kick back and watch the router dial when it's supposed to.

On the other hand, if you're using a device that requires your server to initiate the connection, you've got a bit more work to do. Let's say you want your Exchange server to send outbound mail immediately and receive inbound mail when the connection's already up. Sending is no problem, since the IMS will bring up the connection; but if new mail arrives at the ISP while the connection is down, it'll sit there in the ISP queue until you dequeue it.

In Exchange 5.0, prior to SP1, the only way to send an ETRN to your ISP's mail host, when you are not using the Dial-up Connections tab's features, is with an external program. With Exchange 5.5, you have another option—there's a new registry key that forces the IMS to automatically send an ETRN whenever it connects to deliver outbound mail. The effect of this setting is that any connection to deliver outbound mail will also cause the IMS to pick up queued mail. The one requirement here is that you use the "Forward all mail to:" option for your outbound mail. This will be the server to which Exchange sends the ETRN to trigger the mail delivery. To turn this feature on, add a new `REG_DWORD` value named `AlwaysUseETRN` to the `HKLM\SYSTEM\CurrentControlSet\Services\MSExchangeIMC\Parameters` registry key. Set it to 1 to force the IMS to always send `ETRN`s; set it to 0 to turn it off. This will cause mail to be dequeued from the ISP every time outbound mail is sent from your system; this may not be regular enough to meet your inbound mail requirements, so you may need to force the issue by scheduling the delivery of a dummy mail message at the frequency that you desire. One alternative is to use a link monitor to generate the test message. Another alternative is to use a scheduling package like *at* or *winat* to run a command-line utility that sends the mail message.

If your ISP does not support `ETRN`, both you and the ISP should select a mutually agreeable dequeuing method, perhaps using the list of dequeuing resources mentioned in "Using Dequeuing," earlier in this chapter.

Dynamic IP addressing

I said earlier that dial-up *requires* a fixed IP. I wasn't entirely lying. Typically, SMTP mail delivery requires a fixed, or dedicated, IP address. This is due to the mechanisms used to route and deliver mail on the Internet. SMTP mail relies on DNS MX records to direct mail for a domain to a destination. The MX record points to a DNS A record, which contains a static IP address. If you don't have an A record (and you won't, if you get a new dynamic IP every time your machine dials your ISP), you'll be out of luck.

While it is possible for the ISP to devise a solution to this issue, it has been very uncommon. In fact, most ISPs don't bother to try. Microsoft came up with a WINS-based solution for the Small Business Server Edition of Exchange, but that's no help for those using the Standard or Enterprise editions of Exchange. If you want to use your Exchange server for Internet mail, and your ISP can't or won't give you a fixed IP address, you have some alternatives:

- If the ISP is running Exchange, you can use the SASL-authenticated `TURN` option to dequeue mail without a fixed IP.

- There are a couple of dynamic DNS registries like monolith (*www.ml.org*) available on the Internet. Every time you connect, you tell the service what your current dynamic IP address is, and the service updates its own DNS A record for you and publishes it. Your ISP maintains the MX record that points to the A record at Monolith, or wherever. I haven't seen this used with Exchange in practice, but it works in theory.

- If your ISP supports PPTP (Microsoft's software VPN solution, which is also supported by a number of other VPN vendors), there's another creative solution. Using a modem or dial-on-demand router, you can make the standard dial-up connection to the ISP, which assigns a dynamic IP. You then use RRAS to set up a PPTP session to a PPTP server at the ISP. Over the PPTP connection, the ISP can allocate a fixed IP address out of a private, nonroutable range (see RFC 1918) and configure it to be dedicated to your account. You then use **ETRN** to dequeue the mail over the VPN connection. I have seen this used in production before, and it works well even though at first blush it seems rather complicated.

Rejecting Spam

If you get mail, you probably also get spam. Way back in 1992, a pair of lawyers in Tucson, Laurence Cantor and Martha Siegel, started blasting ads for their immigration services to USENET groups. The idea caught on, and now my mailbox gets anywhere from two to twenty spam messages a day, advertising everything from pornography to golf balls.

To users, spam is an annoyance; to mail administrators, it's a burden. Not only do your servers have to handle the incoming spam load; you'll probably find yourself having to answer user questions about what the mail is and where it came from. Luckily, Exchange 5.5 includes some features that allow you to reduce the amount of spam delivered to your server; these features were enhanced in SP1 and SP2.

 If you want to know (lots) more about spam, check out O'Reilly's *Stopping Spam*, by Alan Schwartz and Simson Garfinkel. This section teaches you only how to use Exchange to cut back on inbound spam, not how to help stamp it out permanently.

The Message Filtering... button in the IMS Connections tab is your gateway to Exchange's spam-fighting features. By using the Exchange message filters, you can reject mail based on the RFC 821 "MAIL FROM" address (the "from" address on the message envelope). When you open the Message Filtering dialog, you'll see that you can give the IMS a list of specific domains whose mail you never want to see. Like other domain-specification dialogs, you can specify absolute domains, or wildcard domains, like this:

```
@foe.com// reject mail from foe.com or any subdomain
#@foe.com// reject mail from foe.com, but not a.foe.com
```

When filtering mail, you can choose either to have the mail automatically deleted or saved in what Exchange calls a *turfdir*. You can always go back and look in the *turfdir* to see what kind of harvest your filters have gathered, but there's a twist. The IMS will automatically create the registry key that specifies where the *turfdir* is, but it doesn't create that directory. To change the location:

1. Create a *turfdir* directory where you wish the messages to be stored (e.g., *D:\ exchsrvr\imcdata\turfdir*).

2. Use the registry editor of your choice to find the **TurfDir** value under the following key in the registry:

   `HKLM\System\CurrentControlSet\Services\MSExchangeIMC\Parameters\`

3. Highlight the **TurfDir** value, select Edit → String, and enter the full path (including the drive letter) to the *turfdir* you want to use.

4. Quit the registry editor.

5. Restart the IMS.

Performance and Registry Tuning

In high-traffic environments, moving the IMS to a standalone system is the best way to improve its performance. Moving DNS resolution and content conversion to a dedicated server frees up the mailbox server to do its primary job. You can also spread IMS traffic over multiple systems. Beyond moving things around, there are some tweaks you can apply that may or may not help performance. Except in extreme circumstances, you should stick with what the Performance Optimizer configures and avoid fiddling with these parameters. If you decide to change any of these settings, be very methodical in your changes and measurements. It is entirely possible to throw the balance off and end up worse off than you started. It is also possible to change too many things at once and not know which had what effect.

The IMS, like the rest of Exchange, has its most commonly used configuration features in the GUI. There are, however, several registry keys that may be useful to know, all of which live under the **HKLM\SYSTEM\CurrentControlSet\ Services\MSExchangeIMC\Parameters** registry key:

AcceptMalformed821Adrs

Setting this **REG_DWORD** value to 1 will cause the IMS to accept invalid addresses. Some older mailers use characters like "=" in their addressing, which requires an exception to the RFC-defined addressing rules.

AlwaysUseETRN

This **REG_DWORD** forces the IMS to always send **ETRN** commands when its value is set to 1; set it to 0 to turn it off. This will cause mail to be dequeued from the ISP every time outbound mail is sent.

DestinationDomainThreshold

By default, the IMS caches up to 1000 DNS resolution queries for performance reasons. However, there are situations where this is undesirable, such as load-balancing smart hosts. This REG_DWORD key can be used to shrink the size of the cache, or disable it completely by setting its value to zero. Be aware that this may cause a significant performance hit if your Exchange Server is using DNS for mail delivery, as configured on the Connections tab.

DisableResolverSearchList

The IMS may incorrectly process the DNS search list before attempting name resolution if you are using wildcard MX records. As described in KB article Q150969, the use of the search list can be disabled by setting this REG_DWORD value to 1.

DisableReverseResolve

By default, the IMS will attempt a reverse DNS resolution of each host or client that connects to it. In environments with large communities of POP or IMAP users whose addresses aren't in the DNS server, this will cause connection times for sending outbound mail to be quite long (1–5 minutes). This action can be disabled by setting this REG_DWORD value to 1. If at all possible, the better solution to the problem is to get the clients correctly registered in DNS. The Windows NT WINS service provides a method for registering DHCP addressed systems automatically, too.

RerouteViaStore

This value (a REG_DWORD) controls whether the IMS will send message traffic to the private IS for message journaling (see "Message Journaling" in Chapter 7 for more details on how journaling works). If you don't add this value and set it to 1, IMS traffic won't be included in the journal.

ResolveP2

With P2 resolution on, Exchange will attempt to resolve the recipient of inbound mail to the appropriate Display Name from the GAL. This can hide the fact that the mail originated outside the Exchange system and make it more difficult to recognize forged mail. P2 Resolution is off by default in Exchange 5.0 and later, but was on by default in Exchange 4.0. If your server has been upgraded from Exchange 4.0, this is most likely still enabled; set this REG_DWORD to 0 to turn it off.

There are also four settings that you shouldn't change manually. You can increase their values to increase the number of available threads if your server is heavily loaded; however, it's best to let the Exchange Performance Optimizer do the work. These values are exposed in the verbose mode of Performance Optimizer (as described in Chapter 18, *Managing Exchange Performance*, and Appendix B, *Useful Performance Monitor Counters*):

InboundThreads

The InboundThreads value is a REG_DWORD that controls the number of threads used by the Inbound MAPI process for content conversion and queue management.

InOutThreads

The InOutThreads value controls the number of threads shared by the Inbound MAPI and Outbound MAPI processes.

OutboundThreads

The OutboundThreads value, also a REG_DWORD, controls the number of threads used by the Outbound MAPI process for content conversion and queue management.

ThreadsPerProcessor

The ThreadsPerProcessor setting determines the number of inbound and outbound SMTP delivery threads active on the server. This is distinct from the number of connections values that are configured through the Connections Tab.

9

Managing the Directory

The new phone book's here!
The new phone book's here!
—Steve Martin
The Jerk

Knowing how to control what the Exchange Directory Service does is critical to keeping your server operating properly, because every message and item that passes through the MTA or the IS must have its addressing information checked by the directory. In addition, the directory contains an astonishing number of invisible objects whose presence is crucial to Exchange's normal functions.

Directory Management Basics

The phrase *directory management* covers a multitude of sins in this chapter. Naturally, one important management task is putting information into (or removing it from) the directory. For the most part, this happens automatically when you create or remove mailboxes, custom recipients, DLs, and so on. You can also import information by using Exchange Administrator's directory import function, as discussed in Chapter 5, *Using Exchange Administrator.*

That's too simple a definition, though, because it ignores the concept of sharing directory information between multiple servers. So let's expand our horizons a bit by defining a few new terms. *Directory replication,* or just *replication,* is the process of completely or partially replicating directory information between two or more Exchange servers. *Directory synchronization,* or *dirsync,* is the process of synchronizing changes between Exchange and a foreign system. The two processes are obviously similar, but there are some subtle differences in their Exchange implementations, not to mention some pitfalls to watch out for when planning and implementing a replication or dirsync system.

Replication Nuts and Bolts

While it's not necessary to understand all the mechanics that underlie the replication mechanism, it's certainly helpful. Mail-based and RPC replication operate the same way; the differences lie primarily in how container data are replicated and how the replication messages travel.

Tracking what needs to be replicated

The directory uses a variety of indicators to keep track of which items need to be replicated, which items have been replicated, and what has been changed. These indicators fall neatly into three separate categories: naming contexts, naming context replication attributes, and object replication attributes.

Naming contexts provide a scope for their subordinate objects. Each scope has its own DN; for example, the Organization naming context has a DN of o=*OrganizationName*. There are five naming contexts in a single-site organization: Organization, Address Book Views, Site, Configuration, and Schema. Those who were awake while reading Chapter 5 will probably recognize that there are containers in Exchange Administrator with these same names—that's because a naming context is the directory equivalent of a container. For example, the *USA* site in the *RobichauxAssociates* organization represents both the container for the site and a naming context for that site.

As you might expect, each of these naming contexts has attributes that control whether, when, and how objects that live in that context are replicated to other servers. Table 9-1 shows the naming context attributes and explains what they're for. Note that since these attributes are attached to individual naming contexts, different contexts can have different attribute values.

Table 9-1. Naming Context Replication Attributes

Attribute	What It Does
Period-Rep-Sync-Times	Dictates when the DS will request changes from servers on the current Reps-From list.
Replicator notify pause after modify (secs)	Registry value (living in `HKLM\System\CurrentControlSet\Services\MSExchangeDS\Parameters`) that controls how often the DS will notify servers on its Reps-To list that changes have been made to the local directory. Change this value to override the default five-minute replication timer.
Reps-From	Lists all the servers from which this particular DS will accept updates.
Reps-To	Lists all the servers this particular DS will send naming context changes to.
Reps-To-Ext	Lists the servers from which this DS will accept incoming requests for replication data.

If you look at the Reps-From and Reps-To attributes in Exchange Administrator's raw mode, you'll see that there are some additional flags like Periodic sync, Init sync, and Mail replica. These flags appear on each naming context's attributes, and the DS uses them to tell whether that naming context should be replicated via RPC (to other servers in the site) or mail.

Directory objects themselves have their own set of attributes. These attributes make it possible for the Exchange DS to tell when any directory object has been changed, and whether the version in its local directory is newer or older than the version its replication partner is offering. Each object has what Microsoft calls a *unique sequence number* (USN). The USN of an object in a local directory is incremented every time that object is changed. Each object's USN may be different in different directories: the USN for my mailbox on one server isn't necessarily the same as the USN on the same object on another server or in another site.

There are six key object replication attributes; you can see any object's replication attribute values by running Exchange Administrator in raw mode and opening the object's properties dialog. Table 9-2 lists the attributes and explains what they do.

Table 9-2. Object Replication Attributes

Attribute	What It Does
Obj-Dist-Name	Identifies the complete distinguished name (DN) of the object, including all naming contexts in which it participates. Every object in a directory must have a unique DN; the DN is the master identifier that Exchange uses.
Object-Version	Identifies how many times the object has been changed. Change number 1 happens when the object is created; after that, each time the object changes, this value is incremented. If replication completes normally, this value will be the same for all copies of a single object in a site, because the object has been changed the same number of times no matter what server directory you look at.
DSA-Signature	Identifies which server directory made the most recent change to the object. This attribute value is actually an Invocation-ID, a unique ID assigned to each directory in a site.
USN-Changed	USN value assigned by the local directory when the most recent change was made to the object.
USN-Created	Preserves the USN-Changed value that was current when the object was first created.
USN-Source	Copies the USN-Changed value the object had on the server where it was changed. The USN-Source value tells you what USN value the object had before it was replicated to your server.
When-Changed	Indicates when the object was changed.

There are some interesting subtleties to how the Exchange DS uses these attribute values:

- You can always tell which directory was the last one to touch an object by looking at the object's DSA-Signature value. To find the matching directory, look at each directory's raw properties until you find the Invocation-ID that matches.

- Be aware that the USN-Created value never changes once it's assigned. If it does get changed, bad things will happen, so never tamper with it in raw mode.

- USN-Source doesn't change when an object is locally modified, but only when the object is modified because a change arrived from another server.

Replication messages

Now you know how the directory keeps track of which items need to be replicated; it knows how often the object has been changed (by the object's Object-Version attribute), what the last replication change was (by the object's USN-Source attribute), and what the last local change was (by the object's USN-Changed value). The DS uses this information to collect changes for replication, but the actual replication process involves a three-step mating dance between the two replication bridgehead servers. Note that this process takes place separately for each naming context that has changes in it, and that the messages I'm discussing can pass via either RPC or mail.

The first step is for the sending server to generate a *notification* message, which goes to whatever servers are listed in the naming context's Reps-To attribute. The only thing in the notification message is the name of the naming context and server that have been changed. All this message does is alert the receiving servers that changes exist.

The receiving server generates a *request* message to ask for replication changes. The request message may come in response to a newly arrived notification message, because the time specified in the Period-Rep-Sync-Times value of the naming context has arrived, or because you used Exchange Administrator to force the DS to ask for a replication update. In any case, the request message names the server and naming context from which changes are being requested, along with the USN value of the last change for that context that the requesting server received. This allows the sending server to determine which changes have already been sent in a previous replication message.

When the request message arrives back at the sending server, it knows what naming context the requestor is interested in, so it starts packaging changes into a *response* message. RPC responses can contain a maximum of 100 changes; mail responses can hold up to 512. The sending server will build as many responses as necessary to send all the changes back to the requestor. Each response message contains the name of the server that's sending the changes, the naming context to which the changes apply, and a list of objects to be replicated. To avoid attribute mismatches, each replicated object includes all of its attributes, not just those that have changed.

Resolving replication collisions

What happens when the same object is modified at the same time in more than one server in a site? For example, let's say you have a distribution list that includes all managers. At the same time, two of your administrators modify the distribution list membership to reflect a new hire in Dallas and a retirement in Chicago. Since the same object has been modified in more than one place, and since the changes are different, the DS has to figure out what to do. Here are the steps that the DS uses to decide:

1. It compares the Object-Version of the replicated object to the copy already in the local directory. If the replicated object's version is higher, it's loaded into the directory. If it's lower, the replicated item is ignored, since it's older than the existing object.

2. If the Object-Version values are identical, the DS compares the DSA-Signature values of the incoming and local objects. If the signatures match, the replicated object is loaded into the directory.

3. If the signatures don't match, the DS compares the When-Changed values of the two objects, and the most recent change is loaded into the database.

Replication

Each Exchange server maintains its own local directory. When you use Exchange Administrator (or another mechanism, like ADSI or the Exchange Administrator directory import feature) to make changes to directory information, that change is first made to the target server's local directory. If you add a recipient to a server, then throw it out the window, that change will be lost, because it was only made to the local directory on the server, which is now spread all over the pavement below your office window.

However, if you have a site with multiple servers, replication may save you. Intrasite replication is completely automatic: every server in a site has a connection to every other server. When you make a change to a directory object on a server, within a specified time (which defaults to five minutes, but see Table 9-1 earlier for details on how to change it) that server will start sending RPC notification messages to other servers in the site. Each server that receives a notification can then request a directory update from the originating server. The originator sends the update (again using RPC) and the receiver records the new data in its local directory. After a short interval, the change will have been propagated to the local directories of all servers in the site.

To enable replication between sites, you must first set up and configure mail connectivity. That's because intersite replication data travels as mail messages, so unless the two sites are able to exchange ordinary mail messages, directory replication won't be possible. You must also set up and configure directory replication connectors, as discussed in Chapter 7, *Managing Connectors and the MTA*. These connectors, which run on the directory replication bridgehead server in each site, monitor changes to the local directory on that server. Every so often, they package all changes made to the local directory since the last update and send a message over whatever transport the directory replication connector is using. Intersite directory replication is always point-to-point: the replication bridgehead server in one site talks to another site's replication bridgehead, and that's it. If you want to link more than two sites, each pair of sites has to have its own set of replication connectors. Changes received by a server go into its local directory; from there, the changes are copied to other site servers through the normal intrasite replication process.

Obviously, replication is the way to go if both you and the people you need to talk to are running Exchange and you're in the same organization. If you need to replicate directory information between two organizations, you're out of luck. Exchange 5.5 SP2 adds a new tool called the InterOrg Replication Utility, but, despite the promise implied by its name, it handles only public folder replication, not directory replication. If you must replicate data between organizations, first read the next section to see whether directory synchronization will meet your needs; if that doesn't convince you, see the section "But I really want to replicate between organizations!," later in the chapter.

Dirsync

Directory synchronization sounds just like replication, but it isn't. Replication is simple-minded mirroring of changes from one directory to another, but *synchronization* implies a basic difference: when you synchronize two directories, you're not just making them clones. Instead, you're actually making changes to *both* directories so that the data in them matches. For example, let's say you work for an engineering services firm whose biggest client accounts for 85% of your business. Since most of your firm's work is done with one client, it's reasonable to want to have access to their directory data, and vice versa.

Of course, nothing says you have to synchronize the *whole* directory. In fact, there are very good reasons not to. Many companies consider their internal organizational structure to be sensitive, since knowing that Joe Blow is the manager in charge of Project X can be useful data to a competitor. Likewise, most organizations don't need or want to synchronize all of their DLs, custom recipients, and public folder information to their synchronization partners. Exchange lets you control what specific directory items get transferred via dirsync.

A shocking true story: I used to work for a company that made X.500 directory software. We were approached by someone from a Very Secret Agency. They wanted to synchronize their directory data with another Very Secret Agency, but in such a way that only the names would be mirrored. That way, if Mr. X wanted to send Ms. Z a message, he could, because Ms. Z would be in his GAL; but none of her organizational information would be mirrored. There's more, too: [censored].

The old-style way to implement this would be to periodically export all the data from your directory and send it to your client; they could import it into their mail system, then send you their directory. The difference between this approach and Exchange's dirsync is like the difference between washing your car by hand and taking it to the car wash. Either way, your car gets clean, but one approach is a lot easier on you and much easier to repeat when needed.

There are some dirsync-related issues that don't pose problems for replication. By definition, dirsync involves synchronizing dissimilar directories, so the first evident problem is that the formats and schemas of the two directories may be very different. For dirsync to work well, the dirsync connection must be smart enough to avoid creating duplicate entries, and there must be some relatively easy way for each end of the connection to control what goes over to the other side. Let's see how you can address these requirements using Exchange's dirsync tools.

I'm not addressing cc:Mail or Microsoft Mail dirsync in this chapter. The Exchange documentation covers them in great detail.

Point-to-point dirsync

Point-to-point dirsync involves two systems: your Exchange servers and a single foreign directory. This is the most common type of dirsync. In Exchange, point-to-point dirsync is implemented by connectors, including the Notes, cc:Mail, MS Mail, OfficeVision, and Verimation MEMO connectors (the last two are actually handled by the SNADS connector). The specific items that get synchronized vary between connectors; for example, you can configure the Notes connector to include or exclude specific attributes.

You can tell Exchange which specific directory attributes it should replicate between Exchange sites using the Attributes tab of the DS site configuration properties dialog.

In general, point-to-point dirsync is fairly easy to set up and administer. You have to tell Exchange what directory objects and attributes you want to send to the other side; if the connector you're using allows it, you may be able to configure it so that you control how foreign and Exchange attributes are mapped to each other. (The Notes connector allows this; other third-party packages may also.) You can also use trust levels to control which items are replicated. First, you apply a trust level to each individual mailbox, recipient, or DL; then you set a trust level on the connector. Only items whose trust level is equal to or smaller than the connector's trust level will be replicated.

One-way dirsync

You can easily describe one-way dirsync as a way to get address information from foreign systems into the Exchange GAL. Since it's unidirectional, changes propagate in one direction, from the foreign system into Exchange. There are several different ways you can implement one-way dirsync, depending on the foreign system's capabilities. These methods share five basic steps.

First of all, you have to find the data source you're going to use. This might be an LDAP server (if your foreign system has one), a Unix *passwd* file or Network Information System (NIS) database, or some other collection. Nothing says the data source has to be a file; it could just as easily be your corporate phone book or your human resources department's database.

 Here's a handy suggestion: use the Trust Level field on mailboxes, DLs, and custom recipients to screen out stuff you don't want replicated. Although Exchange doesn't pay attention to this field unless you're doing an MS Mail dirsync, your own scripts and tools can be made to replicate only those items whose trust level is high enough to meet your requirements.

Once you've identified the source, the second step is to extract data from the data source and format it in a way that Exchange can understand. The least common denominator approach to one-way dirsync is to export a list of directory objects from the foreign system into some kind of delimited ASCII file, then slice and dice it with a Perl script, Excel macros, a Visual Basic application, or whatever else you're comfortable writing. The processing script has to take the data from the foreign system and make it conform to the format Exchange Administrator's directory import functions expect to see. (This is exactly what the Exchange Migration Wizard does when you run it: it extracts the foreign system's address data, makes it into a CSV file, and slurps it into the local site's local directory.)

For this step to be successful, you'll need to understand what attributes are available in the Exchange directory, because you may find that there are fields in your data source that you want to keep but that don't have direct Exchange counterparts. In that case, you can hark back to the coverage of custom attributes in Chapter 5 and set up custom attributes for whichever fields Exchange doesn't already support. If you don't have any clue what attributes you want to use, see the discussion of the Import Header Tool in Appendix A, *BORK Tools*.

For efficiency's sake, you might want to make your processing script smart enough to skip data that hasn't changed since the preceding day. For example, if every day you import a 15,000-item address list from PROFS into your Exchange server, and only 15% of the items in the list have changed, why not skip processing the 12,750 items that haven't changed? One simple way to do this: keep two days worth of data, then use *diff* or a similar tool to cull everything that's not a change.

The third step is actually moving the data from the originating system to your Exchange server. This may be easy or hard, depending on how the two systems are interconnected, if at all, and whether they share any type of network or physical media connectivity (for instance, you can't write a FAT floppy with an IBM S/390). You can use network connections if you have them, bearing in mind that some of the information, like U.S. Social Security Numbers, hire dates, and so on, may be sensitive. For example, it's not hard to schedule an FTP session to automatically move the files nightly.

The fourth step is importing the new data into the server. If you've successfully completed the preceding steps, this step is easy: just use Exchange Administrator to import the data. You may find that your work from the second step needs to be redone if you and Exchange disagree on the data's format or the attribute names you specify for loading. That leads me directly to the fifth step.

What's the fifth step? Being able to automate and repeat your synchronization when necessary, of course. Most organizations change over time: people join and leave, get married or divorced, change their names, get promoted, and so on. (In fact, Microsoft estimates that around 20% of their directory changes are due to employee moves and name changes!) That's why it's a good idea to develop a script for step two; even if it's a pain in the neck to get it written, once it's written you can use it over and over and over. You can also use scheduling tools (like *cron* on Unix or *at/winat* on NT) to automate the processing, transfer, and loading of the data. That way, you can schedule synchronization the same way you'd schedule replication.

Any-to-any dirsync

Point-to-point dirsync is all well and good, unless you're some humongous corporation like GE or British Aerospace. In that case, it's very likely that your Exchange systems will need to exchange directory information with many different systems. It's also likely that some or all of those systems are running on big mainframes. If this describes your situation, there's good news and bad news. The bad news is that Exchange itself doesn't offer you any direct help. The good news is that there are solutions, but they all come from third parties.

The first is to hire Microsoft Consulting Services (MCS) and get them to install the Exchange Enterprise Directory Connector. This grandly named product (formerly sold by LinkAge under the name "LinkAge Directory Exchange") pulls directory data from a source you specify, stuffs it into a Microsoft SQL Server database, and uses the recorded data to synchronize your Exchange directory with any number of foreign systems. I confess to not knowing how much this solution costs, but I'm sure it's expensive. Microsoft says that average implementation time varies from 5 to 20 days, so draw your own conclusions.

The second method is a little more convoluted. Since you can use the one-way methods described above to import data from anywhere,* you can construct a chain of one-way synchronizations that pull data from the various and sundry systems you need to import from. The downside to this approach is that you can quickly get stuck in the tar pit of daily maintenance. Most of us have better things to do each day than laboriously verify that all ten of our synchronization scripts ran and that the changes made it into the site directory. While on the surface this method would seem to be cheaper than the Enterprise Directory Connector, ask yourself how the number of man-hours necessary to maintain the two solutions compares, say, over a two-year period. That may make the MCS solution a lot more palatable.

But I really want to replicate between organizations!

All right, I admit it: I used misleading language earlier. The truth is that you *can* synchronize directory information between organizations, but all your choices have constraints. Basically, you can choose between expensive but supported, cheap but unsupported, or roll-your-own solutions.

Let's start with the expensive-but-worth-it tool: the LDAP Synchronization Utility (LDSU) from Compaq/Digital. LDSU runs on a server somewhere in your organization and uses the LDAP protocol to synchronize two directories. As long as you can arrange LDAP access between the two organizations you want to synchronize,

---

* Anywhere, that is, that you have access to, providing you're savvy enough to get data out of it and massage it into Exchange format before it hits your server.

LDSU will do the work for you. Basically, once it's set up, you can just leave it alone; it has earned a reputation as a very stable and robust product. The bad news: it costs U.S. $20,000 just to get started—see *www6.service.digital.com/ems/ ldsu/* for full details. You may find, though, that having a stable automated process is cheaper over the long term than a solution with lower up-front costs. Of course, you can use the Enterprise Directory Connector I mentioned earlier to link Exchange organizations, as well as whatever other systems you may have to contend with.

Now, on to the cheap-but-risky category. The BORK includes a tool called the InterOrg Synchronization Tool (or IOST; it's covered in more detail in Appendix A). It's instructive to note what Microsoft says about it:

> Inter-organizational directory synchronization is a complex process and should be undertaken only by certified Microsoft Exchange specialists. In addition... [this tool] is provided separately and with little or no support.

That's Microsoft shorthand for "here there be dragons." To use IOST, you must have SMTP connectivity between replication bridgehead servers in the two organizations you want to link. One bridgehead acts as the *master*; the others act as *requestors*. Each bridgehead server sends its updates to the master, which collects them and stores them in a JET database on the master server. Every so often, the master updates its master copy of the directory and sends it back to the requestors. This architecture is similar to the one used for intersite replication, but it can span two or more organizations. (Interestingly, the master also acts as a requestor, sending its local site's updates to the master database, which has nothing to do with the bridgehead server's local directory.)

To set up IOST, you have to do a number of things to the master and each requestor:

1. Install IMS on each bridgehead if it's not already there and add two mailboxes to each server: one for the master and one for the requestor. Test the IMS to make sure you can use it to send SMTP mail back and forth between the master and each requestor.

2. Run the IOST installer from the BORK on each server. The installer will let you choose whether you want the target server to be a master or a requestor.

3. On the master, use the IOST property pages to tell the master IOST which requestors it has permission to talk to.

4. On each requestor, use the IOST property pages to tell the requestor what to synchronize (mailboxes, custom recipients, and/or DLs), what master to talk to, and which Recipients container to use for export.

There's a mind-numbingly complete document, "MS Exchange Inter-Organization Directory Synchronization Planning Guide," that covers the specific details of setting up IOST on the MS TechNet CD (look in the Technical Notes section of the Exchange materials).

Once the IOST is running, it will send updates every 24 hours. You can request an immediate synchronization and set the time and days you want synchronization to occur, but there's no way to synchronize more frequently. You can also force the IOST master to send a complete copy of the directory to a requestor, or you can force a requestor to ask for a complete copy; to do either of these, use the Export and Import USN fields on the requestor property pages. You do, however, have some periodic maintenance tasks to do. Most notably, you'll need to periodically clean up the requestor and master mailboxes on all servers; outgoing directory data gets filed in the Sent Items container, and imported information is moved from the Inbox to the Deleted Items container. You'll need to run the Mailbox Cleanup Agent (described in Appendix A) or use the Exchange Administrator Tools → Clean Mailbox… command to get rid of the old messages.

What about those homegrown solutions I mentioned earlier? In addition to these tools, you can always adopt some form of the one-way synchronization process I described earlier to transfer data between organizations. For example, you could write a script that would query one organization's server via LDAP, make a CSV file from the result, remove any duplicates, and insert the new data into a second organization's GAL via the Exchange Administrator directory import function. If you're handy with a modern scripting language, and have some time to play, this may be a viable alternative for you.

Replication Topology and Scheduling

In Chapter 3, *Exchange Planning*, you learned about the hub-and-spoke and mesh site models. Normally, your directory replication topology will match your site model, because it's easy to add DRCs atop whatever site-to-site links you already have in place. There's no law saying it has to be that way, though, and a good understanding of replication topology may help you choose a more effective model.

Consider the site model shown in Figure 9-1. It's a mesh, but with a twist: each site is only connected to one other site. Any change made to the local directory in the *ATL* site has to be propagated through the *STL*, *MSY*, and *DEN* sites before it reaches the *SFO* site. Even if the DRCs are set to "always" (which means they replicate every 15 minutes), at best it will be an hour before any change makes it from

ATL to *SFO*. If the replication schedule is longer, updates will take correspond-ingly longer to get where you want them to go.

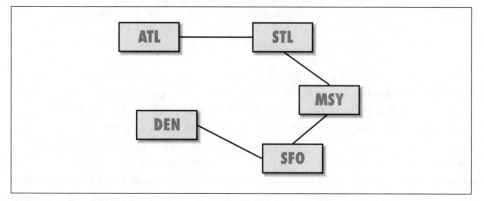

Figure 9-1. A mesh topology with no intervening links slows replication

You're probably thinking that *you'd* never design your organization that way. Check out Figure 9-2 for a somewhat improved version of the same organization's topology.

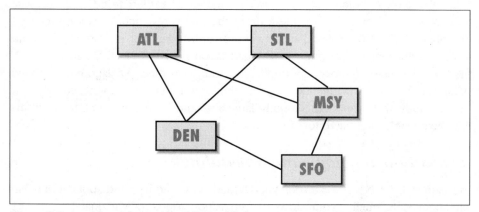

Figure 9-2. A mesh topology with additional links

This seems a little better, since now replication updates from *ATL* can get to *SFO* via either *STL* and *MSY* or a single hop through *DEN*. However, consider the cost in bandwidth. *STL*, for example, can receive replication updates from three other sites; every update it gets from any of those sites can potentially go to the other two, even if they could have gotten them from a "nearer" site. If nothing else, this arrangement uses more bandwidth for notification and request messages.

Now look at Figure 9-3. The same set of sites are now in a hub-and-spoke config-uration. Any change at one of the spoke sites goes to the hub, thence to the other spoke sites. This reduces the amount of bandwidth used for replication, since all sites get their data from the hub. A change to data at any spoke site will take only two replication cycles to propagate outward. Pretty good, right?

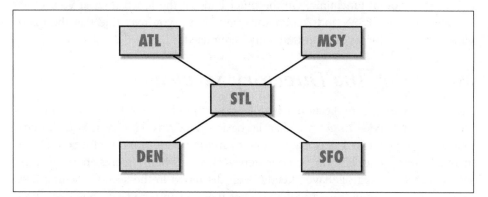

Figure 9-3. Hub-and-spoke topology improves overall replication efficiency

Maybe, but maybe not—the schedule you set for the DRCs on these servers controls how long each replication cycle is. For example, let's say that you set the hub DRC to push updates out at 8 p.m. every night, and you set the spoke DRCs to push their updates out at 11 p.m. This seems reasonable at first glance, but it really means that a change at any spoke won't make it to any other spoke until 8 p.m. the next day! Let's say I change a mailbox in *DEN* at 5 p.m. The hub replicates to *DEN* at 8 p.m., and *DEN* returns the favor at 11 p.m. That means my change doesn't get to the hub until 11 p.m., and it won't go out to the other spokes until the following night's hub replication.

Now, consider swapping the order so that the hub replicates at 11 p.m. and the spokes go at 8 p.m. The change is made at 5 p.m., it goes to the hub at 8 p.m., and the hub sends its changes to the other spokes at 11 p.m. The round-trip time for the change dropped from 27 hours to 6 hours!

You might infer from this that it's a good idea to schedule replication very frequently, maybe even using that tempting Always radio button on the Schedule tab. Don't, because every replication cycle causes traffic even if there's nothing to replicate. That traffic takes time and resources to process, meaning that your MTA will waste time handling unnecessary messages. In fact, in a hub-and-spoke model, excessively frequent replication can send your MTA into the replication death spiral discussed in Chapter 7—enough spokes working together can quickly flood the hub MTA.

How do you choose a reasonable schedule? The biggest driver is normally how much latency you can tolerate in directory updates. Is it okay if updates made one day in one site don't arrive until later in the day, or even very early the next day?

You also have to consider how the load on your network and servers varies during the day and during the week. For example, at sites where the users tend to be gone for lunch more often than not, you might be able to get away with scheduling a replication at lunchtime. On the other hand, if the lunch hour at your office is really the "visit ESPN and Dilbert web sites" hour, you may find that the bandwidth you need for replication is already being used.

Managing the Directory Service

Apart from setting a replication schedule, you don't have to do a whole lot with the Directory Service to get it to handle basic operations. However, you can customize its behavior to a reasonable degree, and there are some useful controls for manually forcing replication or consistency checks when circumstances warrant. The server-level controls have already been discussed in the section "Setting DRC properties" in Chapter 7, so I won't go over them again here (with one exception; see the later "The Knowledge Consistency Checker" section). The DS Site Configuration object in the Configuration container allows you to set properties for the DS on all servers in your site.

The General Tab

The General tab of the DS Site Configuration object's properties dialog is pretty boring, but I've included it in Figure 9-4. Naturally, it includes the standard display and directory name fields; it also lets you control two aspects of directory maintenance that we haven't discussed before now.

When a directory object is deleted, the Exchange DS replaces it with a *tombstone*. Actually, all it does is flip the Is-Deleted attribute on the object, but any object with that attribute set is referred to as a tombstone. Just as in real life, the tombstone marks the passing of an object so that it won't go unnoticed. The tombstone's purpose is to be replicated to other sites; when you delete an object in one site, the tombstone is replicated instead of the deleted object, and it replaces the actual object in other sites. The "Tombstone lifetime (days)" field in the General tab controls how long tombstones stay active. The default of 30 days is intentionally generous, since it may take a while for replication to complete in a network that has lots of sites, poor design, or slow links. You can safely decrease it to 7 or 14 days in most cases, although there's no real reason to do so.

Deleted items in the public and private IS have tombstones, too, but they're handled by the IS, not the DS.

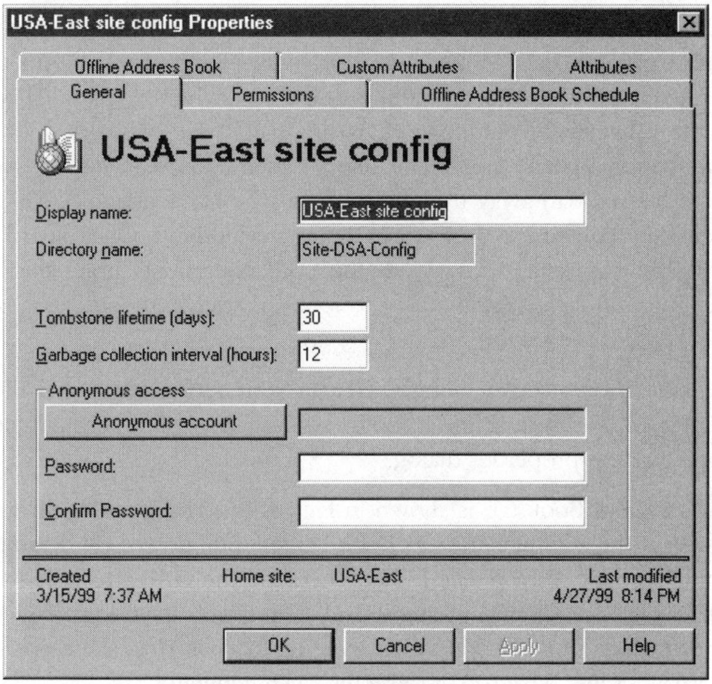

Figure 9-4. The General tab of the DS site configuration properties dialog

The "Garbage collection interval (hours)" field controls how often the DS goes through the directory and actually deletes items whose tombstone lifetime has passed. During garbage collection, the DS deletes tombstones and removes deleted objects. The default setting is to run the garbage collection task every 12 hours, which is fine. There's no way to control what time it runs, just how many times per day.

The "Anonymous access" group might seem out of place, but it's there for a reason. When you allow anonymous access to an item, you specify which account the IS should use to gain access to the item. Every access requires a valid account, even if you're not requiring valid credentials from the user on the other end of the wire. However, the DS needs access to its database, too. The "Anonymous account" button and the corresponding password fields allow you to choose the account that the DS will use for access when an anonymous client comes calling. Whatever account you choose here can be given permissions on various objects in the directory; for example, to enable anonymous access to an ABV, just grant the account you specify here Search permission on the ABV's Permissions tab.

Using Offline Address Books

Offline address books (OABs), are a neat feature that Exchange Server offers for mobile and roaming users. Normally, to resolve an address in the GAL (or even to browse it), you'd need a network connection to your home server. This is fine if you're in the office and your network is up, but it doesn't work so well when you're stuffed into one of those little teeny coach-class seats on US Airways or when you're on the road away from your office. The DS generates OABs from one or more recipient containers, then stores them in a hidden public folder.* When an Outlook or Exchange client downloads the OAB, the client copies the OAB data and caches it locally, allowing the user to look up stuff in the address book without out a connection to the server.

There are two aspects to generating OABs on your server: regulating the generation process itself, and scheduling it. Both tasks are controlled through tabs on the DS site configuration properties dialog.

The Offline Address Book tab is shown in Figure 9-5. The most significant control for most sites is the "Offline Address Book server" pull-down. By default, the first server in the site will be responsible for generating the OAB. However, OAB generation can suck up a significant amount of time if you have lots of recipients in your GAL or recipient containers. To balance the load on your site servers, use this control to assign a less-busy server to be the OAB generator.

The Address Books list shows you which recipient containers your server will generate OAB information for. Most of the time, you'll want to generate an OAB for the GAL and leave it at that. However, with the Add and Remove buttons, you can customize the list so that OABs are built for any combination of recipient containers and ABVs in your site. This is useful when you've segregated your GAL by using ABVs, either to keep one group from seeing others' addresses or to keep from cluttering up your clients. The Generate All button does what you'd guess: it forces the DS to generate OABs for all specified containers right this minute.

Finally, the "Microsoft Exchange 4.0 and 5.0 compatibility" button owns up to a problem introduced with Exchange 5.5: it generates OABs that older versions of the Exchange client can't read. If you know or suspect that some of your users will be using these older versions, check this box; there's no penalty for doing so, since all versions of Outlook can read the older format.

Now, on to scheduling. The Offline Address Book Schedule tab contains the same grid schedule control that you've seen in other schedule tabs, and it works the

---

* The OAB folder lives on the first server installed in each site. See Chapter 4, *Installing Exchange*, if you want to remove the first server, or else your OAB data will sleep with the fishes.

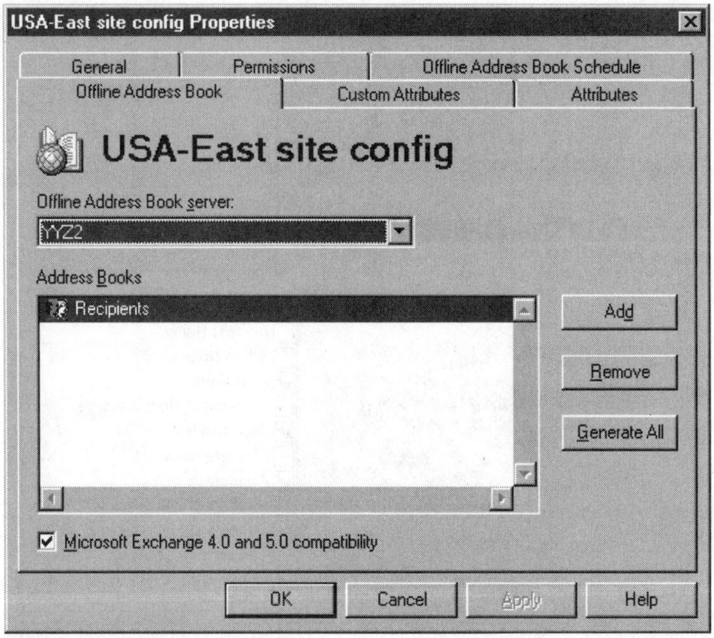

Figure 9-5. The Offline Address Book tab of the DS site configuration properties dialog

same way. You can pick any combination of one-hour slots and weekdays to schedule OAB generation. It's a good idea to schedule it so that it occurs *after* directory replication takes place. There's not much point in generating an OAB, then having a bunch of new changes added to the directory that potentially make parts of the OAB invalid.

Managing Object Attributes

Each directory object has attributes; the exact set varies according to the object's type. As you may have picked up by now, Exchange Administrator is really just a fancy frontend that gives you a pretty interface for changing these attribute values. There are lots of internal Exchange objects whose attributes you shouldn't change, and which aren't normally visible to users; however, users do want to see attribute values for things like mailboxes and DLs.

The Attributes tab

The Attributes tab of the DS site configuration properties dialog (shown in Figure 9-6) lets you control which specific attributes are made visible for a particular group of objects.

Figure 9-6. The Attributes tab of the DS site configuration properties dialog

 You use the Attributes tab to control which attributes are visible, but you can't control which items are replicated during intersite replication between Exchange servers.

There are three sets of controls in this dialog:

Configure

This list lets you choose which DS requestors the settings you make apply to. The choices are all self-explanatory, although it's interesting to note that you can't control what attributes are replicated within a site.

Show attributes for

This pull-down lets you choose which objects your choices apply to. You can screen attributes for DLs, mailboxes, public folders, custom recipients, or all of them together.

The scrolling list

This shows all available attributes for whatever you select in the pull-down. You can check and uncheck attributes until you've set the ones you want to be available. Note that the contents of this list will change depending on the item type you choose from the pull-down.

The Custom Attributes tab

The Custom Attributes tab is pretty straightforward: it shows ten custom attributes and gives you fields to enter the attribute names you want used for those attributes. For example, you can define custom attributes for employee ID, birthday, and mail stop. One Microsoft demo I saw had attributes for heel height and shoe size—what you put in the attribute fields is entirely up to you. Once you add custom attributes, they'll immediately be available for mailboxes, custom recipients, and DLs on the local server, but replication has to finish before they're available elsewhere in the site.

Exchange treats the data you put in these fields as blobs, and it replicates the data in the fields without replicating the field names! If you set Custom Attribute 1 to be "Birthday" in your site, and I set it to be "Favorite Football Team" in my site, when our sites replicate each of us will see data that doesn't seem to match our field definition. If you're using custom attributes across multiple sites, be sure to coordinate your attribute definitions so that all sites use the same names for the same attributes.

 Remember, you can customize the search templates that MAPI mail clients see (see Chapter 5 for details). That makes it easy for users to find people based on a custom attribute value, in addition to searching on fields like last name or phone number.

The Knowledge Consistency Checker

The Knowledge Consistency Checker (KCC) is in charge of synchronizing the directory's listing of servers and sites with the actual set of servers and sites out in the world. For example, if one of your servers or sites is removed from the network, the directory won't know it's gone until the next KCC is completed. The KCC is also required because you might need to add a new server while other servers or sites are down. You can manually start a KCC with the Check Now button on the General tab of the server's Directory Service properties dialog; the DS automatically runs it every three hours.

The KCC uses a multistep process to discover the state of your Exchange organization and make any necessary directory updates. To begin, the KCC connects to the local server's directory and gets a list of all servers in the local site. This list of local servers turns out to be very important to the KCC process. The process then continues:

1. The local server chooses a server in the local site and binds to it. It then compares that server's name to the names on the local server list. If the server name isn't on the list, it synchronizes the site configuration naming context in both directions. This step is repeated until either a matching name is found or all servers in the local site have been contacted.

2. The local KCC process searches the local directory for all of the naming contexts it has write access to. For each one it finds, it verifies that the naming context has entries for each server in the site in the context's Reps-To and Reps-From attributes. These are required for intrasite replication. If any context is missing data, the KCC repairs it.

3. The local server looks for connectors in the local site's Directory Replication container. For each connector it finds, it checks to see whether there's a corresponding remote connector; this tells the KCC whether this site and the remote site have a two-way connection. If the connector is two-way, it updates the inbound site list on the local connector so that it matches the outbound site list on the remote connector.

4. The local server iterates over the list of all local DRCs to build a list of all sites that are replicated into this site. Armed with this list, the KCC checks to make sure that each outbound connector replicates the right set of sites: all inbound sites except the ones coming in on that connector, plus the local server.

5. The local KCC checks the local directory for non-writable replicas of other servers' naming contexts. These replicas are informational copies of other sites' data maintained by replication, but the local site isn't allowed to change them.

6. Once the KCC has built a complete list of replicas, it compares it with the list of naming contexts delivered by the inbound connectors. If the KCC list has any replicas that are no longer replicated, they're removed from the directory; contrariwise, any replicas that should be in the directory, but aren't, are added.

7. The KCC builds a list of all the authorizations it can find in the directory, then traverses the list, throwing away any credentials not used by the installed connectors.

8. The KCC verifies that each intersite replica arriving at this server is replicated to all other servers in the local site. Any replicas marked for nonexistent servers are ditched.

9. If there are any objects in the local directory whose Invocation-ID attribute shows that they were last modified by a server that's no longer in the site, the KCC assigns a new Invocation-ID matching one of the local site's servers. It chooses a server at random each time, so one server won't end up owning all the newly relabeled objects.

Providing Directory Access with LDAP

The Lightweight Directory Access Protocol (LDAP) is an Internet-standard protocol designed so that clients and servers from different vendors and on different platforms can share directory information. Exchange 5.0 offered some LDAP support; Exchange 5.5 improves on that foundation by allowing authenticated clients to write data back to the LDAP directory.

What's LDAP good for? Well, for one thing, it's the best way to share the contents of your directory with users who aren't running Outlook or OWA. Eudora Pro, Netscape Messenger, and other IMAP4/POP3 clients, including Microsoft's own Outlook Express, support LDAP as a means of finding addresses for people whose names you already know. The Exchange LDAP implementation allows you to support these clients with GAL-like functionality; in fact, Outlook 97, 98, and 2000 also support LDAP as a means of finding directory information.

LDAP is one of the four Internet protocols for which Exchange 5.5 provides native support. Before you can serve LDAP data to anyone, you'll have to enable the protocol at the site or server level. To do this, you'll need to turn on the "Enable protocol" checkbox on the LDAP Site Defaults object (it's in the Protocols container of the site Configuration container) or the LDAP Settings object, which lives in the Protocols container beneath each individual server. Once you've turned LDAP on, clients may immediately access it.

If you want to follow the default behavior of most other Unix LDAP servers—that is, anonymous clients can connect on TCP/IP port 389 and see everything in your directory, and authenticated clients may modify data in accordance with their permissions—you can stop reading here. If you want to change these defaults, keep reading; you've come to the right place.

Basic LDAP Configuration

The first thing you'll probably want to configure is whether LDAP is available to clients or not. You can use the "Enable protocol" checkbox I mentioned earlier to turn LDAP on and off on individual sites and servers. As with the other Internet protocols Exchange supports, you can turn off the protocol at the site level, then enable it on individual servers, or vice versa, provided that the "Use site defaults for all properties" checkbox is not checked. This checkbox does exactly what its name suggests: when it's checked, all of the server's LDAP settings are taken from the site configuration. You can still use the server-level properties dialog to inspect properties on an individual server, you just can't change properties until you clear the site defaults checkbox.

The site- and server-level LDAP properties dialogs are so similar that I'm going to pretend only the site-level dialog actually exists. I'll mention any significant differences.

On with the configuration: the General tab of the site's LDAP Site Defaults properties dialog lets you specify whether LDAP is enabled or not and what TCP/IP port the server listens on. If you change this port number from its default value of 389, clients won't be able to connect unless their port number settings are changed to match. This can be a cheap and reasonably effective way to make your directory data available to users who need it without opening it up to everyone; however, this sort of security through obscurity usually doesn't hold up for very long, so you should probably consider using authentication instead.

Enabling Authentication

Speaking of which, the Authentication tab of the properties dialog gives you six choices for authentication methods. You can enable or disable each method independently. Actually, there are only three methods:

Basic (Clear Text)
>   This method uses a username and password for authentication; the "Clear Text" part of the name comes from the fact that those credentials are transmitted without any encryption or even obfuscation, so an eavesdropper can easily see them.

Windows NT Challenge/Response
>   This uses NT's built-in authentication method. When a client connects, the server sends a challenge message to the client, which must process it and send it back so that the server can verify its credentials. This method is more secure than basic authentication because the client encrypts its password before answering the challenge, but it only works with Microsoft clients.

MCIS Membership System
>   This is designed for use with Microsoft's Commercial Internet Server (MCI... get it?) system. If you're running MCIS, you'll need a whole different book to figure out how to get its authentication working.

Why did I list only three methods after I said there were six? Simple: each of these methods comes in two flavors, with and without Secure Sockets Layer (SSL) encryption. When you use SSL, connections between the client and server are automatically encrypted. Once the encrypted connection is set up, Exchange and the client use whatever authentication method they both support. Clear-text authentication over SSL is secure, so don't hesitate to use it if your LDAP clients can make use of it.

What about clients that don't provide any authentication data at all? By default, the Exchange LDAP server allows anonymous users to browse and search the directory. You can control anonymous browsing in two different ways. First of all, you can turn it off altogether with the Anonymous tab of the properties dialog—just clear the "Allow anonymous access" checkbox. You can also restrict what anonymous users can see by selecting an anonymous access account on the DS general properties page (see Figure 9-4 earlier in the chapter), then restricting the Search permission on some containers to limit what the anonymous access account can see.

Setting Search Limits

On to searching—coincidentally, that's the next tab in the properties dialog. Part of the LDAP specification is a filter language you can use to build fairly complicated queries. Most clients hide that complexity by letting you search for names without giving you the ability to make arbitrarily complex queries. Part of the responsibility for searching falls on the server; the Search tab of the LDAP Site Defaults properties dialog is where you control how the Exchange DS handles searches. There are three radio buttons on this property page that control how the DS interprets wildcard searches.

Let's say you use an LDAP client to search for everyone on a server whose last name starts with "st." A well-written client will encode that search as a search for all items whose "common name" attribute starts with "st". A poorly written client will search for all items that have the substring "st" in the common name attribute, then it'll throw out all the ones that don't fit. Here's what the Search tab radio buttons do:

Treat "any" substring searches as "initial" substring searches (fast)
Makes a search for "|mit|" act like a search for "mit*." This search will find "Mitchell" and "Mitterand," but not "Smithers." This is the default.

Allow only "initial" substring searches (fast)
Tells the DS to ignore any substring search that isn't an initial substring search. This saves your server some work, but may reject some legal searches from clients that don't know any better.

Allow all substring searches (slow)
Tells the DS to allow any type of search, even if it's slow.

This tab also contains a field that allows you to control the maximum number of found records returned to a client. By default, most LDAP servers return a maximum of 100 records, so that a client who tries a search on some excessively broad term like "*e*" won't end up with the entire contents of your directory. You can throttle the maximum number of result records up and down according to taste.

Using LDAP Referrals

One cool feature of LDAP is that it supports automatic referrals. If you've configured your server properly, it will automatically hand off any search it can't handle to another server. For example, if your Exchange organization spans multiple companies, you can set up LDAP referrals so that a query for a company B employee sent to company A's server will bounce to company B's server. Referrals are commonly used on Unix LDAP servers, since they make searching a lot nicer for the user. Exchange supports this feature through the Referrals tab in the Site Defaults properties dialog; you can provide up to 350 referral servers.

To configure a referral server, you need four pieces of information: the DNS name or IP address of the server, the DN of the organization it serves (say, "c=US, o=RobichauxAssociates"), the TCP/IP port number it's listening on, and whether you connect to it via SSL or not. Armed with that information, you can add the referral server by using the New... button on the Referrals properties page, then filling in the appropriate fields. You can edit and remove referrals, too, by using the corresponding buttons. You can also select which referral server is used when no results come back from a referral search; just select the referral server you want and click the Default Referral button.

Using Address Book Views

An Address Book View is just a set of predefined search criteria that groups and selects addressable objects according to whatever limits you select. When you look at it in Exchange Administrator or a mail client, it looks like a separate recipient container, even though it's not. Once you create an ABV, it's stored in the directory and automatically propagated throughout the entire organization. A maintenance task periodically scans the GAL and updates any ABVs you've defined to keep them reasonably current.

ABVs are stored in the directory and regenerated periodically, but you create and manage them using Exchange Administrator. Since they're directory objects, I decided to talk about them here instead of in Chapter 5.

ABVs and Views Explained

Once you create an ABV, you'll notice that it expands to include subcategories. Let's say I built an ABV for O'Reilly & Associates, sorted by city. The container pane of my Exchange Administrator session with an O'Reilly server would show the Address Book Views container, under which there would be a child container, most likely named "City." In this case, "City" is actually an ABV container; it contains child containers named "Cambridge," "Köln," "Sebastopol," and so on, one for each city defined anywhere in the directory. For simplicity's sake, I'll call these children "views" for the rest of this section, even though they're really containers. Selecting any one of these views shows the recipients who match that view's attributes as though they were hosted there, even though they're not in separate containers. Deleting or changing the properties of the City ABV container affects all its child views, although you can adjust some properties separately.

Creating a New ABV

To create a new ABV, use Exchange Administrator's File → New Other → Address Book View… command. The ABV properties dialog will appear, and the first thing you have to do is provide a display name and directory name for the new ABV; until you do that, Exchange Administrator won't let you switch to the other, more interesting tabs. The Group By tab (shown in Figure 9-7) is where you tell Exchange Administrator how you want the ABV entries to be grouped. Each successive level of indentation represents an additional subcategory; in the figure, you can see that this ABV groups first by country, then by state, city, and department, in that order.

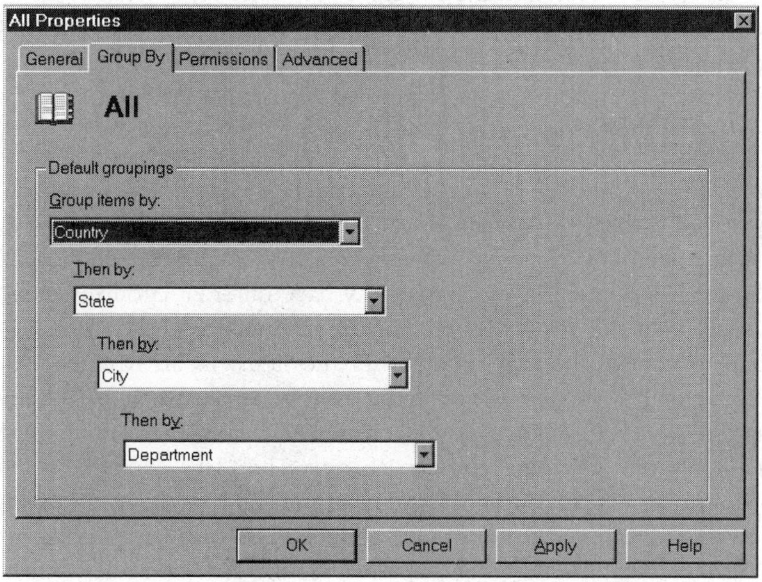

Figure 9-7. This ABV groups recipients by four criteria, in descending order

The Advanced tab of the ABV properties dialog appears when you create or show the properties of an ABV container. It contains two checkboxes and one button, all of which are useful.

Promote entries to parent containers

>   This checkbox lets you decide whether you want low-level groupings to prop-
>   agate upward. When this setting is off, recipients stay in the lowest-level ABV
>   that they match. Let's say you set up an ABV like the one in Figure 9-7. When
>   the option is off, people in the marketing department of the Kansas City office
>   won't appear in the Kansas City, Missouri, or U.S. ABVs—only in the Market-
>   ing view under US/Missouri/Kansas City. When the option is on, that depart-
>   ment's employees will appear in all ABV containers in the path, from US on
>   down.

Show this view in the client address book

>   This checkbox is pretty self-explanatory. If you turn it off, you'll still see the
>   ABV and all its containers in Exchange Administrator, but mail clients won't
>   see it in the GAL. This is handy if you want to use ABVs for managing recipi-
>   ents but don't want to expose them to your users, for whatever reason.

Remove Empty Categories

>   This button does what you'd expect, after you confirm your choice: it removes
>   any child view of the ABV that has no recipients in it. To revisit the city/
>   department example, if you don't have a marketing department in your Chi-
>   cago office, and therefore have no mailboxes with a Department value of mar-
>   keting and a City value of Chicago, clicking this button will make the Chicago
>   Marketing view vanish.

Changing ABV Grouping Properties

You can edit the properties of an ABV container or view object in the usual way.
As I mentioned earlier, the Advanced tab only shows up when you open the properties dialog of an ABV container; however, all ABV containers and views have the
Group By tab. The only problem is that they have different Group By tabs! You've
already seen what the Group By tab for a container looks like (see Figure 9-7);
you use it to control the sort order of all the items in an ABV container. The
Group By tab on a view object is different, as you can see in Figure 9-8. Instead of
the hierarchy of sorting choices found on the ABV container Group By tab, this
dialog has only one grouping you can change. The "This container" field shows
you what attribute was used to group items in this view, and the "Grouping value"
field shows what value of the attribute produced the view. A quick glance at the
figure shows you that Country = Switzerland was the grouping rule for this view.

The Sub-containers pull-down normally shows what attribute is being used to
group children of this view object. In the ABV container that owns the view
shown in the figure, the sort order was Country, State, City, Department. But Switzerland doesn't have states; instead, it has cantons, which aren't an attribute you
can select by default. Instead of selecting by state, which would be meaningless

Figure 9-8. The Group By tab for a view object lets you change how subcontainers are sorted for this object

since there aren't any mailboxes in this view with that attribute, I told Exchange Administrator to skip creating any subviews by setting the Sub-containers value to none. Of course, I could define a custom attribute, name it Canton, and sort by that instead.

The point of this pull-down is that it lets you change how subviews of the current view are grouped on a one-by-one basis. In this case, the Switzerland view's subgrouping was removed, but you could just as easily add a new subview grouping by picking a different attribute from the Sub-containers list. For example, if you have a particularly large department in one city, you could break that one city's "by department" view down further, perhaps by using a custom attribute to indicate project assignments. As an administrator, you might also find it helpful to build ABVs that group people by home server so you can quickly see only those people on a particular box.

Creating Extra ABV Containers

You can always create new ABV view objects. This is a useful (and quick) way to add arbitrary subdivisions to an existing ABV container or view object. The File → New Other → Address Book View Container... command is available when you select an ABV view or container; when you use it, you'll see the same dialog as the one pictured in Figure 9-7, earlier in this chapter. All you have to do is fill in the directory and display names, then use the Group By tab to select the subcontainer and value you want to use for the grouping. By default, whatever you enter in the Display Name field on the General tab is used as the value in the Group By tab; for example, if you create a new entry named SJC-West and select Home Server in the Sub-containers pull-down, the default value will group users who have a home server named *SJC-West*.

A Sneaky Way to Do Bulk Attribute Changes

Here's a slick trick I learned at Microsoft's Exchange Conference: you can quickly change the value of one or more attributes in many records in an unexpected way. Let's say that you work for a medium-size company with offices in several cities throughout North America. Because the regulatory environment in California is oppressive, your West Coast office moves from Los Angeles to Colorado Springs. You could open the properties dialog for each mailbox and change the city manually, but that's a loser idea because it takes too long and involves a lot of boring repetition. Your second alternative is to do a directory export of all the mailboxes that are moving, edit the CSV file, and reimport the data—still not a very streamlined solution.

Instead, try this: open the Recipients container that holds the mailboxes you want to change. Select the mailboxes, then use the Tools → Add to Address Book View command. A dialog will pop up; in it, you'll see a list of all the currently defined ABVs. In your case, all you have to do to make the move happen is expand the ABV container, select the Colorado Springs ABV, and click OK; Exchange Administrator will process each mailbox you selected and add it to the ABV, which in turn changes the value of whatever attributes the ABV selects by. For example, if you've got an ABV that groups first by department, then by city, when someone transfers from the operations department in Sunnyvale to the marketing department in Fairfax, you can use the command to update both attributes at once. Try it—I promise you'll like it.

Nifty Directory Tricks

By now you understand how to manage the DS, but there are a few tricks that may not have occurred to you.

Using Container-Level Search Controls

Sometimes circumstances force you to combine several different organizations under the umbrella of a single Exchange organization. For example, you might have built an organization that includes several different subsidiaries of a parent company. As long as you want to share all of the address book data for all the organizations, you're fine. But what if you want to limit each organization to seeing only its own GAL? This is often the case if you're providing Exchange services to more than one organization at a time. One of my clients is a holding company with several independent business units that don't have much in common; setting up a separate GAL for each of them without setting up separate Exchange organizations was the way to cleanly separate each unit's data.

How do you do it? Since this section falls after the ABV section of the chapter, you'd be right if you guessed the solution had something to do with ABVs. In essence, this procedure requires that you segregate your domain accounts into groups based on their membership in each business unit; you then create ABVs and grant permission on them to the groups. Here's the scoop:

1. Use the DS Site Configuration object's General tab to assign an anonymous account for the DS to use. Any account will do, but you must specify one.

2. Use User Manager to create one global group for each group you want to have its own GAL. For example, I had to create four global groups, one for each business unit.

3. Put each domain account into the appropriate group. Normally, you'll put an account in the group that the account owner "belongs" to.

4. Create a new ABV, grouping it by whatever attribute is appropriate (usually Company, Department, or a custom attribute). This step creates a separate searchable list for each organization, containing only the mailboxes and other objects you want that organization to see; but at this point, everyone can see it.

5. Select the new ABV in the Exchange Administrator container pane. You'll notice that it expands to show each of its subdivisions.

6. Select the first subdivision of the ABV (department, division, business unit, or whatever), then open its properties dialog and switch to the Permissions tab.

7. Use the Permissions tab to give the appropriate group from step 2 Search permission on the ABV. Repeat steps 6 and 7 for each subdivision.

8. Use Exchange Administrator's Tools → Options... command to make sure that the "Show Permissions Page for all objects" and "Display Rights for Roles on Permissions page" checkboxes are turned on.

9. Open the Exchange organization object's properties dialog, then switch to its Permissions tab. Give the Exchange service account Search permission on the object.

Why does this work? In Exchange 5.5, granting the Search permission to a specific account turns off the default "everyone can search" permissions for that object. As soon as you give any account search privileges, you've immediately restricted access to only the accounts or groups that hold the permission. Microsoft did it that way on purpose, because in 5.5 the Search permission can be used for access control, although it seems counterintuitive—adding a permission doesn't normally remove other permissions!

Monitoring Replication

It can be useful to monitor how many inbound and outgoing replication messages your bridgehead servers are generating, but there hasn't been any good way to do it. Microsoft recently released a hotfix for systems running Exchange 5.5 SP2 that adds two new Performance Monitor counters: "Incoming Inter-Site Replication Updates/sec" and "Outgoing Inter-Site Replication Messages/sec." These two counters measure what their names imply, so you can quickly establish a system for monitoring replication traffic and alerting you when it's abnormal. See Chapter 18, *Managing Exchange Performance*, for more on using Performance Monitor.

These counters are available as a hotfix; you can contact PSS to get them, or you can download them from Microsoft's FTP server at *ftp.microsoft.com/bussys/ exchange/exchange-public/fixes/eng/Exchg5.5/PostSP2/DIR-fix/*. They'll be bundled in Exchange 5.5 SP3 when it ships, and likely in Platinum, too. Note that this hotfix also fixes several directory-related problems, so you should obtain and install it even if you don't want the counters.

Once you've gotten the hotfix files, you have to install them. You can use Microsoft's *hotfix.exe* utility, or you can manually remove and replace the old files. There are four files that must be replaced: *dsamain.exe* is the DS executable; *dsactrs.ini* is a parameter file for the DS Performance Monitor counters; *perfdsa.dll* contains the counters themselves, and *dsactrnm.h* is a C header file that defines the counter names and identifiers. Here's what to do:

1. Stop the Exchange services on the server you're updating.

2. Go to the (*exchsrvr\bin*) directory, where your Exchange executables are stored.

3. Use the `unloadctr` command to unload the existing set of DS counters:

   ```
   unloadctr MSExchangeDS
   ```

4. Rename the four files; I usually tack on an extension of *.old* so I can back changes out later if I need to.

5. Copy the hotfix files into the *exchsrvr\bin* directory.

6. Reload the new counters with the `loadctr` command:

   ```
   loadctr dsactrs.ini
   ```

7. Restart the Exchange services.

Extending GAL Search Capabilities

Depending on the tools you use to search the Exchange directory, it can be easy or hard to find the recipients you're looking for. Back when the Exchange client was Microsoft's darling, you could type in part of a recipient name, hit CTRL-K, and see whether Exchange could clairvoyantly figure out whose name you meant to type. Outlook 97 and 98 are smarter about doing name matching, but sometimes you want to search by an attribute that's not directly available. One way around this is to use LDAP, but that's not always possible. The following sections describe some ways to extend your available search capability.

Enabling name resolution by first name

This is a nifty trick if your organization is pretty informal. If you typically assign mailbox names like "bob" and "sherry" instead of "rbjones" and "slwinkler," turning on first-name searching makes it easier to quickly find the recipient you're looking for. Doing so, however, requires you to make a schema change using Exchange Administrator's raw mode on every server in the site, so it's not to be done casually. Here's what to do:

1. Open Exchange Administrator in raw mode, then use the View → Raw Directory command. This forces Exchange Administrator to show the Schema container.

2. Double-click the Schema container, then use the View → Refresh command or the F5 key to force Exchange Administrator to update its display.

3. Open the properties of the First Name object under the Schema container, either by double-clicking it or using the File → Raw Properties... command.

4. When the Object Attributes dialog appears, select the Search-Flags attribute from the list. Set the attribute value to 2 by typing 2 into the Edit field, then clicking the Set button.

5. Click OK to close the Object Attributes dialog, then quit Exchange Administrator and stop and restart the DS.

Enabling searches on custom attributes

Custom attributes can be really handy, assuming you use them in accordance with the advice I gave earlier in this chapter. You can use the trick I mentioned in the previous section (with a few twists) to make custom attributes searchable. This is a great way to find people by employee ID, building number, shoe size, or whatever other criteria you've set up as your custom attributes. To make it work, here's what you need to do:

1. Open Exchange Administrator in raw mode, then use the View → Raw Directory command. This forces Exchange Administrator to show the Schema container.

2. Use the Custom Attributes tab of the DS site configuration properties dialog to give the custom attribute the name you want it to have.

3. Open the properties of the newly renamed custom attribute by selecting it (it's under the Schema container).

4. When the Object Attributes dialog appears, set the Search-Flags attribute value to 2, then click OK to dismiss the dialog.

5. Quit Exchange Administrator, then stop and restart the DS.

You still have two other things to do: you have to update the search dialog template so that users can actually request a search using the new attribute, and you have to update the mailbox details template so that clients who display a mailbox's properties will see the attribute. See "Customizing Address Templates" in Chapter 5 for more details.

10

Managing Public Folders

I am a great friend to public amusements;
for they keep people from vice.
—Samuel Johnson
James Boswell's *Life of Samuel Johnson*

Public folders are shared workspaces that any or all of your users can access. You can use them to hold discussions, post policy or status information, schedule meetings, and read Internet news. Most sites that use public folders find that they're easy to use as archives, too, but using them this way requires careful attention to their management. In particular, you must be careful to set up a replication topology, replication schedule, and aging policy that matches your users and their usage patterns.

Public Folder Basics

Public folders are like mailboxes, in that they can hold an arbitrary number of messages, each of which is stored in a database. As you'd expect, public folders live in the public IS database, and the settings that control access to and replication of public folder data are all controlled through the public IS object's properties pages.

What Can You Do with a Public Folder?

You can do anything you want—a public folder can hold all the same datatypes as a mailbox. In particular, many organizations use public folders to hold Outlook contact data, in effect making the public folders a shared contact database. Each public folder has its own mailbox address, taken from the name of the folder, plus the server, site, and organization names, all adjusted according to whatever proxy address generation settings you've imposed. As a result, you can send mail to a public folder, which makes it easy to use to archive mailing list traffic. This is particularly useful when you have a high-volume mailing list (like the *msexchange* mailing list hosted at *www.swynk.com*, which generates about 150 messages per day) or one whose contents you want to share with more than one reader. Just subscribe the public folder to the list and watch the mail pile up.

Public folders also serve as the backbone of Exchange's collaboration features. Apart from being able to store documents so that everyone in a workgroup or team can read them, you can also write applications that use public folders to store and route data. For example, you can build (or buy) workflow routing applications that use public folders to move work items between the groups that must process or approve them.

In a less formal vein, you can use public folders for discussions. Each public folder can have permissions attached to it, so you could easily set up folders to facilitate discussions that might otherwise go on only in private email. These permissions are the same as those listed in Chapter 2, *Exchange Architecture*, so it's possible to grant read access to a folder to one group and modify access to another group. One benefit of using public folders for discussions is that it allows secure discussions (say, about Human Resources policies) to take place without requiring items to be stored in individual users' mailboxes. This is especially handy since many organizations are seeking to strictly limit the use of email for confidential material, fearing accidental or legally compelled disclosure in the future. If all your sensitive material is in one place, it's much easier to make sure that your email retention policy is being carried out.

 You should probably exercise firm control over who you allow to create folders and what names you allow, or your public folder hierarchy will quickly turn into a big mess. Having a naming standard in place helps make sure that everyone can find the data they're looking for.

Public folders are also where the Exchange Internet News Service puts the news articles it retrieves. Managing the INS is covered in the next chapter, but in the remainder of this chapter, I'll point out public folder management issues that have special relevance to news folders.

How Do Clients Get Public Folder Data?

The answer depends on how your Exchange organization is configured. If you're using a single server, users get their folder data from that server, and that's it. As soon as you have multiple servers or sites, the sharing process becomes more important. We've already outlined the sharing process in the section "Planning public folder distribution" in Chapter 3, *Exchange Planning*, but a brief recap can't hurt.

There are two components to public folder information that live in the public IS. The first is the public folder hierarchy. It's just a list, with ownership information, of the folders in the public IS; MAPI, NNTP, and IMAP4 clients use this hierarchy to display the list of public folders, complete with names and access controls. The data in the public folders is stored separately. The practical effect of this split is that the folder hierarchy is automatically replicated throughout the Exchange organization—but the data isn't! That means that clients anywhere can see a list of all folders, but they may not be able to read the data inside the folders.

Public folders are first created on a single server. This server is called the public folder's *home server*. Interestingly, you can't create public folders through Exchange Administrator; you can create them only with clients, though you can use Exchange Administrator to set permissions that restrict who can create them. Each folder can have one or more replicas; any public folder server in an organization may have zero or one replicas of any folder in the organization. Replicas are all treated as equals; each one is an exact copy of all the others, with no central master copy. A change made to any replica is always copied to all other replicas, so (disregarding replication latency for a minute) all the folders eventually end up with the same contents. However, the home server is responsible for receiving messages sent to the public folder's address, as well as for notifying folder contacts when replication conflicts arise.

When a client tries to open the public folder hierarchy, the request goes to the client's home server DS. When the client opens a specific public folder, the request also goes to its home server's DS. The DS doesn't hold any public folder data, but the home server may or may not have a public IS, and the DS knows where the public IS for the server is, and it knows where the nearest replica is and what affinity rules apply.

Public folder permissions

Each public folder can have its own distinct set of permissions. These permissions govern which mailboxes may view and modify items in the folder, though it's important to note that they don't control who can see the folder in the hierarchy list. When you create a new folder, it inherits permissions from its parent folder; you can use Exchange Administrator to modify those permissions as necessary. Users can also set permissions on public folders, assuming you've given their mailboxes the necessary permissions.

The owner of a public folder can apply access controls to any mailbox, DL, or public folder in the GAL; custom recipients can't have public folder access controls because they don't have public folder access. The permissions you can apply are shown in Table 10-1.

Table 10-1. Public Folder Permissions

Permission	What It Allows
Create items	Holder may create messages in a folder, but not in subfolders.
Create subfolders	Holder may create subfolders in this folder. Newly created subfolders inherit permissions from the parent folder, and the user who creates them gets Owner permission on them.
Delete items	Holder may remove items from the folder, according to the scope granted: "None" means the holder can't delete anything, "Own" allows the holder to delete items he created, and "All" allows the holder to whack any item in the folder.
Edit items	Holder may edit items in the folder, according to the scope granted: "None" means the holder can't edit anything, "Own" allows the holder to edit items she created, and "All" allows editing of any item.
Folder contact	Holder receives notification of things that happen to the folder, including when the folder goes over its permitted maximum size or when there's a replication or design conflict.
Folder owner	Holder owns this folder and has full control over it. The name of the last owner is never removed from the folder's access control list.
Read items	Holder may read any item in the folder. Without this permission, a user can't open the folder at all.
Folder Visible	Holder can see that the folder exists.

Normally, you apply permissions to folders by assigning users to particular roles. These roles aren't related to the Exchange Administrator roles you learned about in Chapter 5, *Using Exchange Administrator*, but they work on the same principle. Each role bundles two or more permissions together, so you can quickly assign privileges to one or more users without sweating the details. Table 10-2 shows the roles you can use on public folders.

Table 10-2. Public Folder Roles

Role	Included Permissions
Owner	Create items, Read items, Create subfolders, Edit All, Folder owner, Folder Visible, Delete All
Author	Create items, Read items, Edit Own, Delete Own, Folder Visible
Publishing Author	Author permissions plus Create subfolders
Nonediting Author	Author permissions minus Edit Own; this role can create new items, but not edit existing ones
Editor	Create items, Read items, Edit All, Folder Visible, Delete All

Table 10-2. Public Folder Roles (continued)

Role	Included Permissions
Publishing Editor	Editor permissions plus Create subfolders
Reviewer	Read items, Edit None, Folder Visible, Delete None
Contributor	Create items, Folder Visible, Edit None, Delete None
None	Folder Visible, Edit None, Delete None

Which replica do you see?

I've already alluded to affinity: you configure it to allow users in one site to access public folders in another site. There are some additional twists that govern exactly how the client and public folder data get together. When you attempt to open a public folder, the client and public IS on the server go through the following set of steps to open a replica of the folder:

1. If there's a replica of the folder on the server when your client got its copy of the public folder hierarchy, the client retrieves the folder contents from that server's public IS.

2. If there's no replica on that server, and if your home server is part of an Exchange location, the home server public IS will look for a replica of the folder on any server in the location. This step only searches for replicas in the named location that your server belongs to, like "Paris" or "Building 3."

3. If no replica is available at your location (or if your server isn't in a location), the next search target is the special location named *. If you want to group several servers in an organization, just put them all in the * location, and clients will be sent there. If more than one server in the * location has an available replica, Exchange will randomly choose one so that overall load is balanced across all servers in *.

4. If a replica still hasn't been found, Exchange will look for one on all servers in the site.

5. If the local site doesn't have any replicas available, Exchange will turn to sites that have affinity with your home site. If your site doesn't have any affinity relationships, you won't be able to see the folder. If the site does have affinity with other sites, Exchange uses the available replica with the lowest cost.

Since affinity between sites is specified as a cost (as you'll see in a bit, when I tell you how to set it), you can force your servers to prefer a specific affinity site. Figure 10-1 shows an Exchange organization with four sites. Lines drawn between the sites indicate the existence of an affinity relationship, and the number next to each line indicates the cost.

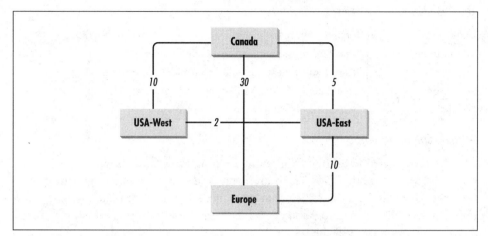

Figure 10-1. An affinity example

Here's some of what this diagram tells you:

• Clients in the *USA-East* site can access folder replicas in their home site, in *Canada*, or in *Europe*. In order, clients will check *USA-West*, *Canada*, and *Europe* if they can't find a replica after executing the steps above.

• Clients in *USA-West* can look for replicas in *USA-East* or *Canada*, but not *Europe*.

How do you choose affinity costs? Normally, they're assigned on the basis of resource usage, since when a client follows an affinity link it's going to generate network traffic. In the same way that you assign connector costs to reflect the relative costs of the network links they run on, you assign affinity costs to guide traffic over the paths of least resistance.

Replicas or affinity: which is right for you?

When you use replicas, you distribute your folders. When you use affinity, you centralize them. Which approach works for you depends on a number of factors, not least of which is whether your own organizational culture favors centralized or decentralized information access. That's your problem, though, and since it doesn't really have anything to do with Exchange, you're on your own.

The difference between the two approaches is subtle, because both allow you to provide access across an organization; they just differ in mechanics. Replicas copy folder information to multiple places. This means that every change made to any replica is guaranteed to take up bandwidth as it's replicated around. Affinity allows you to force users to use particular replicas. Bandwidth and server resources are used only when a user wants to look at or change a particular item. However, depending on how your sites are physically connected to one another, you may find that the bandwidth requirements of an affinity setup are too much for you.

Most of the time, the proper solution is a mix of the two approaches. For folders that are seldom viewed or changed, it doesn't matter whether you replicate them or use affinity, because their overall traffic will be low. If your architecture has multiple sites with high-bandwidth LAN or WAN connections, spreading replicas around will give users fast access to folder contents because each site will have a replica; but this is a bandwidth-intensive approach, so it won't work well everywhere. In general, you'll probably find that using affinity to grant access to folders that are frequently modified, and thus generate lots of replication traffic, will reduce the overall network load. The nice thing is that there's no penalty for switching things around; you can add and remove replicas and affinity costs with ease.

Managing Public Folders

Not only do you have to design and implement an architecture for your public folders, you also have to take care of them, in the same way that you have to care for a houseplant, house cat, or house. There's some ongoing maintenance required, both at the public IS and individual folder levels. In fact, you can monitor and set public folder properties across the entire site or on individual servers.

Setting Site-wide Public IS Properties

The Information Store Site Configuration object, available in the site Configuration container, is where you set defaults that you want to apply to all public folder servers in a site. From this object, you can choose what container public folders are stored in, who may and may not create new top-level folders, when storage warning messages are generated, and what affinity costs you want applied to folders.

The General tab of this dialog is straightforward, so I won't show it here. The only interesting item on it is the Public Folder container group. By default, public folders go in the Recipients container on their home server. You may find it useful to put them in their own container; that makes it easier for people to find them in the GAL, and it simplifies the process of creating an ABV that contains only public folders. Use the Modify... button to specify which container you want newly created public folders in this site to go into. Note that you can only select an existing container (so create a new one before clicking Modify..., if you haven't already) and that this change doesn't affect existing folders, just new ones.

Now, on to something a bit more interesting. The Top Level Folder Creation tab, shown in Figure 10-2, lets you control which mailboxes have permission to create new top-level folders. This has nothing to do with who can create new subfolders in an existing folder; that's controlled by permissions on the parent folder. This setting applies only to creation of new folders in the specified container. By default, everyone can create top-level folders. To allow or restrict individual mailboxes or DLs, use the appropriate radio button in the "Allowed to create top level folders" or "Not allowed to create top level folders" control groups, followed by the corresponding Modify... button. You can fill both lists at once. In fact, if you want to put a DL on one list or the other, but you want to exclude particular DL members, you can do it. Let's say I have a DL named "Product Group Mgrs" and I want to let them all create top-level folders except for one manager who's a contract employee: I'd put the DL in the "Allowed" list but the excluded manager's name in the "Not allowed" list.

Figure 10-2. The Top Level Folder Creation tab

Public folders can have storage limits on them, just like regular mailboxes. The IS on each server runs a task every so often that scans the list of public folders on that server and generates "your public folder is too big" messages to the folder contacts if the folder exceeds the size limits. You can use the Storage Warnings tab to control how often this task runs. Most sites find that the default setting, which runs the task once per day, is plenty, but you can use the schedule grid on the tab to schedule warning generation any time you like.

Setting site public folder affinity

The Public Folder Affinity tab lets you set affinity costs for public folders in your site. You have to set these costs at the site level because of the process each server uses to find the cheapest replica of a user-requested folder. The tab itself is pretty boring: it contains two lists and a couple of buttons. The left-hand list, labeled "Sites," shows all sites in your organization. The right-hand list, labeled "Public folder affinity," shows which sites have defined affinity relationships with your site. You can use the Add and Remove buttons between the two lists to move sites from one list to the other.

When you put sites in the right-hand list, you can select a site from the list and use the Set Value button and the field next to it to assign an affinity to that particular site. Type the affinity cost you want in the field, then click Set Value; you'll notice that the change is reflected in the Cost column of the list.

Setting Server-Specific Properties

As it turns out, there are a bunch of server-specific properties you can strap onto a public IS with the server's Public Information Store object. There are a total of 12 property sheets in this dialog. Some of them are things we've seen before in other contexts, including the stuff controlled by the Permissions, E-mail Addresses, and Diagnostics Logging tabs. Some others, like the Server Replication Status and Folder Replication Status tabs, duplicate items in the server's Public IS container, which we talk about below. The remaining tabs, though, offer you control over how the public IS handles folders.

The E-mail Addresses tab is worth a look, since you can add extra addresses for each public folder. For example, if you have a folder for customer feedback, you can add an extra SMTP address (like *feedback@somewhere.com*) that points to the folder. Don't delete the X.400 address, though; the MTA needs it.

The General tab

The General tab may look a little sparse, but it has some of the most commonly used controls of any IS properties page. General tab controls specify deleted item recovery on public folder items and the size at which storage limits are issued for public folders.

The Item Recovery group contains two controls: the "Deleted item retention time (days)" field lets you specify how long deleted items linger in the dumpster before they're actually deleted, and the "Don't permanently delete items until the store has been backed up" checkbox tells the store not to delete messages from the dumpster until the store has been backed up. It's important to realize that this setting can trump your deleted item retention period. Let's say you've chosen a retention period of 3 days, then checked the "Don't permanently delete" checkbox. If you back up your store once per week, deleted items will not be permanently removed every three days—they'll go away every seven days, after the store is backed up.

The Storage Limits tab contains two controls. The "Issue Warning (K)" checkbox tells the store whether to issue storage warnings or not. Check it to turn this feature on, then fill in the size (in kilobytes) that the folder must reach to trigger the warnings. Warnings are generated according to the schedule you set in the site IS Configuration object.

The Instances tab

Earlier in the chapter, I told you how public folder replication works. However, I didn't tell you how to create public folder replicas—you use the Instances tab on a particular server. When you switch to the Instances tab, you'll see something like Figure 10-3. The Site pull-down in the bottom-left corner controls which site's folders you see in the dialog. The "Public folders" and "Folders on this Information Store" lists together contain all the folders in the site. Folders that have replicas on this server are shown on the right; folders that exist on other servers but not this one appear on the left. You can use the Add and Remove buttons to move folders from one side to the other. When you move a folder to the right-hand list, you're creating a new replica of the folder on your server; when you move it to the left, you're removing the local replica.

When you create a new replica, it's not instantly available; you have to wait for the replication process to copy the folder's contents over to the new replica. How long this takes depends on your public folder replication architecture. You can also use the Replicas tab of an individual public folder to control that particular folder's replication, as discussed later in the section "Creating new public folder replicas."

The Age Limits tab

If you let your public folders grow without limit, pretty soon they'll start to look like an abandoned factory—you know, the kind with brambles, bushes, and weeds totally covering what was once a useful structure. It's possible to set age limits on public folder contents, both at the server and individual folder levels. Whenever the public IS maintenance task runs, it goes through each folder and removes items that are older than the specified age limit.

The Age Limits tab allows you to specify two kinds of age limits. The first kind applies to all folders on this particular server: there's a checkbox labeled "Age limit for all folders on this information store (days)," along with a text entry field. To set

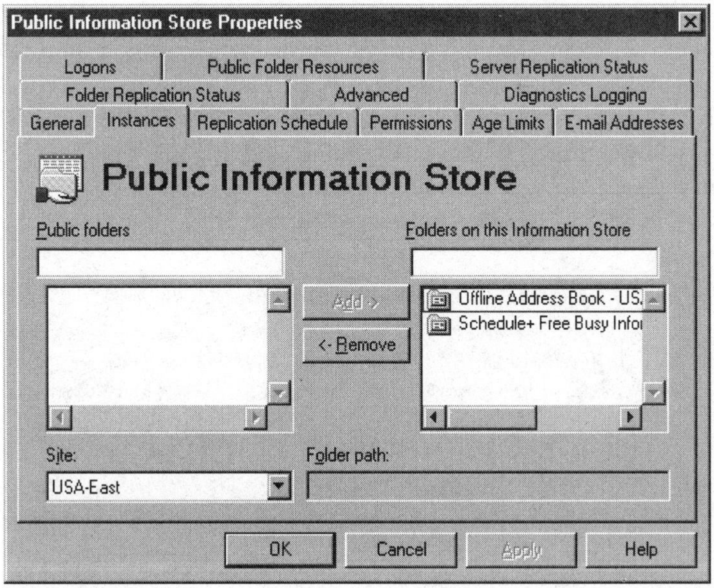

Figure 10-3. The Instances tab

a uniform limit for all folders on this server, just check the box and enter the age limit you want to use. The bottom part of the tab shows you a complete list of all folder replicas on this server. Table 10-3 shows you what data items you'll see for each replica. By default, all the columns are shown, but you can change the displayed set with the Columns... button.

Table 10-3. Columns Displayed in the Age Limits Tab

Column	What It Shows You
Folder	Name of the public folder.
This Replica (days)	Age limit set on this particular folder replica. Overrides the "All Replicas (days)" setting for individual folders.
All Replicas (days)	Default age limit set for all replicas of this folder.
Removed Older Than	Date of oldest message in the public folder; all messages older than this date have already been removed.
Total K	Total size, in kilobytes, of all nondeleted data in the public folder.
Folder Path	Complete path (starting at the root public folder) to this folder.
Delete Pending	Whether the folder is about to be deleted. If you've marked this replica for deletion, its status will show up as true, but it won't actually be deleted until the next public folder replication.

When you select a folder and click the Modify… button, you'll see the Modify Age Limits dialog (see Figure 10-4). This dialog lets you tweak the age limits for one or all replicas of the folder. The top third of the dialog shows you the folder's name and the date before which all items have been removed. The two checkboxes in the center of the dialog allow you to specify an age limit for the replica hosted on the server whose public IS you're tweaking and for all replicas of the folder throughout the site. You can set both or neither from this dialog.

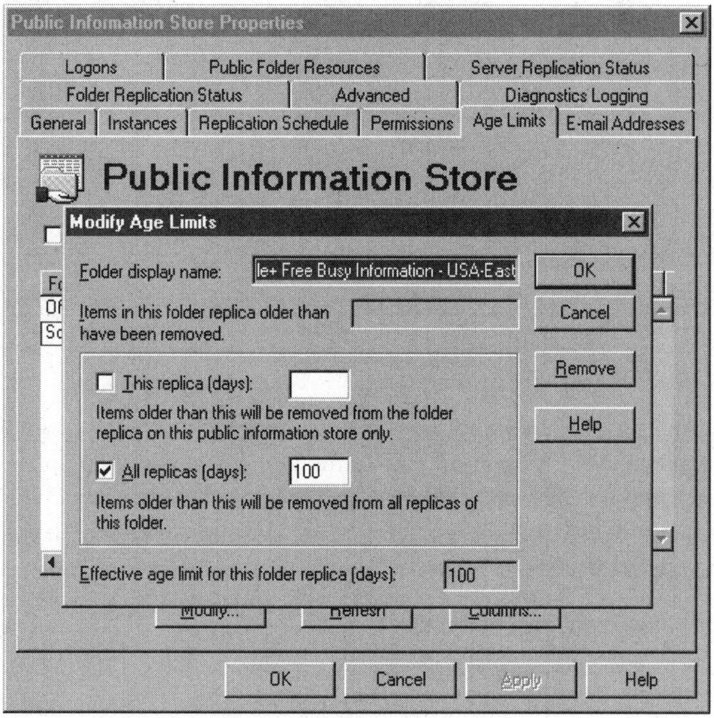

Figure 10-4. The Modify Age Limits dialog

The last field of the dialog, "Effective age limit for this folder replica (days)," is a handy guide that shows you what age limits apply to a particular folder replica; there can be more than one limit shown.

The Advanced tab

This tab should really be labeled the Extra Replication Stuff tab, since that's what's on it. There are three controls here, one of which is a button that restores the other two controls to their default values. The "Replicate always interval (minutes)" field lets you specify what "always" means in the context of public folder replication. By default, if you specify that replication can always happen,

Exchange takes that to mean that every 15 minutes it should look for, and replicate, the folder hierarchy and any changes to contents. You can adjust that interval up or down, although setting it to less than 15 minutes may result in a lot more replication activity than you expect. The other control, "Replication message size limit (K)," lets you set a maximum size for outgoing replication messages. The default of 300KB is adequate; if you lower it, you'll generate more replication messages, but each one will be smaller (conversely, raising it will give you fewer, larger messages).

Setting Properties on Folders

Even though it doesn't look like it, a public folder is really just a mailbox. If you don't believe me, you have only to look at the properties dialog for a folder and note how many of the tabs correspond to the tabs in a mailbox properties dialog! In Exchange Administrator, folders are stored in a Folders container at the organization level, although you can create new folder containers, as discussed in the section "Setting Site-wide Public IS Properties," earlier in the chapter.

 The Distribution Lists, E-mail Addresses, Custom Attributes, and Permissions tabs work just like their mailbox counterparts, so I won't talk about them here. See Chapter 6, *Mailboxes, Recipients, and Distribution Lists*, if you need a refresher.

Setting General properties

The General tab of the public folder properties dialog has several seemingly unrelated items in it. You can use the Folder Name field to rename the folder, and you can use the "Address book display name" group to specify a new name for this folder's GAL entry. The Alias name field can be used to specify a friendlier alias for the public folder; clients can use the alias as an addressee when they're sending mail to the folder.

The remaining controls are the interesting ones. If the folder you've selected has subfolders, the "Propagate these properties to all subfolders" checkbox will be visible. When you check it, any changes you make to the parent folder's properties will automatically be blasted onto all subfolders. The "Limit administrative access to home site" checkbox allows you to control who may administer the public folder. When it's checked, only users who have administrative permissions on the public folder's home server can create new replicas or rehome the public folder to another server. When it's cleared, any administrator can do so. The Client Permissions button is covered in its own section, since it's arguably the most interesting item in the entire public folder properties dialog.

Setting client permissions

When you click the Client Permissions button on the General tab of the folder properties dialog, you'll see the Client Permissions dialog shown in Figure 10-5. The area at the top shows which client permissions apply to the folder; for newly created folders, this will reflect whatever client permissions the folder inherited from its parent folder. For top-level folders, there will only be three items listed: "Default" indicates what permissions everybody gets, and "Anonymous" indicates what access anonymous IMAP4 or NNTP users get. Whoever created the folder will be listed as the owner.

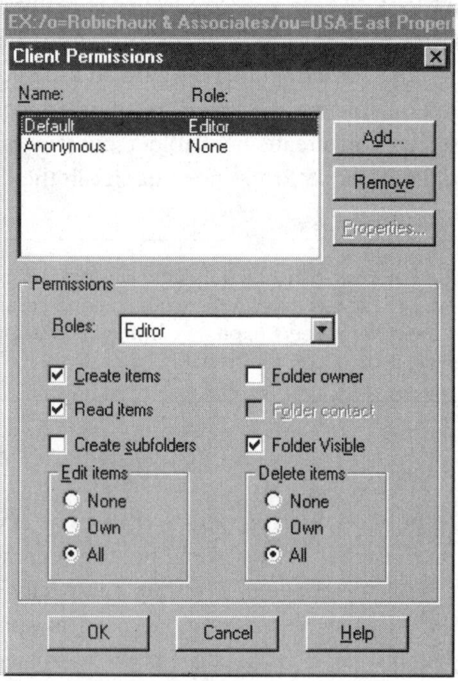

Figure 10-5. The Client Permissions dialog

You can use the Add…, Remove, and Properties… buttons to control who appears in the top list. When you add a new mailbox or DL to the list, it appears with a role assignment of "None". To change roles for an item in the list, just select it and pick the role you want it to have from the Roles pull-down. If none of the existing roles suits your needs, you can build a custom role for the selected entity by choosing whatever combination of permissions you want it to have.

Changes you make here take effect immediately on the folder's home server; since folder permissions are stored in the directory, along with the folder hierarchy, the permissions change may take time to propagate to all servers in your site or all sites in your organization.

Creating new public folder replicas

You can create additional replicas of any folder in the site with the Replicas tab of that folder. When you switch to this tab, you'll see two list boxes. The one on the left shows all servers in the site that currently don't have replicas of the folder, while the list on the right shows folders that do contain replicas. You can use the Add and Remove buttons to move servers from one side to the other. When you move a server to the left-hand list, that removes the current folder's replica from that server unless it's the last replica of the folder in the site, in which case you can't remove it. Conversely, when you move a server to the right-hand list, that causes Exchange to create a new replica of the folder on the selected server, though its contents won't be filled in until replication completes.

Remember, you can also use the Instances tab of the server's Public IS object to control what replicas are hosted on a particular server.

Setting storage and retention limits

The Limits tab of the public folder properties dialog is slightly different from the mailbox Limits tab. The biggest difference is that you can set age limits on replicas of the folder; however, you can't prohibit receiving or sending mail when the public folder goes over its size limit, as you can with mailboxes. It's important to note that the settings on this tab only apply to the selected folder replica, not to other replicas of the folder in the site or organization.

The "Deleted item retention time" control group lets you specify whether you want this folder to use the default retention time set in the public IS property page. If so, check the "Use information store defaults" checkbox; otherwise, fill in the text field with the number of days you want to cache deleted items in this replica. The "Information store storage limits" control group lets you control the storage limit for the folder, either by applying the IS default (by checking the "Use information store defaults" checkbox) or specifying the folder size that you want to trigger size warnings.

The "Age limits" control group is where you apply age limits to a particular replica. Recall that you set store-wide age limits on the Age Limits tab of the server's Public IS object; this tab lets you override those limits on a per-replica basis. When you set a limit here, it applies to all replicas of the selected folder, no matter what server they're on. You can see the effective age limit on any folder by selecting it in the Public IS object's Age Limits tab; this is really the only way to resolve the confusion of simultaneous store, folder, and replica age limits.

Scheduling replication

Normally, you'll set a replication schedule for the entire public IS and leave it alone. Sometimes, though, you need more flexibility. For example, you might want to reduce the frequency at which your NNTP news folders are replicated, or you might want to make a folder replicate more often so that its contents are available with less latency. Each folder's properties dialog has its own Replication Schedule tab, sporting the familiar schedule grid control. The big difference is that the radio buttons you use to specify a schedule have a new family member: "Use Information Store Schedule." When this button (the default) is selected, this replica will use the server-wide schedule, but if you choose any of the other buttons (Never, Always, or Selected times) you can override the replication schedule for the selected replica.

Setting advanced properties

The Advanced tab combines some of the controls you first saw on the mailbox properties dialog's Advanced tab with some new controls that are specific to public folders. "The Simple display name," "Directory name," "Container name," and "Trust level (0-100)" controls are old friends by now, so let's skip them and move on to the new stuff:

Replication msg importance

This pull-down lets you control what priority outgoing public folder replication messages carry. The default setting, Normal, means that replication messages are queued just like every other kind of message, so they don't get any special treatment. If you want to speed up or slow down replication message traffic, you can use the Urgent or Not Urgent settings, respectively.

Home server

This pull-down shows you what server this folder is homed on; it contains the names of all servers in the site that already have a replica of this folder. To rehome the folder, choose another server, and this replica will be moved to the server you select. This moves the existing replica off your server, so if you want to create a new replica, use the methods described earlier in the chapter.

You might wonder why you'd want to rehome a folder. Normally, you do this because the folder is living on one server, but has most of its active users on another server. Since the home server receives all messages sent to the folder, it makes more sense to have the folder homed where most of its users are; thus, you'd probably want to rehome it.

Hide From Address Book

> This checkbox, which is turned on by default, keeps this public folder's addresses from appearing in the GAL. You can still send mail to a public folder whose address you know, but hiding it makes it harder for random users to post messages to it using their mail clients.

Container name

> This field shows you what container the public folder lives in. Unless you've changed it as described earlier in this chapter, you'll normally see "Recipients" in this field.

A Word About Newsgroup Public Folders

When you install the Exchange Internet News Service (INS), you'll find out that it expects to dump incoming NNTP articles into your public folder hierarchy. When you install INS, you get a new top-level public folder called *Internet Newsgroups*; whichever newsgroups you tell your INS to carry will appear in a hierarchy below that top-level folder.

The good news is that all the standard tabs you've learned about apply to Usenet newsgroups stored in public folders. It's good news, because that means you can apply storage limits and aging to keep the relentless flow of inbound news from choking your server. There's an additional tab in the properties dialog of newsgroup public folders: the NNTP tab lets you see the group's full name (like *hsv.general* or *comp.os.mswindows.windows-nt.admin*) and choose which character set it uses.

For more on the details of administering the INS, see Chapter 12, *Managing the Internet News Service.*

Viewing Folder Status and Resource Usage

Oftentimes you'll want to see what's happening with your public folders. For example, you might want to know whether a particular server has been replicating like it's supposed to, or how much storage space a certain folder occupies. You can use the following four views (described separately in the next several sections) to find out what's happening with your public folders:

- Folder Replication Status
- Logons view
- Public Folder Resources view
- Server Replication Status view

You can get this data from several places:

- The properties dialog of individual folder instances includes a tab for the Folder Replication Status view. This view shows the status of all servers that host replicas of the selected folder.

- The properties dialog of the server-level Public Information Store properties dialog has tabs for the Public Folder Resources, Server Replication Status, and Folder Replication Status views. These views show data for all replicas hosted by the selected server.

- The Public Information Store container at the server level in Exchange Administrator contains leaf objects for all four views. These leaf objects work like the mailbox resources view you've already seen. Selecting the leaf object fills the right half of the Exchange Administrator window with the selected view's data. The leaf objects show all data for the selected server.

The Folder Replication Status view

The Folder Replication Status view shows you the replication status of each folder replica on this server. By default, the view contains four columns, though you can customize the view with the View → Columns... command. The Display Name column shows the replica's name; the Last Received Time column shows you when the last replication message for this folder arrived, and the Number of Replicas column shows how many replicas of the folder exist in the site.

 If you're looking at any of these views inside a properties dialog, use the Columns... button to customize the view, since the menu won't be available inside the properties dialog.

The Replication Status column shows you whether there are unreplicated changes in this replica or not. A status of "In Sync" means that this replica's contents match other replicas in the site, and that all changes have been replicated with no conflicts. A status of "Local Modified" tells you that your replica has changes in it that haven't been replicated to other sites yet.

The Logons view

The Logons view shows you who's currently logged on to the public IS on the selected server. By default, the view shows you the username and NT account name for each user, along with the time they logged on and the time they last communicated with the store. If you use the View → Columns... command, you'll find that there are a ton of other items you can view, including the host address, the number of open folders, attachments, or messages, and the number of various types of database operations.

The Server Replication Status view

This view shows the overall status of replication activity on the selected server. The default view shows you the server's name, the replication status (either "In Sync" or "Local Modified," as in the Folder Replication Status view), and the arrival time of the last incoming replication message. Two other items are also shown by default: the average transmission time required to send updates from the local server to the server you're looking at, and the amount of transmission time required to send the most recent replication update in the same direction.

The Public Folder Resources view

This view is a one-stop summary of what's in your public folders. The default view shows you the total number of items in each folder and how much space they take up; when the folder was created, when it was last accessed, and how many accounts have the Owner and Folder Contact roles assigned.

If you use the View → Columns... command to customize the view, you'll see that you can also see the total space used by deleted items that are currently in the deleted items retention store, the folder name, the full path to the folder, and the total number of messages like forms, views, and templates in the folder that actually belong to the system.

 Don't forget that you can use the File → Save Window Contents... command to save the contents of any of these views as a CSV file.

Enabling Anonymous Folder Postings

Anonymity makes it easier to say things you might not say if your name were attached to your message. Thomas Paine used it to great effect, as did Benjamin Franklin. On the current Internet, it's used both for good and evil. What does this have to do with you? You can configure your Exchange servers to allow anonymous posts to one or more public folders. This may be desirable or undesirable, depending on how you view it. In general, anonymous public folders are useful for the same types of things as a locked suggestion box—reporting safety hazards, fraud, waste, and abuse, and the like. By setting up an anonymous public folder and then giving read access only to those with a need to know, you can provide this functionality to your users with a minimum of fuss.

To make this work, you'll have to install the Anonymous Posting NT service, which comes on the Exchange CD (*setup\i386\sampapps\server\anon*) and configure an account for it to use; you'll also need to create the anonymous public folder. The service accepts messages sent to the public folder, makes them anonymous, and posts them in the public folder without any identifying information.

Here's how to install and configure the service:

1. Use User Manager to create an account for the service to run under. This anonymous service account must have "Log on as a service" permission, and it must be a member of a group that has Administrator privileges in Exchange; if it's not, the service won't be able to log on to the Exchange database.

2. Create a mailbox named Anonymous and assign its primary Windows NT account to the account you created in step 1.

3. Use Exchange Administrator to give the anonymous service account Administrator privileges on the organization and site objects.

4. Use Outlook to create the public folder to which you want anonymous posts to go.

5. Edit the folder properties with Exchange Administrator. Make the following changes:

   a. Give the anonymous account from step 1 Editor privileges on the folder.

   b. Use the Administration tab of the public folder properties dialog to create a new rule on the folder. The rule should accept mail from the anonymous service account and forward it to the public folder.

   c. Select the new rule in the Folder Assistant dialog, then click the Edit Rule button. When the Edit Rule dialog appears, click Delete.

   d. Click the Advanced... button; when its dialog appears, make sure the "Only Items That Do not Match These Conditions" checkbox is selected. This creates a rule that deletes any items that don't match the rule from step b.

   e. Dismiss the public folder properties dialog.

6. Install the anonymous posting service by copying all files from the *setup\ i386\sampapps\server\anon* directory on the CD to some location on your disk, then running the *instanon.exe* installer.

As long as the service is running, any messages posted to the folder will appear as anonymous messages. When the server is not running, you can still post messages, but they won't appear in the folder until the service is next started.

Controlling Public Folder Replication

Public folders are a great way to disseminate information, not to mention that you can build pretty sophisticated collaboration tools on top of them. However, there's a tricky balancing act required to make good use of folders. On one hand, you could just lump all your folders on one server in a site, then let users go there to get their data. This eases management and eliminates replication traffic, but that poor server is responsible for serving all clients, which can hurt its overall performance. Clients still have to use bandwidth to get to the folder contents, though. On the other hand, you can replicate every folder to every site, ensuring that users can always get a local replica of any folder they want, but guaranteeing a ton of perhaps unnecessary replication traffic.

You'll have to find a happy medium between these two extremes; exactly what you end up with will depend on several factors. The good news is that it's fairly easy to change your mind!

Picking a Replication Strategy

So, how do you decide how many replicas you need and where to put them? The best strategy is to carefully analyze three things: what's in the folders, who needs access to it, and how often it changes. These factors will vary from place to place. For example, one client of mine uses public folders to distribute the contents of the employee handbook. Since this doesn't change very often, and since it's not accessed frequently, there's only one replica of that particular folder; the customer feedback and project tracking folders and the folders that hold Outlook schedule information are replicated more widely.

The more often items in a folder change, the more replication traffic occurs. This traffic will be generated even if no one's interested in the folder contents. By contrast, a nonreplicated folder won't generate any traffic until a client actually comes to look at it. The heuristic you should take away from this dichotomy is simple: use fewer replicas of folders that change often but aren't frequently accessed, and use more replicas of folders that are heavily accessed. Of course, this is only a heuristic, not an ironclad principle.

Understanding replication conflicts

A *replication conflict* occurs when the same message is edited in more than one replica at the same time. If there's only one replica of a folder, there's no problem: only one user can record changes to a single item at a time, no matter how many accounts have permission to do so. When a folder has multiple replicas, though, conflicts can occur. Let's say that the folder in question is set to replicate twice per day, at noon and midnight. On Monday morning, my editor and I both modify our local replica's copy of a public folder message. At noon, when the replication kicks off, both our servers notice that there are actually two separate and incompatible changes to the same item, and the home server for the folder notifies whoever is designated as the folder contact.

How does this work? The public folder replication agent (PFRA) is the part of the public IS charged with replicating public folder data. Each item in each replica has its own unique change number that specifies how many changes have been made to the item. The PFRA also maintains a set of *predecessor change numbers* that keep track of which versions of the item existed on the replica in the past. As you edit an item in a public folder, the change number is updated.

When a message is replicated from one site to another, the receiving PFRA can compare the change number of its copy of an item to the change number of the incoming item. If the existing item's change number appears on the predecessor list of the incoming item, the store knows that the new item really is newer than the existing copy. If the existing item's change number isn't on the new item's predecessor list, that means that the incoming item is older than the local item, which signals a replication conflict.

Conflicts have to be manually resolved by the folder contact; however, once the contact has fixed the problem, the resolved message can be replicated normally.

What affects replication bandwidth usage?

Lots of things affect replication volume. As you've already seen, the number of changes to items in the folder is one factor. Every change to an item generates replication traffic to all replicas of the folder, so if you change one item three times that's actually three separate replication messages! The problem multiplies if your public folder architecture allows users in multiple sites to make changes to their local replicas. You can have multiple changes to the same item from each site, which in turn generates replication conflict messages.

The amount of data in the folder is important, too. Exchange treats every item independently, whether it's a 25MB PowerPoint presentation or a 1KB message. Any change to an item causes the entire item to be replicated, so changing one title in that large PowerPoint file will cause the whole file to be replicated to all folder replicas. If you have items that will be modified often, it's usually better to break them up into the smallest possible pieces. For example, you might store individual sections of a book manuscript instead of storing entire chapters or (horrors!) the entire book as a single file. Newsgroup folders are notorious for growing large, too, especially for folders that carry popular Usenet groups. The more data in the folders, the more bandwidth replication will require.

Of course, the replication schedule you choose also has a profound influence on how much bandwidth your replication will occupy. Since replication data travels in normal messages, if you clog your connectors with tons of replication messages, real messages won't be able to get through. How do you choose an appropriate schedule? Read on.

Choosing a Reasonable Schedule

One good way to throttle back the amount of replication bandwidth is to adjust the replication schedule to reflect how often folder contents change. (Remember, you can't adjust the schedule used for replicating the folder hierarchy.) By default, replication is set to "Always," which means that every 15 minutes, your servers will start chattering to each other. To start with, dial back the replication frequency so that noncritical folders are replicated less often. While this increases latency and thus raises the chance that replication conflicts will occur, the savings in bandwidth may make up for it. You can adjust the schedule so that replication happens only at particular times of the day, plus you can limit replication to particular days of the week.

In most cases, limiting replication of noncritical folders to nighttime hours on weekdays can do wonders. Since public folder data is replicated via mail messages, there's no point in replicating public folders more frequently than the underlying connector. If your public folder schedule is set to replicate every two hours, but the connector you're using only activates every six hours, you're wasting cycles and bandwidth to generate updates that will just sit in the queue.

Why Backfill Is Your Friend

If your network and servers all run perfectly 100% of the time, every replication message that one server sends will arrive at all its destinations. For those of us who fall short of that ultimate reliability, there's replication backfill. Backfill might sound like landfill, but it's not—the term comes from the construction industry. When you build a retaining wall in your yard, and you pile dirt up next to it after the wall is upright, that's backfill. Hold that thought while I explain how Exchange does it.

Exchange attempts to backfill public folder data whenever it detects that it hasn't gotten all the replication updates for a public folder. These updates are packaged into what the PFRA calls *folder content packets*. The missing packets may be missing because one or more replication messages were smashed in transit by a foreign gateway or misbehaving MTA; it might also be necessary to backfill a server that crashed and was restored, because the server will miss any public folder replication traffic sent while it's down.

When the PFRA notices that it's missing one or more packets, it creates placeholders in the public IS. These placeholders indicate that some real public folder data should be present, but isn't. The PFRA waits for a while to see whether the missing packets show up on their own, as they might if the problem is a delayed update rather than a missing one. At the end of that waiting period, the PFRA issues a backfill request to two other servers that hold replicas of the folder. The request identifies which content packets are missing. When the PFRA on another server sees the backfill request, it bundles up the requested folder content packets and sends them to the server that needs the backfill.

There are two related situations to consider. First of all, what happens when you add a new replica? The replica doesn't have any data in it at first, so the PFRA on the replica's server sends a backfill request for the folder's contents. When it arrives, the folder contents are backfilled, and everyone's happy. The other situation is the reverse: what happens when a backfill packet arrives for a folder that doesn't exist, as it might if a recent change was made to the public folder hierarchy? In that case, the PFRA queues the packet and waits to see whether a corresponding change to the hierarchy arrives within four hours. If it doesn't, the packet expires, and if the server wants the update, it'll have to request it via another backfill request.

Replicating Between Organizations

Exchange 5.5 SP2 adds a nifty new tool for replicating public folder data between organizations. This tool's called the Interorg Replication Utility (IRU), and it allows you to selectively replicate some or all public folder data (including free/busy data) between servers in two organizations. To use IRU, you have to install the IRU services on a server, then make a few minor configuration changes to each organization's Exchange servers.

IRU basics

Let's start with some terminology that Microsoft's defined just for this product. Figure 10-6 shows a made-up configuration using IRU to join two organizations, cleverly named A and B. In the diagram, you'll see that A is labeled as a *publisher*, B is labeled as a *subscriber,* and there's a *replication agent* between them. Let's decode these terms:

Publisher
> Owns the folders and exports folder contents outside the organization.

Subscriber
> Receives content from a publisher. You can allow changes made by a subscriber to be replicated back to the publisher, or not.

Replication agent
> An NT server that connects the publisher and subscriber. The agent can be located in either the publisher or subscriber domain; it logs on to both sides' Exchange servers using appropriate credentials.

The replication agent connects to the publisher's public folder server, copies some or all of that server's data, and packages it for delivery to the subscriber organization. In the opposite direction, changes made to the replicated data on the sub-

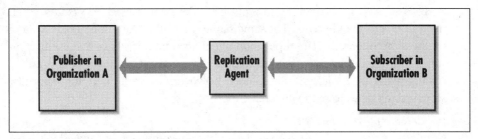

Figure 10-6. A simple IRU configuration

scriber side can be packaged up and sent back to the publisher, where they're injected into the public IS just as though a user on the publisher network had changed it.

Replicating free/busy information

Free/busy information is stored in a separate, hidden public folder. You can use IRU to replicate it so that you can effectively schedule resources and appointments between two organizations. However, you can only publish free/busy information in one direction. If you want two organizations to be able to schedule items on each others' calendars, you'll need to set up two separate publishers, one on each side, and two replication agents.

Setting up the IRU

To use the IRU, you have to complete five steps: you must prepare the publisher and subscriber servers, set up the replication agent, create a replication configuration file, and set up the replication service itself. The first three steps are fairly easy to accomplish; let's see what's involved:

Setting up the publisher server

This requires you to set up a mailbox and NT account for the replication agent service to use, so we'll call this the *replication agent account*. You need to grant this new account Owner permission on each folder you want to publish. Alternately, you can grant the account Publishing Editor permissions, but the Default and Anonymous permission settings on the folder won't be replicated.

You also have to create a new public folder for the replication agent. Use your Outlook client to make a new folder named *ExchsyncSecurityFolder* under "All Public Folders," then grant Folder Visible permission to the replication agent account. Don't assign any Anonymous or Default permissions to this folder.

Configuring the subscriber server

You need to create a replication agent account on this server, too, and to create the *ExchsyncSecurityFolder* folder. You also need to create root folders in the subscriber public folder hierarchy for each set of folders you're subscribing to. Let's say you're subscribing to a public folder named *Open PSS Issues*; you'd need to create a folder with that same name under the "All Public Folders" item on the subscriber side. The replication agent account must have Publishing Editor or Owner permissions on the folders. If you don't set this up, the public folders won't be replicated. Subfolders, however, are replicated automatically, so you don't need to manually create them.

Setting up the replication agent

Normally, you run this service on the publisher computer, but you don't have to. The only requirement is that the computer on which you put the agent must be a member of either the publisher or subscriber domain. The replication agent machine must be running NT 4.0 SP3 or later and Outlook 97/98, along with Exchange 5.5 SP2. To install the replication agent, create a directory somewhere on your machine (I usually use *\exchsrvr\replagent*) and copy the files from the *server\support\exchsync\i386* directory on your SP2 CD or distribution directory to the new directory. The two files you need are *exscfg.exe* (the configuration utility) and *exssrv.exe* (the replication agent itself).

Configuring the replication agent

Now that you've set up the publisher and subscriber machines and installed the replication agent, it's time to configure the agent to do what you want—this is the fourth step in the five-step IRU setup process. You do this with *exscfg.exe*, the replication agent configuration utility. Once you launch it, here's what to do:

1. Use the Session → Add... command. A dialog will pop up asking you to indicate whether you want to replicate free/busy information or plain folder contents. Select the appropriate radio button and click OK. The dialog shown in Figure 10-7 will appear.

2. Fill in the Title field with whatever name you want this configuration to have.

3. Adjust the Maximum Tasks field to set the appropriate number of threads for the replication agent. You should allocate one thread per site you're replicating with if you're doing free/busy replication, and either 2 or 4 threads (4 is better) when replicating public folder information.

4. Use the Schedule... button if you want to schedule times for the replication agent to run. By default, the agent runs every 30 minutes throughout the week, but you can limit it to particular days of the week or time ranges.

5. If you want to log replication events to a text file, which I recommend until you're confident that everything's working right, click the Logging... button and check the Enable checkbox.

6. Use the controls in the Publisher Organization group to specify the server and replication agent mailboxes you want to use on the publisher machine. Next, you can use the Advanced button to specify the NT domain credentials you

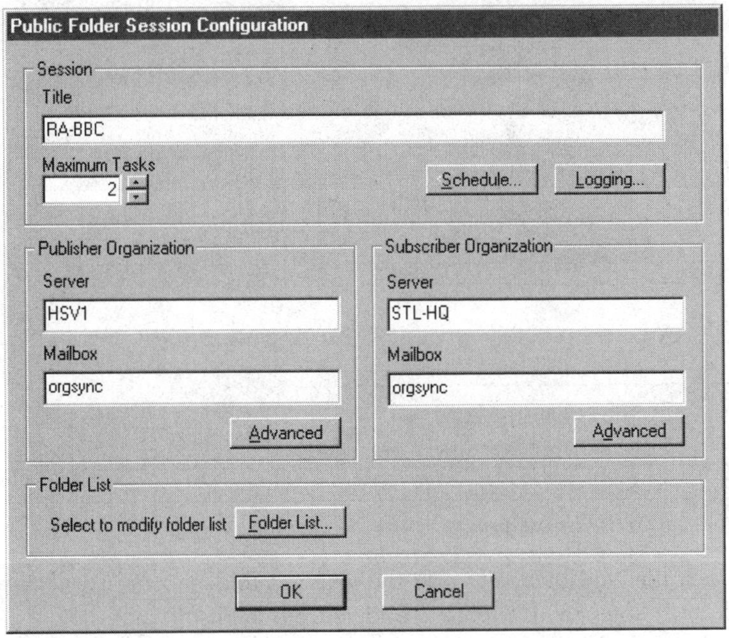

Figure 10-7. The IRU configuration dialog

want the agent account to use when it logs on to the publisher. Fill in the controls in the Subscriber Organization group the same way.

7. If you're creating a replication configuration for free/busy information, you won't be able to do this step. Otherwise, you can click the Folder List... button to see a dialog that shows all the public folders on each side. The dialog itself is divided into several sections, as shown in Figure 10-8.

Fill these sections out as follows:

— The folders available on the publisher and subscriber sides are shown in the top half of the dialog. The Logon buttons let you log on to the respective machines to get their folder lists. Log on to both machines before proceeding.

— Select each folder you want to replicate from the list on the left, then use the controls below the folder list to specify where each published folder is replicated to.

— The row of four buttons gives you control over what happens when the selected folder is replicated. Click Subfolders to replicate subfolders of the selected folder; click Deletions to replicate deleted messages and folders, and use the Default and Anonymous buttons to control whether those sets of folder permissions are replicated, too.

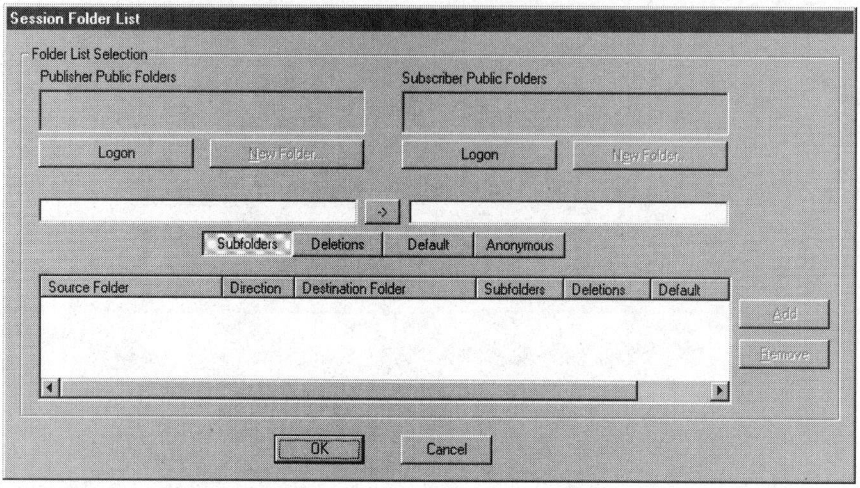

Figure 10-8. The IRU folder list dialog

— Click the Add button to add the selected folder to the replication list. Of course, you can also remove folders from the list if necessary.

8. Click OK to dismiss the session configuration dialog, then save your configuration file using the File → Save... command or the toolbar button. Close the configuration tool.

Configuring and starting the replication agent service

The fifth and final step is to install and configure the replication agent service. When you run *exssrv.exe* for the first time, you'll need to use the Install button in its main window to specify the replication account credentials you want to use and the location of the configuration file you saved in step 8 above. You can optionally have the replication agent started at boot time by checking the "Automatic start at system boot" checkbox, or you can start it manually using the Services control panel, the Server Manager, or the NT command line.

11

Managing the Information Store

You learned how to manage the public IS in Chapter 10, *Managing Public Folders*, but I cleverly disguised the material as a discussion of public folder management. In this chapter, you'll learn how to manage the private IS. Since it doesn't take much management, this is a short chapter.

The private IS database stores user mail, and that's all it does. The IS service itself is responsible for delivering mail sent between recipients on the same server, and it works in conjunction with the MTA (and perhaps the IMS) to deliver mail to recipients on other servers. There's no way to adjust that aspect of its behavior, though you can tweak some settings that pertain to user mailboxes.

Most of the time, when people want to configure the private IS, what they're really trying to do is control mailbox behavior. The things they want to control typically include one or more of the following:

- Setting deleted item retention periods

- Setting storage limits to restrict how much mail users may store in their mailboxes

- Granting one user permission to use another user's mailbox (as you'll see in Chapter 13, *Managing Exchange Clients*, you usually do this from the client, although you can give any mailbox User permission on another mailbox, as discussed in Chapter 6, *Mailboxes, Recipients, and Distribution Lists*)

- Backing up and restoring individual mailboxes (covered in Chapter 17, *Recovery and Repair*)

Other aspects of mailbox management, like setting options for individual mailboxes, are covered in Chapter 6; this chapter will focus on the first two items.

IS Basics

From reading Chapter 2, *Exchange Architecture*, you know how the IS and DS databases work, how transactions are logged, and so on. Understanding the database mechanism is important, since every change made to the private IS must be recorded for your database to remain consistent. Instead of rehashing that stuff, I will talk about some features unique to the IS.

IS Maintenance

The IS databases require periodic maintenance. This is no different from any other kind of database; as items are inserted into and removed from the database, the tables used to store those items expand. The only way to make the tables shrink is to compact them by actually removing deleted items, but this takes time. When the contents of one table changes, there may be changes necessary to other tables, and so on, *ad infinitum.*

Don't confuse the routine IS maintenance I'm talking about here with emergency maintenance, which you do using the tools described in Chapter 17. Routine maintenance is automatic; the IS does some tasks on a schedule you set with the server properties dialog's IS Maintenance tab (see Chapter 14, *Managing Exchange Servers*, for more on this tab), and it does other tasks on its own. Emergency maintenance is more like taking your car to the body shop after getting rear-ended; you don't do it unless you have to, and it doesn't happen automatically.

Scheduled maintenance

Six tasks take place during scheduled IS maintenance: two of them run on both the public and private IS databases, and the other four run only on the public database. Every 15 minutes, the master maintenance thread in the IS checks to see whether that interval is marked as a maintenance start time in the schedule on the IS Maintenance tab. If it is, the master thread fires up a single maintenance thread, which runs at below-normal priority, so that it doesn't interfere with processing mail. The maintenance thread performs each of the six tasks in series. Each task has a minimum period associated with it that you can't change; if that period hasn't been reached when the maintenance thread starts, the thread won't perform that particular task until the minimum period has been reached. This prevents the IS from wasting time on a task that was recently completed and doesn't yet need to be run again.

Here's what the six tasks do. To learn how to control them, see the section "Controlling IS Maintenance," later in the chapter.

Index aging

The IS maintains a separate set of indices for each client. These indices cache table information to make displaying messages in a particular view faster. After a certain period of time, indices belonging to views that haven't been used in a while are removed.

Tombstone maintenance

As you may remember, when an item in the IS or DS is deleted, it's not immediately removed; it's marked with a tombstone and left in the database for a while. Every 24 hours (the minimum interval, which can't be changed), the tombstone maintenance task ages tombstones and removes items whose tombstones have reached their age limit.

Public store message expiration

This process zips through the public store and deletes public folder messages that have reached the effective age limit set for that folder (remember, there's one limit set on the entire public IS, but there may also be a limit on any individual folder). The default minimum interval for this task is 24 hours, but you can adjust it in the registry.

Public store folder tombstone aging

If the IS just let tombstones lie around after the items they mark were deleted, pretty soon the public IS database would be clogged with unnecessary tombstones. Every 24 hours (the minimum interval for this task, which you can't change), the tombstone aging task removes any tombstone older than the aging limit, which is 180 days by default but can be adjusted. This process keeps the number of tombstones from growing without limit by pruning old tombstones that have already been replicated. Note that this process affects only folder tombstones; message tombstones are handled by the tombstone maintenance task.

Public store server version updating

Each Exchange server has a version number that comes from the version of Exchange running on it. The DS stores the version number of each server so that newer versions of Exchange can be made to interoperate with older versions; distinguishing new from old depends on these numbers. Every 24 hours, this task updates the public store's copy of these version numbers.

Public store article index expiration

This task only runs if you've installed and configured the INS to put NNTP news in your public folder hierarchy. At the minimum interval (60 minutes, by default, but you can change it), this task removes expired articles. Articles expire after seven days, unless you change the expiration period; expiring an article is effectively the same as deleting a public folder message.

Nonscheduled routine maintenance

Apart from the regularly scheduled maintenance tasks outlined above, the IS does a variety of other background maintenance tasks at varying intervals. You can't schedule these tasks; they run at intervals determined by the IS. In some cases, you can adjust how often they run, but that's not true for all tasks.

There are four nonscheduled tasks:

Background cleanup

The background cleanup task recovers space in the database files by completely removing items whose lifespan has ended (i.e., items whose deleted item retention period has passed, transient objects created by the IS and DS, and so on). You can think of this task as the one that actually empties the dumpster.

Database compaction

Database compaction, more properly called online defragmentation, shuffles pages in the database so that the database file is contiguous. This task normally runs after the background cleanup task, so that space marked as available during that task can be compacted during this task.

Storage warning generation

This task isn't scheduled as part of IS maintenance; you schedule it with the Storage Warnings tab of the IS Site Configuration object. When this task runs, it looks for mailboxes or public folders that exceed their size limits, then takes the appropriate action. This task runs as a separate background thread, but the nonscheduled maintenance thread is in charge of launching it when the schedule dictates.

Periodic maintenance

Every ten minutes, the IS starts a background thread to perform some necessary tasks, which run at varying intervals. Some tasks run every ten minutes, while others run once per day. These periodic tasks do the following:

— Reload the current IS storage quotas from the directory

— Flush the current cache of table row counts back to the IS database file

— Flush any cached directory information that needs to be written to the DS database

— Reload per-mailbox storage quotas from the directory for use in the storage warning task

The Dumpster

Exchange 5.5 added a neat new feature: deleted item recovery. Once this feature is enabled, users can undelete messages they've deleted. Once a message is deleted, it stays in the IS, but is marked as deleted. Exchange treats these deleted items as though they were in a virtual container, which Microsoft calls the *dumpster*, until the deleted item retention period is reached. For example, if you've set the retention period to 30 days, a message you delete on March 1 will stay in the dumpster until March 31. When the SA runs its database maintenance thread, one task of that thread is deleting any messages in the dumpster whose retention periods have been reached.

The private and public IS give you a further safety valve; if you check the "Don't permanently delete items until the store has been backed up" checkbox in the corresponding property page, the maintenance thread won't remove anything from the dumpster until after a successful backup, meaning that as long as you have a good backup, you can restore a deleted item even after the retention period is over by restoring the entire backup to a recovery server, as described in Chapter 17.

Client dumpster support

Apart from having Exchange 5.5, you must use particular revisions of Outlook. Outlook 97 8.03 was the first version to incorporate dumpster support, so you must be running that version or a newer one (including Outlook 2000). The MacOS Outlook client supports deleted item recovery, as does the OWA client. Unfortunately, POP3 and IMAP4 clients don't support recovery by default, because of how deleted items are handled.

How items get in the dumpster

When you delete an item from within Outlook, Outlook moves the item to a special folder in your mailbox called Deleted Items. Items in the IS dumpster don't count toward your mailbox storage limit, but items in your *Deleted Items* folder do.

Clients that use POP3 or IMAP4 don't know about the *Deleted Items* folder, so they just ask the store to delete the message, meaning that it never goes to the dumpster. The same holds true when you use the Shift-Delete accelerator in Outlook, because that tells it to remove the selected items immediately without putting them in the dumpster. However, the store doesn't actually delete these items. Instead, it marks them as deleted, but leaves them in place until the next time the system's database maintenance thread runs. That means you could still potentially recover them, but Outlook only enables the Tools → Recover Deleted Items… command when you select the *Deleted Items* folder.

Using DumpsterAlwaysOn

You can force Outlook to turn the recovery command on in more folders by adding a new REG_DWORD value called DumpsterAlwaysOn beneath the Outlook registry key at HKLM\SOFTWARE\Microsoft\Exchange\Client\Options, then setting its value to 1. With this switch on, Outlook will allow you to use the Recover Deleted Items... command on any mail folder, but not on contacts, tasks, or journal items.

To automate this change on all your machines, add it to your system policies so that it's automatically distributed to clients.

What about POP3 and IMAP4 clients? They still don't know about recovering deleted items, but by using Outlook to log on to an individual mailbox, you can still recover items that someone has accidentally deleted. As you'll see in Chapter 17, restoring an individual mailbox to the server is a big hassle, so it's a lot easier to use this trick to let users recover their own mail.

Configuring the IS

There are two types of IS settings you can adjust: the settings Microsoft exposes in Exchange Administrator, and those that require you to fire up a registry editor and get your hands dirty. For the most part, the adjustments you can make from within Exchange Administrator will be sufficient, but I'll cover the others, too.

Configuring Server-Level Properties

In Chapter 10, you learned how to configure the site Configuration container's IS Site Configuration object. In that object, you schedule storage warning generation, regulate who can create public folders, and so on—there are no settings that pertain strictly to the private IS. You configure the private IS through each server's Private Information Store object. When you expand a server object in Exchange Administrator's container pane, you'll see that the Private IS object has two leaf nodes below it: Logons and Mailbox Resources. They're covered in the next section; the real action is in the properties dialog for the Private IS object itself.

The General tab, shown in Figure 11-1, lets you control the two items mentioned earlier in the chapter: deleted item recovery periods and storage warning limits. The Item Recovery group lets you specify the deleted item retention period for this server's private IS (the setting you make here has no effect on the public IS, or on any other server in the site). Use the "Don't permanently delete items until the store has been backed up" checkbox to force the store to hang on to items in the dumpster until the next backup successfully finishes; it's checked by default.

The "Storage limits" group lets you set mailbox quotas for all mailboxes on the store that don't have storage limits specified. By default, there aren't any limits

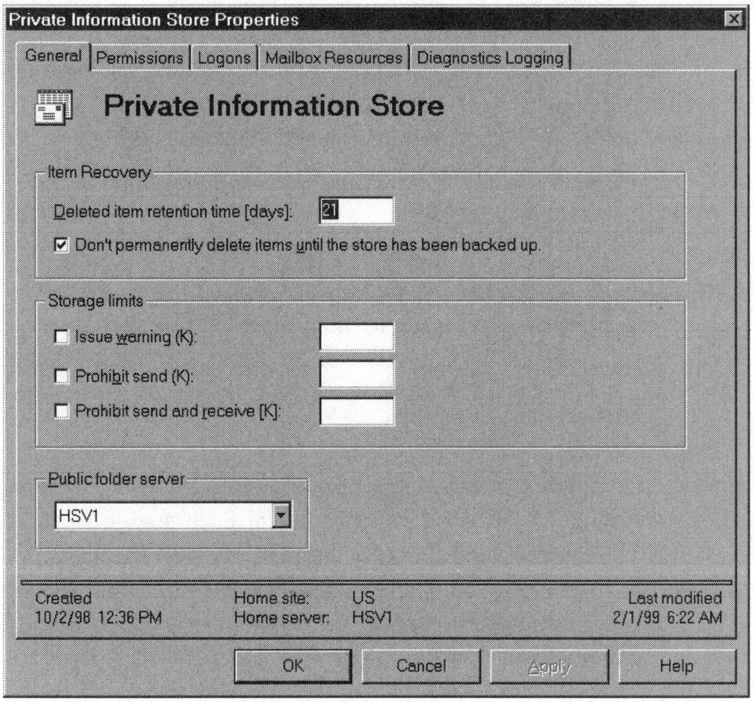

Figure 11-1. The General tab of the Private Information Store Properties dialog

imposed. There are three levels of limits. The "Issue warning" controls set the limit
at which the SA will send a polite message (which you unfortunately can't customize) to the user saying, basically, "your mailbox has too much stuff in it, so clean
some out." The "Prohibit send" controls specify the mailbox size limit that will
keep people from sending out new mail; likewise, the "Prohibit send and receive"
controls will stop MAPI users* from sending or receiving mail until their mailbox
size drops below the limit.

The "Public folder server" pull-down allows you to tell the IS which public IS
server is handling public folder data for mailboxes on this server. If you're using a
server that already has a public IS on it, this pull-down will contain your local
server's name. To remove the public IS, just use this pull-down to specify another
public folder server for user mailboxes, then use Exchange Administrator to delete
the public IS.

---

* These controls have no effect on outbound messages sent by POP3, IMAP4, and OWA users, but the
  inbound limits still apply.

Controlling IS Maintenance

Despite the bewildering number of options, buttons, and property pages in Exchange Administrator, not every parameter you can tweak has a corresponding user interface setting. This is especially true of the IS maintenance process, which you should leave alone, for the most part. However, there may be times when you want or need to adjust these settings.

 All the keys I mention in the rest of this section are stored under the `HKLM\System\CurrentControlSet\Services\MSExchangeIS` key, so all paths are given relative to that location.

Controlling index aging

There are three index aging settings you can modify; the IS maintains separate versions of these settings for the public and private IS. Each setting is a `REG_DWORD` that lives in either `ParametersPublic` (for the public IS) or `ParametersPrivate` (for the private IS). If you want to change these settings from their default values, you'll have to use a registry editor to add the value you want, since the defaults are used when the related value doesn't exist.

`Aging Clean Interval`
> This interval specifies how often the IS should scan through the cache looking for old items that can be deleted. The default interval is 24 hours, but you can supply a new one as long as you calculate it in milliseconds.

`Aging Keep Time`
> This value specifies how long a view will be kept after its last use by a client. The default is 8 days; if you're modifying this value for Exchange 4.0 or 5.0, it's in milliseconds, but if you're using Exchange 5.5, you have to specify it in seconds; don't forget to multiply by 86,400 to convert from days to seconds. Microsoft recommends lengthening this interval if public folder performance suffers on large folders, since it takes longer to recreate a view that's been aged out of existence than to fetch it from the cache.

`Reset Views`
> If this setting exists, and if its value is not 0, the IS will remove all cached view indices the next time the aging task runs. Once the index aging finishes, this value will be set back to 0. Use this setting if you want to completely flush the view cache.

You can also turn on diagnostic logging for the index aging process by adding a `Views` value to the private or public IS diagnostic logging keys in the registry:

`Diagnostics\Private\General\Views` and `Diagnostics\Public\General\Views`, respectively. Acceptable settings for these values match the standard diagnostic logging settings: 0 means "none" and 5 means "maximum."

Controlling message expiration

By default, the expiration task runs every 24 hours, but you can provide your own interval, in milliseconds, by adding a new value named `Replication Expiry` to the `ParametersPublic` key.

You can also turn on diagnostic logging for the expiration process by adding a value named `Diagnostics\Public\Replication\Expiry` and setting its value to the desired logging level, from 0 to 5.

Controlling public folder tombstone aging

The `ParametersPublic\Replication Folder Tombstone Age Limit` key controls the lifetime of public folder tombstones. This value should be in days; if you don't add this value, the default of 180 days will be used.

Controlling article expiration

You can control NNTP article expiration in two ways. The first is controlling how often the cleanup occurs; you make this change by adding a value named `ParametersPublic\NNTP Article Cleanup Interval` and setting it to the number of milliseconds indicating the interval you want the task to run at. The default value is 60 seconds, or 60,000 milliseconds.

You can also control how old an article can be before it's subject to expiration. The default value here is 7 days, but you might need to adjust it down if you have a large amount of traffic on your server, or up if you want to keep articles around longer. Either way, you'll have to add the `ParametersPublic\NNTP Article Expiry` value, which holds the expiration interval in milliseconds.

Controlling background cleanup

You can regulate the frequency at which the public and private background cleanup tasks run by adjusting the `ParametersPublic\Background Cleanup` and `ParametersPrivate\Background Cleanup` values. Adjust them (using values in milliseconds) to reflect the interval at which you want the background cleanup tasks to run.

Viewing IS Resource Usage

The IS tracks some aspects of its resource usage for you. In particular, you can see who's logged on to the store at any point in time (the Logons view), and you can see what resources individual mailboxes are using in the store (the Mailbox Resources view). Like the public IS, the private IS resource views are available in two places: there are tabs in the Private IS Properties dialog, and the Private IS object in Exchange Administrator has leaf nodes whose names match the view names.

The Logons View

The Logons view is pretty similar to the corresponding view for the public IS; it shows you who's logged in to the private store, what time they logged on, and so on. The default view shows six items: the user and mailbox names, the NT account used to log on, the logon time, the last time data in the mailbox was accessed, and the version of the client used for this logon. The Columns... button (on the Logons tab) or command (when you look at the view in the Exchange Administrator contents pane) lets you see more data, including the number of folder, messaging, and I/O operations; the DN of the mailbox and user; and the number of folders, messages, and attachments the user has open.

 The number of logons you see may not correspond to the number of clients actually logged on. That's because the IS uses separate logons for the public and private IS databases; third-party services you add may also require logons of their own.

The Mailbox Resources View

The Mailbox Resources view gives you a summary of how much space each mailbox is using, along with some other useful goodies. The default view shows you the mailbox name, NT account, the time of the last logon and logoff, how many items are in the mailbox, and how much space the mailbox is using. You can add four other columns: the amount of space used by this mailbox's dumpster, the full DN of the mailbox, whether the mailbox is below or above its storage limit, and the number of associated messages (e.g., how many of the messages in the mailbox are shared by other mailboxes).

I've seen a number of people complaining online that the "Total K" and "Total no. items" columns in the Resources view are inaccurate. They're accurate, but the totals include some items you may not expect. Besides mail messages and attachments, these totals include all Outlook folders and contents—journal items, notes, contacts, deleted items that aren't in the dumpster, and sent items.

12

Managing the Internet News Service

It is better to be making the news than taking it.
—Winston S. Churchill

The Internet News Service (INS) is an optional Exchange component that enables your Exchange server to send news articles to and receive them from other Internet news servers, including other Exchange servers running INS. INS makes it possible for your users to read and post Internet news messages using the familiar public folder interface.

Let me preface the meat of this chapter by saying that it won't teach you how to use, much less administer, Internet news. If you want lots more detail on Usenet organization and administration, check out the Nutshell Handbook *Managing Usenet*, by Henry Spencer and David Lawrence (O'Reilly & Associates). This chapter focuses on installing and managing the INS.

Having said that, let me digress to lay out a few basic definitions. *Usenet* is the term used to name the Internet's news system. It's made up of many individual, interlinked, distributed *news servers*, each of which can send articles to and receive them from any other. Just like the Web, Usenet doesn't have a central server; instead, individual servers exchange messages, or *articles*, with one another. Articles are organized by topic; each topic group is called a *newsgroup*. News server administrators can choose what newsgroups their servers carry.

When a user posts an article to a newsgroup, he's actually sending to a news server, which can then replicate the article to its peers. Those servers then replicate the article to their peers, and so on. The overall replication process is similar in effect to (but much different from) that of public folder replication.

You're free to set up INS servers on your Exchange machines just to share articles inside your network—nothing says that your INS machines must exchange articles with the worldwide Usenet. In fact, that's how most Exchange sites use the INS.

Understanding the INS

The INS serves as a connector that can send and receive messages in the standard format that other news servers expect to see. That's all it does; message storage and retrieval are handled by the public IS. In particular, the INS is responsible for the following tasks:

- Maintaining the list of newsgroups that this particular INS carries

- Accepting inbound articles from other news servers and delivering them to the public IS for storage

- Retrieving new messages from the public IS and passing them to other news servers

- Performing content conversion on inbound and outbound messages

Key Protocols and Standards

The key protocol used by the INS is the Network News Transfer Protocol (NNTP). The original Usenet system relied on point-to-point dial-up connections to transfer news articles; in the mid-1980s, the original NNTP specification was published as RFC 977.

NNTP

NNTP describes a stream-based protocol designed for transferring news articles between two peer servers. According to RFC 977:

> NNTP is designed so that news articles are stored in a central database allowing a subscriber to select only those items he wishes to read. Indexing, cross-referencing, and expiration of aged messages are also provided.

See *www.faqs.org/rfcs/rfcsearch.html* for the full version of the RFC.

To be a little more specific, NNTP specifies three basic capabilities. First of all, NNTP allows pushing newsgroup information. A *push feed* is where one server contacts another to deliver articles. NNTP implements this as an exchange of control messages:

- The IHAVE message is sent by the host that initiates the feed; its purpose is to let the receiving end know what articles the sending end has available.

- The receiver responds with a SENDME message containing a list of articles it doesn't already have.

- The original sender transmits each article listed in the SENDME message.

NNTP also supports pulling newsgroup information with a *pull feed*, in which a server sends a request to a remote news server for a specific set of articles. This request is often just a request for articles that have arrived after a specific date and time. The local news server then initiates connections to download those articles, with the exception of any articles that the local server already has in its cache. To the remote news server, a pull feed looks just like a client reading news, so as long as you can get newsreader access to the remote server, you can use a pull feed.

The third basic NNTP function is interactive news reading, which allows newsreader software to retrieve and post articles to a news server. Messages are posted with incomplete header information; the header information is then completed by the news server before articles are transferred between sites. The header information enables the system to identify articles and recognize duplicates.

RFC 977 describes in detail each of the commands that are used by NNTP, so I won't present them here. If you'd like to look at them, go to the reference URL given earlier.

Other standards

NNTP depends on some other standards, four in particular:

RFC 822
> Specifies the format for mail and news messages. You first encountered this standard in Chapter 8, *Managing the Internet Mail Service.*

RFC 1036
> Specifies the format in which Usenet articles are presented.

RFC 1123
> Amends the original RFC 822 specification.

RFC 1153
> Specifies the digest format that some newsgroups use.

Usenet architecture

Usenet is actually a collection of individual sites, or *nodes*. Each site may contain one or more servers; in turn, each server can receive one or more newsfeeds. A site may act as either a *hub* or a *leaf*. Hub sites feed news to other *downstream* sites; leaf sites are those that accept articles for local posting and return them to a hub. Hub sites replicate with other hubs and leaf nodes; leaf nodes only replicate articles with the hub that provides their newsfeed.

The INS can act either as a hub node, combining multiple newsfeeds and making them available to other hubs and leaves, or as a leaf node that accepts local posts and replicates them back to an upstream node.

Two types of hosts are used in replicating Usenet information between sites. The first is an *outbound* host. This host receives or accepts a newsfeed from an upstream Usenet site. The other type of host is called an *inbound* host; inbound hosts actually provide newsfeeds to downstream Usenet sites. Both outbound and inbound hosts can be separate news servers, but usually they are the same machine.

INS or Something Else?

The INS isn't the only way to provide Usenet access to your users; most sites have a choice of three alternatives:

Allowing users to have direct newsreader access to your service providers' Usenet news server, perhaps by using a proxy server
> This requires no server administration on your part, but it means that each user has to obtain, configure, and use a newsreader, and there's no way for you to control what Usenet content users are reading.

Setting up your own news server, perhaps using a low-cost server like Linux (free) and the inn news server (also free)
> This approach requires you to configure and maintain a news server, but you gain a great deal of control over which groups your server carries, how clients may connect (including whether you allow users outside your organization to connect), and so on.

Using the Exchange INS
> This provides the same functionality as a separate news server box, without the additional hassle of configuring and maintaining a separate server. The INS service allows Exchange to act as a full-fledged Usenet host, providing both inbound and outbound posting, push and pull feeds, or a combination of both. You can also use it as a hub node to combine multiple newsfeeds, then provide them to remote leaf node sites.

Exchange sites that have to manage a large volume of news articles usually choose one of the first two options, because the overhead of maintaining, archiving, and cleaning up Usenet-size public folders is nontrivial. Don't let that discourage you, though; if you only want to carry a small subset of Usenet, or if you want to move your own internal traffic, the INS will do a fine job.

INS advantages

One major advantages of using INS when you're already using Exchange is that you can use the existing Exchange or Outlook client software for reading and posting newsgroup messages. In Outlook and the Exchange clients (but not in Outlook Express), Usenet newsgroups appear as public folders, and you can access them like any other public folder. You can even use OWA to get to the newsgroups; in addition, assuming you've given them permission, clients can create newsgroups just as they can create public folders.

You retain complete control over the location, availability, and naming of newsgroup folders. This includes easy delegation of public folder permissions for access control. You also have the option of allowing standard newsreader access to existing public folders in your organization; this is an often overlooked but very nice feature of the INS, since it allows you to open your public folders to people who aren't using the MAPI Outlook clients without installing OWA.

Lastly, the INS provides support for the use of the rich HTML and MIME formatting recognized by browser software or Exchange and Outlook client software. Articles posted in rich content can be converted to straight text for viewing by standard newsreader software.

INS also allows you to easily configure newsgroup availability in two ways: you can control which newsgroups your Exchange users can see, read, and post to, and you can control which newsgroups carried on your server are available to anonymous users or users on the Internet. You can configure access for the outside world differently than for the users on your LAN. When you open up availability of your Exchange newsgroups to the outside world, such as the Internet, the newsgroups can be accessed by standard newsreader software. In fact, you can use standard newsreader software to access newsgroups on the local network, if you want to.

The INS also allows you to regulate the amount of bandwidth your feed uses. Since bandwidth is finite, and most networks always seem to need more than they have, this is a welcome feature. As I mentioned earlier, a full Usenet feed can be as much as 2GB of new articles every day, day in and day out, that have to pass over the network and be stored somewhere. You can limit which newsgroups your INS carries, thus limiting both the amount of bandwidth it takes to get the articles and the amount of disk space and bandwidth required to replicate them through your organization. In addition, you can schedule INS connections so that they occur only when other activity is relatively low.

Reasons not to use the INS

By no means is INS the ultimate news server; it has some limitations that may make it unsuitable for some uses. First of all, if your news usage is light, you'll probably be better off letting your users talk directly to your provider's server. INS has relatively little overhead, but that's not the same as saying it never requires administration or troubleshooting.

At the opposite end of the spectrum, if your newsfeed is large, or if you're going to be providing large downstream feeds, the amount of disk space, CPU, and bandwidth that INS will consume to do the job may be prohibitive, especially considering that you can get a cheap 386, 486, or Pentium and use it with Linux to act as a dedicated news server.

There's another good reason: news servers are pretty much self-healing. If the spool gets damaged, you can just ask your upstream provider to refill it. That's a far cry from mail, which you normally need to protect and preserve. If you commingle news articles and real public folder data, you may find yourself spending time to back up stuff that's not really important to your everyday operations but that still takes up backup time and space.

Getting a Newsfeed

Before you can install and configure the INS, there are some prerequisites you need to meet. First of all, you need an Exchange server with a public IS and enough space to hold the desired set of newsgroups. You'll also need Internet connectivity, either through RAS or a direct connection. (See Chapter 8 for more details on using RAS to connect to the Internet.) You'll need to arrange for a newsfeed from somewhere. Finally, you'll need to decide how you're going to configure your INS.

Arranging Your Newsfeed

If you're not interested in providing Usenet service with the INS, you can skip the rest of this section. On the other hand, if you want your users to have Usenet access, finding a newsfeed is critical. Most ISPs offer newsfeed service to their customers; if your ISP carries the groups you want, all you have to do is ask. Nothing says you have to get your newsfeed from your ISP, though. There are service providers like SuperNews who do nothing but Usenet, and you can often find a local site that has an NNTP feed and is willing to pass on a subset of it. If you find someone who's willing to do that without charging you, they deserve to be treated as if they're doing you a favor, because they are!

Regardless of the newsfeed origin, you'll have to negotiate the type of feed (push or pull) with the administrator of the Usenet site you're connecting to. If their news server recognizes the newnews NNTP command, a pull feed is an option. If it doesn't, a push feed is your only alternative.

Choosing a Feed Type

Before you get ready to install the INS, you need to answer some basic questions about how you want your newsfeed to work. These answers will determine the type of feed you get, and they'll influence how much impact your news service will have on your Exchange configuration.

Push feed or pull feed?

In a push feed, some other server connects to your INS, tells you what groups and articles it has, and sends them to you. With this feed type, the other server controls which newsgroups and articles you get (although you can control which ones you accept), as well as the schedule at which connections are made. The remote host begins the exchange by connecting to port 119 (the default NNTP port) on your server, then sending messages to the INS over that port. Push feeds use the IHAVE/SENDME protocol: the remote host compiles a list of all the articles it has and sends them to the INS server, which compares the IHAVE list with its own message cache. The INS then compiles a SENDME message containing the message IDs of the messages it doesn't already have. The remote server returns these articles to the INS; once that's done, the INS will retrieve any queued local postings from the public IS and deliver them to the remote site.

Pull feeds require more involvement from the INS, because the INS has to contact the remote server. The INS starts by asking for the current time and date. Once it has that, the INS constructs a request (using the newnews command) that says "send me a list of all the news articles you have that were posted after this date and time." Any articles not appearing in the local host's history file are then downloaded. Pull feeds also require more CPU time on the server that's doing the feeding, since it has to build a list of articles stored since the last feed took place. Many sites disable the newnews command for this very reason.

 The Exchange history file, *ics.dat,* is what the INS uses to track the messages it knows about, including messages posted from the local host and what messages are currently in the public IS.

Which type of newsfeed you choose will depend on what your service provider can offer. If the provider's news server doesn't support the newnews command (not all do), you'll be stuck with a push feed. If your feed provider does support newnews, you can use a pull feed. INS doesn't care either way.

One-way or two-way?

A one-way newsfeed simply replicates articles from the remote news server to your INS; no articles pass back the other way. Two-way newsfeeds allow both inbound and outbound articles, so your users can post messages to the local news server and have them replicated across the Usenet. Choosing between these two is usually a policy decision; some organizations don't mind employees reading Usenet, but don't want them posting to it.

Full or partial newsfeed

At the time of this writing, a full Usenet newsfeed takes up about 2GB per day, spread over upwards of 38,000 newsgroups (some of which are bogus). That's a lot of data; in fact, it's more than most servers want. You can quibble with the definition of "full," but even if you only get the groups that actually contain active traffic, that's *still* more data than your server may comfortably accept.

You can get an up-to-date list of the full set of Usenet groups from *ftp://ftp.isc.org/pub/usenet/CONFIG/newsgroups*. This makes it possible for you to select the groups you want as part of your planning process.

Almost all organizations using INS choose to get a partial newsfeed containing only the groups they need or want. Usenet has a lot of tasteless, pornographic, and just plain bizarre content, so many companies prefer to limit the groups they carry to those that serve some obvious business purpose. That decision is entirely up to you; the INS can be configured to carry any group that your service provider can deliver to you.

Exchange and News Storage

Now that you've got a newsfeed, you still have to figure out how you're going to get all that news onto your news server and store it.

What about age limits?

You can apply two kinds of expiration limits to INS news. First of all, there are the standard public folder age limits you learned about in the previous chapter. You can use these limits to purge your newsgroup public folders of outdated material just as you do on regular public folders. You can also use the registry settings described in the section "Controlling article expiration" in Chapter 11, *Managing the Information Store*, to force the INS to expire news articles after a certain period of time.

Some newsgroups generate more traffic than others, and the length of time for which each group's content remains useful varies. When you adjust the expiration time, you can set it only for the entire server, but you can apply public folder age limits to individual folders. I recommend setting a default expiration time of 14–30 days, then using individual folder age limits wherever you think the default time is either too long or too short.

How much storage and bandwidth?

The total amount of space you need on your server will vary in proportion to the newsgroups you carry. Because news traffic is highly variable, I can't provide you a good heuristic for estimating how much space you'll need. If at all possible, put the INS on a dedicated machine with plenty of expansion room so you can add more disk space as needed.

You should also be aware of the bandwidth requirements of the feed you choose. If you accept a set of groups whose volume averages 250MB per day, that's 250MB per day less network bandwidth you have available (and don't think that because Usenet volume is usually expressed as megabytes/day that it arrives evenly around the clock; it's actually bursty). If you're using INS only to create a private intranet news service, bandwidth probably won't be a problem.

You can minimize this impact by scheduling when your INS pulls news from its remote peers. If you're using a push feed, you'll have to negotiate with your service provider. But, as mentioned before, if you're receiving push feed, the schedule at which the feed is done will be determined by your provider. It may indeed negatively affect your network bandwidth if the replication occurs during periods of high network usage.

Load balancing

As you plan how you'll deploy the INS, you should consider balancing the load. The machine on which the INS is installed must be able to handle the CPU, I/O, and network overhead imposed by sending and receiving messages, plus any load imposed by NNTP clients that connect to it directly. Unlike public folder clients, NNTP clients expect to connect to a particular server. In order for them to see newsgroup folders on a specific server, NNTP clients must have access to that server. If you want your NNTP clients to have more than one server available, you'll have to replicate your newsgroup public folders.

It's worth mentioning that newsgroup replication isn't the same as (or as smart as) public folder replication. The volume of messages in the newsgroups you carry can swamp low-bandwidth connections, so you may want to consider using public folder replication, instead of NNTP, to transfer news articles to low-bandwidth sites.

Security

The biggest security issue with the INS is permissions: to whom do you give permission to configure the connector? Who has permission to create new newsgroups in your public folder hierarchy? Who has permission to read and post news articles? It's not necessary to completely settle the answers to these questions before installing INS, but you should be mulling them over in the background while setup is running. You can also choose whether individual INS servers will require users to present valid authentication credentials before reading or posting news.

How do you answer these questions? Start by limiting who can configure the INS connector in the same way you limit administrative access to other connectors—by using the connector Permissions tab. Most sites separate their administrators into multiple groups with different permissions, and you may want to consider keeping a separate group of newsfeed administrators that have permission to tweak the INS but nothing else.

The decision about who gets permission to create new newsgroups on your server is pretty easy, too. In general, whoever is allowed to create other public folders should have the same permission for newsgroups. Remember that if you or your users create new newsgroups in one of the standard Usenet hierarchies, your downstream servers may not accept those groups. There's a formal procedure for creating new Usenet groups; see the *news.announce.newusers* newsgroup for an introduction. You don't have to follow it for newsgroups internal to your network, but it's critical that you follow it if you want to create a new group for use out in the wilderness.

In general, my advice on the "who gets news access" question is to be permissive. Many companies fear that unfettered Usenet access will be a productivity drain. My answer: if you can't trust your employees to do their work instead of reading news, why'd you hire them in the first place? Regrettably, this decision may not be up to you. There's no real technical reason to restrict news access when you use INS, especially since most of your users will probably be using MAPI clients anyway.

Hooking up with your provider

Your Usenet service provider will need some information from you to set up your newsfeed. In particular, if you have a permanent Internet connection, they'll need to know the IP address and DNS domain name of your INS servers, since most providers allow news access to their permanently connected customers without requiring authentication. If you're connecting via dial-up, they probably will have the IP and DNS information they need from their remote access system; if you want to use authentication on your end, you'll need to give your provider a set of credentials they can use to reach the server.

What do you need from the service provider? Obviously, you'll need the IP addresses and DNS names of the news servers that will be providing your feed, whether it's a pull or push feed. Depending on your network configuration, you may need to make changes to your firewall and routing architecture to allow that traffic to pass. If your newsfeed provider requires your servers to provide logon credentials, you'll need those as well. Finally, you need to find out how to get a copy of the *active file*, which specifies which groups the provider's servers carry. The provider may give you a copy via email or FTP; the INS can also download it as part of its installation.

Installing the INS

You install the INS with Exchange Administrator's File → New Other → Newsfeed... command, which starts the Newsfeed Configuration Wizard (NCW). Once you've completed the NCW steps, there are some clean-up steps you should complete before your newsfeed gets heavily used.

Using the NCW

When you first launch the NCW, it reminds you to gather the information discussed in the preceding section; once you proceed to the second page, the actual configuration process begins.

Page 2: Selecting the server

You can install the INS on any server in your site; the second page of the NCW lets you pick the target server. You also need to provide the full DNS name of that server, which it labels as the Usenet site name. Note that this isn't the same as your Exchange site name, though the NCW fills in that value. For example, when I installed the INS on a server named *YYZ2* in a site named *Canada*, the NCW helpfully suggested *canada.robichauxassociates.com* as the server name, even though that's not the server's name! Make sure you fill in the actual DNS name of the server on which you're installing the INS.

Page 3: Selecting the feed type

The third NCW page lets you select the type of feed you're setting up. There are actually two sets of controls. The upper set lets you choose whether your newsfeed is outbound, inbound, or both; there are appropriately named radio buttons for each choice. If you choose either "Inbound and outbound" or "Inbound only" newsfeed options, you will be required to select whether the inbound leg of the feed is a push or pull newsfeed; there's a radio button group at the bottom of the page for making this choice. Those controls will be disabled if you select "Outbound only."

Selecting the "Inbound and outbound" newsfeed option allows you to pull messages from your Usenet provider's host computer, or you can accept messages that are pushed to your Exchange server from your Usenet provider. You could also push messages posted to newsgroup public folders on your Exchange server to your Usenet provider's host computer. One other thing to remember is that if you want a remote host computer to pull messages from your Microsoft Exchange server, you only have to configure the NTTP client access on your Exchange server. The remote host computer can then pull messages acting as though it were an NNTP newsreader.

Page 4: Selecting a connection type

The INS can exchange news over permanent or dial-up connections. If you're using a permanent connection (or one available over your LAN), just select the "Connect using my LAN" button, and you're done. If you want to use a dial-up connection (which requires that you have the RAS service installed and configured before you run the NCW), select "Connect using my dial-up connection," then tell the NCW what phone book entry, username, and password you want to use for the connection.

Page 5: Set a preliminary schedule

This step allows you to tell the INS how often it should connect to your newsfeed provider. Note that you'll see this screen no matter what feed type you select, but it only applies to inbound pull feeds. Your choices range from the default of connecting every 15 minutes to connecting every 24 hours. After the INS is installed, you can change this schedule.

Page 6: Specifying the remote site

This page is where you specify the Usenet site name of your remote provider's site. Notice that this doesn't necessarily have to be the same as the DNS name of the computer. Your provider will give this to you.

Page 7: Specifying the remote server address

Your service provider will give you the IP addresses and DNS names of the news servers you can use. However, you can only enter one server on this page, though you can enter either an IP address or DNS name.

Page 8: Providing authentication credentials

Use this page to specify what credentials your server will use when it tries to authenticate itself to the remote server, as well as the credentials you want the remote server to use when it contacts you. If you're not using authentication, you can skip this page with no ill effect.

To configure a pull feed, fill in the "Log in to remote servers as" and Password fields with the credentials your service provider supplied. To configure a push feed, use the Change... button to pick the mailbox or custom recipient that you expect the remote server to authenticate as when it opens a connection.

The "Require secure connection (SSL)" checkbox allows you to specify that you want your news traffic encrypted with the SSL protocol. You can use SSL with push or pull feeds, but the server on the other end has to have SSL enabled as well. Once the INS is installed, you can select additional authentication types.

Page 9: Getting the service account password

The real page 9 tells you that the NCW is ready to install the INS; when you dismiss that page, another page (which I call "9 junior") pops up so you can enter the site service account password. The NCW needs this so it can install and start the INS, which actually runs as an NT service alongside the SA, MTA, IS, and DS services. Of course, if you get the password wrong, you won't be able to continue with the installation, since the INS has to be running to proceed.

Page 10: Identifying the administrator

Whichever mailbox you designate as the Internet news administrator will own all the Internet news public folders. The administrator also gets any status or bounce messages generated by the INS. This step is mandatory. Just as with the IMS, I recommend creating a separate mailbox for the news administrator and naming it *usenet*, the de facto standard name used by Internet news servers for their administrator.

Page 11: Supplying the active file

On page 11 of the NCW, you specify where the active file is located. This file is nothing more than a big list of the newsgroups that your provider's server carries; it doesn't contain any information about messages in those groups. Think of it as a menu—its contents determine which groups you can choose to carry on your servers. This page gives you three choices:

- If you already have a copy of the active file, choose the "I have the active file. Import it from:" radio button, then use the Browse... button to locate the file for the INS.

- If you want the INS to download the active file from your news provider, use the "Download the active file from my provider now" button; this tells the NCW to immediately fetch the active file, which might take a while over a slow link.

- If you want to set up the list of groups later, use the "I'll configure my newsfeed later" button.

If you choose to download the active file, you'll get a dialog box indicating the progress of the download.

Page 12: Choosing newsgroups for your server

If you told the NCW that you have (or want it to get) an active file, the next step of the install process displays a dialog showing all the newsgroups in the active file. You can navigate through the list, choosing which individual groups or hierarchies you want to carry by using the Include and Exclude buttons. When you've got a complete list, and you click the Next button, the NCW creates a new set of public folders under the *Internet Newsgroups* root folder; there will be one folder for each level in the hierarchy. For example, if you choose to carry the *comp.risks*, *soc.religion.mormon*, and *hsv.general* newsgroups, your hierarchy will look like Figure 12-1.

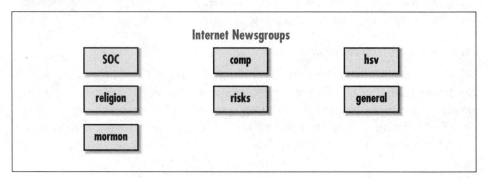

Figure 12-1. Each level of the Usenet hierarchy you carry gets its own folder in the Exchange public folder hierarchy

Testing Your Installation

After you finish running the NCW, you'll see your newsgroup folders appear in the public folder hierarchy almost immediately. They won't have any articles in them for a while, depending on your feed type and scheduling. Verifying that NNTP feeds are working can be tricky, because a lack of incoming articles doesn't necessarily mean that anything's wrong—the newsgroups might just be quiet.

If you lack the patience to wait and see whether articles appear in your public folders, you can turn on diagnostic logging for the NNTP protocol (use the Diagnostic Logging tab of the server's NNTP properties dialog, located in the server's Protocols container). Setting the Connections category to Medium logging is usually sufficient; if you're using a pull feed, you can also turn on logging for the NNTP Pull Newsfeed category.

With a pull feed, it's easy to determine if your configuration is working or not—just stop and restart the INS. When it restarts, it will immediately try to open a pull connection, and you'll see news start flowing if all is well. Even if it's not, you'll get messages in the event log indicating what's happening with your server. One fairly common message is event ID 13084, which indicates that the remote server doesn't support the **newnews** command. If you see this, you'll have to create a new push newsfeed or somehow get your provider to start supporting **newnews**.

Once you've got inbound news flowing, the next step is to see whether articles posted from your site can make it out into the world. Use an NNTP client or Outlook to post a message to the newsgroup of your choice, then check the event log. If you see event ID 13054, your article was posted successfully; the event message shows the article ID and the receiving host. If you don't, the most likely cause is that the remote site isn't accepting your posts because it's been instructed not to; this is normally something you have to resolve with your provider. For more specific troubleshooting information, see "Troubleshooting the INS" in Chapter 15, *Troubleshooting Exchange Server.*

Managing the INS

The NCW does almost all of the work of setting up an INS newsfeed for you, but you'll still need to make some adjustments to keep your newsfeed in working order.

It's important to understand the distinction between INS properties, which apply to the one INS running on your machine, and newsfeed properties. Since each INS can handle multiple newsfeeds, some settings apply to individual newsfeeds, while others apply to all newsfeeds. Most of the properties that apply to all newsfeeds are set through the registry, so let's start with the items specific to individual newsfeeds.

Setting Newsfeed Properties

You adjust settings for an individual newsfeed from its properties dialog. Newsfeeds appear in the site's Connections container.

The General tab

The General tab doesn't have much of interest on it. You can change the newsfeed's display name, and you can see the newsfeed type, which tells you whether the newsfeed was configured as a push or pull feed. As noted earlier, though, you can't change this setting; to change the newsfeed type, you have to delete the connector and then recreate it. The "Enable newsfeed" checkbox is slightly more useful; you can use it to turn the newsfeed on or off when necessary. Apart from these items, the only other useful control here is the Administrator's mailbox group, which shows you who the designated administrator for this feed is and allows you to change the administrator if necessary.

The Messages tab

The Messages tab should probably be named the Limits tab, since that's what it does: you use it to set limits on the maximum size you'll allow for outgoing and incoming messages. By default, there's no limit on incoming messages, but outgoing messages are capped at 1024KB. The incoming message size controls will only appear if you have configured the newsfeed for inbound traffic.

It's a good idea to set inbound and outbound limits just as a preventative measure. Most users won't attempt to post very large messages to your newsgroups, but some might, and there's never any telling what other Usenet users may be posting.

The Hosts tab

This tab lets you see and change the Usenet site and host names for a particular newsfeed. Normally, you won't change either of these unless your provider tells you that they're changing their machine names. You can also use the "Additional inbound hosts" control group to add additional hosts for a newsfeed: you use this option when you're running an inbound push feed and your provider uses multiple hosts. If you want to pull news from multiple hosts, you need to establish separate newsfeeds for each host.

The Connection tab

The INS can connect via either your LAN connection or a dial-up connection. The Connection tab lets you switch between these two on a newsfeed-by-newsfeed basis, which is nice. If you choose the "Connect using Dial-up Networking" radio button, you'll have to specify a DUN phone book entry and a set of account credentials to use when logging in. Note that these may or may not be the same credentials you use to authenticate to the news server, depending on how your provider has set up their security.

The Security tab

The Security tab features three sets of controls. The first one you'll see is the "Require secure connection (SSL)" checkbox, which is off by default. If you enable it, the INS will use an SSL connection for this newsfeed's communications with other news hosts. There's no way to turn this on or off for individual hosts; while enabling it does add security, it also imposes a stiff performance penalty, which worsens as more traffic passes through your feed. There's also no way to enable SSL in one direction; if you turn it on on your server, your provider has to enable it too.

The "Outbound connections" group is where you specify what username and password the INS should use when connecting to an upstream host and feeding articles to it. Your provider will tell you what credentials to use here. If your provider doesn't require authentication, just leave these blank.

The "Inbound connections" group allows you to specify the account you want inbound connections to authenticate as. This is the account information you supply to your Usenet provider if you require them to authenticate. You can use any mailbox or custom recipient from the GAL, as long as it's not hidden. The Remove button clears your choice and returns the INS to its default state of not requiring inbound authentication.

The Schedule tab

The Schedule tab is only useful for pull newsfeeds. Like every other Schedule tab you've seen thus far, it offers a grid with either 15- or 60-minute resolution that you use to schedule when you want pull connections to be initiated. Selecting Never will force this newsfeed to never attempt to pull articles from the other site; this is a useful way to shut down a newsfeed temporarily or permanently.

One other thing: if you schedule your pull sessions too closely together, one session may not finish before the next one starts. This does no harm, but it makes more sense to schedule your sessions far enough apart so that one session finishes before the next one starts.

The Inbound and Outbound tabs

These two tabs let you specify which individual groups you want to propagate. The Inbound tab controls which groups your server accepts from inbound feeds, and the Outbound tab controls the groups whose articles you want to propagate in your outbound feed. Both tabs work the same way: they display a tree of newsgroups through which you can navigate by clicking. When you want to include or exclude a specific group or hierarchy, you can do so with the Include and Exclude buttons. By default, the groups listed on the Outbound tab match the set listed on the Inbound tab.

Whether or not you selected the groups you want to carry in the NCW, you can change those settings at any time with the Inbound tab. When you include a new group, you'll start getting articles in it the next time your INS talks to the remote server, but when you exclude a group, the articles in it don't immediately disappear; you have to wait for them to expire normally.

When you use the Outbound tab, you're telling your server which newsgroups you want to propagate to the outside world. If you don't want your users to post news articles to the Internet, don't include any groups on this tab. Your users will be able to talk to each other via posts in the newsgroups, but those posts won't show up in the outside world. Of course, you can select particular groups to replicate, or not, depending on your environment.

The Advanced tab

The Advanced tab only has one button on it: "Mark All As Delivered". Normally, when the INS talks to another server (no matter the feed type), it will request any articles it thinks it doesn't have. This may result in a deluge of articles, since your upstream server may keep a large spool of past articles. A quick check of my provider's spool shows some groups with more than 2,000 articles just from the last 7 days; if their expiration time was longer, there would be more. If you want to prevent the INS from fetching all these articles, click this button; it effectively updates your INS history file so that the INS thinks it's caught up on your current list of groups. Any new articles that arrive at the remote server after you click this button will still be transferred, but any whose timestamp is before the button click will be ignored.

If the Exchange active file, *ics.dat*, is ever corrupted or damaged, the INS will automatically create a new, empty file, which will make the INS decide that it needs to refetch every article your upstream servers have. If this happens, use this button to stop the excess replication.

> There's another situation where this button is useful: if your provider ever has to rebuild its news server's news spool, its list of article numbers may be reset. When that happens, the remote server will tell the INS that all of the articles it has are new, meaning you should rush to click this button to keep the remote server from sending you duplicate copies of the articles you already have.

Setting NNTP Properties

Unlike the newsfeed connector object, which you configure in one place, you can configure NNTP settings in two places: at the site level, and at the server level. The main difference is that the server's NNTP properties page has a Diagnostic Logging tab and the site version has a tab that allows you to accept or reject Usenet control messages. Any settings you specify at the site level are propagated down to all INS servers in the site, but each server can override any or all site defaults.

The Diagnostics Logging and Permissions tabs are identical to the ones we've already covered for other components, so I won't go over them again here.

The General tab

The General tab allows you to see and change the display name for the NNTP object, create or change the administrative note displayed with the object, and turn the NNTP protocol off or on. The most important controls on this form are the

"Enable protocol" and "Enable client access" checkboxes; they allow you to control whether the protocol is enabled or not and, if so, whether clients can connect to use it. On the server properties dialog, there's also the familiar "Use site defaults for all properties" checkbox.

On the site version of this tab, you'll also see the Administrator's mailbox group, which shows you the designated administrator for this feed and allows you to change the administrator if necessary.

The Newsfeeds tab

This tab displays all the newsfeeds configured on Exchange servers within your site. Selecting a newsfeed here and double-clicking it or using the Properties... button, takes you to that newsfeed's properties dialog. The Create Active File... button allows you to create an active file on the site-level tab, but not on individual servers. This file lists the newsgroups that particular newsfeed server carries; you'll usually send an active file to the downstream news servers you'll be feeding. You can also use the Usenet site name field to change this server's site name; if you do, make sure to notify any downstream hosts your server feeds news to.

The Authentication tab

You can require clients to provide authentication credentials to use your NNTP server, or you can allow them anonymous access. If you want to require authentication, you do it from this tab. The six authentication methods available from this tab are identical to those available for the IMS: clear-text authentication, Windows NT challenge/response authentication, and MCIS authentication, and each of these types with SSL.

The Message Format tab

The NNTP and RFC 822 standards were originally designed to work with plain 7-bit ASCII text, but Usenet has grown to embrace languages and content types that require 8-bit characters, multiple character sets, and MIME encoding. In particular, the advent of Netscape's (and Microsoft's) newsreader packages has caused the spread of MIME HTML news articles.

 The Message Format, Idle Timeout, and Anonymous tabs appear at the server level, but their controls are disabled unless you uncheck the "Use site defaults for all properties" checkbox on the General tab.

The Message Format tab allows you to control how outgoing messages are format-ted. Not coincidentally, the settings here correspond to the Internet Mail tab of the IMS properties dialog, since both the INS and IMS use the IMail protocol engine in the IS for content conversion. For news articles, you can choose from the follow-ing encoding methods:

MIME

This radio button tells the INS to encode articles as MIME objects. MIME is now standard for transporting multimedia messages in Usenet groups, but some newsreaders still aren't MIME-capable, so not everyone will necessarily be able to see multimedia attachments or message parts. Most clients can han-dle this, though, and MIME is definitely the best way to encode attached objects for transport, so leave it turned on.

With the MIME setting active, you have two additional choices:

Provide message body as plain text

Tells the INS to leave the message body as a plain text part, so that even non-MIME newsreaders can see it.

Provide message body as HTML

Instructs the INS to encode the message body as HTML.

If you check both of these boxes, each outbound message will actually have two body parts, encoded as a MIME multipart/alternative message. While this doubles the message size, it also allows the use of rich content in your news-group postings—just remember that not everyone can see that content. Since many Usenet users are still stuck with clients that can't understand HTML body parts, I recommend sticking with the plain-text option.

UUENCODE

This radio button makes the INS use uuencoding for any attachments to news-group articles. This encoding is the old de facto standard for news articles, so using it gives you maximum compatibility at the expense of including rich content that MIME-aware newsreaders can see. You can optionally turn on BinHex encoding for Macintosh clients, but MIME is a better choice if you know Macintosh users will be reading your articles.

Clients support S/MIME signatures

This checkbox tells the INS that you want to leave S/MIME signatures alone, both on inbound and outbound articles. Checking this box allows you to send and verify S/MIME signed messages; unchecking it causes the INS to strip the signature information.

The Idle Timeout tab

To avoid bogging down your server, you'll need to specify limits on how long an inactive NNTP connection can remain open. By default, the INS closes inactive connections after ten minutes of inactivity, but you can change that interval or force it to leave idle connections open. To drop idle connections, select the "Close idle connections" radio button and specify an idle time in the "Timeout (minutes)" field. For most users, a time ranging between 20 and 40 minutes is long enough. Alternatively, you can allow idle connections by choosing the "Do not close idle connections" button. However, even after polling several news administrators I work with, I can't come up with a good reason to select this option, and leaving it unselected will leave more resources free for active users.

The Anonymous tab

If you want to allow anonymous users to access your NNTP server, as is usually the case inside a firewall, use the "Allow anonymous access" checkbox on the Anonymous tab. When this option is set, you can still restrict access to individual public folders by setting permissions on their properties pages; if you want to restrict access to authenticated users only (the default setting), just uncheck this box.

The Control Messages tab

Control messages are an in-band signaling mechanism; they're news articles that act as instructions to news servers that honor them. Control messages can be used to request the creation or removal of newsgroups, the cancellation of individual articles, or the approval of posts to a moderated newsgroup.

In the old days (until about 1995), almost all news servers trusted control messages and would automatically honor their contents. However, since they don't carry any authentication, it's easy to abuse control messages, and that's just what happened: renegade sites (or, more precisely, jerks) would flood Usenet with bogus article cancellations and group creation and removal messages. As this control message flooding continued, most sites switched over to queuing control messages so a human could review them before processing.

Exchange implements this mechanism. All incoming control messages go into a queue, which is visible in this tab. You can review queued messages at any time and either accept them (in which case the changes they specify are made) or reject them. Whether you accept or reject a message, once you evaluate it, the message will be removed from the queue.

 Exchange doesn't generate control messages when you create or remove newsgroups in your public folder hierarchy. It does properly update the active file, though. If you create a newsgroup that you want to propagate outside your organization, the servers you feed will need an updated copy of your active file.

Note that this tab does not appear in the NNTP protocol object properties dialog box at the server level—it's only visible on the site object.

Other Useful Management Tricks

Unlike the IMS, the INS doesn't usually require a lot of adjustment once you finish running its wizard, but there are some other administrative tasks you'll probably need to perform at some point during your stewardship.

Setting up NNTP client access

To make the public folders on your server accessible to NNTP clients, you must include them in the server's newsgroup hierarchy. The Tools → Newsgroup Hierarchies... command in Exchange Administrator allows you to select which portions of your public folder hierarchy end up looking like newsgroups. By default, the *Internet Newsgroups* root folder will appear in this dialog; you can use the Add... and Remove buttons to selectively include any folder and its children. You can set up an existing public folder hierarchy for NNTP client access even if you don't set up a newsfeed connection. If you set up a newsfeed connector, the newsgroup public folders will automatically be included in the newsgroup hierarchies.

Once you add folders using this dialog, you should set permissions on them using Outlook. (In fact, it may not be a bad idea to set permissions on the real newsgroups, too.) Right-click any newsgroup public folder in Outlook, open the properties dialog, switch to the Internet News tab, then make sure "Publish this folder to users of newsreader software" is checked.

Configuring NNTP access with Microsoft Proxy Server 2.0

Most organizations that connect their networks to the Internet employ some type of firewall to protect their internal resources from outside dangers.[*] Since proxy servers allow content caching (and thus bandwidth conservation), a number of vendors combine firewall and proxy server functionality into one product. Microsoft's Proxy Server 2.0 (PS2) is one such product. If you're using PS2, you have to make some adjustments to its configuration to allow outside users to get to your INS, whether they're reading news or exchanging a newsfeed with you. If you're using another type of firewall, the overall process is the same, but the individual steps may be different.

The first thing you need to do is to install the Winsock proxy client on your Exchange server, unless PS2 is running on the Exchange server itself. This makes it possible for the Exchange server to communicate with the proxy server. You can

---

[*] If you're connected to the Internet, and don't use a firewall, please put this book down right now and go get one. Seriously.

install the proxy client by running the *Winsock* client *setup.exe* application from the *mspclnt* share on the proxy server.

The second thing you'll need to do is to modify the proxy configuration file, *wspcfg.ini*. When you install the proxy, you get a default version of this file. Normally, the Exchange IS expects to make outbound connections directly to port 119 of whatever NNTP server it's talking to; you need to modify this file to tell the IS to connect to port 119 on the proxy server instead, so the proxy server itself can make the connection to the outside world.

Open *wspcfg.ini* with Notepad or another text editor and add the following text to it, then save the file in the same directory that *store.exe* is in (usually *exchsrvr\bin*, unless you've moved things around):

```
[STORE]
ServerBindTcpPorts=119
Persistent=1
KillOldSession=1
```

After you have added this text, stop and then restart the IS service.

You can configure the proxy to pass other protocols across the proxy server—just add the port numbers to the `ServerBindTcpPorts` line. To bind the ports for SMTP, NNTP, IMAP4, and POP3, respectively, the line would look like this:

```
ServerBindTcpPorts=25,119,143,110
```

To enable LDAP access through the proxy port, a slightly different entry is required because LDAP isn't part of the IS. The LDAP standard defines port 389 as the standard service port, so the appropriate code looks like this:

```
[DIRECTORY]
ServerBindTcpPorts=389
Persistent=1
KillOldSession=1
```

Disabling pull newsfeeds

You may want to consider eliminating the availability of pull newsfeeds on your INS server. Pull feeds can cause considerable use of bandwidth and slow response for NNTP clients. You can disable support for pull newsfeeds by creating the following `REG_DWORD` registry value and setting its value to 1:

```
HKLM\SYSTEM\CurrentControlSet\Services\MSExchangeIS\ParametersSystem
NNTP NewNews Disabled
```

This essentially turns off the **newnews** command; any remote host attempting to pull a newsfeed from the Exchange server will be refused access.

Creating a moderated newsgroup folder

Some Usenet groups are moderated: all new posts to the group must be sent to a moderator for approval before they appear. You can turn any of your newsgroup folders into moderated folders by adjusting the appropriate settings with Outlook. Open the target folder's properties dialog, then switch to the Administration tab and click the Moderated Folder button. The Moderated Folder dialog (see Figure 12-2) will appear.

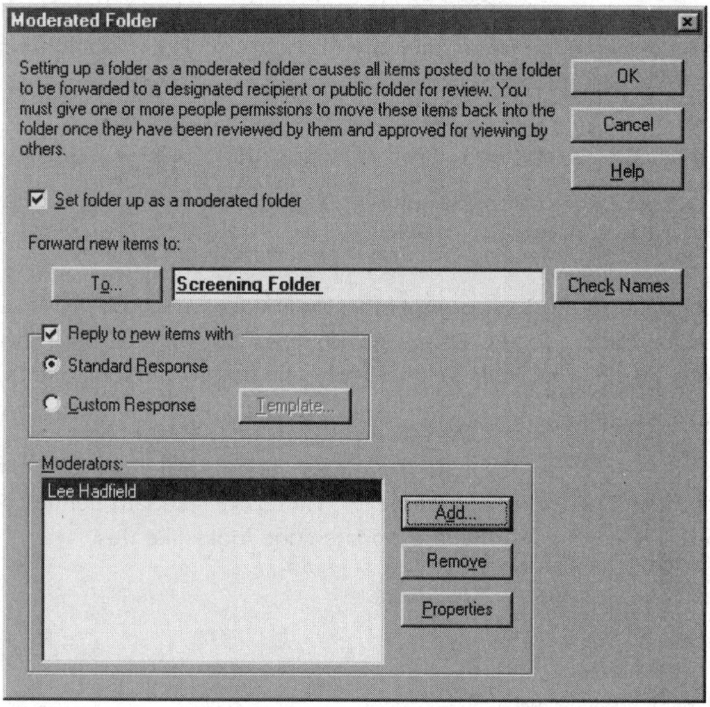

Figure 12-2. Use this dialog to turn an ordinary folder into a moderated one

You use this dialog to establish your desired moderation settings. Here's the deal:

1. Check the "Set folder up as a moderated folder" checkbox to turn this into a moderated folder.

2. If you want to automatically send all posted messages straight to one or more moderators, use the To... button to select a mailbox, custom recipient, or DL from the GAL. You can also type names in the field and use the Check Names button to verify them.

3. If you want newly posted items to get an automatic response, check the "Reply to new items with" checkbox, then select whether you want the

canned Exchange response, which explains that the item must be approved before posting, or a slightly more custom version, which you create by clicking the Template... button and typing the message text you want used as the reply.

4. Using the Moderators list, add the moderators you want for this particular group. You can specify any number of visible entries from the GAL as moderators for a group; make sure the moderators you specify have permission to move approved items back to the newsgroup public folder.

Changing the Moderator

In addition to changing the group's moderator with the Exchange or Outlook client, you can also modify the list of moderators stored in the *exchsrvr\add-ins\INS* directory. Moderator information is stored in a file called *moderatr.txt*; the file contains the SMTP addresses of the newsgroup moderators for each moderated newsgroup. Each entry in the file maps one newsgroup to one moderator address, although you may use wildcard patterns. The first matching moderator is used, and you can use the **%s** escape sequence to insert the group name. For example:

```
ra.*: %s@robichaux.net
comp.risks: neumann@sri.com
*: %s@uunet.uu.net
```

This establishes three moderators: one for the *ra.**hierarchy, one for the *comp. risks* group, and one for all other moderated groups. Don't make changes to the moderator settings for groups you get from Usenet unless your news provider instructs you to; you're free to change the moderators for your own groups as often as you like. You must stop and restart the INS to make it notice the changes.

Using the instimes.exe utility

The *instimes.exe* utility is used to backfill newsfeed messages that were posted before the newsfeed was configured. For example, if you configure a newsfeed today, but want articles from two weeks ago, you could use this utility to fetch those articles from the remote host, provided they still existed in the remote spool.

When INS connects to another NNTP server, it checks the time on the remote host; it requests only articles that were posted since the last time it connected. The most recent connection time is always based on the remote host's time, never on the Exchange server time. This information is stored every time replication occurs. *instimes.exe* essentially allows you to manipulate the Exchange stored time so you can rewind (or fast-forward) your news collection to a particular point in time.

The *instimes.exe* utility is located on the Exchange Server CD in the *server*
support\utils directory. Copy it from there to somewhere on your local disk (I suggest *\exchsrvr\bin*), then run it. You'll see the dialog shown in Figure 12-3.

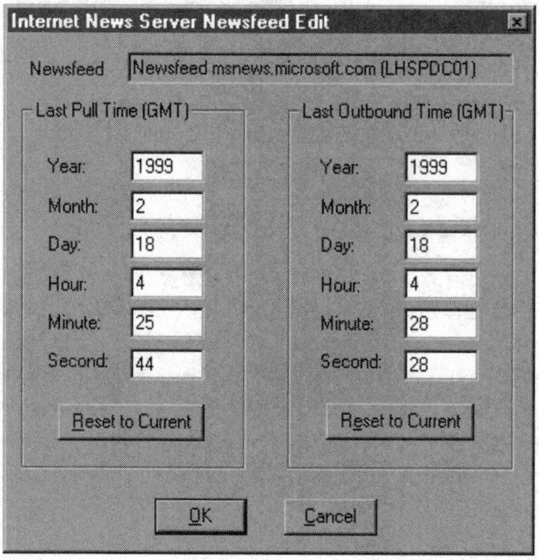

Figure 12-3. The instimes.exe utility allows you to backfill newsgroup articles

The "Last Pull Time (GMT)" and "Last Outbound Time (GMT)" control groups let
you edit the times in the dialog box to suit your needs; to force your server to
ignore news until some future date, set the date forward. To backfill from the
remote site, adjust the date backwards.

13

Managing Exchange Clients

Good counselors lack no clients.
—William Shakespeare
All's Well That Ends Well, I, ii, 115

The preceding chapters of this book have talked about various aspects of Exchange Server while mostly glossing over the fact that servers exist so clients can use them. Now it's payback time! This chapter will examine how you install, configure, and manage the Outlook client; along the way, I'll touch on some issues pertinent to sites using POP3, IMAP4, or Outlook Web Access clients in addition to, or instead of, Outlook.

Exchange Client Basics

You're faced with a number of choices when you want to provide a way for users to connect to your Exchange server. Which client you choose will depend on what your users need to do and where they need to do it from. If all your users are running Windows 95/98/NT on your LAN, there's no reason not to use Outlook, since it has a nice feature set and a lot of administrative tools you can deploy. If you have users who are using Macs or Unix machines, you might need to mix in some OWA or IMAP4/POP3 clients; likewise, if you have mobile or roaming users, the standard Outlook client may not be the best choice.

Available Clients

Clients you can use with Exchange fall into two basic categories: MAPI clients use the Microsoft MAPI interfaces to talk to the server, and Internet protocol (Internet) clients use IMAP4 or POP3 instead. Some clients can do both; most, however, are stuck in one camp or the other.

Microsoft Outlook

Microsoft Outlook is easily the most powerful of the Exchange clients. It includes support for email, calendaring, scheduling, tasks, journal keeping, public folders, automated processing of messages and meeting requests, the ability to work with custom forms, and many other features. The trade-off for all this power is size. Outlook 2000 is a full-fledged member of the Microsoft Office suite and, as such, isn't recommended for use on machines with less than 32MB of RAM. With the default features installed, Outlook 2000 will occupy upwards of 12.8MB of hard drive space. Keep in mind that a full installation of Outlook can easily balloon to well over twice that amount!

Versions of Outlook are available for Win32 (Windows 95, 98 and NT), Win16 (Windows 3.x), and Macintosh, but the Win32 version is indisputably the most powerful, so users on other platforms may notice a distinct lack of capability.

Outlook currently comes in three flavors: Outlook 97, Outlook 98, and Outlook 2000. All three can act as either MAPI or Internet clients; in fact, you can use them to simultaneously send and receive mail using both protocols. However, many of the best features, like calendaring, offline folders, and rules, require you to use MAPI mode. Outlook 97 is widely available as a free download in the U.S., but you must purchase Outlook 98 and Outlook 2000.

Microsoft Outlook Express

There's a lot of confusion among users and administrators about the differences between Outlook and the unfortunately named Outlook Express (OE). Outlook is the full-featured desktop information manager and Exchange client; Outlook Express is a POP3 and IMAP4 email client that also supports reading NNTP news. OE is included with Internet Explorer versions 4 and later, on both the Macintosh and Windows platforms. Because it's an Internet client, OE can't directly take advantage of some Exchange features; as far as Exchange is concerned, OE is just another POP3/IMAP4 client (though it does support S/MIME).

Outlook Web Access

Outlook Web Access (OWA) isn't a client application—it's a web page. When you set up OWA on your Internet Information Server (IIS), and configure Exchange to allow HTTP access, clients can connect to the OWA page and use a set of Active Server Page (ASP) scripts that talk to the Exchange server.

OWA has the advantage of being highly portable. It can be accessed from any machine in the world that has an Internet connection and a relatively recent browser such as Netscape Navigator 3.x or Internet Explorer 3.x or later. The interface looks remarkably similar to Outlook (which is why it's called "Outlook Web Access," even though there's no common code between OWA and Outlook).

There are some disadvantages to Outlook Web Access, though. Its user interface is a little clunky compared to the Outlook client family: messages aren't marked as read when you've read them, and the process of refreshing your inbox isn't as smooth as it could be. OWA requires that you host a web server at your site with inbound access, and it's somewhat more limited than regular Outlook. For example, while you can check your email and your calendar through OWA, you can't access your *Contacts* folder. In addition, some sites have found that OWA is unstable under heavy user loads, although Microsoft is fixing OWA bugs at an impressive clip.

Microsoft Exchange Inbox

Also known as the ubiquitous Inbox, this Microsoft messaging client may be familiar to the many users of Microsoft Fax who have not previously installed Outlook. Windows 95, 98, and Windows NT used to install this client by default; because the name was confusing, it was quickly renamed "Windows Messaging" instead (that name is confusing, too, but it lives on).

The advantages to using this client to access Exchange are that it's free and already installed on most Windows 9x and NT machines, plus it's relatively simple to use and support. However, it's really only good as a MAPI client, and its feature set lags far behind current POP3/IMAP4 clients, not to mention Outlook itself.

Microsoft Exchange Client

This client actually shipped with Exchange 4.0 and 5.0; it's a more robust version of the Exchange Inbox. It adds the ability to utilize rules and additional folders. As a bonus, it can support multiple mail profiles, so a single Exchange Client can retrieve mail from MS Mail, Exchange, and POP3 servers, putting it all in a single inbox. For those stuck in the early 1990s, there's actually a DOS version of this client that will run under DOS 6.2.

POP3 clients

POP3 clients like Eudora Pro (and Light), Pegasus, Pine, and the built-in mailer included with the PalmPilot can talk to Exchange as long as you've enabled the POP3 protocol. You can use POP3 clients only for email, though, because POP3 doesn't provide any way to support calendaring, contact management, and so on. In addition, POP3 is a receive-only protocol; POP3 clients use SMTP to send outgoing messages. Many sites that have to use POP3 because they have client platforms that can't run Outlook or an IMAP4 client combine OWA with POP3 access; this allows users to send and receive mail while still having some access to calendaring and public folders through OWA.

If you're planning to allow POP3 to contact your Exchange Server from the Internet, make sure that your firewall leaves port 110 open.

IMAP4 clients

IMAP4 is POP3 done right; it allows remote mail access like POP3 does, with the added benefits of folder synchronization and filtering, plus better authentication. Its advantages are that it's fairly fast for remote access and that a variety of clients are available for various platforms (including OE, Netscape Communicator, Eudora Pro, and PowerMail). IMAP4 doesn't support calendaring or contact access; however, you can configure Exchange so that IMAP4 clients can access public folders, and you can use IMAP4 in conjunction with OWA, if needed.

As with POP3, to use IMAP remotely you'll need to leave a port open on your firewall—in this case, port 143. As with POP3, there may be security consequences to opening your firewall, so carefully consider whether that's the best way to solve your problem. You may want to consider using RAS or PPTP to get to your internal network from a remote client using IMAP.

Managing Outlook

Outlook is Microsoft's entry into the once-crowded Personal Information Manager (PIM) field formerly dominated by products like Sidekick, Lotus Organizer and Ecco. In the short time since Outlook was introduced it has, perhaps largely by virtue of being included in the Microsoft Office 97 suite, gathered an impressive market share and following. Don't make the mistake of thinking that Outlook's success has been entirely on the coattails of its suitemates; Outlook has gathered its own impressive industry reviews and has gained a significant user following. However, to get full benefit of Outlook's features, you need to run it with an Exchange server. In this configuration, Outlook adds a significant new feature to the traditional PIM: email. Microsoft likes to position Outlook as a "messaging and collaboration client" rather than a mere PIM. In this chapter, I'll ignore all the PIM features. If you want a good book on using Outlook, try *Outlook Annoyances*, by Woody Leonhard, Lee Hudspeth, and T.J. Lee (O'Reilly & Associates).

What's New in Outlook 2000?

The latest member of the Outlook family, which as of this writing is due to be in consumer hands by the second quarter of 1999, is Outlook 2000. Outlook 2000 builds upon the strong foundation laid by Outlook 97 and its less prominent follow-up, Outlook 98.* Table 13-1 summarizes the features that Outlook 2000 adds or enhances to the Outlook 97/98 feature set; I assume you're already more or less familiar with the Outlook 97/98 feature set as a basis for comparison.

Table 13-1. New and Enhanced Features in Outlook 2000

Feature	Description
Increased integration with Internet Explorer	Outlook 2000 allows you to add links to web pages to your Outlook bar and even browse web pages directly in the folder window.
Preview pane	Introduced with Outlook 98, the preview pane now supports HTML viewing and hyperlinks, as well as signed and encrypted mail.
HTML email from any Office 2000 application	User can send a document, spreadsheet or other file directly from the application in HTML format so that the recipient doesn't need the item's original application in order to view it.
Run Rules Now feature	Users can manually have any Rules Wizard rule execute at any time and on any folder.
Enhanced receipts tracking	See all received receipts for a message and print the receipts log if desired.
Save as Web Page	Personal or team calendars can be published to HTML for posting on an Internet or intranet site.
Direct booking of resources	Users can now schedule resources like conference rooms or AV equipment without a designated delegate machine running.
Use of distribution lists in meeting planner	Users can now expand a distribution list in the meeting planner to see the free/busy schedule of each individual member of a list or group.
Quick synchronization options	Users can specify collections of folders to synchronize based upon the speed of the connection.

One of the biggest tangible enhancements in Outlook 2000 is its improved speed. Outlook 98 introduced the "Outlook Today" view, which is designed to be a quick overview screen of a user's *Calendar, Inbox,* and *Task* folders. Users complained that it was sluggish on most machines; in Outlook 2000, Microsoft has sought to resolve this issue as well as improving the performance of startup, shutdown, and switching between folders. Another significant change in Outlook 2000 is the

---

* This is not to imply that Outlook 98 was an inferior product; far from it. It was more of an interim release that hasn't been as widely distributed or installed as Outlook 97. However, it was the first Exchange client that really made offline synchronization work right.

ability to add any file, application, or even web link to the Outlook bar; simply drag and drop it. Also, customized toolbar buttons and even menubar items are simple to add and modify.

The final change I'll mention here is the introduction of adaptive toolbars and menus. What that means is that frequently used commands and buttons appear on the menu or toolbar, while rarely used ones are not displayed unless the user pauses for an unusually long time on a menu, double-clicks to open the menu, or deliberately clicks to obtain more commands or buttons. Using a feature or command will result in its automatically being added to the appropriate menu or toolbar, while a less-used feature will be dropped off. Accordingly, your most recently (and generally most frequently) used commands will dominate the menus and toolbars.

Installing Outlook 2000

There are a couple of different ways to install Outlook 2000, depending upon your situation. The most familiar way is to take the CD to a machine, sit down, and perform the installation. I'll highlight a couple of points to be aware of during a CD installation, but the step-by-step process is obvious enough that I won't cover it in detail here.

What if you don't want to visit all 2,000 machines on your network? You can install Outlook 2000 by using Microsoft Systems Management Server to do a network installation or by using the Outlook Deployment Kit (ODK) to create a custom installation. We'll cover these methods in more detail than the standard CD installation.

Before you install Outlook

Before you install Outlook 2000 there are two things you should take care of to make your installation go more smoothly:

Make sure that your client can correctly resolve the address of the Exchange server it will be talking to

> You can configure the client system to use a DNS or WINS server, or you can simply add an entry for your Exchange server to the *HOSTS* or *LMHOSTS* file. Making sure that name resolution works before installing Outlook speeds the process of configuring Outlook to use the Exchange server by allowing it to easily and quickly find the server on your network.

Create the mailboxes for this user before you start

> Outlook will want to connect to the mailbox, so naturally it's easier if there is an existing mailbox for it to connect to.

Installing Outlook

When you run the Microsoft Office Installation in Custom mode, you have several Outlook components to select from and a couple of new ways to install those components. The feature selection window is shown in Figure 13-1; it allows you to pick individual Office components, including Outlook 2000 and its support items. There are four different installation options:

Run from My Computer
> Installs the files to your local hard drive; has the advantage that when a feature is needed, it is close at hand and can be quickly used.

Run from CD/Network
> Installs the files to a shared network point. This saves on disk space, but requires you to be connected to the network in order to utilize that feature. Also, running a feature from the network tends to impose a little performance penalty.

Install on First Use
> This new feature first appeared in Office 98 for the Macintosh. It adds the feature to all toolbars and menus, but doesn't actually install the feature until the first time the user attempts to run it. This can save disk space and installation time and can be a good option for things like Help files that might never get used. A word to the wise, though: when you do try to run that option, you'll need to have your Installation CD or Shared Network Installation point available to you, or you'll be out of luck. This is not something you want the CEO to discover from an airplane at 30,000 feet.

Not Available
> This is essentially the same as not installing the feature at all. It won't appear on menus or toolbars.

Not all options are available for all components. The Help files, for example, cannot be set to "Not Available."

"Run from CD/Network" depends on the nature of your installation. You'll only have the option to "Run from CD" if you're doing the install from the CD. Likewise, "Run from Network" is only available if you're installing from a Network drive.

The Importers and Exporters should be installed if you anticipate moving data to or from other programs, or if you use a Timex Datalink watch. If you're not sure if you'll use these features, and are sure you'll have the Office CD or Network Installation point available, you can install these as "Install on First Use."

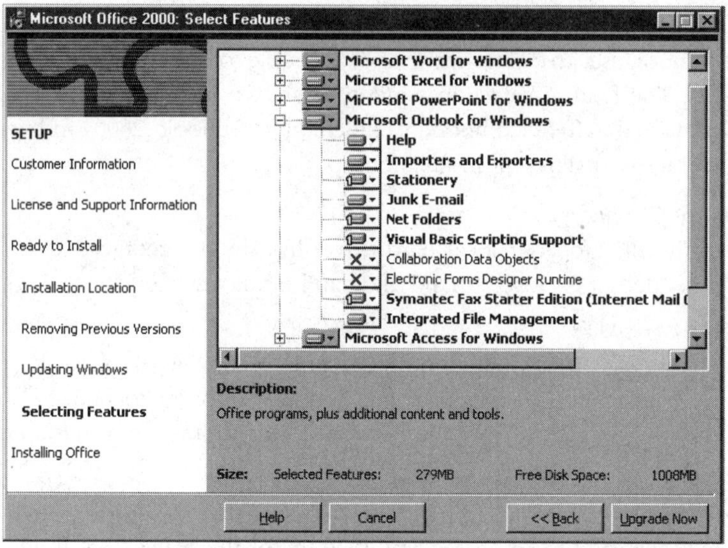

Figure 13-1. The Windows installer allows you to choose how components are installed

The Stationery feature is useful if you plan to do a lot of HTML mail and want the custom templates; otherwise, you can skip installing that feature. I recommend installing the Junk E-Mail filter; it's a handy tool for screening incoming mail and automatically filtering out mail that meets certain criteria as spam.

Most users with a Corporate/Workgroup installation of Outlook (i.e., one that includes the Exchange Server service) will skip installing Net Folders. Net Folders are a tool for sharing data among multiple users, but they cannot be used to share a folder that is in an Exchange Server mailbox.

If you plan to do a lot of custom forms with Visual Basic Scripting, install the Visual Basic Scripting Support. It's a handy debugging tool to help you develop the scripts and forms. Likewise, if you want to do Collaboration Data Objects (CDO) programming, you'll want to install the Collaboration Data Objects component.

If you have forms that were created with the Electronic Forms Designer, you'll want to install the Electronic Forms Designer Runtime to enable access to these forms; otherwise, you can skip installing this module.

The Symantec WinFax Starter Edition is only available for Internet Mail-Only installations of Outlook. If you're in Corporate/Workgroup Mode, you must use Microsoft Fax (or a third-party faxing solution).

The Integrated File Management component enables the built-in file and folder viewing such as "My Computer," "My Documents," and so forth. I usually don't install this component, because I prefer to do such work with Windows Explorer.

Configuring Outlook for Exchange

Outlook, like the Exchange Client, depends on *profiles* and *services* to get mail to you. A user must have at least one Microsoft messaging profile on her workstation in order to use Outlook or the Exchange Client, even if the client is using Internet protocols. The profile defines who the user is, what account he's using, and what services the profile owner wants to use. Each service defines a communication or storage method for Outlook. Outlook 2000 includes the services shown in Table 13-2.

Table 13-2. Outlook 2000 Services

Service Name	What It Does
Exchange Server	Allows Outlook to connect (via MAPI) to an Exchange server, and to store and retrieve mail from the server's private IS.
Personal Folders (PST)	Creates a personal folders (PST) file on your local hard drive or on a shared drive. Inbound mail may be stored in the PST file instead of the Exchange IS; PST files may also be used to store archived mail. The PST looks very much like an Exchange mailbox: it includes all of the typical folders (*Calendar, Inbox, Contacts*, etc.). There are many good reasons *not* to use PST files as your default delivery location, as you'll see later in the chapter.
Microsoft Fax	Outlook will utilize Microsoft Fax to send and receive fax traffic from your computer.
Microsoft Mail	Allows Outlook to communicate directly with MS Mail post offices, without requiring you to set up the MS Mail connector on your Exchange server.
Outlook Address Book	Allows you to use the contents of the Outlook *Contacts* folder for email address books and/or for mail merging in Word.
Personal Address Book (PAB)	A holdover from previous Outlook versions used for storing email contacts and their addresses. Office 2000 is moving users away from storing email contacts in the limited Personal Address Book (PAB), preferring instead to have all contacts go into the *Contacts* folders.
Microsoft LDAP Directory	Allows Outlook to find information in LDAP directories, not just in the Exchange GAL.
Internet E-mail	Allows you to connect to a POP3/SMTP Server to send and receive email.
Microsoft Outlook Support for Lotus cc:Mail	Allows you to connect to cc:Mail post offices to send and receive email.

To use Outlook as an Exchange client, you must install the Exchange Server service on the Outlook client. For an existing Outlook installation, follow these steps:

1. In Outlook, select the Tools → Services... command.

2. Add the "Microsoft Exchange Server" service.

3. The Microsoft Exchange Server dialog box will appear, as shown in Figure 13-2. Fill in the name of your Exchange server and mailbox on the General tab.

4. Verify your connection to the server and the mailbox name by clicking the Check Name button. This forces Outlook to contact the Exchange server and verify that a mailbox with the name you've specified exists and is accessible. If Outlook underlines the server and usernames you've entered, then you have a successful connection. Otherwise, you'll get an error message. Double-check your server and mailbox names. If you're sure that both are correct, the error could indicate a problem either with name resolution to the server or with the mailbox on the server.

If you have multiple Exchange servers in your organization and you're not sure which server the mailbox is homed on, you can simply type the name of any Exchange server in the same organization; Outlook will automatically resolve the correct server for the mailbox you specify. Note that this only works if the servers are in the same Exchange organization.

---

5. Select your connection state in the "When starting" control group:

   — If you want Outlook to attempt to figure out whether you're connected or not, use the default setting of "Automatically detect connection state." Outlook will automatically set itself to offline or online mode, depending on whether it thinks you're connected to a LAN.

   — If you want to explicitly tell Outlook what type of connection to use, choose the "Manually control connection state" button. If you want to set a default state and change it only when needed, use the controls in the Default connection state group. If you'd rather have Outlook prompt you for a connection type each time you start it, select "Choose the connection type when starting."

   How do you choose the right connection type? If you have a machine whose connection state rarely changes, your best bet is to pick the connection type and use the "Manually control connection state" setting to keep Outlook from wasting time trying to deduce the correct connection method. If you're using a laptop or another machine that's sometimes on

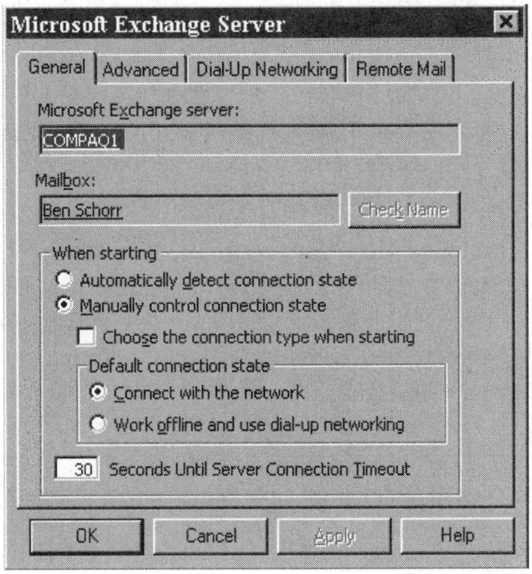

Figure 13-2. The General Tab of the Exchange Server service properties allows you to configure your connection to the server

the network and sometimes off, use the "Choose the connection type when starting" checkbox to give you manual control.

6. Use the Advanced tab to do any or all of the following:

— If you want to open additional mailboxes as part of this profile (assuming you're the owner or have been granted permission by the owner), you can add those mailboxes to the list here. This feature is especially useful when you want to give one user access to another user's *Calendar* or *Contacts* folders.

— If you're concerned about security, you can set Outlook to encrypt data when you're connected via the network and/or when you are working remotely. This option forces Outlook to encrypt all the RPC messages it exchanges with the server.

— The Logon network security option lets you tell Outlook to use your NT logon credentials to authenticate you to Exchange. If you like, you can set Outlook to prompt you for your username and password each time you start the program by setting the logon network security option to None. This is useful if you often wish to log into your Exchange server with a user account other than your NT domain logon account.

— If your machine is a notebook, or not always connected to the Exchange server, you can enable the Offline Folder feature. According to options you specify, Outlook will store copies of your Exchange folders in an Offline Folder File (OST) that you can use when you're not connected to the server.

— Checking the "Enable offline use" checkbox, then clicking the "Offline folder file settings" button lets you configure how Outlook handles your OST settings such as filename and encryption, as well as a handy button to compress your OST file to save on disk usage.

The Dial-up Networking tab lets you configure the phone number and log-in options that Outlook will use if you have "Work offline and use dial-up networking" selected as your default connection state on the General tab. The Remote Mail tab lets you schedule remote mail sessions and configure which mail messages will be processed during the connection.

 You must restart Outlook for any of these changes to take effect.

After you've installed Outlook

One of the mistakes that people commonly make after installing Outlook is thinking that they can uninstall the Exchange Messaging client. Don't do it! If you remove the client, you'll also remove Outlook's messaging capability. You can delete the *exchng32.exe* file if it really bothers you to have it there, but it's handy to be able to run the original Exchange client for troubleshooting, so I recommend you leave it.

If you installed Outlook 97 and would like to change the Inbox icon on your desktop to Outlook, there is a utility called *chnginbx.exe* in the *\valupack\patch* subdirectory of your Office 97 CD that will do it for you quickly and painlessly. Outlook 98 and 2000 will do this automatically.

Using PST files

A Personal Folders File (PST) is a datafile that resides on your local computer and contains all the data that would ordinarily be in an Exchange mailbox: the *Inbox* and *Sent Items* folders, calendar and contact data, and so on.

The conventional wisdom is that you should avoid PST files as if they were radioactive. Why? The data they hold is difficult to manage centrally and rarely gets backed up, especially if your users store their data on their local machines. You thus lose the benefits of Exchange's robust database, including single-instance storage, and it's much easier for users to lose their mail data. In fact, PSTs use at least twice as much space as the IS, since they store two copies of each message: one as plain text and one in rich-text format (RTF).

Server-based rules will not work on PST data, and PST files can't be opened for shared access, so they may not get backed up when you expect. Outlook is supposed to close the PST file after 30 minutes of inactivity, but if other MAPI clients are running, scheduled backups won't get the file because it's still in use. As if those weren't sufficient reasons, there's at least one more: users whose calendars are stored in PST files can't share their calendars with server-based users, meaning that you lose most of the benefits of being able to use calendaring in Outlook.

As a general rule, I recommend that Outlook users avoid using PSTs as the default mail delivery location. There is one case where PST files can be useful: for storing older, noncritical messages or archived items that no longer need to be stored on the server. Since those messages are basically archival material, they won't change terribly often, they can be backed up less frequently, and they generally won't need to be shared among multiple users.

If you choose to disregard this advice and use PST files as your primary mail storage method, here are a few things to be aware of:

- Be very careful to note what the client's Default Delivery Location field says (check the Delivery tab in the dialog that appears when you use the Tools → Services... command). If you're using an Exchange mailbox, you will, in almost every instance, want the default delivery location to be the mailbox in the IS. If you set the default location to a user's PST file, all of the mailbox's mail will be moved to the Inbox of the PST file.

- Reminders will fire only from the root folders of the default delivery location. If you have the default delivery set to the Exchange mailbox, reminders for any tasks or calendar items that user puts in the PST folder will never activate.

- It's very easy for users to get confused about which version of the *Inbox* or *Calendar* they are looking at. Caution them to be careful not to inadvertently post or schedule into the wrong set of folders.

Deploying Outlook en Masse

If you're rolling out Exchange and Outlook together, you'll probably find that installing and deploying Exchange isn't the hard part, since you can use the tools described in Chapter 4, *Installing Exchange*, to automate much of the installation. Besides, there are usually many more clients than servers, so the more difficult task is getting Outlook installed and configured on all your desktops.

Easy Access to Your Archived Data

Once you set storage limits, your users will eventually be forced to archive their mail. Outlook offers the AutoArchive tool, which periodically pops up and offers to archive old mail by putting it in a PST file. Some users like this tool; others prefer to archive mail manually. Anyway, once the mail has been archived, what if the user wants to see it again?

This is easy to do: just add a Personal Folders service that points to your *archive.pst* file. Use the Tools → Services... command, then click the Add button and select a new PST file. Name this file *archive*, or something equally meaningful to you; when Outlook prompts you for the location of this file, enter the path and filename of the file that AutoArchive created for you. If you're not sure where the file is, back up: use the Tools → Options → Other → AutoArchive command and note the path and filename. Once you've entered this in the Personal Folders setup and clicked OK, you're done!

Now you can open your folder list and you'll see your archive folder and all of the archived data right there for easy access any time you want it.

The ODK

The Outlook Deployment Kit (ODK) is a collection of tools, utilities, and documentation that Microsoft has assembled to ease mass deployment of Outlook. It's not available for retail purchase or download; you can only get it from the Microsoft Developer Network (MSDN), Microsoft's Select or Open licensing programs, or a Microsoft Certified Solution Provider.

The centerpiece of the Outlook Deployment Kit is the Outlook 97/98 Deployment Wizard. Essentially, this tool allows you to preset all the installation options for Outlook so that your users can do the installation without having to make many (or any) choices, and you can have a standard configuration across a department or across your entire organization. The output of the ODK is a customized installer that your users can run from a CD or a network share.

The Office Custom Installation Wizard

Outlook 2000 doesn't use the ODK; instead, it introduces the Office Custom Installation Wizard (OCIW), a tool used to create customized installations of the entire Microsoft Office suite, including Outlook. The OCIW is only available on the Office 2000 Resource Kit CD. The OCIW generates two types of files, which the Office 2000 installer uses to perform the actual installation:

MSI (installer package) file

A database of files and configuration settings for Office. The installer extracts the components it installs from this package. The default MSI file is *install.msi*, and it's never altered; whenever you make a new installation package, you get a new MSI file.

MST (transform package) file

Lists the changes that need to be made to the settings in the MSI file for this installation. This file is generated by the OCIW.

By running the OCIW, you can preconfigure the files and settings that you want your Outlook clients to end up with, then save those selections as an MST file. One strength of the OCIW is the ability to create multiple MST files for different types of users. The Accounting department might have different needs than the Engineering department, so the OCIW allows you to create an MST file for each group of users with the unique settings that group needs.

Because the OCIW is designed to let you control all aspects of Office 2000 installation, it's worth a book on its own. I'll focus on what you need to know about using OCIW to install Outlook, not on what-all it can do.

To install the Office Custom Installation Wizard, insert the Office 2000 Resource Kit CD and run the *\ciw\setup* application. That will install the OCIW, Office Profile Wizard and Internet Explorer Administration Kit (IEAK) onto your workstation; you can then run OCIW from the Office 2000 Resource Kit group in the Start menu. Here's what will happen once you do:

1. After telling the OCIW the location of the Installer Package file (typically *install.msi*) you plan to use, you'll be prompted to open an existing MST file. Answering "No" tells OCIW to create a new MST file. Be aware that if you try to open an MST file created with a different package file, you'll get an error message telling you that the two files do not correspond, and the OCIW will ask you to either specify a different MST file or create a new one. You can create a new MST file with the same name as the old one (which overwrites the old one), but none of the settings from the previous MST file will carry over.

2. Once you've confirmed the path and name of the MST file you wish to use, OCIW will prompt you for the default location of the installation. Typically, you would want to leave the default (*drive:\Program Files\Microsoft Office*) path as it is, but if your company policy is to install to a different path, or if you want to preserve components of a previous Microsoft Outlook or Office installation, then you'll have to specify a different path for the installation.

3. The next wizard page in the OCIW allows you to have Setup remove specific previous versions of Microsoft Office products such as Access 95 or Word 97 as part of the custom installation process. This is a handy way to prune any old versions you don't want to use.

4. Next, you can specify how you would like the product installed. Your choices include "Run from My Computer," "Run from Network," "Install on First Use," or "Not Available," as described earlier in the chapter.

5. The next step is to tell the OCIW how to migrate the user's existing profile information into the new installation. If no previous settings exist, the OCIW will use Microsoft's default profile information. If you prefer, you could also have the OCIW create a new profile for that user from an Office Application Settings Profile (OPS) file that you saved with the Office Profile Wizard.

   One of the best uses for the Office Profile Wizard is to migrate a user to a new machine. Rather than force the user to reconfigure all user settings, you can have the Office Profile Wizard from the Office 2000 Resource Kit take a snapshot of the settings on the user's old machine. You can then have the OCIW include that OPS file (the snapshot) in the Transform (MST) file and incorporate the old settings into the installation on the new machine.

6. You can have the OCIW add any extra files you want installed to the user's computer as part of the setup. This can be a handy way to automatically copy a standard *HOSTS* file, custom macros or templates, or a special *readme.txt* file that you want on the user's computer. These files will be stored in the MST file when you complete the OCIW configuration.

7. In the same vein, the next step allows you to use the OCIW to add any new registry entries you wish during the setup. Alternatively, you can stuff these settings into a system policy file using the NT System Policy Editor.[*]

8. Still more customization: in this step, the OCIW prompts you to add, remove or modify any shortcuts you'd like changed or added on the target machine. This can be a handy way to distribute a standard set of shortcuts or perhaps add a shortcut to a standard office document like an online policy manual.

9. If you have multiple network installation servers, you can specify them on the next screen. The advantage here is that if one server is busy or offline, the installation can proceed from another. Of course, this presumes you have multiple servers you want to use for installation.

10. On the next page, you may specify that you want Setup to run other programs after the Microsoft Office installation is complete. Note that the only

---

[*] For lots more detail on system policies, see Chapter 6 of my book *Managing the Windows NT Registry* (O'Reilly & Associates).

programs it won't run are Windows installer programs such as Microsoft Office's *setup.exe* or the *msiexec.exe* program.

11. Finally, we get to an Outlook-specific page (see Figure 13-3). This page lets you preconfigure Outlook for your end user. You can specify usernames, servers, which services you want installed, and other settings. Doing this now saves you from having to instruct your users on what settings to use, or (worse yet) having to run from machine to machine configuring Outlook settings.

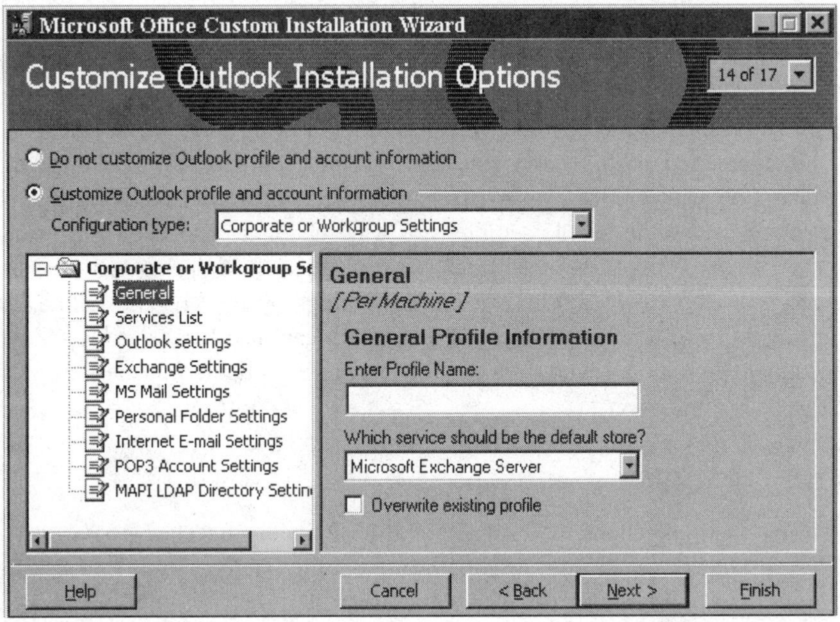

Figure 13-3. The Office Custom Installation Wizard allows you to preconfigure your Outlook settings

12. The next OCIW page gives you options for installing Internet Explorer 5.0. You can opt not to have it installed at all, but be aware that this may cause problems with Outlook responding properly when *mailto:* URLs are clicked on. Also, don't be tempted to install IE5.0 in Minimum configuration. Outlook requires at least Standard installation of IE5.0 for it to work properly.

13. The final page allows you to add, remove, or modify any of the installation properties. For a complete description of these properties and what they do, see the *setupref.xls* file in the Office 2000 Resource Kit.

To run Microsoft Office 2000 Setup using your MST file for the settings, you should use the **transforms** command-line switch with *setup.exe* like this:

```
setup.exe transforms="F:\public\install\accounting.mst"
```

Consider adding the /qn+ switch to the end of your command line; this runs the installer in silent mode, with a confirmation message when the installation completes. This gives you an elegant installation solution: the user doesn't have to watch the setup happen or interact with it, but he's notified when the process is completed. Note that the confirmation message at the end won't display if Setup needs to reboot the machine after the installation completes. The Office 2000 Resource Kit has complete documentation on command-line switches you can use with the Setup executable.

Microsoft Office Profile Wizard

The Office Profile Wizard (OPW) is a simple tool; it does only two things. You can save newly created profiles, and you can restore saved profiles. You might use it in conjunction with Outlook as an Exchange client: configure a station with Outlook, specifying all the profile settings you want clients to use, then run the OPW and save those profile settings. Later, if you discover that settings have been changed, you can easily restore the correct settings by running the Office Profile Wizard again to restore your saved OPS file. You can also have the OCIW tell the setup utility to utilize a saved OPS file for the profile settings in a new installation of Office 2000.

16-Bit Outlook

The 16-bit Outlook client is a subset of the 32-bit client. This is probably due mostly to limitations in the underlying operating system, but I suspect that Microsoft has a vested interest in encouraging all those 16-bit Win 3.x users to upgrade. The stated minimum client requirements to run the 16-bit Outlook client are 8MB of RAM and 12MB of hard drive, though 12MB+ of RAM and 22MB+ of hard drive are recommended.

Installation is a straightforward process, so I won't talk about it in detail. There are some functional limitations in this version of the client that you should be aware of before you install it:

- Though you can respond to voting messages (messages with voting buttons in them), you won't be able to create and send new voting button messages.

- There is no Internet Mail Service for the Windows 3.x product; it's intended as an Exchange client only and doesn't support IMAP4 or POP protocols.

- If you want to view the calendar of an Outlook 32-bit user, you'll have to install the Schedule+ Exchange Transport DLL, which is located on the Exchange 5.5 Client Pack CD in the *\support\msoutl\win16* directory. Note that this is only to view the calendar directly—you can still view the free/busy information without this extension installed.

- Forms created with the Outlook 32-bit version's built-in forms design tool will not be accessible with the 16-bit client. The solution to this is to create the forms using Active Server Pages and Exchange Collaboration Data Objects (CDO) so that they can be viewed as HTML in a web browser.

  These types of forms are supported in the 16-bit client that ships with Exchange 5.5 through a bit of smoke and mirrors. When an Outlook form is sent to a 16-bit (or Macintosh) user, 16-bit Outlook automatically starts an associated HTML form (created using ASP and CDO) using Outlook Web Access. In a manner of speaking, you're using the OWA client for viewing and filling out the form. As you can guess, for this to work there are two important prerequisites:

  — You must use ASP and CDO to create the forms, and you must associate the ASP version with the corresponding Outlook form. ASP/CDO forms are not automatically generated when you create the Outlook form.

  — You must have Outlook Web Access installed and configured on the server.

 Microsoft views the Windows 3.x and Macintosh Outlook clients as "stepping-stones" to the Outlook 2000 (32-bit) version, and recommends that users who don't plan to migrate from Windows 3.x/Macintosh in the near future consider using Outlook Web Access (OWA) instead.

- Remote Access from a Windows 3.x client is accomplished by using the Shiva-Remote software included on the Microsoft Exchange Server CD. Note that you will have to set up your NTRAS server to accept either clear-text or regular encrypted Authentication (not Microsoft encrypted authentication) for the connection to succeed.

Outlook for Macintosh

The Macintosh client has always been the weakling of the non-Win32 bunch. Fortunately, in Exchange SP2 it got a badly needed boost—SP2 includes Outlook for Macintosh version 8.1. With a few minor differences, it's substantially the same as the Windows 3.x client.[*]

---

[*] Most Macintosh users don't consider parity with Windows an improvement, but the old client really was junky.

Here are some things worth noting about the Outlook for Macintosh client:

- If you want to use Macintosh Outlook with S/MIME-based message security, you'll have to use the SP2 version on a PowerMac, since the 68K version doesn't support S/MIME.

- As with the Windows 3.x client, there's no Internet Mail Service for the Macintosh. If you wish to send Internet email from your Macintosh client, you'll have to do so through an Exchange server running the Internet Mail Service. The Macintosh client also lacks a Microsoft Mail service.

- *Calendar*, *Contacts*, and *Tasks* are available, but are essentially the same as Schedule+ version 7. Though they are accessible from the Outlook bar, these folders will display in a separate window (unlike Outlook 2000, where each of these folders displays within the Outlook folder window). Interoperability between the Macintosh client and Win32 clients is limited to seeing free/busy information.

- If your Macintoshes are running MacOS 8.0 or 8.1, you must have the SP1 or SP2 clients. MacOS 8.5 support wasn't added until the SP2 version.

- You can't use the standard ODK to package and deploy the Macintosh Outlook client.

- You can't buy Outlook for Macintosh separately; it comes with Exchange 5.5.

- You cannot share PST and PAB files between the Macintosh and Windows clients. They aren't compatible.

- To connect your Macs remotely to an Exchange server, you'll have to use a third-party solution like Apple Remote Access or a PPP connection into your LAN.

The minimum system requirements for the Macintosh client are a PowerPC processor, system 7.6.1, and at least 8MB of RAM. Microsoft recommends that you have at least 16MB of RAM if you're planning to run Outlook and the Calendar.

Delegating Folder Access

Sometimes you need to give other users access to some or all of your folders. This can be an important part of collaboration, and it's frequently done in situations where users need to share information but a public folder isn't a good solution. A common example of this would be a secretary who needs to access the boss's calendar to add and manage appointments. There are two basic strategies for arranging this *delegate access*. Which strategy you choose depends upon how often you anticipate accessing the other user's folders.

If the delegate only needs occasional access, the File → Open → Other User's Folder command is probably an adequate solution. This command lets one user open another user's folders, provided the folder owner has granted that account permissions. For this to work, the owner must use the Permissions tab of the folder's properties dialog to add the user, or users, that should get delegate access. You can make setting permissions a bit easier by using the predefined roles Outlook offers. Setting a user's role to Reviewer, for example, allows that user to see the folder and read any items in it, but not to add items or to edit or delete any items in the folder. Once the folder owner has added delegate users, those users will be able to open the folders and operate within the permissions granted.

If the delegate needs more or less constant access to the owner's folders, this solution is not very efficient. Fortunately, Outlook and Exchange enable you to access the folders of other users and add them to your Outlook bar right along with your own folders. For this to work, the owner has to grant delegate access to the root mailbox folder. This isn't quite as ominous as it sounds, because granting access to the mailbox doesn't automatically give delegate access to subfolders unless it's explicitly granted. For example, if you give your secretary access to your mailbox, he will not have access to your *Inbox* folder unless you specifically grant it.

One word of caution: even though granting access to the mailbox doesn't grant any permissions to the existing folders, it does automatically grant that user permissions to any new folders that you create. If you create a new folder that you don't want delegates to see, you'll need to go into the permissions for that new folder and specifically remove the delegate from the permissions list.

To grant access to a specific folder, right-click it and select the Permissions command, then use the permissions dialog to grant delegate access to the specific users you want to have access. You can do this for other individual folders, like *Calendar* and *Contacts*, if you need to.

The delegate user still needs to add your mailbox to his Exchange Server service so that it will be opened automatically when he starts Outlook. This allows the delegate user to access your mailboxes' folders from his Outlook bar. Follow these steps to add a mailbox:

1. On the delegate user's machine, select the Tools → Services... command.

2. Select the Microsoft Exchange Service from the list, then click the Properties button.

3. Go to the Advanced tab and click the Add button next to "Open these additional mailboxes." Type the name of the user whose mailbox this delegate has been granted access to, then click OK.

4. The other mailbox name should now appear on the list of additional mailboxes. You can add more mailboxes, or click OK to finalize the process.

You may have to restart Outlook for this to take effect, but once you restart, you will discover that if you open your folder list you will see the other person's mailbox listed there. You can then click the + sign next to their mailbox to expand the list of folders and drag and drop any available folders to your Outlook bar, as desired.

 If you get an error message that a mailbox could not be found when you try to expand it, that usually means that the mailbox owner has not yet, or not correctly, granted you permissions to that mailbox.

Logging into another user's mailbox

If you need to log on to Exchange with someone else's user credentials, there's an easy trick to speed it up. Use the Tools → Services... command, open the properties dialog for the Exchange Server service, and switch to the Advanced tab. Once you're there, set the Logon Network Security group to None. This makes Outlook prompt you for a username, domain name and password each time you start it with this profile. As long as you know this information, you can log in as any user you wish and access that user's mailbox. Before you worry about the possible security breach, note that you need to know the user's password to get into a mailbox this way.

Providing Remote Access

Outlook supports several different options for remote access to mailboxes on an Exchange server. Your choice of option will depend upon the type of connectivity you have between remote users and the server and the frequency with which you expect any particular user to connect remotely.

Connect and work online

If you often have a reliable connection to your Exchange server (running at 28.8Kbps or better), you can use Outlook as if you were connected directly on your LAN. First establish your connection to the network via Dial-up Networking (or however you're configured to connect), then start Outlook as if you were connected. You'll be able to do anything you can do locally because you are connected to the Exchange server and using the mailbox directly. Keep in mind that, depending on the speed of your connection, performance may be substantially worse than what you're accustomed to at the office. Outlook uses MAPI, which in turn uses RPCs. As you probably remember from earlier chapters, RPCs are highly sensitive to network speed and latency, and dial-up connections tend to be relatively slow and to have relatively high latency.

Work offline with synchronization

This is one of the most commonly used options because it allows you to use Outlook normally without having to stay connected during the entire Outlook session. In essence, you use this option by configuring Outlook for offline use (as described in the section "Synchronizing Data for Offline Use" later in the chapter), connecting to the Exchange server, synchronizing your folders, and disconnecting from the server. When you restart Outlook—this time without connecting—you simply tell Outlook to work in offline mode. This mode gives you full access to all the data and folders you synchronized, as though you were connected to the server. When it's convenient, you can reconnect to the Exchange server and resynchronize your folders; this sends any changes and messages you've created to the server and downloads any new messages or changes back to your local folder cache.

Fast, Cheap, Secure: Pick Two

With the proliferation of virtual private networks (VPNs), many companies are taking advantage of VPNs to give their remote users better access to Exchange resources.

Windows NT and Windows 95/98 include the capability to set up remote access over an Internet connection by utilizing the Point-to-Point Tunneling Protocol (PPTP). To establish a PPTP connection, remote users connect to their ISP via normal modem connections, then start a second Dial-up Networking session that has been configured to use the virtual VPN adapter. This "connection" actually encapsulates data bound for the remote VPN service in ordinary PPP packets. To the ISP, or any other node the packets touch, they look like ordinary packets; when the PPTP data reaches the VPN's server (which can be an NT machine running RAS), the server accepts and authenticates the connection.

Once that connection is established, remote users start Outlook as if they were connected locally. The result is a connection that can be as fast as the local Internet connection, via a local telephone call to a provider that may offer unlimited access for just $20 or so per month. There's no need to maintain multiple hosts or modems at the home office, and there are no long-distance bills or slow modem connect speeds for the remote user.

For most companies, reducing their per-user remote access costs to just $20 or so per month would be a tremendous cost savings. There's a drawback, though: if you don't configure your VPN properly, you may accidentally allow unauthorized users to connect to your servers over the Internet. There's a good paper explaining the underlying issues at *www.counterpane.com/pptp.html*.

Remote mail

This is the least powerful of the remote-access options bundled with Outlook, but also one of the simplest and best suited to extremely slow connections. Remote mail will only send and receive email; it won't synchronize your calendar, tasks, or public folders.

You configure remote mail access with the Remote Mail tab of the Exchange Server service properties dialog. You can set it to dial in at selected times (using the connection you specify on the Dial-up Networking tab), or you can use it manually with the Tools → Remote Mail menu item. Once connected, it can retrieve all marked messages or items that meet certain criteria you specify, such as all messages that are unread or all those from a specific sender.

Remote mail has the additional advantage that you can preview your message headers before deciding which messages to download, so you can tell Outlook not to download any messages that have attachments, thus saving time over a slow link.

Synchronizing Data for Offline Use

It's not always convenient for your users to be connected to your Exchange server, particularly if they're using notebook computers or a machine outside your office LAN. Outlook provides for offline use by means of an Offline Folder, or OST, file. By synchronizing this file either manually or automatically, you can ensure that any changes made on either side of the connection are reflected in both places.

The most common use of synchronization is for private folders: your *Inbox*, *Calendar*, *Contacts*, and *Tasks* folders, and so forth. Synchronization of public folders is possible (and useful, since the alternative is either staying connected or downloading tons of public folder information) but it requires a bit more effort; you must drag the public folder you want to synchronize into your *Favorites* folder.

Before you start configuring your desired synchronization settings, make sure that you have configured Outlook for offline use. You do this by choosing the Tools → Services... command, selecting the Microsoft Exchange Service item, and clicking the Properties button. Once the properties dialog opens, switch to the Advanced tab and make sure that the Enable Offline Use checkbox is marked. The first time you check this, Outlook will complain that it can't find the indicated OST file and ask if you want to create one. Click the Yes button and an OST file will be created.

Synchronizing private folders

To synchronize a private folder, select it and open its properties dialog, then switch to the Synchronization tab, as shown in Figure 13-4. The controls in the

"This folder is available" group control whether the folder is synchronized or not. The default choice, "Only when online," means that nothing in the folder will be synchronized. To mark the folder so that it can be synchronized, click the "When offline or online" button. You can then use the Filter... button to specify specific criteria for synchronization, like ignoring messages over a certain age or size.

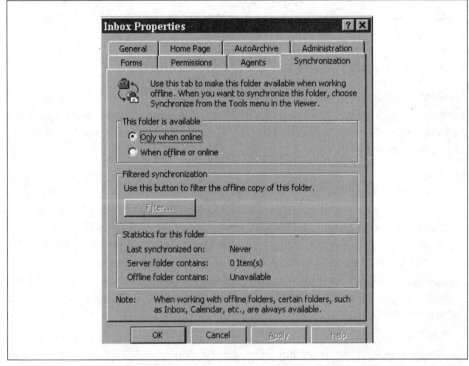

Figure 13-4. The Inbox Properties Synchronization tab allows you to enable or disable offline use and shows some useful statistics

Once you've marked the folder as synchronizable, use the Tools → Options... command; in the options dialog, switch to the Mail Services tab and configure how often you would like the synchronization to occur. If the machine in question is a laptop that's occasionally connected to the LAN, you might want to set it up for "When online, synchronize all folders upon exiting." That way, your laptop users can get their offline folders automatically synchronized whenever they're connected to the LAN.

To manually synchronize one or all folders, use the Tools → Synchronize... command from the main Outlook menu screen.

Synchronizing public folders

Synchronizing public folders is a bit more complicated. You can't just right-click the public folder and synchronize it as is; first, you have to copy that folder to your local *Favorites* public folder. Open the folder list, then open the Public Folders subtree and use your mouse to drag any public folders you wish to synchronize to the *Favorites* folder immediately above. You can then right-click on the version of the public folder that appears in your *Favorites* folder and configure the synchronization settings as you do for private folders.

Improving Outlook Performance

Outlook 2000 is, overall, noticeably faster than Outlook 97/98. Compared to Exchange (or even NT), there's relatively little you can do to improve Outlook's performance, but that doesn't mean that there's nothing you can do. Here are some suggestions:

- The number one performance complaint: Outlook takes a very long time to start up. Most of the time, when users have this beef it's because the RPC binding order is set wrong. This value (which lives in the `HKLM\SOFTWARE\ Microsoft\Exchange\Exchange Provider` registry key) tells Outlook the order of protocols to use when connecting to the Exchange server. If the protocol you're using isn't at the head of the list, the client has to try each protocol in the list until it finds one that works. To set TCP/IP as your first protocol, edit the value so that `ncacn_ip_tcp` comes first. You should also remove any reference to protocols you don't use.

- The number two performance complaint is that the Outlook client is slow when sending and receiving messages. If you use TCP/IP as the network protocol to reach your Exchange server, you may be able to fix this problem by making sure that name resolution is properly configured on your system. You should be able to get quick responses when you ping your Exchange server by name and IP address; if you don't, make sure your DNS (or *HOSTS* file) is properly configured.

- Outlook 2000 sucks up RAM just like the other Office applications. You should consider 32MB as a reasonable minimum for Office 2000, but I strongly encourage you to get as much RAM as you can afford, especially if you're using Windows NT.

- If Outlook is performing sluggishly while connected to your Exchange server, make sure that your network (or the server itself) isn't overloaded with traffic.

- If you're running the Windows 3.x client, make sure that your Windows 3.x machine has the latest TCP/IP protocol stack and client software.

- If you're running the Outlook for Macintosh client with a 24-bit color display, you may find that you're low on memory. Reducing the display resolution can sometimes improve performance by freeing up additional memory.

- Another Macintosh tip: if you're in an environment where the Exchange server is local to the user and bandwidth is plentiful, you may find that running AppleTalk instead of TCP/IP yields some performance improvements.

- Encourage your users to keep their mailboxes cleaned up. Deleting or archiving old messages can help to keep things running fast. Also remind users to empty their *Deleted Items* folder periodically if they don't have it set to automatically empty.

- Set AutoArchive to move old items to a PST file located on a network drive or the local hard drive of the user's PC. They can be easily accessed if needed in the future, and moving them out of the Exchange Information Store may provide better response times.

- If you're not using the journal (most users don't even know it's there, much less use it), turn off the AutoJournal feature. (In Outlook 2000, use the Tools → Options → Journal Options command.) Just uncheck anything you don't want journaled.

- Remove Microsoft's FindFast "utility" from your startup group.

Managing Outlook Web Access

Outlook Web Access (OWA) is a very clever new feature from Microsoft. A derivation of the Active Server Components web-based messaging client that was in Exchange 5.0, OWA is really just a custom web application hosted by IIS and using the Exchange server as its data source. OWA's strengths include:

Accessibility
   It's accessible from any browser that supports frames on any platform. This allows users to access their Exchange mailboxes by using OWA from web kiosks, Macs, PCs, Unix machines, or even PDAs, as long as the host browser supports frames.

Portability
   It's completely portable. No configuration or mail data is stored on the host, so users can log in from a different machine every time, if desired.

Speed
   It's relatively fast over a slow connection.

Installation/Configuration

To use OWA, you don't have to install anything on the client, just on the server. OWA requires the following components:

- Windows NT 4 or later with Service Pack 3 (SP3) or later installed

- Microsoft Internet Information Server (IIS) 3.0 or later

- IIS Active Server Pages (ASP) components

- Exchange Outlook Web Access components

The server that hosts the Outlook Web Access does not have to be the same machine that hosts the Exchange server; however, if they are on separate machines IIS must be configured for anonymous access and clear-text authentication.

Installing OWA

Installation is a simple procedure; in fact, you may already have installed all the necessary components. If you're not sure, pop back to Chapter 4 and follow the instructions to add the OWA components to your existing installation. There are also a few configuration steps necessary to make OWA work right:

- Any users who are going to use OWA must have the Log on Locally right (granted with the Policies menu of User Manager).

Granting Log on Locally gives every user so assigned the ability to walk up to your NT server console and log in, so make sure you've accounted for the physical security of your NT server.

- Only the Internet Explorer browsers support NT challenge/response authentication. If you want to use other browsers, make sure that you've also enabled some other type of authentication.

- On the IIS server, be sure that the *IUSER_Servername* account has been granted the Log on Locally right and that you're using the same password for this account in User Manager and in the Internet Service Manager.

- NT challenge/response authentication will only work if Exchange and IIS are running on the same machine.

- It is always a good idea to review the latest Knowledge Base articles, release notes and white papers to ensure that you're aware of all of the latest developments and requirements for installing a component like OWA.

OWA and Firewalls

Depending upon the configuration of your system, you may have a firewall either in front of, or behind, your IIS server.

If your firewall is behind your IIS server

The firewall is going to want to deny connection attempts to any ports that you haven't told it to leave open. Since Exchange, by default, assigns two random port numbers to use for communicating with the IS and DS there is no way to tell your firewall ahead of time which two ports to leave open.

The solution is to tell Exchange to assign two specific ports, instead of random ones, so that you can configure your firewall to allow access. To do this you will need to edit the registry on your Exchange server and then configure your firewall appropriately:

1. On your Exchange server, open the registry editor of your choice.

2. Go to the DS registry key at `HKLM\System\CurrentControlSet\Services\MSExchangeDS\Parameters` and add this value:

   ```
   Name: "TCP/IP Port"
   Data Type: REG_DWORD
   Value: 000004C9(1225)
   ```

   This tells Exchange to use port 1225 for the Directory Service.

3. Go to the IS registry key at `HKLM\System\CurrentControlSet\Services\MSExchangeIS\ParametersSystem` and add this entry:

   ```
   Name: "TCP/IP Port"
   Data Type: REG_DWORD
   Value: 00000004CA(1226)
   ```

   This tells Exchange to use port 1226 for the IS.

4. Close the registry editor.

5. Configure your firewall to allow TCP connections to be made to ports 1225 and 1226.

6. You will also need to make sure that port 135 is open and available between the IIS and Exchange server machine so that the RPC port mapper can do its job. (For more on TCP/IP port assignments and firewalls, see Chapter 16, *Exchange Security*).

Of course, you can use other port numbers instead of these two. The important thing is to make sure that you make this change on your Exchange servers *and* on the firewall.

If your firewall is in front of your IIS server

This case is much easier. If your IIS server and Exchange box are on the same side of the firewall, all you have to do is instruct your firewall to allow inbound connections on port 80, the default HTTP port, and port 443, the default SSL port. This allows external users to get in. Whenever possible, you should use OWA with HTTPS to prevent eavesdropping on your mail users.

I should also mention that you can change these default ports if you wish; they don't have to be 80 and 443, but in most instances you'll want to just leave them at the defaults. If you do change them, make sure to update your firewall and give correct port numbers to your users.

14

*Managing
Exchange Servers*

*The management of a balance of power is a
permanent undertaking, not an exertion
that has a foreseeable end.*
—Henry A. Kissinger
White House Years

Exchange offers some unique capabilities compared to other email systems, but those capabilities come at a price. To get maximum reliability, stability, and performance, you must be proactive in managing your organization's servers, because if you just wait for something bad to happen, it may be too late to recover. Careful planning of your server configuration and ongoing maintenance is required to ensure that your environment is optimizing your server usage, with minimal data loss risk and best performance.

Messaging is all about information flow—people communicating with people, both inside and outside an organization. Getting to know user habits, activities, and trends is critical to delivering a messaging system that meets user needs. You should have evaluated user needs before you deployed Exchange; now it's time to see how those considerations affect server management.

Server Management Basics

Before we go into the details of the Exchange server management tools, let's talk about philosophical issues that affect what you do to your servers. There's no gray area when it comes to uptime and performance—more is better—but other management areas offer a little more flexibility.

Microsoft has positioned Exchange as a one-size-fits-all solution for every customer from the small office market to very large corporate mail systems, but these markets have different concerns. In particular, storage management, replication, and high availability features such as clustering are much more important to large sites than to small ones. Also consider that the smaller customer has to deal with the same backup complexity and data growth as a larger customer, but often with fewer staff.

Most ongoing management of server hardware revolves around the I/O subsystem. For most applications, Exchange isn't particularly CPU-bound, and there's not much you can do to manage RAM except to add it when necessary. Because of dynamic buffer allocation, which you first encountered in Chapter 1, *Introducing Exchange Server*, Exchange 5.5 will productively use as much RAM as you install. Database backup and maintenance issues are a significant part of your day-to-day work, as are troubleshooting and (hopefully) implementing proactive fixes to problems before they bite you.

It is important to distinguish between managing servers at the site level and at the individual server level. Exchange abstracts much of what you would associate with a single server in other products up to the site level, leaving mostly practical tasks like managing disks and backups. For many higher-level messaging functions, like limiting the use of connectors and message sizes, the site is the best level to work on, since site-level changes can apply to multiple servers.

Centralized Storage: Pro and Con

The most sophisticated form of Exchange implementation is a centralized storage model, where all user mail and public folder data is stored on the server instead of on individual machines. In this model, clients just view mail; they don't keep their own local copies. As you learned in Chapter 13, *Managing Exchange Clients*, remote, low-bandwidth, or offline users can use Outlook's offline synchronization features to keep their local and server-based mail caches synchronized.

Pro

Centralized storage allows you to concentrate all your management efforts at the server level, not on the clients. When clients store their own mail data, you have less assurance that it's protected from loss, damage, or compromise than you do if it's on a stable, secure, managed server. Do you want to back up hundreds of clients or a single server?

There are some compelling reasons for using centralized storage management:

- Exchange is built from the ground up to support centralized storage as a way of managing information flow and retention. It's designed to support very large Information Stores and to let you juggle mailboxes and servers to spread the load gracefully.

- In a typical office environment, users want to be able to do their (often non-computer-related) job without concern for backups, disk storage, growth management, and so forth. Forcing each user to keep track of their own mail interferes with their real jobs.

- With centralized storage, you gain the benefits of single-instance storage, plus the management benefits of having all your data stored in, and available from, a small number of servers.

- PST files are fragile. They're easily corrupted and subject to loss or damage by other applications on the workstation. There's no way to recover accidentally deleted messages from a PST. (See "Using PST files" in Chapter 13 for more details on why most seasoned administrators say "PST BAD.")

Con

Centralized storage isn't perfect. There are three major arguments against centralizing all your mail data on your servers:

- It's possible to build such a big centralized store that you can't efficiently back it up or restore it. It's very difficult to deal with the practical backup and recovery solutions for a 100GB or 200GB store; it would literally take days to run database tests, and the need to backup and restore the entire file makes it difficult to recover quickly from any sort of failure. You can empirically test how long backup and recovery takes on a test server loaded with a copy of your database; in some cases, upgrading your backup system can get you out of this particular problem.

- If you use centralized storage, you'll be held to a higher standard for reliability and availability; when your server's down, users are prevented from using their mail at all, not just from sending and receiving new mail.

- Server redundancy is critical. The centralized storage model tempts many people to build one big server with lots of mailboxes, but if anything happens to that one server, you're dead in the water. You can fix this problem to some extent by using a larger number of smaller servers, thus distributing both load and risk.*

Choosing the proper solution

If there's any way you can avoid it, don't use PST files. If you use PST files, you lose all the benefits of centralized storage, including ease of backup, single-instance storage, and centralized security. If your users insist on keeping their own

---

* Ed Crowley points out that if you split one server into two, you've doubled the overall odds of a failure, but when the failure occurs it will only affect half as many users.

local replicas of mail, strongly encourage them to use offline folders (if they're using Outlook) or IMAP (if they're not), since both of these allow each client to keep a local store that mirrors the contents of the client's mailbox on the server.

If you must allow PST files, restrict their use as much as possible, and educate your users about the potential pitfalls, so they'll know what limitations PST files impose. Then be prepared for complaints and help requests once the inevitable happens and someone loses, or can't open, a PST file. You've been warned.

Small Doesn't Always Mean Harder

It might seem ridiculous to plan for 24/7 availability and uptime for a small Exchange implementation of 10 to 100 users. Users at small sites, though, don't need their email any less than users at big companies. Email has entered the mainstream, and users expect and demand that email be as available and reliable as the public telephone system.

The good news is that it's often easier for small organizations to follow good server management policies. Smaller organizations usually find it less expensive to update clients, provide training, and so on. Small Exchange sites usually don't have to wrestle with the complexities of multisite networks, which is a savings both in administrative cost and hassle for the administrative staff.

Two heads are better than one

At a minimum, consider splitting the workload at your site—even if it's a very small site—across two Exchange servers. This may mean that you redefine what a server looks like. Chapter 3, *Exchange Planning*, gave some pretty detailed guidance about the best kinds of hardware for running Exchange, but you may find a larger group of less-capable servers is better for your individual needs than a small number of bigger servers. I'm not suggesting trying to host 1500 users on a Packard Bell box you bought at Sears, but not every server application requires a stout server with lots of RAM and fast RAID storage.

The former Soviet Union's strategy for military supremacy was to build large numbers of robust but feature-poor weapons, as opposed to the Western strategy of building a small number of highly capable but fragile weapons. While the theory was never tested in battle, you may find that the Red Army approach works to your advantage even if you're running a large Exchange site. Consider a server that runs the IMS or other connectors. These connectors are typically CPU-bound. As long as you don't store any public folder or mailbox data on them, disk redundancy and performance are relatively unimportant. Two good-quality desktop systems may actually provide better overall performance and redundancy than one larger connector server. Having two independent systems also makes it much easier to do scheduled maintenance on either machine. However, adding servers also adds hardware and maintenance costs, so there's a tradeoff to evaluate. In general, whenever possible, I like to put connectors on their own server in each site.

Scheduling Maintenance Time

Microsoft's claims notwithstanding, Windows NT is not quite perfectly stable. If you put all your mail and Exchange resources on a single server, you run the risk of unplanned downtime caused by NT problems. Even if you don't run into NT problems, you're still guaranteed to have to reboot the system when you make configuration changes and do upgrades. Although Windows NT 4.0 Service Pack 4 is much better than previous versions in this regard,* ancillary services like Internet Explorer and IIS tend to offset SP4's improvements by requiring reboots when you update or reconfigure them.

Since Exchange lets you do online backups without stopping its services, if you don't change the configuration of your servers, and if fortune smiles on you by keeping your hardware from breaking, you can run Exchange for months on end without shutting it down. However, it's important to factor scheduled maintenance like installing product upgrades or service packs, or even doing an offline defragmentation of the store, into your availability plan. Don't just take the server down at random intervals to install hardware or software upgrades; instead, make a schedule and stick to it. This minimizes your unplanned downtime and lets you plan updates and maintenance on your own terms.

Managing Large Stores

When the combined size of your public and private store files starts getting up around the 12GB mark, the practical matters of backup, recovery, and storage management start to get a lot more important. The Standard Edition of Exchange is limited to 16GB per store file, but Enterprise Edition doesn't have any limit on the store size. However, there are practical limits to how much stuff you can physically back up. Let's say you have a 54GB store that you can back up at 6 GB/hour. That means that every full backup will take 9 hours, and restores will take up to twice as long, depending on how recent your backup is. If your server fails, you're looking at 9 to 18 hours just to reload the backup from tape and patch the databases! It could be worse if you have to spend time tracking down a replacement computer, installing Windows NT and Exchange, and doing whatever else is required to correct the actual cause of the problem.

---

* Microsoft's quantitative data suggests roughly a tenfold improvement in mean time between unscheduled reboots, and I have seen nothing to disprove this.

You can plan for this eventuality in two ways. One way is to take advantage of Exchange's strengths and distribute your data: you can split your public IS across many servers by distributing folder replicas (see Chapter 10, *Managing Public Folders*, for details), or you can move user mailboxes to better distribute the load. The second way, upgrading your backup hardware, is initially less expensive, but it doesn't give you the same flexibility and redundancy as adding servers.

Managing the Managers

It's essential that everyone responsible for administering your Exchange servers agree on policies and procedures. It's far too easy to accidentally make undesirable changes, and in a multisite network those changes may quickly be replicated. How to coordinate server management depends on your organization: if you're the only Exchange administrator, or if you're in a position to develop and enforce a set of guidelines, management is easy. If you must build a consensus, reaching agreement and maintaining discipline to work together are a little harder. You can use the rest of this section to formulate a policy sensible enough for all your administrators to agree on.

Controlling changes

When you have multiple servers in a site, it's preferable to have all directory changes made to a single server. This lowers the risk of replication conflicts created by changes to more than one replica of the directory. Since you can install Exchange Administrator on any NT 4.0 machine, it's usually pretty easy to agree on centralizing directory changes. Of course, practically everything you can change in Exchange Administrator is a directory change, so be specific about what kind of changes you'll allow.

It's also a good idea to keep changes to permissions on directory objects to a minimum. The less often you change permissions, the less chance you have to make a mistake. One way to centralize permission management is to replace the permissions given to the account you used to install Exchange with those of a Windows NT global group, then put whomever you want to have administrative access in this group. This keeps changes to the Exchange Directory hierarchy permissions to a minimum: you just assign permissions to the group once, then add and remove accounts as necessary.

To make this change, create the Windows NT group using User Manager, populate it with the proper accounts (including the account of the administrator making the change), and log off. Log back on as a member of the group, then use Exchange Administrator to make the appropriate changes to the organization and site Configuration container permissions.

Controlling who has administrative access

Speaking of changing permissions, there are three objects in the directory whose permissions are particularly important: the organization, site, and site Configuration containers. To control who has administrative access to your servers, you can adjust permissions on these objects. Normally, after you install Exchange, there will be two accounts with permissions on these objects: the site service account and the account you used when installing Exchange. By opening the Permissions tab on these three objects, you can modify which groups and accounts have permissions on these objects.

Modifying permissions on these three objects is particularly important because many items in the Exchange directory inherit permissions from one or more of these objects. If you haven't made any permissions changes since installing Exchange, these are the only objects that need to be changed, given this inheritance. On the other hand, if you have made changes, it would be prudent to spot-check other objects, especially the default Recipients container.

Remember, the Exchange Administrator application won't show the Permissions tab on most objects unless you use the Tools → Options... command to force it to do so.

You can assign permissions to individual containers and leaf nodes. For example, you can set permissions so that a particular account or group could change connector settings and view their queues without giving that account or group permission to make changes to mailbox objects.

Documentation!

Mainframe, minicomputer, and database administrators are usually pretty good about keeping detailed records of their system configurations and software loads. However, many NT and Exchange administrators don't have that background, so it's likely that your network is a little lacking in this respect. At a minimum, you should be keeping track of the following:

How is NT installed on your Exchange servers?

This should include information on what hardware is installed on the server, what its network settings are, any special drivers, the way hard disks are partitioned, what service packs are installed, and anything else you think you'd need to know to reconstruct a failed machine.

How was Exchange installed?

> What is the service account? Which server was the first one installed in the site?

What connectors are you using?

> What remote systems do they talk to? Who can you call if the server on the other end of the connector starts acting up?

What's your disaster recovery plan?

> A plan is never easy to produce (see Chapter 17, *Recovery and Repair*, for some hints), but having one on hand makes an actual recovery much less stressful.

Apart from this workaday documentation, you should also outline your anticipated needs for future storage and upgrades, when possible. Try to decide when major upgrades like Windows 2000 and Exchange 6.0 will be deployed, and document your reasoning. Try to define your rules governing when a server is too old or too slow and how to decide what to replace it with.

Last, but certainly not least, write down your strategy for incremental Exchange Server and client upgrades. Do you apply new service packs 15 days after they ship, or do you wait 6 months until they're stable? When Outlook 2001 ships, will you upgrade immediately, or wait for Outlook 2002?

Storage and Growth Management

It's an old chestnut that data expands to fill the space available, and this happens to be true when it comes to email systems. Users, by and large, don't do a good job of removing old email. The fault's not all theirs, though; email is seeing increasing use as a transport and storage mechanism for other kinds of data, like voice mail and faxes. Between public folders and the ability to file personal mail into organized trees of folders, Exchange has become many users' tool of choice for filing medium-term data.

Even if your users are well organized and diligent about cleaning up their mailboxes, and even if you impose storage limits to keep folder and mailbox sizes within reason, you'll probably find that the volume of messages and average message size are larger than you expected. As Exchange becomes more popular in your organization, you'll probably also find that mail system usage increases as people get more comfortable with the product and find new applications for it, like booking shared resources or holding votes.

Managing the growth of your servers requires careful planning and forethought; namely, you must decide how big you'll let a server get before you start moving mailboxes and services to other servers. You'll have to set your own thresholds, but I can suggest a few ways to help you determine what those thresholds might be.

Normally, you'll probably let a server grow to the size you feel comfortable with. You may be constrained by the amount of disk space on a server or the perceived risk inherent in hosting lots of mailboxes or folders on a single server. More likely, you'll be limited by how much data you can back up and restore in the amount of time you have available. For example, if the best backup system you have available can back up a 10GB store in 7 hours, you might be better off capping the store size at about 7GB (since at that rate you can back up 7GB in about 5 hours and restore it in about 10) by moving some users and data to other servers.

You can use empirical data to tell you how fast the store on your server is growing: capture the Mailbox Resources and Public Folder Resources views to a text file once per month, and you've got an instant baseline for comparison. You can also use the Performance Monitor counters discussed in Chapter 18, *Managing Exchange Performance*, and Appendix B, *Useful Performance Monitor Counters*, to keep track of the load on your machines, including the average number of active users on a server and the inbound and outbound message traffic rates.

When you add new servers to a site, Exchange imposes zero penalty on you, but the servers have to work a lot harder to move mail between users in diferent sites. Exchange components have been designed to allow you to spread the service load across multiple machines: connectors on one server, public and private IS databases on separate machines, and so on. My normal recommendation is to allow your servers to grow to around 70% of their capacity before expanding them or shifting some load elsewhere. For example, if you have a server equipped with 15GB of space, when the combined size of your public and private IS database files hits around 10.5GB, I'd start looking for a new place to move some mailboxes and folders. The same is true for response time: if your server starts bogging down because there are too many concurrent users for it to handle, move some mailboxes to another server.

Knowing Your Users

It's important to study traffic patterns on your servers, especially with regard to when users are most likely to receive and read their email. Some environments are strictly 8-to-5 (although they can receive incoming mail at any time of the day), while others have users who connect and actively use the server at all hours of the day and night.

It's also valuable to spot-check the Mailbox Resources view of the private IS to see which mailboxes are growing the most in items or bytes. You can use Exchange Administrator's File → Save Window Contents... command to save snapshots of this view every so often, comparing versions to see where growth is happening. Check the volume and size of public folders, distribution lists, and Usenet groups on your servers to help you understand how users are actually using the system.

If you have users who subscribe to Internet mailing lists, you may find significant benefits in subscribing a public folder to those lists. This centralizes storage of list mail and makes its contents available to a wider range of people without any additional load on your server or the mailing list host. Microsoft has a white paper titled "Subscribing Public Folders to Internet Mailing Lists," available at *www.microsoft.com/exchange/55/gen/Subscribe.htm.*

One more suggestion: in Chapter 3, I suggested putting users who work together on the same server so they can exchange mail most efficiently. Consider how you can track and measure how often users are sending to each other; proper placement is beneficial to both you and the users, and it's easy to move mailboxes between servers when you need to. One way (albeit an imprecise one) to get this insight is to look at the Single Instance Ratio counter of the public and private IS objects (see Appendix B for a full explanation of these counters). Of course, it's not hard to send out a short survey to all the users on a particular server (hint: create an ABV or DL to group users by the server they're on) and just ask them how often they mail other users on the same server; while unscientific, this type of user poll can shed valuable light on what your users are doing.

Mailbox Moving Magic

One of Exchange Server's best-kept secrets is that it doesn't care what server is holding a particular mailbox. All addressing and security is based on an object's place within the site, not the server's name. It's possible to introduce a new server, move some or all users to that server, and decommission the original server or servers. Here's the best part: this can be done without stopping the servers or touching the clients, and if everything is done with planning and proper sequence, users will never know the difference.

When you use the Tools → Move Mailbox... command in Exchange Administrator, it moves the mailbox—including all its content and user settings, like inbox assistant rules, permissions, and so on—to another server in the same site. You can use this function to rename a server, swap users between servers, or even deliver a zero-downtime upgrade from an old Exchange 4.0 box to Exchange 5.5.

As an example, here's how you can use the Move Mailbox function to replace an old server:

1. Install a new server into the same site as the old server. Give it a different name from the old server.

2. Replicate your public folders from the old server to the new server. Set the folders to replicate, monitor replication progress until they're synchronized,

then remove all replicas from the original server. Use the Replicas tab on the server's Information Store objects to track progress.

3. Make sure any specialty site functions are relocated to another server, including the routing calculation server designation and the system's hidden public folders (see "If you're removing the first server in a site" in Chapter 4, *Installing Exchange*, or Knowledge Base article Q152959, for more on these folders).

4. Remove and recreate any messaging or directory replication connectors hosted on the old server. It may be safer to duplicate and overlap some connectors, such as the IMS, while you reconfigure the affected systems. The overall process for moving connectors is intuitive if you remember how Exchange calculates routing costs:

   a. Create the new connectors between the machines you want to connect.

   b. Raise the cost of the old connectors higher than the cost of the new connectors so that Exchange will prefer the new connectors when making routing decisions.

   c. Force Exchange to recalculate its routing table by using the Recalculate Routing button on the General tab of the server's MTA properties dialog. Once the routing table has been rebuilt, new messages should start flowing over the new connector instead of the old one.

   d. When there's nothing queued up for the old connector, delete it on both ends of its original connection.

   e. Recalculate the routing table again to remove references to the old connector.

5. Use the Move Mailbox... command to move each user as the opportunity presents. One way to accomplish this is to monitor logons and wait until a user is no longer accessing her mailbox (although you can just go ahead and move mailboxes without most users ever noticing, especially during lunch hour). Use the Recipients container under the Server object in Exchange Administrator to track progress and easily identify which mailboxes are on a given server.

6. Using a MAPI mail client such as Outlook 98, the next time a user whose mailbox has been moved tries to connect to the old server, it silently tells the client "hey, your mailbox has moved over here." If the old server isn't running when the client tries to reconnect, you'll have to update the user's profile manually.

7. Keep the old server online for a while. Someone could be on vacation, or a user may have additional clients on laptop systems or at home.

8. In a month or so, unplug the old server from the network and double-check everything to make sure that you didn't forget to move or rehost anything important.

9. When all is correctly rehosted, decommission the old server. The server can then be deleted from the site.

The best thing about this procedure is that none of these steps, except for the last one, are irreversible, and you can do each step or part of a step at your leisure and comfort level. There is one thing to be aware of: when you move one or more mailboxes, Exchange Administrator does the move message by message, so moving large mailboxes can take a long time and generate a large volume of transaction logs. A single 200MB mailbox (consisting of around 30,000 items) can easily take 45 minutes to move; a large group of large mailboxes could take a day or more to relocate. Keep an eye on the amount of free space on your log disk during the move; you may need to do a full online backup during the migration to clear the logs.

Managing Disks

During installation, the Exchange Server setup application puts all of its executable, database, and log files on the same disk partition. As you saw in Chapter 3 (and will see again in Chapter 18), this usually leads to suboptimal performance and recoverability, since the installer doesn't pay attention to disk speeds or configurations. Your best course of action is to run Performance Optimizer, but not until after you've finished installing and configuring any additional connectors.

When do you need to add more disk space to your server? That depends. If you have room, you can just add another drive, then run Performance Optimizer to let it move files to the optimum locations. If you're using a hardware RAID controller, you may or may not be able to expand the array by plugging in another drive; some controllers will automatically expand the array onto the new drive, while others make you rebuild everything from scratch. Of course, you always have two other alternatives: add another array, or move some users and public folders off the server so your disk space requirements are reduced.

Speaking of disk space requirements: don't forget to consider storage limits on your mailboxes. One popular approach is to give every mailbox the same limit, then grant exceptions on a user-by-user basis. It's easier to start out with storage limits than to impose them after users have grown accustomed to having zillions of messages in their mailboxes. In a no-limit environment, at least spot-check the mailbox size every so often so you can see who's using the most space.

Ensuring adequate maintenance space

The Exchange database maintenance tools (which you'll learn more about in Chapter 17) require extra workspace to do their jobs. In general, you'll need somewhere between 100% and 200% of the size of the largest store file on your system. If you need to do an offline defragmentation (or, worse, a repair) of your 14GB *priv.edb* file, you'll need at least 14GB of free space. This is a pretty hard requirement to meet unless you have a separate recovery server; fortunately, the maintenance tools will work fine (albeit slower) if their workspace is on a network drive.

Disks, backup, and restore

It's important to have hard data that tells you what kind of backup and recovery time to expect for a given store size. When this time gets too long, you should either upgrade your backup solution or move some data off the server. The best way to estimate how long backup and restores will take is to try one: make a file that approximates the size you expect your store to reach, then back it up and restore it, using your production backup environment. See how long it takes, running the test at least three times and averaging the results, then factor in the extra restore time required for Exchange to replay transactions, and so on. Don't forget to allow for differences in time if you're doing backups over the network; some systems are slower and some are faster when using the network.

Increasing Availability

Exchange is like a big set of Tinkertoys; you can combine its parts in a wide array of configurations, some of which are more stable and useful than others. Choosing the right combination of components for individual servers helps you boost the availability* of your Exchange machines. You have a range of options, from moving problem-prone components to less critical servers to moving your services over to a cluster group.

Distributing Server Tasks

You can make a good case that your mailbox server should be dedicated to serving users, and you can dump other stuff like connectors and OWA onto other servers. This approach reduces the number of things that can break on the mailbox server, and it eliminates the need to take the system down for upgrades or maintenance of components unrelated to message storage and retrieval.

---

* I define "availability" as "time when a server is available to answer requests." This isn't very precise, but it'll do for our discussion here.

IMS and OWA

The Internet Mail Service and Outlook Web Access components are ideal candidates for moving somewhere other than your mailbox servers. Consider the following factors:

- OWA and IMS are both CPU-intensive. In addition, OWA requires IIS, which itself often requires special product patches and has its own set of security concerns.

- Putting these components on one or more separate servers means you can update, repair, replace, or move them without incurring any major impact to the mailbox server.

- New features, such as VPN technology and updates to prerequisite services, may be desired sooner than features on core storage servers. For example, Windows 2000 will introduce a new version of IIS, so it would be nice to be able to upgrade your OWA servers without touching your core servers.

- Since IMS and OWA are normally used to communicate with the public Internet, putting them onto their own servers allows you to put them outside your firewall without exposing your mailbox servers (although it's best to put your IMS in the DMZ of your network, not outside the firewall).

- The IMS has the potential to generate lots of unplanned activity, especially if someone mailbombs your domain or accidentally generates a looping message. If the IMS is on a separate server, these events won't affect your mailbox servers as much, except for the server that holds the mailbox.

- When offline maintenance or server recovery is being performed on a mailbox server, Internet mail can still be accepted and held until the store server is operational.

The downside is that it costs more money to put these components on separate machines; however, since you don't need the high disk performance or redundancy you'd want on a mailbox server, you can usually get by with a less expensive computer system. Licensing cost is a factor, too, because you have to have additional server licenses for Exchange and NT Server.

Connector servers

It's usually a good idea to use dedicated connector servers, and not just in organizations that have high message volume to particular destinations. Connector servers are a more general form of IMS- or OWA-only servers: they can host whatever set of connectors you put on them. Servers that run the DRAS or X.400 connectors often require special services like RAS or X.25 drivers. Exchange's connectors aren't updated as frequently as the IMS and OWA, but most of the other benefits listed in the previous section still obtain.

Critical and high-demand users

All users and departments aren't created equal. The 80/20 rule (the old saw about 20% of the users generating 80% of the load) may not hold in your organization, but it's likely that some of your users are more demanding, or more important, than others. For example, your webmaster probably sends and receives more email than most other users, and your CEO and CFO probably expect that their mail needs will take priority over everyone else's.

You can solve both problems by putting critical users and high-demand users on their own (preferably separate) servers. For example, use the Mailbox Resources view to find the people with the largest mailboxes, then put all of them onto a single server.

External addresses that are critical to your business, like your *support@company. com* or *sales@company.com* addresses, are best tied to public folders. The data in these folders can then easily be replicated and shared, and it's easy to set up multiuser access so that all members of the group responsible for an address can get to incoming mail. You can create custom forms to automate filling in the FROM: field of a message, allowing groups of users to easily respond without giving out their personal email addresses. You can even use the message flag feature so that one user can indicate to others in the group that a message has already been responded to, is being worked on, or has not yet been checked.

Archiving data

Wouldn't it be nice to have the best of both worlds? When someone leaves, most organizations just delete their mailboxes. This means you lose any chance to get valuable or useful data from the mailbox once its owner departs. Instead, consider establishing an archive server whose function is to hold mailboxes that are no longer accessed on a daily basis. In fact, this archive server can hold old public folder data, too. To really get something nifty, consider using public folders to store old mailbox data. Public folders are better than PST files because they can be secured so that only authorized persons can access the archived data, and replicating the data is easy. You can use a low-performance server with lots of disk space (like that old server you just replaced) as an archival server, and you can even make management changes, like doing less frequent backups.

Clustering

You can loosely define a cluster as an assembly of more than one computer system that shares responsibility for a software task. Clustering is different from component-level hardware redundancy, which seeks to maximize availability of commonly failing components by using redundant components in a single system, error-correcting RAM, and fault-tolerant disk storage. Clustering works at a system level, not a component level; with properly configured clustering, any part of a single computer, or the entire computer, could fail without interrupting service. Once the failed system is repaired, it can rejoin the cluster.

Clustering also promises to ease the administrative and upgrade tasks associated with a server. In theory, you should be able to apply service packs, upgrade NT and its applications, and replace or upgrade hardware without affecting what your users are doing. A cluster network typically supports a controlled shutdown that shifts all users off an individual system in the cluster, allowing it to be serviced.

Microsoft and a number of third-party vendors offer NT clustering solutions, but NT clustering is still in its infancy. Currently, if you want to deliver clustering functionality on Windows NT, you have to invent your own mix of smart planning and turnkey solutions. Typically, customers who have experience with large systems and who can't tolerate downtime are experimenting with these early releases. Windows NT's infrastructure doesn't currently support mainframe-style clustering that transparently handles node failover and load balancing. Microsoft is still learning how to deal with these issues (in part by buying up NT clustering products from Valence Research, Tandem, and others) and has indicated that clustering is very important to its large corporate customers, so I expect NT clustering to get better.

The Microsoft Cluster Server (MSCS)

In general, clustering is an excellent, if expensive, way to provide high availability, but Microsoft Cluster Server (MSCS) has some flaws that make it unsuitable for many applications. In particular, MSCS only supports cluster-aware applications. The Enterprise Edition of Exchange is cluster-aware, provided you run it with MSCS and the Enterprise Edition of Windows NT Server. Unfortunately, using Exchange with MSCS requires you to share one set of disks between the two nodes in a cluster. Exchange's biggest availability weakness is the relative difficulty of recovering a damaged IS or DS database, so the lack of a true clustered disk is a pretty serious roadblock. In addition, MSCS only supports two-node clusters in which one machine runs Exchange and the other machine sits there, waiting for the first one to fail—not an ideal use of the second server.

MSCS does have promise, so some organizations have adopted it for its long-term payback. With these limits in mind (and don't forget hardware costs), here's a short list of things you should know before using MSCS and Exchange:

- The two computer systems should have similar CPU and RAM characteristics, as a registry replication agent clones the Exchange settings. When you run Performance Optimizer, it runs on only one system, and the second system receives a copy of those settings. If the systems differ substantially in CPU or RAM factors, the configuration Performance Optimizer suggests will be wrong for the second system.

- Don't even think about building a clustered system unless *every* component of both nodes is on the Windows NT Hardware Compatibility List (HCL).

- Most components of the OS are not shared, so damage to Windows NT is likely to be contained on only one system. For example, if NT crashes because you installed the wrong version of a new video device driver, it probably won't impact the second system.

- The shared disk is the most critical component in the cluster, so damage to the shared disk will definitely impact both systems.

- Failover—when the active system fails and the other takes over—takes somewhere from 30 to 60 seconds. In some circumstances, Exchange can't fail over automatically, so someone must watch for failures. Users will need to reconnect to the server after it fails over.

- OWA and the Lotus Notes and cc:Mail connectors aren't supported on clusters. In addition, some services (notably the KMS) don't automatically fail over.

This list is short because clustering, like migration, is an area where it often pays to hire an experienced consultant and let them steer you clear of the many pitfalls. Since clustering requires two very similar (better yet, identical) systems, plus two additional copies of NT Server and Exchange Enterprise Edition, a cluster represents a substantial investment, and there are so many subtleties and potential obstacles that we can't cover them all here. At a minimum, before trying to set up your own cluster, read the MSCS documentation, read the *cluster.doc* document on the Exchange CD, and visit the unofficial MSCS web site at *www.i405.com/ MSClusters.*

If the database becomes corrupted or inconsistent, the IS service won't start on either node. Likewise, to perform an offline recovery attempt with *eseutil* or *isinteg*, the services must be stopped, which impacts both cluster nodes.

Until Exchange Server supports mirroring of the mailbox data to multiple systems, clustering's benefits will be rather limited. I recommend that if you've got the money to spend on a cluster, spend it on solid redundant hardware, including RAID, hot-swappable disks, redundant power supplies and network cards, and a striped backup array.

Windows NT Load Balancing Service

Microsoft is offering Windows NT Load Balancing Service (WLBS) free to customers who have licensed Windows NT Enterprise Edition.* WLBS is based on Valence Research's Convoy Clustering products, and supports 2 to 32 nodes, with excellent

---

* As of this writing, you can get it from *www.microsoft.com/ntserver/nts/downloads/winfeatures/WLBS/ default.asp*, but that location may change.

scalability. No special hardware is required, as special network drivers enable all the clients to share a single IP address. To outside clients, your WLBS cluster looks like a single system. You define a single IP address for a particular service, like SMTP or HTTP, and the WLBS service takes care of allocating incoming requests to individual machines within the cluster.

You can use WLBS to handle OWA and SMTP traffic, since they're both based on TCP/IP. SMTP traffic requires that you tell WLBS to listen on port 25, after which it will automatically distribute incoming messages to the least loaded IMS in your cluster group. For OWA, you have to tell WLBS to listen on port 80 (for HTTP) and port 443 (for SSL), and you have to use the WLBS affinity setting to instruct it that all connections from a single client should stay on the same server.

Microsoft doesn't seem to officially support running OWA atop WLBS, but I attribute that to WLBS being a fairly new acquisition. Check the MS Knowledge Base for up-to-date documentation.

Managing Your Server

Exchange Server is so focused upon organizations and sites that it's easy to overlook the Server objects in the Exchange Directory. Don't overlook this area, though; most of the properties you set here aren't available anywhere else, and they're important to the ongoing stability and performance of your servers.

Setting Server Properties

Let's start with the ubiquitous General tab. Apart from showing you the version of Exchange installed on the selected server (which is a handy thing to know), the only useful control on this tab is the Server location pull-down. You can use this pull-down to establish subsites, or locations, that group servers according to their physical location. This gives you two useful capabilities:

Better control over public folder replicas
> When you have multiple copies of a public folder within a site, you can group servers using the location field (as described in Chapter 10). This allows you to regulate how a client connects the user to a replica, overriding the normal selection process.

Improved connector control
> As described in Chapter 7, *Managing Connectors and the MTA*, you can apply restrictions on the address space properties page of any connector; these restrictions allow you to limit use of a connector to servers in a particular location, giving you better control over which users are using your connection resources.

The Services tab

The Services tab of the server properties dialog lets you configure which services can be monitored by local or remote server monitors. Server monitors are discussed in detail in the section "Monitoring Your Servers," later in this chapter, but for now, you should know that the monitor gets information about which services to monitor from this tab.

The Services tab contains two lists. The Installed services list shows all Windows NT services installed on the server, starting with the Alerter. You can monitor any of these, not just the Exchange services. The Monitored services list shows which services will be monitored, and the Add and Remove buttons between the two lists allow you to change the monitoring set. There are also buttons that clear the monitoring list, add all services to it, or set up a monitor set with just the default services (the DS, IS, and MTA).

By default, new monitors will monitor only the DS, IS, and MTA. That's sufficient for most servers; on critical servers, however, you should also monitor the SA, and on servers running the IMS you might also want to monitor the SA. You may also find it useful to monitor other services like *netlogon* and the IIS services. In general, you need to monitor any service whose failure will affect your users' ability to use your services.

The Locales tab

Microsoft spends an impressive amount of effort localizing its applications into various languages. Users who don't speak U.S. English appreciate the opportunity to run a version of the application that uses their native language. With a server application like Exchange, you might wonder how localization works, since each client already has a language. Locales are the answer: they determine how date, currency, and time values are displayed, as well as how text is sorted and what folder titles are displayed.* When a specific locale, such as German, is selected for installation on a server, clients of that language connecting to the server see information that is properly sorted and formatted in that locale's language. Without installing this on a server, German clients connecting to this server would be stuck with U.S. English.

The Locales tab of the server properties dialog controls which locales are installed on your server. You can install as many or as few locales as you want, from Afrikaans to Ukrainian. The tab uses the familiar two-column format you've seen before: the left-hand list shows all available locales (though the list says "Installed

---

* I recently got mail from an administrator who'd installed the German version of Exchange and wanted to know why all his English-language users were getting mail in a folder named *Eingang*. Locales were the culprit.

locales") and the right-hand list shows which locales are actually installed and available for users. Use the Add and Remove buttons to move locales between the two lists.

The Database Paths tab

The Database Paths tab of the server properties dialog shows the paths to this server's databases and transaction logs. Normally you'll use Performance Optimizer to move these files, as described in Chapter 18 (whether you choose the location or Performance Optimizer does). However, I recommend that you familiarize yourself with the locations of your databases and logs and keep this information in your records; it's beneficial if you have to recover a server.

Moving databases or log files manually is a *terrible* idea. Don't do it. If you have to move either set of files, take a full online backup, run Performance Optimizer to move the files, then do another full online backup.

The IS Maintenance tab

The IS Maintenance tab lets you schedule the tasks discussed in the section "IS Maintenance" in Chapter 11, *Managing the Information Store.* You can allow the maintenance tasks to run whenever Exchange thinks they're needed (the Always radio button) or at selected times, scheduled in 15- or 60-minute increments.

Note that backups will interrupt the online defragmentation, so take care to schedule your backups and IS maintenance so that there is time to do both. It's better to schedule maintenance before backups.

The Advanced tab

The Advanced tab allows you to make one of the most important choices of your Exchange administrator career: whether circular logging is on or off. The circular logging scheme and its pros and cons are covered in both Chapter 2, *Exchange Architecture*, and Chapter 15, *Troubleshooting Exchange Server*, so there's no reason to belabor the point. I strongly advise turning circular logging off for both the directory and IS.

The Advanced tab also features a dangerous but occasionally useful button: the DS/IS Consistency Adjuster... button. The consistency adjuster compares the contents of the DS and IS and recreates directory entries for objects that are in the IS but not in the directory.

Normally, you use this for disaster recovery, as discussed in Chapter 17 (see the section "Restoring Exchange to a Different Computer"). In particular, you use the adjuster when you have a good backup of the IS but not of the DS. The adjuster performs four separate tasks:

- It creates new directory entries for any mailbox, DL, or public folder that's in the IS but that doesn't already have a directory entry.

- It resets any mailbox ACLs that contain references to missing objects. For example, if your mailbox has a permission entry for the mailbox JoeD, and that mailbox isn't in the IS, that ACL entry will be removed.

- It rehomes any public folders whose home server or site can't be found. Since the DS won't contain any data from its replication partners, all servers and sites will be unknown until replication completes normally after you run the consistency adjuster.

- It resets ACLs on public folders homed in unknown sites. If you later recreate a connection to the original home site, the new server's copy of the folder permissions will overwrite the correct version, and your users' permissions will get whacked.

Exchange 4.0 and 5.0 always do all four of these steps; Exchange 5.5 allows you to choose which steps the adjuster completes. Don't run the adjuster unless you're doing a disaster recovery, and then only if you've read and understood the notes on its use in Chapter 17.

The Diagnostic Logging tab

The Diagnostic Logging tab on the server allows you to quickly review all of the server's various diagnostic logging settings. This provides a redundant path to the same settings available on individual objects on the server. It's a good idea to periodically check these settings to ensure that they match the logging levels you want, especially if you have several administrators working on your machines. It's all too common to have someone increase logging levels while trying to solve a problem and then leave them there for weeks or months. Excessive event logging activity will slow down the server and fill your event log with meaningless junk

Routine Maintenance Tasks

Just like a car, an airplane, your heat pump, or any other relatively complex artifact, Exchange requires routine preventative maintenance. Some of what you have to do is proactive, like making sure your databases are holding up. Other tasks, such as upgrades and patch applications, don't necessarily happen at predictable intervals, and they often involve some unknowns.

Periodic Maintenance

Certain forms of maintenance can be scheduled. Tasks in this class don't need to be done immediately, but they are generally predictable; you can anticipate that they'll be needed and schedule them when it's convenient. At least every three months or so, schedule an evening during which you can take your servers down for maintenance. In larger environments, this may be a full weekend each month, depending on how many servers you have to manage. If you've split up your users and server roles, you can maintain one server at a time without stopping incoming mail or affecting users whose home servers aren't being worked on.

Here's a good start on a list of basic maintenance functions you may need to perform on Exchange and your servers:

- Upgrading firmware/BIOS for the computer system, disk controllers, SCSI hard drives, and other hardware components.

- Adding RAM and disk space.

- Upgrading Exchange Server with service packs, hotfixes, or version upgrades.

- Upgrading Windows NT with service packs, hotfixes, or version upgrades. Note that some of these upgrades may take longer than an evening, especially if you're migrating to Windows 2000 or reinstalling NT from scratch.

- Upgrading products that support Exchange, like backup software, IIS, Internet Explorer, and so on.

- Running an IS integrity check with *isinteg* (although I'd recommend doing this on a backup copy of the database stored on a recovery server).

- Doing an offline defragmentation and backup of your IS on your recovery server. This gives you an additional check on store integrity.

Daily and Weekly Activities

It's important to keep on top of your Exchange systems. When everything's going well, these checks may seem unnecessary, but failures (or your users) can quickly cause problems you're better off knowing about as soon as possible. There are two classes of regular tasks: those you should do every day, and those you should do weekly or monthly. Let's start with the everyday stuff:

- Check the status of your backups daily. Spot-check how long backups took, how much total space was used, and so forth. Any substantial increase in time from one day to the next could be a symptom of a server or network problem; for example, I've frequently seen problems with switched Ethernet components improperly being set to the wrong duplex setting. The components still operate, but with 10 to 100 times less performance. This kind of problem can sneak up on you.

- Check the postmaster mailbox you've defined for the IMS and INS. Other mail administrators may be trying to contact you concerning your server, one of your users, or other issues.

- Check the application event log on all Exchange servers you manage, to scan for unusual activity or errors. You should strongly consider the purchase of a monitoring utility like Ipswitch Software's (*www.ipswitch.com*) WhatsUp, which automates the process of scanning and summarizing your event log files.

The following tasks are better done weekly:

- For multiserver environments, work out a weekly report to gauge general server activity and growth. For example, you might want to know the public and private IS sizes for each server, along with some of the performance data you'll learn how to gather in Chapter 18.

- It's not a bad idea to reboot your servers periodically, especially if you're using OWA, which has gained notoriety for memory leaks and other stability-robbing behavior. Once you install NT 4.0 SP4 and Exchange 5.5 SP2, you'll probably find that OWA is much better behaved than in prior versions.

There's quite a bit of debate on this last point in the Exchange community. One camp points out that Unix servers routinely stay up for months or even years with no need for reboots, and that there shouldn't be a need for periodic reboots. The other camp points out that Windows NT and Exchange aren't as mature as Unix and that all the bugs aren't out yet. Some Exchange problems are easily cured by a reboot, like memory leaks in components that eventually eat up all available RAM, or a long-running series of problems with the IS that suddenly make it suck up 100% of the CPU. These problems are pretty infrequent, and rebooting an entire server just to restart a single service seems like a drastic solution. However, sometimes a reboot is the only way to fix problems, even after you try more conventional methods. Don't go out of your way looking for excuses to reboot, but don't be afraid to do so when you think it's necessary.

Automating reboots

If you feel better having your machines rebooted every so often, you can use a tool included in the Windows NT resource kit: the *shutdown.exe* program will shut down a server. For example, you could use the Windows NT Scheduler service to schedule a reboot at 1 a.m. every Sunday, as follows:

```
AT 01:00 /EVERY:Sunday "C:\winnt\system32\shutdown.exe /L /R"
```

You have to supply the correct path to your local copy of the shutdown utility, and you may want to pick another time to actually do your reboot.

In light of the previous section, you might wonder why you'd want to schedule a reboot. The best reason I can think of is OWA: the combination of NT SP4 and the Exchange 5.5 SP2 version of OWA is a huge improvement over the stability of previous versions. Having said that, OWA is still probably the least robust Exchange component, and if you run it with large user loads, you'll probably find it advantageous to reboot your server nightly to clear out leaks and transient problems.

Stopping Exchange services on demand

Many users have found that it's actually quicker to stop the Exchange Server services before scheduling a reboot. You'll also need to stop the services to do an offline backup or restore, and it's a good idea to stop services any time you don't want users logging onto a particular server. You can use a simple batch file to stop all the core services in order:

```
ECHO Stopping Exchange Server Services...

net stop MSExchangeIMC /y
net stop MSExchangeMTA /y
net stop MSExchangeIS /y
net stop MSExchangeDS /y
net stop MSExchangeSA /y
net stop MSExchangeSA /y
net stop MSExchangeSA /y
```

If you're using other services that you need to stop, like the MS Mail or Notes connectors, you'll have to stop those services before you stop the Exchange MTA service. In general, you need to stop all the connectors before you stop any of the core services.

Note that in this file, the services are listed in an order that's the reverse of the service start order. You have to stop the SA last because it's normally the first service to start. If you reverse the order of these lines, you can build a batch file to use when restarting Exchange.

Removing user accounts

Most administrators delete the mailbox of any user who leaves their organization. While this is a simple and obvious way to turn off mail access for that user, it frequently results in the administrator having to waste time restoring the entire IS to recover mail from the deleted mailbox. There's another procedure that works better and accomplishes the same end result:

1. Make sure deleted item retention is turned on for the mailbox.

2. Hide the mailbox from the GAL so no one can send mail to it.

3. Put the termination date in the Notes field for your own reference.

4. Remove the SMTP addresses from the mailbox, so that outside users can't send mail to it through the IMS.

5. Remove any permissions assigned to the mailbox; change the Primary Windows NT Account setting for the mailbox to the departed user's manager.

Once you've completed these five steps, all you have to do is wait a while (30–45 days is usually adequate) before deleting the mailbox. During that interregnum, the departed user's manager can still recover items from the mailbox, but no one can send new mail to it. As soon as you're certain that no one will need anything from the mailbox, you can safely delete it.

Applying Upgrades, Service Packs, and Hotfixes

Many administrators are reluctant to install product upgrades, service packs, or hotfixes, and in general, you should only apply hotfixes that resolve a current problem. Installing every hotfix you can find is similar to taking unlabeled medicine you find in the back of your medicine cabinet in the hope that it will cure your cold—maybe it will, and maybe it won't, since it's probably not cold medicine.

There are good business reasons not to upgrade your Exchange server, including the fact that version changes usually require upgraded licenses (licenses never seem to get cheaper) and that new versions frequently require upgraded hardware. If you depend on third-party products like voice mail or fax integration tools, you'll probably want to delay installing upgrades until you're certain that the upgrades and your third-party products can coexist.

The real reason administrators are sometimes skittish about installing upgrades is their fear that the upgrades will introduce new problems. This fear stems from past performance of some Windows NT service packs and hotfixes, but it's worth noting that the Exchange team has historically done an excellent job of testing their service packs prior to release. In fact, they even held back Exchange 5.5 SP2 when a bug was found the day before its release.

Don't let unnecessary fear slow you down. In general, a reasonable policy is to wait two weeks after the release of a service pack and install it once you understand the changes it will make. You can find a wealth of discussion about service packs and hotfixes on mailing lists like the ones discussed in Chapter 15. Another alternative that might work for you is to install SPs and hotfixes on systems in a test lab or somewhere else that's not part of your production environment. That way, you can see what's likely to happen to your production systems before making any actual changes.

Changing Your Server Configuration

If you have more than one server, it's likely that sometimes you'll have to make changes to your servers' participation in Exchange or Windows NT. Some of these are routine changes, like changing the service account password. Other changes, like moving servers between domains or organizations, require more advance planning.

Small Changes

Some changes are pretty minor, either because Exchange does the work for you or because the change itself is small.

Changing the service account password

The best way to accomplish this change is to let Exchange do the work for you. Changing the service account password is a big pain in the neck if you do it manually, since you have to change it for every service on every server. Instead of doing that, use the Configuration object's properties dialog. Go to the site whose password you want to change, select its Configuration object, and open its properties dialog. When you do, you'll see that there's a tab labeled Service Account Password; click it, then enter the new password you want Exchange to use.

Once you've done so, you'll see a progress dialog as Exchange Administrator changes the password on each server in the site. When it finishes, you'll see a dialog warning you to run the User Manager on a PDC or BDC and change the service account password to match the value you gave it in Exchange Administrator. Do so, then stop and restart the Exchange services on each server, perhaps by rebooting. Now you can see why I suggested changing the password as part of your scheduled maintenance and not on a whim!

Cleaning up after a password change

I'd be remiss if I didn't point out that changing the service account can have unintended consequences. For example, if you use DRAS, site, or X.400 connectors to join your site with another, have you specified the other site's service account on the connectors' Override tab? If you have, when the other site changes its service account password, your connector will stop working.

As soon as you change the service account password, notify the remote side that you've done so. If you suddenly notice that your site, DRAS, or X.400 connectors aren't moving mail like they should, verify that you have the correct service password for the site you're talking to.

Adding a backup service account

Throughout this book, I've warned you about the dangers of losing your site service account password. Guess what? There's a way to insure yourself against that loss. You can create one or several backup accounts and use them only if you need to. Here's what to do:

1. Run User Manager on a domain controller.

2. Create the backup site service account. Make sure the "User cannot change password" and "Password never expires" checkboxes are marked.

3. Optionally, put the new account into a group that has administrative rights on either the local computer or the domain. This makes it easier for you to administer Exchange and NT at the same time, while logged on with the service account.

4. Give the new account the special rights that the existing account has. Use the Policies → User Rights… command to grant the backup account the "Logon as a service," "Restore files and directories," "Act as part of the operating system," and "Change the system time" rights.

5. Launch Exchange Administrator on a server in the site, then add the new account to the Permissions tabs on the organization, site, and site Configuration containers. Grant the new account Service Account Admin rights.

When you need to use this account (say, because you've lost the existing service account password, or because some helpful but undertrained person has deleted the existing account), just go to each server in the site and use the Services control panel (or Server Manager) to update the site service account, then stop and restart the services.

Medium Changes

This section covers some things you might need to change that take a little more effort and caution than the simple changes already covered.

Changing the domain of a server

You may need to move a server from one Windows NT domain to another. It's very likely that you'll need to do this as you get ready to move to Windows 2000, and you may find it necessary before then if you need to change your domain structure to accommodate organizational changes. Microsoft recommends you call its product support group to get help with this procedure, but making the change is relatively straightforward, so you may be able to get by without help.

Here's what you need to do:

1. Make a full (not incremental or differential) backup of your Exchange server, since you'll be using Exchange Administrator in raw mode to modify the directory schema.

2. Create a trust relationship between the new domain and the existing one: make the old domain trust the new one. Don't join the new domain yet.

3. If you're not keeping the old domain around, create a new service account on each server in the new domain. Use User Manager to give the account the necessary rights: "Log on as a service," "Act as part of the operating system," "Back up and restore files," and "Change the system time."

4. Start Exchange Administrator in raw mode, then add the new account to the organization, site, and Configuration containers. Give the new account Service Account Admin permissions. Don't remove the existing service account.

5. Use the View → Raw Directory command to turn on raw display, then select the Schema object in the site container. Open its Raw Properties dialog with the File → Raw Properties command.

6. In the Schema properties dialog, select the NT-Security-Descriptor item, click the Editor button, and pick the NT security descriptor editor.

7. In the security descriptor editor dialog, add the new account, then use the Roles pull-down to give the new account Service Account Admin permissions.

8. Shut down the System Attendant service, then use the Services control panel to specify that the new service account owns the Exchange services.

9. Use the Network control panel to join the new domain, then reboot the server.

10. Remove any trust relationships with the old domain.

11. Run Exchange Administrator in raw mode again, then remove the original service account from the organization, site, Configuration, and Schema containers.

 The Move Server Wizard, covered later in this chapter, can automatically move users from one domain to another while moving a server or changing a server's membership. Consider using this wizard if you are changing more than just the domain.

Changing the service account

Sometimes people want to change over to using a different account as the service account. Microsoft's official stance on this procedure is that you need to call PSS for help before attempting it yourself. They have good reason to say this, because if you make a mistake while changing service accounts, you may not be able to fix it, especially since you have to do the following steps on every server in the site.

If you feel adventurous, and if you have a good backup of every server in your site, you can attempt the following procedure, which is basically what Microsoft support will tell you to do if you call them:

1. Using User Manager, create the new Windows NT account that will be the service account. Assign the necessary rights to the account.

2. Start Exchange Administrator in raw mode, then add the new account to the organization, site, and Configuration containers. Give the new account Service Account Admin permissions. Don't remove the existing service account.

3. Use the View → Raw Directory command to turn on raw display, then select the Schema object in the site container. Open its Raw Properties dialog with the File → Raw Properties command.

4. In the Schema properties dialog, select the NT-Security-Descriptor item, click the Editor button, and pick the NT security descriptor editor.

5. In the security descriptor editor dialog, choose the new account, then use the Roles pull-down to give the new account Service Account Admin permissions.

6. Shut down the System Attendant service on all servers in the site. This has the effect of forcing all Exchange services in the site to stop.

7. Once everything's stopped, use the Services control panel on each server to specify that the new service account owns the Exchange services. Don't restart any services until you've done this step on all servers in your site.

8. Run Exchange Administrator in raw mode again, then remove the original service account from the organization, site, Configuration, and Schema containers.

9. Stop all the services for all the servers in the site.

10. Manually change every one of the Exchange account services using Server Manager or the control panel Services applet.

11. Restart all the services, one server at a time.

12. Once you've confirmed that everything is working, remove the permissions in the directory for the old service account.

 There are two things to watch out for: make sure none of your connectors depend on the service account, and be certain that no other sites are sharing your site service account. Site connectors and DRAS connectors may use the account, even across domain and site boundaries, so you may need to inform other sites of the change.

Moving a user from one site to another

There is no automatic way to move a user from one site to another. If you want to do this, you'll have to delete the mailbox in the original site and recreate it in the new site. Although the email addresses that are visible to the outside world (like SMTP and cc:Mail addresses) don't need to change, Exchange uses the internal directory name—a DN that contains the name of the site—as a reference to the mailbox. This means that the mailbox's distribution list memberships, public folder permissions, and shared calendar folders have to be reassigned by hand; there's no direct way to automate this, unfortunately.

Preserving the mailbox's data is simple: use the Outlook client to copy all the messages you want to save to either a PST or a public folder. Delete the old mailbox, create the new one, and reimport the mail. You can also use the *exmerge* tool, discussed in Appendix A, *BORK Tools*, to automate this process. You can even use the directory import/export feature of Exchange Administrator to delete and recreate the mailbox, but remember that this won't move the mail in the mailbox, but only the directory entry for the mailbox.

Upgrading from Standard to Enterprise Edition

I've already discussed the differences between the Standard and Enterprise editions of Exchange. To recap: the Enterprise Edition removes the 16GB store size limit and includes some connectors that cost extra with the Standard Edition. Upgrading from Standard to Enterprise is straightforward: make a good backup, then follow the steps in Chapter 4. Alternatively, you can install Exchange Enterprise on a new server, then move data over to it as discussed in the section "Mailbox Moving Magic," earlier in this chapter.

Using the Move Server Wizard

Some changes to your Exchange infrastructure are major and require a lot of forethought and prior backup action. The biggest change you can make is one that would have been impossible until recently—moving an Exchange server from one organization to another. Shortly after the release of SP1 for Exchange 5.5, Microsoft released the Move Server Wizard (its codename was Pilgrim, but I'll call it MSW for short). As you might suspect from its name, the MSW automates the process of moving a server from one organization or site to another. This is a huge improvement over the old way of moving a server, which was basically to create an entirely new server, then migrate every individual user's mailbox over using *exmerge* or PST files.

It's important that you carefully review the MSW documentation before you try to move anything. This section provides a comprehensive overview, but the devil is in the details.

What the MSW does

If you're accustomed to moving NT servers and workstations between domains, you might not think that moving an Exchange server between sites would be particularly difficult. You'd be wrong, though. Every object in the directory has a distinguished name that includes the organization and site under which the object was created. Moving a server means that you have to rename every object in the directory on the server you're moving; you also have to adjust the old site's directory to reflect the absence of objects that were moved along with the server. There's never been any way to do this manually, since most of the objects whose names need to be adjusted aren't visible in Exchange Administrator.

If all you want to do is rename a server, move it to another domain, or add a new server in an existing site or organization, Exchange can do that without the MSW.

The MSW handles the task along with all of the collateral adjustments that have to be made. Here's what the MSW does:

1. Updates every object in the server's directory to reflect the new site and organization to which the server is going. Each object gets a new distinguished name and a placeholder address. Objects' old addresses are kept so that the objects can still get mail at either address after they move; the MTA is responsible for resolving the addresses and getting the mail delivered to the proper location.

2. Updates the messages stored in the private IS on the server so that all stored messages have the correct address for any item modified in step 1.

3. Checks for duplicate names or objects, since moving one server into another organization may result in some duplication.

4. Removes the server from the original site (and possibly organization), removing references to that server's objects from the original directory.

5. Adds the server to the new organization and site, creating them if necessary. This capability lets you split one organization into two by using MSW to move a server to a new organization that doesn't exist yet.

While the MSW is a quantum leap in capability over the *status quo ante*, it's not completely automated. You have some tasks to perform once the MSW finishes its work; for example, you have to restart the MTA on the server you've moved, clean up public folder replicas, reset permissions, and so on.

The MSW can do four things, each of which is useful under some circumstances:

- Rename a site by moving the last (or only) server in the site to a new site with a new name.

- Split an existing site by moving one server out of a multiserver site into a new site with a new name.

- Move a server from one multiserver site to another one without removing the original site.

- Merge two sites with different names into a single site. For example, when two companies merge and their existing organization names aren't the same, one company can use MSW to join the other company's organization, then both companies can create sites in the same organization.

In general, renaming and merging sites depend on you having only one server in those sites. To accomplish this, collapse your site into a single server by moving mailboxes, connectors, and public folders to one server in the site and removing the others. Once that's done, you can disconnect the site from its organization and use MSW to create a new site in the organization, rejoining the organization when it's done.

As a final bonus, the MSW can also change the Windows NT domain and service account information for a server, whether you're moving it or not.

What the MSW can't do

There's a fairly long laundry list of things the MSW can't do, and you need to know what's on the list before proceeding. The good news is that the MSW checks for and warns you about most of these limitations, shown in the following list, before it proceeds:

- The MSW can't be used to move servers running Exchange 4.0, 5.0, or 5.5 without SP1 or later. You also have to upgrade all servers in the original site, as well as any bridgeheads in the destination site, to version 5.5.

- The MSW can't move the IMS or KMS, nor can it move any connectors or gateways, including third-party gateways and extension products. You must remove connectors or gateways before you do the move.

- The MSW can't be run on computers linked in an MSCS cluster.

- The MSW can't be run in the middle of a replication cycle; you should only run it after replication has completed.

- You can't change languages when moving. If you want to move a German server, use the German MSW, or all of your localization information will be lost.

- Messages that are queued when the MSW runs may be bounced, so you can't effectively run the MSW when you have a large queue of pending messages.

- The MSW can't move encrypted mail. Actually, it can, but users won't have access to their keys after the move, so they need to decrypt any stored mail before the move.

- The MSW doesn't update a number of things in the private IS, including message signatures, public folder permissions, public folder contents, and client-side Outlook rules.

- The MSW doesn't update things that depend on the server name, including link and server monitors, OWA, and NNTP newsfeeds.

Before you touch anything

It's critical that you understand the limits of what the MSW can do and the tasks you have to perform manually before you start moving anything. When you run the MSW, you'll see a plethora of warning dialogs, checklists, and validation steps. Occasionally, you'll have to click on buttons labeled "I Understand" to show that you've been paying attention to what the wizard is trying to tell you.

First off, you need to be aware that any third-party packages you're using (particularly integrated fax or voice mail systems) may depend on custom extensions to the directory. If you're using one of these products, it's likely that MSW will upset it. Contact your vendor before you do anything.

You may find it beneficial to do the actual move in stages. For example, let's say you're splitting up an existing organization into a number of separate organizations, one for each division. Assume that there are currently three servers in the site and organization; let's call them *A*, *B*, and *C*. You want to move *A* to a new organization first. One way to accomplish this while still minimizing downtime and risk is to take the following approach:

1. Install a new server named *D*. When you install it, give it the new site and organization name you want the new division to have.

2. Remove any public folder replicas on *A*. If there are folders whose only replica is on *A*, create replicas on *D* before removing them from *A*. You can also use NNTP to replicate any public folders that you want moved from the existing site to the new server on *D*.

Nonconformity Considered Harmful

MSW was released after SP1. It was rereleased with SP2. Does that make sense? It didn't to me, either. The basic upshot is that you can use the post-SP1 version to move SP1 servers and the SP2 version to move SP2 servers. You can't use the SP1 version to move an SP2 server, or vice versa; the wizard will warn you and refuse to work.

Apart from meaning that you have to keep track of two separate versions of MSW, are there any larger implications here? Yes. In general, the minicomputer and mainframe worlds would never tolerate the mishmash of software and firmware versions common at most NT sites. "Real" data centers typically pick a configuration (including hardware, firmware, and software), then install it on all their servers. When they upgrade one server, they upgrade all of them, and they keep detailed records about what got upgraded and when.

In your Exchange network, why not adopt a similar strategy? You don't gain anything from having a patchwork set of different software versions (especially if you're mixing Exchange 4.0, 5.0, and 5.5), and you can waste an astonishing amount of time troubleshooting problems that arise because two seemingly identical servers have a slightly different configuration. Choose a baseline configuration for your servers, then stick with it, even if it means having to bite the bullet and upgrade some of your older servers. The money you save in reduced overhead and troubleshooting cost will more than recoup the expense of the upgrades.

---

3. Create any connectors that the new site will need on *D*.

4. Verify that all the public folder content is getting where you want it to and that the connectors are behaving properly.

5. When you're ready to do the actual move, use MSW to move *A* to the new site and organization.

It's a good idea to clean up as much clutter as possible before you move anything. When possible, consolidate users and public folders onto the smallest possible number of servers so you don't have to move lots of servers. Doing multiple moves can be a time-consuming process, since the site directory has to be essentially rewritten each time through. It's also a good idea to take this opportunity to clean up user mailboxes and perform an offline defragmentation of the public and private IS databases.

Why all this caution? When you use MSW, you're using it on live, production servers. This is sort of like a military live-fire exercise; any carelessness on your part may result in unintended casualties. Unlike moving mailboxes between servers within a site, MSW moves are generally irreversible, and it will probably be too late when you discover a planning or execution mistake.

 If you're planning a move and don't have someone experienced with MSW to advise you, I strongly recommend that you set up some lab computers and simulate your intended changes to make sure there aren't any unintended side effects.

Preflight checklist

There are some things you must do (or not do) before you can successfully run the MSW:

- You must turn off the Exchange event service if it's running. If you don't, the MSW will fail.

- You need a ton of free disk space, up to twice the current size of the *dir.edb* file, plus 15% of the size of your private IS and 1.5KB for each object you're moving (that adds up if you're moving lots of mailboxes).

- Close any Exchange Administrator sessions (including link, server, and performance monitors) attached to the server you're moving.

- Don't try to move a directory replication bridgehead server unless it's the last server in the site. If you move the bridgehead before moving all other servers in the site, you'll stop replication for the entire site, and messages will start piling up. If you absolutely must move the replication bridgehead, configure another site server as a bridgehead first, then update all the other sites so they talk to the new bridgehead.

- If you're moving a server with connectors, you must update any other servers that use the connectors. For site connectors, make sure no other server lists the server to be moved as a target; for X.400 connectors, make sure no other server specifies the server you're moving as a remote partner. Be sure to let replication complete after you reconfigure the remote connectors but before you remove the connectors on the server you're moving.·

- If the IMS is installed on the server you're moving, install the IMS on another server in the site, remove it from the server being moved, and recalculate the routing table before attempting the move.

- Don't move a server that's set up to generate OABs or to act as a routing calculation server. If necessary, just assign another server to that role before the move.

- Don't try to move a server that's running KMS; MSW doesn't know how.

A word about public folders

If the server you're moving contains public folders, there are some additional steps you must complete before the move:

1. Get a list of which replicas are hosted on the target server.

2. Identify which folders exist on other servers in the current site and which ones live only on the target server.

3. On the target server, remove any replicas that have other replicas in the site.

4. Decide what you want to do with each public folder that's only homed on the target server. If you want a replica to remain in the current site, create a replica on another server. If you don't, don't do anything.

Once you've completed these steps, wait one full replication cycle to allow the changes to propagate throughout the site.

Using MSW

The MSW follows the standard conventions you'd expect from a Microsoft wizard, with a few twists. When you run it, the first page you see lists four categories of information you should already have reviewed: what you should do before running MSW, what your users need to do, what the MSW does and doesn't update, and what you and your users have to do after the wizard has finished. Until you click the I Understand button, you can't proceed to the next wizard step.

Next, you'll see a summary screen telling you where the MSW plans to create the temporary files it needs, along with an estimate of the amount of disk space it expects to need. You can change the temporary file location, if necessary.

The next step is to tell the wizard how you want to move your server (see Figure 14-1). You can do the same two things as when setting up a new server: you can join an existing site or create a new site and/or organization. To move your server to a new site, use the "Create a new site" radio button but specify the same organization name, and the MSW will ask you to confirm that you want to create a new site. To move your server into an existing site, pick "Join an existing site" and choose a target server in the site.

The next step is to specify the service account you want the server to use once it's moved. Depending on where you're moving the server, you may need to specify the same service account that's already in use or a new one; if the wizard can figure out which account to use, you'll only have to enter the password.

Next, the MSW asks you what to do about custom recipients in the site. You can move them from the original site to the new one, and you can optionally choose to remove them from the original site after the move finishes. However, since you'll probably want to use the same set of recipients in both sites, it's easier to

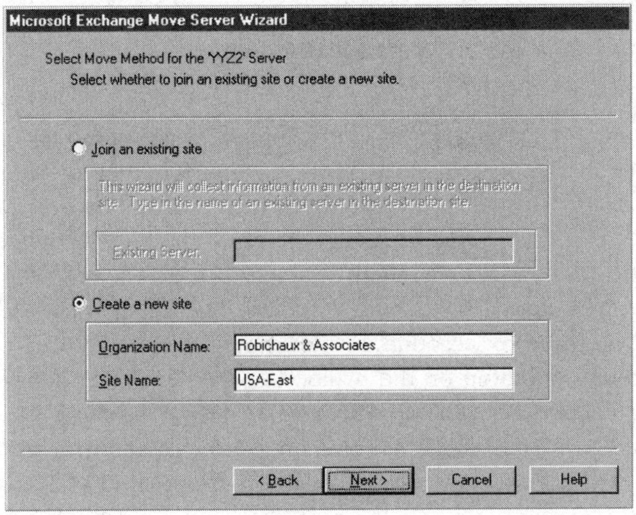

Figure 14-1. You can move a server into an existing site or a new one

use the directory export commands described in Chapter 5, *Using Exchange Administrator*, to export and remove the custom recipients from the original site, then reimport them to the new site, especially since there's no mailbox or public folder data associated with custom recipients.

Your next decision is what to do with DLs in the original site. Like custom recipients, DLs can be moved, or you can export and reimport them. The MSW gives you three radio buttons on the next wizard page:

Do not move distribution lists with this server
Tells the MSW not to make any attempt to move DLs; use this button when you're going to move the DLs yourself, or if you don't want them moved at all.

Move only distribution lists that have owners who are moving along with the server
Moves DLs whose owning mailbox is hosted on the server that's moving. This option preserves ownership links for DLs that are moved, so use it if you only want to move DLs whose owners are moving.

Move all distribution lists in this site
Moves all DLs in the original site, whether their owners' mailboxes are moving or not.

In the latter two cases, the MSW leaves a set of placeholder objects in the original site so that replies to old messages stored in site users' mailboxes will go to the correct destination even after the DLs are moved.

You can also choose two other DL-related options: you can tell the MSW to move mailboxes for DL members who are moving along with the server, and you can specify that you want the DL objects deleted after they're moved (this option is automatically turned on when you choose to move all site DLs).

If you're moving an existing server into a new domain, you can have the MSW move the mailbox accounts as well. This is most useful when moving a server into a new site that just happens to be in a different domain; however, you can cheat and run MSW twice if you want to stay in the same site but change domains: run it once to move to a new site, then run it again to move back to the original site. While this involves quite a bit of time and effort, it may still be easier than manually changing the mailbox accounts to the new domain, using the "Primary Windows NT Account..." button on the mailbox properties dialog. However, this feature requires that the domain already have matching accounts. For example, a mailbox owned by *RA\paulr* can has its ownership changed to *ROBICHAUX\paulr* if that account exists before you run MSW, but not to *ROBICHAUX\paul*.

Once you've completed the preceding steps, the wizard starts its heavy lifting. It has to map the old and new directory objects to see what matches between the two servers. You'll have to wait a while for this process to finish, though the wizard is helpful enough to provide an estimated completion time for each step. Tony Redmond estimates that the wizard does its work at around 3–4GB/hour, though this rate varies according to your hardware setup. Once the wizard finishes, you'll see a summary dialog that tells you what you're doing and warns you of anything you need to know (see Figure 14-2).

> Take advantage of the fact that the MSW will warn you of anything that needs to be fixed before the move. Fix whatever it warns you about, then run it again, repeating the run-and-fix cycle until you get no warnings.

The MSW also creates several report files in a folder named *mvsrvdat*, created in the location you specified for temporary files. The *report.txt* file contains the summary information presented in the report; the *mailbox.csv*, *cstrecipt.csv*, and *distlist.csv* files contain lists of the mailboxes, custom recipients, and distribution lists moved by the wizard.

> Once you click the I Understand and Finish buttons, you've crossed the Rubicon; there's no undoing what the MSW will do next.

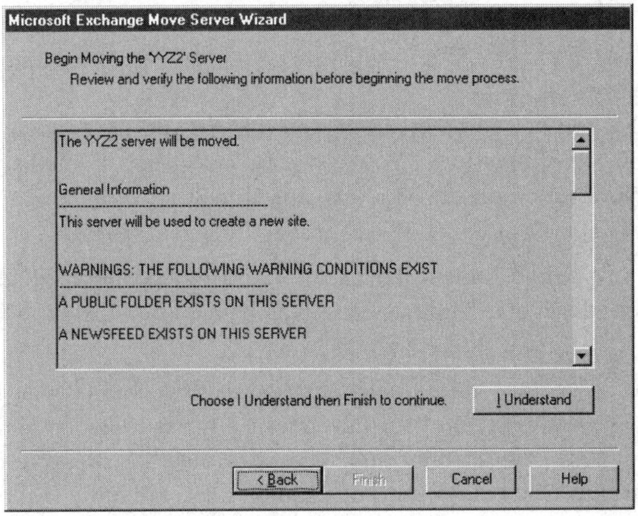

Figure 14-2. The Move Server Wizard summary of changes

After the DS and IS have been modified, the MSW stops the Exchange services, installs the modified databases, and restarts the services. At this point, if you've joined an existing site, the MSW will kick off an intrasite directory replication cycle, and you'll have to wait for it to finish.

Once the MSW is done with the move, you'll get another summary dialog that lists several categories of tasks you and your users need to perform. You can click on each category's button to get a complete checklist. Once you're satisfied, clicking the Finished button restarts the Exchange services (except for the MTA), and the new server is up and running.

Post-move cleanup

Just because you managed to get the MSW to move your server, don't assume that there's nothing left for you to do. There are still a number of critical housekeeping tasks you must perform to get your servers back to their original operating condition:

Reinstall connectors

> Until you've reinstalled any required connectors, you won't be able to send mail or replication messages between previously existing servers and the new server. Do this first.

Restart the MTA

> If you're creating a new site, you can start the MTA immediately (there's a checkbox on the last MSW page, so the MSW can do this for you). If you're

joining an existing site, let intrasite replication finish before starting the MTA; otherwise, the replication process won't have up-to-date address information for servers outside the site.

Start directory replication

Until replication has completed for both the old and new sites, your GAL will have duplicate entries in it. You can start replication immediately using the Request Now button on the Sites tab of each DRC.

Clean up your public folders

Rehome any public folders that need to be moved because of your server move, then reassign any permissions that changed because of the move.

Clean up directory links

The MSW creates several files that track directory object links. For example, the "Managed By" attribute is a link because it ties together a mailbox or DL and the address of that entity's manager. You need to preserve these links to keep your directory consistent. For example, if I move my mailbox, the mailboxes of all the people who report to me need to be updated to reflect my new address.

The MSW records links that use the "Manager," "Members," "Accept messages from," "Reject messages from," "Alternate recipient," and "Can send on behalf of" attributes. The wizard creates two separate files: *lnkfixup.csv* contains links that point to servers in the original site or organization, and *sitename.csv* contains links from other servers in the original site that point to the server being moved. There's also a batch file named *lnkfixup.bat.* To do the actual fixup, just run the batch file with the name of the server you want the information loaded onto. You can also specify which *sitename.csv* file you want loaded.

Remove duplicate addresses and ABVs

When the MSW finds a duplicate email address, it adds it to the *proxyfixup.csv* file. To remove duplicates, you have to import this file using the *proxyfixup. cmd* file, but you have to do it more than once. First, import the file into one server in each site that originally hosted a duplicate name. Once you've done that, you need to import the file onto the server you just moved. In between these two steps, you'll need to edit the file to specify which of the duplicates you want to leave alone and which you want to get a new address.

There may also be duplicate ABVs; if so, you need to remove them using Exchange Administrator.

Restore permissions

If you've moved your server to a new domain, you may need to manually change or add Windows NT permissions on the accounts. You should also verify that the moved server has the permissions you want on the organization, site, and Configuration containers.

Do a full online backup

This is a key step. You have to do a full backup to make sure you capture the complete state of the directory; incremental and differential backups won't do the trick.

What users have to do

Each user whose mailbox was moved must do all of the following tasks:

- Delete any OST files the client had been using. Users who are using Schedule+ or the old-style Exchange client must delete their Schedule+, or SCD, files also.

- Each client must recreate a new user profile that points to the new server. Don't try to copy or edit the existing profile, because it won't work, though it appears to. The new profile should point to the mailbox name on the new server. Don't try to do this before removing the offline folder and Schedule+ files, or the new profile won't work right, either.

- Exchange and Schedule+ users need to manually recreate their offline folder and Schedule+ files, since creating a new profile doesn't do that for you.

- If the user has been using private folders, permissions on those folders will probably need to be adjusted.

- Any mail that users decrypted prior to the move can be safely reencrypted with *sectool* (see *"Using sectool"* in Chapter 16, *Exchange Security*).

- Outlook 98 users who had inbox rules in their profiles will find that these rules conflict with rules stored on the server during the move. They'll have to tell Outlook to use the server versions. When the Rules Wizard complains that it needs help resolving the conflict, select the Server button in the error dialog to make this change stick. In addition, users may need to update their rules to reflect changes made to the rule sources or targets.

- Clients will have to download the updated version of the organization OAB, and they'll have to update their personal address books as well.

Monitoring Your Servers

Exchange Server includes two types of built-in monitors that let you monitor server availability and uptime. These monitors act in addition to whatever other monitoring systems you may have in place. There are two types of monitors: *link* monitors and *server* monitors.

Link monitors periodically test the connection between two servers. When you create a new link monitor, the source system periodically polls the target system to see how it responds. At every polling interval, Exchange sends a test message to the other end, which may or may not be an Exchange server. The source server watches for a response from the target machine; if a response doesn't arrive within a predefined interval, the monitor is triggered.

Server monitors watch the state of a set of services. By default, monitors watch only the DS, IS, and MTA services, but you can monitor any Windows NT services, whether they're part of Exchange or not. When you start a monitor, it periodically makes RPC requests to the target server, so you can only monitor servers to which you have RPC connectivity. Each request should trigger a response from the monitored server; you can configure what happens if no response arrives. A single monitor can watch multiple servers in multiple sites.

Both monitor types run only when Exchange Administrator is running, so it might be a good idea to establish a monitoring workstation you can use for nothing but monitors.

The Exchange Administrator controls for starting, stopping, and pausing monitors from the command line are covered in the section "Exchange Administrator Command-Line Switches" in Chapter 5.

The first step in configuring either type of monitor is simple: you create the monitor using the File → New Other → Link Monitor or File → New Other → Server Monitor... commands. You'll then see the General tab of the corresponding monitor properties dialogs (the General tabs are actually identical, as you'll see in a minute). The next step in configuring your monitor is to fill out the properties dialog.

Configuring Common Monitor Properties

The three tabs common to both monitor types are described in the following sections.

The General tab

The General tab, shown in Figure 14-3, is pretty simple. You have to enter a display name and a directory name, as usual on this type of tab. You can specify a log file if you want one; if you do, the monitor will log each successful and failed connection or service test. You can also specify two polling intervals in seconds, minutes, or hours. The Normal interval controls how often the monitor performs its check; the "Critical sites" interval tells the monitor how often to monitor servers or links that have already progressed to a critical or warning state.

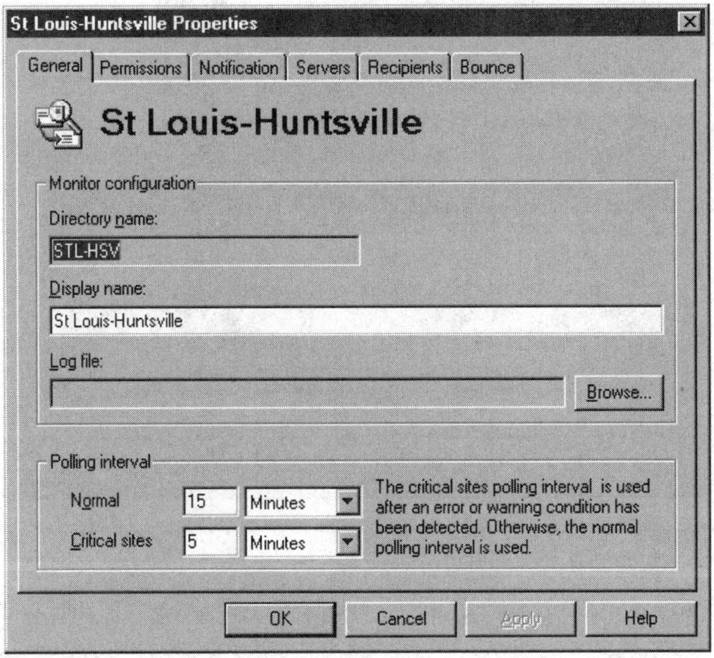

Figure 14-3. The monitor General tab

The Notification tab

The Notification tab allows you to control when the monitor reports an exception or error condition. There are two separate levels of notification. The *warning state* represents the first level of exception: think of it as what happens when a monitor request is late. The *alert state* is the second, more severe, level: it's the state your monitor will show if a response is very late in arriving.

You can create multiple notifications using this tab (see Figure 14-4). Each notification can have one of three associated actions: it can run an arbitrary command-line executable (great for getting pager notification of problems), it can send a mail message (not so great, because depending on what the problem is, the mail may not reach you), or it can send a Windows NT alert to a computer you specify. Each notification also has its own interval, so you can set up an escalating set of notifications. Mine are set to send me an alert after 15 minutes and page me after 45 minutes; that way, I don't get paged for transient problems.

It's worth reiterating that a single monitor can watch several servers or sites, but each monitor can have only one set of notification actions. For example, let's say you set up a monitor that watches all connections to and from your home office in Boston. If you set up a group of notifications that alert your system managers in

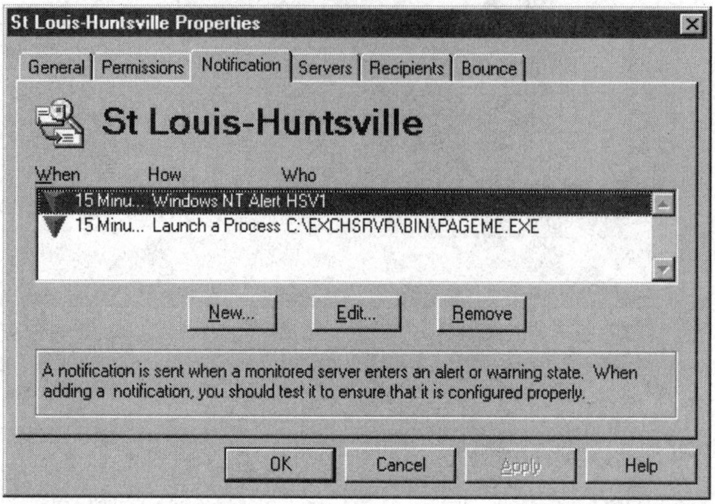

Figure 14-4. The monitor Notification tab

Boston, you cannot also set up a separate set of notifications that will alert the
staff of a regional office without creating a separate monitor just for them.

The Servers tab

Use this tab to specify what you want the monitor to watch. This tab uses the now
familiar two-column format: the left side shows all the servers in the current site,
along with a pull-down that lets you choose between sites in your organization.
The right-hand list shows which servers you're actually monitoring. In between,
there are two buttons you can use to move servers between the two lists.

Configuring Server Monitors

Server monitors have two additional tabs you can use to configure them, described
in the following sections.

The Clock tab

You might wonder why Exchange includes a time monitoring feature, especially
when the Network Time Protocol (NTP) makes it easy to synchronize system
clocks. The answer is that Exchange depends on accurate times to keep track of
message arrivals and replication. The Clock tab of a server monitor's properties
dialog allows you to set monitor and alert states if the time on a monitored system drifts more than a specified interval away. By default, you get a warning when
the clock drift exceeds 15 seconds and an alert if it goes above 60 seconds; in

both cases, the default action is to reset the remote system's time to match the system running the monitor.

I recommend that you turn this feature off and use either an NTP service or a command file (scheduled with at or winat) that uses the net time command to synchronize the clock with a given server. If you use the Exchange time synchronization feature on a server whose clock is wrong, the wrong time will be propagated throughout your organization. It's better to make each server responsible for getting the correct time from a trusted source.

The Actions tab

The Actions tab allows you to cross the line between monitoring and interacting with your servers by configuring actions that take place when a monitored service stops. This is really more of a product marketing feature than a useful tool. Why? Exchange services don't normally stop all by themselves. Does it make sense to use an automated attendant to keep restarting a service that keeps failing? Without knowing the cause of the failure, is that attendant providing you with a useful service, or just a Band-Aid?

For most environments, automatic service restart isn't a very good idea. If someone is stopping the services on purpose (probably for maintenance), having the monitor restart them isn't going to help anyone. If the service is genuinely failing, restarting it (or the entire server) isn't going to help you figure out what's wrong, and it may make the problem worse. Consider carefully whether you really want to use automatic restart.

Configuring Link Monitors

Link monitors automate the sending of test messages to remote servers. This is akin to checking your telephone line by picking it up every so often and seeing if you can call your mom. Like the public telephone network, link monitors don't test any particular path; they just test that a message can get from point A to point B.

Apart from configuring the three common tabs, you don't have to do much to get a new link monitor up and going. You need to specify bounce intervals, and if you're monitoring a connection to a foreign system you need to specify recipients for the test messages.

The Bounce tab

The Bounce tab of the link monitor properties dialog is used to specify the threshold times for entering the warning and alert states. As with other link monitor durations, you can specify these times in hours, minutes, or seconds. The default settings put your monitor in the warning state after 30 minutes and the alert state after 60 minutes. Personally, though, I find that my users balk at mail delays of 30 minutes or more, so I've turned the warning state down to 5 minutes and the alert state to 15 minutes. However, a longer setting is appropriate if you're monitoring slow or congested links during peak usage periods.

When you set these durations, make sure they match the schedule of the connectors underlying the link. For example, if you've scheduled a link monitor to watch your IMS, and the IMS schedule limits it to connecting every 45 minutes, don't schedule your monitor with a shorter duration or you'll see bogus failures.

The Recipients tab

There are three ways for the link monitor to communicate with the server on the other end of the link. If you're checking the link to a remote Exchange server, the monitor will automatically ping the remote server's SA service. You can send mail to an address that will trigger a program or script on the remote end, forcing it to return a message back to the monitor. Finally, you can specify a bogus recipient address and let the monitor send mail to it; as long as the remote end will generate a recognizable NDR, this approach works well for most non-Exchange systems. This latter method is useful for monitoring MS Mail systems, which is why it's included.

The Recipients tab lets you use the latter two methods; you don't have to use it when you're monitoring the link to an Exchange server. The tab itself contains two lists. The "Message subject returned from" list shows addressees that will return the complete subject line of the original ping message. Exchange, and some Unix systems, return the entire message subject (usually with a keyword like "Undeliverable" or "Failed") when bouncing a message. The "Message subject or body returned from" list is for systems (like most of those running sendmail) that return bounces with a different subject line, but will include the original message in the NDR. These lists work like the allow/deny lists you've already seen: each one has a pair of buttons marked None and List, which you use to control whether that category is used or not, and a Modify… button that lets you add specific addressees to the corresponding list.

15

Troubleshooting Exchange Server

*You're either part of the solution
or part of the problem.*
—Attributed to Eldridge Cleaver

Exchange troubleshooting is not for the faint of heart, because Exchange itself is a complicated product, and it interacts with Windows NT in sometimes unpredictable ways. If your Exchange server is part of a multiserver site or a multisite organization, that adds even more complexity. This chapter won't even attempt to cover every potential problem you might encounter; instead, it will explain the most common problems and their solutions, along with general strategies and techniques for both preventing and solving Exchange problems.

The Art of Troubleshooting

Depending on your mindset, tracking down an Exchange problem can be an interesting puzzle or a nightmare. The goal of troubleshooting is to determine and correct the cause of a problem—fixing only the symptoms of a problem hides the underlying cause, making the problem more difficult to identify, and ultimately making things worse. You should continually ask yourself whether the corrective action you're planning to take addresses the cause of the problem or its symptoms. To compound things, users often report symptoms and ask you to fix them, without understanding or having any information about what might have created the problem.

Troubleshooting Exchange requires the strict application of logic, deductive reasoning, and the scientific method. Approach a problem like Sherlock Holmes, if you want to find out what's really going on: collect evidence, follow the chain of cause and effect, identify the possible variables, rule out those that make no sense, then methodically change only one variable at a time. If you change a bunch of stuff all at once, how do you know what was really wrong and how to fix it if it happens again?

Six Steps to Success

Microsoft teaches a six-step troubleshooting process in the official courseware for MCSE certification. While I don't want to go to jail for plagiarism, I think the overall approach is a sound one, so I'll present the six steps in the following sections.

Diagnose the problem

With Exchange, the problem is usually pointed out to you, so you don't have to go looking for it. Sometimes, though, you do need to look; for example, a user complaint that sending mail from Outlook is slow gives you the symptom of the problem, but not the root cause.

Explore the problem

This step involves gathering as much knowledge as possible about when the problem occurs, including what (if anything) has changed in the system configuration, what the system was doing when the problem occurred, and whether you can duplicate the problem or not. During this step, I recommend you check TechNet and the Microsoft Knowledge Base to see if the problem is known and if a fix exists, in which case you can usually skip the rest of the steps.

Identify potential solutions

If you know what might be causing the problem, you can start brainstorming possible solutions. List all potential root causes, plus at least one solution for each cause. Once your list is complete, put the causes in order of probability. Don't do anything with your list yet.

Try the solutions

Start by applying the first solution on your list. Be sure that you have good backups or recovery plans before taking any action that might cause data loss.

Did that fix it?

Did your solution fix the problem, and not just the external symptoms? If it did, was this a one-time fix, or could this problem occur again in the future? If it could happen again, do you have a plan for either preventing it from happening or fixing it the next time? Your plan might be something as simple as educating users what not to do, or as complex as adding a complete recovery server.

Record your knowledge

Once the problem is fixed, document your solution. What was the root cause of the problem? How did you identify the cause, and what made you certain of your diagnosis? Was there anything you would have done differently? Write all this stuff down and store it where you can easily get to it. Don't put it in your mailbox or in a public folder, or you might not be able to access the information when you most need it.

Classifying Problems

Problems break down into several categories. Having a mental framework to categorize problems helps you narrow down their causes and identify solutions. I suggest the following categories:

Architectural

These problems occur because there's something wrong with the design of your messaging system. For example, if your replication makes you fall into the death spiral discussed in Chapter 7, *Managing Connectors and the MTA*, that's an architectural problem: the system is doing what it's supposed to do, but your configuration is making it impossible. These problems are usually pretty hard to fix without adjusting the underlying architecture.

Site-wide

These problems affect all servers in a site, or even all sites in an organization. For example, if Internet mail sent to your users bounces, that's a site-wide problem, even though the specific cause may be limited to a single server. Fixing site-wide problems is usually a priority, since they affect lots of users at once.

Single-server

These problems occur when something is amiss on one server in a site—perhaps its IS won't start, or mail hangs in its MTA queue. Because these problems affect a single machine, they also affect users on that machine, but to a lesser extent than site-wide problems.

Single-user problems

These problems are every administrator's nightmare: your CEO deletes his mailbox, someone in Accounting changes permissions on a public folder and needs you to help change them back, and so on. This category also includes legitimate problems that strike users through no fault of their own.

While it may be a hassle for you to fix the problem (especially if the user cops an attitude about it), always look at these problems as opportunities in disguise, because what your users do wrong can tell you a lot about whether your training, data recovery procedures, and administrative setup are up to the task or not.

Administrative

> This category covers stuff you do wrong. For example, if you put your users into multiple Recipient containers, and then find out that you need to move some of them between containers, that's an administrative problem. The software didn't cause it, nor did the users. If you follow the advice in this book, administrative problems should be few and far between.

Mail flow

> This category is intentionally broad; it can include one or several of the above categories. Anytime mail doesn't go where you want it to, that's a mail flow problem.

Eight Problem-Solving Questions

Along with familiar precepts like *"Cherchez la femme,"* "Follow the money," and *"Cui bono?,"* there is a specific set of questions to ask when you're trying to isolate an Exchange problem. The eight questions I present here are targeted at helping you identify and resolve mail flow problems; most mechanical problems like corrupt stores or failing services don't require a lot of deep introspection.

When someone reports that mail they send isn't getting where it's supposed to, you can ask these eight questions to help identify the problem's location and cause:

1. Did the message even leave the client's outbox? If not, why not?

2. Is it stuck on the first server it was sent to? If so, is it in an MTA queue, waiting to go to the connector? Is it stuck in a connector queue? Is it even being routed to the right connector, or is it being routed somewhere that has a connection schedule or restriction that makes it get stuck?

3. Is the GWART up to date? Are there any replication problems that might indicate problems with mail flowing over the same route?

4. If the message makes it across the first hop, is it getting stuck on a remote server? Where is it on that server?

5. Is it stuck on a connector to a remote system? Is there a problem with the remote system the connector delivers to? For example, if you're trying to troubleshoot a problem involving a recipient on a foreign X.400 system, can you tell whether the message made it there or not?

6. Were any NDRs generated along the way? If so, what systems generated them? If any of them came from Exchange, what service on what server sent the NDR, and why? What do the NDRs tell you?

7. Are there pertinent event log messages on the server where the message is stuck?

8. Have you used message tracking and the appropriate diagnostic logs to look for further evidence?

Duplicating Problems

We've all heard the old Zen koan that asks whether a tree falling in the forest makes a sound if no one is there to hear it. Does a problem exist if you can't duplicate it? You might not think so, but your users will probably disagree. One key part of isolating a problem is getting it to happen on demand. This is easier with some problems than others, but it's always worth making the attempt. There are some tried-and-true strategies you can use when you need to duplicate a problem:

- If the problem involves data in a mailbox, try accessing the mailbox from a second system and see if the same problem occurs. See if you can reproduce the problem with an older (or newer) client than the one giving the trouble.

- If the problem relates to the IS databases, you can backup and restore the IS onto a clone machine, then isolate the cause of the problem there while keeping the production system running.

- If the problem involves a client, try another identical version of the client, either by cloning the problem system or by finding another machine with an identical loadout.

Gathering Problem Information

When you get ready to try to solve an Exchange problem, the first step is to arm yourself with as much information as possible about the servers and clients involved. If you've been documenting your setup as you go (as suggested in Chapter 14, *Managing Exchange Servers*), this will be easy, but it's worth doing even if you have to scratch around to find the answers.

The first question I always recommend asking is simple: did the thing that's broken work before, or is this the first time you've attempted to use it? Something that was working but is now inoperative suggests different root causes than something that hasn't ever worked.

At a minimum, you'll probably want to know the following:

- What versions of the client and server software are you currently running? Server versions are available from Exchange Administrator's Servers object (select the object and look in the contents pane); client versions are available through the Mailbox Resources view.

- What version of Windows NT is installed? What service packs and hotfixes are installed?

A Little Help from Your Friends

For the most part, you should be able to handle the everyday problems you'll run into. You may find extraordinary problems every now and then, and you're certain to be better equipped to solve them if you take part in one or more of the Exchange community forums scattered around the Web. The very first time you see someone else warning against doing something you were about to do—thus saving your bacon—you'll be glad you did.

Not surprisingly, there are a number of mailing lists and sites dedicated to Exchange administration and management. Before you start asking questions on any of them, you should take the time to find the frequently asked questions (FAQ) list and read it thoroughly. There's nothing like reading a FAQ looking for the answer to one question and finding answers to several others in the process! The following are some recommended lists and sites:

- The MS Exchange list is now hosted by Stephen Wynkoop at *www. swynk.com*, but it has been around since 1994 or so, and was formerly hosted by Peter Bowyer at *www.msexchange.org*. Volume varies (as does the technical difficulty of the questions and answers), but it seems to average around 150 messages per day. There are a number of Microsoft engineers and PSS people who hang out here.

- Slipstick Systems offers a terrific resource site for Exchange and Outlook clients at *www.slipstick.com/exchange/index.htm*. The site, hosted by Sue Mosher, covers literally everything you might ever want to know about Outlook 97, 98, and 2000.

- The Microsoft Clustering list (*msclusters@ed-com.com*, or *www.i405.com/ MSClusters/* for subscription information) carries discussion of Microsoft's Wolfpack clustering solution, including its use with Exchange.

- The MAPI-L list (see *peach.ease.lsoft.com*) carries discussion of developing or automating MAPI operations. Though it's not limited to Exchange discussions, most of the members are using Exchange Server. The list membership includes many hard-core programmers, including some of Microsoft's Exchange developers.

- The WinNT-L list (also at *peach.ease.lsoft.com)* is a heavily active mailing list for discussions related to Windows NT management and installation.

There is also a wealth of Usenet groups that carry useful discussion about Exchange. Microsoft maintains the majority of them (all of which fall under the *microsoft.public.exchange* and *microsoft.public.outlook* hierarchies). If your provider doesn't carry these, you can get them straight from Microsoft's news server at *msnews.microsoft.com*. You may occasionally find the *comp.mail.** hierarchy useful, too.

- Are there any other Microsoft products (especially BackOffice components or the MS proxy server) installed on the same machine? If so, you'll need their version information, too.

- Are there any third-party Exchange add-ins on your server, particularly virus protection or content-management packages?

- What other programs are running on the server? In what order were these programs installed?

- If the problem is with the client, does the problem happen when you use OWA or an Internet protocol client? If the problem is with an Internet protocol client, what happens if you try a different one?

If you can, you'll also need to check the system's event log to see whether there are any messages pertinent to the problem. To make this easier, use the Event Viewer application to increase the size of the application event log beyond its default size of 512KB, which enables you to maintain a better audit trail of past event messages.

Using the Knowledge Base

Microsoft's Knowledge Base (KB) is a terrific tool when you're trying to troubleshoot a problem. Since it's fully indexed and searchable, you can enter a description of the problem, an ID from the event log, or keywords describing the failure and see whether it's a documented problem or not. For example, plugging "–1018" into Microsoft' search engine will net you at least 11 articles explaining what that event ID means (it's bad; see Chapter 17, *Recovery and Repair*), what might have caused it, and how to fix it.

I strongly encourage new administrators to get in the habit of checking the Knowledge Base when they're trying to identify a problem. If you find a succinct description of your problem, you'll have saved time and effort; if not, you may still find some related information that can help you solve your problem. At worst, you'll be out the two or three minutes it took to do the search. Here are some tips for getting the most use out of the KB:

- If you know the specific article number you want, send mail to *mshelp@microsoft.com* with a subject line containing the article number (or multiple article numbers, separated by commas). Their mailbot will send back the articles you request.

- If you search for a specific article number and can't find it, that means Microsoft has retired the article. Try searching by the keyword or title from the original article; you may find that a new article on the same topic has been issued.

- Regularly use the search tool on the main KB page to glance at the list of new articles posted over the last 30 days; you may find fixes for problems that have been bothering you for a while.

Eek! A Bug!

Before spending any time to document and report a bug, assess how serious it is and how much impact it has on you. Be sure you can reproduce the bug. The more time you spend isolating the circumstances of the problem, the more quickly a solution will be reached, especially since your dealings with Microsoft support are likely to be over the phone or Internet, not in person.

Every software product has bugs. More precisely, they all have *faults* and *flaws*. A fault is when something bad happens during processing, like when a transaction can't be committed to the store. It's a transient event that may or may not happen again, and from which the system may or may not be able to recover. A flaw is a mistake in the program code.

Search the Microsoft Knowledge Base and TechNet database. Try to find an exact match for your configuration; if you see a flaw or fault reported for Exchange 5.0 and you're using 5.5, that's probably not a good match. However, many articles that describe procedures for making something work are labeled as applying to old versions of Exchange even though they apply to 5.5 as well.

If a client or server service pack exists for the release you're using, it's best to install it. Sometimes Microsoft includes fixes for problems without acknowledging those fixes in the KB or release notes.

It's easy to jump to the conclusion that a problem you're having is a defect in Exchange or NT, but chances are excellent that the problem is due to a misconfigured system or some other fault or flaw. Keep up with service packs, bug fixes, and peer resources; it's likely that you won't ever be the first person to find a defect.

If you think you've found a real, bona fide flaw in Exchange, you should take some preliminary steps before calling Microsoft's support group:

- Be prepared to slowly explain everything you have done. Writing up the problem and details of your environment ahead of time will save you considerable time. Even when you do everything right, a real bug, if you're the first to encounter it, can take days or weeks to get resolved.

- Start by thinking through a problem to determine why you're having a problem but other customers aren't. Are your users unique? Do you have unusual hardware or software on the server? For example, antivirus programs and specialized server monitoring programs can cause problems.

When Your Server Stops

One of the worst things that can happen is that one of your Exchange servers just stops working, usually right in the middle of the workday. Choosing good hardware and taking good care of it will lower the risk of server crashes, but there are always unforeseen or unavoidable circumstances. Chapter 17 covers server recovery, but sometimes you don't have to do a full recovery; this section explores some causes of server crashes and suggests where to look for a fix.

Windows NT Blue Screens

Windows NT is the foundation for the server processes of Exchange Server. Fortunately, Exchange does not include any drivers, and none of its components run in the kernel's address space. Almost every time I've ever seen an NT Blue Screen of Death (BSOD) on an Exchange system, it's been because of a hardware or NT problem that had nothing to do with Exchange (particularly when the system includes third-party products like non-Exchange-aware virus scanners). Of course, this is small comfort when your server crashes, but it's important to understand what usually causes the BSOD to appear and ruin your day.

Anecdotal evidence suggests that the most common BSOD Exchange administrators encounter revolves around disk controllers, particularly RAID controllers. It's critical that you have the correct NT 4.0 drivers installed for any mass storage device. That goes double for SCSI controllers and double again for RAID controllers. One administrator I know who works at a government site recently told me about a problem she'd had on one of their servers. They'd get periodic BSODs on one machine but not on the others, even though their configuration was identical. It turns out that the firmware on the SCSI RAID controller of the problem machine was one revision out of date—and that was enough to cause a problem.

Antiviral software is another particularly common cause of BSODs on Exchange servers. Some virus checkers only work with very specific NT configurations, so upgrading your server from SP3 to SP4* can break things spectacularly. The same is true of any other third-party system extensions you install; be sure to follow their installation requirements closely and be prepared for problems if you deviate from them.

Other problems may appear tangentially related to Exchange. For example, if your NTFS partition becomes corrupted, you may observe that the system crashes when the IS is started. Checking the integrity of the IS database won't tell you anything, because Exchange isn't the cause of the problem, but running chkdsk will help locate the problem.

---

* SP5 came out as this book was going to press.

It's critical that you develop your NT troubleshooting skills, because if you get a BSOD, it indicates a serious problem, especially since BSODs can cause your IS or DS to become corrupted. If you've recently changed your hardware or software configuration, start looking there first. If you haven't, you may need to use the NT setup disks to repair your system configuration, or even move your Exchange services to another server and reinstall NT.

When NT won't boot

After a sufficiently bad crash, you may not be able to boot your NT installation. You can use the standard Microsoft emergency repair procedure, or you can try some shortcuts first. One shortcut is to install Windows NT Workstation with no networking or accessories, which only takes about 10 minutes when run from CD. Once it's installed, you can boot into it and recover the data you need, even if you need to run ntbackup. As long as the disk that has your data on it is still available, you'll be in good shape.

You can also do some detective work if you suspect that NT won't boot because of a driver problem. The *boot.ini* file on your boot partition controls the boot loader: by adding the right switches (as shown in Table 15-1) you can force it to tell you what drivers are being loaded. You can also use the remote debugger included on the NT Server CD (you'll also need a null modem cable) to inspect the problem machine's boot process from a second machine.

Table 15-1. Switches You Can Add to the boot.ini File

Switch	What It Does
/basevideo	This switch forces NT to boot with the standard $640 \times 480 \times 16$ VGA driver. You can always use this option to force NT to ignore whatever display driver you've installed; that makes it possible to boot when your driver or display card are misconfigured.
/baudrate=X	Specifies the baud rate to be used for a serial debugging connection. The default is 9600 baud if a modem's connected and 19200 baud if a null modem cable is connected. When you specify this switch, it also turns on the /debug switch.
/crashdebug	Turns on the automatic recovery mode normally enabled through the Recovery group in the Startup/Shutdown tab of the System control panel.
/debug	Tells the kernel to activate the remote debugger so you can isolate problems using a second computer.
/debugport=comX	Specifies which serial port (COM1, COM2, and so on) to use for a debugging session. Forces the /debug switch on.
/nodebug	Don't load the kernel debugger. This provides a slight performance boost.
/sos	Display the names of drivers loaded during the boot. By default, only dots are shown on the blue screen; adding this option forces NT to identify which drivers are being used.

Dr. Watson Errors

BSODs are unlikely to be caused by Exchange, but user-mode exceptions are a different story. When a user-mode application crashes (or, more properly, throws an exception), the Dr. Watson debugging tool (*drwtsn32.exe*) runs. It maintains a log in the *%systemroot%\drwatson.log* file that contains details about the application's environment at the time it crashed.

 If you install programming or development tools, they may replace Dr. Watson with their own exception handlers. In general, those kinds of tools shouldn't be on your servers, anyway.

If there are ongoing or repeating problems, or if your server has a large number of users, it may be a good idea to install the debugging symbol files for your Exchange executables. These symbol files provide more specific information about which piece of code was running when the exception occurred. Most sites don't install these files until a problem occurs, and then only after Microsoft support requests more specific information, since having the symbol files installed imposes a space and speed penalty. I don't recommend installing symbol files as a matter of course, but you should know how and when to do so.

Be aware that there are at least two separate symbol sets: you have to install symbols for NT, and there are separate symbol sets for each service pack. Exchange also has its own set of symbols, so if you're running an NT 4.0 SP4 machine with Exchange 5.5 SP2, you'll need the NT4, SP4, and SP2 symbols. The processes for installing symbols for NT and Exchange are slightly different, but the overall process is easy enough:

1. Install the symbols for NT 4.0 itself. On your NT Server CD, run the **expndsym** utility (it's in the *support\debug* directory) and tell it where your NT system installation lives, like this:

   ```
   expndsym f: c:\winnt40
   ```

   The first drive letter should be the correct letter for your CD drive. This creates a new directory in your system directory called *symbols*, and the symbol files themselves are installed.

2. Install the symbols for whatever service pack you're running. If you have the CD for your service pack, the *support\debug* directory has a *symbols* subdirectory for each processor type; just copy the files from the appropriate directory on the CD to the *symbols* directory in your system directory. If you downloaded your SP from Microsoft's web site, you'll also need the matching symbol file: *nt4sym3i.exe* for SP3 on x86, *nt4sym3a.exe* for SP3 on Alpha,

sp4symi.exe for SP4 on x86, or *sp4syma.exe* for SP4 on Alpha. Run the appropriate installer and tell it where your symbol file directory is.

3. Run the Exchange symbols installer, *server\support\symbols\setup.exe*, from your Exchange CD, then install symbols for whatever service pack you're using.

4. Set Dr. Watson as the default debugger by running it with the –I option.

> Make sure you always maintain enough space on your system partition so you can install symbol files and debugging tools. This means you'll need around 300MB of free disk space, but it's invaluable when you need it.

When the IS Won't Start

I hate it when this happens. You will, too. Fortunately, not all instances of IS startup failures are fatal. Anytime the IS detects that the *priv.edb* or *pub.edb* files are in an inconsistent state, it refuses to start. This inconsistency may be because a transaction couldn't be committed, because the database file is corrupt, or because the moon is in the wrong phase; there are too many possible causes to enumerate here.

The key to identifying why the IS won't start is the system event log. Whenever a startup failure occurs, the IS will log an event with a source of ESE97. In most cases, the error message logged is self-explanatory. For example, here's what the error message for event 193 says:

> MSExchangeIS ((424)) The database engine failed with error –510 while trying to log the commit of a transaction. To ensure database consistency, the process was terminated. Simply restart the process to force database recovery and return the database to a consistent state.

As error messages go, that's a great one: it tells you what happened, what the consequences are, and how to fix it.

> There's a great list of Exchange event IDs at *www.ncgroup.com/abu/exchange/xevents.htm*; the material here was culled from the MS Knowledge Base, TechNet articles, and just plain poking around.

Common causes of start failures

In general, the Information Store will keep running without incident. There are several common reasons why the IS fails to start:

- If you move the database files by hand, the transaction log files won't match the database and the IS won't start. Don't do it. Use the Performance Optimizer (as described in Chapter 18, *Managing Exchange Performance*) to move databases if they need moving.

- The IS requires at least 10MB free on the transaction log and database partitions. If they're on the same partition, that means you need 20MB free. Make sure you have enough free space. If you get a mail loop (especially if you have the IMS's archiving feature turned on), or if it's been a long time since your last backup, this can quickly fill up your disk without your knowledge.

- If you're running the Standard Edition of Exchange, and your public or private IS is very close to the 16GB limit, the IS will shut down instead of growing beyond that limit. If this happens, do an offline defragmentation of the database (see Chapter 17 for details) to reclaim the database whitespace, then restart the IS. If the database is already compacted, then you may have to consider upgrading to Enterprise Edition to get the store to start. A call to Microsoft support is in order.

- The IS will shut down if it can't write to the NT event log. This usually happens because the event log is full; its default size limit is only 512KB. Before this bites you, increase the event log size using Event Viewer. It is recommended that you set the Application log to overwrite as needed.

- If you restore the databases from an offline backup, when you try to restart the IS, it will fail with error −1011. That's by design: after doing an offline restore, you have to use the `isinteg –patch` command to fix up the database, as discussed in Chapter 17.

There are other causes to consider, too. If the SA doesn't start (usually because someone has changed the service account credentials), the IS can't run; in addition, if core NT services fail because there's a problem with a low-level driver or component, that may cause the SA or a service that depends on it to fail.

Don't panic

What if your store won't start and none of the problems listed above is to blame? Relax. First, stop all the Exchange services on your server, then reboot it. Make sure to allow adequate time for the services to stop normally; if you forcibly reboot the server before the services have stopped, you will worsen any underlying database problems. The IS automatically tries to restore the database to a consistent state when it's started after a reboot, so as long as you shut down the services cleanly, the IS will have a chance to play back any logged transactions that haven't been stored in the database. (If the IS stopped cleanly, there won't be any unlogged transactions.) Make sure you wait long enough for the IS to replay the logged transactions, and don't forget that the Services control panel won't automatically update its display to show what services are currently running if a service starts or stops while it's open.

If rebooting doesn't restart the store properly, surf over to the Microsoft Knowledge Base to look for possible causes before you panic and make the problem worse with a hasty recovery attempt. The Knowledge Base is currently located at *support.microsoft.com/support/search/c.asp?FR=0*, but it seems to move around on Microsoft's site from time to time.

Search for the specific error number you see in the event log. That will almost always lead you to an article detailing the root cause for that particular failure so you can fix it. Before you try to fix anything, make a full offline backup, including all the log files and databases. This is critical, since you may need the backup information to restore your server later.

If your IS won't start after a crash

If your server has suffered from OS or hardware crashes, including sudden loss of electrical power, it's possible that the IS or DS database files may be damaged. It's critical that you carefully review any messages in the event log to determine what's wrong with the store before you attempt to recover it. In some cases, it can be best to move your mailboxes and public folders to another server before attempting to repair a damaged store, assuming you can restart it; if you can't, you won't be able to move anything. See the section "Recovering Your Data" in Chapter 17 for more details.

Troubleshooting Server Problems

Even when your server doesn't fail outright, there will undoubtedly be cases when it starts acting funny, or when something that was working fine suddenly quits.

Installation Problems

Exchange Server installation is pretty simple, but you may encounter problems. The most typical problems occur when Setup can't overwrite a file that's already in use, or when it can't connect to an existing site to join it.

Problems during setup

Setup problems are typically related to the system's software configuration. As discussed in Chapter 4, *Installing Exchange*, the setup process itself is pretty fault tolerant. There are four primary things to check when you have problems installing Exchange or a service pack:

1. You must have enough disk space. The Setup program checks to make sure you have enough space, but if you're upgrading an existing installation or reinstalling some components, the space calculations may be wrong.

2. No other application can be using any of the DLLs or other files that Setup replaces. Make sure Outlook and all other MAPI applications are closed before running Setup; in fact, you should follow Microsoft's advice and make sure that all applications are closed. When applying an Exchange service pack, you also need to ensure that there are no Performance Monitor, Event Viewer, or Exchange Administrator monitors pointing at the server you're upgrading. If you still get errors complaining that a particular DLL is in use, just rename the offending file and tell Setup to retry.

3. You must have all the prerequisite products and drivers installed in the right order. That means NT 4 SP3 or later, plus any hotfixes you need. If you're running any other BackOffice products, check the Exchange 5.5 *readme.wri* file to make sure there aren't any conflicts; for example, IIS 4.0 has an SMTP server that needs to be removed if you intend to install the IMS, and the Internet Locator Service for NetMeeting conflicts with Exchange's LDAP server.

4. Make sure all antivirus and backup services and programs on your server are disabled.

Problems when joining an existing site

There are really only two things that can go wrong when adding your server to an existing site. First of all, you have to verify that your server can see the target server you specify (see the next section, "Checking Network Connectivity"). If the two servers can't establish an RPC connection, you won't be able to complete the installation. This usually manifests itself as an error dialog reporting a DS_E_ COMMUNICATIONS_ERROR.

The second usual problem area is directory permissions. Both servers must share the same security context, and the account you use to do the installation must have appropriate permissions in the target site. Make sure you've set up your site service accounts properly and specified the correct account during setup. DS_E_ INSUFFICENT_ACCESS_RIGHTS is the error you'll see when directory permissions problems occur.

Checking Network Connectivity

Exchange is completely dependent on network connectivity. If something goes wrong with your network, your clients and servers won't be able to talk to each other; shortly thereafter, your MTA and connector queues will start growing as outbound messages get stuck.

Things that make you say "duh"

Ordinarily, I wouldn't point out the basic steps of checking to make sure that your server's NIC is connected to a cable, that the cable is connected to a hub, that the hub has power, and so on, but a depressing number of reported network problems happen because something was accidentally or purposefully unplugged and not plugged back in. These problems are particularly common when your server is sitting out in view of the general public instead of being in a nice, safe server room. The first thing you should check is that all your cabling is properly in place.

One reviewer told me that her site had recently upgraded to 100Base-TX and had found that some of their NICs were set to always use 10Mbps links. This made the machines with those NICs drop off the network. Consider this one more thing to check.

Once you've checked the cabling, there are some other simple tests you can perform; if one of these indicates the problem, you'll save a lot of time and trouble by skipping the rest of the tests in this section:

- If possible, make sure the machine you're trying to connect to is powered up and on the network.

- See whether you can use NetBIOS services at all. For example, open up the Network Neighborhood and see what's in it, or try mapping a drive in Windows Explorer. This can help tell you whether your physical network hardware is working okay.

- Try using the `ping` utility to ping the IP address of the remote machine. Consider that some network devices block the ICMP packets required for `ping` testing; if pinging fails, it doesn't necessarily mean that the connection is bad, but it may indicate that it is.

If any of the above tests fail, your problem is outside the scope of this book.

Checking name resolution

Assuming that the underlying network is working, the next thing to check is name resolution. Exchange can use both NetBIOS and TCP/IP name resolution, so you'll need to check both of them, starting with NetBIOS:

1. If you're using a *HOSTS* or *LMHOSTS* file, verify that there's an entry for the machine you're trying to reach, and that the associated IP address is still correct.

2. If you're using WINS, make sure your WINS server is up and on the network and that its database hasn't been corrupted. If necessary, reboot the WINS server. Also, check that there haven't been any changes to your network configuration that might prevent WINS packets from reaching your WINS server.

3. Verify that you can use `ping` to ping the remote server using only its WINS hostname, then repeat the check from the remote server to make sure it can see your server.

You must do the same types of tests for DNS name resolution:

1. Verify that your DNS server is answering requests and that its address is properly specified in the Network control panel.

2. Be sure that nothing is obstructing the flow of packets to your DNS server. You can test this from the command line by using the `nslookup` command to look up the address of a well-known host like *www.oreilly.com*. If you don't get a response, something's wrong with your DNS configuration.

3. Verify that you can use `ping` with the full domain name of the host you're trying to reach.

 There are some additional steps involved in checking that resolution is good enough for the IMS; see the section "Troubleshooting MTA and Connector Problems," later in the chapter.

Checking RPC connectivity

Once you've verified that your underlying network connection is okay, check whether RPC packets are making it between points A and B. MAPI clients use RPC to talk to Exchange, and Exchange servers within the same site (or joined by a site connector) use RPC to communicate.

The first step is to see whether you can connect to the other server's *IPC$* share. This hidden share is used for some types of RPC communications; if it's not working, you won't be able to RPC anywhere. You can use the **NET USE** command to try attaching to the other server's share; in this example, replace *server2*, *domain2*, and *serviceAccount2* with the server name, domain name, and service account for the remote server:

```
NET USE \\server2\IPC$ /USER:domain2\serviceAccount2
```

If this works, you can check to see whether you can mount shares on the remote server; if it doesn't work, it means the underlying network isn't passing RPC packets, so you'll need to fix it.

You can also use the rpcping utility (located on the Exchange Server 5.5 CD-ROM in the *Server**Support**RPCPing* directory) to test RPC connectivity to a remote site. rpcping comes in two components: a server that must be run on the Exchange server, and a client (there are 16- and 32-bit Windows clients, plus a DOS version, and even source code, on the CD).

The client application for rpcping is pretty simple: you run it, tell it which server you're trying to reach, and tell it to start pinging. As each ping packet is sent to the server, you'll see whether the server received it or not. In order to accurately duplicate what Exchange is doing, you need to run the client and server portions of rpcping while logged in as the Exchange service account. Here's the lowdown:

1. Log in as the Exchange service account on the remote server and run the rpcping server.

2. Log in as the service account on your server and run the rpcping client.

3. Choose the server you want to talk to, use the Number of Pings group to pick a number of ping packets, and make sure the Run with Security checkbox is filled; this forces rpcping to use the encrypted RPC mechanism that Exchange uses.

4. Click the Start button, then watch the status area at the bottom of the client window. You'll see a ping-by-ping account of whether the ping attempts succeeded or failed. If they succeeded, the problem isn't with the underlying network; if they fail, you need to double-check your RPC configuration (see KB article Q165324 for more details).

5. Start over at step 1, but reverse the client and server locations to test pinging in the other direction.

Diagnostic Logging

The Diagnostic Logging tabs scattered around Exchange Administrator control how much information Exchange components write to the NT application event log. With Exchange, logging is pretty much an all-or-nothing proposition: you get either too little information or too much. However, when you do have a repeatable problem logging can be of considerable use in helping determine the circumstances of a problem.

Even when you have logging turned off, various components log warning and alert messages. Some of these alert messages are normal: for example, the IS logs messages when it starts and stops. When you turn diagnostic logging on for a particular component, you'll notice the component starts logging increasingly small events. For example, when you enable maximum logging on the X.400 connector, you'll see that it logs practically every byte it exchanges with a remote system.

Leave diagnostic logging off until you suspect or identify a problem with an individual component. At that point, you can increase the logging level on that component and look over the logs to find out what's wrong.

Troubleshooting MTA and Connector Problems

The MTA and connectors come into play as soon as you try to send messages from one server to another. Most such problems fall into two categories: network problems and improperly formatted or corrupted messages. There are some other things to watch out for along the way.

Message Tracking

Exchange has the capability to track messages from their initial delivery to an Exchange server somewhere in your organization to their arrival at the addressees' mailboxes. This tracking can be very useful when you're trying to find out why mail doesn't get where it's supposed to go; however, it only tracks mail messages until they leave your Exchange organization.

Internally, Exchange Server assigns each message a unique identifier composed of the organization name, server name, and a date-derived series of numbers. The overall message tracking process consists of two steps: find the message you desire, then track it using Exchange Administrator's Tools → Track Message... command.

Enabling message tracking

You have to turn on message tracking; it's never on by default. If it's off, your options for tracking problems are cut back significantly, so turn it on. You enable tracking on the General tab of the MTA site configuration properties dialog and on the General tab of the IS site configuration properties dialog. You must also enable tracking on the IMS if you want to use it there; other connectors may also require you to enable tracking in their individual properties dialogs.

The amount of disk space and processing required is low relative to the value of this information. Although it is generally difficult to define an "active server," a moderately active server with 100 users would generate between 1MB to 4MB of message tracking logs per day.

Maintaining the logs

Every day at midnight, Exchange creates a new log file for that day, then uses it to record information about every message generated on the server: mail, public folder replication, and directory replication traffic are all included. You can purge the tracking logs when necessary; by default, Exchange will retain seven days worth of log files. These are normally stored in the server's *exchsrvr\tracking.log* directory. Each Exchange server also creates a Windows NT file share called *tracking.log* that points to this directory. You can change this directory by stopping the SA, putting the directory name you want to use into the `HKLM\System\ CurrentControlSet\Services\MSExchangeSA\Parameters\LogDirectory` value, then restarting it.

If you want to change the retention interval for tracking log files, use the General tab of the System Attendant object on each server. You should back up these files, and you should use the same interval for all servers in a site to avoid losing tracking information when messages traverse servers whose retention intervals are shorter than the rest of the site.

What's in the logs

The key to understanding tracking is knowing that Exchange Server routes based on sites, not servers. For example, if a site has six servers and a single site connector linking it to a second site, any of the six servers could process an outgoing message. In a similar example, if three of the six servers are running the IMS with equal routing preferences, outbound messages from the other three, non-IMS servers could go out any of the three outbound servers.

This routing scheme is why you have to turn on tracking on the MTA and the IS: the IS only handles tracking messages that originate, or are delivered to, the IS on a particular server, while the MTA can track messages sent between servers and sites. To get a complete picture of a message's path through your system, you need to enable tracking on every service that touches it. Once you do, you're ready to examine the log contents.

Each entry in the tracking log has an event ID number; Table 15-2 shows the most common event numbers and their meanings (Chapter 17 of the *Exchange Administrator's Guide* on the Exchange CD has a complete list).

Table 15-2. Message Log Event IDs

Event ID	What It Means
0	A message arrived from a connector or server.
4	A local client (MTA, user, DS, etc.) submitted a message for delivery.
7	The IS or MTA transferred a message to another Exchange component.
9	The IS delivered a message to one or more local recipients.
26	The MTA expanded a DL as part of delivery processing.
28	A message was bounced to some recipient other than one of the original addressees.

Table 15-2. Message Log Event IDs (continued)

Event ID	What It Means
1010	The IMS accepted and enqueued an inbound message.
1011	The IMS successfully delivered a message to its destination host.

Using Message Tracking

The Message Tracking Center, which appears when you use Exchange Administrator's Tools → Message Tracking... command, is the heart of Exchange's tracking abilities. The first step is to choose a server to use as a tracking host; you can use any server on which you have administrative permissions. Exchange Administrator actually attaches to the *tracking.log* share on the server you specify, so the account you're logged in as must have permission to use that share. It's best to start with the server the sending mailbox was located on, if possible, since that's where the logs start.

Once you've chosen a server, the Select Message to Track window appears. You can only find messages by the sender and recipient addresses; you can optionally specify how many days back you want to search. Once you fill out the search criteria and click the Find Now button, Exchange Administrator will start searching the logs. As it finds messages, they're displayed in the bottom portion of the message tracking window. You can see the properties for individual messages by selecting a message, then clicking the Properties button; the properties dialog that appears shows you the event type, who the sender and recipients are, what time the message was originated, how big it was, what its priority was, and where it was transferred.

Once you select a message in the search results list, the Message Tracking Center appears, as shown in Figure 15-1. This window gives you the message ID for the message you've selected, and it shows the tracking history at each point in the message's lifetime.

Click the Track button to see where the message has been. The tracking history will indicate when the message was delivered to each recipient, or you can use the "Find Recipient in Tracking History..." button to look up specific recipients.

A typical message will show that it was submitted and delivered; some messages will also show processing by MTAs or connectors within the site. Note that the log analysis is done from the system where you run Exchange Administrator, so it may be slow over dial-up or underpowered WAN links. Figure 15-2 shows the tracking history for a single message.

By selecting any item in the "Tracking history" list and clicking the Properties button, you can see the properties of the message at that point in time, which is useful when you're trying to locate where a message ended up.

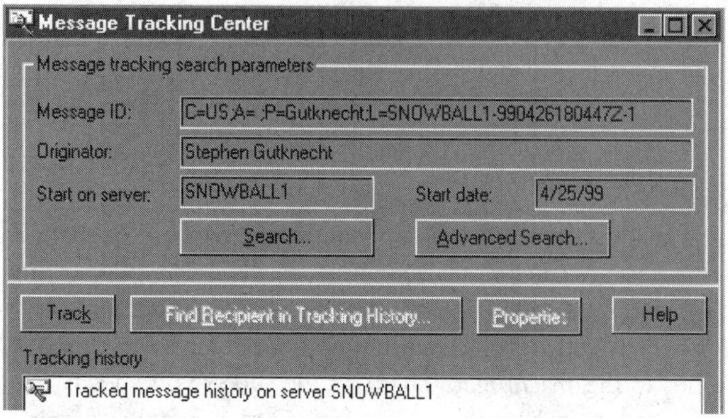

Figure 15-1. The Message Tracking Center shows the selected message

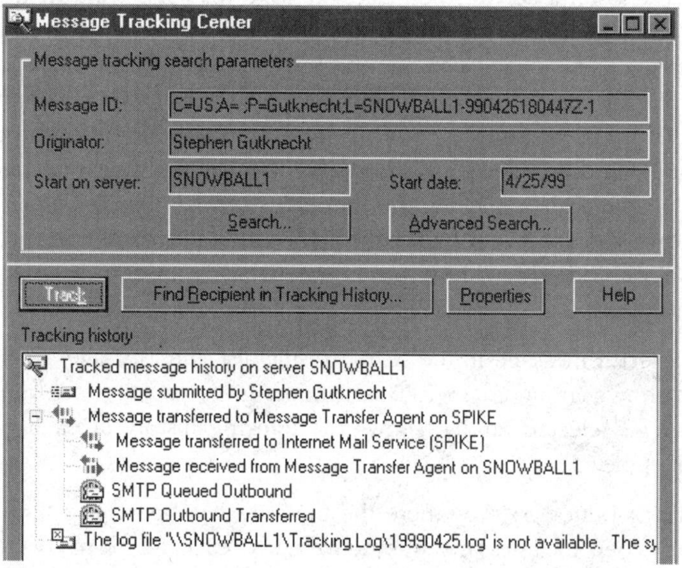

Figure 15-2. The message tracking log for a single message

Troubleshooting the MTA

The most visible symptom of MTA problems is that your MTA queue length (as exposed in Performance Monitor) gets longer and longer. This happens because services pass messages to the MTA for delivery, but when the MTA can't deliver them, they stack up in the queue. Note that this doesn't necessarily indicate a problem with your MTA; it may be that the receiving MTA is down, so messages pile up in your queue until the receiving MTA is ready to accept them.

When the MTA stops or won't start

Most MTA queue backlogs can be attributed to failed network connections or multiroute dead-ends. However, it's also possible that the MTA might stop abruptly:

- The MTA will stop if it runs out of disk space. Make sure there's enough free disk space (e.g., at least 10MB) for the MTA's scratch area. You can confirm that this is the root cause of the problem by checking the event logs for event ID 9411.

- The MTA depends on the DS and SA services. Since no other service depends on the MTA, it's possible that the MTA may not start because one of these prerequisite services fails to start. Use the Services control panel to verify that the SA, DS, IS, netlogon, and RPC services are all running.

- If the MTA database becomes corrupted, the MTA won't start. This can happen when a connector passes a malformed or illegal message to the MTA, or when the database becomes corrupted through random bad luck. Use mtacheck to fix this problem.

- Verify that the files in the *mtadata* directory aren't read-only. If the MTA can't create its log files in this directory, it won't start.

When MTA queues grow too long

When MTA queues get backed up, it's because messages are flowing in faster than they can be passed to other MTAs. This can happen for a number of reasons, most of which are easy to check and fix:

- If the link to the other site is down or flaky, your MTA won't be able to transfer messages. Make sure you have good connectivity to the other site.

- If the other site's MTA is down, you obviously won't be able to send messages to it. Verify that all the MTAs you're trying to talk to are up and going.

- The connector you're using to pass MTA traffic may not be scheduled often enough to clear out the backlog. Try increasing the connection frequency to flush out the backlog, then gradually decrease it as far as you can without raising your queue length unreasonably.

- If you've turned on directory replication, you may have inadvertently entered the replication death spiral. See the sidebar "The Replication Death Spiral" in Chapter 7 for details on how to fix this.

The mtacheck utility

When the MTA starts after an abrupt shutdown, it automatically runs a utility called mtacheck, which scans the MTA's internal queues and databases looking for objects that are damaged or malformed. Any defective objects it finds are stored in files for you to inspect; once it's done scanning, `mtacheck` rebuilds the queues so the MTA can be restarted.

Although `mtacheck` can remove data from your MTA queues, there's normally no reason to run it manually. If PSS advises it, you can run `mtacheck` according to their directions, but I mention it here only to alert you to its presence, not to encourage you to run it.

Troubleshooting the X.400 Connector

Once you get the X.400 connector running, it's pretty easy to maintain and very stable. Most X.400 problems relate to getting things properly connected and working in the first place; in second place are problems caused by a change on one end of a connection that's not reflected on the other end. If you're having trouble getting your X.400 connector going, here are some things to check:

- The X.400 address spaces must match on both ends of the connector. They're case-sensitive, and you have to remember not to overlook the `a=` entry (that's "a=" followed by a single space) when connecting to another Exchange Server system.

- If you get the IP address or DNS name wrong on the Stack properties page, you won't be able to connect to the other end. Use the IP address instead of the DNS name so you'll be protected against DNS problems. The X.400 connector is extremely intolerant of slow DNS resolution or timeouts.

- If something is blocking traffic on TCP port 102 between you and the remote system, your X.400 connector will fail. If you or your remote peer are using a firewall, you have to open that port. If you've changed the default port number as described in Chapter 16, *Exchange Security*, you must change it on every MTA your MTA talks to. You can use `ping` or `telnet` to see whether you can establish a session to the remote system.

- The local MTA name on your server may or may not match the NT name of the server. All remote MTAs you talk to must have the right name for your local MTA. This is also true in the reverse direction: if you specify the wrong name or password for a remote system, you won't be able to talk to it.

- The MTA you're talking to may not be completely X.400 compliant, or it may have some quirk that prevents it from communicating with an Exchange MTA. The only way to fix this is to get in touch with your counterpart at the remote site and find out what MTA they're using and which conformance mode it expects to be in.

The X.400 connector does a good job of logging error and exception messages to the event log, so check there before attempting to repair the problem.

Troubleshooting the IMS

The Exchange 5.5 IMS is tightly integrated with the IS. That's good and bad: it gives the IMS a significant performance boost, but it also means that a problem with the IMS can kill the IS too. IMS problems fall into two general categories: problems transferring mail with other sites and problems which make the IS stop.

Name resolution and network problems

If your IMS can't connect to remote hosts, it won't be able to send any of its queued mail. You'll generally be able to tell whether the problem is on your end or the remote end; if it's you, some or all of your outbound mail won't leave your servers. If the remote end is the problem, you'll notice that mail to a particular domain fails but mail to other domains gets through.

There are actually two separate types of IMS name resolution problems. One type happens when you're using the DNS and routing your own mail; the other happens when you're using a smart host and letting your IMS route through it. Let's deal with DNS problems first:

- Verify that the other site has valid MX and A records. You can do this with `nslookup` by giving it the `set type=MX` or `set type=A` commands before typing the server name you're looking for.

- Make sure you can resolve the remote domain; if you can't, test another DNS server to see whether you can resolve the domain with it instead.

- If you're seeing bounces to a particular domain, make sure that the domain name exists and that the failed messages are properly addressed. For example, it's relatively easy to misspell my last name, so mail to *paul@robicheaux. net* will bounce even though it looks right to most people.

- Use the `restest` utility (it's on the Exchange CD in the *server\support* directory) to duplicate the IMS name resolution process.

You should also verify that your direct or RAS connection to the Internet is working, and that you can successfully establish an SMTP connection to the outside world.

If your mail is routed through a smart host, you must ascertain whether your IMS can look up the smart host's address and establish a connection to it; you should also verify that the routing host hasn't been renamed or given a new IP address. Make sure to distinguish trouble that occurs when your IMS can't deliver to the smart host from trouble that occurs when the smart host can't route and deliver the message.

Fixing incoming failures

The most common causes of inbound mail failures with the IMS are easy to find and fix:

- You must have a DNS MX record for your domain that points to your Exchange server, along with a corresponding A record. If you don't, outside hosts won't be able to find where you want mail sent.

- Make sure you've configured the IMS to accept messages from the domain that's trying to send you mail.

- The IMS must be set to accept incoming mail, not to "Outbound only" or "Flush queues."

- The object you're trying to send mail to must have an SMTP address in the directory. While this seems obvious, sometimes people remove, change, or forget to add SMTP addresses for mailboxes or DLs, then wonder why they can't send to them.

The nature of SMTP routing means that some incoming failures will be transient. For example, while writing this chapter, I wanted to answer a question that a reader had mailed me, but mail to his site was bouncing because a recent change to his DNS records hadn't propagated to me. The next morning, the mail went through normally.

Removing corrupt messages

When the IMS gets a message that's not formatted according to its expectations, it normally quarantines the message in a folder named *Bad* in the IMS's mailbox, and that's the end of it. Depending on what's wrong with the message format, though, the IMS may fail while trying to parse it. Though Microsoft tries to make the IMS robust, it's impossible to anticipate every type of creative misformatting that Internet mail clients and servers can generate.

When the IMS sees a misformatted message, it will generate one of two events in the event log. Event ID 4116 means that the IMS found a bad message while processing items from its internal queue, so it stored a copy of the faulty message in the *Bad* folder. Event 4117 means that the IMS noticed that the message was bad during its SMTP conversation with another server.

Whenever you see one of these events, it's a sign that there's a bad message in your IMS queue. Unfortunately, there's no way to identify exactly which message is at fault. You can use a text editor to look at the files in your *imcdata\in* directory, but you have to have a good understanding of the RFCs discussed in Chapter 8, *Managing the Internet Mail Service*, to spot the problems by hand. If you can't find the bad message and manually remove it, you have three choices:

- Stop and restart the IMS, in the hope that it will have better luck processing the malformed message.

- Remove some or all of the files from *imcdata\in* until you get the IMS to restart normally. By trial and error, you can isolate the bad message, as long as there aren't too many messages to test. You can also whack the entire contents of the directory; that will flush the queue and allow the IMS to start, at the expense of losing the queued inbound mail.

- Use the *mdbvu32.exe* utility to peek inside the *Bad* folder and identify the bad message so you can remove it.

This third option is the most flexible way to find out what's wrong, but it's more complicated than the other two. I'm sure you can handle the details of the first two steps, so I won't go into them any further, but mdbvu32 is worth more exposition.

mdbvu32 lives in the *support\utils* directory of your Exchange 5.5 CD. Before you can use it, you have to copy it from the CD and create a MAPI profile that it can use. Microsoft warns against using an existing profile with mdbvu32, so you have two choices: you can use the profinst utility, or you can copy an existing registry profile by creating a new key, saving an existing profile, and loading the new profile into another key. The following list gives the steps for using profinst.

 If you're just investigating, stop the IMS before you start poking around in the *Bad* folder. If you're following these steps because your IMS is stopped, you're okay.

---

1. Log on to the server where the problem IMS is installed. You can log on as an Exchange administrator, but I recommend logging on as the site service account to make sure you have adequate permission to do what you need to do.

2. Run profinst, which takes three parameters: the name of the MAPI service you want to use, the name of the profile, and the profile type. Since mdbvu32 requires a gateway profile, that's the kind you'll need to create. Here's a sample that creates a profile named DebugIMS:

   ```
   profinst /service=MSExchangeIMC /name=DebugIMS /type=gateway
   ```

   You only need to do this step once; keep the profile around when you're done, in case you need it in the future.

3. Start mdbvu32. When its logon dialog appears, as shown in Figure 15-3, select the MAPI_EXPLICIT_PROFILE checkbox, but leave the others alone.

4. Once you've filled out this dialog, mdbvu32 will pop up the standard profile selection dialog. Pick the debugging profile you just created. Nothing exciting happens when you do; all of mdbvu32's goodies are hidden in its menus.

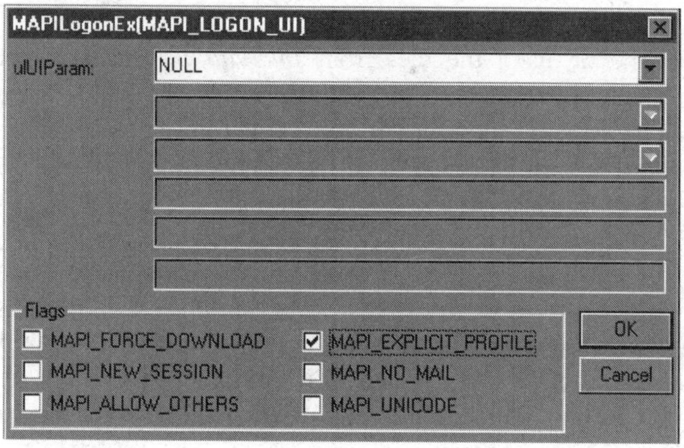

MAPILogonEx(MAPI_LOGON_UI)   ☒

ulUIParam: NULL   ▼

                                                                       ▼

                                                                       ▼

Flags
☐ MAPI_FORCE_DOWNLOAD   ☑ MAPI_EXPLICIT_PROFILE   OK
☐ MAPI_NEW_SESSION   ☐ MAPI_NO_MAIL   Cancel
☐ MAPI_ALLOW_OTHERS   ☐ MAPI_UNICODE

Figure 15-3. The mdbvu32 startup screen

5. Use the MDB → Open Message Store... command. It will ask you whether to open the private store or the public store; you need to open the private store. You'll then be back at the blank and uninteresting mdbvu32 root window.

6. Use the MDB → Open Root Folder command. You'll see a window like the one in Figure 15-4. The Child Folders list shows you all folders inside the mailbox you have open, while the "Messages in Folder" and "Associated Messages in Fld" lists show you child items of the selected child folder.

   By double-clicking a child folder, you can open a separate window that shows messages inside the folder. In your case, you'll want to double-click the *Bad* folder, after which you'll see a list of the messages in that folder.

7. The "Operations available" pull-down lets you select what you want done to the selected message. You can choose lpFld → OpenMessages() to open the selected message and see what's in it, which will hopefully clue you in to what's wrong with the message. If you choose lpFld → DeleteMessages() instead, you can delete the selected message. No matter what command you choose, nothing happens until you click the Call Function... button, but once you do, action is immediate.

Make sure you don't delete any folders in the mailbox, even though mdbvu32 will happily allow this.

8. Log off with the Session → Log Off... command.

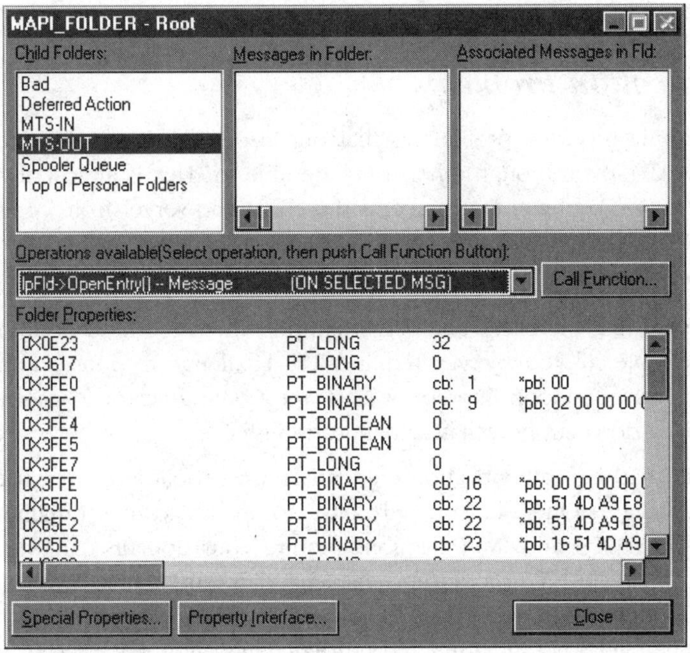

Figure 15-4. The Root folder of the IMS mailbox

Troubleshooting Internet Protocols

The Exchange IMail protocol engine, discussed in Chapter 8, acts as a conduit between the IS and clients that use the NNTP, POP3, and IMAP4 protocols. In addition, the INS uses the NNTP protocol on its own (its interfaces don't use the IMail engine). In general, the troubleshooting process for these protocols varies a little from what you've seen earlier in the chapter. That's because the client is often at fault; the Internet protocols Exchange supports are defined by RFCs, but client and server developers don't always interpret the RFCs in the same way. This leads to subtle (and sometimes blatant) incompatibilities between Microsoft and non-Microsoft clients and servers.

The first thing I recommend when a user reports an Internet protocol-related problem is to make sure they're using a client that works properly with your configuration. It's easy to isolate problems by trying a different client and seeing whether the problem recurs with that client. If the problem recurs, it's probably not the client's fault. If it doesn't, it's most likely to be something about the client's interaction with Exchange that's causing the trouble. It's not uncommon to see differences in client behavior depending on the exact revision of the client. Internet

Explorer 4.01 with SP1 is different from plain old IE 4.01, and IE 5 is a totally different animal.

Authentication Problems

One commonly reported problem is that one user can't log on to get mail with POP3 or IMAP4, even though other users are able to. This is almost always due to an authentication problem that prevents the client and server from communicating correctly. You'll know that's the problem if users can log on and get mail with OWA or Outlook, but not with their POP3/IMAP4 client. Here's what to check:

1. Make sure that the client and server support the same kind of authentication. For example, if your server requires NT challenge/response authentication, you can't use Outlook Express or Netscape Communicator to get mail from it, since they don't support that authentication type.

2. Be sure that the authentication credentials are supplied in the proper format. When you use Outlook, you only have to specify your username and password, but POP3 and IMAP4 logons require your domain name and mailbox alias, too (if the NT account and alias are different). For example, to use my Palm III to pick up mail from my server I have to use *ra\paulr\paul* as my username. Since not all POP3 and IMAP4 clients allow backslashes in user credentials, you can use either forward slashes or backslashes; Exchange doesn't care.

3. If you're using a multiserver site, make sure your users are connecting to the proper home server.

 You can use NT's built-in `telnet` utility, along with the port numbers for POP3, IMAP4, NNTP, and SMTP traffic, to do some basic troubleshooting. If you can successfully establish a connection from the client's machine to the Exchange server, you can rule out any network-related problems, and you can check authentication with the appropriate commands.

Troubleshooting NNTP Problems

There are two kinds of NNTP problems: problems involving the INS's communication with other systems, and problems with NNTP clients that are trying to talk to the IS. The latter are rare, since the wide variety of Unix NNTP servers means that client developers have to be pretty good about adhering to the letter of the RFCs. Authentication problems with NNTP are common, though, so if you've turned on NNTP authentication don't forget to check there.

Enabling NNTP protocol logging

If your INS refuses to talk to another NNTP server, you can turn on diagnostic logging for the INS by editing a registry value. Although other components expose diagnostic logging in a handy tab, this is the only way to change the logging level. Set the value of the `NNTP protocol logging level` value under the `HKLM\SYSTEM\CurrentControlSet\Services\MSExchangeIS\ParametersSystem` key. A value of 0 tells the INS not to log anything; values from 1 to 4 correspond to the range of log settings from minimum to maximum.

You can also adjust the location of the log file by editing the `NNTP Protocol Log Path` value under the same `ParametersSystem` key you just saw.

NNTP clients receive "502 no permission" errors

Authentication is usually to blame for this class of problems. If you allow anonymous access, you won't ever have this problem; if you require authentication, these problems usually occur when your users try to use the news server anonymously or mistype their credentials. To prove that this is the problem, you can `telnet` to port 119 of the Exchange server, then use the `AUTHINFO` command combined with the account name, mailbox alias name, and password to see if you can get permission for access:

```
AUTHINFO domain\account\alias password
```

"502 no permission" errors when talking to remote NNTP servers

When attempting to do a newsfeed transfer to a remote Usenet provider, you may receive the same kind of error message, indicating that the remote server doesn't accept your credentials. This is usually because your news service provider has set restrictions on which IP addresses are allowed to access its news server. If your machine is not included in their access list, the remote server may refuse to talk to you. To fix this, make sure that your server's IP address is correctly registered with your Usenet provider.

Event ID 1165 in the application log

Heavy NNTP client loads may trigger the IS to register event ID 1165 in the event log. This event number indicates that the IS does not have enough database sessions for the threads in the store process that are serving the clients; this adversely affects performance of the Exchange server as a whole, since it has to wait for database access. You can adjust the number of sessions the IS makes available to clients by adding a new `REG_DWORD` value called `Sessions` to the `HKLM\SYSTEM\CurrentControlSet\Services\MSExchangeIS\ParametersPublic\` subkey. The value you specify here is interrelated with two other registry settings that control the total number of threads available to the IS (see the section "The most important settings" in Chapter 18 for more details). You can calculate the optimum number of sessions as follows:

```
Sessions = (((maxThreads * 3)/4 + backgroundThreads) * 3)/5 + 1
```

The default value for **maxThreads** is 20 and the default for **backgroundThreads** is 25, but the actual values may differ; if you've run Performance Optimizer, it may have replaced the defaults with its own calculated values. Once you've altered the Sessions value, stop and restart the IS. If you still get 1165 events in your event log, you can gradually adjust the session count upward, being careful not to exceed the number of threads allocated by the other thread values.

Slow response for NNTP clients

If your NNTP users complain that things are slowing down, there are a couple of adjustments you can consider. The first is to increase the number of threads the IS can spawn; when clients have to wait for a thread, that slows them down, so by adding more threads, you improve overall client performance at the expense of other operations. The number of client threads is controlled by the **MaxPoolThreads** value under the `HKLM\SYSTEM\CurrentControlSet\Services\MSExchangeIS\ParametersNetIf` key. You can adjust this value upward in small increments until your user response time reaches an acceptable level.

The other adjustment is a little more complicated. The IS tries to buffer database tables whenever it can; when it can't, it keeps tables open to speed subsequent accesses to the table data. If you increase the number of tables that the IS can keep open, that speeds access to newsgroup data, but it costs you some buffer space. Every eight open tables take up the same amount of space as one buffer. The two keys you can adjust are both stored in the `MSExchangeIS\ParametersSystem` subkey; the **Preferred max open tables** value controls the number of open tables, and the **Max buffers** key controls the number of open buffers. Every time you increase the number of open tables by eight, be sure to decrement the buffer value by one. How do you know where to set the number of tables? You should increase it to somewhere above the number of active newsgroups you carry, since each newsgroup requires more than one open table. You'll probably have to experiment to find the optimal balance between the number of open tables and buffers, since buffering speeds some operations.

Troubleshooting POP3 and IMAP4

If you find that authentication isn't the problem with your POP3 or IMAP4 connection, and if you can successfully use `telnet` to make a connection from the client machine to the server, you can turn on diagnostic logging for the protocols and look over the logs that the IS generates. The registry keys that control diagnostic logging are located in the `HKLM\SYSTEM\CurrentControlSet\Services\`

`MSExchangeIS\ParametersSystem` key: `POP3_Protocol_Logging_Level` is a `REG_DWORD` whose value (from 1–4) sets the logging level, and `IMAP4_Protocol_Logging_Level` does the same for IMAP. In addition, you can control where the log files for these protocols are written by modifying the `POP3_Protocol_LogPath` or `IMAP4_Protocol_LogPath` values (both `REG_SZ`s).

The log files themselves contain information about the back-and-forth negotiation between the client and the server; you can review them to see which end is generating the error that's stopping your mail from flowing.

Troubleshooting Outlook Web Access

OWA has gained a reputation for being unstable and a resource hog. While early versions probably deserved these labels, the version shipped with Exchange 5.5 SP2 is pretty solid, provided you've installed NT 4.0 SP4 and the IIS 4.0 hotfixes. That doesn't mean it's problem-free, though.

The first and best suggestion I can make for OWA troubleshooting is actually a preventative step: put OWA on its own server, with or without IIS 4.0. That way, if you do have problems, you can restart the server or make other changes as needed, without affecting anyone's stored mail, while preserving mail access for non-OWA users.

The dreaded "Failed to Get Inbox" message

OWA says "Failed to Get Inbox" anytime it can't log on to a specific mailbox. This may be because the user has mistyped her credentials, or it may be because something else is wrong; unfortunately, the error message doesn't tell you specifically what's wrong. There are some basic things to check, though:

- All the accounts you want to have OWA access must have "Log on locally" right on the machine where OWA is running.

- If OWA is running on a member server (e.g., it's not a PDC or BDC), users who authenticate to that OWA machine have to enter the domain name with their username in the OWA logon page (using, say, *RA\paulr* instead of just *paulr*). This is because IIS only checks the local account database unless you provide a domain for it to check.

- OWA can't handle mailbox aliases that contain spaces; you'll have to rename them.

- If you have your IIS server set up to use NT challenge/response authentication, remember that only Internet Explorer for Windows supports that type of authentication. Macintosh, Unix, and other platform users can only use basic authentication, even if they're running Internet Explorer.

Microsoft recommends using SSL as part of IIS to provide adequate security for OWA logons. If you don't want to pay VeriSign their $350/year to get a server SSL certificate, try visiting Thawte (*www.thawte.com*), since they charge less money for the same service. Their certificates are perfectly good for use with OWA; in fact, you can just generate your own with the IIS 4.0 certificate server if you don't need a certificate that outside entities can verify.

- Verify that the problem account has permission to use the Exchange mailbox the user is trying to log on to.

- Verify that the problem account can successfully log on to OWA when running from the IIS server. If it can't, it's most likely that the username and password are wrong.

- If your user is using Windows 95/98, try logging on from another machine or switch to a different browser on the same machine. If either switch succeeds, delete the user's cached password (PWL) file, log off, and log back on to force Windows to create a new file.

File permissions and security

Outlook Web Access creates a variety of temporary files and requires MAPI DLLs that a normal IIS machine doesn't require. For example, OWA creates temporary MAPI message files for each user who logs in; by default, these files will be created in the Windows NT system directory. A competently secured installation of NT will have ACLs set on the system directory, so ordinary users can't write to it, and users won't be able to get or send mail via OWA. To fix this, you'll need to specify an alternate location for the temporary files:

1. Using your favorite registry editor, open the `HKLM\Software\Microsoft\Windows Messaging Subsystem` key.

2. Add a `REG_SZ` value named `ProfileDirectory`, then set its value to the directory where you want the temporary files to go. Note that the Authenticated Users group and whatever account you've specified as the IIS anonymous user should have write permission to whatever directory you name here.

I can't quote any hard and fast rules for securing OWA's installation, because OWA installs files throughout the NT system hierarchy. I recommend that you install it, reapply the permissions you had set before the installation, and see whether OWA works. If it does, try adjusting the permissions to be slightly more restrictive; if it doesn't, loosen them up some. Your goal should be to get the most restrictive permissions possible.

Troubleshooting Client Problems

Client problems are funny, because most users assume that anything that goes wrong is a server problem. It's hard to separate legitimate problems from user-education problems. For example, Outlook has a rich set of tools for building customized views. You can build views to sort and categorize your mail, but if you turn on the "only show unread mail" view, all your read mail seems to disappear! I can't count the number of times users have asked me, "Where'd all my mail go?" The first principle of client troubleshooting: educate your users about the features of their mail clients and teach them whatever else you can that will lighten your support burden.

Genuine Client Problems

There are a number of legitimate client problems you'll probably run across; let's start with those.

Using the Inbox Repair tool

Occasionally, problems including sluggishness and instability in an Outlook system running a Personal Folders file can be traced to corruption in that file. Running the Inbox Repair tool, *scanpst.exe* (found under the System Tools group in the Accessories item in your Programs group on the Start menu), can be an easy way to verify, and sometimes restore, the integrity of the PST file. When you use this tool, it's best to run it several times on the PST file in question; sometimes the second or third run will detect problems that eluded the utility on the first run.

Fixing a corrupted OST

If you end up with a corrupted or damaged OST file, consider it disposable. Assuming there's nothing wrong with your Exchange mailbox itself, it's usually faster and easier to just delete your OST file, create a new one, and resynchronize from your mailbox. Try this procedure:

1. Open the Microsoft Exchange Service properties dialog and disable offline mode for your client.

2. Find your OST file and delete it.

3. Reopen Outlook, then go back to the Microsoft Exchange Service properties form and reenable offline mode. Outlook will ask you to confirm that you want to create a new OST file.

4. Synchronize your mailbox as usual. Keep in mind that since it has to completely repopulate an empty OST file, this may take a little longer than usual.

Recovering a damaged Exchange mailbox with an OST file

Here's a little-known fact: you can use an OST file to restore a damaged or accidentally deleted Exchange mailbox, as long as you haven't changed the profile for that mailbox. To accomplish this very handy feat, start Outlook in offline mode, then export all of your folders from the OST file into a new PST file. Once you've done so, you can reload your mailbox from a backup (or create a new mailbox) and import the PST file's contents into the new mailbox.

Stopping a runaway client

In general, it's not a good idea to shut down Outlook by killing its process, but sometimes you have to. When you forcibly shut down Outlook with the Task Manager (brought to you by the Ctrl-Alt-Del key combination), it's not guaranteed to properly close all connections to the server or its MAPI sessions; the problem seems to be worse under Win9x than under NT. This can cause later problems if you try to relaunch Outlook before your next reboot. One way to reduce the odds of having problems is to kill off the MAPI spooler process, *mapisp32.exe*, before attempting to relaunch Outlook; the other way is to reboot your machine.

Frozen clients

Outlook is very tightly integrated with Internet Explorer. That's good and bad: Outlook has many of the capabilities of IE, but if you install a version of IE that's not known to work with your version of Outlook, you may notice that your Outlook client session seems to freeze while IE is doing something intensive like starting Java or an ActiveX control. Be sure that you install matching versions of IE and Outlook. I strongly caution my clients against installing beta versions of IE on their production machines for precisely this reason.

Mail sticks in the outbox

When you send a message with the MAPI version of Outlook, Outlook actually hands it off to the MAPI spooler, *mapisp32.exe*. At that point, Outlook considers its job done; the spooler is responsible for delivering it to the IS, which in turn handles further routing of the message, as described in Chapters 1 and 2. The first thing I usually check when users say their mail is stuck is that their local copy of *mapisp32* is running and that they haven't recently force-quit Outlook.

If the spooler is running, the next thing to check is the addressees on the message. If one of the addressees is a type that Outlook can't deliver (say, a fax addressee using a local fax transport like AtWork), the message will stick until Outlook can resolve and deliver to all the addressees. If the message is addressed to a DL, the MTA must be running on the server, or it can't expand the DL and the mail will just sit there.

There's another common cause: if a user is working offline, and opens an item in the *Outbox* folder then closes it again, the mail will be held in the outbox. The proper procedure is to open the message and hit the send button, not to close the message again. Of course, users who are working in offline mode won't be able to send mail; new messages they create will stay in the outbox until those users go back to online mode.

It's a Feature

In contrast to the legitimate problems you will be called on to solve, some problems users report aren't real problems, but misunderstandings of how things work. If you're aware of potential misunderstandings and ready to deal with them, you'll be better prepared for the inevitable requests to solve these un-problems.

Understanding message recall

Imagine being able to retract a message you accidentally sent to the wrong person, or one written in the heat of anger. The idea behind message recall is great: it's designed to let you recall a message that you sent so recipients who haven't yet seen it won't see it. The implementation, though, leaves something to be desired. Recall only works under the best of circumstances: if the recipient is logged in and hasn't read or moved the message, the recall will work. However, if you try to recall a message when the recipient is not logged in, when they log on later, they're likely to find in their inbox not only your original message, but also an automated message indicating the recall request. If your recipient is anything like me, the first thing they'll do when they see the recall request is open the message you were trying to recall to see what was so scandalous that someone didn't want you to see it! There's no good workaround for this problem, other than to tell your users to think twice before sending mail.

Mystery floppy access

Sometimes users will complain that Outlook is accessing their floppy drive for no good reason. There are a few possibilities to check here:

- Check the PST and PAB services to make sure Outlook doesn't think that there's a PST or PAB file on the floppy drive.

- Check the AutoArchive settings (with the Tools → Options → Other → AutoArchive command) and make sure that Outlook doesn't think the archive file is on a floppy.

Removing PST passwords

PST files can have their own passwords; however, users tend to forget them. In the old days, losing a PST password meant the user was out of luck. Officially,

Microsoft still says that there's no supported way to unprotect a PST file. Unofficially, you can use the *pstupg19.exe* tool (to find it, try doing an AltaVista or Excite websearch). This program strips the password from a PST file, leaving it unprotected. You can also check out vendors like Access Data (*www.accessdata.com*) and Passware (*www.lostpassword.com*) if you want a supported solution.

Excessive prompting for passwords

If your users complain that they're being asked to enter logon credentials every time Outlook starts, Exchange doesn't recognize the credentials it's getting from Outlook and is asking for a new set. Here are the two most common reasons this happens:

The user mistyped their password during their initial logon
> If you mistype your password the first time, Win95 tells you of the error and prompts you to correct it. You then type your password correctly and are granted access to the system. For some reason, however, Exchange doesn't recognize the corrected password and still will prompt you to confirm your identity. The solution is to be very careful logging on so that you don't mistype your password.

You have Logon Network Security set to None
> While this is occasionally helpful, it introduces the requirement of providing credentials every time you launch Outlook. Go to the Advanced tab of the Microsoft Exchange Service properties dialog, then make sure that Logon Network Security is set to NT Password Authentication.

My mail is gone!

Outlook has a ton of shortcuts and ways to move and delete messages, which make it awfully easy to do something accidentally with a message. I'm sure that I'm not the only administrator who's found stray messages dropped into public folders, for example.

Sometimes your users will contact you and tell you that an important message is missing. Oftentimes, the user will admit to having seen the message recently. If possible, it may be worth asking them to reconstruct what they were doing. With their permission, you may want to open their mailbox, either in their office or while you're talking to them on the phone, and see if you can find the message somewhere. Use Outlook's Advanced Find feature (right-click on the Outlook Today object in Outlook and you'll see the command) to search for any text that the user can remember. You should also search their local hard drive for the MSG files that Outlook creates when users save a message to disk.

Finding hidden messages

Sometimes lost mail hasn't really been lost or moved—it's hidden. Outlook makes it easy to instantly make some or all of your mail disappear, leading to an inordinate number of frantic help desk calls. For example, clicking on one of the headers at the top of the mail window makes Outlook sort by that field, meaning that mail you just saw can suddenly move elsewhere in the inbox. Outlook's canned views and filters are also a rich source of potential misbehavior; for example, with a few clicks you can hide all mail older than seven days, all mail you've already read, or any number of other variations.

You may also find the user has created rules with the Inbox Assistant or the Rules Wizard that automatically process incoming messages, perhaps deleting some messages or moving them to a subfolder.

Having the date and time set wrong on a client system will have all kinds of odd effects, including unusual timestamps on messages in the receiving user's folder.

Using alternate clients

One approach to resolving problem behavior or data in a mailbox is to access the mailbox from another client. This may allow you to delete a problem message, find out where something has gone, and so on. For example, there's a flaw in Outlook that sometimes causes it to go crazy and present hundreds of calendar reminders at once. (Hint: don't set your system clock forward for Y2K testing unless you want all your reminders to go off at once.)

In general, anytime you encounter a problem that occurs only with one mailbox the quickest way to pinpoint the problem is to test that mailbox with another client. For example, Microsoft recommends using the Exchange/Windows Messaging client (*exchng32.exe*) to troubleshoot profile and rule problems; if the problem occurs on both Outlook and Windows Messaging, it's not a problem with the client installation or configuration.

16

Exchange Security

To keep your secret is wisdom;
but to expect others to keep it is folly.
—Oliver Wendell Holmes,
Chief Justice of the U.S. Supreme Court

Way back in Chapter 2, *Exchange Architecture*, I discussed some fundamentals of Exchange's security architecture, promising that they'd be covered in more detail later in the book. This chapter will delve into the process of securing your Exchange server, its mail traffic, and its stored mail against disruption, destruction, and eavesdropping.

Understanding Exchange Security

Windows NT was designed with integrated security controls. These controls allow resource owners and administrators to limit who can use objects in the system; the corresponding auditing mechanism provides an evidentiary trail showing who did what when. Exchange builds on this access control and auditing framework by providing its own controls. One point is worth reiterating: Exchange permissions and NT permissions are totally distinct. For example, accounts in NT's Domain Admins built-in group don't have permission to modify Exchange objects unless you manually grant that group permissions on the appropriate containers.

Access Controls

Exchange access controls are enforced by the IS for mailboxes and public folders and by the DS for other objects. You specify these controls with the Permissions tab on each individual object. It's critical to remember that objects inherit permissions from the parent containers; if you look at the Permissions tab of a typical directory object, you'll see that the site Configuration container and the organization object may have contributed permissions over and above what you've manually specified. For example, a quick check of the NNTP Site Defaults object shows that the service account has the Service Account Admin right and my administrators domain group has the Permissions Admin right, both of which were inherited from the site Configuration object.

In practice, this means that you must be very careful about who has permissions on three objects: the organization container, the site container, and individual server containers. By default, a new install of Exchange will grant permissions on these containers to two accounts: the account you used to install Exchange will have Permissions Admin rights, and the service account will have Service Account Admin rights.

If you use the "Display rights for roles on Permissions page" checkbox in the Permissions tab of the Exchange Administrator options dialog, you can see that there are individual rights assigned to each role. These rights are listed back in Table 2-1; by customizing the roles you assign to individual accounts, you can selectively grant some accounts the permissions you want them to have. For example, you could assign a mailbox Send As permission on a DL, or grant someone you trust to manage DL settings Permissions Admin rights to that DL and nothing else.

Connection Security

Connection security means that you maintain good control over whom your systems talk to and how they communicate. Accordingly, most connection security concerns revolve around your Exchange servers' connections to computers outside your organization:

Do I allow any unnecessary connections from outside?
Do you have your IMS and INS configured properly? If you want to allow anonymous connections to your DS, have you created a new account with limited privileges and assigned it as the DS and LDAP anonymous account? If you're allowing anonymous access to NNTP, did you mean to?

Are my connections using appropriate authentication?
The IS, IMS, and INS allow you to specify particular authentication methods for clients and servers who want to connect and exchange data with your servers. At a minimum, you should allow both clear-text and NT challenge/response authentication so that clients can use challenge/response authentication if they are able to. If you're using the INS to feed news to other providers, make sure they have authentication credentials.

Am I using SSL and IPsec where appropriate?

Protecting your connections against hijacking and eavesdropping is part of connection security. SSL imposes a performance penalty, but it provides good authentication, so I recommend that you make it available to OWA and NNTP users.

Resource Security

Resource security means that the resources on your Exchange server are available only to those people authorized to use them. This security category covers spam-proofing your servers (see Chapter 8, *Managing the Internet Mail Service*), protecting your servers and clients against viruses (discussed later in this chapter), making good backups (see Chapter 17, *Recovery and Repair*), maintaining good physical security procedures, and any other measures that protect the availability and integrity of your data.

In general, a good Exchange resource security plan will answer several questions:

Is my server adequately protected against physical damage, tampering, or theft?

A surprising number of sites leave their Exchange servers sitting next to someone's desk, where practically anyone can spill a diet Coke on them, kick out the power cord, or take them out of the building. I'm not going to discuss physical security here, but it's worth thinking about. A server that gets flooded, zapped by lightning, or stolen won't provide good service to your users.

Is my server adequately protected against data loss due to hardware failure?

In particular, do I have an adequate backup plan, and am I confident that my backup tapes actually have usable data on them? Do I know how to restore my server from my backup tapes? Have I ever tried to do it?

Is my server protected against unauthorized access?

Do you have good, hard-to-guess passwords on key accounts? Have you limited the number of accounts that have administrative access to your servers to the minimum number necessary? If you're connected to the Internet, have you used the spam controls discussed in Chapter 8 to keep from being a relay host?

Have I been keeping up with service packs for NT and Exchange?

NT 4.0 SP4 has a ton of security-related fixes, as does Exchange 5.5 SP2. If you don't have both of these (or their successors) installed, you should. In addition, you should make regular visits to Microsoft's security web site (*www. microsoft.com/security/*) to keep apprised of new patches and updates.

Am I practicing good security hygiene?

At a minimum, you should be following the guidelines given in this section so that you have good control over permissions, good connection security, and appropriate use of advanced security.

Common Exchange Security Mistakes

A number of security mistakes are so common they're worth mentioning here. I can't guarantee that not making these mistakes (or fixing them, if you've already made them) will make your installation 100% secure, but I can promise that your overall security setup will improve if you follow the recommendations and avoid the pitfalls in this section.

Not securing Windows NT adequately

If you don't secure the underlying operating system, Exchange will still apply its own security measures, but their usefulness may be reduced. After all, if the service account or administrator passwords are compromised, an attacker can gain full access to your Exchange server, and there are documented cases where a poorly secured NT installation has allowed crackers to access and modify Exchange servers. While a complete treatment of Windows NT security is outside the scope of this book, here are the minimum measures you or whoever handles your NT security should take:

- If you're on the Internet, make sure your NT machines are behind a properly configured firewall. A number of easy attacks can greatly speed up the compromise of Internet-connected machines; all of these can be blocked by proper firewalling.

- Protect your administrator account credentials. Don't give more access than necessary, especially on your Exchange servers.

- Keep up with security patches and hotfixes. Spend some time every week surfing NT security sites like Bugtraq (*www.ntbugtraq.com*) to keep current with what's going on.

- Protect access to your emergency repair disks and backup tapes, as well as to your servers. An attacker who can get any of these can get an unencrypted copy of the SAM database, which can easily be cracked by password crackers. Consider using the `syskey` protection utility built into NT 4.0 SP3 and later. I covered these issues at length in Chapter 8 of *Managing the Windows NT Registry* (O'Reilly & Associates).

Installing Exchange with the wrong account

The account you use to install Exchange gets permission on the site and organization containers, meaning that it ends up with access to most of the objects in the configuration tree. Although Exchange Setup requires an account with Administrator permission, don't use your primary administrative account to install it; use a secondary account instead. Name it something like *ExchangeAdmin*, then limit access to those folks who need it. If you've already installed Exchange with an inappropriate account, you can always fix it by changing the site, organization, and Configuration container permissions.

Losing or changing the service account password

The service account is critical, since all the Exchange services use it to authenticate themselves to NT. If you lose the password and can't recover it, you'll have to change the service account password on all servers in your site, and possibly in other sites, if you're using a single common domain to provide the account credentials. Sometimes the password will get changed out from under you, usually by a well-meaning but undertrained administrator. You'll know when this happens because your services won't start after a reboot.

> If you use the User Manager for Domains to turn on auditing for security policy changes (use the Policies → Auditing... command), the event log will reflect password changes. You'll be able to see that the service account password was changed—just look for event ID X.

If you lose the service account password, you'll have to change it, using the steps in the section "Changing the service account password" in Chapter 14, *Managing Exchange Servers*. If someone accidentally changes the password, you're in the same boat. One way to protect your password: write it down, seal it in an envelope, sign the envelope's sides and flaps (so you can see if it's been opened), then lock it up where it can be recovered in case of emergency.

Losing the KMS password

There are actually two kinds of passwords you need to keep track of. The first is that long string of letters and numbers (my old one was "PGZEWRXZSABJWSQ") that the KMS requires at startup. The second kind is passwords you assign to individual KMS administrators to do things like enroll new users or revoke certificates. If you lose the KMS startup password, you're hosed; there's no way to recover its data, so you have to remove it, reinstall it, and reenroll all your users. You might consider the sealed-envelope solution for your KMS startup password, even if you're using the floppy-storage option.

Compromising the KMS or service account passwords

If your KMS password is compromised, an attacker can issue new security keys or revoke existing ones. If the service account password is compromised, an attacker can do just about anything else. Protect those passwords! Make them hard to guess; use the NT 4.0 SP3 *passfilt.dll* to enforce password checking, and don't give passwords out unnecessarily.

Forgetting to turn off SMTP relaying

If you leave relaying turned on, your server will eventually be used as a spam relay. The cretins who use spam as a marketing tool continually scan blocks of IP addresses looking for servers that have relaying capability. While spam may not seem like a security problem, the flood of mail you'll get after your server is used to send spam out to the world can overwhelm your connection—assuming complaints to your upstream ISP don't get your connection cut off first. Stopping spam is a good thing to do, both for your own good and for the Internet community.

Inadequate backups

You must have good backups of your Exchange databases, period. The repair tools you'll learn about in Chapter 17 can help restore your database files in some circumstances, but you're much better off if you can restore your databases and log files from tape than if you have to cross your fingers and pray that the recovery tools will do the job. If your store is too big to allow you to make backups on a regular schedule, split its data onto multiple servers and back them up separately.

Security Policy and the Wonderful World of Jurisprudence

The subject of how much access employers legally have to employee email messages is a very sticky one, and it has not yet been fully settled by U.S. law. (Note that I am not an attorney; nothing I say in this section is legal advice in the U.S. or anywhere else, and I am not familiar enough with law or custom outside the U.S. to say anything coherent about it.) On one end of the spectrum, some employers insist that any traffic carried on their system—whether it's a note to your boss, your wife, or your mom—is their property and subject to their inspection at any time. The other end points out (rightly, in my layman's opinion) that if the company doesn't tell you they're going to inspect your mail then they have no legal right to do so. Of course, there are all sorts of intermediate positions; I once worked for a NASA contractor that kept email and phone calls private, but would open any postal mail sent to company facilities. On the other hand, my most recent employer had only two firing offenses: discussing your salary with others and attempting to read other people's mail.

One of the key tests seems to be whether employees have a "reasonable expectation of privacy" when they use a company email system. Some aspects of your security policy, like whether you support S/MIME and whether users have been told that their mail may be monitored, can influence whether employees have this expectation; that's why this section is here instead at the end of the chapter.

Inspecting Mail for Legal Reasons

Let me start with a suggestion: never look at anyone's mail unless you are forced to. When I say "forced," that's what I mean. Never accept a verbal request to "glance at" someone's mail. If your manager, or some other agent of your employer, requires you to look at the contents of someone's mailbox, get it in writing. Once you have written direction, don't ever do the job in private. Make sure that a representative of the company (ideally, someone who is legally responsible at the company, like the general counsel or a corporate officer) is present. If you're being asked to inspect a mailbox because of pending or current legal action, make sure that an attorney for the other side is present, so there can't be any later distortion of what happened. Consider having the whole thing videotaped.

This may sound terribly paranoid, but it's not. The question you should be asking isn't whether your company has the legal right to look at mail or not; it's whether your company will defend your actions in a court of law, and whether any third parties may be able to take issue with what you did or how you did it. You need to be able to document what you saw, when you saw it, and who was present at the time—not to protect your employer, but to protect yourself.

Let's take a simple example: suppose your boss comes to you and says she's concerned that someone in another department has been harassing one of her employees. You obediently open up the victim's mailbox, find some mail that looks harassing, and show it to your boss. She manages to get the harasser fired, at which point he files suit for wrongful dismissal, naming you as a codefendant. Feel free to substitute other scenarios: you learn that someone's embezzling, you learn that your company is doing something illegal, you learn that someone's having an affair, or whatever.

Before you shake your head and dismiss the idea of facing legal action, think again: this kind of stuff happens every day in corporate America. You have only to look at the Microsoft trial, or the recent case in which a major Wall Street firm fired several employees for exchanging pornographic pictures in email, to see widely publicized cases where the actions of email administrators have been under scrutiny.

In the course of regular system maintenance, as when looking at the NDRs sent to your Administrator mailbox, you may be exposed to other people's mail. Most companies have an email policy stating that mail may be monitored as an incidental part of regular system maintenance. If your company doesn't have such a policy, consider getting one drafted and approved; it will help protect you from unintended consequences if you see, and report, something you shouldn't have seen.

Complying with discovery requests or subpoenas

What do the Clinton administration, the Bush administration, and Microsoft have in common? I tried to think of a good punch line, but the truth is that they've all suffered legal woes because of their email retention policies. When you're served a subpoena or search warrant, you are legally obligated to produce the records it calls for, to the best of your ability. That doesn't mean you should destroy evidence, but it does mean you can't produce records that you don't have. This argues in favor of having a policy in place to limit the amount of archived email that may come back to haunt you later. Of course, if your company is perfectly ethical, you should keep mail around as long as possible to bolster your defense, if necessary.

Virtually all large companies already have policies that specify how long vital records should be kept, particularly sensitive records like employee performance reviews. Many companies have adapted this policy to email; for example, one large aerospace company has an email policy that requires the deletion of all mail more than 14 days old, period. Again, I'm not providing legal advice. However, it seems prudent to spend some time doing two things: studying how your records retention policy applies to email (if it does), and deciding whether your email system is in compliance. For example, what do you do with old backup tapes? If you allow PST files, are you backing them up somewhere? How confident are you that your Exchange configuration is keeping pace with that policy?

One area that's particularly unclear is whether you (either as an individual or as a corporate entity) can be compelled to decrypt stored email and provide the decrypted version under subpoena. The legal arguments both pro and con seem to be well-reasoned, but in the absence of a court decision, it's safe to say that the topic is unsettled; don't depend on encrypting your email as a defense against having to produce it in a trial.

Adding Disclaimers

For some bizarre reason, one of the most popular questions I see in Exchange discussion lists involves adding an automatic disclaimer at the end of every mail message leaving a site. I'm not sure why this is such a popular idea, since the disclaimers are so vague as to be basically meaningless. Here's a sample (I didn't make it up, but I have removed some identifying information):

> This email is confidential. It may also be privileged or otherwise protected by work product immunity or other legal rules. If you are not the intended recipient please notify the sender IMMEDIATELY, by telephone on XXX XXX XXXX, and delete the message from all locations in your computer; you should not copy the email or use it for any purpose, or disclose its contents to any other person: to do so may be unlawful.

Email is an informal method of communication and is subject to possible data corruption, either accidentally or on purpose. For these reasons it will normally be inappropriate to rely on advice contained in an email without obtaining written confirmation of it.

A list of the names of the partners and their professional qualifications is open to inspection at XXX. The partners are either solicitors or registered foreign lawyers.

Most of the people I see asking about this work for either financial services firms (including brokerage houses and investment bankers) or law firms. Draw your own conclusions. There's not much more to say about this particular topic, because Exchange doesn't support any way to add a global disclaimer. You can force all your clients to put the disclaimer in their signatures, but that's not usually foolproof enough for the people who want this capability. The only way to achieve this result in Exchange 4.0, 5.0, or 5.5 is to use a third-party product like MIMEsweeper (*www.contenttechnologies.com*).

A better solution might be to ask whether having a disclaimer like this really buys you anything. The preceding example says that email is confidential, which it normally isn't, and that you can't rely on it. Does adding a 2KB block of meaningless boilerplate text to every outgoing message actually accomplish anything productive?

 If you absolutely must have disclaimers on Internet mail, there's a tool that can do the trick called the IMS Extension. See *www.dbsinyc.com/DBSI/exchange.htm* for a copy; be forewarned that you can only configure it through the registry.

Scanning and Filtering Mail Content

In Chapter 8, you learned how to use the IMS to protect your users from (some) spam; however, certain sites want more active filtering. In particular, I often see questions about whether it's possible to filter incoming or outgoing mail based on message contents, not just on origin or destination.

The answer is "sure, if you want to spend some more money." Exchange doesn't support any kind of content filtering, but third-party products like MIMEsweeper and Trend Micro's VirusWall can be instructed to block messages that contain specified keywords. By specifying a string of common keywords, you can, in theory, block the majority of inbound spam, and you can use outbound filtering to keep mail about Project Wombat from getting out to your competitors. Most filtering tools can also restrict message attachments, so you could prevent people from sending your users MPEG movies, ActiveX controls, PowerPoint documents,* or whatever else you want to screen out.

These filtering tools are reasonably smart, but they can be fooled, and when you use them you're adding overhead to your IMS, since the filter must run on every incoming or outbound message. If you just want filtering to keep people from mailing off-color jokes to your employees, I think it's reasonable to question whether the resource and purchase costs are worthwhile. On the other hand, your management may insist on it.

Requiring message security

If you want to force all your users to use advanced security on messages they send out to the world, you'll need a different kind of scanner. For example, Network Associates makes a scanner called the PGP Policy Management Agent (PMA; see *www.nai.com/products/security/pma/pma.asp*); you set up your network so that the PMA is designated as your organization's SMTP server, and it scans all outgoing mail to make sure it's signed, encrypted, or both. You can require that mail to particular users or domains be protected in particular ways, and you can use the PMA to provide key recovery if you find that desirable. There are similar products from Worldtalk and other vendors, if you need them.

Using Advanced Security

Exchange's advanced security (AS) has come a long way since its original incarnation. As of Exchange 5.5 SP2, it supports the S/MIME message security standard and X.509 version 3 security certificates, meaning that it can interoperate with S/MIME products from other vendors, at least in theory. The AS system provides end-to-end message protection: messages are digitally signed or encrypted before they leave the client, and they remain protected until the recipient decrypts or verifies them. This is good, since it means that the mail is protected between the time it's sent and the time it's read, including while it's in transit between servers.

How Advanced Security Works

In Chapter 2 I briefly discussed the general steps to get advanced security up and going. Before I move on to a more detailed discussion of those steps, it's important to know how the entire advanced security process works, and what the key components do, so you'll understand what actually happens when you enable advanced security and your users start using it.

---

* Judging by the large number of mind-numbingly dull PowerPoint presentations I've had to sit through, this might be a significant kindness to your users.

You are now in France

France has laws that prohibit the import of any kind of cryptographic software, including S/MIME clients and servers. The U.S. and many other countries have laws that restrict the export of such software. Without getting into a lengthy rant about the absurdity of these laws,* it's time to point out that Microsoft is subject to them. Accordingly, the strength of the cryptography you can use with Exchange advanced security varies according to your location. (Using a form from the BORK, in *\exchange\winnt\i386\security\selfcert.doc,* you may legally export U.S.-strength cryptography on a laptop you take with you and bring back on international trips.)

In the U.S., you can buy, sell, and use any strength cryptography you want; you just can't export it. Because the U.S., Canada, and Mexico have reciprocal trade laws, vendors can sell U.S.-strength cryptography throughout North America, and Microsoft does. However, if you live outside North America, Microsoft can't legally sell you anything stronger than 40-bit RC2-40 or 64-bit CAST, which are the weak for-export algorithms included in Exchange Server.

Why is this stuff important? Exchange implements the actual cryptography modules on the client, not on the server. You can tell the server what key length and algorithms you want it to use for clients inside North America and for those outside. If you manage to get a North American client out of the country (it's illegal, but possible), the server doesn't know the difference. In practical terms, this means you have to be careful when you order or download Exchange, Outlook products, or service packs. For example, there are two separate versions of the SP2 CD. You might wonder why this is so: since cryptography is implemented on the client, why have two different versions of the server? The answer is that the SP CDs include a separate client CD.

If you're in North America, order, install, and use only the North American versions. Be careful when installing service packs, since the downloadable clients always have low security. If you're using the high-security versions, update them only with high-security versions of the service packs, whether for NT, Exchange, or the client.

One more thing: the reason for this section's title is that Peter Gutmann, a noted cryptographer, devised an attack to lower the security of Windows NT's built-in cryptography. The Microsoft CryptoAPI modules check the locale information maintained by NT to see what services to offer. It turned out that writing a small program that silently reset the locale to French also made CryptoAPI dumb down to 40-bit cryptography. That's been fixed, but it was too good a title to pass up.

---

* See the Electronic Frontier Foundation's *Cracking DES* (O'Reilly & Associates) if you want more details on these laws and how they obstruct legitimate commerce while doing little of use.

Public, private, and bulk keys

There are three types of keys involved in advanced security. The section "Exchange Advanced Security" in Chapter 2 explained a bit about private and public keys, but more detail might be helpful. First, remember that public-key systems depend on the existence of two related keys: a public key, which you can freely distribute, and a private key, which you can't.

Let's say you have a post office box. Anyone at the post office can stuff mail into the back of the box, but only you can retrieve mail by unlocking the door at the front of the box. That's how public-key encryption works: anyone can send you an encrypted message using your public key, but only you can read it, because only you hold the corresponding private key. Public-key signature operations work the same way, but in reverse: you encrypt a fingerprint of the message using your private key, and anyone can verify the signature using your public key.

If you live in the U.S., you've probably seen the lockboxes used by real estate agents when they sell a house. The agent has a master key that fits all her lockboxes, and each lockbox contains a key for an individual property. These individual keys are analogous to bulk keys: each encrypted message uses a new, randomly generated bulk key, which is never reused. Bulk keys are superencrypted with the recipient's public key to protect them. Public-key operations are slow, but secret-key operations are fast, so using the public key to encrypt the small bulk key instead of the entire message is much faster.

Certificates

An X.509 certificate is a binary blob that contains some attributes and a signature. A *certificate authority* (CA) takes the attributes, which can include anything from your name to your public key, bundles them into the X.509 format, and signs them with its own key, which is contained in a *root certificate*. In essence, the CA is certifying that the attributes are valid, even though it may not actually do any checking. Because the certificate is signed by the CA, no one can tamper with it after it's been issued.

 A CA may directly issue certificates to end users, or you can construct a hierarchy of CAs. For example, you might have a root CA for your entire organization, then subordinate CAs for each division. These subordinate CAs would issue certificates to users, but would depend on the root CA for signatures. When a client wanted to verify a certificate's integrity, it would verify both the subordinate and root CA signatures.

Let's say that Alice wants to send Bob an encrypted job offer. To do so, Alice needs to encrypt the message using Bob's public key, which she doesn't have. Certificates solve that problem. As long as Alice trusts the CA that issued Bob's certificate, and as long as she has access to an Exchange directory that has that certificate, either directly or via LDAP, she can get the certificate and use it.

Exchange uses separate certificates for signing and encrypting messages. Every time you send a signed message, your signing certificate is included in the message so that recipients can verify it even if they don't have direct access to your directory. Public encryption certificates are stored as a mailbox attribute in the directory, and they're included in the GAL and OABs, so anyone who can download an OAB, or see the GAL directly, can get your certificate and send you encrypted mail.

Certificate revocation lists

Sometimes it's necessary to revoke a certificate after you issue it but before it expires. Normally, you do this for one of two reasons: either the private key associated with the certificate is (or may have been) compromised, or the person who holds the private key has left your organization. Either way, the purpose behind revoking a certificate is to mark it as no longer trusted, ensuring that it won't be used for future transactions.

A certificate revocation list (CRL) is just a list of certificates and timestamps; the list is signed by the CA that issues the CRL. Any certificate that appears on the CRL is assumed to be revoked as of the time contained in the corresponding timestamp. The S/MIME standard specifies when clients should (and must) check the CRL to see whether a certificate has been revoked before using it; in general, it's allowable to use revoked certificates to verify messages signed before the revocation but not after.

The Exchange KMS keeps its own CRL up to date; if you've chosen to import and trust other CA certificates, you can also import their CRLs. Any CRL you import manually will be stored in the organization directory so that all your clients have access to it.

Key components

The KMS, the client, and the CA are the three most important pieces involved in Exchange advanced security. Each has its own set of responsibilities:

- The CA signs newly issued advanced security keys with its own key, turning them into certificates. It also embeds policy attributes that specify whether the key pair can be used for signing, encrypting, or both. Exchange 5.5 SP1 and later depend on the Microsoft Certificate Server, which runs under IIS 3.0 or 4.0, as a CA, but your clients can freely exchange mail with users whose certificates are signed by other CAs as well.

- The KMS issues temporary keys that the client uses to communicate securely with the KMS during the enrollment process. Once the client gets the temporary keys, it generates a certificate request that is sent to the CA for processing. The KMS also maintains a list of which keys have been revoked. In older versions of Exchange, the KMS acted as a CA that could issue X.509 version 1 certificates, but there's a separate CA in 5.5 SP1 and later. This CA is also included as part of the NT Option Pack, which means you'll be forced into installing IIS 4.0 if you want to use it.

- The client uses temporary keys to talk to the KMS and request a permanent set of keys. Once the KMS has issued the keys, the private key is transferred back to the client, which encrypts and stores it for later use. When you want to send a protected message, or read a message someone's sent to you, the client does all the work.

Processing protected messages

Table 2-3 provided a brief overview of the four basic public-key operations that Exchange and its clients support, but more detail might help at this point. Suppose Anne and Bill want to exchange a series of secure messages, and they're both enrolled in advanced security in the same Exchange organization.

Anne composes her initial message in Outlook. When she sends it, Outlook computes a cryptographic hash of the message, yielding a 128-bit fingerprint. The hash is encrypted with the sender's private key and added to the message. Outlook then builds a structure containing the message, the encrypted hash (which is really the signature), and the sender's public certificate, and that's what gets delivered to the recipient.

When Bill gets the message, his Outlook client computes the message's hash, then decrypts the encrypted hash sent with Anne's message. Remember, her hash was encrypted with her private key, so her public key, which is included with the message, can be used to verify it. If the two hashes match, that means the signature is valid and the message hasn't been tampered with; if they don't match, the message isn't valid.

Bill wants to answer Anne's message with his own encrypted message. When he sends his reply, his Outlook client generates a new bulk encryption key and uses it to encrypt the message. It then encrypts the bulk key with Anne's public key, so that her private key can decrypt it. The encrypted message, and the encrypted bulk key, leave Bill's computer and go to the Exchange server for delivery.

When Anne opens the message, her client uses her private key to decrypt the bulk encryption key; next, it uses the bulk encryption key to decrypt the actual message text. If Bill signed the message before encrypting it, Anne's client will automatically verify the signature after the decryption succeeds.

Installing Advanced Security

Microsoft made a significant change to Exchange advanced security in Exchange 5.5 SP1. Prior versions of Exchange used a dedicated KMS to issue certificates; the new and improved version uses the Microsoft Certificate Server (part of the NT 4.0 Option Kit and the IIS 4.0 distribution) to do the job, because the original KMS only supported X.509 version 1 certificates. While no less secure than the newer version 3 certificates,[*] version 1 certificates can't be made to interoperate between organizations. Outlook 98 and Outlook 2000 (as well as Netscape Messenger and other S/MIME clients) support either type of certificate, but you'll need to use X.509v3 certificates if you want to exchange secure mail with the outside world. Exchange 5.5 always installs the KMS components, even if it doesn't activate them, but you have to manually install the CA.

There's no requirement that the CA and Exchange be on the same machine; in fact, more often than not, they're on separate machines. There are good security reasons for this; normally, CAs are dedicated machines protected by stringent physical security so no one can tamper with them.

The overall process

To get advanced security up and going, a number of steps are necessary. None of them are particularly difficult, but it's crucial they be done in the right order. Here's what you need to do:

1. Install the KMS on one Exchange server in your organization, no more. Follow the instructions in Chapter 4, *Installing Exchange*; choose Complete/Custom setup, then select the KM Server component.

2. Prepare your certificate server for use. This step is made up of several smaller steps, so it's covered in the next section.

3. Install the Microsoft Certificate Server package on your certificate server, then install the Exchange policy module for it. The policy module tells the certificate server what rules to use when issuing new certificates.

4. Tell your KMS where your certificate server is.

5. Enroll mailboxes in advanced security, either individually or in bulk.

Preparing your certificate server

The certificate server computer must be running NT 4.0 SP3 or later. Since SP4 has so many security fixes in it, I recommend using SP4. In addition, the certificate

---

[*] In a move very typical of CCITT standards, the certificate format went from version 1 to version 3.

server needs both Internet Information Server 4.0 and Internet Explorer 4.01 or later (it's included in the IIS and SP4 installations, fortunately).

Once you have these prerequisites up and running, there's another required step: you must create a shared directory in which the server can store certificates. This directory must be accessible to all authenticated users, so give it Everyone:Read privileges. Although Microsoft's documentation doesn't spell it out, you should create this share on an NTFS partition.

Installing the CA

To actually install the Certificate Server, you'll need the NT 4.0 Option Pack (NTOP) CD. The installation process isn't that hard, but I wouldn't necessarily call it straightforward, either. Here's what to do:

1. Start the NTOP setup utility. Go through the Microsoft licensing mumbo-jumbo.

2. Select the Add/Remove button. When the list of components appears, select Certificate Server to mark it for installation, then click the Show Subcomponents button.

3. Make sure the Certificate Server Certificate Authority item is marked. You may also check the documentation and web client items if you want them installed, but neither is mandatory.

4. In the Microsoft Certificate Server Setup window, use the controls in the Configuration Data Storage Location group to specify the shared folder where certificates should be stored. Make sure the Show Advanced Configuration checkbox is marked, then click Next.

5. When the advanced options page appears, change the default hash algorithm from its default of MD5 to SHA-1.*

6. If you're installing a CA as your organizational root CA, make sure the Root CA radio button is selected. If you want to install a subordinate CA, select the Non-Root CA button and see the section "Installing a subordinate CA."

7. Click Next, then fill out the CA identification form with your organization name and location. When you click Next, the NTOP setup installer will configure and install the CA.

8. Shut down and restart your server.

---

* S/MIME supports both MD5 and SHA-1, but MD5 has some security weaknesses that make SHA-1 a better choice.

Installing a subordinate CA

Microsoft's Certificate Server can function as either a root or subordinate CA. What you get depends on the radio button you select in step 6 of the preceding section. When you install a subordinate CA, that CA can issue certificates and CRLs, but it doesn't sign the certificates it issues; the root CA signs them. This implies that you have to establish a trust relationship of some kind between the root and subordinate CAs. The Microsoft CA expects to see a signed CA certificate, or it won't start. Root CAs can sign their own certificate, but subordinate CAs need a certificate signed by the root before they'll run.

First, though, you have to install the subordinate CA. That process is identical to the instructions in the preceding sections, including the part about creating a shared directory for the subordinate CA to put its certificates into. Once you've done that, you're ready to generate a signed certificate for the subordinate CA to use. Here's how to do it:

1. On the subordinate CA computer, go to the *certs* directory and copy the *.req* file (its name will vary, but it will always have that extension) to a floppy. This file contains a canned certificate request that the root CA can process. Take the floppy to your root CA.

2. At the root CA, log in as an administrator and stop the Certificate Authority service.

3. Use the registry editor of your choice to change the `ValidityPeriodUnits` value (in `HKLM\SYSTEM\CurrentControlSet\Services\CertSvc\Configuration\`*caName*) to 5. This tells the root CA to issue a certificate valid for five years. Of course, if you want your subordinate CA certificates to have a shorter lifetime, you can use a smaller value.

4. Restart the Certificate Authority service.

5. From a command prompt, ask the root CA to sign the subordinate CA using the following command. When you finish this step, the floppy will contain the original request and the newly issued certificate:

   ```
   certreq a:\filename.req a:\filename.crt
   ```

6. Copy the root CA's certificate from the shared certificate directory to the floppy. This file is named after the root CA computer and the name you gave the root CA. For example, mine is named *HSV1_RA CA 1.crt.*

7. Reset the `ValidityPeriodUnits` value back to whatever it was before you changed it in step 3 above, then restart the Certificate Authority service.

8. Take the floppy back to your subordinate CA server, then copy the root CA's certificate to the *%systemroot%\system32* directory. You must name the file *rootca.crt.*

9. Copy the signed certificate (*.crt*) file from the floppy to the shared certificate directory on the subordinate CA. This file will be named after the subordinate CA computer and CA name. For example, my subordinate CA is named *STL1_RA SUB1.crt*.

10. Use your favorite registry editor to change the `HierFileName` value (creating it as a new `REG_SZ` value if it doesn't already exist) under the CA configuration key, `HKLM\SYSTEM\CurrentControlSet\Services\CertSvc\Configuration\`*caName*. Set the new value to the full path and name of the subordinate CA's request file, minus the *.req* extension. For example, on my machine, the value would be set to *d:\certs\STL1_RA SUB1*.

11. Run the `certhier` program from the command line. It establishes the certificate hierarchy on the subordinate CA.

12. Start the subordinate CA's certificate service.

After installing the CA

Once you've installed the CA, you still have some work to do:

1. Stop the Certificate Server service on the certificate server.

2. If you're already running NT 4.0 SP4 or later, skip this step; otherwise, download and install the certificate server hotfix from *ftp://ftp.microsoft.com/bussys/iis/iis-public/fixes/usa/certserv*, following the instructions in the included *readme.txt* file. (In brief, you must do a full backup of your certificate server data, uninstall it, reinstall the hotfix version, and reload your backup.)

3. Copy the Exchange policy module, *expolicy.dll*, from the *eng\server\support\kms\expolicy* directory on your Exchange SP1 or SP2 CD to the *%systemroot%\system32* directory on the certificate server. Note that if you downloaded the service pack, or if you got the non-North American version of the CD, you'll have source code files instead of a DLL. Thank the U.S. Department of State for that.

 Once you install the Exchange policy module on a CA, that CA can't be used for anything other than Exchange. This argues in favor of setting up a subordinate CA, as described in the section, "Installing a subordinate CA."

---

4. Register the policy module with the *regsvr32* command:

```
regsvr32 c:\winnt\system32\expolicy.dll
```

5. If your certificate server is a different machine than the Exchange server that's running KMS, you'll need to link the KMS and the certificate server by doing the following:

— Install Internet Explorer 4.01 on the KMS machine if it's not already there.

— Establish a persistent drive mapping to the shared certificate storage directory on the certificate server. The mapping must be persistent so the share will always have the same drive letter; the KMS will get confused if it changes.

— Stop the KMS, then use the NTOP setup utility to install the Certificate Server web client component on the KMS machine. Once you've rebooted, restart the KMS.

Setting CA Options

You can set two separate sets of options, both of which live in the site Configuration container. The CA object holds settings specific to the site servers' interaction with the CA, and the Site Encryption Configuration object holds settings that determine what encryption algorithms clients may use. The latter object is covered in the later section, "Setting Site-Specific Options."

Before you can open the CA properties dialog, the KMS must be running, since it handles access requests for the CA. In addition, you must be logged on using credentials that appear in the CA's administrator list. The account you used to install Exchange will be the only one on this list until you edit the list as described in the later "The Administrators tab" section.

The General tab

The General tab is pretty uninteresting. As usual, you can see the display and directory names for the CA object, and you can edit the display name. The Certificate Server field shows which CA is designated for use in this organization. You can't change it on machines where you've installed the KMS; once you specify a CA, you're stuck with it. On machines that don't have their own KMS, this field will be blank. When you change it, you'll get a dialog showing all installed KMSs in your organization. Once you choose one, you shouldn't change it.

The Administrators tab

You can designate any number of administrators for your CA. Start with one, and add any Windows NT account to the list, not just mailboxes. The accounts you designate may come from any domain with which the server's home domain has a trust relationship. These accounts have permission to manage the CA and the Exchange KMS, so they can enroll users and add or remove root certificates from the certificate trust list. Only administrators on this list can manage the CA, and even they must log on to the CA when they try to open the CA properties dialog.

 By default, the KMS sets the initial password for all administrators, including the default administrator described earlier, to "password." Make sure you change this *immediately*.

In addition to the list of administrators, there are three buttons of interest. The Add Administrator... button lets you choose an account to add to the list, while Remove Administrator does what you'd expect. The "Change My KM Server Password..." button lets you change the password associated with the selected administrator. This isn't the same as that account's NT password, and you should avoid using the NT account password for the CA password, to prevent potential compromises.

The Passwords tab

Normally, the CA allows a lone administrator to do anything. You may choose to require that two or more administrators provide credentials before performing some tasks. For example, the U.S. military requires the concurrence of two launch officers to fire a nuclear missile.* While the CA isn't a strategic nuclear power, a careless or malicious administrator could cause significant damage, for example, by trusting other CAs you don't want to trust, or by adding new but untrusted administrator accounts to the CA list.

The Passwords tab allows you to specify the number of administrators you want to require for five separate categories:

- Adding or removing administrator accounts or changing the number of administrators required to perform a particular CA action
- Recovering a user's signature and encryption keys
- Revoking a user's certificate
- Trusting or untrusting another CA's root certificate
- Changing the default certificate format used for newly enrolled mailboxes

You can set different thresholds for any or all of these; each action can require any number of administrators from one to the number of accounts you've defined. In general, I recommend setting these parameters to 2 or 3; higher values make it difficult to get the required people in the same place when you want to make a change.

---

* In fact, the "two-man rule" is entrenched in the U.S. strategic nuclear forces and many sections of the cryptography and security community.

The Enrollment tab

The Enrollment tab, shown in Figure 16-1, controls the options in effect for enrollment of new users, but it's not where you actually enroll users.

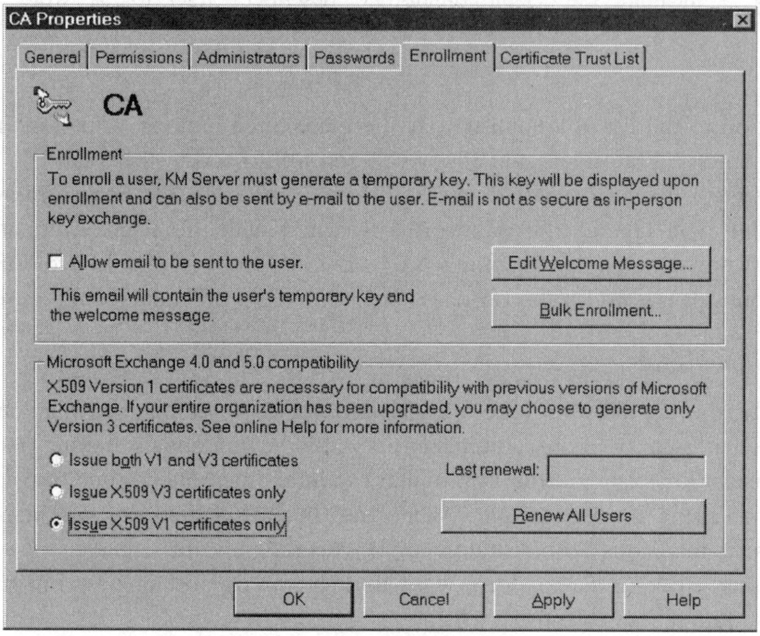

Figure 16-1. The Enrollment tab controls enrollment options

The Enrollment control group contains three controls:

Allow email to be sent to the user

> This checkbox tells the CA that it's okay to send temporary keys to the user when they're generated. This is definitely more convenient than meeting the user in person to deliver the key, but there's no way to email the temporary keys securely; doing so imposes a small, but real, security risk. If you don't check this box, you can't send temporary keys to individual users.

Edit Welcome Message...

> This button lets you edit the welcome message that's mailed with the temporary keys when you allow temporary keys to be mailed. This is a good way to tell your users what to do with the spiffy new keys you just mailed them.

Bulk Enrollment...

> This button opens a separate dialog that allows you to enroll all users in a particular container at once. This can be a real lifesaver if your organization adopts advanced security when you've already got a passel of users. With this

dialog, you can choose a recipient container to enroll, and you can choose whether to mail temporary keys to the new users, save them to a text file, or do both.

The "Microsoft Exchange 4.0 and 5.0 compatibility" group is only interesting if you've been using older versions of Exchange with the KMS in the past. If you haven't, you can safely ignore these settings. If you have, you have three choices:

Issue both V1 and V3 certificates
This button tells the CA that when you generate a new user certificate, you want to generate it in both V1 (the old format) and V3 (the new, preferred, format). This allows newly enrolled clients to share their public certificates outside your organization while still making them available to older clients.

Issue X.509 V3 certificates only
This button forces the CA to issue only version 3 certificates. If all your clients are Outlook 98 or later, and you have no older Exchange servers or clients anywhere, this option allows you full interoperability without the excess baggage of an unnecessary V1 certificate.

Issue X.509 V1 certificates only
This button, which is selected by default, tells the CA never to use the newer format. This is apparently the default because existing sites that use the old-style KMS are fairly common; however, since Microsoft is making a concerted effort to spread Outlook 97/98/2000 everywhere, these old clients will die off reasonably soon in most environments.

When you change this setting, you'll see a confirmation alert telling you that some clients may not be able to interoperate after the change; once you dismiss it, you'll be asked to choose a certificate server. You must pick a certificate server that has the Exchange policy module installed on it; if you don't, Exchange will catch your mistake and refuse to use that CA.

The Renew All Users button lets you reenroll all current clients with the settings you've selected. When you click this button, clients will be notified that they need to request a new certificate; but this happens without any manual intervention on your part. You'll need to do this if you've changed the default format used for securing messages on the Site Encryption Configuration object, or if you've changed the certificate type. The "Last renewal" field shows you the last time a mass renewal was performed.

The Certificate Trust List tab

This tab takes a little explaining. You may remember my earlier mention that you can choose to trust CAs outside your own organization. When you do so, you're really saying that you want to treat a certificate signed by a CA you trust just as though it were signed by your own CA. In effect, you're delegating authority for deciding who you trust to another entity.

For example, I used to work for LJL Enterprises, a company that makes S/MIME software. I know and trust them. Accordingly, I added the root key for their CA to my Exchange trust list. That means that any time one of my users gets a message with an LJL certificate, they can verify it as though it were signed by my CA. The client checks the sender's certificate and the LJL CA certificate; since the LJL CA appears in my organization's trust list, the client can see that I trust it.

Most organizations trust large issuing authorities like Verisign and GTE; you can choose to add their CA certificates to your trust list, as well as adding other CAs that you have business reasons to trust. For example, let's say your organization has its own CA, plus individual CAs for each business unit. You could add the root CA certificate and each business unit CA certificate to your trust list to ensure that you can exchange secure mail with users throughout the other business units. Why not just add the root CA certificate? Because CA signatures form a chain, with the client certificate at the bottom and the root at the top. Let's say you have a certificate from Joe Smith at BigCorp. If BigCorp has a single CA, Joe's certificate chain will be `cn=Joe Smith; o= BigCorp; c=us`. If Joe's in the WidgetGroup business unit, his chain might be `cn=Joe Smith; ou=WidgetGroup; o= BigCorp; c=us`. This second chain requires two CA certificates for a full verification: one for BigCorp and the one for WidgetGroup.

The Certificate Trust List tab shows you which certificates you currently trust, along with some parameters: whether the signature chain is valid, the name of the certificate, the DN of the issuer, when the certificate expires, and when its CRL expires. The four buttons below the list let you manipulate the list:

Import...

> This button lets you import a CA certificate or CRL from a file. The certificate or CRL must be in a plain binary file, not in the PKCS#7 format you get when you export a certificate from Netscape Messenger, Outlook, or Outlook Express.

Trust or Untrust...

> This button lets you change the trust level of a certificate. Either you trust a certificate or you don't; there aren't any intermediate levels. You must untrust a trusted certificate before removing it, or you won't be able to go back and untrust it later.

Remove...

> This button lets you remove a CA certificate, the associated CRL, or both. Normally, you'll remove certificates when they expire, when you no longer trust the issuer, or when you accidentally import a duplicate.

Properties...

> This button brings up a dialog box that shows you the guts of the certificate: its issuer and holder DNs, its serial number, its fingerprint, the algorithm used to sign it, its expiration date, and whether it's valid or not.

Setting Site-Specific Options

The Site Encryption Configuration container lets you set two groups of options. The first group is located on the General tab; as usual, that tab contains the display and directory names for the Configuration object itself, plus a field showing the primary KM server for the site. Once you select a KMS, you lose the ability to recover users' keys, so changing it is intentionally difficult. I won't cover the procedure here.

The Algorithms tab, shown in Figure 16-2, is a bit more interesting. There are two sets of algorithms that you can specify: one for Exchange 4.0 and 5.0 clients, and one for S/MIME clients. Within each set of algorithms, you can individually specify which algorithms you prefer for clients inside and outside North America. This segregation is necessary because, as mentioned previously, U.S. law forbids the export of strong cryptography. While you can certainly dumb down your North American clients, I recommend choosing the strongest possible encryption for North American clients (CAST-64 for older clients, and 3DES for S/MIME users). It's safe to use strong encryption, because S/MIME clients are required to look at the set of algorithms available to the recipient before encrypting a message, so it shouldn't ever be possible for you to generate a message that a client in another country can't read.

The remaining control group on this tab is for selecting the default format used for message security. Set this to S/MIME unless you have older clients you want to include in advanced security; if you have older clients, you should strongly consider upgrading them, since S/MIME clients offer a ton of useful security features not present in the old Exchange clients. If you change this format setting, you'll need to force your clients to renew their certificates as described in the section "The Enrollment tab," earlier in the chapter.

Everyday Advanced Security

Now that you know how to install and configure the CA and KMS, what do you do with them? On a daily basis, probably not much. The bulk of your work will probably be enrolling new users and occasionally revoking old ones. Don't forget about making backups, either!

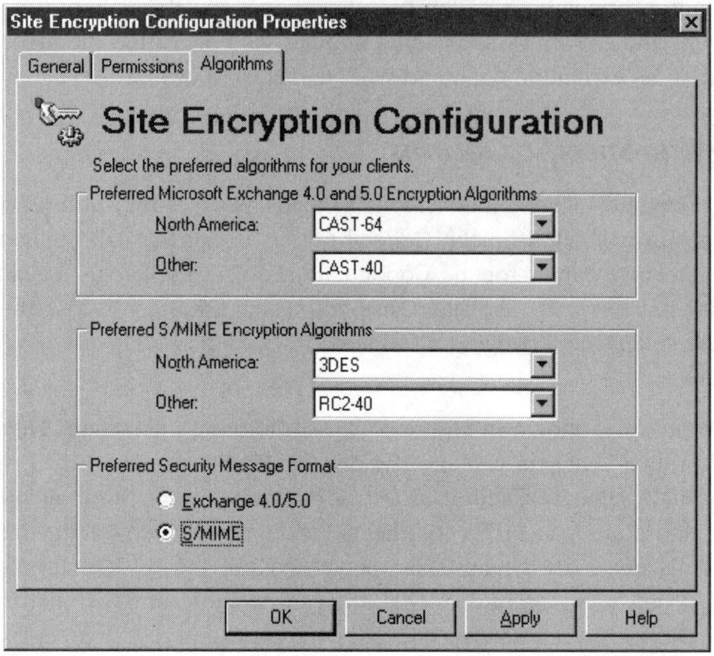

Figure 16-2. The Algorithms tab lets you specify what algorithms clients should use

Managing users

To enroll users *en masse*, use the Enrollment tab. In addition, you may need to enroll individual users from time to time. You do this with the Security tab of the mailbox properties dialog. When you open this tab, you'll see something like the tab pictured in Figure 16-3.

The contents of the fields in this tab, and which buttons are enabled, vary depending on the current status of the mailbox. There are four key status indicators you need to recognize. "New" means that the mailbox has been enrolled in advanced security, but the mailbox owner hasn't yet used her client to request a certificate. "Active" means that the mailbox has been enrolled and the owner has requested a certificate, which may or may not have been issued. "Revoked" means that the certificate for this mailbox has been revoked, and "Undefined" means that the mailbox isn't enrolled in advanced security.

Before I talk about specific tasks you can perform in this dialog, let me point out what the Forget Remembered Password button does. If you check the appropriate box in the KMS logon dialog, the KMS can cache your logon credentials for up to five minutes. Clicking this button makes the KMS empty its cache so that you'll have to log on again. This protects you from making an advanced security change,

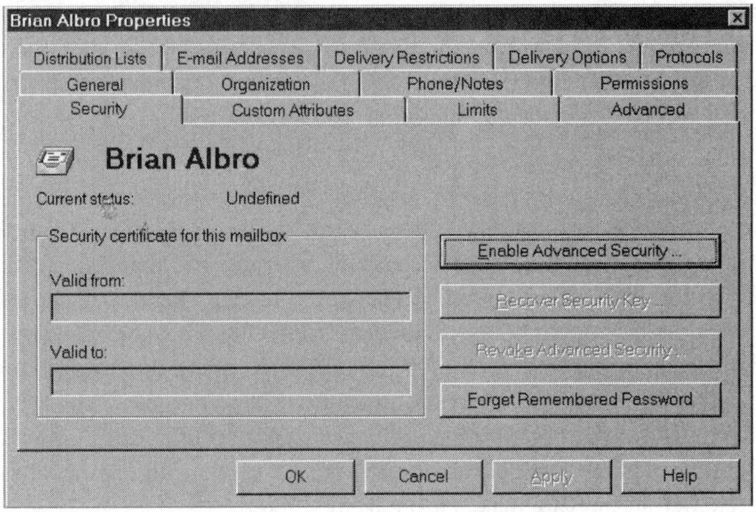

Figure 16-3. The mailbox Security tab details the mailbox's advanced security participation

then having someone else sneak in behind you while your credentials are cached and making some other change.

Enrolling a user

The Enable Advanced Security... button will be visible when the mailbox's certificate status is shown as Revoked or Undefined; when you click it, after logging on to the KMS you'll get a security token to give to the user. The token is a twelve-letter code that enables the client to generate a key it can use to talk securely to the KMS. Once you've gotten the token to the user, either via email or in person, she can use the Tools → Options... command in Outlook to set up the client for advanced security, and once the CA has issued the certificate, the user will be able to participate in security.

Recovering a user's keys

If one of your users forgets the security password for his certificate, or if the private key is lost due to a disk crash or some other loss that doesn't involve a compromise, you can recover it. Key recovery* protects you against malicious employees, too. You can always recover a key and use it to read encrypted mail after someone leaves.

---

* Don't confuse *key recovery* (you can get your own keys back) with *key escrow* (someone else can get your keys without your knowledge).

Once you click the Recover Security Key... button, you'll find that the recovery process works just like the initial enrollment. You log on, the system provides a twelve-letter token, and you give the token to the user. When he uses the token in his client, the keys are recovered from the encrypted store maintained on the server, the certificate is updated, and all is well.

Revoking a user

Revoking a user's security privileges is easy: just click the Revoke Advanced Security... button. You'll see a confirmation dialog warning you that the certificate will be added to the CRL; when you click OK, you'll have to log on to the KMS, then the revocation will appear to be immediate. Actually, it's not immediate; there's some nonzero time lag involved. The revocation request has to get to the CA, which has to revoke the certificate and update its CRL. Then the CRL has to be distributed throughout the organizational directory. Bottom line: don't count on revocation being instantaneous, because it can take up to one full organizational replication cycle before the CRL makes it out to the hinterlands.

Moving mail

When you move a server using the Move Server Wizard, the wizard blithely moves all the mail in the server's store, which is what it's supposed to do. Since the encryption keys needed to read encrypted mail are on the client, clients can still read their mail after the move, but you'll lose the ability to do key recovery on those messages after the move unless you make users decrypt them first. This happens because once you move the user mailboxes and their contents, you have to re-enroll the users in advanced security at the new server location.

If you move mailboxes with Exchange Administrator's Tools → Move Mailbox... command, there's no impact, so users will still be able to read their mail.

Changing the KMS password path

When you install the KMS, you either provide a floppy for the KMS startup password or you get a long password that you have to write down and manually enter in the Startup Parameters field of the Services control panel. If you want to switch between these methods, you can. The `MasterPasswordPath` value, a `REG_SZ`, lives under the `HKLM\Software\Microsoft\Exchange\KMServer` key. When it's present, the KMS will look in that path (it has to be a full path, including the drive letter) for a file named *kmserver.pwd*. The file has to contain the KMS password on the first line, and nothing else.

To switch from using a floppy to entering the password manually, remove this value, open the *kmserver.pwd* file, and write down the password. To switch in the other direction, create a new file, put the text password into it, put it on a floppy, and add the `MasterPasswordPath` value.

Don't put your KMS password directly on your server. As your KMS password is exposed, an attacker could potentially start your KMS and use it without your knowledge. The risk of this happening is lessened if you've chosen good passwords for the KMS administrators, but it's still worth guarding against.

Backing up and restoring keys and certificates

You can use the `certutil` tool bundled with the Microsoft Certificate Server to back up and restore the keys and certificates generated by the CA. Note that this tool doesn't do anything with the log files or databases the certificate server itself uses; it just stores the certificates and keys that the CA uses for signatures and verification. `certutil` takes two command-line flags:

```
certutil
        -backup password keyFile
        -restore password keyFile
```

password

Specifies the password that should be used to encrypt or decrypt keys and certificates before they're stored in the file. `certutil` uses the PKCS#12 standard for encrypting the data (see *www.rsa.com/rsalabs/pubs/PKCS/html/pkcs-12.html* for more details).

keyFile

Specifies the file to encrypt or decrypt.

One wrinkle about using these commands: you have to install the Certificate Server package to get `certutil` and its DLLs. That means that if you need to recover a failed server, you must install the CA, restore the keys, uninstall the CA, and reinstall it again, telling it to use the existing keys in the process.

If you need to restore CA data to a different computer than the one on which it was created, see Knowledge Base article Q185195, which outlines the lengthy procedure required.

Backing up KMS data

The KMS keeps its data in a subdirectory named *kmsdata* under the *exchsrvr* directory. When you use **ntbackup** or another tool to back up your Exchange databases, this directory isn't included, and you won't be able to back it up manually as long as the KMS is running. To do a backup or a restore, make sure the KMS service is stopped, then back up all the files in the directory using whatever backup tool you choose. Note that this isn't the same as backing up or restoring the CA's data store.

Protecting Against Viruses

The best way to provide virus protection in Exchange is a hotly debated topic. The range of opinion varies from one extreme to the other: one camp holds that virus protection isn't needed on servers, since NT is relatively secure against viruses, and the other believes that you need several layers of antiviral defense. I happen to belong to the second camp, so I'll start this section by explaining why.

In this section, I'm going to pretend that viruses, malicious ActiveX controls, and malicious Java applets are all the same. If you're really concerned about ActiveX and Java, make sure the products you choose handle them appropriately; however, in my opinion, viruses are a much more pervasive and serious threat.

What, Me Worry?

It's hard to accurately estimate the real impact of virus damage. There's a lot of hype surrounding the issue: vendors who sell antiviral products (particularly Network Associates) are prone to overstating the threat, because scaring people helps sell their products. Many organizations that suffer isolated virus infections don't realize the scope of the problem; many organizations that have widespread outbreaks try to keep the fact from becoming public.

The cost of antiviral software, however, is easy to quantify. For adequate protection, you need it installed on every desktop, laptop, and server on your network. Depending on how many machines that is, and what software you choose, that can amount to a substantial sum. In the absence of hard data to quantify what risks you run, and in the cold presence of cost figures for protection, should you bother with it? Absolutely! Consider the following:

Viruses spread

A single virus that enters your network on one machine can easily be spread to other machines, and so on, until your entire network is compromised. Since each infected machine may have many infected applications or files, the time and cost of recovering these machines can quickly add up. Email provides another transmission path for viruses; it's easy for people to exchange infected files.

Some viruses are extremely malicious

We've all heard stories about annoying viruses, like the plethora of bother-some-but-harmless Word macro viruses. However, there are some real nasties out there, and if one of them gets loose in your network you can lose quite a bit of data.

Viruses make you look stupid

A number of otherwise respectable software vendors have recently been pub-licly humbled because they accidentally shipped product CDs with viruses on them. Imagine the impact of sending a new client a file that infects several of their machines—not exactly the most positive impression you could make!

If your duties only involve administering email, you might not be too worried about these points, but you should be, because your personal machines and your servers may be vulnerable. Since viruses may enter your network via email sent from the outside world, you need to know how to protect the systems you're directly responsible for.

There's a great page called "Computer Virus Myths" at *www.kumite. com/myths*. It's well worth reading, because it points out some exam-ples of egregious misbehavior by the media and antiviral vendors.

Types of Antiviral Tools

There are three primary types of antiviral tools. More precisely, there are three places where antiviral packages can usefully be installed. A complete discussion of how these tools work is outside the scope of this book; it's enough to understand that almost all virus checkers depend on a set of signatures supplied by the ven-dor. These signatures are supposed to uniquely identify the presence of a virus in a file. Virus checkers scan data and executable files looking for these signatures; if a signature is found, the checker may or may not be able to disinfect the file and remove the actual virus.

Firewall or gateway tools

The ideal solution would probably be to stop incoming viruses before they could ever get to your clients. (Of course, this ignores the fact that the clients them-selves usually bring viruses in!) Firewall or gateway virus checkers are designed to offer a first line of defense; they sit at the interface between your LAN or WAN and the Internet and scan every incoming or outgoing message for viruses. This is a pretty resource-intensive task, since the scanner has to accept each message, un-MIME or uudecode each attachment, decompress any compressed files, and scan them; normally, you'll want to establish a configuration like the one shown in Figure 16-4. In this example, a single machine runs the virus scanning gateway; any messages it approves are passed to the IMS in site *A*, which then routes messages to recipients in other sites.

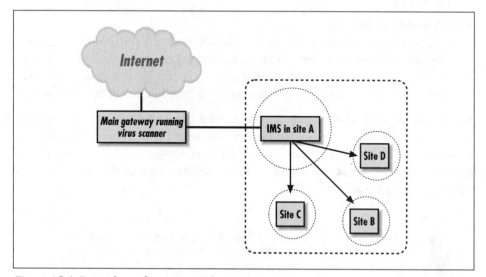

Figure 16-4. Example configuration with a gateway scanner between you and the Internet

Does it make sense to use a firewall virus scanner? It depends. It's certainly better to stop viruses before they make it to your servers or clients, and a gateway scanner can help do that. Many products, including MIMEsweeper and Trend Micro's VirusWall (*www.antivirus.com*) also add content filtering and other useful services I've already talked about. However, your overall mail traffic flow will be slowed by the presence of a firewall scanner, and they can be expensive. Carefully consider whether the added protection is worth the added expense for your own particular site.

Server-based tools

These tools actually install on your Exchange server. Their purpose is to scan every incoming message, whether it comes over a connector or from a user attached to that server, and make sure it doesn't have any viruses before the message goes into the store. Some of these checkers run as services and periodically inspect the store; others masquerade as MAPI clients that register interest in every mailbox on the server.

Exchange's single-instance storage model is both a blessing and a curse when it comes to virus protection. Since shared messages are only stored once, that means you only have to disinfect each message once, no matter how many recipients it has. On the other hand, a single message that doesn't get disinfected can potentially infect a large number of client PCs. This complicates the choice of server-side virus checkers, since any one that runs as a service or as a MAPI client can potentially miss incoming messages. If you think about how messages are processed when they arrive, you'll see why this can happen: when the store has a new message for a MAPI client that's currently connected to the store, it sends a MAPI notification to that client, which then turns around and asks for the new mail. If the recipient mailbox and the virus scanner both get the notification, it's possible for the client to get the unscanned message before the scanner does. Bad.

To work around this, most antiviral packages designed for Exchange play tricks with the MAPI interface or other parts of Exchange. As a result, you're forever playing roulette with your server: when you get ready to install an NT or Exchange SP, it may or may not install a different version of some component that the scanner depends on, so the scanner may or may not keep working. Some scanners are more vulnerable to this kind of breakage than others, but in general, adding a server-based scanner means you're adding one more variable to an already complex configuration.

Having said that, I recommend that you purchase and install a good-quality scanner on your servers (more on that in a bit). My current favorite is ScanMail, from Trend Micro. It's robust, stable, and fast, and it seems to be fairly tolerant of operating system and Exchange upgrades. However, be aware that all server-based scanners impose some performance overhead, though the benefits they offer are worth it.

Client tools

This one is a no-brainer. Since users are always trading software, sticking in floppies of dubious provenance, and generally displaying poor information hygiene, your clients definitely need to be running antiviral software. While you may think that providing server- and firewall-based virus scanners reduces the need for client scanning software, it doesn't, for three reasons:

- Your client machines probably have floppies and CD-ROMs, which means they're perpetually vulnerable to infection, even if they aren't heavily used for email.

- Your client machines are most likely running Windows 95 or Windows 98, both of which are much more vulnerable to virus infections than Windows NT.

- The server and firewall scanners aren't guaranteed to catch every incoming virus. For a good time, read any antivirus vendor's license agreement and warranty; by no means do they promise protection, or agree to accept responsibility for failure.

Which client antiviral package you use is up to you. There are too many contenders for me to make a one-size-fits-all recommendation. On machines I'm responsible for, I use and recommend Symantec's products, and avoid the McAfee family, but you're on your own for this one—it's almost as bad as choosing between vi and emacs.

Providing defense in depth

Astute readers will have noticed that I recommend using more than one category of scanner. That's because the best overall way to protect your system is to provide a multilayered defense. Just for a minute, assume that you had an unlimited budget. (Ahhhh! Isn't that a nice feeling?) You'd get maximum protection from using a combination of a gateway scanner, a server scanner, and scanners on each of your clients. If each layer stops 95% of the viruses that enter your network, you'd be in good shape: your firewall would catch 9,500 of 10,000 incoming viruses, the server would catch 475 of the remaining 500, and your client would catch 23.75 of the final 25, letting through 1.25 viruses, for an overall protection rate of 99.999875%.*

Even if your budget is more limited, implementing more than one layer of virus defense is a good idea. At a minimum, you have to protect your users' machines, since they're vulnerable to other infection vectors besides email. If at all possible, a server scanner should be your next acquisition. Despite their limitations, a good server scanner adds a significant degree of protection by limiting the spread of viruses; even if it doesn't catch every one of them before delivery to the client, but catches most of them, you'll be better off. If you can afford it, a firewall or gateway scanner is a nice addition, especially if you have to do something like add a disclaimer to all outgoing mail or scan incoming mail for keywords.

Useful Security Tasks

Apart from the process of setting up advanced security and occasionally changing permissions, Exchange requires relatively little security administration once you get everything set up properly. However, there are some tasks you may need to perform that don't fit neatly into the rest of the material in this chapter, so I've moved them here.

---

* You could argue that these numbers are bogus, since they ignore the fact that virus arrivals aren't evenly and randomly distributed, but I think the overall analogy is still sound.

What Melissa Should Have Taught Us

As I was writing this chapter, the Melissa virus was released into the wild and started hammering Exchange sites around the world. Microsoft and most anti-viral software vendors responded quickly by releasing scanning tools and updates to server- and desktop-based scanners. The earliest firsthand reports of infection that I saw came out late on a Thursday; some sites had appropriate scanners and tools in place by midday on Friday, so they were able to continue operations normally. The media, up to and including the *New York Times*, was full of stories about sites that had longer-lasting problems. Why was there such a big difference in the impact?

- Melissa only infected sites that were using Microsoft Word and Outlook; that's because it was written using Word's built-in macro language. The virus author hardcoded the virus to depend on Outlook as a mail transport. Sites that weren't running Word and Outlook weren't affected.

- Word includes a way to set security policies for documents that contain macros. Microsoft and most security experts recommend that you turn on the warning feature that pops up a dialog telling you that a new document contains macros and asking you if you want to enable them or not. The initial infection apparently came when a message containing an infected document was posted to a pornography group on Usenet; when the first Word/Outlook user downloaded the document and opened it, the race was on. It appears that the infected users either had macro security turned off or ignored the warnings.

- Sites that were using server-side virus scanners were able to stop users from logging in to the store, clean it with the scanner, and fix things up relatively quickly. Sites that were using client-side scanners only had to simultaneously propagate the necessary updates to all their clients at once.

- Some large sites, including Microsoft, quickly shut down their IMS servers to prevent infected messages from going in or out of their servers until their virus scanners were updated.

You can derive several practical recommendations from these points:

- Get a server-side virus checker, preferably from a company with good customer service and support. On the *msexchange* mailing list, a number of administrators praised Trend Micro for their rapid release of a Melissa signature for their scanner; NAI was also quick to respond.

- If you use a desktop virus checker, make sure it can scan for macro viruses.

—Continued—

- Know how to use the `isscan` tool described in this chapter.

- Turn on Word's macro virus protection, using the General tab in the Tools → Options… dialog. Try to educate your users so they know what the warning means and that it's not something to casually dismiss.

- Pay attention! Subscribe to Microsoft's security alert list (*www.microsoft.com/security*). If your antiviral vendor has any kind of automatic update or subscription service, consider using it.

- Make a plan. If your site is hit by a major virus infection, how will you contain its spread?

Scanning the IS for Forbidden Content

I recently got an intriguing question from an Exchange administrator at a government site. He wanted to know if there was some way to scan the entire IS for messages containing a certain forbidden word. Some classified projects have names that are themselves classified; apparently, someone had accidentally sent out a message using one such name, and this administrator was trying to eradicate all traces of the errant message from his store.

Microsoft's PSS group has several tools that scan the store for a particular message ID or other identifier (like the famous "Bedlam" tool). The recent arrival of the Melissa virus led them to publicly release a tool called `isscan`; it's actually designed to search for the Melissa macro virus, but can be customized to scan for any set of attachments and message subjects you want.

Using isscan

The `isscan` tool is available from Microsoft's FTP site at *ftp.microsoft.com/bussys/exchange/exchange-public/fixes/ENG/Exchg5.5/ISSCAN/*. (There's also an Exchange 5.0 version; both flavors are available for x86 and Alpha processors.) Once you download and install `isscan`, you'll find that it's very simple to use. In its default mode, it's configured to scan for the Melissa virus only, but you'll probably want to customize it.

`isscan` takes a small set of command-line parameters:

```
isscan [-fix ] [ -pri ] [ -pub ] [-test { badmessage,| badattach} ]
   [-c critfile]
```

-fix

Specify this switch to have `isscan` delete any messages that match its pattern list; otherwise, it will generate a log file (*isscan.pri* or *isscan.pub*) listing the results of its scan.

`-pri, -pub`

> These switches control which IS database is scanned; you can specify one or both, but you must provide at least one.

`-test`

> This switch tells `isscan` what to look for. Unless you specify a criteria file, the `badmessage` flag checks for messages with the subject line "Important Message From" and a creation time after March 1, 1999. The `badattach` flag checks for attachments named *list.doc* that have file sizes between 40,000 bytes and 60,000 bytes. Messages that fail the `badmessage` scan are removed. Messages that have an attachment that fails the `badattach` scan are kept, but the attachments themselves are removed.

`-c critfile`

> This switch specifies a criteria file you can use to match other types of messages besides those containing the Melissa virus.

As it comes from the factory, this tool is useful for removing the Melissa and Papa macro viruses from your IS, but you can build a criteria file that lets you customize it for removing future viruses and other unwanted messages. You can specify two types of criteria: attachment criteria tell `isscan` to match files with a particular name and size range, and message criteria specify a portion of the subject line and a creation date. The formats are simple:

```
ATTACH fileName minSize maxSize
MSG subjStart startDate
```

Each parameter is separated by tabs. *fileName* should be a filename, with extension, and the two size parameters should be in bytes. *subjStart* can be an entire or partial subject line; `isscan` flags all messages where the start of the subject line matches what you specify. The *startDate* parameter tells `isscan` to ignore any messages created before the start date. Here's an example that will catch the Melissa virus and some variants:

```
ATTACH list.doc   40000 60000
ATTACH list1.doc  40000 60000
ATTACH new.doc    20000 40000
MSG Important Message From 1999/03/01
MSG New version of virus 1999/03/28
```

Using the Message Store Sanitizer

Realizing that `isscan` won't solve everyone's problem, Microsoft has publicly released the Message Store Sanitizer (MSS). It was originally available only through PSS; as I write this, it's available from *ftp.microsoft.com/transfer/outgoing/bussys/ premier/Melissa/MSS/*, which in turn is listed in Knowledge Base article Q224336. I can't guarantee that it will still be there when the book hits print, but you'll probably still be able to get it from PSS if you need it.

MSS uses the MAPI interface to enumerate all the mailboxes within a designated Exchange container, then compares each message in those mailboxes or folders against the scan criteria you supply. As with `isscan`, you can generate a log of messages that match with or without automatically deleting matching messages. MSS is a command-line utility; it takes its parameters from a command file, usually named *mss.ini*. This file contains four groups of command keywords:

General

> Sets the scope of the search-and-destroy operation. Its command keywords are shown in Table 16-1.

Table 16-1. Commands for the General Group

Keyword	Legal Values	Description
Container	Full path to the container you want to inspect	This keyword is used to specify what container or subcontainer you want to scan. If you specify a container that has subcontainers, the subcontainers will be scanned.
Delete Flag	TRUE or FALSE	TRUE tells MSS to remove messages it finds; FALSE leaves them in the store. In either case, found messages are logged.
Mailbox	Full DN of administrator mailbox	This keyword must specify the full DN (from the organization name on down) of a mailbox with enough permissions to enumerate and open all mailboxes in the store—usually either the service account or your administrator mailbox.
Scope	Server	This keyword's value must always be Server.
Server	Name of server to check	This keyword specifies which server you want MSS to investigate.

Criteria

> Specifies what MSS should look for when sanitizing. You can scan by message subject (using the PR_SUBJECT keyword), message body, creation time (PR_CREATIONTIME), sender name (PR_SENDER), message size (PR_MESSAGE_SIZE) and whether the message has attachments or not (PR_HASATTACH).

Report

> Contains only two keywords: Report File Name tells MSS where to put the report file, and Report Flag should always be set to TRUE.

Report Properties

> Allows you to specify which attributes should be included in the report, using the same property flags as the Criteria group. Set the value of a flag to 1 if you want to see it in the report.

Here's an example of how this looks in practice:

```
[General]
Container=/o=RobichauxAssociates/ou=HSV/cn=Recipients
Server=HSV1
Scope=Server
Mailbox=/o=RobichauxAssociates/ou=HSV/cn=Recipients/cn=administrator
Delete Flag=TRUE

[Criteria]
PR_SUBJECT=Important Message From
MatchType=1

[Report]
Report File Name=mss.txt
Report Flag=True

[Report Properties]
PR_SUBJECT=1
PR_CREATION_TIME=1
PR_MESSAGE_SIZE=1
PR_SENDER_NAME=1
PR_HASATTACH=1
```

This file will scan for messages whose subject line contains the text "Important Message From," a hallmark of messages infected with the Melissa macro virus.

Configuring Exchange's TCP/IP Ports

Packet filters and firewalls are designed to let you limit the range of ports on which clients may connect. If you want to enable your Exchange clients and servers to talk to each other across a firewall, you have to make some adjustments to the firewall configuration. Exchange uses the well-known static port number 135 to listen for client connections. This port is owned by the RPC endpoint mapper service, which is in charge of randomly selecting a port on which to offer the requested service. When the client connects to port 135 on the server, the server assigns two random ports to the client: one for talking to the DS and one for talking to the IS. Since the firewall can't handle random port numbers, the connection won't work. In addition, intrasite replication and connections that use the X.400 or site connectors all depend on a similar port assignment scheme. You can force Exchange to always use the same predefined static port number for these connections by making a few registry changes.

First, configure your firewall to pass traffic on TCP port 135. You may also need to open port 80 for HTTP, port 443 for SSL, port 25 for SMTP, port 110 for POP3, and port 119 for NNTP, if you want your firewall to pass traffic using those protocols as well.

Next, choose a range of port numbers you know no other services on your network are using. Port numbers below 1024 are reserved for the system, so don't use those; frequently, ports from 1024–1150 or so are grabbed by other TCP/IP services. Look at the *%systemroot%\system32\drivers\etc\services* file to see what ports are already in use, then add the port ranges you select to this file.

All the registry keys in this section are REG_DWORDs.

Assigning static ports for the MTA

By default, the X.400 connector uses TCP port 102 for its traffic. You can either open that port on the firewall or assign a new port number. If you choose to do the latter, add a new value named RFC1006 Port Number to the MTA parameters key at HKLM\SYSTEM\CurrentControlSet\Services\MSExchangeMTA\Parameters. Set this value to the port number, in hex, that you want your MTA to use. Remember that all other MTAs that talk to the modified MTA must use the matching port number.

You can also modify the port that the MTA uses for the RPC endmapper service. By default, it listens on port 135; add a new value named TCP/IP port for RPC listens to the MSExchangeMTA\Parameters key, then give it the desired port value. Stop and restart the MTA to force it to notice the change.

Assigning static ports for the DS and IS

The DS and the IS may be assigned static port numbers by adding a new value named TCP/IP port to the appropriate subkey. The DS port is set by MSExchangeDS\Parameters\TCP/IP port, while the IS port is set by adding the MSExchangeDS\Parameters\TCP/IP port value. Stop and restart the affected service when you've made the change.

Allowing remote administration

If you want to use Exchange Administrator to administer a remote server through a firewall, you may do so by adding the same TCP/IP port value to the MSExchangeSA\Parameters key. You should make this change only on the servers you want to administer, and you should very carefully consider whether through-firewall administration is a security risk you're willing to take.

Using sectool

The Bulk Advanced Security Tool, or *sectool.exe*, allows you to encrypt or decrypt all mail stored in a mailbox. The BORK (see Appendix A, *BORK Tools*) contains versions for Windows 95 and NT; you must run the appropriate version for the client OS you're using. You use `sectool` in a fairly limited number of cases, all of which involve some change to your certificate or the set of algorithms available to you. For example, when you use the Move Server Wizard to move users from one organization to another, they may have to use `sectool` to move their mail. Another example is the one included in `sectool`'s documentation, which involves a user moving from North America to an area where only weak encryption is legal.

To run `sectool`, you must have access to the user profile that owns the mailbox you're encrypting or decrypting. When you launch `sectool`, you'll find that it only has two commands: Secure Folder and Unsecure Folder, which do what you'd expect. The procedures for securing and unsecuring folders are very similar. Here's how to use the Unsecure Folder option (which you'll use first):

1. Launch `sectool` and use the Exchange Security → Unsecure Folder... command.

2. Log on to MAPI using a profile installed on the machine (if you haven't already).

3. Choose the message store and folder you want to unsecure from the dialog `sectool` displays.

4. Decide whether you want to unprotect all messages in subfolders, or just the ones in the folder you select.

To reverse the process, use the Exchange Security → Secure Folder... command. The steps are the same, except that you can choose whether you want to encrypt all mail in the folder(s) you select, or only those messages that were encrypted before you unsecured their parent folder.

Setting Filesystem Permissions

Good security practice dictates that you should restrict access to your servers and their files to those who need it. If you're using NTFS on your server (as you should be), you can use its access control lists (ACLs) to limit access to the directories and files on your servers. A complete guide to securing an entire NT installation is outside the scope of this book; Trusted System Services has an excellent guide at their web site (see *www.trustedsystems.com/NSAGuide.htm*), so refer to it if you need help understanding your NT installation or how to accomplish it.

Table 16-2 shows Microsoft's current recommendations for ACLs on Exchange; these are likely to change with future releases of the product.

Table 16-2. Microsoft's Exchange ACL Recommendations

Path	What to Do
\exchsrvr\tracking.log	Remove permissions for Everyone.
\exchsrvr\add-ins	Remove permissions for Everyone.
\exchsrvr\connect\msmcon\maildata	Remove permissions for Everyone.
\exchsrvr\connect	Remove permissions for Everyone.
\exchsrvr\address	Remove permissions for Everyone.
\exchsrvr\res	Remove permissions for Everyone.
\exchsrvr\bin	Remove Everyone: Full Control permission.

The last item, *exchsrvr\bin*, is worthy of special mention. Just removing Everyone:Full Control permission is a good start, but you should consider setting permissions restricting access to the accounts that actually need to run the executables and DLLs in the *\exchsrvr\bin* directory. The problem is that it may take some experimentation to get the permissions set just right, since many of the files in that directory are used by system accounts and processes.

17

Recovery and Repair

I do not believe in recovery.
—Lillian Hellman
Scoundrel Time

In some organizations, email has become more important than the telephone—consider how a business like Microsoft or Amazon.com would operate internally without email. Microsoft and its partners have been pushing hard to make Exchange into a single messaging source, unifying voice mail, fax, and email into a single inbox. This unification makes disaster recovery even more critical.

Disaster recovery is a complicated topic. I'm not going to address the basics of recovering a crashed NT server, nor will I discuss the low-level preparations (like keeping a copy of your backup tapes offsite) you should already be doing. The Exchange documentation makes very little mention of disaster recovery; instead, the BORK and two white papers are usually cited as canon. I'll outline what you need to know about the fundamentals of disaster recovery and explain where you can find specifics for unusual tasks like recovering one system in a cluster.

Understanding Server Recovery

Let me begin with a simple but often overlooked truth, which I've formatted as a warning to catch your eye if you're just skimming.

 If you don't have good Exchange backups, your ability to recover your servers will be *extremely* limited. You *must* make sure your backup procedures work, and you must continually monitor the process to ensure that your backups are usable.

Exchange Server's normal backup procedures are primarily geared toward single-server disaster recovery; they're designed to help you replace an entirely failed member server, no matter what caused the original loss. The IS and directory databases are highly specialized, which is what gives them so much functionality, but the recovery and repair procedures necessary to fix a downed server are very specific to Exchange. You can't just pop in a tape, run ntbackup, and go.

Exchange is easy enough to set up and configure that it's possible to overlook some fundamental steps that ensure your configuration will be recoverable if something happens. There are three key requirements:

- Plan your recovery strategy to make sure you have everything you'll need to do a recovery: hardware, software, and backups.

- Understand the specifics of your configuration and how to best recover it.

- Practice recovery procedures so that when it's time to do a real recovery, you're not flustered or frazzled by the unfamiliar procedures.

Planning Your Recovery Strategy

Failure to plan is the most common cause of permanent Exchange data loss. Why? Consider a typical single-site environment with two servers. One server is lost in a fire. Its backup tapes were sitting next to it on a desktop instead of in an offsite (or even fireproof) vault. Oops. That server's not recoverable, because its administrator didn't plan adequately, not because the server got roasted. The key points you have to consider when planning your recovery strategy are straightforward:

How long can I afford for my server to be down?
Later in this chapter, you'll learn how to estimate backup and restore times; on top of that, you have to factor in the time it takes to run Exchange's database repair tools, if needed, plus any time to get hardware set up and organized.

Do I have adequate replacement hardware?
If your primary server is a large quad-processor box with a 60GB store, what happens when you need to restore all 60GB of data to another machine? The best possible outcome is to keep a clone of your standard server configuration in your test lab so that you can use it as a recovery server (this implies that you have to budget accordingly, as discussed in Chapter 3, *Exchange Planning*).

This also extends to backup hardware. For example, if you back up your servers to DLT, you'd better make sure you have more than one DLT drive, because if your sole drive fails you won't be able to back up or restore until it's fixed or replaced.

Am I making regular backups?

Do they happen often enough to capture all the changes made to my server? Do they include system information like the domain SAM and server registry?

Are my backup tapes secure?

Ideally, you should have multiple sets of backup tapes, some of which should be stored in a secure offsite location. See the Nutshell Handbook *Windows NT Backup and Restore*, by Jody Leber (O'Reilly & Associates) for more details.

Am I making the right kind of backups?

There's a difference between offline and online backups, and in general online backups are more useful and easier to restore. Do you know what kind you're making right now?

Steal this white paper

Microsoft has prepared a terrific 84-page white paper titled "Exchange Disaster Recovery." It was originally written for Exchange 4.0 by a group from Microsoft Consulting Services; since then, it's been updated several times and is still the canonical source of disaster recovery knowledge. One reason it's so long is that it consolidates in one place much of the information spread throughout this book.

Stop reading this book right now and go get the white paper; it's available from *www.microsoft.com/exchange/55/whpprs/BackupRestore.htm*. Once you've got a copy, come back and resume reading; I'll be making reference to the white paper throughout the rest of this chapter, and it's a very handy reference to keep right next to each of your servers.

Estimating recovery space requirements

Some recovery procedures use more space than others. In particular, any time you have to run the `isinteg` or `eseutil` tools, it's likely that you'll need a significant amount of extra disk space. A good heuristic is that you should always have at least as much free space as your largest store file; some repairs require twice as much space as your largest database file, so be prepared to juggle things around or use a network shared drive, as described later, to leave yourself enough room.

Don't forget that this extra storage is required for most database maintenance tasks, too; if you plan to do offline defragmentations or inspections with `isinteg`, you'll need the extra space.

Estimating recovery time

To know how long it'll take to recover your system, you first must know how long it will take to physically move your backed-up data to the recovery system. Once your store gets bigger than about 5GB, recovery time is driven primarily by the speed of your I/O subsystem. Even with a Fibre Channel RAID array, an 18GB file copy between two separate controllers and disk arrays can take more than an hour. Over a 100Mbps switched full-duplex network, a 16GB file copy time still takes around 90 minutes. When you consider the sad fact that restoring data takes at least as long as backing it up, and that running the Exchange utilities can push the total recovery time to twice as long as the original backup requirement, knowing how long things take is critical.

It's prudent to establish a baseline for the speed of your network and servers. I recommend the following tests, using at least a 2GB store file:

- If you intend to run `eseutil` or `isinteg` on the same disk partition as the databases, do a disk-to-disk copy on that partition.

- If your system has multiple controllers, do a disk-to-disk copy between the two controllers on one server.

- Do a disk-to-disk copy between two unique servers; this will tell you what sort of network throughput you can reasonably expect during a restore.

- Back up your stores from disk to tape using your backup software. For best performance, put your tape drive on a different controller than your database disks. With some systems and backup software, local backups will be faster than doing backups over the network; on others, CPU load and other overhead will actually make a local backup slower.

- Back up your stores from their home on one server to a tape drive on another. This offers you superior flexibility when it's time to restore, since you aren't limited to restoring onto a machine with a tape drive.

These tests take time to run, but one late night or Saturday spent doing them provides real-world data on how long restores will take in your environment. These tests will tell you how long it takes to restore the data, but not how long it takes to play back the log files. There's no really good way to estimate that, since many short transactions take longer to play back than an equal-size block of a few large transactions.

 Note that these tests may show that your I/O system isn't well optimized for copying large files. That's okay, since most Exchange I/O is made up of small (4KB to 64KB) requests. See Chapter 18, *Managing Exchange Performance*, for more details.

One interesting note: Exchange 5.5 has been tuned to make the database backup APIs significantly faster. Microsoft claims that Exchange supports speeds up to 30GB/hour, so if you can't back things up that fast the problem is likely that your backup hardware can't keep up.

Logging and the Databases

Chapter 2, *Exchange Architecture*, covers database transaction logging in detail, including a general overview of backups; you may find it helpful to flip back there if you need a refresher. The logs often actually grow faster and consume disk space faster than the database files themselves. Every transaction generates a log entry. For example, if you send a message containing a 24MB video clip to your inbox, then delete the message, you'll have generated more than 24MB of log files: one set of log data records the new message, while a separate set records its deletion.

The biggest stumbling block to successful Exchange recovery is circular logging; when you enable it, you're giving Exchange permission to throw away log data. With circular logging off, as long as you have a good copy of your transaction logs, you can restore your database to a consistent and correct state. If being able to recover your data is more important than the cost of having to buy enough disk space, turn circular logging off on your IS servers. There's no excuse for leaving it on when you can buy a 10GB drive for U.S. $150 or less.

A recovery scenario

Even if you lose the entire public or private IS—say the single disk it's on crashes beyond repair—you may still be able to restore the server with no data loss. For this to happen, there are two ironclad requirements:

- You must have a complete backup: either a full backup or a full backup combined with appropriate incremental and differential backups. If you use differential backups, all the differential tapes must be available and complete.

- Circular logging must be turned off, and you must have access to the log files either on their original disk or from a recent backup. (Remember, according to what you learned in Chapter 3, your logs should always be on a separate disk from your IS databases.) Exchange 5.0 and 5.5 turn circular logging on by default, so you must manually turn it off.

As long as you meet these requirements, data loss can be zero. Let's say that the primary server for your workgroup is highly active; it has a 24GB *priv.edb* and logs grow at a rate of about 40MB per hour. A full backup is performed each night, starting at 11:00 p.m. and ending around 12:30 a.m. The logs and databases are stored on separate drives.

At 3:05 p.m. on Tuesday, a cleaning lady is working in the server room and accidentally pulls the power cord out from the back of a server. This happens right when Exchange is updating a table in the private IS, so the IS ends up corrupted. Upon reboot, the IS service fails to start. You review the event log and determine that the IS won't start because the database is corrupted. You opt to restore from your backups.

Although the IS is down, the DS and SA services are running. You start `ntbackup`, pop in last night's backup tape, and select to restore the *priv.edb* from last night and start the restoration. Approximately 70 minutes later, the file is restored.

Now, let's stop to consider what's happened so far. Your Exchange server now has a *priv.edb* from 12:30 a.m. on Monday, but the server last saw activity at 3:05 p.m. Hundreds (if not thousands) of new messages, sent items, and user changes have altered the database in those 14 hours and 35 minutes. There's good news, though: since you still have pristine copies of the log files, once you restart the IS, it begins to play back the approximately 560MB of log data that has accumulated since the backup finished. Each transaction in the log is rerecorded in the private IS, so when the IS finishes its job, your store is returned to its exact pre-unplugging condition.

How likely is this scenario? Very! If the drive with your IS had failed, or if you had to repair some other component, you'd still be able to restore things the same way. Even if you have to rebuild a server from scratch, as long as you have good backups, you'll be able to make things right. Note that this recovery wouldn't have been possible without proper planning and execution, and time was still required time for the recovery itself.

> Depending on what caused the original corruption, it's conceivable that replaying the logs will lead to the identical circumstances and again corrupt the store. Be sure to pin down the cause of failure before you try to recover from it.

It is worth noting here that a $200 call to PSS for a helpful walkthrough of the recovery process may be the cheapest insurance you ever buy. If you don't practice recoveries regularly, and if you don't have a detailed plan written by you and customized for your environment, it is cheaper to get help beforehand than after a bungled restoration.

Backing Up Exchange

Exchange is designed to be backed up while running. These online backups give you maximum access to your data, since you don't have to stop Exchange's services to do a backup, provided you use an Exchange-aware backup product. (See the sidebar "Third-Party Backup Tools" for more on that touchy subject.) Before you start making backups, though, you need to know what to back up.

What to Back Up

How do you know what to back up? You can go the easy route and just back up everything on your server; even then, you need to understand what specific items are most important. You may also want or need to be more selective about what you preserve on your backups. Here's a suggested list:

- The public and private IS databases and the directory database. To do a successful online backup, you must use an Exchange-aware backup tool.

- Transaction logs. The public and private databases share one set of logs, so they are backed up together, but the directory logs are separate.

- The Key Management Server database. You must stop the KMS before you back up its data, then restart it when you're done. Remember that the KMS data is stored in its own directory, and that it's not backed up as part of the Exchange backup process.

- Other miscellaneous files in the Exchange directory trees, including MS Mail and other connector files, the GWART files, IMS archive messages, and so on.

- The Windows NT registry on the Exchange server. `ntbackup` includes a checkbox you can use to specify that you want this backed up; you should also keep your emergency repair disks current.

- The Windows NT SAM database. Exchange depends on Windows NT security information for the service accounts and user access to mailboxes, so to restore a server you must have access to the SAM context it formerly lived in.

- If you're allowing your users to use PST or OST files, and if you're storing them on a central server, be sure to back them up, too. Better yet, don't allow your users to use them.

Backup Considerations

Exchange Server supports three forms of backup: full (also known as normal), incremental, and differential. If you insist on using circular logging, you can only do full backups; incremental and differential backups depend on the log files.

Full

A full backup, as the name implies, is a complete backup of the data: everything you specify is backed up in its entirety. All Exchange recovery depends on having a full backup plus any incremental or differential backups you use. Since a full backup captures everything on your server, it has the advantage of being complete, but the disadvantage that each full backup requires the same amount of time.

Exchange-aware backup applications purge the transaction logs after the backup completes; that's safe, because by the time the backup finishes, all logged transactions have already been applied to the store and backed up to tape.

Differential

Differential backups capture only those changes since the previous full backup. Exchange-aware products implement differential backups by storing only the log files that have changed since the previous full backup, not any of the IS or DS database files themselves. Differential backups don't purge the log files.

Because differential backups preserve all changes since the previous full backup, you don't have to keep all of them together. Let's say you do a full backup every Sunday and differentials Monday through Friday. You can use the full backup plus any one of your differential backups to do a complete restoration. This means that as the week progresses, your differential backups will take longer.

Incremental

Incremental backups are similar to differential backups, with a major twist: at the end of the backup, the transaction log files are purged. This is a lot more aggressive than differential backups, since if anything goes wrong with your backup media, you no longer have log files! Incremental backups have to be used together; if you make a full backup on Sunday and incrementals the rest of the week, restoring a server that fails on Wednesday requires the full backup plus Monday and Tuesday's incrementals.

Choosing the right backup strategies

Instead of focusing on saving tapes or labor when doing the backup, focus on saving yourself trouble and effort when you need to restore your servers. That's when the availability of the right backup data really pays off. If doing a daily full backup takes too long or uses too many tapes to be feasible for your site, get new backup hardware. When the time comes to do a restore, the last thing you want to worry about is chasing down all the incremental or differential tapes you need.

If you can't do full backups every day, do a couple per week and do differentials on the other days. If your disk space situation forces you to use incremental backups, you can do so, but I'd only recommend it until you can get a bigger drive for your log files.

Safeguarding your backup tapes

While a complete discussion of the pros and cons of tape rotation and offsite storage doesn't belong in this book, I can give you an abbreviated version: use three sets of tapes, which I'll call A, B, and C. Each week, rotate the sets. For example, if you use A this week, then B should be in a fireproof vault at your facility, and C should be in a similar vault in a different location. Next week, you'd start using C, you'd move B offsite, and you'd put A in your office vault. This shuffling may seem like a terrific hassle, and it is, but it's also excellent protection against losing or damaging one set of tapes.

I also strongly recommend that you establish a periodic audit of your backup procedures and their implementation. Check to make sure that your scheduled backups are actually happening, that data is being written to the tapes, and that you can restore it. I once was called in to restore a system that had failed; the system's tape drive was slightly out of alignment, so that it could read tapes it had written, but other drives couldn't. That put a quick stop to the restoration until we figured out what was wrong.

Content considerations

In some environments, email requires special attention for backup procedures and data recovery ability. For legal and business liability reasons, efforts may be made to ensure that long-term backups are not retained. In the United States of America, it is not uncommon to hear of companies who have policies on how long tapes may be kept. The contents of email "conversations" can be used in legal proceedings, from sexual harassment cases to establishing that an organization had a specific intent during dealings with a partner company.

Using ntbackup

Exchange includes a version of the ntbackup utility that has been modified to understand how to find Exchange servers in an organization, connect to them, and back up their data without stopping the server's Exchange services. When you install Exchange or Exchange Administrator on a machine, you get this modified version of ntbackup. You can tell when you have it because there will be a new Microsoft Exchange… command in the Operations menu.

What ntbackup can do

Although it's not as sophisticated as some of the available third-party products, ntbackup is still my favorite solution for backing up Exchange servers, because its integration with Exchange is seamless: to back up a server's DS or IS, just pick the server and items to back up, then sit back and relax. You don't have to stop your Exchange services or otherwise fiddle with things.

ntbackup supports a wide variety of IDE and SCSI tape devices, but it doesn't support removable media or hard disks, so you can't use it to do an online backup to another disk somewhere. In addition, ntbackup doesn't have a lot of fancy tape management features. It doesn't know about autoloaders, striped DLT arrays, or other exotica. However, it's robust, reasonably fast, and free.

Using the GUI

ntbackup is pretty easy to use, so I'm not going to spend time explaining its basic functionality. The online help is good, and you can learn a lot from just poking around. Instead, let's dive into the Exchange-specific changes.

When you run ntbackup and select the Operations → Microsoft Exchange… command, you'll see a window split into two panes, just as in Exchange Administrator. The left pane shows your organization, sites, and servers. When you select a server in that pane, the right pane shows what items you can back up for that server. The DS and IS are shown separately, but no distinction is made between the public and private IS files.

To specify a server or database to back up, just click the checkbox next to it. Once you've selected everything you want to back up (bearing in mind that recovery will be easiest if you back up each server separately), you can click the Backup button or use the Operations → Backup… command to start the festivities. The familiar Backup Information dialog will appear; it looks just like the standard ntbackup dialog, except that you'll see each server's DS or IS as a separate backup set labeled "Microsoft Exchange" plus the server name (for example, "Microsoft Exchange: Information Store \\HSV1"). You can use the Backup Type pull-down to select a backup type of normal, incremental, or differential. If you're running ntbackup on the Exchange server itself, you can use the Backup Local Registry checkbox to force it to back up your registry as part of the session. When you're done specifying what you want backed up, press the OK button and the backup will begin. As things progress, the Backup Status window will show you which organization, site, and server it's backing up, and it will log any errors it finds.

 Don't assume that your entire backup will fit on a single tape; it might not, and ntbackup will dumbly sit there waiting for the next tape. In the meantime, incoming transactions will pile up in your Exchange server's database.

Exchange-specific command-line switches

ntbackup has a bunch of command-line switches, all of which are well documented in its online help. Oddly, the Exchange-specific switches aren't documented at all. Since you need them to do command-line backups, this is a pretty major omission, but there are only two pertinent switches: DS and IS. These work as you'd expect: in your ntbackup command line, you use the switches along with the machine name you want to back up. For example, this command line backs up drives *c*, *d*, and *e*, along with the DS and IS, on the server named *HSV*:

```
ntbackup backup c: d: e: DS \\hsv IS \\hsv /v /d "HSV DS/IS/drive" /b
    /t Normal /l c:\backup\daily.log
```

Testing your backup

You can and should verify the integrity of your backups. Microsoft's recommended approach is covered in Knowledge Base article Q178308; in brief, they recommend that you do the following:

1. Set up a test server onto which you can restore the backup.

2. Restore the backup onto your test server.

3. Stop the IS and DS services on the test server.

4. Use the `eseutil /g` command (described in the later "eseutil" section to verify the integrity of the restored data. You'll need to run it three times, once for each of the database files.

If the restore was successful, none of the above steps will report any errors. I also recommend some basic sanity checks on the database content: consider checking mailboxes or public folders with known content to be sure everything is there. You could also use Outlook's Advanced Find command to search for random strings on the entire mailbox, searching both subject and body; this is a good test of the IS random-access indices. When you're done, check the test server's application event logs for any unusual errors.

Restoring from your backups

Restoring from a backup made with **ntbackup** is pretty easy; it's the other steps involved in the recovery process that are tricky, like knowing when to start the Exchange services. To restore from an online backup, run **ntbackup**. When the Tapes window opens, double-click your backup tape or use the Operations → Catalog... command) to force it to catalog the tape. Once the catalog has been loaded, use the Tapes window to check the databases you want to restore, then use the Operations → Restore... command to start the restore. The Restore Information dialog will appear, and you'll need to fill it out properly:

- You can only restore a DS to the server it was backed up from; by filling out the Destination Server field, you can restore an IS to another server.

- You can restore the private and public IS databases separately by checking the appropriate boxes.

- If you check the "Erase all existing data" checkbox, **ntbackup** will replace the existing databases on the target server with the new ones you're restoring. Use this option only when you're sure you want to overwrite what's already on the server.

- The "Start Service After Restore" checkbox lets you choose whether to automatically restart the DS or IS service once the restore finishes. Don't check this unless you're sure you don't need to run `isinteg`.

Once you've set the restore options the way you want them, click the OK button and the restore will start. Since `ntbackup` has to stop the Exchange services before doing the restore, it will ask you to confirm that you want them stopped.

Offline Backup

If the Exchange IS service is cleanly stopped, then the *priv.edb* and *pub.edb* files will be closed normally and all logged transactions will be correctly posted. Once you've done this, it's possible to save the *priv.edb*, *pub.edb*, and *dir.edb* files to disk or tape, in effect making a backup using the filesystem as a backup tool. Since the Exchange services aren't running while you do this backup, it's called an *offline* backup.

Generally, online backups are best; they preserve your ability to back up your data while still keeping your server operating. However, there are circumstances where offline backup and recovery are useful, as when you're constructing an alternate server or running tests that require a complete copy of the database files.

The critical ingredient to doing a successful offline backup is to make sure that the IS is correctly shut down. If the stop attempt fails, or if the service stops as the result of a crash, the database files will not be suitable for an offline backup. At a minimum, you should restart the IS and stop the service correctly before making a copy of the files.

If you're using a third-party backup solution that doesn't support Exchange, you may be tempted to rely on offline backups as your primary safety net. I don't recommend it. Offline backups don't delete the log files, as online backups normally do. In addition, Exchange-aware backup programs run a page-level integrity check on the database as each page is backed up. When an offline backup is performed, the database pages are not checked; the file is just copied, so database damage can go unnoticed until you need to restore from your offline backup.

 If you keep daily watch on your event logs, you'll notice any unusual developments associated with the backups before they can do permanent harm. Microsoft Knowledge Base article Q188646, titled "XADM: Unable to Back Up Exchange Server 5.5 with Event ID 105," explains what to do when you encounter underlying database problems while doing a backup.

Restoring from an offline backup

There are four key steps to successfully restoring from an offline backup:

- Safeguarding the existing database files, in case you want to undo the restore. To accomplish this, copy the contents of the *exchsrvr\mdbdata* directories on all your system drives to a safe location.

- Finding the correct location for the IS and DS databases and logs. These paths are stored in the registry: the `HKLM\System\CurrentControlSet\Services\` `MSExchangeIS` key has separate entries for the database log path (`ParametersSystem\DB Log Path`), public IS database (`ParametersPublic\` `DB Path`), and private IS database (`ParametersPrivate\DB Path`); there are separate entries for the directory in the `MSExchangeDS` key.

- Copying the files from wherever you backed them up to back to the correct location. The public and private IS databases, IS log files, directory database, and directory logs can all be in different directories, and it's critical to get them in the correct location.

You can't restore log and database files to a different path than the ones they came from, because they contain internal signatures; you can, however, restore them to different drives, as long as the relative path remains the same.

- Running `isinteg -patch` after the restore finishes, but before you try to restart the IS. See the section "Using the –patch switch" for more details.

Maintenance and Repair Tools

As discussed in Chapter 11, *Managing the Information Store*, Exchange can perform many database maintenance tasks either on its own or according to a schedule you set. These tasks include tombstone cleanup, online defragmentation, index expiration and aging, and other tasks associated with regular preventative database maintenance. However, there are times when offline tools are required for database compaction, testing, and repair.

Don't use offline tools unless absolutely necessary. Like firearms, they're irreplaceable when you really need them, but they can be dangerous in careless or untrained hands.

Third-Party Backup Tools

Many of the enhancements on the backup management front aren't particularly beneficial to Exchange administrators. For example, for normal Windows NT file backups, it may be desirable to have a web interface to the backup program allowing a user to search hundreds of thousands of files to specify which one to restore. One area where third-party backup tools really look good is hardware support. Many products support autoloading tape drives, multiple tape drives configured in striped arrays, or backup devices that `ntbackup` doesn't support. Apart from hardware support, many larger organizations have chosen backup solutions that can handle multiple operating systems or special needs like hierarchical storage management.

While third-party products can often do things that `ntbackup` can't, many of them have a history of problems with their Exchange support interfaces. Microsoft has provided a set of API routines that third-party products can use to scan the IS, but not every vendor has been able to successfully decipher Microsoft's documentation and build a usable backup tool.

Most third-party products that advertise Exchange support are usable, provided that you're careful. Make sure you get the correct agent or plugin module to properly back up Exchange, and make sure that the version you're using is the right one for the combination of Exchange, NT, and service packs you're running. Spend some time researching the *msexchange* list archives, the Microsoft Knowledge Base, and your peer network to find out whether other sites with similar configurations have had good luck with the solution you want to use.

No matter what else you do, always test your backup and restore setup on a complete copy of your database (with a recovery server, of course). It's imperative that you find problems with your backup software or hardware in the controlled environment of your test lab, not during a real service outage.

eseutil

`eseutil` is a command-line program that performs a variety of functions on the database, including compacting, testing and repair. It operates on individual 4KB database pages, not on messages, mailboxes, or folders. Exchange 5.5's version of `eseutil` can check database integrity at about 10GB/hour and repair databases at 8–10GB/hour; `isinteg` can defragment databases at 4–5 GB/hour.

 `eseutil` replaces `edbutil`, the utility program used on Exchange 4.
0 and 5.0 databases. In Exchange 5.5 SP1 and later, it is located in the *winnt\system32* directory instead of in *exchsrvr\bin*.

When to use it

Ideally, you'd never run `eseutil`. I always cringe when I see people running it as a preventative maintenance tool. This is somewhat like doing preventative maintenance on your car with a welding torch: it gets the gunk off, but one wrong move and your engine will be a melted lump of slag. There are only three circumstances in which I recommend running it:

- When you want to check the integrity of a database, either *in situ* or from a backup.

- When you need to defragment a database to free up disk space. For example, if you move several dozen mailboxes to another server you can reclaim their space by an offline defragmentation. Don't do this routinely, however; there's no reason to do so, since the online defragmentation process runs daily.

- When you need to fix a corrupted database because you can't restore it from a backup, or because Microsoft tells you to.

I can't overemphasize that this is not a tool for casual or everyday use. It can be dangerous, especially in repair mode.

How to use it

`eseutil` works in six distinct modes. For most Exchange systems, the only modes you'll be interested in are the defragmentation, integrity check, and repair modes. The six modes are described individually in the following sections.

The first thing you have to cope with are the mode switches that control what `eseutil` does, shown in Table 17-1.

Table 17-1. eseutil Command-Line Switches

Switch	What It Does
/D	Defragmentation mode: copies the specified database to a new file, then defragments the file to make its data contiguous. When defragmentation finishes, copies the new file back to the original location.
/G	Integrity check mode: validates checksum and header information against the actual database contents. Nondestructive.
/M	File dump mode: dumps the database file's contents in (mostly) human-readable form.
/P	Repair mode: validates the database table structure and links, truncating or changing things where necessary. May cause data loss. Use as a last resort.
/R	Recovery mode: attempts to put databases in a consistent state by repairing bad table links, but doesn't truncate or otherwise modify data in the tables.
/U	Upgrade mode: rarely used, since it's designed to update an older database schema to the current revision. Normally, Exchange's setup and service pack installation programs do this.

Here's a complete breakdown of the `eseutil` options:

```
eseutil
     | /D database [/L logPath] [/S systemPath] [/B backupName]
        [/T tempName] [/P] [/O]
     | /G database [/T tempName] [/V] [/X] [/O]
     | /M[mode] fileName
     | /P database [/T tempName] [/D] [/V] [/X] [/O]
     | /R { /IS | /DS } [/L logPath] [/S systemPath] [/O]
     | /U database /D dllPath [/B backupName] [/T tempName] [/P] [/O]
```

Defragmentation mode

Exchange normally defragments the IS databases while the IS runs. However, you can do an offline defragmentation with `eseutil`; since the services aren't running, the utility can do a better job of compacting the database. Microsoft recommends that you do a full online backup after doing an offline defragmentation, because any outstanding log files will have the wrong database signature after the defragmentation finishes. In my opinion, you should do one before the defragmentation, too, just in case something goes wrong.

Defragmentation mode has its own set of switches:

```
eseutil /D database [/L logPath] [/S systemPath] [/B backupName]
        [/T tempName] [/P] [/O]
```

database

Specifies the database you want to defragment. Use /ds, /ispub, or /ispriv as the database name to tell `eseutil` to look up the database name and path in the registry, or provide the full path and database name.

/L logPath

Specifies the location of the transaction log files for this database. Defaults to the current directory if not specified; not required when using the /ds, /ispub, or /ispriv switches.

/S systemPath

Tells `eseutil` where to find the checkpoint file. Defaults to the current directory.

/B backupName

Forces `eseutil` to make a backup of the database being worked on, using the specified name and path.

/T tempName

Specifies a name for the temporary database that `eseutil` creates. Useful for redirecting the temporary database to another disk where you have more space. Defaults to *tempdfrg.edb* in the current working directory.

/P

> Tells `eseutil` to preserve the temporary database, so it will create it but not replace the original with the newly created file. You would then need to manually replace the original file with the newly created temporary file.

/O

> Suppresses the `eseutil` version and copyright message.

Integrity check mode

`eseutil` can verify the low-level integrity of the database and its pages. Note that this is different than `isinteg`, which checks the integrity of message and mailbox items in the database. This mode is nondestructive, but it assumes that the database is in a consistent state when you run it; if not, you'll get an error. Integrity check mode has the following syntax:

```
eseutil /G database [/T tempName] [/V] [/X] [/O]
```

database

> Specifies the database you want to check. Use /ds, /ispub, or /ispriv as the database name to tell `eseutil` to look up the database name and path in the registry, or provide the full path and database name.

/T tempname

> As in the defragmentation mode, specifies where to store the temporary file.

/V

> Turns on verbose mode, which provides a wealth of information about what the utility is doing.

/X

> Forces `eseutil` to provide detailed error messages instead of its usual terse ones.

/O

> Suppresses the `eseutil` version and copyright message.

Dump mode

The dump mode tells `eseutil` to print some information about either the database header or the checkpoint file. It's mostly useful if you're curious about what's in those files or if you're asked to dump the files during a call to Microsoft support. The dump mode has the following syntax:

```
eseutil /M[mode] filename
```

mode

> Specifies the dump mode you want to use. The K modifier specifies a check-point dump, and the H modifier (the default value) specifies a header dump.

filename

> Specifies the full path and filename of the file whose contents you want to see.

Repair mode

eseutil can attempt to repair a damaged database by checking the database's links between various tables of information and fixing those links if it can tell that they're bad. This repair operation is nondestructive, but it's not guaranteed to return the database to a consistent state when you run it. Repair mode has the following syntax:

```
eseutil /P database [/T tempName] [/D] [/V] [/X] [/O]
```

database

> Specifies the database you want to repair. Use /ds, /ispub, or /ispriv as the database name to tell eseutil to look up the database name and path in the registry, or provide the full path and database name.

/D

> Specifies that eseutil should test the database for errors without repairing it.

The /T, /V, /X, and /O switches have the same function here as in the previous modes.

Recovery mode

The recovery mode is scary because it can cause data loss. When you tell eseutil to recover a database, it will freely truncate any database page it can't cleanly recover. While this will normally restore your database to a consistent and usable state, it will also normally cause you to lose some message and/or mailbox data. Don't use this mode except as a last resort. If you run an integrity check and it shows errors, always run a repair first. If that doesn't fix everything, you have two choices: restore from a good backup (hopefully with no data loss), or run a recovery. Any time you're tempted to choose the latter option, call Microsoft support first to see whether there are any other alternatives for recovery. Microsoft has an array of specialized tools to fix specific problems, but these are available only if you call them. Recovery mode has the following syntax:

```
eseutil /R { /IS | /DS } [/L logPath] [/S systemPath] [/O]
```

The interesting switch here is the one that controls whether the recovery runs against the IS or DS. You can specify either, but not both, and eseutil will automatically look up the location of the log and database files in the registry; you can't manually override those values. The /L, /S, and /O switches work the same way here as in the other modes.

Update mode

The update mode is rarely used. Microsoft's documentation says its use will usually only be required "with the release of a major, new revision of Microsoft Exchange Server." Update mode has the following syntax:

```
eseutil /U database /D dllPath [/B backupName] [/T tempName] [/P] [/O]
```

database

Specifies the database you want to upgrade. You have to give the full path and database name; there aren't any shortcut switches.

/D dllPath

Specifies the full path to the database DLL for the version of Exchange you're upgrading from.

The /B, /T, /P, and /O switches work the same as in other modes.

isinteg

The isinteg utility does two things:

- It can test the IS databases for logical errors and fix them. In this mode, it verifies the integrity of information in the database, not of the database itself (that's eseutil's job). To do this, it cross-checks information in about 20 tables to determine what state the database is in. More specifically, it searches the IS databases for table errors, incorrect reference counts, and orphaned objects, none of which should exist in a consistent database.

- It can patch the IS after you restore it from an offline backup. This is necessary because restoring an offline backup of the IS databases doesn't restore some internal fields of the database, but the patch mode will.

Microsoft recommends against using isinteg to fix database errors unless they tell you to. As with eseutil, there's some risk involved with running isinteg; however, I think it's reasonably safe to run it if you know what you're doing. However, be forewarned that running isinteg may cause data loss, so don't do it unless it's necessary.

When to use it

The most common use for isinteg is to patch the store after running an online backup, as discussed in the "Using the –patch switch" section. Apart from that, any time the IS won't start, you should run isinteg in test mode so it can check the IS for errors, particularly if you see IS errors in the event log.

There are other circumstances when you might suspect that something's amiss:

- An inconsistent message count on private or public folders. For example, a folder may show five new messages when only three exist. `isinteg`'s reference count tests are used to address such issues.

- An unexplained crash of the Information Store when a user accesses a given folder or message.

- A user is unable to access a message or folder from any client due to client error. Event log entries may also be present on server containing messages.

It never hurts to run `isinteg` in test mode; however, you should only run it with the `-fix` switch if you've got a recent backup.

How to use it

The full set of `isinteg` options looks like this; they're explained in Table 17-2:

```
isinteg [-pri] [-pub] [-fix] [-L [logFile]] [-detailed]
    [-verbose] [-test { alltests | testName} ] [-dump] [-[patch]
```

Table 17-2. isinteg Command-Line Switches

Switch	What It Does
-detailed	Provides additional detail on any database problems found.
-dump	Verbose dump of store data. Interesting, but not always useful.
-fix	Fixes problems found during the integrity check. Without this switch, a read-only check is performed.
-L	Specifies the name of the `isinteg` log file. Defaults to *isinteg.pub* or *isinteg.priv* in default directory.
-patch	Patches Information Store after an offline restore.
-pri	Specifies that `isinteg` should check the private Information Store, *priv. edb* (it gets the file's location from the registry).
-pub	Specifies that `isinteg` should check the public IS, *pub.edb.*
-T	Specifies path to database files; normally extracted from registry.
-test	Specifies which tests will be performed. `-test alltests` is recommended, since it runs all tests in sequence. You can also name individual tests. The following tests are named: *Folder/message tests*: `folder, message, aclitem, delfld, acllist, timedev, rowcounts, attach, morefld, global, searchq, dlvrto, search, dumpsterprops, namedprop` *Private IS only*: `rcvfld , mailbox, oofhist` *Public IS only*: `peruser, artidx, newsfeed` *Reference count tests*: `msgref, msgsoftref, attachref, acllistref, aclitemref, newsfeedref` (public only), `fldrcv` (private only) `fldsub, dumpsterref` *Groups tests*: `allfoldertests, allacltests` *Special tests*: `deleteextracolumns`
-verbose	Provides verbose progress messages.

Using the -patch switch

`isinteg` is also used to patch the database when you restore it from an offline backup. This is necessary because of how the IS allocates object IDs: each object in the public and private IS databases has a globally unique identifier, or GUID. Object GUIDs are derived from the base GUID of the store they live in. Microsoft uses GUIDs in Exchange to uniquely identify an object's location and creation time. When you do an offline restore, you're reloading an "old" version of the database: in effect, you're turning back time. If you don't change the store's base GUIDs, newly created objects could accidentally get GUIDs that match items already in the store, which would cause major trouble for replication.

When you do an online backup, `ntbackup` fixes the GUIDs as it does the restore; for an offline backup, you must manually fix them by running `isinteg -patch`. If you don't run this command after doing an offline restore, the IS won't start, and it will record error −1011 in the event log. The message for that event says (paraphrased) "You restored an offline backup. Go run `isinteg -patch` or I won't start."

To use the `-patch` switch, make sure that the DS and SA services are running, then run `isinteg -patch` from the command line. It will replace the GUIDs, after which you can safely restart the IS. Note that you can't patch one IS or the other; `isinteg` will always patch both databases.

Recovering Your Data

Chapter 15, *Troubleshooting Exchange Server*, covers basic troubleshooting of the Exchange Server environment; it is a good reference point to start from. Once you've determined what's wrong, how do you fix it? Understanding how to fix specific problems is useful only if you can match your specific problem to the corresponding solution. Table 17-3 summarizes common problems and their solutions; the rest of this chapter will discuss the solution steps in detail.

Table 17-3. Troubleshooting Guide

Problem	Server Condition	Procedure
Directory database (*dir. edb*) damaged or missing	NT installation is okay. Exchange installation is okay. The server's directory is corrupted or unavailable (including disk failures).	Restore the directory database from a known good backup.
Public and/or private IS database damaged, logs okay	Windows NT and Exchange are undamaged. The *priv.edb* and/or *pub.edb* files are lost or damaged. Circular logging is off. You have a usable backup.	Restore the IS and log files to the failed server. Restart the IS to force it to play back the log files.

Table 17-3. Troubleshooting Guide (continued)

Problem	Server Condition	Procedure
Private IS damaged or lost, no logs	Windows NT and Exchange are undamaged. The *priv.edb* and/or *pub.edb* files are lost or damaged. Full logs are unavailable (log drive has failed, backup is bad, or circular logging was on). You have a usable backup of the IS.	Prepare for data loss! Restore from most recent full backup, then restart IS to play back any remaining log files. Some changes made since full backup will be lost.
Public IS damaged or lost, no logs	Windows NT and Exchange are undamaged. Replicas of the public folders exist.	Restore the old public IS database, then allow public folder replication to bring the contents up to date.
Single mailbox deleted by human error	Server is undamaged. No OST is available.	Create a new mailbox for the user on the production server, then see the section "Recovering Data from One Mailbox."

One of the more challenging aspects of dealing with recovery is the combination of losing Windows NT and Exchange Server at the same time. There are basically only a few considerations:

Is the hardware working, or was it the cause of the failure?

If the hardware is safe, the cause of the problem was human error, software, or some other factor that was removed. If the hardware caused the failure, are you reusing the old hardware, or do you need to acquire new or spare hardware?

Can the data be recovered from the system?

If the database files can be copied off, you may wish to bypass any tape restoration solutions and jump right to a offline restoration. If the system won't boot to access NTFS, one technique to get to the *.edb* files is to boot up from a Windows NT CD-ROM and install a second copy of NT on another partition to get NTFS access long enough to copy the files. Options here depend on the specifics of the failure and the disk layout. I've also seen drives moved off one computer and connected to a controller of a different computer. Consult your NT experts, as this is just a simple file retrieval; when the Exchange services aren't running, *.edb* files are just like any other files on a Windows NT system.

How long do you have?

If rebuilding a server will take time, do you have another suitable machine already running that could either join the domain or be renamed in the domain?

Recovering Data from One Mailbox

The biggest surprise to most new Exchange Server administrators is the inability to easily restore a single mailbox, folder, or message. In fact, the Exchange design requires that an entire *priv.edb* or *pub.edb* file be restored at once. Practically speaking, this means that the entire server's mailbox contents must be restored to retrieve a single user's deleted mailbox.

To recover a single message in a single mailbox or public folder, you have to restore the entire private or public IS—a huge amount of effort. Exchange 5.5's deleted item recovery feature means that most of the time you can get away without having to go through the whole process, so I recommend that you turn this feature on and give it a liberal retention period. (Note that it won't help you if the client is using PSTs, POP3, or IMAP4.)

What if you need to recover an item that has been removed but isn't in the dumpster? You can't restore the IS to your production server, because that'll overwrite changes to everyone else's mailbox. Instead, you need a separate recovery server. A separate server will come in handy for other recoveries, too, so if at all possible, you should keep one handy.

The recovery server

Your recovery server needs to have enough disk space to install NT and Exchange with all the service packs you use on your production servers, plus enough space to restore the private IS. It can be on the same LAN as your production network; however, if you leave the recovery server up you must be sure that it doesn't try to participate in directory replication.

Before you can recover anything, you must prepare the server appropriately:

1. Install Windows NT and any service packs. This computer can be a PDC, BDC, or member server; its network name is unimportant because you will only be restoring the IS, not the DS.

2. Install Exchange. When prompted, create a new site, using the organization and site name from the server whose backup you're restoring. Don't join the existing site.

3. Install whatever Exchange service pack was installed on the server at the time of the backup. For example, if you're restoring from a backup made while SP1 was installed, install SP1 on the recovery server even if you've since upgraded your production machine to SP2.

4. Install the Exchange or Outlook client on the recovery server.

You may or may not need to repeat these steps in the future; if you have a dedicated recovery server, you may be able to leave it alone once it's set up, or you may have to reinstall Exchange or even NT to match the configuration of the server you're trying to restore from.

Recovering a single item

Once your recovery server is up and going, the actual recovery is straightforward. The following steps assume that you've logged on to the recovery server as an administrator:

1. Restore the IS to your recovery server, either from an offline or online backup. Make sure the IS starts when you're done.

2. Run Exchange Administrator, then start the DS/IS consistency adjuster. (It's in the Advanced tab of the server's properties dialog). This is required to populate the directory, since you didn't restore it.

3. Open the Recipients container, find the mailbox you want to restore, and open its properties dialog. Use the Primary Windows NT Account button to select the account you logged on with as the mailbox owner.

4. Configure a messaging profile for the new user account, making sure to add the Exchange and Personal Folder services to it.

5. Launch the Outlook or Exchange client. If you're using the Exchange client, select the user's folder and copy it, then paste it to the Personal Folders item. If you're using Outlook, use the File → Export... command to export the desired data to a PST.

6. Deliver the PST to the original client, or move the PST contents into the user's mailbox. Warn the user sternly not to lose any more data.

These steps work whether you want to restore an individual message or an entire mailbox.

Restoring Data When Your Machine Is Okay

Restoration is where backup solutions test their mettle. You are strongly advised to test your backup solutions as much as you can tolerate, as there is no point in doing a backup if the restore is unsuccessful. All too often, automated backup solutions get out of hand and errors are not caught until it is too late.

The act of restoring itself can present a risk. Accidentally restoring over an active server can have disastrous results. In fact, Microsoft's documentation advocates a dedicated recovery server as a primary means of recovery. The following excerpt is from the documentation:

> When a mailbox or information store is corrupted, you can use backups to recover the information store to a dedicated recovery server and then restore the mailbox

or information store to the production server. When a server fails, you can use backups to restore the server's information store, directory, and configuration to a recovery server and then place the recovery server in production to replace the failed server.

Before attempting any restore or recovery efforts, make copies of all the existing database and log files. In fact, it may be simplest to stop all of the Exchange server programs, then **xcopy** the various *exchsrvr* file trees, which may be on multiple partitions. With large stores, this could take some time, but it could be of considerable use if the restoration is problematic or in determining the cause of the failure.

Restoring from a failed database drive

This is probably the easiest type of recovery, because if you have a good backup and a good copy of the log files, Exchange can cleanly repair itself. If you lose the public or private IS or directory databases because the drive they're on fails, here's what to do:

1. Use the Services control panel to disable and stop the SA service.

2. Replace the failed drive. Create a new logical drive with the same name as before, then format it.

3. Create a directory structure for Exchange identical to the one on the failed drive (you can cheat and look in the registry to get the correct structure). Normally, this means you need to create the *exchsrvr* directory with subdirectories named *mdbdata* and *dsadata*.

4. Restore the databases from your last backup. If possible, use an online backup. Don't worry about restoring the transaction logs (if they were on the same drive, you'll need to follow the steps in the next section).

5. Enable the SA service, then start the SA, DS, and IS services. When the IS starts, it will replay the transaction logs and bring the restored IS or DS up to date.

6. Check the event log to make sure everything went smoothly.

Restoring from a failed log drive

When your log disk fails, you're probably going to end up losing some data unless your most recent backup is very recent indeed, although you may be able to recover some data using a separate procedure that I'll get to in a minute. First, here's what you need to do when you lose the disk with the IS logs on it:

1. Use the Services control panel to disable and stop the SA service.

2. Replace the failed drive, then create a new logical drive with the same name as before.

3. Format the new disk and create a directory structure for Exchange identical to the one on the failed drive. In particular, you need the *exchsrvr\mdbdata* directory.

4. Back up the IS databases, either online or offline.

5. Restore the most recent online backup of your IS databases.

6. Enable the SA service, then start the SA, DS, and IS services. When the IS starts, it will contain only the data from the time of the last backup.

7. Check the event log to make sure everything went smoothly.

 When you lose the DS log disk, you're in better shape because the directory can repair itself via replication. All you have to do in that case is fix the broken disk (following steps 1–3 in the previous list), back up your existing directory, then restore the most recent online backup of *dir.edb*. Once you do that, and restart the SA and DS services, the normal replication process will backfill any missing data.

If you want to try your luck at extracting additional data from the IS itself, you can. Some data that would normally be available from the logs might be available in the IS, in which case you can retrieve it by using the consistency adjuster. However, you must attempt this on the recovery server, not your production machine.

1. Set up your recovery server using the instructions in the section "The recovery server," earlier in this chapter. As in that section, be sure to use the same organization and site names as the production server, but don't join an existing site. Create a new site with the same name.

2. Make a backup copy of all files in the *exchsrvr\mdbdata* directories on your server.

3. Copy the private and public IS databases from the production server to the recovery server.

4. If necessary, use `isinteg` and/or `eseutil` to repair the databases. Once the databases are consistent, start the IS.

5. Run the DS/IS consistency adjuster. This may make changes to your IS and directory, which is what you're hoping for.

6. Use the exMerge tool (covered in Appendix A, *BORK Tools*) to merge whatever data the adjuster adjusted from the recovery machine back to your production server.

Restoring Exchange When NT Is Damaged

As long as you can accurately recreate the underlying NT configuration of your Exchange server, restoring to it is not significantly harder than restoring when a disk fails. Restoring the IS is exactly the same, in fact; the difference is that you normally need to restore the DS as well, and that's a little more complicated. There are two new requirements that you must be able to meet to successfully restore the directory:

- The recovery server must have the same organization, site, and server name as the original machine.

- You must have access to the original domain's SAM database.

Of course, the server you're restoring onto has to have adequate capacity to hold the databases, enough disk space to install Exchange and Windows NT, and so on. Be careful to accurately replicate the server's original NT configuration: install the same hotfixes, service packs, and third-party services in the same order as the original installation.

Restoring domain controllers

You have to be especially careful during recovery if you've installed Exchange on a domain controller, because having access to the domain SAM is a prerequisite for a successful recovery. If your failed machine was a BDC, you're in good shape; as long as the PDC or another BDC is still on the network, you can reinstall NT on your Exchange server as a BDC, and you'll be okay. The same is true if the server you were restoring was a member server.

The sticky part comes when you try to restore Exchange onto a machine that was formerly a PDC. If you reinstall NT as a PDC, it will create a totally new SAM database that won't match the original; although you'll be able to restore the IS and DS from a backup, you won't be able to start the Exchange services or use the restored directory, since it depends on the original security context. Without a directory, you can't do anything except restore individual mailboxes.

The key is to make sure that you have an available PDC when you do the restore. It may be a BDC that you've promoted (in which case you make your newly reinstalled server a BDC and promote it later), or it may be the original PDC. As long as one domain controller is available, you won't have any problem.

Restoring Exchange

The steps involved in restoring Exchange to a server that has been reloaded with a fresh copy of NT are as follows:

1. Remove the computer's old domain account on the PDC/BDC, then add it back.

2. Log on to the target machine as a domain administrator.

3. Run Exchange Setup using the /r switch. (See Chapter 4, *Installing Exchange*, for details.)

4. Make sure the server name matches the original server name; it should, as long as the NT names are the same.

5. Create a new site using the exact same site and organization name as the original server. Upper- and lowercase letters are different to Exchange, so make sure you have the capitalization right.

6. When prompted, use the same service account as the original server.

7. Install the same connectors that were on the original server.

8. Install the same Exchange service pack as was on the original server.

9. Configure the IMS, INS, MS Mail connector, and any third-party connectors, since they may store their configuration parameters in the registry instead of the directory.

10. Run Performance Optimizer.

11. If KMS was installed on the original machine, reinstall it.

12. Install Outlook or the Exchange client.

Don't start the Exchange services. At this point, you've got a fresh installation of Windows NT and Exchange, but you still have to reload your data from your backups.

Restoring your data

The restoration procedure varies slightly, depending on whether you have an online or offline backup and whether you have any log files generated after the original backup. I'll note the differences where they occur. Here's how to restore your data:

1. If you have transaction logs generated after the original backup, copy them to the log directories of the recovery server.

2. If you have an online backup, restore it using ntbackup. Tell ntbackup to back up the private and public IS, turn on the "Start Services After Restore" checkbox, and make sure the "Erase all Existing Data" box is checked unless you have transaction logs from after the original backup.

   If you have an offline backup, stop the Exchange services on the recovery server and copy the database and log files to their proper locations, then restart the DS and SA and run isinteg -patch. Once that finishes, restart the IS.

3. If you're running KMS, stop the KM service and restore its data, then restart it.

4. Verify mailbox account associations by opening a mailbox's properties dialog and checking the Primary Windows NT Account field. If you used the correct domain SAM, you should see that the account is correct.

5. Use the client software you installed in step 11 of the previous section to make sure that you can log on as a user, see calendar data, and exchange mail with other users.

6. Repeat the previous step using someone else's workstation.

7. Reconfigure Exchange and NT to match the original configuration:

— Increase the size of the application event log.

— Make sure the page file is set to the correct size.

— Turn off circular logging.

— Add any alternate service accounts.

— Set diagnostic logging levels, INS, and IMS settings as desired; they're stored in the registry, not the directory.

Restoring Exchange to a Different Computer

There are circumstances where you may be willing to lose configuration data but are more concerned with mailbox (*priv.edb*) content. As long as you keep the server name the same and get a new domain account for that name, you can restore Exchange to a new server. But what if you want to move it somewhere else? Perhaps your Exchange installation is damaged, but the server is still able to run other services, and you are unwilling to rebuild the entire system; instead, you want to move Exchange to another system with a new name.

This is not an ideal solution, as configuration data will be lost, all clients will need to be told about the new server, and so forth. It is best suited for testing of restore procedures, single mailbox restore, and other data-only restores where clients and other servers never directly connect to this restored data.

One variation of an offline restore is an alternate server restore. The normal Exchange restore procedure doesn't allow you to create a *priv.edb* or *pub.edb* file directly. To accomplish this, you would need to restore your database to an alternate server, stop that server, and manually copy the file you desire. If you do this, the server name and other aspects of the server won't be identical to the one you intend to deploy the store database on.

The fastest way to do this is to do a restore as outlined above. When you try to restart the IS, Exchange will complain via event log entries, including event ID 143, that the logs and the databases don't match. Your only possible response to that is to remove the log files, then restart the IS. This costs you the data in the log files; whether that's acceptable or not depends on what you're trying to do; be sure not to do anything until you have a good backup of the log files!

Once you've restarted the IS, you still need to use the DS/IS consistency adjuster to bring the directory in line with what's in the mailboxes. Figure 17-1 shows the DS/IS Consistency Adjustment screen. In this case, we want to synchronize the private IS and the directory, so the "Synchronize with the directory, and create new directory entries for mailboxes that do not have a corresponding directory entry" box is checked. It exactly describes our situation, as we used the restoration from tape to put the mailboxes in place without restoring the directory.

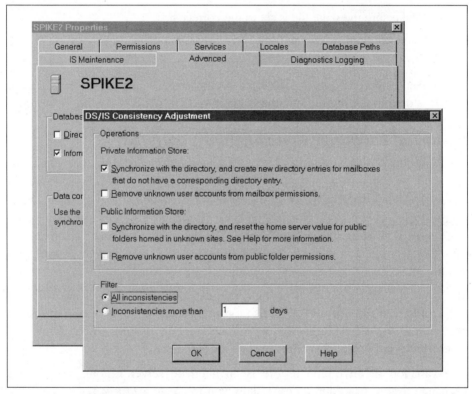

Figure 17-1. DS/IS Consistency Adjustment screen, options selected to discover users from the alternate server priv.edb file

One last step is to change the Filter setting to "All inconsistencies" from the default of "Inconsistencies more than 1 days." Press OK to start the adjustment. After the adjuster finishes running, the directory entries will appear. You will notice that the directory entries are missing all their normal fields; most of the mailbox information is stored in the directory, and we didn't restore it. However, the information that was restored is enough to allow you to recover data from the mailbox and print it, look it over, or whatever.

Directory Recovery

Complete recovery of the database is often not as much of an issue. Given the directory's relatively small file size and its replication with other servers in the same site, most directory issues are not related to total file loss or corruption.

This is not to say that problems do not exist: since the directory is central to the server's behavior, it is critical to take care in changes or actions that impact the directory. For specific recovery procedures, the Microsoft white papers and Knowledge Base articles should be referenced. In particular, Knowledge Base article Q196406, titled "XADM: Replication Fails After Disaster Recovery," covers much more than the title implies. It includes a further reference to KB Q15960, titled "XADM: Rebuilding the Site Folders in a Site."

Another good reference is KB Q162353, titled "XADM: Restoring an Exchange Directory," which outlines a strategy to rebuild the directory. Although this article somewhat oversimplifies the operation, it does emphasize how basic tools such as file copy and directory import/export can be used when proper backup solutions fail. When no copy of the directory is available, data in the IS can still be recovered. A call to Microsoft support or consultation with someone who has done this procedure is in order for such a situation, as there are several options and version-dependent concerns.

One of the most important steps is to quarantine the server. If new mail delivers or directory replication takes place, irreversible changes can be made.

Preventative Medicine

How can you ensure that your recovery goes smoothly? Practice makes perfect, but adequate documentation and good configuration control helps, too. You should maintain the following items and audit them periodically to make sure that the documentation and the real-world implementation match:

- If you're using a TCP/IP environment, keep *HOSTS* and *LMHOSTS* files for all the Exchange servers, backup servers, domain controllers, and other critical systems the Exchange server system may require.

- Keep documentation on backup locations and procedures, including where offsite tapes are stored and how to get to them. Include details such as contact information for all responsible persons and companies.

- Export the entire directory to a CSV file every week or every night as a precaution.

- Make sure records of each server installation, including the service account username and password, are available. This information should be secured, but it is also important to ensure that the current service account password is available for server recovery.

- Make regular (at least weekly) registry backups. Be sure to make additional backups after hardware, operating system, or Exchange configuration changes.

- Verify the backups at least once after every Exchange Server service pack, version upgrade, or other major change.

- Put your databases and logs on separate physical disks.

- Turn off database circular logging.

- Consider procedural issues when a mailbox is terminated. For example, hiding a mailbox for 30 days before deletion could prevent the need to restore the mailbox if an employee returns or a replacement staff member requires access to content.

- Have a basic plan on how to react if a database becomes corrupted or a system needs to be otherwise restored. For example, do you want to take the time to do a full file-by-file tape backup of the system before you start any attempts to recover or restore? This could be of use later, when attempting to find out why the failure took place.

- Have a suitable null modem cable on hand at all times, and familiarize yourself with use of the kernel debugger to trace system boot-up. This will be valuable one day when you find that your NT server won't boot due to a device driver, hardware device that failed, or corrupt system file.

- Make sure you run `rdisk` after each configuration change. It may be best to do so weekly or daily as part of routine maintenance.

As I mentioned at the start of this chapter, when your backups are properly planned and implemented, the next challenge is to help cut the recovery time down to the minimum. You can do this by buying backup hardware sized appropriately to the task at hand; in some cases, you may want to consider splitting up large private or public IS databases by moving some of their data to another server. Chapter 14, *Managing Exchange Servers*, discusses some of these issues and explains what solutions and practices make sense.

Offline Defragmentation

If you are concerned that the store may have minor problems, one way to regain assurance is to run an offline defragmentation or integrity check on your recovery server. This is also a good way to establish performance baselines for a particular system.

If you do decide to defragment your store, you must make a full online backup after the defragmentation finishes. When the offline defragmentation process runs, it changes the signature on the database, making it incompatible with older log files.

Reducing the Risk of Mailbox Loss

What can you do to reduce the risk of losing mailbox data? Assuming you have good backups, and that you've turned on deleted item retention to guard against accidental deletions, what else can you do? There are several potential solutions, some of which are pretty creative:

- Use scripts or an alternate mail client to copy the mailbox contents on a message-by-message basis. Exchange 5.5 does not support server-to-server replicas of a mailbox, but you can deliver this type of feature with some clever scripting.*

- For mailboxes with critical data, consider offering users their own public folder for longer-term storage. Most users create various folders for storage based on projects, work areas, and other organizational methods. By leveraging the Outlook shortcut bar and the public folder Favorites category, you can make it easy for them to use a tree of individual public folders instead of mailbox folders. Part of this solution involves overcoming the literal meaning of "public folder" by establishing a good tree structure and proper permissions to make these folders as secure as the mailbox. One big advantage of this solution is that public folders can be replicated, limiting the bulk of the mailbox and simplifying backup and recovery.

- Use the alternate recipient features to tie the mailbox to a second mailbox on another server or a public folder. This provides a backup copy of the mailbox contents; one trick is to create a public folder, set the permissions to default write, unhide the folder from the Global Address List, then put that public folder in as an alternate recipient.

- Use Outlook's ability to clone the user's mailbox contents with an OST. With a little scripting, you can establish a way to automate opening the mailbox, selecting all folders, synchronizing them all, then copying the OST to a safe location. This way, just the OST can be restored.

- Use a third-party product that supports mailbox-by-mailbox, or "brick-level," backup. These backup applications actually open each mailbox and download individual items. The restore process involves an automated fetching of the mail and uploading it back into the mailbox. These applications are slow, and they often don't work very well, but they may be worth investigating if none of the other alternatives meets your needs.

---

* Especially considering that the Win32 version of Perl supports MAPI!

18

Managing Exchange Performance

*If there is nothing really wrong on your system,
there probably will be after you manually change
half the parameters in Performance Optimizer.*

—Identity withheld,
"Understanding the Microsoft Exchange Server
Performance Optimizer" white paper
(*http://support.microsoft.com/support/exchange/
content/whitepapers/perfopt.asp*)

How many angels can dance on the head of a pin? That's the sort of almost theological territory you start getting into when you venture into discussing computer system performance. Major vendors like Hewlett-Packard, Dell, Compaq, Microsoft, Oracle, IBM, and Intergraph know all the tricks of tweaking benchmark applications to put their products in the most favorable light.

Since you're reading a book about Exchange, there's no point in discussing its benchmark numbers. Instead, this chapter will teach you what factors influence Exchange performance, how to measure your own real-world performance, how to simulate various loads on your servers, and—best of all—how to tune your Exchange network for optimal performance. It doesn't matter how many users a vendor says you can put on one of their servers; what matters is what you can do with your users. Let's start with a few basic definitions:

Throughput

A measure of work done per unit of time. For example, if you measure how many inbound SMTP messages your server can process in an hour, or how long it takes your backup process to completely back up your IS, those are measures of throughput. This measurement is useful when you want to know how long it takes to do something or how many tasks a particular configuration can do in a work day. Two common Exchange throughput measures are transactions/second and messages/second.

Response time

Measures how long it takes the server to respond to a request, such as an incoming SMTP connection request, or a logged-on Outlook user who has just double-clicked a new message in her inbox. One way to set performance goals is to decide on an acceptable average response time, then size your servers and network accordingly. Normally, as you add users (and thus load) to a server, the average response time for each request increases.

Bottleneck

This is just what it sounds like: a choke point that restricts stuff on either side of it. In performance tuning lingo, a bottleneck is a system resource or task in high demand that slows down or restricts performance when it's unavailable. For example, if your disk I/O queue is always longer than the number of disk spindles in your system, that indicates that your disk subsystem is a bottleneck, since every item read or written has to sit in the queue and wait its turn. Sometimes bottlenecks are layered; if you add a second CPU to your server, that may fix one bottleneck but reveal that your server is now hampered by a lack of RAM.

What Influences Exchange Performance?

The first step in effectively managing your Exchange servers' performance is to understand what affects that performance. There are so many different influences that it's hard to enumerate them all. To save you the trouble, this section will do it for you.

Software Architecture

The design principles that underlie Exchange and Windows NT exert a profound influence on how Exchange performs. NT was designed to support scalable applications, so it includes multithreading and multiprocessing support. Exchange takes advantage of these capabilities, but your design decisions can also have an effect on bottom-line performance.

Windows NT

Windows NT offers several architectural features that can affect Exchange performance. The most obvious is probably multiprocessor support. NT automatically spreads system and application tasks across however many processors you have; applications that are multithreaded, like Exchange, stand to benefit the most from multiple processors. When NT was first shipped in 1993, there were very few multiple-processor machines available for it to run on. Thankfully, that's no longer the case. Most server vendors now offer 2- and 4-processor machines, and there are 8-, 10-, 12-, and 16-CPU machines available if you need a bigger box. The relationship between processors and performance isn't strictly linear. You might expect that a 2-processor server would be 100% faster than a single-processor machine, but it's not: the best you can expect is an improvement of roughly 70% per additional processor, which is still nothing to sneeze at. Exchange handles its own thread pooling, in combination with the NT thread scheduler, and it expects that you won't try to help it along by manually setting thread priorities or affinities. Doing so can have a negative impact on overall performance.

NT also makes heavy use of virtual memory. The virtual memory manager is designed to ruthlessly prune the working set of any process that lets its pages lie idle, guarding against processes that grab RAM but don't use it. However, Exchange 5.5 is optimized to use as much RAM as you can stuff into your computers—the more, the better. That argues in favor of making sure that your page file is correctly sized for the amount of RAM you have; Microsoft recommends that your page file be set to the amount of physical RAM in your server plus 125MB. The Exchange IS will use as much physical RAM as possible for buffering, so you need to leave adequate page file space for other applications and components.

Finally, NT is able to use RAID storage two ways: with a hardware controller and the appropriate drivers, and through NT's built-in RAID software. As you'd expect, using NT's software RAID imposes a performance penalty, though it can make up for it somewhat by providing increased redundancy, even when you don't have a RAID controller. The actual penalty varies, and it applies mostly to mirroring, as NT's striping is surprisingly efficient. The penalty applies to write operations; you can reduce it by building your software RAID sets on disks controlled by separate controllers.

For maximum performance and redundancy, use a good-quality hardware RAID controller with battery backup. It's instructive to note that every server vendor that sells RAID controllers configures them similarly. RAID really can make a huge difference in performance, depending on whether you set it up properly or not; you'll learn more about that in the section "Which RAID level should you use?" later in the chapter.

Exchange

Microsoft has tailored the BackOffice suite of server products, of which Exchange is a member, to take full advantage of NT's built-in features. All of the Exchange executables are fully multithreaded and multiprocessor-aware, although some of them, notably the MTA, depend on single critical threads that can act as performance bottlenecks in some configurations. Exchange 5.5 and later also can take advantage of very large amounts of physical RAM. Exchange 5.0 could productively use up to 256MB; Exchange 5.5 can use up to 2GB, or 3GB if you're running NT Server Enterprise Edition.

Even if your hardware doesn't scale to such impressive heights, you'll find that Exchange lends itself quite well to load balancing and redundancy. Let's start with the basic notion that you can spread user mailboxes and public folders across many servers, which makes it easy to regulate the load (and thus the throughput and response time) on any particular server. Adding servers and moving users around is a time-tested way to decrease average response time. You can also move connectors around and change which servers act as bridgeheads, giving you even more flexibility in load management.

The Exchange store is particularly sensitive to disk speed and configuration. This is an artifact of the store's design, as you learned in Chapters 1 and 2: the exact mix of striped, mirrored, and plain volumes you use can have a dramatic effect on performance, because of Exchange's logging architecture. Since every incoming or outgoing message can generate several disk I/O operations, as the message load on a server increases, the disk load increases, too, but at a higher rate.

The type of connectors you use can also have a noticeable impact on overall performance. For example, the site connector expects to have at least 64Kbps of permanent bandwidth available to it. If you run a site connector over a slower connection, you'll notice that message transfer performance over the connector may be poor, because the site connector's architecture depends on having enough bandwidth to handle RPC connections. By contrast, the X.400 connector thrives on low-bandwidth and error-prone connections, because it's designed to run over those types of links. If your connectors' performance is poor, you'll quickly find that directory and public folder replication performance are poor, too, since replication changes are packaged as mail messages.

Hardware Configuration

The hardware configuration of your machines is important, and it's the factor you have the most control over, since it's hard to regulate what your users do, and you often have no influence over how your network is laid out or what services it provides. As the Exchange administrator, though, you'll probably be in charge of specifying the hardware you need, so now's a good time to get familiar with how hardware choices influence Exchange performance.

What kind of CPU?

In the consumer world, faster CPUs are always better; that's why you see all the major box vendors rushing to be the first ones out with new machines whenever Intel bumps up the CPU speed. This rule isn't strictly true for NT, though. Why? There are two reasons, one obvious and one subtle. The obvious reason is that you'll probably get better overall performance from two 233MHz CPUs than a single 400MHz CPU. On a single-processor machine, Exchange and NT have to share

Why Best Buy Doesn't Sell Exchange Servers

Budget pressures sometimes tempt administrators into using inappropriate boxes for servers. You probably know someone whose primary or backup domain controller has a Packard Bell logo on the front, for example, or whose entire IIS farm consists of a matched pair of no-name Pentium II machines from the local Best Buy. Moving up a notch, there are lots of sites running critical services on desktop machines from Dell, Hewlett-Packard, Intergraph, and so on, even though the machines they're using aren't designed or marketed as servers.

Why shouldn't you do the same thing for your Exchange server? There are several reasons, some of which you may not have considered:

Limited expandability

This isn't so bad for something like a domain controller, but for an Exchange Server, it's the kiss of death. When your users eat up all the disk space on your server (they will; it's what they do best), and you want to add more space but can't, you're looking at a major hassle.

Unsuitable architecture and design

A single-processor machine with a slow bus isn't the ideal platform for Exchange, no matter who sells it. CPUs with very small on-chip caches (notably Intel's Celeron) run NT slowly, and machines with limited bus widths or IDE-based controllers will be noticeably pokey if you run Exchange on them. Top that off with the fact that desktop machines usually don't have hot-swappable power supplies, RAID bays, and so on— all the things you need in a critical server.

Limited or nonexistent NT support

Microsoft maintains a list of devices that have been tested for compatibility with various versions of NT (see *http://www.microsoft.com/ntserver/ showcase/hwcompatibility.asp?RLD=34*). If your machine or any of its components aren't listed here, you may find that NT won't run at all, or that it's unreliable. The first question you're likely to hear when you call Microsoft is "Is your hardware on the compatibility list?" If you say no, they won't help you. That brings me to the next item on the list.

Vendor support

When you buy an NT server from Dell or Intergraph, if you have a problem with NT, you can call the vendor for help. If you buy a box and a retail copy of NTS, when you need help, you have to call Microsoft, which may or may not be a good way to get your problem fixed.

—Continued—

Secret gotchas

Dell was selling a machine last year for home use. Its specifications looked mostly identical to one of their office desktop machines, but, as luck would have it, there was a slight difference between them that drastically slowed network throughput on the home machine. I don't think the difference was deliberate, but the home machine was never marketed for office use, so how can you complain if the box you buy at Circuit City has some hidden flaw or incompatibility when you install NT and Exchange on it?

While all this may sound like a thinly veiled ad for server manufacturers, the bottom line is that people buy servers from HP, IBM, and so on for a reason; the servers are designed to do the job. Skimping on your hardware may save you a few bucks now, but it's almost guaranteed to cost you more in the end. As confirmation of this principle, ask yourself how often you see a professional tradesman like a contractor, plumber, or dentist using consumer-grade tools from Sears or KMart.

---

the CPU, but since they're both multithreaded, they can take advantage of the second processor to distribute the load, providing better overall performance. In general, the more CPUs you can provide for Exchange to use, the better. However, for most Exchange servers, the CPU isn't the bottleneck.

The second factor is cache size. NT is very sensitive to (and benefits from) large on-CPU and level L2 caches. That's why the Pentium Pro and Pentium II Xeon processors do so well in NT benchmarks. Despite the Pro's relatively slow clock speeds, its large on-chip cache suits NT just fine, and the Xeon combines fast clock rates with large caches. The performance advantage is diminished on machines with more than four processors, because large caches are more difficult to keep coherent; that's part of the reason SMP boxes with more than four x86 CPUs aren't commodity items. You'll probably find that most of the servers you evaluate have 512KB of L2 cache, plus whatever on-chip cache is provided in the CPU itself.

How much RAM?

Exchange 5.5 can use as much RAM as your server can hold. Depending on your server load, it may not need that much, but it will attempt to use as much as its internal DBA rules decide it can productively use. Since RAM is still relatively cheap, try to put at least 192MB in all your servers (leaving 64MB for NT and 128MB for Exchange itself), then add another 16MB for each connector on the server. If your budget allows, make provision to add more RAM later if you notice that VM paging is getting excessive. Note that the Exchange 5.5 Performance Optimizer has a flaw that causes it to do a poor job of optimization on systems with more than 1GB of RAM. Make sure you install SP2 before running Performance Optimizer if you fall into that category.

Disk and I/O Configuration

All other things being equal, the best place you can spend your money when buying an Exchange server is on the I/O subsystem. That's because a few extra bucks spent here can make a tremendous difference in overall performance. There are four fundamental parameters to consider when you're trying to evaluate your I/O system's performance:

Capacity

How much stuff can your storage system hold? The raw capacity of the drives in your system may or may not accurately reflect the capacity: six 9GB drives in a RAID array don't yield 54GB of capacity. In addition, you always need to reserve room for Exchange's maintenance tasks; once you hit about 80% of your disk capacity, it's time for an upgrade.

Data rate

How many megabytes of data can be read or written per unit of time? Data rate is most often expressed as megabytes per second, or MB/sec. As the overall data rate of your system improves, you'll see improved backup and restore performance.

Request rate

How many I/O requests can be satisfied per second? Each user request to send, retrieve, open, delete, or edit a message generates several read and write requests. As the number of users on your server increases, if you can manage to keep the average disk queue length below the number of disk spindles, you'll see constant (or even improved) response time as the load grows.

Response time

How long does a user have to wait for something to happen? This isn't really an I/O performance parameter, but it's a good way to measure your system performance, since it's how users will judge things.

Which RAID level should you use?

Notice that the title of this section is not "Should I use RAID?" The answer to that question is a loud yes. Here's why:

- If your private IS reaches a certain size (currently about 23GB, since that's the biggest disk that you can buy, as of this writing), you'll need RAID to hold everything. You can also create very large logical volumes that are split across multiple physical disks; this aids expandability.

- RAID offers load balancing across multiple disks, so you can exploit the response rate multiplier effect I will discuss in the next section. As a bonus, it lets you avoid bottlenecks on any one disk, like the one that holds your log files.

- A properly configured and equipped RAID array offers protection against hardware failures. Since disk drives tend to have lots of moving parts, which are the parts most prone to failure, this alone is a pretty compelling reason to consider RAID.

Now that you're (hopefully) convinced to use RAID, let's talk about which RAID level is appropriate. There are five levels of interest to most administrators, as shown in Table 18-1.

Table 18-1. RAID Levels

RAID level	Description	Read Performance Characteristics	Write Performance Characteristics	Redundancy Characteristics
JBOD	Just a bunch of disks: no redundancy.	Identical to individual disks.	Can provide up to (number of disks 5 individual I/O per second) response rate.	Nothing special; each disk can fail independently.
0	Striping: writes are distributed across multiple drives so that one write operation is split across multiple spindles.	One stripe on each spindle can be read concurrently, so read performance in an N-drive array can theoretically be N times better than a single drive.	All stripes written simultaneously; with hardware, identical to single-disk writes (but caching has major effect).	Loss of any disk in the stripe set is fatal to the entire set.
1	Mirroring (a.k.a. duplexing): all writes are made to two or more drives in parallel.	Identical to individual disks, since read may be done from any disk in the mirror set.	If hardware mirroring, identical to individual disks. If software mirroring, performance penalty.	All disks in an N-disk mirror set are identical, so $(N-1)$ disks can simultaneously fail with no downtime.

Table 18-1. RAID Levels (continued)

RAID level	Description	Read Performance Characteristics	Write Performance Characteristics	Redundancy Characteristics
5	Striping with parity: writes are striped across multiple spindles, and parity is spread across all drives. Offers best cost-per-megabyte ratio.	Short reads (those less than the RAID chunk size) can be handled in the same amount of time as a single read operation. Longer reads take proportionally longer.	Writes take the same amount of time as a single write operation. However, since the write is spread across multiple disks, the actual completion time may be delayed if one of the disks is busy.	Loss of any disk in the set is survivable, since the replacement can be rebuilt by recalculating parity. Loss of any disk during a rebuild (except the one being rebuilt) is fatal.
0+1 (also called RAID-10	Mirroring plus striping. Offers best ratio of cost to I/O per second. Minimal performance penalty for using software RAID; no penalty if the controller does the work.	Best performance: reads are distributed across spindles with no need for parity checking.	Identical to RAID-5, minus the overhead of parity calculation.	Identical to RAID-0.

How do you choose the RAID level that's right for you? If the I/O mix is 30–50% read operations (the range where Exchange typically operates), then RAID 0+1 is from 65–80% more efficient than RAID-5. However, using an equal number of disks, RAID-5 gives 50–90% better utilization of disk space. The big tradeoff is whether you're better off spending money to boost performance or to boost capacity. Since disk drives keep getting bigger and less expensive, my vote goes with the RAID 0+1 solution.

What about log files? As it turns out, log files are only read if something bad happens. Remember, each new transaction is posted to the log file immediately and to the store (or directory) database when load permits. Since log files are always written to sequentially, there's no real reason to put them on a striped array, though mirroring them does make good sense, as it provides additional redundancy. Microsoft recommends that you put your log files on the fastest disk in your server; the Performance Optimizer will do this for you automatically.

How should you partition storage?

Is it better to have one big drive or several smaller ones? The answer turns out to be somewhat counterintuitive. It might seem that a single large drive would provide better I/O throughput, but it turns out that having several drives allows the controller to distribute the I/O load by scheduling multiple reads and writes at once. Table 18-2 shows five different configurations for a 36GB disk array. Notice that as the number of drives rises, the total number of I/O operations possible per second increases linearly. These results argue strongly in favor of splitting your storage across multiple drives for performance reasons, since every drive you add multiplies the total request rate the subsystem can handle, assuming you're using a good controller.

Table 18-2. I/O Operations per Second in a 36GB Disk Array

Drive Size	# of Spindles	I/O per Second per Drive	Total I/O per Second
23GB	2	70	140
18GB	2	100	200
9GB	4	100	400
4.3GB	9	100	900
2.1GB	18	100	1800

When you build your RAID sets, there are some things to be concerned about, though. First and foremost is the data rate you can squeeze from the array. This directly affects your backup and restore performance. If your array is so big that you can't back it up or restore it in a reasonable time, then it's too big; get another server and start migrating users to it.

If you're using a RAID level with parity, you need to be concerned with array rebuilds, too. The rebuild time is proportional to the number of drives in the array and the size of the drives, and any drive failure during a rebuild will render the entire array useless. If you go this route, make sure you have hot spares on hand and that you have assured yourself of your backups' integrity.

How do you estimate the I/O load?

Pierre Bijaoui of Compaq introduced a set of numbers for estimating I/O during his excellent presentation on Exchange I/O performance at the 1998 Microsoft Exchange Conference. I haven't found any grounds to quibble with them, although they may vary slightly from what you observe on your own servers. He claimed that IS activity for an active user results in an average of 0.1 to 0.15 I/O operations per second, and that log file activity adds another 0.02 I/O per second. Both figures can reach peak values 10 to 15 times higher on a 500-user server.

Let's do some conservative back-of-the-envelope math: say you want to build a 500-user server with a 50GB store, yielding a 100MB/user storage quota. If you expect all 500 users to be active at once (first thing Monday morning, say, or maybe right after lunch), you'll need an average of (0.15 × 500) = 75 I/O per second for the IS, plus another (0.02 × 500) = 10 I/O per second for the log files. Sound easy? Sure, but don't forget the peak expansion: to guarantee response time, you actually need to provide 1,125 I/O per second for the IS and 150 I/O per second for the log files. Assuming that you can get 100 I/O/second/drive without too much shopping around, you'd still need an 11-drive array to satisfy the maximum peak loads. If you assume a somewhat more optimistic peak load factor of 10 times the average, that puts you at a mere 750 I/O per second, which is somewhat easier to achieve.

What about caching?

Disk caching is often misunderstood as a one-size-fits-all solution for boosting performance. It's actually more subtle than that, because several levels of disk cache are active when Exchange is running. Exchange caches as much of its own data as possible, subject to the amount of RAM it has to work with. Below that, NT has its own disk caching mechanism; further down, the disk controller and individual drives have their own caches. For purposes of this discussion, I'm going to ignore the NT and Exchange caches; since you can't turn them off or control them, you can't control their influence on your system performance. Hardware disk caching is another matter entirely.

There are two basic types of caching: *read* caching and *write* caching. Read caching stores data in the cache as it's read from disk; subsequent requests for the same data can be fetched from the cache instead of requiring another read I/O request. Read caching's overall performance effect depends on how often requested data is found in the cache (the *cache hit rate*). Paradoxically, if the read cache is too large, reads slow down: the controller has to find the requested data in the (large) cache table, and the hit rate tends to be low. A variant of read caching, known as read-ahead caching, allows the controller to pre-fetch data it expects to be read. Read-ahead caching helps a lot if your application accesses data in a predictable sequence, as during a backup operation, but for normal random I/O, it reads—and fills the cache with—a lot of extraneous data, lowering the hit rate. Read-ahead caching can lower Exchange performance: it lowers the maximum request rate available for a desired response time, and it raises the response time required to answer a constant request rate. The magnitude of the performance effect depends on the controller and disk configuration, but it can range as high as 40%.

Write-back caching (WBC), on the other hand, is a great way to boost performance, especially for Exchange's transaction log files. When WBC is active, write requests made by applications or NT are buffered by the controller. As far as Exchange or NT can tell, the write happens instantaneously, because the controller stores the data and writes it when convenient. The uncoupling of the write request from the actual write makes it seem as though writes have zero response time; however, this magic depends on having an adequately sized cache. The WBC cache has to be large enough to handle the largest group of I/O requests the application can generate, and the disk subsystem has to be fast enough to flush data from the cache faster than it arrives. These requirements translate to a WBC cache of 32–64MB for a large Exchange server. Some WBC controllers also perform *write gathering*, a technique that collects multiple writes (either to the same location or different locations) and consolidates them into a single physical I/O request; this further speeds up write operations.

What's the downside to WBC? There's only one, but it's a big one. If the controller cache becomes corrupt or unavailable, the data on disk won't match what the application thinks is on disk. This is the kiss of death for an Exchange server, since the IS and DS depend on a variety of internal structures that are updated every time a transaction is logged. If even one transaction's data is lost in a cache failure, the results can be impressive, in the same sense as an earthquake or burst dam.

What can make the controller cache fail to write its data safely to disk? The obvious example is loss of power. The solution is easy: use an uninterruptible power supply, make sure it works properly, and put a battery backup unit on your controller. The backup battery will preserve cached data even when there's no electrical power available. As long as the battery doesn't run out, the controller will immediately write out the cached data next time the machine boots. If the controller card itself fails, too bad—you lose. The only way to prevent this particular failure is to use dual controllers and mirror the entire RAID set, but this soon gets expensive. A better solution is to make sure your backups work correctly, since controller failures are extremely rare and you need good backups anyway.

Network Configuration

The topology, usage patterns, and bandwidth of your network have a profound impact on Exchange performance. After all, every incoming or outgoing message has to pass over the network somewhere, even between users whose mailboxes are on the same server. It's not always possible to structure your network for Exchange's benefit, but knowing what does benefit Exchange can come in handy.*

What topology?

Microsoft's Exchange planning documents claim that up to 80% of email in an organization is sent between people in the same workgroup. Even if that figure is a bit high, it's a good idea to try to put people who need to exchange mail frequently on

---

* Tony Redmond, a well-known Exchange deployment guru with Compaq, once said that no consultant knows your network configuration and loading better than you do, and that's true of authors too!

Using Dell's PowerMatch Tool

Dell makes PowerMatch, a nifty tool for sizing your Exchange server needs. PowerMatch (available for free from *wwwapp.us.dell.com/filelib/download/index. asp?fileid=962&libid=14*) allows you to get a decent estimate of what size Exchange server you need. While it only suggests Dell hardware (surprise!), it does a pretty good job of matching the workload you suggest with an appropriate configuration.

Once you download and install PowerMatch, when you run it you'll be asked to supply several pieces of data:

- The number of users you expect to use the server, from 30 to 10,000.

- The percentage of light, medium, and heavy users. Light users send seven messages and receive 20 per day; medium users send 20 and receive 66, and heavy users send 39 and receive 119.

  PowerMatch assumes storage quotas of 20MB for light users, 50MB for medium, and 100MB for heavy users, but you can adjust this.

- Whether your users are mostly going to run Outlook or an Internet-based client (including OWA).

- What type of disk array (none, RAID-0, RAID-1, or RAID-5) you plan to use.

- How much you expect your Exchange user base to grow over the next year (from 0% to 200%).

- Whether you want special features, including redundant power supplies and fans, clustered systems, or hot-swappable disks.

When you have answered these questions, PowerMatch suggests a system, including the disk configuration. In my case, leaving all the defaults as Power-Match presented them yielded a recommendation for a Dell PowerEdge 2300 with five 9GB disks (two as a RAID-1 array for the OS and logs, with the other three in a RAID-5 array for the databases). This system has a single 400MHz Pentium II processor and 256MB of RAM. It's interesting to note that for 200 users, that's about the same configuration I'd have chosen manually!

Since the tool is free, I suggest you nip over and get a copy, then run it to see what Dell suggests for your existing user load; you might be surprised by the results.

the same mailbox server, and, when possible, to put those users and their servers on the same subnet. By doing this, you can localize most traffic for that server on its local subnet: messages from one user in the accounting department to another won't have to go to the engineering server and back again. Getting all the users on the proper servers can be difficult and time-consuming, but getting most of them in the right place will still provide you some benefit.

One arrangement that works well and is relatively inexpensive is to use a higher-speed backbone to connect your Exchange servers. For example, one network I configured used switched 100Base-T to connect the Exchange servers to one another. Each server's mailbox clients were connected to it via 10Base-T. This allowed us to segregate client-to-server and server-to-server traffic, leading to faster server performance and better user response time. (Dell was even running a promotion at the time we bought our servers, so the 100Base-T hardware was free! Don't you love e-commerce?)

What usage patterns?

Now we're back to trying to figure out how your network is actually used. You should be able to estimate how many other applications are competing with Exchange for bandwidth, and approximately how much bandwidth they use. Many organizations with branch offices have the branches connected to the central office with a single 56Kbps or ISDN channel, so Exchange has to share that bandwidth with logon validation requests, file and print service traffic, Web browsing, and who knows what else.

It's probably not feasible to change your users' usage patterns (unless you suddenly install a proxy server to keep them away from the *Playboy, Cosmopolitan,* and ESPN web sites), so this factor falls into the category of useful knowledge that doesn't necessarily lead to any action. Sometimes, though, changes in your business processes will lead to changes in your network usage patterns. For example, one client of mine recently changed a human resources forms catalog into a set of web forms. Instead of little brown intraoffice mail envelopes, the network now carries all that traffic. Be aware when things change, since a sudden increase in non-Exchange network usage will steal bandwidth from your Exchange servers.

How much bandwidth?

More bandwidth is good. Less bandwidth is bad. If my editor would let me, I'd leave it at that, because anyone who's spent more than a few minutes using Exchange, Outlook, or the Internet already knows that. Why? Exchange makes extensive use of network remote procedure calls (RPCs) for communication between MAPI clients (including Outlook 97/98) and the server, as well as for interserver communications and Exchange Administrator sessions. RPCs are bandwidth intensive and can tolerate very little latency, so a low-bandwidth network will probably cause RPCs to time out, hampering server and client performance.

The amount of bandwidth you need is hard to estimate, because it depends on your user loads, connector configuration, and network topology. Outlook and

Exchange clients can run in remote mode over standard modem lines, so you can get by with 14.4Kbps or better connections for client-to-server communications. If you've properly configured offline folders, your users will be able to synchronize and download only what they need. Server-to-server connections are the same way: if your servers rarely need to pass messages to one another (remember that message traffic from replication counts), you can easily join servers with DRAS connectors running over modems, or even with 9600bps X.25 connections running with the X.400 connector. If you want to use the site connector, have lots of replication traffic, or have high interserver mail loads, you'll need more bandwidth. Your public folder architecture is important, too: if you use replicas, there is more replication traffic, but if you don't, every time a user opens a public folder item, it has to be fetched from the home server and transferred across the network.

Your Applications and Users

Of all the things that influence performance, this one is probably the hardest to quantify. Usage patterns are maddeningly hard to categorize, and it can take a while to understand the impact of your users' daily work patterns. You can draw some generalizations: it's likely that you'll see more mail moved on Monday and Friday than on other days, and you'll notice a decline in mail volume on weekends and holidays. However, these generalizations aren't very helpful; you'll have to study the mail volume in your system (using Performance Monitor or other measurement tools) to see exactly where the peaks and troughs are.

Microsoft defines three vague classes of users: light, medium, and heavy. The specifics of the definitions aren't important; what's important is that you can use the same categories to group your own users. Sometimes it's hard to slot people into categories by their job description, since they may be heavy mail users even if their job doesn't necessarily require it. For example, if you've set things up so users can subscribe to Internet mailing lists, or if you run your own internal distribution lists, you may find that even a supposedly light user still gets a ton of messages. You can get some idea of mail usage by looking at the number of items and size of users' mailboxes. A quick way to gather this information is to open the Mailbox Resources view for the private IS on the server you're interested in, then use the File → Save Window Contents... command to save a tab-delimited version of the view.

The applications you run on your Exchange servers have a definite impact on performance. If you're using just plain vanilla email, with no scripting, routing, calendaring, Internet news, or other resource-sucking features, you'll probably get better performance from your servers than a site with the same hardware and user loads that runs one or more of these additional services. For performance tuning purposes, you should consider OWA, POP3, and IMAP4 as separate services, since they're not part of the core Exchange MAPI services. In fact, OWA really counts as a separate application if you also run IIS on your Exchange server.

Measuring Exchange Performance

Measuring the performance of your Exchange server is relatively easy; interpreting the results is the difficult part, until you know what to look for. The point behind doing performance measurement at all is to gather a baseline of performance data during your servers' normal operation. In the future, you can compare the current performance against that baseline and see how your servers are doing. This proactive approach to monitoring is critical to preventing server bottlenecks; if you wait until users start complaining, it'll be harder and take longer to isolate the problem and plan a fix.

The primary tool for monitoring Exchange performance is the NT Performance Monitor. Apart from a very brief refresher, I'll assume you already know what the Performance Monitor is and how to use it. NT models every distinct thing (like a printer, a user account, or a CPU) as an object. In Performance Monitor, NT objects whose performance can be monitored, like a network card, a group of threads, or the Exchange MTA, appear as Performance Monitor objects. Some objects exist alone; others, like threads or CPUs, may have peer objects of the same type. These peers are called *instances*. For example, if your server has four CPUs, Performance Monitor will display one CPU object with four instances.

Each instance has one or more parameters, or *counters*, that you can monitor. That means that you can watch the same counter on multiple instances of an object at one time, which is very useful for monitoring things like how much CPU time the Directory Service is using or how many I/O requests are arriving each second.

The Canned Monitoring Sets

To ease the process of trying to separate the performance sheep from the goats, Microsoft has included seven Performance Monitor workspaces that can show you much of what you need to know about your servers' performance and health:

Microsoft Exchange Server Health
> This workspace shows a chart view, updated every second, with six counters: % Total Processor Time; % Processor Time for the DSA, MTA, store, and MAD process instances; and Pages/sec. These counters provide a quick snapshot of the overall server health: you can see whether any one process is sucking up too much CPU time, and you can see the system's overall CPU and virtual memory loads.

Microsoft recommends adding two disk-related counters to the Server Health workspace: the Logical Disk object's Disk Bytes/sec and % Disk Time counters. (First, you must enable these counters with the `diskperf -y` or `diskperf -e` command). These two will tell you what kind of disk load your servers are subject to, and that's an important health parameter.

Microsoft Exchange Server History

This workspace is a chart view updated every 60 seconds. It includes only three counters: the MSExchangeIS object's User Count counter, the MSExchangeMTA object's Work Queue Length counter, and the Memory object's Pages/sec counter. These three counters give you a good long-term view of what your server has been doing.

Microsoft Exchange Server IMS Queues

This workspace presents a histogram, updated every second, showing the inbound and outbound queue lengths for both the IMS and MTS queues. It's a useful way to monitor the overall message load the IMS is handling, so you can spot queue backups before they get too large.

Microsoft Exchange Server IMS Statistics

The IMS Statistics workspace is updated twice per minute; it displays the total number of inbound and outbound messages handled by the IMS.

Microsoft Exchange Server IMS Traffic

The IMS Traffic workspace includes five counters: Messages Entering MTS-IN, Messages Entering MTS-OUT, Messages Leaving MTS-OUT, Connections Inbound, and Connections Outbound. This combination gives you an overview of the traffic flow in and out of the IMS. The workspace is updated every second.

Microsoft Exchange Server Load

This workspace provides an overall view of the total load on the server. It includes the Message Recipients Delivered/min and Messages Submitted/min counters from the MSExchangeIS Public and MSExchangeIS Private objects, the Adjacent MTA Associations counter from the MSExchangeMTA object, the MSExchangeIS object's RPC Packets/sec counter, and four counters from the MSExchangeDS object: AB Browses/sec, AB Reads/sec, ExDS Reads/sec, and Replication Updates/sec. This workspace is an excellent way to see the big picture of the load imposed on your server, though it doesn't give you information about any specific bottlenecks.

Microsoft Exchange Server Queues

This workspace, updated every ten seconds, shows a histogram representing the size of five queues: the MTA's work queue, the public and private IS send queues, and the public and private IS receive queues.

Microsoft Exchange Server Users

This workspace only shows one counter: the MSExchangeIS object's User Count value. It's displayed as a histogram and updated every ten seconds. You can easily resize the workspace window to get a constant readout of how many users are on your server at any time.

What Should You Monitor?

Before you start monitoring stuff willy-nilly, it's a good idea to plan what you're going to monitor. The various components of NT and Exchange offer literally hundreds of performance parameters you can chart, graph, and get reports on, so you can quickly drown in a volume of relatively useless data unless you know what to look for. There are three separate (but partially overlapping) sets of counters and objects you can monitor, depending on what you're trying to accomplish with your monitoring.

Tracking load trends

One reason to monitor your servers' performance is to gather data about their performance under load. As the load placed on them grows, you'd ideally like to find that the load is heading towards the maximum allowable range well before it actually gets there. Watching the load trends on your servers allows you to see the number of messages and users the servers are handling; more importantly, you can extrapolate the load trends based on these values.

Nine key counters you can monitor will give an excellent overall picture of a server's burden; they're listed in Table 18-3. (Note that the message submission and delivery rates won't match, since each message may have several recipients.) If you're running the IMS service, you should probably also watch the MSExchangeIMC object's Inbound Messages/Hr and Outbound Messages/Hr counters, which tell you how many messages the IMS is processing. Likewise, if your server is handling an NNTP feed, check the Newsfeed Messages Sent/sec and Newsfeed Messages Received Rate on the MSExchangeIS object.

Table 18-3. Key Load Trend Indicators

Object	Counter	What It Tells You
MSExchangeIS	User Count	How many users have been on the server since its last restart.
	Active User Count	How many users have done something in the last 10 minutes.

Table 18-3. Key Load Trend Indicators (continued)

Object	Counter	What It Tells You
MSExchangeIS Private	Messages Submitted/min	How many messages per minute your users are sending.
	Message Recipients/min	How fast the IS is delivering submitted messages.
MSExchangeIS Public	Messages Submitted/min	How many messages per minute users are submitting to public folders.
	Message Recipients Delivered/min	How fast the IS is delivering messages to public folders.
MSExchangeMTA	Messages/sec	How fast the MTA is processing inbound and outbound messages.
	Message Bytes/sec	Divide this by the Messages/sec value to get the average message size being processed.
	Work Queue Length	How many items are waiting for processing at the MTA.

Of course, you can also get a good deal of useful load trend data from the Microsoft Exchange Server Load workspace. However, that workspace doesn't tell you how many people are using your server or what message size the server has to deal with; on the other hand, it gives you some information about what users are doing with the directory.

Tracking responsiveness

Along with monitoring server loading and using that data to predict future loads, you should also plan on monitoring server responsiveness under the load. It's hard to quantify exactly what is "responsive" and what's not; however, you can monitor some key parameters that tell you how long the various service work queues are (see Table 18-4). The longer the queue, the longer it takes to process newly submitted items, and the longer it takes a user's mail to be delivered to its eventual destination.

Table 18-4. Key Server Responsiveness Trend Indicators

Object	Counter	What It Tells You
MSExchangeIS Private and MSExchangeIS Public	Send Queue Size	How many items are queued for delivery. Normally, this should be close to zero. If it stays above zero for short periods, that usually indicates a peak in demand; if it stays there for a long time, that indicates the IS isn't keeping up with the message load.

Table 18-4. Key Server Responsiveness Trend Indicators (continued)

Object	Counter	What It Tells You
	Average Time for Delivery (public IS) or Average Delivery Time (private IS)	How long it takes the public or private IS to deliver a message. If this value keeps drifting upward over time, that indicates your servers are losing their ability to handle the load.
	Average Local Delivery Time (private IS) or Average Time for Local Delivery (public IS)	How long it takes the server to deliver a message to recipients on the same server as the sender. Watch this value over time; when it starts trending up, it means your server is starting to fall behind.
MSExchangeMTA	Work Queue Length	How many items are waiting for the MTA. If this value stays above zero, that indicates the MTA can't keep up with the load; short bursts of activity may drive it up, but it shouldn't stay there.

Tracking raw performance data

The two preceding groups of settings tell you when your servers' load or response times look like they're trending upward, but then you need to find out why. The answer is most likely to come from looking at the objects and counters that give you a direct look at the server's inner workings (see Table 18-5). These counters, both individually and together, will tell you what server subsystems are doing, how many resources they're using, and where the bottlenecks are likely to be found.

Table 18-5. Monitoring Raw Performance Counters

If You Want to Monitor...	Look at This Object: Counter	What You'll Find Out
CPU usage	System: % Total Processor Time	This counter tells you how much of the system's total processor time is being used. If the CPU usage stays above 80% or so for long periods, or even hits 100% and stays there, it's time to consider a faster CPU or additional processors. You can reduce CPU load by moving services, including Exchange connectors, to other machines or by distributing some Exchange tasks, like distribution list expansion and public folder hosting, to other servers.
	Process: % Processor Time	By monitoring the CPU usage of individual Exchange processes like the IS (*store*), the DS (*dsamain*), and the MTA (*emsmta*), you can see whether any one process is consuming an unusual amount of CPU time.

Table 18-5. Monitoring Raw Performance Counters (continued)

If You Want to Monitor…	Look at This Object: Counter	What You'll Find Out
	System: Context Switches/ sec	This counter tells you how often the system switches between threads in different contexts. As this number increases, it indicates that the system is spending more and more time switching contexts and less time actually doing useful work.
	System: Processor Queue Length	This queue length tells you how many threads are waiting for processor time. Its usual values are 0 or 1; if the counter stays at or above 2 for sustained periods, it means that threads are being forced to wait for a turn at the CPU, and your server might benefit from a faster CPU or additional processors.
Memory usage and performance	Memory: Pages/ sec	This counter tells you how many virtual memory pages are being written to or read from disk each second. Since each page read or written adds to the load on the disk, the pages/second value tells you how many I/O operations per second VM is adding to the disk system's workload.
	Memory: Page Faults/sec	This counter tells you how many times per second the VM system has to go to disk to load a page it needs. This counter is mostly interesting when you're running other services besides Exchange; you can use it in conjunction with the Page faults/ sec counter for individual instances under the Process object to see which processes are faulting the most. Armed with that knowledge, you can make adjustments to each application's memory usage to optimize overall performance. Generally, page fault rates of more than 20 per second indicate excessive page faulting, which can be cured by adding more RAM. Note that if this value is high, but the Memory:Pages/sec value is low, you're okay; the combination means you have lots of page faults but that most of them are being serviced from RAM and not from disk.
	Process: Working Set	A process' *working set* is the set of all VM pages it's currently using. The NT VM manager continually adjusts the size of each process working set to keep it as small as possible without triggering excessive faulting. The values for each process instance's copy of this counter tells you how big that process working set is (in bytes). This tells you how much RAM a particular process is actively using at a given time, which helps you know whether you have enough RAM to adequately supply all the processes you're running.

Table 18-5. Monitoring Raw Performance Counters (continued)

If You Want to Monitor...	Look at This Object: Counter	What You'll Find Out
	Memory: Committed Bytes	This counter indicates how many bytes of RAM NT has allocated to applications and system services. You must have at least this much space in your paging file. If this value continuously hovers near the size of your paging file, make it bigger.
	Memory: Available Bytes	NT's VM subsystem continually adjusts each process' working set to keep at least 4MB of RAM free. If the processes need more memory, NT will start giving up its 4MB stash, but paging and page fault rates will increase, slowing things down overall. This is an instantaneous value, not an average.
	Database: Cache Hit %	This counter tells you how often the IS and directory were able to fetch data from their respective caches instead of from disk.[a] Microsoft says that a hit rate of 95% or so is desirable: more than that, and you probably could free up some buffer space; less than that, and you could add buffers to get better performance. The Table Open Cache % Hit counters give you similar information about table opens.
Disk usage and performance	Logical Disk: Disk Bytes Written/sec and Disk Bytes Read/sec	These counters tell you how much overall throughput your disk system is providing. Along with the Disk Reads/sec and Disk Writes/sec counters, these counters tell you how close to the manufacturers' specifications your disk system is coming. As these values get closer and closer to the spec values, that indicates you're reaching maximum capacity.
	Logical Disk: Avg. Disk Queue Length	Long disk queue lengths mean that applications have to wait to have their I/O requests answered. If the difference between this counter and the number of disk spindles on your server averages more than 2 or 3, your disk is a bottleneck.

[a] Remember, there are separate instances of the Database object for the directory and IS.

The Physical Disk object has counters you can monitor, but it's harder to use them to get any meaningful data, since they watch individual disk drives and not the whole subsystem. When you're using a RAID controller, the counters essentially monitor the whole RAID subsystem. My advice: don't bother with them; use the Logical Disk counters instead.

Size does matter

When you're building Performance Monitor workspaces to watch over your server, it's important to remember that Performance Monitor can be *too* helpful sometimes. It automatically scales chart views for you: if you monitor two counters, one with a range of 0 to 1 and one with a range of 0 to 100, Performance Monitor will scale the chart from 0 to 100. This feature can make it difficult to see peaks and valleys in the counter values.

There are a couple of workarounds to this problem. First of all, you can use the Options → Chart... command to set an appropriate vertical scale by filling in the Vertical Maximum field. If you need to monitor two counters with different scales, just put them in different workspaces. Part of the reason why several different workspaces are included with Exchange is that Microsoft has segregated counters both by what they measure and by their scales.

Of course, if you miss critical data it might be your fault. When you create a view in Performance Monitor, you can set an update interval for it. Choosing an appropriate interval is important; if you pick one that's too small, you may have trouble picking out long-term trends, since past data will be pushed off the screen too fast. Set an interval that's too large, and you'll miss fluctuations that happen between update times. You may need to experiment with your workspaces until you find update settings that fall between these two extremes.

Performance Simulation

If you go solely by vendor benchmarks, you may be fooled into thinking you can, or should, put 10,000 users on a single server. While it's technically possible to do this, given a very large server and a huge budget, it's not a very good idea, as you learned in Chapter 14, *Managing Exchange Servers*. That leaves open the legitimate question of how to figure out how many users you can put on your server. If you've already got a set of servers in place, you can tell how many users they can handle just by watching their response under load, but what if you want to empirically determine what a server can handle without putting it into your production network?

There are two ways to accomplish this; both involve external performance simulators. I say "external" because both programs run outside of Exchange; as far as the Exchange server can tell, they look like ordinary MAPI clients:

Exchange Load Simulator
> The Exchange Load Simulator, or just LoadSim, is from Microsoft. It's free, and it works reasonably well. You can get it from *www.microsoft.com/exchange/55/downloads/LoadSim.htm*.

Dynameasure

Dynameasure, from Bluecurve (see *www.bluecurve.com/products/download_ msg.htm*) is definitely not free. It's designed as a capacity planning and monitoring tool for NT infrastructures; as part of that capability (which has gotten it into Boeing, GM, Microsoft, and lots of other large NT shops) it can do comprehensive monitoring and prediction for Exchange networks. Dynameasure can do a lot of things that LoadSim can't. For example, it can monitor multiple Exchange servers at once, and it offers an easy-to-use GUI instead of Load-Sim's confusing command language.

Performance simulation is not unlike Olympic track and field competition. In the pole vault and the high jump, you set the bar at a certain height, then attempt a jump: either you clear the bar, or you don't. That's the LoadSim approach. Dynameasure is more like the decathlon: the overall score your server earns depends on a number of factors you select.

Both simulators use clients (Dynameasure calls them "motors") that simulate what a real MAPI user might do. Both allow you to vary the level of user activity: Load-Sim offers canned light, medium, and heavy user profiles, but allows you to adjust the specific amounts of message traffic each profile type generates, while Dynameasure offers a broader range of profiles. You can also influence the overall server load by controlling how many clients are hitting a server. With Dynameasure, you can vary the test time and change the load during the test, thus more accurately simulating a real workload. LoadSim limits you to a constant load, though it randomly distributes activity according to the total limits you specify.

The overall approach to doing tests with either tool is to set up a testing network with enough clients to provide the desired testing load (though Dynameasure works just fine on a production server). You also have to generate a test database of messages; once you've done that, you fire up the clients and let the server run. What happens next varies between the two products; LoadSim produces a score file that tells you whether your server met your response time goals or not, while Dynameasure offers a flexible set of graphs, charts, and text reports that can help make the actual scores more understandable.

One particularly nice feature of Dynameasure is that it can collect data on the server's resource utilization and match it with throughput and response time data. That means, for example, that it can correlate an upward spike in response time with a rise in the disk queue length, making it easy to spot bottlenecks. You can do the same thing manually by running Performance Monitor during your Load-Sim tests and logging the results, but it's a little harder to find bottlenecks when you have to look for them manually.

Are these tools really useful? I have mixed emotions. LoadSim is a good way to benchmark server configurations to see which one is better, but it's not particularly useful for measuring how much load your systems can handle. I've also seen a number of complaints that its results don't match real-world observed performance. Some of these faulty results may be due to poor test procedure (for example, you should do performance tests on a network whose traffic and topology mirror your production network), but some complaints are valid.

Dynameasure is a terrific product: it's easy to use and it produces easy-to-understand results, but it's costly. I'm not sure it will be of benefit for most small sites, but I encourage you to hit the Dynameasure web site and download their evaluation package so you can see for yourself.

Performance Tuning

Now you know how to examine server performance and test it with various loads. It's time to cautiously enter the world of performance tuning. As I mentioned way back in Chapter 1, *Introducing Exchange Server*, Windows NT and Exchange are both designed to be largely self-tuning; the system monitors its ongoing performance and adjusts whatever parameters it sees fit. NT's self-tuning happens all the time, without you being aware of it. Exchange does a bit of self-tuning automatically, but most of its tunable parameters must be adjusted either manually or with the help of the Performance Optimizer.

Just because you *can* adjust these parameters doesn't mean you should. In general, you should plan on leaving them alone unless you can clearly identify a good reason (like advice you see here or from Microsoft PSS) to change them. Sometimes the cure is worse than the disease.

Using the Performance Optimizer

Microsoft included the Performance Optimizer (also called by its filename, *perfwiz. exe* or just `perfwiz`) as part of the standard Exchange distribution in an attempt to help automate the process of deciding how to configure Exchange for best performance. When you set up Exchange for the first time, the setup program makes some assumptions about where to put the DS and IS databases and how to configure things; Performance Optimizer can make any needed changes after everything's been installed.

Performance Optimizer's primary job is to evaluate your system's disk and memory configuration and figure out where to put the DS and IS databases and the MTA and IMS queues. It also asks you how many users will be on the server and what the server will be doing; based on your answers, it may make changes to other configuration settings.

When you install Exchange, the last step in the installation process gives you the chance to run Performance Optimizer to adjust the installed defaults. However, you can run it any time you want to. Apart from its entertainment value (which is minimal), there are times when you should be sure to run Performance Optimizer so that it can adjust your Exchange configuration:

- When you install or remove RAM or processors from your server
- When you add a caching disk controller or RAID array
- When you plan on increasing or decreasing the number of user mailboxes or public folders on a server
- When you add to or remove from the server a connector, gateway, or service (including KMS and OWA)

These changes all seem innocuous enough, but when you change the underlying hardware available to Exchange, or when you change the load placed on the server by adding or removing services or users, Performance Optimizer needs to run so that it has a chance to tweak Exchange parameters to take the changes into account.

You can run Performance Optimizer by running *exchsrvr\bin\perfwiz.exe*; Microsoft also includes an item (look for "Microsoft Exchange Optimizer") in the Microsoft Exchange section of the Programs submenu in the Start menu.

You can run `perfwiz` with the –r switch; that sets it to read-only mode, in which it evaluates your system's performance characteristics but doesn't actually make any changes.

The steps you need to take are outlined in the following sections.

Step 1: The friendly welcome

When you first start the Performance Optimizer, the first page tells you it will "analyze your system to optimize use of hard disks and memory for Microsoft Exchange Server." It then points out that, for Performance Optimizer to do its work, all Exchange services must be stopped. When you click the Next button, Performance Optimizer will attempt to stop the services before proceeding to the next page. Note that this may upset any link or server monitors that are watching the server, so shut them off before running Performance Optimizer.

Step 2: Tell Performance Optimizer about your server load

The second page you'll see when running Performance Optimizer is shown in Figure 18-1.

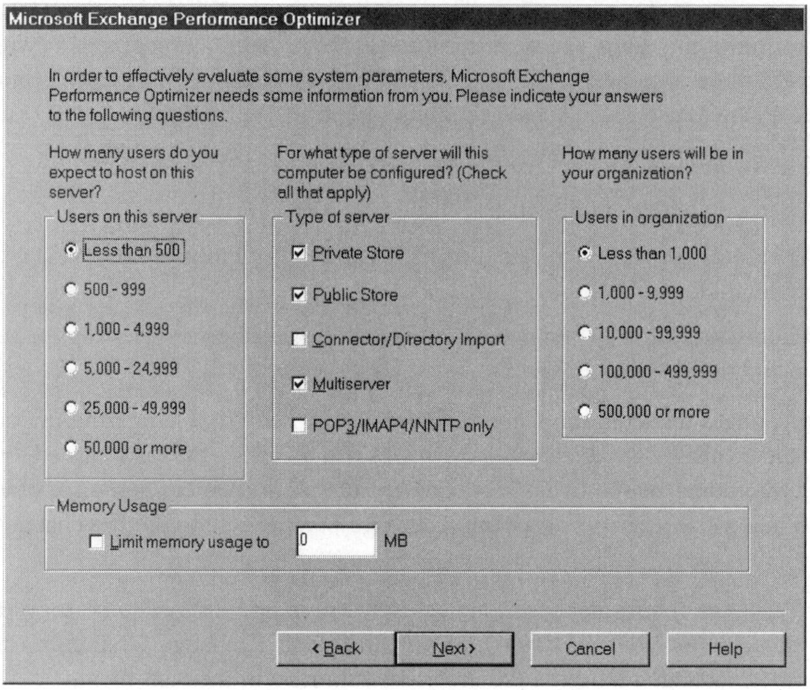

Figure 18-1. The second step in the Performance Optimizer process is to tell Performance Optimizer what your server will be doing

This page contains three questions:

How many users do you expect to host on this server?

> Your answer can range from "Less than 500" to a wildly optimistic "50,000 or more." Exchange uses the answer to determine how much load clients are likely to place on the server and how many resources it should allocate to handle them. In Exchange 5.5, this value also tells the MTA how much space to allocate for caching, so even on servers that don't host any users, it's a good idea to set this value to around one-third the total number of entries in your GAL.

For what type of server will this computer be configured?

> The five checkboxes in the "Type of server" group tell Performance Optimizer something about your server:

> — Check or clear the Private Store and Public Store checkboxes to indicate whether this server has a public IS, a private IS, both, or neither. Your answer here tells Performance Optimizer how to balance resource allocation between the public and private components of the IS.

— If your server will be running any connectors, or if it will be used to import directory information via a gateway or Exchange Administrator, check the Connector/Directory Import box. When Exchange has to run connectors, that adds an extra load on the server, plus it changes the number of threads needed to perform various housekeeping and background tasks.

— If this server will be part of a site that contains multiple servers, check the Multiserver checkbox to tell Performance Optimizer that you want it to allocate resources for intrasite communications.

— If all the clients that connect to this server do so with POP3, IMAP4, or NNTP (that means no MAPI clients or OWA users), check the "POP3/IMAP4/NNTP only" checkbox and Performance Optimizer will reduce the number of buffers and threads dedicated to handling MAPI connections; instead, those resources will be allocated to Internet protocol connections.

How many users will be in your organization?

Your answer tells Performance Optimizer how many buffers to allocate for the DS database, how many DS threads to spawn, and how to configure replication.

The Memory Usage group is actually a hangover from earlier versions of Exchange. Exchange 4.0 and 5.0 would slurp up all available RAM on a server, which would reduce the performance of other services running on the same box. The "Limit memory usage" checkbox and field allowed you to throttle Exchange's memory usage so that it would leave some RAM for other applications. Normally, Performance Optimizer calculates a base amount of RAM (based on the total amount of physical RAM in your server) and uses that to determine how many buffers of each type to allocate. When you specify a value here, Performance Optimizer uses it instead of its calculated value.

Since Exchange 5.5 already has its own scheme for dynamically requesting and releasing memory, there's usually no performance advantage to be gained from using these controls, so you should probably leave them alone. For earlier versions of Exchange, Microsoft recommends that if you decide to use limits, you set the limit to up to 75% of the amount of physical RAM, but not less than 64MB.

Step 3: Disk analysis

When you click the Next button on the page from step 2, Performance Optimizer tests your disks by doing a number of read and write operations that mimic the type of disk I/O the DS and IS need to do. These tests, which usually only take a few seconds, create a number of 4MB files; Performance Optimizer then makes both sequential and random-access I/O requests to all physical disks simultaneously. These tests are run on all the physical disks on your system so that Performance Optimizer can gauge both absolute and relative performance. When these tests are complete, Performance Optimizer tells you to click the Next button to continue.

Step 4: Selecting file locations

Step 4 in Performance Optimizer is where the results of the disk timing measurements taken in step 3 show up. The fourth page of your Performance Optimizer session shows you the current location of six sets of files: the private and public IS databases, the IS logs, the DS database, the DS logs, and the MTA queues. For each set of files, Performance Optimizer shows you where the files are currently located (albeit in a little tiny edit field that's way too short to show the full path) and where it suggests they should be located for best performance. The rules Performance Optimizer uses to make these suggestions are fairly simple: it tries to put the IS transaction logs on the disk with the fastest sequential I/O score and the DS and IS databases on the disk with the fastest random-access I/O score.

You're free to accept or reject Performance Optimizer's suggestions; however, be forewarned that it's not safe to try to move these files yourself: the transaction logs contain references to the physical location of the database files on disk, so moving the databases will render the log files worthless. That's why Performance Optimizer stops the Exchange services before it does anything: all outstanding transactions are committed to the database, so the log file contents are no longer necessary after the services have been stopped.

 If you want to move the database files yourself, you can do so by using the Database Paths tab of the server's properties dialog in Exchange Administrator. After you confirm that you really want to move the paths, Exchange Administrator will stop the Exchange services, move the files, and restart the services.

Step 5: Moving the files

Step 4 is where Performance Optimizer presents its suggestions to you; the following step asks whether you choose to accept them or not. This page contains a single checkbox that says "Move files automatically," along with some explanatory text that tells you to check the box if you want Performance Optimizer to move the files for you. Since you can't move the files manually, what you're really choosing is whether you want to move the files or not, not whether you want to do it automatically or manually. If you select the checkbox, when you click the Next button, Performance Optimizer will move the files for you; if not, they'll stay in their current locations.

Performance Optimizer recommends that you make a full backup of the database files before having it move them. This is a good idea; in fact, you should make sure you have a good full backup *before* you run Performance Optimizer at all, since it has to stop the Exchange services.

Step 6: Restarting the services

Whether you moved the files or not, when you hit the sixth Performance Optimizer step you're almost done. This page congratulates you (because "Microsoft Exchange has been optimally configured for use on this computer," naturally). The page also lists all the Exchange services Performance Optimizer will attempt to restart when you click the Finish button; if you prefer, you can check the "Do not restart these services" checkbox to leave the services stopped. There's no way to choose individual services to restart; it's an all-or-nothing deal.

It's worth noting that no actual changes to the system's registry are made until you click the Finish button, but the database files are moved. If you realize that you provided an incorrect answer in step 2, you can hit the Finish button and rerun Performance Optimizer later, use the Back button to go back and change your answers, or click the Cancel button; but no matter what, your database files will be rehomed.

Checking what Performance Optimizer did

Performance Optimizer records what it finds and the changes it makes in a log file, *%systemroot%\system32\perfopt.log*. Here's an example that Performance Optimizer generated when I ran it on one of my test servers immediately after installing Exchange 5.5 Enterprise Edition. This particular box is a big Dell PowerEdge 2300 with two CPUs, a RAID array, and 512MB of RAM.

```
Detected 2 processor(s)
Detected 536268800 bytes physical memory
Found fixed logical disk C:
Found fixed logical disk D:
The database file C:\exchsrvr\MDBDATA\PRIV.EDB is consistent.
The database file C:\exchsrvr\MDBDATA\PUB.EDB is consistent.
The database file C:\exchsrvr\DSADATA\dir.edb is consistent.
Performance Results
(Smaller values better)
Disk  RA(ms)    Seq(ms)
--------------------------------------------------------------------
--
C:    2703      1953
D:    1812      1969
Microsoft Exchange Server Private information store file was moved from
    C:\exchsrvr\MDBDATA to D:\exchsrvr\MDBDATA
```

```
Microsoft Exchange Server Message Transfer Agent log files was moved from
    C:\exchsrvr\mtadata to D:\exchsrvr\mtadata
Microsoft Exchange Server Public information store file was moved from
    C:\exchsrvr\MDBDATA to D:\exchsrvr\MDBDATA
Microsoft Exchange Server Directory service database file was moved from
    C:\exchsrvr\DSADATA to D:\exchsrvr\DSADATA
Set # of information store buffers from 1000 to 130925
Set # of directory buffers from 1000 to 130925
Set Minimum # of information store threads from 8 to 10
Set Maximum # of information store threads from 20 to 50
Set # of directory threads from 48 to 50
Set # of background threads from 25 to 37
Set # of heaps from 4 to 8
Set # of information store gateway in threads from 1 to 2
Set # of information store gateway out threads from 1 to 2
Set Buffer Threshold Low Percent from 5 to 3
Set Buffer Threshold High Percent from 15 to 3
Set Maximum # of pool threads from 10 to 50
Set # of dispatcher threads from 1 to 2
Set # of transfer threads from 1 to 2
Set # of kernel threads from 1 to 3
Set # of database data buffers per object from 3 to 6
Set # of RTS threads from 1 to 3
Set # of concurrent MDB/delivery queue clients from 3 to 10
Set # of concurrent XAPI sessions from 80 to 30
Set # of MT gateway clients from 8 to 10
Set # of retrieval queue clients from 2 to 10
```

You can tell what Performance Optimizer does from looking at this log file, even if you skipped the preceding sections. The very first thing it does is count resources: CPUs, RAM, and physical disks. Next, it checks the public IS, private IS, and directory databases to make sure they're internally consistent. If those checks succeed, it runs timing tests. In my case, it discovered that the RAID array was significantly faster than the single boot disk for random access disk I/O but scored the same on the sequential I/O tests.

Based on the timing and resource results, you can see that Performance Optimizer made a ton of changes: 21 out of the 60 or so Performance Optimizer settings were adjusted. Once the optimizer detected how much RAM the machine had, how I'd answered the questions from step 2, and what speed the disks ran at, it decided to move the private and public IS files, the directory database, and the MTA logs. Whenever you run Performance Optimizer, it's worth reviewing the log file to see exactly what it did.

Do-It-Yourself Tuning with Performance Optimizer

Performance Optimizer supports a verbose mode, selected with the –v option. In this mode, you have access to six pages worth of additional controls that give you very fine-grained control over the settings that Performance Optimizer normally adjusts on its own. You make these changes at your own peril, but sometimes good sense, your own experience, or Microsoft will dictate that you make a change, so it's a good idea to know how.

A word to the wise

Performance Optimizer uses some very sophisticated tuning algorithms based on Microsoft's intimate knowledge of the relationships between different Exchange components. Performance Optimizer can adjust around 60 parameters, any one of which may depend on (or affect) any number of others. Making blind changes to the 40 parameters you can manually adjust in Performance Optimizer is a good way to screw up your servers. Accordingly, here are some suggestions about how to safely use Performance Optimizer:

- If it ain't broke, don't fix it. Unless you can pinpoint a specific reason to adjust a specific parameter, don't touch it.

- Watch your server performance before you make a change. Once you've clearly identified that something's amiss, work on one issue at a time. Don't try to make one big sweep through Performance Optimizer to simultaneously improve your MTA, IMS, and disk performance; if you do, you won't have any way to identify which changes helped performance and which may have hurt.

- If your hardware is inadequate, Performance Optimizer changes won't fix the problem. Most of the time, if your system performance is poor, there's nothing Performance Optimizer can do to fix it.

- Extreme changes in the values of any setting may make your server less stable. Microsoft recommends making incremental changes of no more than 10–20% of the current value.

- If you're not sure what effect a change might have, don't make it! You can use the information later in this section or articles in Microsoft's Knowledge Base and TechNet services to find out what a change's effect might be; you can even call PSS to get more information.

Differences between verbose and normal mode

The first visible difference between normal and verbose modes in Performance Optimizer is that you can choose whether to perform the disk timing analysis tests or not. The verbose-mode version of the third Performance Optimizer page features a checkbox labeled "Analyze hard disks" that you can use to skip the tests altogether, along with a list box that shows all the physical drives in your system. You can use this list to selectively analyze one or more disks instead of doing them all; however, since Exchange issues concurrent I/O requests to all disks it tests, you're better off analyzing all disks at once to get a truer picture of your overall disk performance.

The other major difference appears after step 5. Instead of going straight to the final step, as you would in normal mode, the verbose mode of Performance Optimizer presents a total of six additional pages that show the current state of some 40 Exchange parameters. You can change any of these values; when you hit the final page, you can either finalize or discard your changes, just as you can in normal mode.

The most important settings

In *Animal Farm*, George Orwell pointed out that even when all animals are equal, some are more equal than others. This is also true of Performance Optimizer settings: of the 40 settings you can manually adjust, there are 14 values that have particular impact on your server performance. In the following list, I've grouped related settings together:

# of information store buffers
# of directory buffers

> These values tell you how many buffers have been allocated to the IS and DS. The values may be the same, or they may differ, with the IS value usually being larger, unless your server doesn't have any user mailboxes. These values are both extremely sensitive to the amount of RAM you have installed. If you find that you're running out of buffers, don't just adjust these values upward, install more RAM and rerun Performance Optimizer.

Minimum # of information store threads
Maximum # of information store threads

> These settings control the minimum and maximum number of threads allocated for handling communications between clients and the IS. Don't change the minimum. Upping the maximum value may allow more clients to be handled at once, but spawning too many threads will mean that most threads have to wait for execution time, making service slower than it would be with fewer threads. If you do change the maximum value, you'll also need to change the "# of directory threads" setting.

# of directory threads

> This setting governs how many threads the DS spawns for all its work, including client requests like address book lookups and server requests like replication. You can use Performance Monitor to see how many threads the DS currently is using: check the Process object's Thread Count counter on the *dsamain* instance (you can also look at the *store* instance to see how many threads the IS is using). If your check of Performance Monitor shows that you're often hitting the maximum thread count, you may want to add more threads—but don't go hog-wild. Instead, increase the value in small jumps (say, between 5 and 10) until the actual usage averages just a bit less than the

Buffer Allocation Explained

Exchange is RAM-hungry, but this isn't due to poor coding practice on Microsoft's part. When Performance Optimizer runs, it looks to see how much RAM is available to Exchange, either by calculating how much RAM is available or by honoring the limit you specify. Out of this available RAM, Performance Optimizer first allocates small buffers for the most critical system services, ensuring that they always have enough RAM. Once these small allocations are made, Performance Optimizer divvies up the remaining RAM for the database to use. These database buffers, which Microsoft persists in calling *JET buffers,* after the original Joint Engine Technology database system Exchange used, are used by the DS and IS to do their database work.

On earlier versions of Exchange, Performance Optimizer allocates between 3000 and 4000 buffers for the first 64MB of RAM, then 1,000 buffers per 7MB of RAM after that. Exchange 5.5 doesn't use any fixed buffer allocation strategy; its dynamic buffer allocation (DBA) scheme allocates as many buffers as possible. For example, the 512MB of RAM in the Dell PowerEdge server I used while writing this chapter resulted in Performance Optimizer allocating a maximum of 130,925 buffers each to the DS and IS. Since these buffers are 4KB each, that means that the DS and IS could each potentially get almost the entire 512MB of RAM! In practice, DBA would ensure that each subsystem shares its buffer space both with other Exchange subsystems and with other applications on the same machine.

Performance Optimizer calculates the number of buffers it should allocate based on the estimates you give of how many users will use the server and what the server will be doing. If your user load or server roles change, you'll need to run Performance Optimizer again to readjust the buffer settings. When you run Performance Optimizer with the –v switch, you can see the effect these settings have on buffer allocation by doing the following:

1. Launch Performance Optimizer with the –v switch.

2. Choose a number of users, a set of server roles, and a memory limitation from the appropriate Performance Optimizer page, then use the Next button.

3. Skip the disk analysis test.

4. Check the values shown for the "# of information store buffers" and "# of directory buffers" parameters. If you changed any of your answers in step 2, you'll probably notice that the old and new values for the number of buffers are different.

5. Continue on through the remaining Performance Optimizer pages to apply its suggested changes, or use the Cancel button to bail out without changing anything.

maximum count. Microsoft's rule of thumb for manually tuning this parameter is to multiply the number of processors by 50 and add 30 to get the thread limit; unless your server is frequently reaching that limit, there's no need to allocate that many threads.

Maximum # of concurrent read threads

This is the maximum number of DS threads used to answer incoming replication requests. These threads are counted as part of the "# of directory threads" setting. Normally, you'll want to have one thread for each server you have to replicate with, so you may need to manually adjust this value to the number of servers in your site plus one, which means you may also need to bump up the "# of directory threads" settings to avoid taking threads away from other directory functions.

# of background threads

Background threads are Exchange's invisible worker ants. While IS threads are busy handling client requests, background threads do the heavy lifting of linking the IS with the MTA and other Exchange components. These worker threads also handle scheduled maintenance tasks, including message expiration, issuing storage limit warnings, online defragmentation, and regenerating offline address books. These threads tend to use significant amounts of memory to get their work done, so raising the value of this parameter can prevent the IS from getting enough memory to run (or even start!). If you're going to change this setting, do it in small increments of one or two threads, then carefully monitor your server's performance. If your background maintenance is generating event log messages, try changing the schedule to allow maintenance to happen more often instead of adjusting the thread count.

# of private information store send threads
# of private information store delivery threads
# of public information store send threads
# of public information store delivery threads

The private and public IS send and delivery threads handle communication between the MTA and the IS. Normally, there are at least two of each of these threads: one controls all threads of the same type, and the others do the actual work. Don't lower these values below 2. If your IS queues seem to be permanently constipated (as shown on the MSExchangeIS Private or MSExchange-Public objects' Send and Receive Queue Size counters), adding extra threads, one at a time, may help. Each thread you add here is a new background thread, so make sure to adjust "# of background threads" to add as many threads as you add here; you may also need to adjust the "# of submit/deliver threads" setting discussed later. If settings of 3 or 4 threads don't clear your thread backlog, you need to plan on upgrading your server or doing something to move some load off the server.

# of submit/deliver threads

The MTA's submit/deliver threads work in partnership with the IS send and delivery threads. When the MTA and IS need to exchange messages, whichever one is sending data spawns a sending thread, and the receiving end spawns a matching thread. By using Performance Monitor to look at the MSExchangeMTA object's Work Queue Length counter, you can see how many objects are waiting for a thread. If you increase the number of MTA submit/deliver threads, you also have to increase the IS send and delivery threads, and vice versa. Because of the interrelationship between the MTA and IS delivery threads, you might be best off to leave them alone.

# of information store gateway in threads
# of information store gateway out threads

The IS gateway threads handle communications between the IS and external gateways like the Lotus Notes connector and the IMS. You can think of the IS-to-MTA send and delivery threads as a special type of gateway threads. You may find that adjusting the number of gateway threads helps resolve backlogs that occur between the IS and your gateways, but the same caveats apply: you'll need to adjust the number of background threads, and you may need to adjust the "# of submit/deliver threads" to boot.

Max # of RPC calls outstanding

This parameter lets you manually adjust the maximum number of concurrent RPC calls the MTA will tolerate. If your event log shows that the MTA is experiencing RPC errors, boosting this value may clear up the problem; however, almost all RPC failures are the result of improperly configured or overloaded networks. Microsoft warns you to never set this value higher than 50.

The other settings

Now that you know about the big 14, you might think that's all, but it's not. There are a number of other settings you might be interested in changing when circumstances dictate.

The first verbose mode page contains eight settings, seven of which were covered in the preceding section. The eighth, "# of heaps," controls how many allocation heaps are allocated to various services. Each heap is used to provide RAM to services that need it; the more heaps you have, the less RAM is available for database buffer allocation. Leave this setting alone unless PSS tells you to change it; Performance Optimizer can do a better job of setting it.

The second verbose mode page contains nine settings. The first six are discussed above (meaning that you've already seen thirteen of the first seventeen settings that Performance Optimizer shows you). The remaining three are shown in Table 18-6; the settings for remaining pages appear in Tables 18-7 through 18-11.

Throughout this section, I talk about default values; these defaults appear on the servers I used, but Performance Optimizer may choose different defaults for your machines depending on your configuration. In general, the best strategy to follow is to leave defaults alone unless you have a good reason not to.

Table 18-6. Performance Optimizer Parameters on Verbose Mode Page 2

Parameter	What It Does
Buffer Threshold Low Percent	Exchange maintains a buffer threshold counter. When the number of free buffers falls to this percentage of the total, the DS and IS start flushing their buffers to disk. Small values (like the default setting of 3%) limit the amount of disk I/O, but performance will suffer if clients have to wait for a buffer.
Buffer Threshold High Percent	The preceding value tells Exchange when to start flushing; this one tells Exchange when to stop. For example, if this is set to 15%, Exchange will continue flushing buffers until 15% of buffers are free. For best performance, Microsoft recommends setting this value equal to, or slightly higher than, the Buffer Threshold Low Percent value (or you could just let Performance Optimizer do it for you).
Maximum # of pool threads	This counter sets the maximum number of threads allocated *per processor* for handling IMAP4, POP3, and NNTP connections. If you have lots of these clients, you can raise this value, but don't raise it above 50.

Table 18-7. Performance Optimizer Parameters on Verbose Mode Page 3

Parameter	What It Does
# of information store users	This parameter value comes straight from the radio buttons in the "Users on this server" group. Normally you shouldn't need to adjust it, since Performance Optimizer uses your answer to set it.
# of concurrent connections to LAN-MTAs	Controls the number of concurrent associations the MTA may open to other MTAs on the LAN. This number should generally be twice the value of "# of LAN-MTAs."
# of concurrent connections to RAS-MTAs	Controls the number of concurrent associations the MTA is allowed to open to MTAs connected via DRAS.
# of LAN-MTAs	Controls the maximum number of LAN MTAs that the MTA will attempt to connect to at once. If you change this, make sure to adjust the "# of concurrent connections to LAN-MTAs" parameter, plus the control block parameter for whatever network protocol you're using.
# of X.400 gateways	Indicates the maximum number of remote X.400 gateways that will talk to this server over TCP/IP, TP4, or X.25 network connections.
ds_read cache latency (secs)	This value controls how long a directory entry can live in the DS read cache before it expires. The longer an item can stay in the cache, the more likely it will be used instead of forcing a read from disk; however, since the cache is of finite size, setting this time too high prevents new items from being cached.

Remember, when you increase the number of threads used for a particular function, you may need to increase the number of background or client threads allocated to avoid starving other subsystems of the threads they need.

Table 18-8. Performance Optimizer Parameters on Verbose Mode Page 4

Parameter	What It Does
# of dispatcher threads	This value indicates how many threads are to be used for message routing. You must have at least two; adding more threads may help speed message delivery, depending on how complicated your GWART is.
# of transfer threads	This value specifies how many threads the MTA uses to transfer messages hither and yon. The default value of 2, which you shouldn't lower, is normally plenty.
# of kernel threads	Kernel threads process requests from the MTA OSI protocol stack. The default value of 3 is fine; leave it alone.
# of submit/ deliver threads	Remember the public and private IS submit/deliver threads? This value tells the MTA how many submit/deliver threads it may use for transferring messages to remote MTAs. If you change this value, do it carefully.
# of RAS LAN-MTAs	This value indicates the maximum supported number of DRAS-connected MTAs the MTA should expect to handle. It's unlikely you'll need more than the default value of 10.
# of database data buffers per object	Each message stored in the MTA cache (which holds messages until the MTA is certain that they've been acknowledged by the destination IS or MTA) will normally have several JET buffers allocated to it. The default value of 6 is fine—don't fool with it.
# of RTS threads	The Reliable Transfer Service (RTS), which you first met in Chapter 7, *Managing Connectors and the MTA,* can use several threads to process and send messages; this value governs the maximum number of threads RTS may use.

Table 18-9. Performance Optimizer Parameters on Verbose Mode Page 5

Parameter	What It Does
# of concurrent MDB/delivery queue clients	Controls the maximum number of IS and XAPI clients that the MTA will talk to at once. A single client can have multiple sessions; as you change this parameter, make sure to change "# of concurrent XAPI sessions" accordingly. Don't lower this value below 2: there must be at least one connection each for the private and public IS.
# of concurrent XAPI sessions	Reflects the maximum number of XAPI and IS client sessions the MTA will allow. These sessions include retrieval queue and gateway clients.
Max # of RPC calls outstanding	As discussed earlier in the chapter, this setting is the maximum number of RPC calls (and thus the maximum number of RPC threads) the MTA will handle at once.

Table 18-9. Performance Optimizer Parameters on Verbose Mode Page 5 (continued)

Parameter	What It Does
Min # of RPC threads	This value sets a floor on the number of RPC threads.
# of MTA gateway clients	This value is the maximum number of gateways the MTA will communicate with at once. Its normal setting of 10 is plenty.
# of retrieval queue clients	This value sets the maximum number of XAPI mail retrieval queue clients the MTA will talk to at once. Leave it alone.
# of TCP/IP control blocks	This value sets a maximum for the number of TCP/IP connections the MTA may make. The standard rule is to allocate 10 blocks for each connector that uses TCP/IP; if you're running a pre-SP2 Exchange 5.5, you'll need to allocate more blocks to work around a bug in the MTA block handling code.
# of TCP/IP threads	The number of TCP/IP threads the MTA may use to connect to other MTAs. The default of two is plenty, so you should leave this setting alone.

Table 18-10. Performance Optimizer Parameters on Verbose Mode Page 6

Parameter	What It Does
# of TP4 control blocks	This value controls the total number of TP4 connection blocks; like its TCP/IP counterpart, it can be adjusted if you need more connection blocks.
# of TP4 threads	The number of TP4 threads the MTA may use to connect to other MTAs. Leave it alone.

If you've installed and configured the IMS, a seventh page will appear with settings as shown in Table 18-11.

Table 18-11. Performance Optimizer Parameters on Verbose Mode Page 7

Parameter	What It Does
# of inbound threads	The number of threads the IMS can use for handling inbound messages; these threads convert incoming messages to Exchange's format and move it from the IMS to the IS.
# of outbound threads	Outbound threads convert mail from Exchange format to MIME and move it from the IS to the IMS queues; this value specifies how many outbound threads the IMS will use.
# of InOut threads	InOut threads can do either inbound or outbound message transfer.
# of threads per processor	Reflects the number of threads the IMS may allocate to each system processor.

Running Performance Optimizer in Batch Mode

Microsoft has thoughtfully provided a way to run Performance Optimizer in unattended mode, so that you can install and optimize Exchange on a new server without having to sit there and push the Next button in dialog after dialog. This greatly speeds setting up a new server, especially since you can save the answer files you use for the setup process and reuse them when you need to install Exchange again.

Performance Optimizer can be run in unattended mode in two ways: the −s switch tells it to look for a settings file named *perfopt.inf* in the *exchsrvr\bin* directory, and the −f command lets you specify the full path to the options file. For example:

```
c:\exchsrvr\bin\perfwiz -f c:\config\standard.inf
```

This code runs Performance Optimizer with the specified settings file. What goes in the settings file? It's just a plain text file with seven lines in it; each line contains one Performance Optimizer keyword. All seven lines don't have to be present, although any setting you don't include will default to a value you might not want. Table 18-12 shows the keywords, their permissible values, and their defaults.

Table 18-12. Parameters for Performance Optimizer's Unattended Mode

Keyword	Legal Values	Default Value	Notes
Users	0, 1, 2, 3, 4, or 5	0	Corresponds to the radio buttons asking for the number of users this server will host: 0 = 1–25 users, 1 = 26–50, 2 = 51–100, 3 = 101–250, 4 = 251–500, and 5 = more than 500.
Org Users	0, 1, 2, 3, or 4	0	Corresponds to the radio buttons asking how many users are in the entire organization: 0 = less than 100, 1 = 100–999, 2 = 1,000–9,999, 3 = 10,000–99,999, 4 = 100,000 or more.
Server Type	Any combination of flags (will always be in the range 0–15)	0	Add the flag values for your server combination. For example, if your server has a public IS and connectors, use a value of 5. Public server = 1 Private server = 2 Private and public server = 3 Connector/Directory Import server = 4 Multiserver site = 8 POP3/Internet = 16
Dont Restart	TRUE or FALSE	FALSE	Controls whether the Performance Optimizer should restart the Exchange services when it completes.
Analyze Disks	TRUE or FALSE	TRUE	Controls whether the disk analysis step is skipped or run.

Table 18-12. Parameters for Performance Optimizer's Unattended Mode (continued)

Keyword	Legal Values	Default Value	Notes
Move Files	TRUE or FALSE	TRUE	Controls whether Performance Optimizer moves the database files if the `Analyze Disks` option is turned on.
Limit Memory Usage	Positive numeric values	N/A	Sets the memory size limit for Exchange processes; if no value is specified, Exchange will use DBA.

A

BORK Tools

This appendix is a start at explaining what's on the BackOffice Resource Kit (BORK) CD-ROMs. There are about 100 tools on the CDs, but not every tool is either useful or safe. The BORK tools are a mix of useful tools designed for administrators and one-of-a-kind tools built by Microsoft's Exchange engineering and support groups. If you don't see a tool listed here, you should assume that it's dangerous and not run it unless PSS tells you to.

The bulk of this appendix is split into three tables, each reflecting the contents of a separate CD: the *BORK Part One*, the *BORK Part Two*, and the *BORK Second Edition*. (The *BORK Third Edition* is in beta as I write this in April 1999; it should be in stores sometime reasonably soon.) You can legally get these tools in a number of ways:

- You can buy the BORK; the list price of $200 seems awfully high, but you can get it for about half that price by using discount bookstores like Bookpool (*www.bookpool.com*). It's worth every penny. The bookstore version of BORK comes with a thick stack of printed documentation that's (to me) easier to browse than the online version.

- You can subscribe to Microsoft's TechNet service, which includes the BORK tools and an electronic version of the documentation.

- You can subscribe to Microsoft's Development Network (MSDN), which includes the BORK CDs but not the printed material that accompanies them.

Some of the BORK tools can be freely downloaded from Microsoft's web site at *www.microsoft.com/exchange/reskit.htm*. The Exchange group maintains a set of useful tools for Exchange at *www.microsoft.com/technet/appfarm/* and *backoffice. microsoft.com/downtrial/moreinfo/exchresource.asp*. Patches and updates to the BORK tools can be found at *ftp://ftp.microsoft.com/bussys/backoffice/reskit*.

This appendix isn't a detailed how-to guide; it's intended to give you a rundown on the tools available to ease your life as an administrator. The most useful tools are covered in their own sections. What about the others? Some of the tools are very simple, and only do one small thing (*header.exe* is a good example); others require expertise above and beyond that of the average administrator. Because BORK tools are generally unsupported by Microsoft Product Support Services, be sure you have a good backup of your server and registry before making any changes to your configuration, because neither Microsoft nor I can promise that the tools won't totally whack your machine.

If you don't find this appendix meaty enough, some of the tools are described in more detail in the *Exchange Server 5.5 Resource Guide*, which comes with both the electronic and bookstore versions of the BORK. In many cases, Microsoft also provides TechNet and Knowledge Base articles that describe the proper use of these tools; they're noted in the tables below when they're particularly helpful.

 When you see *I386* in the following sections, feel free to substitute another CPU type (like *alpha*) if you're not using an x86-based server.

The Rules-Based Distribution List Tool

How many times have you wanted to create a distribution list by providing a criteria like "every manager in Houston" or "every employee outside North America?" Exchange doesn't provide a way to do this automatically, but the Rules-Based Distribution List (RBDL) tool does. It's not part of the *BORK Second Edition*, but it should be in the *Third Edition* when it's released, and it's available from *www. exchangecode.com* in the meantime.

In brief, you use RBDL by creating a DL and supplying a query string that defines how RBDL should select mailboxes and DLs for membership. Once you've done that, you can run RBDL manually or automatically, and it will use LDAP to interrogate the Exchange directory and update the DL according to its criteria.

To use RBDL, you must have an Exchange 5.5 server in your site; on the machine where you want to run RBDL, you must have the Active Directory Services Interface (ADSI) and Microsoft Data Access Components (MDAC) runtime components. Both of these are available from Microsoft's web site, on TechNet, and on MSDN. Install them according to the directions on their web pages, then download and install RBDL.

Building a DL with RBDL

The actual process of creating a new DL is pretty straightforward:

1. Use Exchange Administrator to create a new DL.

2. Open the DL's properties dialog and go to its Advanced tab.

3. Put the query string you want to use, prefixed by RBDL=, into the Administrative Notes field.

4. Run RBDL to build the DL.

Steps 1 and 2 have already been covered in previous chapters; the other two need some further explanation.

Building a query string

The query string that RBDL expects to see looks somewhat like a URL, with some extra stuff added. Here's an example:

```
RBDL=<LDAP://HSV1/o=RobichauxAssoc;(objectClass=organizationalPerson);
    cn,adspath;subtree>
```

The first part of the query specifies the protocol (LDAP), the server name (*HSV1*), and the Exchange organization (RobichauxAssoc); the remaining three parts specify the query string, what attributes to use when querying, and whether to look in subcontainers or not (**subtree** turns on subcontainer searching, while leaving it out suppresses subcontainer searching).

How do you construct a query string? Since they're made up of the same kinds of queries you can use for LDAP queries, you can check the RFCs that define the LDAP protocol and its query strings (RFC 2251 and 2254). You can also use Exchange Administrator's raw mode to get the names of attributes (for example, st is state) and use them to construct a query filter.

Running RBDL

When you run RBDL, you must specify the full path to the container you want it to process, along with the /**container** switch. For example:

```
RBDL /container:"LDAP://HSV1/o=RobichauxAssoc/ou=USA-East/cn=Recipients"
```

would run RBDL once on the Recipients container in the USA-East site of the RobichauxAssoc organization. You can specify any named container; whatever container you specify will be processed along with all its subcontainers. RBDL will look at every DL in the container and update those with RBDL query strings in their Administrative Notes fields.

You can also use the /pause switch to have RBDL spawn a process that wakes up after the number of minutes you specify to update the lists. For example, this command will fire up RBDL to rebuild all my rule-based DLs every 12 hours:

```
RBDL /container:"LDAP://HSV1/o=RobichauxAssoc /pause:720"
```

You can also schedule RBDL with the *at* or *winat* commands, or run it as a service with the *srvany* tool from the NT Resource Kit.

The Storage Statistics Tool

This MAPI application, better known as *storstat*, is designed to gather statistics from your users' mailboxes, send them to a central location (in this case, a mailbox you've created named StorStat), then compile the statistics so you can get a realistic view of how your users actually use their email. The tool can be distributed to all of your users; I've found that the easiest way to make it accessible to everyone is to put it into a public folder every user can access. Then you point your users toward it, and shazam!—your statistics are waiting for you in the StorStat mailbox. Data collected will include the average number of items sent and received daily and the number of folders and rules belonging to each user.

Next, you'll want to use what the documentation calls "Administrator Mode." To so this, you'll need to first ensure that you have administrator permissions on the StorStat mailbox, and set the mailbox as the default profile for your email client. From a command prompt, you'd then type storstat -a. As the tool works, you'll see the progress bar move until the tool has completed its analysis. Save these results in order to export the data into MS Excel. The Visual Basic macro *statmac.xls* is included with the tool to help you decipher the data in the StorStat mailbox. This information will give you a good view of your users' collective messaging habits.

Some caveats you're better off knowing about now:

- Make sure that the StorStat mailbox is created before asking your users to run the utility!

- Take the documentation seriously: don't overload your server by having everyone run the tool at once. I found that while 80 users at a time can run the tool successfully, 800 users running the tool at once broke StorStat for one of our clients. The send portion of the MAPI function is broken and doesn't seem to be fixable, so the tool no longer sends to the StorStat mailbox. If we come up with a solution for this, we'll post it on this book's web site (*http://www. oreilly.com/catalog/managexsvr*), but don't hold your breath.

- If all your users aren't saving their mail to their *Sent Items* folder, the data you collect on items sent per day will be skewed.

The Mailbox Cleanup Agent

The Mailbox Cleanup Agent runs as a service on Exchange servers; you define when you'd like it to do its job, and your lifelong quest to keep mailbox sizes from growing uncontrollably will finally be satisfied. It's similar in many ways to the Tools → Clean Mailbox... command presented in Chapter 5, *Using Exchange Administrator*, but it has some additional features. In particular:

- You can schedule it to clean mailboxes regularly.

- You can choose whether cleaned messages are deleted or moved to a special folder called *System Cleanup* in each user's mailbox.

- You can choose which mailboxes are cleaned and which are left alone.

- You can control what types of messages are cleaned.

Once you install the MCA, it appears as a service in the Services control panel, and as an item in the Recipients container. Use the control panel to start the service; by default, it's set to manual startup, but you can enable automatic startup by adding a `REG_MULTI_SZ` value named `DependOnService` to the MCA's key, located at `HKLM\System\CurrentControlSet\Services`, and give it a value of `MSExchangeIS`. Some versions of the MCA use a key named `MSExchangeMCA`; others use `MCAserverName`.

The current version of MCA, 1.93, replaces the tool by the same name found in the *BORK Part Two*. MCA 1.93 is available from Microsoft's web site or on BORK3, coming soon.

When you open the MCA item in Exchange Administrator, you'll see that it has three tabs:

Configuration
>   This tab lets you set parameters for how cleanup occurs: you can set separate age limits for the *Inbox* and *Sent Items* folders, choose whether you want to delete items immediately or move them to a folder named *System Cleanup* in the user's mailbox, and specify how many days may pass before items in the *System Cleanup* folder go to the *Deleted Items* folder. The Exclude Mailbox button on this tab lets you supply a list of mailboxes that you don't want cleaned.

Schedule
>   This tab lets you control what time of day the MCA starts (it defaults to midnight), how often it runs, and when it runs. For example, you can run it every 15 days, every two weeks on Friday, or on the first Sunday of every other month.

Notification

> This tab allows you to control whether users get a mail message when MCA processes their mailboxes, and (if so) what that message says. The default message tells them that their mailbox has been cleaned, but you can customize it.

By default, MCA 1.92 and later won't remove data from the *Outlook Calendar, Contacts, Notes, Journal,* or *Tasks* folders. However, some of these folders (notably *Journal,* which many users have turned on without realizing it) can accrue lots of junk. To allow MCA to purge additional item types, you can edit the `KeepMsgClass` registry value (a `REG_MULTI_SZ`) under the `MCAserverName` registry key. For example, if you remove the `IPM.Contact` value from `KeepMsgClass`, the MCA will purge contacts that meet the settings on the Configuration tab.

If you want to know how much work the MCA is doing, check the event log for event ID 728. This event logs how long the MCA took to run, how many mailboxes were cleaned, how many messages were moved or deleted, and what size those messages were. You can then look at event 1221 from `MSExchangeIS Private` to see how much free space was recovered by the next online defragmentation.

The Public Folder Administration Tool

This command-line tool (*pfadmin.exe,* version 1.3.0, updated from version 1.2.1 on the *BORK Part Two*) makes public folder administration easier, especially when changes need to be made to multiple public folders—just what a busy administrator needs! You can use this tool to rehome multiple public folders at once, replicate public folder Access Control Lists (ACLs), and identify various item types within public folders. Mailboxes can be removed from or added to the permissions lists of public folders *en masse* with this tool; you can also use the tool to create a CSV file listing message types within a public folder tree.

Two separate tools are included in *pfadmin*: the Public Folder ACL Replication tool and the Public Folder Item Class tool. In order to use these tools, you must have an email client installed on the workstation you're using, and you have to log on as the Exchange service account, create a profile named PFProfile on the client and add a valid mailbox and server name to the profile.

The Public Folder ACL Replication tool has several command-line options, and all of these can be enhanced by using switches for more control. More command-line options for the tools are detailed in the BORK documentation. We'll only hit the high points here:

SETACL

> Allows you to set the access control list specifying who has permissions to the folder and who doesn't, and what type of permissions each user should have

SETREPLICAS

> Sets location of replicas of the specified public folder

LISTACL

> Gets a list of who has what permissions on the specified folder

LISTREPLICAS

> Tells where replicas for the specified public folder reside

MESSAGECLASS

> Specifies type of form used in the public folder

The Public Folder Item Class tool examines the message class of every item in a public folder tree, and writes the data gathered to a CSV file that contains one line for each folder's information. The tool is very simple to run: at the command line, you type:

```
pfadmin ? messageclass
```

You get to decide which IPM classes you'd like to track. Messages that fall within a subtype are counted in both the subtype and its parent type, and only one subtype is allowed per parent type. PFAdmin doesn't examine attachments and objects (or any contents) within messages; it just analyzes the type of message.

One thing to remember: after rehoming a public folder, you may need to run the DS/IS consistency adjuster so Exchange notices the change.

The Global Address List Modify Tool

This tool lets users modify their own mailbox properties, thus taking some of the administrative load off your shoulders. Microsoft estimates that approximately 20% of their directory data changes every year as people move around, get married, and so on. This tool is a good way to pass the workload back to the users.

 This tool can be put into a *Tools* public folder along with other tools, such as the Storage Statistics tool mentioned earlier in this appendix. This is useful when you have the kind of users some of my clients have: those who mean well, but often forget where they've stored items.

You don't want your users to muck up your nice clean directory, you say? Well, you can decide which fields you'd like users to be able to modify. The only areas they can modify by default are on the Phone/Notes tab of their mailbox. If you'd like, you can enable them to change their addresses, titles, or other fields. Here's an example using the Title field; the following procedure can be used for most fields on the General and Phone/Notes tabs:

1. Open Exchange Administrator in raw mode.

2. Connect to the appropriate server; you may want to test this on a server that has a small number of users, to start.

3. Use the View → Raw Directory... command to get the full raw view.

4. In the container pane, find and double-click on the Schema object.

5. Double-click on the Title attribute in the contents pane.

6. In the Access-Category area, change the value to 2. (See Chapter 9, *Managing the Directory*, for more on using this trick.)

7. Click on Set, then on OK. You'll get a warning, but just click on OK again and the changes will take effect.

8. Remember to do this for each server you have mailboxes on when you announce the presence of the tool, or you'll have many disappointed users!

If your organization takes advantage of Exchange's ability to let you set up custom attributes, you can allow your users to change those entries, too. Place the *galmodca.exe* tool into public folder we talked about earlier, make any schema changes you'd like (again, on all servers), and you're in business!

The Rest of the Tools

Tables A-1 through A-3 describe the tools on the three BORK CDs.

Table A-1. Tools in BORK Part One

Tool Name	What It Does	Location
AT&T Mail Migration Tool	Allows you to migrate messages from AT&T Mail Access Plus v2.7 or earlier, or PMX Mail systems (StarMail, PC, and Team) into MS Exchange format. Access Plus and PMX messages need to exist either on a local drive or on a locally accessible MS-DOS compatible drive. The target MS Exchange mailbox and profile must exist before migration begins. Encrypted messages must be decrypted before migration; this tool can't decrypt messages.	*Exchange\ I386\Migrate\ AttmWiz*

Table A-1. Tools in BORK Part One (continued)

Tool Name	What It Does	Location
AutoFill Tool	Client tool that changes the way Exchange and Out-look clients resolve addresses in the To, CC, and BCC fields of messages. This is a smart tool that guesses addresses based upon the profile's address-ing history. Registry entries can be made to control how AutoFill works.	*Exchange\ I386\Client\ AutoFill*

Table A-2. Tools in BORK Part Two

Tool Name	What It Does	Location
Acctonme Tool for MS Mail (AKA Acc2nme Tool)	This command-line utility builds (or backs up) the MS Mail post office list files and their shadow files, from the users' global system files.	*Exchange\ Common\ MSMail*
Administrative Mail Agent	Installs as an NT service; allows administrators to create mailboxes by sending a message to the AdminAgent mailbox. An Exchange mailbox needs to be set up for this account before it can work. Useful for automating account creation.	*Exchange\ I386\Admin\ AdminAgt*
ASPiriN Tool (ASN.1 Decoder Tool)	GUI-based ASN.1 (Advanced Syntax Notation One) decoder that allows administrators to view X.409 ASN.1 data from the *\exchsrvr\mtadata* directory. This tool is rarely used; it's for experts only, although it won't do you any harm to run it just to see what it looks like.	*Exchange\ I386\Admin\ Aspirin*
AutoSig Tool	This tool is a registry file that enables a user's signa-ture to roam with the user to multiple Windows 9x workstations.	*Exchange\ Common\ AutoSig*
Backup Tool for MS Exchange	Creates a single daily automated report on the backup status of multiple Exchange servers in an organization. The data contained in the report includes the size of the databases, duration of backup, and whether the backup succeeded or failed.	*Exchange\ I386\Admin\ ExchBkup*
Buddy Drop-per Tool	This tool is most useful in environments where a mix of platforms and/or languages coexist. It allows administrators to automate the distribution of files, applications, and tasks. Also see Dropper Remote Tool.	*Exchange\ I386\Admin\ Dropper*
Bulk Advanced Security Tool	The Bulk Advanced Security Tool enables adminis-trators to encrypt and decrypt messages in folders and subfolders of PST files. A PST file must be used in conjunction with this tool. Best used when a user who's enrolled in advanced security needs to move to a different site within an organization, or even to another organization, such as a sister company.	*Exchange\ I386\Security\ SecTool*

Table A-2. Tools in BORK Part Two (continued)

Tool Name	What It Does	Location
CleanSweep Tool	CleanSweep deletes specific forms, views, or rules reply templates. It also deletes rules and permissions from a mailbox, but it's all or nothing with rules and permissions; there is no granular control over the removal of those items. CleanSweep is commonly used to subdue misfiring Out of Office Assistants. It doesn't work on the Exchange 4.0 client. See KB article Q174045 for instructions on loading and running CleanSweep. Also, read article Q150303 before doing anything, so you don't accidentally whack your users' Inbox Assistant rules.	*Exchange\ I386\Admin\ CleanSwp*
Crystal Reports	Crystal Reports allows you to generate detailed reports on MS Exchange data taken from both the client and the server. Data sources are seen as database tables by Crystal Reports. You can run both predefined reports and custom reports against the Exchange databases. Data from multiple sources can be combined into one report. This is one of the most useful tools for gathering data from MS Exchange. There's too much information on this tool to include here, but there is a lot of information on the use of Crystal Reports available from Microsoft's web site and from TechNet.	*Exchange\ I386\Admin\ Crystal*
DL Import/ Update Tool	Extracts information from previously created Access, Excel, or other data sources and creates distribution lists by importing a CSV file. Also automates updates of Distribution lists.	*Exchange\ I386\Admin\ DLImport*
Dropper Remote Tool (installs with the Buddy Dropper Tool)	Remote Dropper allows you to run commands from remote computers. See the description of the Buddy Dropper Tool.	*Exchange\ I386\Admin\ Dropper*
Dumpfld Tool for MS Mail	The Dumpfld tool is useful when you need to check the contents and/or integrity of a MS Mail folder file. The tool reports on the file's condition, but makes no changes to the file. Will not work on MMF files.	*Exchange\ Common\ MSMail*
Dumpidx Tool for MS Mail	Dumpidx is very similar to the Dumpfld tool, mentioned above; however, this tool does a read-only verification on the condition of folder index files. Still doesn't work on MMF files.	*Exchange\ Common\ MSMail*
Dumpkey Tool for MS Mail	Dumpkey is useful in helping to identify which calendar file is owned by which user.	*Exchange\ Common\ MSMail*

Table A-2. Tools in BORK Part Two (continued)

Tool Name	What It Does	Location
Duplicate Proxy Tool	The Duplicate Proxy Tool lets you search the directory for records containing duplicate proxy addresses. (Duplicate proxy addresses could be created when replication between servers has yet to occur; this is a fairly rare occurrence.) Requires that the LDAP protocol be enabled on your server.	*Exchange\ I386\Admin\ Psearch*
EFD Handcode Agent	Lets you copy and paste your handcode text into your EFD script. This tool is used in conjunction with Visual Basic code.	*Exchange\ I386\Devel－ opr\EFDhandc*
Event Log Scan Tools	With this tool, you can collect details on specific events and services from more than one server at a time; the results are written to text files. For the tool to work, the installation files need to be copied onto a computer that is running the services you want to monitor. Advanced event filtering capabilities are enabled in this tool. You can stop and restart services, run a batch file, or send pop-up or email messages based upon specific events found in the logs.	*Exchange\ I386\EventLog*
Fixfld Tool for MS Mail	Use the Fixfld tool when you suspect corruption in MS Mail 2.1 or later folder files; it attempts to rebuild these folder files based upon their contents at the time the tool is run. Does not work on MMF files.	*Exchange\ Common\ MSMail*
Fixidx Tool for MS Mail	Fixidx should only be used when MS Mail 2.1 or later post offices are corrupt or severely damaged. The tool rebuilds the folder index file; all folder names will be lost when this tool is run. Running this tool will not affect MMF files.	*Exchange\ Common\ MSMail*
Gimport Tool for MS Mail	This is a command-line tool that helps to automate creation, deletion, and modification of post office address groups; works with MS Mail, X.400, SMTP, SNADS, and PROFS users present in the address book.	*Exchange\ Common\ MSMail*
Global Send Options Tool	Allows the user to set default options used for all messages, specifically deferred send time and encoding preference.	*Exchange\ I386\Client\ GloblSnd*
Import Header Tool (a.k.a. Make CSV Tool)	This tool, often referred to as *header.exe*, enables administrators to easily create header files in CSV format for use with Exchange Administrator's directory export and import commands. This tool is very useful when specific directory information needs to be exported from or imported to mailboxes, custom recipients, or distribution lists. It must be run at the Exchange server; it will not work from a workstation.	*Exchange\ I386\Migrate\ Headers*

Table A-2. Tools in BORK Part Two (continued)

Tool Name	What It Does	Location
IMS Sample Extension DLL (a.k.a. IMCert)	Enables the IMS to act as a smart host that can route messages between the Internet and other SMTP hosts. The tool intercepts SMTP messages before they are processed by the IMS, and modifies the envelope addresses, not the message headers.	*Exchange\ Samples\ IMCert*
Internet Idioms Tool	Makes Exchange clients behave more like traditional Internet mail clients; allows users to create automated signatures and prefixed replies, change default read font. This tool is only available in English. The tool works only with the Exchange 4.0 and 5.0 clients, and will cause problems if it's installed when you upgrade to Outlook. See KB article Q166487 for details on removing it.	*Exchange\ I386\Client\ Inetxidm*
Internet Mail Connector Configuration Extractor Tool	This command-line tool extracts configuration data and IMC messages from the Information Store and Directory of an Exchange server; the data can then be restored to another Exchange server. This tool should not be used without the support of MS Product Support Services; it's definitely not for the weak of heart.	*Exchange\ I386\Admin\ IMCExt*
Mailbox Migration Tool	Allows administrators to move a complete copy of an Exchange mailbox, including rules, to a server within a different site or organization. The administrator running the tool needs permissions on both the original and new mailboxes. This tool will only run from Windows NT.	*Exchange\ Winnt\<platform>\MBMigrate*
Mailbox Statistics Tool (a.k.a. StorStat)	This is a good tool to distribute to all of your users; the easiest way to make it accessible to all is to put it into a public folder that every user can access. The results of the mailbox scan will automatically be sent to the StorStat mailbox, and you can then run the tool against the gathered statistics to get a detailed report on your users' collective messaging habits. Make sure that the StorStat mailbox is created before asking your users to run the utility!	*Exchange\ I386\Admin\ StorStat*
MS Exchange Preview Pane Extension	Adds a third area to the client window to allow you to view the body of a message without actually opening the message. Adds other functionality such as reminders and the ability for a user to view the size of their message store. This functionality is built into Outlook 98 and later clients.	*Exchange\ I386\Client\ TriPane*
MS Mail Export/Import Tool	Easily converts Exchange formatted export files into MS Mail format. Also provides the reverse functionality: you can convert MS Mail directory exports to Exchange format.	*Exchange\ <OS>\Admin\ EximWiz2*

Table A-2. Tools in BORK Part Two (continued)

Tool Name	What It Does	Location
MS Mail Export/Import Tool (cont.)	This tool is most useful when you don't actually want to dirsync between MS Mail post offices and Exchange servers, but you still need to exchange directory information: this tool provides manual dirsync.	
MS Mail Proxy to MS Exchange Proxy Conversion Tool	Uses Perl scripts to convert existing SMTP/MHS/X.400 addresses from MS Mail format to MS Exchange format. Addresses may then be added to an Exchange directory as custom recipients.	*Exchange\ Common\ Proxy*
MS Mail Route Change Program	This is a command-line tool that automates route changes to all external MS Mail post offices.	*Exchange\ I386\Admin\ ChgRoute*
MS Mail SMTP Gateway Proxy Migration Tool	Replaces an MS Mail SMTP gateway with the MS Exchange Internet Mail Service while preserving the users' original SMTP addresses as proxy addresses within the MS Exchange directory. The DXA Agent should be stopped when you use this tool.	*Exchange\ I386\Migrate\ MigSMTP*
MS Schedule+ Address Book Assistant	Copies Address Book entries into the user's Schedule+ contact list. Gives Schedule+ users the ability to print a contact list.	*Exchange\ I386\Client\ SchedABA*
MvCal Tool for MS Mail	This tool is helpful to locate a specific user's online calendar file when the file is suspected of being damaged or corrupt.	*Exchange\ Common\ MSMail*
Natural Language Support Configuration Tool	Installs files to support languages not on the default Windows NT language list.	*Exchange\ Common\NLS*
Netdump Tool for MS Mail	This command-line utility can collect and display information on external post offices and gateways.	*Exchange\ Common\ MSMail*
ONDL Tool	This command-line tool can either pull a list of members from a distribution list or show on which distribution lists an account resides.	*Exchange\ I386\Admin\ OnDL*
PF Replication Verifier Tool	Verifies that replication is running normally by comparing folder and message content, and MAPI properties, between public folder replicas.	*Exchange\ I386\PFTools\ Replver*
PF TreeInfo Tool	This client-side tool counts and displays the number of messages and/or the number of subfolders in a public folder.	*Exchange\ I386\PFTools\ PFTree*
Phone Book Search Tool	Enables a user to search through the global address book or a recipients list to locate a user, using a phone number or alias as the search key.	*Exchange\ I386\Admin\ Phone*

Table A-2. Tools in BORK Part Two (continued)

Tool Name	What It Does	Location
Pkicker Tool	This command-line tool allows administrators to add, delete, or update proxy addresses for users without using the Exchange Administrator program.	*Exchange\ I386\Admin\ Pkicker*
Profile Generation Tool (a.k.a. Automatic Profile Generator or *profgen*)	Automates creation of Exchange profiles for roving users by using the login ID to create the profile; especially useful when users often work at different workstations or when several users share a laptop. The tool can be added to the Windows startup group.	*Exchange\ I386\Admin\ ProfGen*
Proxy Update Tool	Automatically converts existing addresses from MS Mail export format to MS Exchange bulk import format.	*Exchange\ I386\Migrate\ Proxy*
Replver Tool	Reporting tool that verifies that public folder information is correctly replicated across sites in an organization. Writes results to a log file.	*Exchange\ I386\PFTools\ Replver*
Revert Tool for MS Mail	This tool resets the "Read" and "Unread" counters in an MS Mail message file.	*Exchange\ Common\ MSMail*
RPC Counter Tool	Monitors the number of remote procedure calls between an application and an Exchange server.	*Exchange\ I386\Developr\RPCCount*
Sentinel Tool	Monitors multiple servers and creates archives of the data collected. Modules for services, performance, and event logs can be configured; each module gathers different types of data. Modules can be distributed to multiple groups of servers configured within the Sentinel tool.	*Exchange\ I386\Admin\ Sentinel*
Server Space Client Extension Tool	This tool is best used when the amount of server space is limited and users will need to keep careful watch over the amount of space they're using. It enables users to display the total amount of space used by the mailbox from the client. This tool provides less detailed results than the Mailbox Statistics Tool mentioned previously in this appendix.	*Exchange\ I386\Client\ SrvSpace*
Simple Mail Handler Tool	This tool works much like the Inbox Assistant (which is included in the Exchange and Outlook clients); however, it does not require a connection to an Exchange server computer for the rules to be created. The tool provides advanced mail filtering capabilities; it allows users to automate archiving of mail from sent and/or deleted items folders. The Simple Mail Handler Tool needs to be added as a service in the client's messaging profile. The tool operates on Greenwich Mean Time; this setting cannot be changed.	*Exchange\ I386\Client\ SMH*

Table A-2. Tools in BORK Part Two (continued)

Tool Name	What It Does	Location
SwitchForms Tool for MS Outlook	Allows users to switch between the Exchange and Outlook clients on one workstation. This tool is best used by staff who need to run both applications, such as administrators testing Outlook while still supporting the Exchange client, or help desk personnel who may need to support both clients. Make sure that your client is closed when you install this utility!	*Exchange\ Win95\Client\ SwitchFm* or *Exchange\ WinNT\i386\ Client\ SwitchFm* as appropriate
UNIX Mail Source Extractor Tool	The Source Extractor works in conjunction with the MS Exchange Migration Wizard to extract email messages from Unix-based systems and then import the mail into an MS Exchange server. This command-line tool is uncompiled source code written in C; a C compiler is required on the host computer for this tool to work. Mail from a user's personal storage and from the spooler will be captured by the tool.	*Exchange\ Samples\ UnixSE*

Table A-3. Tools in the BORK Second Edition

Tool Name	What It does	Location
EXLIST List Server	This is an Exchange-based version of a standard list server; most sites find that a commercial package like LISTSERV is a better choice, because EXLIST is flaky at best.	*Exchange\ Samples\Exlist*
ExMerge	ExMerge enables administrators to merge data from recovery servers to production servers after disaster recovery. This tool can be used to move messages from the Information Store into personal folders (PSTs), or to ease moving a user between Exchange sites or organizations.	*Exchange\ I386\ExMerge*
GAL Modify Tool	This tool can be distributed to users so they can modify their own mailbox properties: users can change their own phone numbers, addresses, and so on. The raw mode of the Administrator program allows you to define which fields the users are able to change. See TechNet article Q186950 for specifics on defining which fields can be modified.	*Exchange\ I386\Client\ GalMod*
GAL Modify for Web Tool	Similar to the GAL Modify tool listed above, but this tool offers web access.	*Exchange\ I386\Web\ GalMod*
InterOrg Synchronization Tool	Allows two or more MS Exchange organizations to exchange directory information via SMTP without constant manual intervention.	*Exchange\ Winnt\InterOrg*

Table A-3. Tools in the BORK Second Edition (continued)

Tool Name	What It does	Location
InterOrg Synchronization Tool (cont.)	Both Master and Requestor InterOrg mailboxes need to be created on each server involved in the exchange of information before the installation of the tool, or you'll end up starting over. Large organizations will want to use SQL as the database, as opposed to Access; things will run much more smoothly if you use SQL. Ensure that you're using the correct versions of the OBDC drivers if there seems to be a problem with the service not processing data. You may need to reinstall the OBDC drivers from the Office 97 CD-ROM.	
Mailbox Cleanup Agent	Allows administrators to delete or archive messages from users' mailboxes based upon message age, in order to regulate the size of your Information Store. This newer version will not remove data from the *Outlook Calendar, Contacts, Notes, Journal,* or *Tasks* folders.	*Exchange\ Winnt\ MBClean* (Replaces version on BORK Part Two)
Mailstorm Tool	This MAPI client tool simulates different levels of stress on the Message Transfer Agent in Exchange; you can force Mailstorm to vomit out thousands of messages at once, which is lots of fun for the server. You can also test message integrity using this tool.	*Exchange\ I386\Admin\ MailStrm*
MAPIndl Tool (a.k.a. MAPI Notes Doc Link Tool)	Allows you to send a Lotus Notes document link (DocLink) using MS Exchange by adding an OLE Automation object to Exchange.	*Exchange\ I386\Developr\MAPIndl*
MAPIsend Tools (a.k.a. Command-Line Mail Sender)	This tool allows you to send mail and attachments through the command line, without using the Exchange or Outlook client. It's useful when you'd like to send email messages from a batch file or script.	*Exchange\ I386\ MAPISend*
PAB-GAL Synchronization Tool	This tool allows users to synchronize the data in their MS Mail personal address book (PAB) with information from the GAL in order to prevent outdated address records from staying in the PAB.	*Exchange\ <OS>\Client\ PabGSync*

B

Useful Performance Monitor Counters

Exchange offers quite an array of objects and counters you can monitor, in addition to the standard NT objects and counters. This appendix lists and explains what each object and counter measures. Generally, the counters in each section appear in alphabetical order (as they do in Performance Monitor), except that I've grouped some related counters together where appropriate.

> In general, any counter whose name includes "/sec" is measuring operations per second, so it's providing an average. Any counter whose name includes "Total" is providing a cumulative count since the last time the service that provides the counter was restarted.

The Database Object

This object has two instances: Directory and Information Store. As you might expect, the counters on this object's instances reflect information about the IS and DS database performance. Since both databases are so heavily used, these counters, described in the following list, can shed some much-needed light on your servers' performance.

> The Database object's counters can all be tweaked with the Performance Optimizer; see the section "Do-It-Yourself Tuning with Performance Optimizer," in Chapter 18, *Managing Exchange Performance*, for details.

Cache % Hit

This counter indicates the percentage of database page requests that could be filled out of the database cache. High rates are good, because they tell you that many requests are being filled without any disk I/O. Low rates indicate that you may need to increase the database cache size.

Cache Page Fault Stalls/sec

The Exchange database caching system can generate page faults just like virtual memory systems do; when a page fault occurs, the database will attempt to replace a free page with the contents of the requested page. When there are no free pages, the requested page can't be immediately loaded; that's a page fault stall. This counter tells you how many page fault stalls occur per second. Ideally, its value should be zero most of the time. If it's not, that indicates you need to raise the clean threshold to allow the cache to more aggressively free up new pages.

Cache Page Faults/sec

Whenever the database file manager tries to fetch a database page from the cache, but finds that the desired page isn't in the cache, it generates a page fault and attempts to put the page in the cache. This counter tracks the number of page faults per second; if this rate is too high, it means that the database cache size is too small.

Cache Size

Speaking of cache size, this counter tells you how much RAM the database cache manager is using. This amount will fluctuate in Exchange 5.5, thanks to the Dynamic Buffer Allocation (DBA) subsystem; in older versions, it will usually stay relatively constant.

File Bytes Read/sec, File Bytes Written/sec

These two counters indicate the rate at which data is read into and written from the database cache. If their values are high, it indicates that the cache is too small, since many I/O operations mean many cache misses.

File Operations Pending

Think of this counter's value as the length of the I/O queue for the database; it tracks the total number of operations waiting for execution. As the number goes up, so does the response time for individual operations, since they have to wait in the queue longer. Large values may indicate that the disk where the database file is stored is causing a bottleneck.

File Operations/sec

This counter represents the number of read and write operations requested by the database cache manager. High values mean that the database cache size is too small, since an undersized cache causes lots of misses and their concomitant I/O requests.

Log Record Stalls/sec

When a log thread wants to add a new log record to its buffer, but the buffer is full, that's a log stall. Stalls are bad because they slow down the logging process. If this value is greater than zero for sustained periods, that probably indicates that your log buffer is too small.

Log Threads Waiting

This counter indicates the number of log threads that are waiting to write their log data to disk. A high value for this counter indicates that the log may be a bottleneck, since making the log threads wait can have a negative impact on performance.

Log Writes/sec

This counter tells you how many times per second the log buffers are written to disk. As this rate increases and approaches the number of I/O operations per second that your server can provide, that indicates that your log device is becoming a bottleneck.

Table Open Cache % Hit, Table Open Cache Hits/sec, Table Open Cache Misses/sec

When the database needs to open a table, it will always try to use cached schema information. If the schema is in the cache, that's a cache hit; if not, that's a cache miss. These counters indicate the rate of cache hits and misses that occurred during table opens. A high hit percentage and high hit rates are good; high miss rates indicate that the table cache is probably too small.

Table Opens/sec

This counter tells you how many database tables the selected instance is opening per second. As this number rises, it indicates an increasing load on your database.

The MSExchange Internet Protocols Object

This object provides counters for the four Internet protocols that Exchange 5.5 supports: POP3, IMAP4rev1, LDAP, and NNTP. Each of these protocols appears as an instance, along with the following counters:

Active Connections

This counter shows the current total number of connections active for the selected instance. This reflects only the number of connections active at the time the monitor's active, not the peak number.

Bytes Received, Bytes Received/sec

These counters tally the amount of incoming data for the selected protocol. The Bytes Received counter is cumulative, while Bytes Received/sec is an average.

Bytes Sent and Bytes Sent/sec

These counters monitor the total and average number of bytes sent using the selected protocol.

Incoming Queue Length, Incoming Queue Size

Respectively, these two counters count the total length of the incoming work queue for this protocol and the size of the objects in that queue.

Outgoing Queue Length, Outgoing Queue Size

These are the opposite of the preceding counters: they count the total number and size of outgoing work queue items.

Outstanding Commands

This counter measures the total number of commands sent by clients that haven't been executed yet. If it helps, think of this counter's name as "Pending Commands," since that's really what it's measuring.

Peak Connections

This counter sums the peak number of connections made using this protocol. This is a useful way to see how many users are connecting to get their mail via POP3 or IMAP4.

Total Commands

This counter measures how many total commands have been sent to the server since it was last restarted.

Total Connections

This counter registers the cumulative total number of connections made on the selected protocol. It's useful in conjunction with the Peak Connections counter.

The MSExchangeDS Object

This object represents the Exchange Directory Service, so its counters reflect access to a variety of directory resources and objects:

AB Browses/sec, AB Reads/sec, AB Writes/sec

These count the average number of accesses to the address book (or GAL) per second. While interesting, this isn't terribly useful for most purposes.

AB Client Sessions

If you've ever wondered how many clients are looking up address data through MAPI clients, this counter will provide the answer (the count of LDAP client connections appears in the MSExchange Internet Protocols object).

Access Violations

Now here's a good one: this counter tells you how many attempted writes to the directory failed because the requestor didn't have appropriate security privileges.

Address Book View modifies/sec, Address Book View reads/sec, Address Book View writes/sec

These counters monitor the average number of accesses to all the Address Book View objects in your organization's directory.

ExDS Client Sessions

This counter indicates how many clients have sessions open to the DS (the "Ex" stands for Extended, not Exchange). Each session represents a connection to the DS from another Exchange component or the Exchange Administrator application.

ExDS Reads/sec, ExDS Writes/sec

These counters measure the average number of directory reads and writes per second. It's a useful way to see how often directory information is being fetched and modified, but since practically every Exchange component does this, knowing the count may not tell you much.

LDAP Searches, LDAP Searches/sec

How many searches were made through the LDAP protocol? These counters will provide the answer to that question. You can find out how many bytes those searches occupied with the counters in MSExchange Internet Protocols.

Objects Replicated Out/sec

This counter tells you the average number of objects per second that the DS was able to identify and package for replication.

Pending Replication Synchronizations

This counter tells you how many directory synchronization changes have arrived from replication partners, but haven't yet been processed.

Remaining Replication Updates

This counter totals the number of replication updates that are sitting in the DS's mailbox waiting for processing. When this value reaches a certain level, you're bound for the replication death spiral.

Replication Updates/sec

This counter provides a handy way to track how well your server is keeping up with inbound replication traffic. It won't tell you how many updates are still pending, but it will tell you how many changes per second the server can handle; combining these two numbers will tell you how long it will take to clear any replication backlog if no new data arrives.

Threads In Use

This counter indicates how many threads the DS has currently spawned to handle its workload. The DS spawns new threads when RPC client requests arrive. By monitoring this value, you can see whether an additional processor would boost your performance: the more threads you see here, the more valuable additional CPUs would be.

The MSExchangeES Object

This object is for the Exchange Event Service (hence the ES in the name). The counters here let you monitor the average and absolute times required to execute a script or process an event, the length of the notification queue for events, how many events and scripts have been processed, and how often the notification timer has fired.

The MSExchangeIMC Object

This object will be present whether or not you've installed the IMS; as you might guess, its instances and counters provide performance data for the IMS and its many inner workings. Since you can schedule IMS connections, you may notice that some of the counters (notably those that count queue lengths) show alarmingly high values between connections, so don't sweat that.

Bytes Queued MTS-IN, Bytes Queued MTS-OUT
> These two counters reflect the total number of bytes queued for inbound and outbound processing. (See Chapter 8, *Managing the Internet Mail Service*, for a refresher on how the IMS queues and transfers items.)

Connections Inbound, Connections Outbound
> These counters show the current number of inbound and outbound SMTP connections the IMS is using.

Connections Total Failed
> This counter indicates how many total connections have failed due to DNS errors, network timeouts, or other errors, not including rejected connections, since the IMS was last started.

Connections Total Inbound, Connections Total Outbound, Connections Total Rejected
> These counters measure the total number of inbound, outbound, and rejected SMTP connections the IMS has seen since its last restart. Rejected connections include connections from sites on the anti-spam list.

Inbound Bytes/Hr, Inbound Connections/Hr, Inbound Messages/Hr
> These counters track average hourly inbound message traffic. Each inbound connection can deliver multiple messages, so the Inbound Messages/Hr and Inbound Bytes/Hr are probably better indications of your servers' workload. There are corresponding counters for outbound messages (Outbound Bytes/ Hr, Outbound Connections/Hr, and Outbound Messages/Hr).

Inbound Messages Total, Outbound Messages Total
> These counters measure how many total inbound or outbound messages have been sent or received since the IMS was last restarted. It's always nice to be

able to casually drop little nuggets like "Gee, our IMS processed 15,000 messages yesterday" when upgrade budgeting time rolls around.

Messages Entering MTS-IN

This counter counts how many messages entered the respective IMS inbound processing queue.

Messages Leaving MTS-IN, Messages Leaving MTS-OUT

Like the Messages Entering MTS-IN counter, but in reverse, these counters measure how many messages the IMS dequeued from each of its work queues. If either of these counter values is lower than the corresponding Messages Entering counter, that indicates a growing backlog.

NDRs Total Inbound, NDRs Total Outbound

These counters tell you just how many NDRs your system is generating and receiving. If these numbers suddenly spike upward, it often indicates a configuration problem of some sort.

Queued Inbound, Queued Outbound

These counters display the current size of the inbound and outbound item queues, showing you how many messages await processing for delivery in each direction.

Queued MTS-IN, Queued MTS-OUT

These counters tell you how many messages are stored in the IMS' internal work queues.

Total Failed Conversions, Total Successful Conversions

The IMS has to do content conversion on inbound and outbound messages, since Exchange's internal format and the Internet standards for message encoding might as well be from different planets. Sometimes these conversions fail; these counters indicate the total number of mangled messages since the last IMS restart, as well as the total number of messages that were converted without incident.

Total Inbound Kilobytes, Total Outbound Kilobytes

These counters register the total amount of data sent into or out of your IMS server since the last IMS restart.

Total Inbound Recipients, Total Outbound Recipients

These counters tell you how many total recipients were processed for inbound or outbound mail since the IMS was last started; this gives you a rough gauge of how many different origins and destinations your Internet mail has.

Total Kilobytes Queued, Total Messages Queued, Total Recipients Queued

These counters show the big picture of outbound delivery: how many different recipients, what data volume, and what total message count were queued up to go to the outside world.

Total Loops Detected

The IMS and MTA examine each address of a message and compare it against data in the GWART in an effort to catch mail loops before they cause problems. Whenever the loop detector identifies a looping message, it generates an NDR; this counter tells you how many such NDRs have been generated.

The MSExchangeIS Object

The IS service maintains a ton of performance parameters, many of which are warehoused in this object. These counters, in conjunction with those in the MSExchangeIS Private and MSExchangeIS Public objects, can tell you pretty much anything you might ever want to know about what the IS is doing. Many of the parameters available through this object come in two slightly different forms. One form indicates the number of currently active items, as in the Active Anonymous User Count counter; the other form indicates the total number of items, as with Anonymous User Count. I've lumped the active and total counters together in this section, listing only the active forms:

Active Connection Count

Records the total number of active connections, that is, connections where the client has made a request or generated some type of activity in the last 10 minutes.

Active User Count

This counter shows how many users are connected to the IS. Active users are those that have requested data from the IS in the last 10 minutes; the User Count counter just shows how many users have connected since the last restart of the IS service.

Active Anonymous User Count

This counter tells you how many anonymous users are currently talking to the IS. If you allow anonymous access, anonymous users can use NNTP and IMAP4 to get public folder and newsgroup access.

Database Session Hit Rate

This counter tells you what percentage of database sessions could be reused. It's more efficient to reuse an existing session than to open a new one, so high values of this counter indicate that your database system is handling the load well.

IMAP Commands Issued, IMAP Commands Issued Rate

These counters record the total number of IMAP4 commands that have arrived from IMAP4 clients, plus the average arrival rate for those commands. This is a good way to measure how much IMAP4 traffic your clients are generating, but not a good way to estimate load; it doesn't tell you what commands the clients are issuing, just how many. There are similar counters for POP3.

IMAP Messages Sent, IMAP Message Send Rate

Want to know how many IMAP messages have been sent to clients? These counters will give you the total number of messages and the send rate. There are corresponding counters for the POP3 protocol.

Maximum Anonymous Users

This counter indicates the peak number of anonymous connections since the last IS restart.

Maximum Connections

This counter displays the peak number of connections, which tells you little apart from how many concurrent requests your IS might conceivably have to handle.

Maximum Users

Use this counter to see the peak number of users on your IS, including anonymous users. This is useful for knowing how many client access licenses you're actually using (don't use it to figure out how many you need, or you may run afoul of Microsoft's license terms).

Newsfeed Bytes Sent, Newsfeed Bytes Sent/sec

These counters tell you the total number of bytes the IS sent to all active newsfeeds, plus the rate at which those bytes were sent.

 You'll still see all these newsfeed counters even if you don't have the Internet News Service installed and active, but they won't give you any data.

Newsfeed Inbound Rejected Messages, Newsfeed Inbound Rejected Messages Rate

These counters tell you how many total messages your newsfeed rejected, along with the time-based rate of rejection. Messages may be rejected because they're duplicates of existing messages or because some kind of transport or format error occurred.

Newsfeed Messages Received, Newsfeed Messages Received Rate

These counters tell you the total number of messages accepted via all your active newsfeeds, along with the rate of their arrival and processing.

Newsfeed Messages Sent, Newsfeed Messages Sent/sec

Oddly, Microsoft missed naming these counters like the others—there's no "Rate" here. Anyway, these counters tell you the total number of outbound messages sent by the IS to your newsfeeds, along with their arrival rate.

Newsfeed Outbound Rejected Messages

If you want to know the total number of this IS's newsfeed messages that were rejected by other NNTP hosts, this counter will tell you.

NNTP Commands Issued, NNTP Commands Issued Rate

These counters measure how many NNTP commands the IS issued to its NNTP partners.

NNTP Current Outbound Connections, NNTP Outbound Connections

These counters tell how many outbound NNTP connections the IS either currently has running or has had since restart. This number will fluctuate according to the schedule you've set for your INS connections.

NNTP Failed Posts, NNTP Failed Posts Rate

These counters measure the number and rate of NNTP message posting attempts that failed. Failed posts aren't the same as rejected posts: a rejected post means the peer server actively rejected the article before attempting to post it, but a failed post indicates that the server tried to post the article but couldn't.

NNTP Messages Posted, NNTP Messages Posted Rate

These counters tally successfully posted NNTP messages, both in total number and posting rate.

NNTP Messages Read, NNTP Messages Read Rate

These counters tell you how many messages the IS has sent to NNTP clients since the IS was started and at what rate they were sent.

Number of article index table rows expired

This counter tells you how many articles have expired from the public store.

Peak Push Notifications Cache Size

This counter registers the peak size of the push notification cache, which the IS uses to cache notices sent to clients who have requested notification when data in the IS changes.

Push Notification Cache Size

This counter tells you how big the push notification cache currently is, i.e., how many clients are currently signed up to get notification of updates.

Push Notifications Generated/sec, Push Notifications Skipped/sec

These two counters indicate how many push notifications the IS generated and how many it didn't send because a notification was already in the cache.

Read Bytes RPC Clients/sec, Write Bytes RPC Clients/sec

These counters indicate the data rate for requests from all RPC clients.

RPC Operations/sec, RPC Packets/sec

These counters give you the RPC throughput rate for individual operations and for overall packet flow. A single operation may require multiple packets.

RPC Requests, RPC Requests Peak

These counters tell you the current and peak number of RPC requests; this is a useful way to judge how busy your servers are.

User Count

How many users can fit on a server? It depends, but this counter will tell you how many users have been on your server.

The MSExchangeIS Private and MSExchangeIS Public Objects

As their names suggest, these objects hold counters specific to the private and public Information Stores. There's a lot of overlap between the two, since many of the interesting values happen to be available for both store types:

Active Client Logons

This counter tells you how many active clients are currently connected. An active client is one that's done something (like opened a message or folder, browsed the GAL, or sent a message) in the last ten minutes.

Average Delivery Time

This counter measures the average time between message arrival at the IS to delivery of the message to the MTA. This average is continually updated so that it reflects the average delivery time of the last ten messages.

Average Local Delivery Time

Local delivery time is the interval between the time the store receives the message and the time it delivers the message to a recipient on the same server. This counter measures the average local delivery time for messages arriving at, and bound for, this server; the average is computed across the last ten messages.

Average Time for Delivery, Average Time for Local Delivery

These are the same as the Average Delivery Time and Average Local Delivery Time, but for the public store. Someone apparently missed the meeting where standards for naming these counters were discussed.

Categorization Count

When a user creates a view filter or performs a search, Exchange must create a categorization and store it in the IS. This counter tells you how many such categorizations currently exist; as the number increases, so does the load on your server.

Client Logons

This counter measures how many clients have logged on since the last IS restart (or since monitoring began). This is a useful way to track usage patterns so you can get a rough idea of how many clients use the server at different times of the day.

Folder Opens/sec

Perhaps you've been curious about how many folders your clients have been opening per second. If so, this counter is for you.

Local deliveries

This counter measures the number of messages delivered to addressees on the server.

Local delivery rate

Like the preceding counter, this one measures local deliveries, except that it calculates the average arrival rate per second.

Message Opens/sec

Slightly more useful than the Folder Opens/sec counter, this one tells you how many messages your clients are opening, on average, per second.

Message Recipients Delivered

This counter indicates how many recipients have received messages since the IS was started. A single message addressed to 15 people will count as 15 delivered recipients, but only as one message for the average delivery time counters.

Message Recipients Delivered/min

This counter records the average delivery rate to message recipients. It's per minute, which seems strange since most of the other counters that measure rates do so by the second.

Messages Delivered, Messages Delivered/min

These counters tally the total number of messages delivered to local and remote recipients, both as an absolute number and as a per-minute delivery rate.

Messages Sent, Messages Sent/min

The IS can hand off messages to the MTA for processing; these counters measure the total number of sent messages and the sending rate.

Messages Submitted, Messages Submitted/min

These counters measure how many messages were submitted by clients to the IS and at what rate those messages were submitted. Once the message has been submitted, the IS can either deliver it locally or hand it off to the MTA.

Number of messages expired from public folders

This counter is specific to the MSExchangeIS Public object; it counts the number of messages expired in the measurement period.

Peak Client Logons

Here's a good counter: it tells you the peak number of clients that have concurrently logged on to your server. If you've planned your servers around assumptions like "X users, only 40% of whom will log on at once," this is an excellent tool for testing whether those assumptions are still valid.

Receive Queue Size, Send Queue Size

These counters measure the current size of the send and receive queues. Note that these queues don't have anything to do with the IMS or MTA work queues; they only reflect the number of messages queued for processing by the IS.

Replication Backfill Data Messages Received, Replication Backfill Data Messages Sent

As you learned in Chapter 7, *Managing Connectors and the MTA*, replication backfill occurs when one site sends another information that originally was replicated to the sending site. These counters measure the number of backfill messages sent and received. Like all of the other replication counters, these counters are only found on the MSExchangeIS Public object.

Replication Backfill Requests Received, Replication Backfill Requests Sent

These counters measure the number of backfill request messages sent and received. Each backfill request message will generate one or more backfill data messages.

Replication Folder Changes Received, Replication Folder Changes Sent

Folder changes are counted separately from other types of replicated data. These counters tell you how many folder change replication messages have been sent and received.

Replication Folder Data Messages Received, Replication Folder Data Messages Sent

These counters tell you how many replication messages containing folder changes were sent and received.

Replication Folder Tree Messages Received, Replication Folder Tree Messages Sent

The public folder hierarchy is replicated separately from the folders and their contents; this pair of counters tells you how many hierarchy update messages have been sent and received.

Replication Message Changes Received, Replication Message Changes Sent

These counters tell you how many messages containing changes to public folders have been sent or received.

Replication Messages Received, Replication Messages Sent

These counters report the total number of replication messages sent and received, including folder change, folder tree, and backfill messages.

Replication Receive Queue Size

It's normal to have a backlog of replication messages; this counter lets you see how big the backlog is so you can take proactive measures to avoid falling into the replication death spiral.

Replication Status Messages Received, Replication Status Messages Sent

Replication status messages are sent separately from other types of replication traffic (remember, each replication message generates an answer). This counter displays the total.

Single Instance Ratio

Pure gold! This counter tells you the ratio (from 0 to 1) of single-instance storage in your IS. The lower the ratio, the less effective your single-instance storage: a ratio of 0 means that every message is stored in a separate mailbox or public folder, while a ratio of 1 means that every mailbox shares the same set of messages. In practice, knowing what this ratio is on a server may indicate whether it would be worth moving some users to group users who get the same messages together, thus increasing the ratio.

Total Count of Recoverable Items, Total Size of Recoverable Items

These counters report on the contents of the deleted item retention cache. Since these are totals, they just summarize the entirety of the private or public IS; if you want totals for individual mailboxes or public folders, you'll have to get them from the appropriate resources view.

The MSExchangeMTA Object

Good MTA performance is vital to the overall performance of your Exchange server. The MTA is intimately involved with most aspects of message transport, so keeping abreast of its health and status is an excellent way to monitor your servers' overall performance.

Many of these counters are identical to the ones offered by the MSExchangeIMC object.

Adjacent MTA Associations

This counter indicates how many associations the monitored MTA currently has open with other MTAs.

Admin Connections

This counter tallies the total number of connections made by Exchange Administrator users to this server.

Admin Interface Receive Bytes/sec, Admin Interface Transmit Bytes/sec

These counters record the average number of bytes received and sent per second on the administrative interface that Exchange Administrator uses to talk to the MTA. Note that these rates only reflect your communications with the server's MTA; if you open Exchange Administrator and don't touch the MTA object, these counters will stay at zero.

Deferred Delivery Msgs

This counter tallies the number of messages whose delivery the MTA had to defer until a later time.

Disk File Deletes/sec, Disk File Opens/sec, Disk File Reads/sec, Disk File Syncs/sec, Disk File Writes/sec

These counters measure the rate of disk I/O operations requested by the MTA. By watching them, you can see what the MTA is doing, and how often.

ExDS Read Calls/sec

The MTA frequently needs to resolve addresses and look up other data in the directory. This counter measures the number of DS read operations the MTA has requested per second.

Free Elements

This counter measures the number of available buffer elements in the MTA buffer pool.

Free Headers

This counter indicates the number of available buffer headers in the MTA buffer pool.

Inbound Bytes Total, Outbound Bytes Total

These counters measure the total number of bytes sent and received by the MTA on all interfaces (including LAN, TCP/IP, and TP4).

Inbound Messages Total, Outbound Messages Total

These counters tally the total number of inbound and outbound messages handled by this server's MTA. This is a good quick check to see what overall load is being placed on the MTA.

LAN Receive Bytes/sec, LAN Transmit Bytes/sec

These counters tell you the rate at which MTA data is being moved over your LAN connections.

Message Bytes/sec, Messages/sec

These counters tell you the rate at which messages are being processed, both by number of messages and their size.

RAS Receive Bytes/sec, RAS Transmit Bytes/sec

These two counters measure transmit and receive traffic rates over your RAS connections; there are similar counters that measure throughput for TCP/IP, TP4, and X.25 traffic.

Threads In Use

This counter shows the total number of MTA threads currently running. This number may be surprisingly high—on a mostly idle server, it hovers around 42. As new RPC requests arrive, the MTA can spawn new threads. By monitoring this value, you can see whether an additional processor would boost your performance: the more threads you see here, the more valuable additional CPUs would be.

Total Failed Conversions, Total Successful Conversions

The MTA has to convert messages between Exchange's internal format and the various formats used by external clients and foreign systems. These counters record the number of successful and failed message conversions.

Total Loops Detected

This is identical to the IMS counter of the same name: it registers the total number of mail loops that the MTA has detected and NDRed.

Total Recipients Inbound, Total Recipients Outbound

These counters indicate the total number of distinct inbound and outbound recipients.

Total Recipients Queued

This counter shows the total number of recipients whose messages are currently queued for delivery.

Work Queue Bytes, Work Queue Length

These two counters count the number of items and the number of total bytes waiting for processing in the MTA work queue.

XAPI Clients

This counter tells you how many clients are connected to the MTA over the XAPI interface. Each client can have one or more XAPI sessions open.

XAPI Gateways

Like the XAPI Clients counter, this counter tells you how many gateways are talking to the MTA over the XAPI interface.

XAPI Receive Bytes/sec, XAPI Transmit Bytes/sec

These counters measure the throughput of data on the XAPI interface.

The MSExchangeMTA Connections Object

This object is distinct from the other Exchange objects because it actually has instances! At a minimum, there will be two instances: one named Microsoft Private MDB and one named Microsoft Public MDB. There will also be one instance for each installed connector. All of the instances have the same counters:

Associations

> The value of this counter indicates how many associations the selected instance has open. The Private MDB and Public MDB will each always have two associations open; other connector instances may have associations open or not.

Connector Index

> This counter's value is the ordinal number of the connector index, which the MTA uses internally. This doesn't seem to have any use, but it's available if you need it.

Cumulative Inbound Associations, Cumulative Outbound Associations

> These counters record the total number of inbound and outbound associations in which the selected connector instance has taken part.

Exchange considers an inbound association to be one opened at the remote end's request; outbound associations are those that your server opens to another MTA.

Current Inbound Associations, Current Outbound Associations

> These counters indicate how many inbound or outbound associations are currently active for the selected connector instance.

Failed Outbound Associations

> It's good to know when outbound associations are failing, since it can indicate a problem with the MTA transport stack, the transport layer protocols, or whatever hardware you're using to connect to the remote system. This counter tells you how many outbound associations have failed for the selected connector instance only.

Inbound Bytes Total, Outbound Bytes Total

> These counters tell you how many bytes the selected connector instance has moved in each direction.

Inbound Messages Total, Outbound Messages Total

These counters give you a way to see how many messages have moved in and out of your MTA in either direction.

Inbound Reject Reason, Outbound Failure Reason

The values of these counter indicate the most recent failure code posted when a message was rejected. Most of the time, these counters will have a value of zero, meaning that no messages were rejected.

Inbound Rejected Total

This counter tells you how many inbound messages were rejected in each monitoring time period.

Last Inbound Association, Last Outbound Association

These counters report the time, in seconds, since the last inbound or outbound association was active.

Next Association Retry

Here's another good one. This counter tells you what time, in seconds since 00:00 on January 1, 1970, this connector is scheduled to try opening an association. Have your calculator handy if you want to decode this.

Oldest Message Queued

This counter indicates how old the oldest message in this connector's queue is: it records the number of seconds since the message was enqueued.

Queue Length, Queued Bytes

These counters tell you how much queued data is waiting for the selected connector instance to process it.

Receive Bytes/sec, Receive Message/sec

These counters indicate the rate of arrival for incoming messages, both by size and number. Remember, they apply only to the selected connector instance.

Total Recipients Inbound, Total Recipients Outbound, Total Recipients Queued

These counters provide a picture of the kind of recipient processing the connector is doing; they report the total number of inbound, outbound, and queued recipients.

Other Objects

Any connector or third-party Exchange component is free to install its own Performance Monitor counters. For example, the MS.Mail, cc:Mail, and Notes connectors all add their own objects and counters, as do many third-party fax and voice messaging products.

Index

About the Author

Paul Robichaux is an experienced software developer and author, and the principal of Robichaux and Associates, Inc. He has worked on Unix, Macintosh, and Win32 development projects over the past six years, including a stint on Intergraph's OLE team. He is the author of O'Reilly & Associates' *Managing the Windows NT Registry*.

Colophon

Our look is the result of reader comments, our own experimentation, and feedback from distribution channels. Distinctive covers complement our distinctive approach to technical topics, breathing personality and life into potentially dry subjects.

The animal on the cover of *Managing Microsoft Exchange Server* is a southern lesser bush baby (*Galago moholi*), so named for its baby-like cries. These chipmunk-sized, brownish-grey South African primates are characterized by foldable ears, elongation of the tarsus (or upper part of the feet), and pads of thick skin on fingers and toes; these pads help them climb trees, where they sleep in nests and hollows during the day. At night, adults forage for insects and acacia gum, then return to the small family groups; the males are very territorial and urinate to scent their territory.

Bush babies usually travel by climbing and swinging through the trees. On the ground, they sit upright and move by jumping around on their hind legs. Their habitat includes woodland, savannah, and scrub desert. They mate every 4–8 months, and after a gestation period of 120 days, females give birth to about two offspring, which mature around 10 months of age and live up to 16 years.

As is the case with many species, the southern lesser bush babies' existence is thought to be threatened as a result of habitat loss.

Madeleine Newell was the production editor and copyeditor for *Managing Microsoft Exchange Server*. Cindy Kogut of Editorial Ink was the proofreader. John Files and Nicole Gipson Arigo provided quality control; Maureen Dempsey, Anna Kim Snow, and Kimo Carter provided production support. Mike Sierra provided FrameMaker technical support. Seth Maislin wrote the index.

Edie Freedman designed the cover of this book, using an original illustration by Lorrie LeJeune. The cover layout was produced by Kathleen Wilson with QuarkXPress 3.32 using the ITC Garamond font. Whenever possible, our books use

RepKover™, a durable and flexible lay-flat binding. If the page count exceeds RepKover's limit, perfect binding is used.

The inside layout was designed by Nancy Priest and implemented in FrameMaker 5.5.6 by Mike Sierra. The text and heading fonts are ITC Garamond Light and Garamond Book. The illustrations that appear in the book were produced by Robert Romano and Rhon Porter using Macromedia FreeHand 8 and Adobe Photoshop 5. This colophon was written by Nancy Kotary.

How to stay in touch with O'Reilly

1. Visit Our Award-Winning Web Site

http://www.oreilly.com/

★ "Top 100 Sites on the Web" —*PC Magazine*
★ "Top 5% Web sites" —*Point Communications*
★ "3-Star site" —*The McKinley Group*

Our web site contains a library of comprehensive product information (including book excerpts and tables of contents), downloadable software, background articles, interviews with technology leaders, links to relevant sites, book cover art, and more. File us in your Bookmarks or Hotlist!

2. Join Our Email Mailing Lists

New Product Releases

To receive automatic email with brief descriptions of all new O'Reilly products as they are released, send email to:
listproc@online.oreilly.com
Put the following information in the first line of your message (*not* in the Subject field):
subscribe oreilly-news

O'Reilly Events

If you'd also like us to send information about trade show events, special promotions, and other O'Reilly events, send email to:
listproc@online.oreilly.com
Put the following information in the first line of your message (*not* in the Subject field):
subscribe oreilly-events

3. Get Examples from Our Books via FTP

There are two ways to access an archive of example files from our books:

Regular FTP

- ftp to:
  ftp.oreilly.com
  (login: anonymous
  password: your email address)
- Point your web browser to:
  ftp://ftp.oreilly.com/

FTPMAIL

- Send an email message to:
  ftpmail@online.oreilly.com
  (Write "help" in the message body)

4. Contact Us via Email

order@oreilly.com
To place a book or software order online. Good for North American and international customers.

subscriptions@oreilly.com
To place an order for any of our newsletters or periodicals.

books@oreilly.com
General questions about any of our books.

software@oreilly.com
For general questions and product information about our software. Check out O'Reilly Software Online at **http://software.oreilly.com/** for software and technical support information. Registered O'Reilly software users send your questions to: **website-support@oreilly.com**

cs@oreilly.com
For answers to problems regarding your order or our products.

booktech@oreilly.com
For book content technical questions or corrections.

proposals@oreilly.com
To submit new book or software proposals to our editors and product managers.

international@oreilly.com
For information about our international distributors or translation queries. For a list of our distributors outside of North America check out:
http://www.oreilly.com/www/order/country.html

O'Reilly & Associates, Inc.
101 Morris Street, Sebastopol, CA 95472 USA
TEL   707-829-0515 or 800-998-9938
       (6am to 5pm PST)
FAX   707-829-0104

International Distributors

UK, Europe, Middle East and Africa (except France, Germany, Austria, Switzerland, Luxembourg, Liechtenstein, and Eastern Europe)

INQUIRIES
O'Reilly UK Limited
4 Castle Street
Farnham
Surrey, GU9 7HS
United Kingdom
Telephone: 44-1252-711776
Fax: 44-1252-734211
Email: josette@oreilly.com

ORDERS
Wiley Distribution Services Ltd.
1 Oldlands Way
Bognor Regis
West Sussex PO22 9SA
United Kingdom
Telephone: 44-1243-779777
Fax: 44-1243-820250
Email: cs-books@wiley.co.uk

France

ORDERS
GEODIF
61, Bd Saint-Germain
75240 Paris Cedex 05, France
Tel: 33-1-44-41-46-16 (French books)
Tel: 33-1-44-41-11-87 (English books)
Fax: 33-1-44-41-11-44
Email: distribution@eyrolles.com

INQUIRIES
Éditions O'Reilly
18 rue Séguier
75006 Paris, France
Tel: 33-1-40-51-52-30
Fax: 33-1-40-51-52-31
Email: france@editions-oreilly.fr

Germany, Switzerland, Austria, Eastern Europe, Luxembourg, and Liechtenstein

INQUIRIES & ORDERS
O'Reilly Verlag
Balthasarstr. 81
D-50670 Köln
Germany
Telephone: 49-221-973160-91
Fax: 49-221-973160-8
Email: anfragen@oreilly.de (inquiries)
Email: order@oreilly.de (orders)

Canada (French language books)
Les Éditions Flammarion ltée
375, Avenue Laurier Ouest
Montréal (Québec) H2V 2K3
Tel: 00-1-514-277-8807
Fax: 00-1-514-278-2085
Email: info@flammarion.qc.ca

Hong Kong
City Discount Subscription Service, Ltd.
Unit D, 3rd Floor, Yan's Tower
27 Wong Chuk Hang Road
Aberdeen, Hong Kong
Tel: 852-2580-3539
Fax: 852-2580-6463
Email: citydis@ppn.com.hk

Korea
Hanbit Media, Inc.
Sonyoung Bldg. 202
Yeksam-dong 736-36
Kangnam-ku
Seoul, Korea
Tel: 822-554-9610
Fax: 822-556-0363
Email: hant93@chollian.dacom.co.kr

Philippines
Mutual Books, Inc.
429-D Shaw Boulevard
Mandaluyong City, Metro
Manila, Philippines
Tel: 632-725-7538
Fax: 632-721-3056
Email: mbikikog@mnl.sequel.net

Taiwan
O'Reilly Taiwan
No. 3, Lane 131
Hang-Chow South Road
Section 1, Taipei, Taiwan
Tel: 886-2-23968990
Fax: 886-2-23968916
Email: benh@oreilly.com

China
O'Reilly Beijing
Room 2410
160, FuXingMenNeiDaJie
XiCheng District
Beijing, China PR 100031
Tel: 86-10-86631006
Fax: 86-10-86631007
Email: frederic@oreilly.com

India
Computer Bookshop (India) Pvt. Ltd.
190 Dr. D.N. Road, Fort
Bombay 400 001 India
Tel: 91-22-207-0989
Fax: 91-22-262-3551
Email: cbsbom@giasbm01.vsnl.net.in

Japan
O'Reilly Japan, Inc.
Kiyoshige Building 2F
12-Bancho, Sanei-cho
Shinjuku-ku
Tokyo 160-0008 Japan
Tel: 81-3-3356-5227
Fax: 81-3-3356-5261
Email: japan@oreilly.com

All Other Asian Countries
O'Reilly & Associates, Inc.
101 Morris Street
Sebastopol, CA 95472 USA
Tel: 707-829-0515
Fax: 707-829-0104
Email: order@oreilly.com

Australia
WoodsLane Pty., Ltd.
7/5 Vuko Place
Warriewood NSW 2102
Australia
Tel: 61-2-9970-5111
Fax: 61-2-9970-5002
Email: info@woodslane.com.au

New Zealand
Woodslane New Zealand, Ltd.
21 Cooks Street (P.O. Box 575)
Waganui, New Zealand
Tel: 64-6-347-6543
Fax: 64-6-345-4840
Email: info@woodslane.com.au

Latin America
McGraw-Hill Interamericana
Editores, S.A. de C.V.
Cedro No. 512
Col. Atlampa
06450, Mexico, D.F.
Tel: 52-5-547-6777
Fax: 52-5-547-3336
Email: mcgraw-hill@infosel.net.mx

O'REILLY™

O'Reilly & Associates, Inc.
101 Morris Street
Sebastopol, CA 95472-9902
1-800-998-9938

Visit us online at:
http://www.ora.com/
orders@ora.com

O'REILLY WOULD LIKE TO HEAR FROM YOU

Which book did this card come from?

_____

Where did you buy this book?
- ❏ Bookstore   ❏ Computer Store
- ❏ Direct from O'Reilly   ❏ Class/seminar
- ❏ Bundled with hardware/software
- ❏ Other _____

What operating system do you use?
- ❏ UNIX   ❏ Macintosh
- ❏ Windows NT   ❏ PC(Windows/DOS)
- ❏ Other _____

What is your job description?
- ❏ System Administrator   ❏ Programmer
- ❏ Network Administrator   ❏ Educator/Teacher
- ❏ Web Developer
- ❏ Other _____

❏ Please send me O'Reilly's catalog, containing a complete listing of O'Reilly books and software.

Name _____   Company/Organization _____

Address _____

City _____ State _____ Zip/Postal Code _____ Country _____

Telephone _____   Internet or other email address (specify network)

Nineteenth century wood engraving
of a bear from the O'Reilly &
Associates Nutshell Handbook®
Using & Managing UUCP.

POST CARD

‖‖‖

BUSINESS REPLY MAIL

FIRST CLASS MAIL   PERMIT NO. 80   SEBASTOPOL, CA

Postage will be paid by addressee

O'Reilly & Associates, Inc.
101 Morris Street
Sebastopol, CA 95472-9902

‖‖‖‖‖‖‖‖‖‖‖‖‖‖‖‖‖‖‖‖‖‖‖‖‖‖‖